THE

JOURNAL

OF

SACRED LITERATURE.

New Series.

EDITED BY JOHN KITTO, D.D. F.S.A.

VOLUME III.

LONDON:

ROBERT B. BLACKADER,

ALDINE CHAMBERS, 13, PATERNOSTER ROW.

AND SOLD BY

SAMUEL BAGSTER & SONS, 15, PATERNOSTER ROW.

EDINBURGH : W. OLIPHANT & SONS.   DUBLIN : SAMUEL B. OLDHAM.

1853.

THE

JOURNAL

OF

SACRED LITERATURE.

New Series.

No. V. — OCTOBER, 1852.

ROMANISM IN FRANCE.

Les Origines de l'Eglise Romaine (On the First Principles of the
Romish Church). By ANDRÉ ARCHINARD. 2 vols. 8vo.
Paris, 1852.

Histoire des Protestants de France (History of the French Protestants). By G. de FÉLICE. 1 vol. 8vo. 1850.

Du Catholicisme en France (On French Catholicism). By E.
DE PRESSENSÉ. 8vo. Paris, 1851.

Dictionnaire Infernal (Infernal Dictionary). By J. COLLIN DE
PLANCY; sanctioned by the Archbishop of Paris. Paris, 1844.

Légendes des Sept Péchés Capitaux (Legends of the Seven
Deadly Sins). By J. COLLIN DE PLANCY. 8vo. Recommended by the Archbishop of Paris.

Le Pélerinage à la Salette (Pilgrimage to Mount Salette). By
the Abbé LEMONNIER. Eighth Edition.

L'Univers, Union Catholique, for the years 1848-52.

Le Ver Rongeur (The Gnawing Worm). By M. l'Abbé GAUME.
Paris, 1852.

ROMANISM in France! What a varied and confused crowd of
ideas does the phrase call up in a mind somewhat acquainted with
the history of the years that have passed away since the days of
Luther. In one sense France may be regarded as the arena in
miniature of the great conflict which his appearance called forth
between the rival powers of authority and free thought. And
there in consequence did Leo and Luther engage in a deadly pas-

sage of arms that marshalled on one side and on the other all the forces of the kingdom—sacerdotal, military, civil—which in their repeated collisions put the whole land into confusion and alarm, and which, after a battle of three centuries, has by no means come to a termination yet. Complicated and wonderful is that web: how deep and various its colours! What grand characters are woven into that national tapestry. There we see and almost fear to look upon the wily and implacable Catharine de' Medici; there we admire that sturdy old Protestant the Admiral Coligny; the Guises come stalking forth on the canvas, haughty and chivalric; proud of their blood, prouder still of their unstained orthodoxy. Mary Stuart we behold now in the lap of a refined sensualism, and now the centre of a Catholic plot designed for the destruction of Elizabeth and the overthrow of Protestantism. Here is Henry IV. perishing under a poniard which Jesuitism has plunged into his breast; and here is Louis XVI. dragged to the guillotine by the insensate fury of unbelief. That stately monarch has left a harlot's bosom to order a dragonade against his Protestant subjects; and that poor wizened Regent enjoys his debauch while he encourages scoffing the most shameless, and infidelity the most extreme. In one part of the picture you see the streets of Paris running with blood at the Catholic massacre of St. Bartholomew; in another part you see them polluted with the sanguinary Saturnalia of revolutionary Atheism. This monarch is Henry IV., who beat Popery on the field of battle, but yielding to the fascinations which it threw around a throne, bartered away his solemn convictions for a mistress and a crown. This monarch is Louis XVI., the only prince of a long series who was really good and pious, and he perishes for the vices of the religion he serves, and the evils accumulated by ancestors with whom he has no sympathy.

In the mazes of that picture there is a unity. Numerous and diverse as the pretences are, two conflicting aims are steadily pursued. All those brooks, rivulets and streams, intersect each other though they do, and various as are the directions in which they seem to run, in reality make their way into two single streams, and these streams seek the ocean towards opposite points of the compass. One hastens to the north,—it is the stream of mental independence; another hastens to the south,—it is the stream of mental servitude. Of the former the philosopher is the self-elected symbol, but its real guardian is the Gospel; the latter is represented by the priest and defended by the soldier. The two powers are in direct antagonism. For more than three hundred years they have been engaged in conflict, and at this moment the battle rages more fiercely than ever.

France is a country of extremes. Its fickle Celtic blood hurries up and down the tube, now resting at fever heat, now sinking below zero. Till recently the latter had been its position for more than half a century. Under the repeated blows of Philophism religion seemed dead in France; dead and buried did it seem; utterly perished, past all hope of revival. The only faith was faith in Voltaire; the only belief was disbelief. Men were sure of nothing except that there was nothing to be sure of. Extinct was all zeal save the zeal for extinction. Religion was not only disowned, it was scorned, laughed at, spit upon. Religion was a token of imbecility, and a topic of impious jesting. Disproved by argument and outfaced by wit, it was scouted as an open cheat or a thinly veiled hypocrisy. Such was the Frenchman's view of religion,—the view of those who set the fashion in the world of thought and speech.

The curtain falls;—in a moment the stage-bell rings, and as the curtain ascends you wonderingly behold a temple where you had seen the hall of a club, and there men are on their knees at worship, where a little before your tearful eyes beheld the orgies of infidelity. What a transformation! Is this worship real? Will that adoration last? will it come to good? These are questions on which some light may be thrown in the course of this essay. First, however, let us make a true report of what we see. The material forces of Romanism in France are apparently very great. Let us recount and measure them.

Speaking in general terms, France may be called a Catholic country. Protestants there are in the land, and among them exclusively may real religion find a home. Equally may it be true that the Catholicism of Catholic France may be little better than the thin coating of ice which you see on the surface of the water in some calm morning of early winter. Nevertheless, in courtesy at least, France must be termed a Catholic country. In religious statistics such is her designation.

Being Catholic, she has of course a Catholic clergy. That clergy before the revolution drew their support from the soil, to one-tenth of the produce of which they had a right, similar to the right of the king to his royalty, and the lord to his rent. Tithes swept away by the revolution left the clergy independent of the state. But independence was not the parent of wealth, and therefore the clergy were ready to receive the annual bounty of the state when Bonaparte saw reason to think that policy required they should be taken into his pay. Since then the clergy appear in the Budget, like the police or any other state officials, and receive a yearly vote of 42,111,050 francs. The franc is tenpence of our money; but as 'the worth of a thing is that which it will bring,' so ten-pence in France is equal to more than a shilling in England. If then we reckon francs as shillings, we find the annual vote for the clergy to amount to more than 2,100,000*l.* sterling.

We must also advert to the enormous capital placed at the service of Romanism for the celebration of its worship. Eighty episcopal sees divide among them 240 diocesan edifices. In France there are 37,013 parishes. Each parish has its church, and, for the most part, each church owes to the state its erection, its repair, and, when needful, its enlargement.

An estimate has been made of the amount of this fixed capital; the interest has been added, and it is found that this second supply is much larger than the former.

We must say a word of the incidental receipts of the French clergy. Means for a general estimate we do not possess. We must confine our remarks to the metropolis. Seventeen churches in Paris annually receive as perquisites from 120,000 to 150,000 francs each; fifteen churches each from 60,000 to 90,000; eight churches each 240,000. Consequently the Parisian churches in all draw from this source an annual income of about 5,000,000 francs, or 250,000*l.* Hence some idea may be formed of the sum received in fees throughout papal France. Let it be observed that this calculation does not include voluntary donations, gratuities, and douceurs.

This huge amount of property is divided among 40,428 ecclesiastics, of whom 681 are canons, 175 vicars general, 64 bishops, 13 archbishops, 6 cardinals, 1 metropolitan archbishop. Besides this large and well marshalled army, volunteer forces, very numerous and in a high state of discipline, execute the will and promote the designs of the Papacy. There is not a considerable city but has several monasteries, several houses of relief under clerical influence, several male or female corporations. These establishments are vast seminaries which spread colonies over the whole surface of the country. Scarcely is there a village which has not one of these colonies. France is thus occupied as if by a vast military organisation. Carmelites, Benedictines, Trappists, Jesuits, Augustins, Visitandines, Ursulins, Sisters of the Sacred Heart— all the various religious orders of the Roman church, have spread over France like the vermin in Egypt. In order to give a precise idea of the organisation and of the mode of operation of these large forces, we shall indicate the principal religious establishments, whence proceed those swarms of nuns and friars who carry out on all sides the doctrine and the influence of Popery. In this list we include not monasteries; they will come afterwards.

Nunneries.	Chief Place.	Number.	Department.
Sisters of St. Joseph	Clermont . . .	30	
The same	Lyon.		
Sisters of the Christian Schools of Pity.	St. Sauveur - le - Vi- comte.	30	
Nuns of the Sacred Heart . . .	Coutances . . .	34	
Sisters of Providence	Portieux	140	
The same	Grenoble.		
The same	Langres	105	
Sisters of Christian Doctrine .	Nancy	420	
Hospitalières of our gracious Lady .	Aix	11	
Daughters of Wisdom	St. Laurent-sur-Sèvres.		
Hospitalières Sisters	Besançon.		
Sisters of Charity du Monitoire .	Bourges	92	
Sisters of St. Paul	Chartres	12	
Sisters of the Cross	Limoges.		
The Saviour's Nuns	La Souterraine.		
Sisters of Mary-Joseph	Dorat	18	} Haute Vienne.
Sisters of the Incarnate Word . .	Azérable.		
Community of Christian Union .	Fontenay-le-Comte.		
Daughters of Wisdom	St. Laurent-sur-Sèvres	176	} Vendée.
Ursulins of Jesus	Chavagnes-en-Paillers	45	
Sisters of the Sacred Heart of Jesus and of Mary.	Mormaison . . .	39	
Sisters of the Good Saviour . .	Caen.		
Sisters of Mercy	Angers.		
Work of the Good Shepherd . .	Do.		
Sisters of Charity of the Congrega- tion of Evron.	Evron	256	} Mayenne.
Sisters of Charity of the Congrega- tion of Providence.	Ruilli-sur-Loire .	90	
Sisters of the Congregation of the infancy of Jesus and of Mary.	Metz	40	
Sisters of St. Charles	Nancy	282	
Sisters of Charity and Christian In- struction of Nevers.	Nevers	240	
Sisters of the infant Jesus . . .	Puy	15	
Sisters of Providence	Ligny-le-Châlet .	43	Yonne.
The same	Nancy	207	
Sisters of Christian Doctrine . .	Do.	107	
Sisters of the presentation of the holy Virgin.	Tours	94	
Sisters of the Trinity	Valence.		
Sisters of the holy Sacrament . .	Romans	. .	Drôme.
Sisters of the Presentation . . .	Bourg St. Andéol.		
Sisters of the holy Infancy.			
Sisters of St. Maur	Privas.		
Nunneries in France .	. . .	2526	

Our list, it will have been seen, is incomplete. The number of establishments of several orders we have not been able to ascertain. Of some the numbers are great: for instance, 'The Work of the Good Shepherd' has establishments everywhere. At least 500 may be added to our total, making 3000 nunneries or insti-

tutions of female ecclesiastics in France. Equally unable are we
to report the number of members in each of these 3000 establishments. The number is considerable. There are 500 'Sisters of
the Trinity;' there are 400 'Sisters of the Holy Sacrament;'
there are 1000 'Sisters of the Presentation.' If we assign on an
average 20 members to each house, we have then another *corps
d'armée* of 60,000 nuns. Yet our list does not include the
capital. At Paris we find—

> Sisters of our Lady de Bon-Secours.
> Infirmerie Marie-Thérèse.
> Sisters of the Sacred-Heart.
> Sisters of St. Michel.
> Sisters of St. Thomas de Villeneuve.
> Sisters Augustines Anglaises.
> Sisters of St. Vincent de Paul.

At least there are 30 convents in the capital. Of one order
alone, namely that of Vincent-de-Paul, there are more than 500
members.

If we now refer to ecclesiastics of the other sex, we need, for
the metropolis, go no farther than the 'General Institute of the
Brothers of Christian Doctrine,' members of which cover the face
of the land. The number of monasteries in France is reported
at 565; multiplying this number by 20, as the probable number
of individuals in each house, we obtain 11,300 monks in France.
Our materials supply the following summary of

The Forces of the Papacy in France.

83	Diocesan Seminaries.
1	Adjoint Seminary.
1	Metropolitan.
188	Ecclesiastical Colleges.
16	Houses of Retreat.
565	Monasteries.
1,012	Pensionnats for Young Ladies.
939	Alms-Houses and Infirmaries.
3,379	Colonies of Nuns.
765	Monkish Schools.
48	Home Missionary Colleges.
40,428	Priests, including Bishops, &c.
60,000	Nuns.
11,300	Monks.
37,013	Parishes and Parish Churches.
80	Episcopal Sees.
240	Diocesan Edifices.
250,000*l.*	Fees in Paris.
2,100,000*l.*	Annual Grant to the Clergy.

These forces serve the papacy in various manners and degrees. The alms-houses and infirmaries are not directly religious establishments; but visited and beset as they are by monks, nuns, and priests, they are, for the most part, in each case a focus and workshop of proselytism. In general this vast army has but one object, namely, the occupation of the entire land in the name of the pope. With a view to that end the several bands, each one duly organised and disciplined, are distributed over the face of the country, with a special reference and adaptation in all instances to the special wants of each locality. The land is mapped out into districts. In the chief place of each district are the seminary or secular college, the ecclesiastical college, monasteries, convents. From the chief places and from the head establishments branches are propagated to the several towns of the district, and thence proceed into the villages and hamlets, minor colonies, or individuals. All these forces are under the hand of the bishop, by whom they have been organised and distributed, and the bishop with his clergy is under the control of the pope.

It may be added, that this vast army of spiritual force is nevertheless not so great as was that by which France was possessed immediately before the revolution, when (in 1757) there were in that country 40,000 curés, 60,000 other priests, 100,000 monks, 100,000 nuns; that is 300,000 persons, or 1 in 67 of the whole population. The actual amount shows however a very great and rapid increase, for in 1829 the clergy of France reckoned 108,000 members, or 1 in every 280 inhabitants. How far the augmentation of the material strength has brought a corresponding increase of spiritual and social influence, is a question which requires mature consideration.

The metaphor of an army badly represents the action of the papal forces in France. Rather may these priests, friars, nuns, brethren, and sisters of all names and kinds be figured as a hive of bees, each employed in his own task; or, as scattered bodies of husbandmen, each tilling his own field and his own plot; or again, as a universal police, of which every individual watches with eyes broad open to detect and apprehend all persons who misdemean themselves in act, in word, aye, even in thought or emotion. But it is only an enumeration of objects that can show how minute is the subdivision of labour, how efficient is the general operation. Nothing is more skilfully calculated and laid out than the entire task which Rome imposes. That task literally embraces the whole of human life; it takes human life in all its conditions and at all ages—the infant, the youth, the adult, the aged; whether sick or in health; whether poor or rich; whether coming into the world or leaving the world; whether in hope of heaven

or in fear of hell; whether in the enjoyment of the smile of the
Church, or under the terror of its frown. By means of the wires
which he has laid down, and which run like bodily fibres through
the whole social frame, the priest, the bishop, the metropolitan,
the pope, can at his will delight or terrify, arouse or soothe, forgive or condemn, pour forth 'airs from heaven,' or 'blasts from
hell;' in a word, smite or heal a parish, a diocese, a province,
a whole nation. First in the series of works performed by the
French clergy, regular and secular, male and female, are their
religious associations, having 'edification,' that is Romanism, for
their aim. Thus, in the year 1848 there was formed with a
special view to the extension of popery, what is termed a 'work
of prayer,' the express purpose of which was to entreat the Almighty on behalf of the salvation of France. This society originated at Saint-Brieux (Côtes du Nord), numbers 40,000 members.
In the same class may be placed the numerous brotherhoods
attached to the different churches. In Paris almost every parish
has its brotherhood. The most important is that of the Sacred
Heart, which some years ago had 50,000 adherents.

Education is an object of special care with these associations.
The work is commenced in the tender and impressible years of
infancy. A very large number of schools are under the direction
of the brethren and sisters of Christian Doctrine. To these must
be added public nurseries and infant asylums. There are in all
parts of France boarding-establishments for girls whose parents
or guardians are possessed of property, such as ' the House of the
Sacred Heart,' at Paris, or the 'Demoiselles d'Instruction,' at
Puy. Small seminaries, free colleges have been multiplied on
every side. They are still multiplying.

While the instruction of childhood and youth receives the
greatest attention, the aged find asylums ready to give them welcome, and to stamp Romanism on their souls. An an example
take the 'Infirmerie de Marie Thérèse,' at Angers. The Hos-
pitalières nuns and the Sisters of Charity fill the poor-houses. A
large number of houses of refuge belong not to the municipalities
but specially to the Romish church. There the sick among the
poor fall under the influence of its officials. For the sick among
the wealthy it has the 'Institut des Sœurs de Notre Dame de
Bon-Secours,' in Paris, where are trained nurses who attend in-
valids at their own homes, and minister at the same time bitter
herbs and bitter doctrine; relieving the body while they enslave
the soul. 'The House of the Good Saviour,' at Caen, may be
taken as the model of the institutions which Catholicism has set
up for the relief of mental maladies. Similar provision is made
by it for the blind and for the deaf and dumb. There are few

prisons which have not their corps of 'Sisters of Charity.' To the
service of captives the 'Sisters of Mary-Joseph' are specially devoted. Everywhere has Romanism opened places of refuge for
women of impure life who are repentant. This branch of practical
benevolence is specially in the hands of the 'Sisters of the Good
Shepherd,' at Angers, who have affiliated institutions in all parts
of France. Catholicism thinks not only of those who have fallen,
but of those also who are in danger of falling. For their assistance workshops are set up and superintended by some of the very
numerous class of 'Sisters.' Infants who are without parents
receive a large share of their kind attention. There are even
houses in which servants out of place find a home. Other establishments make it their business to procure situations for girls and
young women.

Thus for all the needs and all the sufferings of social life a
provision is secured. Equally is preparation made to welcome
those who, under the influence of Catholicism, wish to quit the
world and seek peace in seclusion; to them a refuge is offered by
the 565 monasteries which rise on the soil of France. This is not
all; those who desire to leave society without entering a monas-
tery, are served agreeably to their wishes, in what are called
'houses of retirement,' such as that of Fontenay-le-Comte, in
Vendée.

In a word, all the various works of benevolence which in England and other Protestant countries are undertaken and performed
by the general spirit of Christian goodness, both lay and clerical,
undertaken and performed by the Christian community in general,
are in France in the hands of what may be called a special religious corporation; are almost exclusively ecclesiastical in character
and object; are in aim, tendency, and result far more spiritual
than temporal. This is only to say in other words that in France
benevolence is polluted with sectarianism; that pure benevolence
has scarcely any existence there; that the papacy turns to its own
account all means of usefulness, and all the sympathies and cha-
rities of the human soul. 'Be a papist, and you shall want nothing; or if you are not a papist, I will minister to you in the
hope of making you one.' The chief aim, the preponderating
aim, almost the only aim of benevolence in France is conversion
to popery or confirmation in popery; and did not its administra-
tors hope by their charity to add something to the triumphs of
their Church, the ignorant might remain in ignorance, the sick
would suffer without alleviation, and the dying depart in drear
solitude. Surpassingly fertile in resources is the Propaganda of
Rome. No means does it leave untried. Its zeal is no less ardent
than various.

It has other arms. As yet we have spoken of what may in
England be termed professional efforts, the efforts, that is, of persons who in some sense have entered into Holy Orders and belong
to the clergy. There are other labours in which lay-power is
put into requisition. Thus at Metz we find a '*Military* Association,' whose office consists in giving religious instruction to
soldiers; a 'brotherly society,' which provides the poor with warm
clothing; a 'Society of Maternal Charity,' which assists women
in child-birth. In most towns of France there are institutions
with similar objects. Specially in Paris has this union of benevolence and proselytism grown into large dimensions. We
mention as an instance the 'Society of Saint Vincent de Paul,'
founded among young people. The society is divided into 'Conferences,' each Conference is composed of from 40 to 50 members.
There are 50 Conferences in Paris, severally attached to the
parishes of the city. The association is daily spreading over
France: its object is to relieve the poor. The President of each
Conference every year visits the poor of his parish or district.
Garments are given away; linen is lent. If the poor man has a
cause at law, he is furnished with advice and legal aid. The chief
aim, however, is proselytism. The Society proclaims that while
succouring the poor, its wish is to bring back men to Catholic
piety; such is the final purpose of those visits, those gifts, those
cares. With that view it receives into its arms children at the
earliest age; it follows them with an attentive eye; it takes every
means to inspire them with devotional sentiments. Of apprentices
it becomes the patron; every Sunday they are gathered together
and instructed. The whole day long suitable officials have apprentices under their care; in the morning they are conducted to
mass; there they receive instruction specially fitted to their wants;
nor is even recreation or amusement forgotten: morning schools,
evening schools are opened where they are required. Another of
the labours of the Society of 'Saint Vincent de Paul' is the rec-
tification of the illicit marriages so numerous in Paris. It has
also a branch called the branch of the 'Holy Family,' whose
office it is to collect together in families those who are visited,
in order that as families the people may attend mass and
receive religious admonition; here, too, interest is blended with
instruction. The Society has moreover established 'Libraries for
the Poor;' it publishes religious books of various kinds. No
means is spared to raise the necessary funds; for that purpose
private canvasses are made, charity sermons are preached, even
lotteries are not disdained.

The children of the world are still wiser than the children of
the light. Books overthrew Popery in France; by books, its

advocates feel, Popery must be restored. 'Captain Sword' is, in his way, no less useful than necessary. Nevertheless the services of 'Captain Pen' cannot be safely dispensed with. Hence the zeal with which the production and the propagation of pamphlets and small books are carried on among the contrivances of Papal proselytism in France. Look at the Society of *Saint Victor de Plancy*, 'for the diffusion of good books.' Founded in 1846, in the diocese of Arras, after four years of preparation, it enjoyed special patronage from the Cardinal de Latour d'Auvergne. In March, 1847, it received the sanction of the Pope, who bestowed special indulgences on those who should labour for its advancement. At the present moment it has the patronage of 42 archbishops and bishops. The society commands the power which ensues from a capital of 600,000 francs. It has a vast workshop at Plancy. Its founder, M. Collin de Plancy, conceived the idea at the moment of his conversion in 1841. On that day, in order to repair the evil he had done while fighting on the side of the free-thinkers, he vowed to God to consecrate the rest of his days to the propagation of 'good books.' 'He has faithfully kept his word.' Two works by this gentleman stand at the head of this Article. Those two works circulate under all the sanction they can derive from episcopal authority. They certainly offer a curious contrast to the publications thought fit for the English people by the conductors of 'The Society for the Diffusion of Useful Knowledge.' The very title of de Plancy's book suffices to excite a feeling of commiseration towards a people for whom such an intellectual diet is provided; and yet what diet so well fitted to imbue the heart with superstitious fears, to prepare the mind for any amount of credulity, and so serve the purpose of ecclesiastical and civil despots? We translate the title in full :—

'Infernal Dictionary, or Universal Repertory of the Beings, the Personages, the Books, the Facts, the Things which pertain to Apparitions; Divinations; Magic; Intercourse with Hell; to the Demons; to Sorcerers; to the Occult Sciences; to Magical Books; to the Cabbala; to the Spirits of the Elements; to the Great Work; to Prodigies; to Errors and Prejudices; to Impostures; to the Arts of the Gipsies; to Different Superstitions; to Popular Tales; to Prognostics; and generally to all False, Marvellous, Surprising, Mysterious and Supernatural Beliefs: by J. Collin de Plancy. 3rd Edition, with 250 new articles.'

'The work of the Holy Infancy' is one of the most recent and one of the most flourishing of the means of internal proselytism which the papacy employs in France. On Sunday the 4th of Jan. 1852, a great festival of this society was held in the town of Nancy. All the children connected with the branches of the institution in the vicinity were present. After the archbishop had said mass, a short instructive address was delivered to the children, and a collection was made towards the support of the work. The cathedral was literally filled with little children, who had been brought thither as if under the influence of rivalry by 'Brethren of the Christian Doctrine,' lay instructors, 'Sisters of the Christian Doctrine,' 'Sisters of Saint Charles,' 'Sisters of Saint Vincent de Paul,' and mistresses of boarding schools.

'This multitude of French children, thus welcomed, praying to the child Jesus, and bringing their little offerings for other unhappy children in infidel (Protestant) countries, presented a truly touching sight, and many Christian hearts were moved thereby. The work of the Holy Infancy extends everywhere with a marvellous rapidity. From France it now sends its beneficent branches to the British Isles, Belgium, Holland, the Rhenish Provinces, Bavaria, Poland, Italy, Switzerland, Spain, Asia, North and South America,' &c.[a]

A few days after a similar festival was held at Blois, where nearly two thousand children were gathered together.

'After the holy mass, during which a short address was delivered to this infantine auditory, they proceeded to the most attractive part of the ceremony, the determination by lot of those of the Associates who should be sent into China as missionaries, and what should be given by them to all those thousands of infants whom they should have the happiness to baptise every year.'[b]

Let the reader peruse the following circular addressed by the Archbishop of Paris to his clergy, under date Jan. 18, 1852 :—

'Reverend Sir,—Among the very numerous labours of love established in our diocese, that of the " Orphans of the Cholera," is, without contradiction, one of the most important, and one which deserves all our care. In truth, how should we not be touched with a deep feeling of pity for the lot of that multitude of deserted children, who, after having lost the authors and the support of their days, have no other means of living than the resources of our beneficence? How can we avoid extending to them a helping hand? No, Rev. Sir, we will not repudiate that precious inheritance which Providence has bequeathed to our tenderness, and we will every year renew in favour of these poor orphans, all the efforts of our zeal, all the sacrifices of our pious liberality. For charity, St. Paul tells us, fainteth not; it knows neither relaxation nor discouragement. (1 Cor. xiii.)

'Consequently, with confidence do we renew our appeal to the pitying hearts of our disciples. Our voice we know will be heard. By means of alms put into our hands, and thanks to the intelligent as well as indefatigable zeal of the members of the Committee of the Work, we have been enabled to place in educational establishments, or to assist in their

---

[a] *L'Univers*, Jan., 1852.   [b] Ib., Jan. 25, 1852.

own homes, more than 550 children. It is not only the life of the body which has been preserved for these orphans, but they have received a benefit a thousand times more precious, a moral and religious education, which by nurturing their spirit in truth, preparing their heart for virtue, and forming in them habits of order, industry and piety, has put them in the way to true happiness.

'The period of the Ecclesiastical Year at which we have now arrived, will furnish you, Rev. Sir, in even the mysteries which we honour, the most powerful motives for exciting the generosity of Christian souls. The recollection of an infant God experiencing the infirmities of our nature, as if to train himself for compassion, enduring the severities of poverty, now lying in a manger, now flying in exile,—this picture, so fit to move the hardest hearts, will be set by you before the eyes of your hearers. Cause this divine infant himself to speak; let him solicit the benefactions. He will account as done for himself, that which is done for these little ones; these homeless orphans; those who are his image, and whom he condescends to call his members.

'Our intention then is, that to assist the work of " the Orphans of the Cholera," a general collection shall take place in all the churches and chapels of our diocese, at the morning and evening services, on the day of the Virgin's Purification.'

Whatever may be thought of the result of these efforts, it is impossible not to admire their earnestness; and though the zealotism by which they are prompted must be regretted, and even blamed by Protestants, yet in the religious feelings whence it springs are to be found the chief impulse and the effectual support of these attempts. It may be that a philosophy no less Christian than wise may be compelled to condemn the excess of charity which this zeal displays, and fearing that justice halts where charity runs, be confident that pauperism will spread in the same proportion in which charity is dispensed and accepted. Nevertheless we cannot ourselves assert that we can contemplate all this active beneficence unmoved; and while we are sure that Popery has in these benign exertions selected a very open, easy, and certain avenue to people's hearts, we must regret that Protestantism both in France and in England observes the woes of the humbler classes far too coldly, and need not be surprised if the hearts of many of its adherents are stolen and carried away into the more genial atmosphere of Catholic benevolence. Undoubtedly, Romanism in France has taken the most effectual—perhaps the only effectual—means of winning over the population from the fatuous reveries or monstrous theories of Socialist speculators and revolutionary incendiaries. Wesley is reported to have said that he did not see why the devil should have all the pretty airs. Can any reason be assigned why the worst of religions should display the greatest zeal, and employ the most efficient means? *Fas est et ab hoste doceri.* It is of

special consequence that the motto should be acted on in these
islands, for here, to a great and still increasing extent, the measures of proselytism which have been found to work so well in
France for Romish ends are applied by societies and individuals,
who act not with less effect because, moving under a common
impulse, they work for the most part invisibly. Indeed, the pro-
pagandism which has been recently called into action in France is
only one arm of the immense sea of Catholic zeal which lies round
all the countries of Europe, ever on the point of breaking in on
the land, to carry before it every obstacle. It cannot be too widely
known, it cannot be too deeply impressed on the minds of Protestants, that there exists a widely spread conspiracy on the part
of Catholic powers, which, originated and directed by Jesuitism, is
designed, and night and day labours with all possible resources and
devotedness, to put down mental freedom, to root out Protestantism,
and to make the authority of Rome universal. With special effort
does this conspiracy direct its batteries against England, as being
the stronghold of Protestantism, and as being socially to a great
extent the mistress of the world; in the confident assurance that,
when England has become papal, the conquest of the world will
soon be completed.

The views which the French clergy have entertained, and the
motives by which they have been actuated on this subject, are set
forth in a leading article which appeared in the periodical representative of the Ultramontane party, *L'Univers*, of Jan. 1, 1852:—

'There is an experience which those who have the care of souls find
confirmed every day; namely, the necessity of sanctifying the leisure
hours of the labourer by turning them to some good account, and by
rendering them agreeable. The wish to draw from his habitual pursuits a man addicted to unlawful pleasures, will most frequently prove
abortive, if at the same time you have not devised a means whereby you
may captivate him by enjoyments that are innocent, and that while they
preserve some attraction, do not present the same dangers. When the
domestic sanctuary was held in honour, when in all classes of society,
even in the lowest, the father found his pleasures in the circle of home,
—then, when every Sunday he went to present his children before the
Lord, in order to partake their joy after having partaken their troubles,
instructing them, edifying them, delighting them;—the Church was
able to hold its peace and be satisfied by smiling on what she saw; but
now, when the tavern has taken the place of the church, and when
"friends" stand where the family used to stand, Religion cannot without
grief behold a state of things so deadly in its consequences. Her first
care in recalling the unhappy back into the way of duty, has been to
point out to the labouring man a means for employing his moments of
repose in a useful manner. The spouse of God, who eases the sick
man's couch, the Church, appears in the person of the "Sisters of

Charity," by the bedside of grief; in the person of " the Trinitarian Friar," near him when he is in slavery; everywhere and always she " becomes all things to all men" in order to save souls.   Let us then be assured that in our days she will attempt to enter (so to say) into a concordat with the age, and while she remains unshaken in her doctrine, now, as at all epochs, she will know how to adapt her means of salvation to the exigencies of the times : yes, she will go even to the extreme limits of her conscience, in order to bring back her wandering children to the faith and to good morals.   This is proved by the Evening Schools founded at Rome by our august Pontiff, as well as the special efforts of several monastic orders, and of the secular clergy, with a view to the material and spiritual welfare of the industrious classes.'

We have surveyed the power of Romanism in France, and found it to be immense.   We have reviewed the means by which that power has been attained, and by which its possessors hope to perpetuate and even augment it, and we have seen reason to think those means very efficacious.   Unquestionably, the present condition of Romanism in France has a serious aspect for the religion of the world.   France is a great social power.   The influence of France is felt in the remotest fibre of civilised life.   If France becomes thoroughly and permanently Romish, Rome will have achieved its most brilliant and most valuable victory.   Supported by France, the Pope will advance into the field in better array than ever.   More than once has France in matters of opinion been the dictator of Europe ; and before her example, if she prove really and vitally Catholic, many a Protestant influence will be compelled to bend.

But as yet the whole case is not before the reader.   The political aspect remains to be presented.   The state changes which have recently been effected are no trifles.   In what relation does Romanism stand to them ?

Accustomed as many have been to regard France as an infidel country, they will not be prepared to receive the statement which we are about to make, namely, that the social convulsions of France within the last century have turned on the pivot of religion. On her soil the two great powers of Faith and No-faith have so fought their deadly battles, as to involve in the result the concussion of the whole social frame.   Without speaking of earlier convulsions, the dethronement of Louis Philippe was owing to a re-action in the popular mind against Catholicism.   No sooner had the power which threw off that incubus been put into fetters by the present government, than a system was commenced the designed effect of which was the complete restoration of the power of the clergy.   Into that system Louis Napoleon entered with his whole heart.   Seated in the presidential chair, he looked around for conservative agencies. Religion he saw at his feet in an imploring attitude. He knew her vital potency, and raising her from her lowly position, took her into his embrace; not because he loved her, but because he loved himself, and knew he dared not make her his enemy. Shortly his ulterior views—views long cherished—began to rise in his mind in definite and most attractive forms. The imperial crown dazzled the eyes of his imagination. ' A republic with imperial forms and insignia '—this dream of the disappointed uncle haunted the ambitious nephew's mind. He resolved to convert the fancy into a reality. But a crown without the anointing hand of the Pope!—a pure impossibility, at least in the case of one who had not the staff of military renown on which to rest. The Pope must be gained. To gain the Pope it was necessary to promote Popery. Therefore its adherents and advocates were taken into favour. Of a sudden, and much to their surprise, the army of Jesuits, so often ignominiously treated in France and driven from its borders, found themselves under the sunshine of court smiles and patronage. ' A new era!' they exclaimed. A turning point in the history of France it was; and of that juncture they determined to make the utmost. Forthwith they let forth into open day all their forces :—

> ' ac venti, velut agmine facto,
> Qua data porta, ruunt, et terras turbine perflant.
> Incubuere mari, totumque a sedibus imis
> Una Eurusque Notusque ruunt, creberque procellis
> Africus, et vastos volvunt ad littora fluctus.
> Insequitur clamorque virûm, stridorque rudentum.
> *Eripiunt subito nubes cælumque diemque*
> *Teucrorum ex oculis; ponto nox incubat atra.*
> Intonuere poli, et crebris micat ignibus æther ;
> *Præsentemque viris intentant omnia mortem.'*

Not without a full consciousness of the support he should receive from the Church did Louis Napoleon venture on the daring and sanguinary step of the 2nd of December. But his confidence rested on a broader and deeper basis than the Eurus, the Notus, or the Africus of Romanism. Useful in the turmoil and conflict of a revolution, the subalterns of the Church could neither lay down the plan of the battle nor greatly contribute to secure a victory. Royal Æolus must be secured. Restored to Rome by republican troops, the Pope repaid the service with warm support. Another power could not be disregarded,—the power of the pen. Intending to crush that power in all its adverse manifestations, the ruler of France was very willing to profit by its displays in his favour. And, alas! but too easy was it to hire the crowd of Parisian penmen, who get their daily bread out of the fickle and ever varying air of the French metropolis. Men so small, however, could not have repaid their employer, had they not entered into the labours of others. By two minds of distinction had the crisis been prepared.

Joseph de Maistre, armed with a style at once cutting, biting, highly coloured and picturesque, placed himself before a public with whom style is almost every thing, as the champion of the theocratic society of the middle ages. He fell on the modern notions of liberty and progress in a manner which Frenchmen can least resist. He assailed them with ridicule; he threw scorn upon them; he treated them insultingly. It was Voltaire in a Jesuit's cloak. It was Voltaire undoing Voltaire's work. With equal ardour and with full enthusiasm did he celebrate the absolute authority of King and Pope. Even persecution of all kinds found favour in his eyes, and called forth the admiring tokens of his pen. Having confounded and derided ideas, he assailed institutions. Alas for the republican forms of government which had sprung from the Great Revolution; he overwhelmed them with sarcasm; he handled them as a boxer in his wrath handles a retiring adversary. Read his work on *The Pope;* read his *Evenings at Saint-Petersburg.*

Bonald, less of an enthusiast but more of a metaphysician than De Maistre, professed the same doctrines and aimed at the same objects. Especially did he give them the support of a new basis, derived from his study of languages. He set out on the principle that speech must have been immediately given by God to man. But if speech was given, ideas, of which speech is the representative, were also given: the shell contains the kernel. Hence truth comes from withont. Truth originally rested on the authority of the God who gave it. But our truth is only the old truth with augmentations. Consequently all truth comes from a higher source, namely, God; and depends on the authority of that source—that is, God and his ministers. Here, then, is the function of the Church, and here is its justification. The Church is in God's stead to man. Consequently the Church is the teacher, man the pupil. The very ideas imply supremacy and submission. And as the Church represents God in morals, so does the King represent God in politics. Their law is God's law; their will is God's will. Each perfect and supreme, the two when united are the voice of God and the power of God on earth.

The propounding of these slavish doctrines at first struck society into a maze. It became giddy, it staggered. Recovering from the amazement, it felt repelled and disgusted. In that state of the public mind liberalism gained influence and began to make head. But the intoxicating draughts were renewed. Supplied freely, they began to bewilder. At last the public mind, fully intoxicated, fell into a deep stupor, or was seized with spasmodic ravings. The hour had come. Here was fear and anguish; there was outrageous extravagance; and there, in the great body of society, stolid indifference. Jesuitism in politics and Jesuitism in religion solemnised their nuptials in the decrees which enslaved a nation, and the firing which carried barricades, decimated districts, and slaughtered innocent and unoffending individuals.

No sooner was the blow struck which converted Louis Napoleon from the president of a free republic into the supreme lord of a dictatorship, than the clergy of France gave in their adhesion to the new order of things, and hastened to lend all their aid to the usurped despotism. At the command of the dictator a *Te Deum* was celebrated in all the Romish churches of France. A formal compliance with the decree was perhaps inevitable; but every thing beyond a perfunctory observance of the ceremony was a gratuitous testimony of favour towards the illegality of the *coup d'état*, the butcheries by which it was attended, and the tyranny and persecution that ensued. In Paris the *Te Deum* was sung in the most imposing manner and amid the most solemn pomp, the archbishop himself, the metropolitan of France, and so the representative of its religion, taking the chief part in the ceremony. On behalf of the selfish dictator, and at the very moment when his hands were reeking with the blood of murdered citizens, whose only crime was their adherence to the laws which their sworn conservator had violated, the papal authorities introduced into the prayer *Domine fac* the ill-omened words Ludovicum Napoleonem (Lord, save Louis Napoleon); and after the completion of the supplication, ' the archbishop gave the benediction of the Holy Sacrament with the censer brilliant with diamonds which the emperor had presented to the metropolitan church.' At the end ' his lordship the archbishop in a procession conducted back to the entrance of the cathedral (Notre Dame) the President of the republic, with the same pomp which had accompanied his reception.' [c]

The following extract from a circular issued on the 1st of January to his clergy by the Cardinal Archbishop of Bourges will illustrate the joy with which the usurpation was witnessed by papal France :—

' Solemn thanksgivings are indeed due to the Most High who has saved us from an immense peril. To testify to him our gratitude for so great a benefit, is to draw down on ourselves new favours.[d] You feel this as well as I, and you will not fail, my Reverend brother, to

---

[c] *L'Univers*, Jan. 5, 1852.

[d] A fine instance of the remark that ' gratitude is a lively sense of favours to come ' !!

inspire with the same sentiment those who are intrusted to your care. Let us together beseech the Lord to finish what he (!) has begun, and for that end to preserve the man of his Providence.'

What a profanation of the holiest words and the most venerable of objects! What a degradation forced on religion, to make her an accessory after the deed of the greatest and most outrageous political crime in the annals of the world!

As might be expected, the news of the revolution was welcomed at Rome. On hearing it, Pius IX. exclaimed, 'Heaven has paid the debt which the Church owed to France!' Why what a pair of religionists have we here!—a Pope thrust on an unwilling people by French bayonets, and an usurper raised to the first step of an imperial throne on the dead bodies of fellow-countrymen whom he had slain, and the merit of the first act so great as to call down from Heaven such special aid as might reward it with successful usurpation. Such, in plain English, is the import of the Pope's joyous words.

An extract from an article in the Jesuits' paper, *L'Univers*, will let the reader know how entirely the usurpation was regarded by the Romish church as the act of God:—

'The truth is, Louis Napoleon has understood at once the strength and the peril of society. With the felicitous audacity of good sense, he put that strength in opposition to that peril. Doubtless he dealt profusely in illegality; he would have committed the greatest wrong, if, instead of being president, he had been a mere steward. But society when in peril gives itself chiefs precisely to commit those acts of illegality. For us we never thought Charles X. perjured, and we are thankful to Louis Napoleon for having been less unfortunate. Revolutionary problems are not solved by legality, they are put an end to by claps of thunder. Only the thunder may come from below or from above. If from below, it bursts forth like the earthquake, overturning everything, setting everything on fire. This was the socialist or parliamentary solution. If from on high, it selects the spot on which it will fall. This is the solution of the 2nd of December. It was instinctively foreseen and desired; it has been universally applauded. The prompt adhesion of the clergy has been ascribed to the influence of M. de Montalembert and that of some other catholics. The advice they gave for that end was very well received, but it was not required. The clergy knew the state of society, and knew what was wanted and what was coming. The clergy saw that bloody tide coming in. The wave which at the last overflowed, appeared to it as the instrument of Providence, and it blessed God who sends whom he pleases and when he pleases. We have had letters from all parts of France. Everywhere sound religious and popular sentiment regards the result as grand and glorious.'[e]

Which of the two is worse in this extract, the bad logic or the

---

[e] *L'Univers,* Jan. 9, 1852.

impiety? They are both Jesuitical; which is nearly the same as to say that they are both very bad.

Unquestionably it is true that Louis Napoleon's *coup d'état* was approved generally by the papal clergy. The moment it was accomplished they saw that the long-desired moment had arrived, and that it was now the time to strike a blow for the restoration of religious despotism. All kinds of tyranny are congenial, and between its patrons there is a tacit sympathy and practical understanding which urge them to act in concert at the right juncture, as for a common object. The clergy of France in consequence threw themselves ardently into the conflict; and, next to Napoleon's fire-arms and bayonets, earned the honour of determining the issue. In every parish and corner of the land they employed all their social and personal influence, and all the awful power which superstition has put into the hands of a Romish priest, in order to prepare men to vote agreeably to their wishes; and when at last the day of election came, the clergy in many instances led their ignorant serfs by hundreds to the poll, holding aloft as an electioneering token the cross, the purest symbol of disinterested pity and love!

Immediately consequent on the President's election and the establishment of his power, Popery began to start into new life, and France manifested a desire to become the most Catholic of Catholic kingdoms. Hitherto that country had preserved for itself no inconsiderable share of religious freedom, in spite of all the aggressive attempts of Rome. 'The liberties of the Gallican church' had been gained by costly sacrifices and numberless efforts. Of those liberties the national mind was proud. France prided herself in being Catholic without being Papal. For a time at least the end of that state of things has come. Popery lifts her head boldly in the land, and Jesuitism walks with brazen front by her side. Rather cautious at the first, they are now as bold as men can be in a bad cause; and certainly they have had great encouragement. The President himself unfurled his banner to them by restoring to the worship of the poor peasant girl the church of the patron saint of Paris, St. Genevieve. With an ardour long unknown the churches became crowded by congregations who, if not pious, were at least of decent behaviour. A host of tracts and pamphlets poured forth from the press, not prohibited to diffuse fatuities, fanaticisms, and superstitions. The Abbé Migne set in rapid motion at Mont-Saint-Rouge the wheels of his immense manufactory of Jesuitical folios, of which, after the rate of one per week, he has promised that some two thousand shall appear—doubtless to the imminent peril of Protestantism, and perhaps of religion too. Even persons of rank and distinction obeyed the general impulse, and idled away an hour in church or chapel.   Marshal Soult died; a religious ceremony was com. manded, and, like a *matinée musicale*, the great world hurried thither.   On the 21st of January masses were performed in all the churches of Paris for the repose of the soul of Louis XVI. The sacred edifices were filled.   'See,' exclaimed the Papacy, ' see how repentant every one is for the crime of 1793.'   Long and severe had been the contest between the University of Paris, together with its affiliated colleges, on the one side, and the Papistic clergy of France, headed by the Jesuits, on the other. The booty was the education of the nation—who should have it in their hands?   Various, aforetime, had the issue been ; and ever as it seemed at an end, did the conflict break out afresh.   Now literature prevailed, and now Jesuitism.   In the recent revolution, the latter, feeling its strength and borrowing courage from suc- cess, swaggered up to the University, and while the former stood there with its hands bound, dealt it a blow from which it will hardly recover.   About the same time ecclesiastical associations and proselyting societies, on whose operations police regulations had imposed some restrictions, obtained from the President, too glad to pay homage to the power by whom he was made, relax- ations and privileges which have given them augmented efficacy as well as fresh activity, and will cause them in number and power speedily to surpass the details we have here supplied.

The material prosperity of ecclesiastical despotism in France is not enduring.   Let it be observed that the prosperity *is* material. Such it appears to be in all the data we have set forth.   Super- ficial is the movement from first to last; or if at all it goes below the surface, it descends not to the heart of society.   It does not mingle with the great under-currents of life.   The movement is superinduced, and it lies like oil on the face of the waters, smoothing them for a moment, but liable to be tossed to the winds when the volcanic forces of the inner soul again burst forth.

The prosperity cannot last because it is antagonistic to the public mind.   In the first place the religious despotism is bound up with the political despotism.   The Pope and Louis Napoleon as supreme powers came in together; they will at least for a time reign together; and they will also, when their hour comes, go out together.   Two suppositions may be made : Louis Napo- leon remains firm in his seat, or he is cast out.   If he remains firm in his seat, he will reduce the power of the church as soon and as much as he can; and in this work he will receive effectual aid from the national sympathies and aversions.   If Louis Napo- leon is cast out, a republic of reality is established, or legitimacy is restored.   Let it be a real republic ; a real republic is the very negation, the positive antithesis of Romish despotism.   Instead of a real republic, suppose a legitimate monarch on the throne. The needs of a lawful sovereign are not so great, so numerous, so urgent, as those of a usurper; and a legitimate monarch, from the very fact of his being legitimate, would rule in unison with national recollections and national attachments; in consequence Gallic Catholicism would once more be in conflict with Roman Catholicism, and the evil spirit of Jesuitism would be expelled. In any contingency the existing clerical despotism would be sure to suffer from that reaction of the public mind which comes from the undue pressures of authority in every land, and nowhere with less uncertainty or more revengeful force than in France. Nor must it be thought that the union which now subsists between the Church and the State in France is cordial as well as friendly. United for the moment by a common necessity, the two have ulterior aims and mean different things. Once seated on the imperial throne, which is his real object, Louis Napoleon would treat Pius *IX.* with as little ceremony as his uncle treated Pius *VII.* The nephew imitating, would, in all probability, caricature the uncle here as in other things, and the present Pope might find himself a prisoner in France even at the moment when with his saintly hand he had placed the imperial crown on his patron's brows. On the other hand, the Church has no affection for Louis Napoleon. It is true she is now hand in hand with him; but while her hand is in his, her heart and her eye look and long in another direction. Her ultimate object is the restoration of legitimacy. With a man-made President or Emperor she has no sympathies—she can have no sympathies. Holding Kingship, like Priestship, to be of Divine origin and Divine right, she owes allegiance to one sovereign—one alone. Louis Napoleon is to her a mere makeshift, with whom, for want of a better master, she politically puts up, hoping, by his means, to gain power to bring back the rightful heir. In that purpose she may succeed; but no small adroitness does she require in the part she has to play. The Count de Chambord has issued commands to the effect that his friends should keep themselves free from the impure contact of adhesion to the ruling power. But the Church is salaried by the State. Thus drawn in two opposite directions, the Church tries to keep a medium path. Hating the basis of his power, she supports Napoleon; revering his claims, she practically disowns Henry. Her heart and her hand go the reverse way. What wonder if in the consequent confusion she make a mistake; if, loving the rightful heir much, she serve the occupant of his inheritance less; and if the suspicions which would ensue should engender coldness, and coldness lead to alienation. Then the Prince-President, no longer playing at religion, throws off the mask, and threatens, like his uncle, to turn Protestant, meanwhile driving Jesuitism out of the land.

The present religious movement must be short lived also because it is factitious. Evidence of the assertion may be found among the details already given. Other evidence is at hand. For instance, miracle-mongering has been revived. We do not mean to charge with known falsehood all who are concerned in the frauds or delusions with which Romish writings have recently abounded. Many, we dare say, are dupes of their own fancies and their own desires. But what we wish to mark is, that just at the nick of time when they are wanted prodigies make their bow. If sent for, they could not have arrived more seasonably. Delay, indeed, there has been, but this delay has not arisen from the want of urgent messengers. If miracles in some cases have not come, miracles have been well advertised for. All the excitements of the papal system have been put into play. From Rome, as a centre, the strings of superstition, of old memories, of intense bigotry, of fear, of hope, in all parts, and especially in France, have been pulled, and pulled sometimes with a twitch of impatience. Books full of wonderful stories are in circulation; miraculous tales are recited from the pulpit; religious processions are multiplied; sacred spots are visited; holy relics are displayed; every thing is done by which the imaginations of the ignorant may be made to teem with those fancies which, being projected outwardly, become prodigies. In certain excited states of the public mind prodigies are, so to say, a natural product. A diseased condition becoming for the time a normal condition, produces correspondent effects with unerring certainty. Wishes then assume the shape of realities; fears take a corporal form in some hobgoblin; and even the palsied limb is made rigid and pliable under the vital energy thrown into it by intense and concentrated mental power.

Were it seemly for us to occupy our pages with ridiculous stories, we could abundantly supply instances and details of the efforts which have been made to get up miracles. It must suffice, however, to mention one or two more of the special means employed. The worship of the Virgin has for this purpose been copiously drawn upon, and no means have been spared to kindle thereon and thereby the sensuous and inflammable imaginations of the South. Then a jubilee was proclaimed, offering full pardon of all sins to the faithful and obedient, and special advantages to such as turned to profit the superstitious capital thus supplied. Besides, a speciality has been given to every usual ceremony. The exhibition in Rome at Christmas of the holy relics there preserved of the birth of Jesus and his manger was trumpeted forth as a timely corroboration of the belief of the believing, and a suitable rebuke of the unbelief of the unbelieving; though the event and all connected with it is a part of the ordinary routine of Rome's superstitious observances. The Queen of Spain became a mother; the Pope sent her a set of baby-linen on which he had bestowed his benediction. The two events are common enough; and not long since the fear of ridicule would have made even Jesuit writers throw over the present of his holiness the discreet veil of silence. But times are changing; there is something to be hoped for from self-glorification, and therefore Rome writes thus:—

'On the 4th of January the Holy Father blessed in his private chapel, a set of baby-linen destined for the young princess which the Queen of Spain has just brought forth. The benediction took place in the presence of the palatine cardinals, the prelates of the court, and of the ambassador plenipotentiary from her Catholic Majesty to the Holy See.

'Touching is the custom which this ceremony calls to mind. It goes back to the ages most deeply impressed with the Catholic spirit:—to those ages when *sovereigns willingly lowered the pride of their crown before* THE SUPERIOR MAJESTY *of the pontifical tiara,* and like persons of private rank, asked from the Vicar of Jesus Christ a benediction, both on the government of their kingdoms, and the members of their families:—happy time when faith was the soul of the world, and bent every brow before its empire.

'Spain, so deeply catholic, could not allow a tradition to become extinct, so Christian and so conformed to the pious sentiments which particularly distinguished its sovereigns. The Queen Isabella, in spite of the misfortunes of the times, and the convulsions which have shaken the church in her country, remembered this custom, always dear to the Queens of Spain. She therefore entreated the pope to bless the linen with which the young princess, granted by heaven to her ardent prayers, was to be clothed. With his usual kindness the Holy Father gave a favourable reception to so pious a request, and a magnificent bundle has been sent by his Holiness to the Spanish Queen. Nothing can equal the richness and beauty of the objects chosen to make up this royal present. The linen is of incomparable fineness; the lace of the greatest value; the coverlets of the royal cradle are admirably embroidered in gold; but the most precious object is a reliquary of the richest and most elegant workmanship. It contains a considerable piece of the holy cradle of our Lord, which has been preserved in the church of "St. Mary the greater," called from this circumstance "the cradle-church." This will be an inestimable treasure for the young princess, and the most precious among those which are connected with her birth.

'In the days of anarchy in which we live, in the midst of this universal contempt for authority and for the sovereign majesty, it is of consequence to call attention to the high esteem in which the Church has always held the person and the power of catholic monarchs. Immediately on the birth of a prince or princess destined by inheritance one day or other to carry the royal sceptre, the church surrounds the cradle with benedictions: in some sort it consecrates the clothes which are to cover its delicate limbs, and protect its tender life against the dangers of the first months: it puts under the special protection of heaven this creature so frail, and yet so precious in a religious point of view and for the happiness of the people; it thus gives its most striking token of the respect it has for those whom God destines to become the pastors of his people, and the heads of a part of his earthly kingdom. Once more, it seems to us that this is a lesson very well suited to our wants; may we profit by it, and learn that the depositaries of power have a right to all our respect. There is no doctrine more needful to be restored in our days. This is the foundation of society and of states; this is the surest preservative against the revolutionary spirit which has so long tormented Europe."[f]

What maudlin have we here! Blest baby-clothes a successful antagonist to revolution! Did we not truly describe the present reactionary movement as artificial? What! is there any thing sound, any thing manly, any thing sensible, any thing natural, in this mawkish eulogy put forth in France at the most seasonable moment to encourage the President and outshame the opponents of his power? And what must be the state of that man's mind who could write and put his name to drivelling such as we have forced ourselves to translate? No, no!—in such a state of mind there is nothing that Protestantism need fear: the only fear—and of this there is great fear—is that trumpery of the kind may so damage religion as to produce ere long infidelity as barren and as mocking as any that has gone before.

Moreover, the movement cannot last, because it is of foreign origin. It is not native in its growth. It did not spring spontaneously out of the French heart. It is no outward expression of a deeply felt necessity. Whatever flowers or fruit it bears, the plant is an exotic. Not only does the plant come from abroad, but it has been forced on the French nation. Introduced among them most stealthily, it is contraband. Jesuitism has been smuggled into France, first under the frock of the priest, and then under the gown of the President. Forced on the acceptance of the French, it has been equally forced on their retention. The hand that was opening to cast the hateful thing away, has been seized by the stronger hand of the law, and with a merciless gripe compelled to hold what it has.

And what is this foreign gift? It is Ultramontanism. The word is a revelation as well as a proof to those who are conversant with the history of France. Yes, it is that Ultramontanism which is among the deepest dislikes of the French heart, and which can by no possibility take root therein. In France, Catholicism has

---

[f] *L'Univers,* Jan. 25, 1852.

life in the national life. Catholicism has entered into the system, and been appropriated by its organs. But French Catholicism differs totally from Spanish or Italian Catholicism. And it differs just on those points in which France has ever been ready to differ with Rome. Catholicism, as a religion of the senses, suits the Frenchman, who lives a sensuous existence in the light and joy of his own 'Belle France.' But the Frenchman is a descendant of the *Francs;* and the very name *Francs* shows how freedom is in the heart's blood of the nation. Without liberty, religion has no charms for a Frenchman. Hence that warfare of France with Rome, by which the French church wrested out of the Pope's hands the liberties to which neither the Spaniard nor the Italian of old aspired, and the refusal of which constitutes the very essence of Ultramontanism. Ere the present religious movement in France can sink into the heart of the nation, one of two very unlikely things must take place,—either the genius of the French people must become totally different, or Jesuitism must form an alliance with freedom. It is no answer to this remark to say that France is now held in fetters of iron. The despotism of a few months does not blot out the testimony of centuries. The French love freedom both in church and state ; and freedom in both they will ere long enjoy.

Even at this moment a violent struggle is going on against the attempt to inoculate France with the Ultramontane virus. No sooner had the political horizon been cleared of the smoke of the President's fire-arms than the Jesuitical party began to assail the classics, both ancient and modern, and to call for the introduction into colleges and schools, as manuals of instruction, of selections from the ecclesiastical fathers. The old battle of the ancients against the moderns and the moderns against the ancients was renewed, and is now being fought over again in France. L'Abbé Gaume, with the aid of his pamphlet *Le Ver Rongeur,* not only of a sudden finds himself a notoriety, but has the questionable distinction of dividing French episcopacy into two camps. The respective forces are led by the Bishop of Arras, who supports Gaume and his lite-rary barbarism, and the Bishop of Orleans, who opposes the same. In this issue once more the merits of Homer, Virgil, Demosthenes, Cicero, the merits of Bossuet, Corneille, and Racine, are a moot point. According to the Ultramontanists, not only the pagan authors must be damned for not having been Catholics, but for the same reason their books must be put under the ban, together with those of their French imitators. In education neither the one nor the other must any longer hold a place. Still more, according to the same authorities it is not very certain that St. Thomas Aquinas is not, as a literary model, far preferable to

Plutarch or Tacitus. It is, however, an undoubted fact that the reign of Louis XIV. was less glorious than the reign of St. Louis ; and the authors of what has been called the Augustan epoch are inferior to the writers of the middle ages. The *Univers* declares that that period was the grand epoch of intelligence ; nay, more, that then happiness was more generally diffused in all classes of society than at any other time. The fight grows warm :—

> Les volumes sans choix à la tête jetés,
> Sur le perron poudreux volent de tous côtés ;
> Là, près d'un Guarini, Térence tombe à terre ;
> Et Xénophon dans l'air heurte contre un Laserre.
> Oh ! que d'écrits obscurs, de livres ignorés,
> Furent en ce grand jour de la poudre tirés.

Indeed the points at issue are deeper than they seem. The Jesuits wish to thrust themselves into the schools, in order to suppress Gallicanism, make Ultramontanism triumphant, and so establish their own ascendancy. They aim at nothing less than to roll back the chariot-wheels of society some eight or ten centuries—the more the better, provided always the carriage keeps at a distance from the days of the spirit of Jesus and his apostles. On the other side the French people, though somewhat mystified with the learned dust raised in this scuffle, are not a little displeased that their literary Olympus should be assailed by these ecclesiastical Titans, and are very averse to renounce the heart-homage which they have paid to Fenelon, Boileau, and Voltaire. The glory of the French nation is in one of its aspects identified with the glory of its literature. *Honi sont qui mal y pense.* Some of the French clergy are awakening to the danger of the extremes ventured on by the Ultramontanists. They have grown timid ; the game is too high, the stakes are too large. They are afraid of committing the interests of religion on the cast of the theological dice-box. Their fear is justified. Ultramontanism, even in France, is a game which none but ecclesiastical *roués* would dare to play. It is indeed inconceivable that a great people should allow their children to be robbed of the privilege of reading and studying its own immortal authors.

It would be easy to give other particulars in which the Court of Rome, or the Jesuitism by which it is ruled, manifests its hatred of liberty. To social liberty in general it is adverse. To the progress of which that social liberty is at once the cause and the guarantee it is adverse. To all free speech it is adverse. To a free Bible it is adverse—nay, to any Bible at all. The Bible societies are as hateful to the Court of Rome as is the press. We could load our pages with proofs : they are, alas ! only too abundant. But they would only be echoes of the following extract from the Encyclical Letter of Gregory XVI. :—

‘ Experience has shown from the earliest times that the states which became distinguished by their power, perished solely by this evil, namely, the immoderate liberty of opinions, licence in discourse, and the love of novelties. To that source is referable that deadly liberty which cannot be regarded with too much horror, the liberty of publishing what any one may please. What man retaining his senses would say that poisons ought to be allowed to be dispensed freely, to be sold, to be publicly offered, nay, to be even drunk? From the infected source of indifferentism flows that erroneous and absurd maxim, or rather *that piece of madness, namely, that the state ought to secure and guarantee to every one liberty of conscience.*’

It is thus seen that Rome is set in direct opposition to the spirit and tendencies of the age. While the spirit of the age is proceeding in one direction, Rome is going in the opposite. How can they meet? How can they agree? The two are rival powers; the two are antagonists in actual combat; no common ground have they; no points of union; no mutual sympathies. The war is a war of extermination.

And not only with the tendencies of the age is Rome in conflict, but with the essential laws of our nature and of social life. One of those laws involves improvement and progress as a condition of existence. Every moment old things become effete and pass away, while all things become new. Age is smitten with torpor, palsy, and decay. This is true of institutions and modes of thought as well as human frames. Forbid renewal, you forbid the perpetuation of life. Say there shall be no progress, you say there shall be no existence. In attempting to stereotype the present, you do what you can to render it as barren as the rock. Rome, then, is in conflict with human nature; Rome is in collision with God’s providence. What will the end be? ‘ Rome shall perish.’

The antagonism of which we have spoken has within the last few years been thrown out in bold relief. While Rome was pressed down by the iron hand of the Emperor of the French, she assumed a meek and quiet aspect and humbled her pretensions. And after Napoleon had expiated his own crimes on a barren rock, Rome stood in awe of the spirit of freedom which raised a throne in almost every European nation. And it was only when liberty seemed again in peril, and when despotism seemed once more to have a prospect of rule, that Rome became first bold, and then daring, and at last set up for the universal mistress of the world. Then the Jesuits were recalled and the Inquisition was restored. Then began the deadly conflict in which Europe is now engaged, and which in all probability will be fought out on the territory of France.

Thus we see that Catholicism has become Romanism, and Romanism exists now in its intensest form. In this intense form it is that popery is incompatible with civil and religious liberty. And in virtue of its activity in this virulent condition, popery must either be overthrown and trodden under foot, or the joints and bands of society will be paralyzed, and its feet lose their functions.

In truth, Jesuitism is the great obstacle, as it is the great reproach of Catholicism. Yet let us be just even to Jesuitism, for only such a mother could have had such a son. Catholicism produced Jesuitism, and must bear the blame of its inherent malignity. However that may be, and whether or not at some stage of its development Catholicism must not have given to the world some such monstrous birth, certain it is that at present—nor least in France—Jesuitism is the great obstacle in the way of Catholicism. It is the obstacle of Catholicism by its carrying Catholicism out to its full consequences—by making prominent the very features in Catholicism which require to be softened down or wholly removed. More papal than the Pope, Jesuitism is also more Catholic than the most intense of ordinary Catholicism. Consequently France, which has refused the less, cannot well receive the greater. If it has been found so difficult to Catholicise France, how impossible to Jesuitise it. And that the rather because Jesuitism is from abroad. Jesuitism is of no land; it has no father, no mother, no home, no country. It is a foreigner every where; every where it is an alien—alien in sympathies, hopes, aims, efforts; it rejoices in no man's joy; it sheds no tears of patriotism; its victories are pure selfishness. Jesuitism, consequently, prevents Catholicism from becoming national in France. In the present struggle the cause at issue is not the cause of religion, nor the cause of Catholicism, but the cause of the Pope; and not so much the cause of the Pope, as the cause of the Jesuits, now the Pope's friends, and now the Pope's foes.

That Jesuitism played the part of Mephistopheles to Louis Napoleon may be well conjectured, from the internecine war that the Prince President has since his assumption of power waged against the press, not sparing the highest literature of his country. Here Jesuitism comes out in all its virulence and in its full odiousness. Not even in the days of the worst Roman emperors did there rage such a persecution against literature as that which this man maintains. The expulsion from France of all free thought— of all the higher mind—of the very pride and glory of the nation! The deed is unparalleled—literally there is nothing so bad in the whole career of civil tyranny; we are not sure that any approach to it can be found in the dark annals of bigotry.

And this is the work of Romanism. What! no remonstrance from Rome? None. No remonstrance from the clergy of France, in which body are some men of letters? None. To banish a literature—to root up the very mind of a people, and cast it out as fit only to be trodden under foot of man! No, this cannot last. Terrible reprisals will be made; and then what will be the fate of Popery in France?

The prevalence of Jesuitism is the forerunner of decline. Yes! the show of strength in France is great, is brilliant. But look beneath the surface. Already are dissolving powers at work. If this work is of God, God's spirit will be manifest in unmistakeable signs and tokens. Health and vigour will be seen there; the bright eye; the well-toned complexion; the brawny limb, the firm tread. If the work is not of God, these divine gifts will be absent—and absent they are.

It might be supposed that the literary energy of France, excluded from its proper and ordinary channels, would flow into theology, and produce works of a superior kind. It has not done so; it cannot do so, for between literature and theology there is in France a great gulf. We have referred to the manufacture of Catholic books carried on by the Abbé Migne. The works are ponderous; some of them are learned; a few are reliable and useful. But they are all tinged—most of them deeply tinged—with Jesuitism, for the special support and extension of which they are produced. And at the best they are compilations—nearly all mere compilations, or translations, or reprints. Of creation there is none; none of the higher intellect; no life to inform the mass; a mere aggregation showing the will to achieve a certain result—the will destitute of the power. What, for instance, can be more idle than to collect and republish all the chief defences of Christianity made from very early ages, inclusive of the apologies of Chalmers and Wiseman, for the purpose of meeting the current objects of unbelief, and furnishing answers to such assailants as Hegel and Strauss? One would be tempted to fancy that the directors of this series of works thought a fresh book a conclusive argument, whatever its contents.

For the last few years we have carefully watched the theological literature of Catholic France; with the character of its chief productions we are acquainted. And we are compelled to say that we have seen in it no signs of life; no originality, no power; no breadth of treatment, no comprehension of the subject; no masterly handling whatever;—but in the little that has come forth there is a poverty of thought and a crudeness of expression, or mere verbosity, or mere reproduction; an attempt to ignore the theological questions of the day, or—which is probably the more correct statement—an almost utter ignorance of issues on the determination of which not churches only but Christianity itself depends.

We are not surprised at these signs of decay. Jesuitism strikes every thing on which it falls with an intellectual blight. Jesuitism does not reason ; if it reasons, it is inconsistent. Every argument implies a 'No' as well as a 'Yes.' The alternative cannot be accepted by infallibility. Besides, what is to be gained by reasoning ? Truth is known—all necessary truth is known and possessed and taught by Mother Church. Her word is the final word ; her word is law. If your faith is weak, it may be quickened by coercion or revived by a prodigy : but proof can do nothing for it ; from discussion it can draw no good. Activity of intellect may be a hindrance to faith ; it may bring perils and snares ; but safety it cannot bestow ; safety is ensured, if only you cease to think and learn to acquiesce.

Of course, Biblical studies in general are in a low condition under the frown of Romanism. Little indeed is the Bible studied ; and when studied, it is studied not for new light, but for confirmation in what is established and the confutation of gainsayers. This, we affirm, is not a religious study of the Bible. Such a study can answer no good Christian purpose ; it cannot instruct, it cannot edify : it may suit a theologian ; it is unworthy of a disciple. Even in divinity schools the Scriptures are neglected. Take as a proof these the words of a Catholic priest, famed for his orthodoxy, as they appear in a journal which is pre-eminently Catholic :—

'It is sad and bitter to think that studies so fit to glorify our Lord scarcely exist at all in our seminaries, and are generally disdained by the clergy of France. One can understand that a priest may adduce solid excuses for not being versed in profane knowledge, but will he venture to plead a dispensation from sacred science ? Yet is there one amongst us who every day studies some pages of the scripture ? Indeed, can that study be conducted apart from sufficient exegetical knowledge ? And where does the clergy obtain such knowledge ? Except indeed you take it into your head to dignify with the name of Exegesis the course in sacred scripture which we went through at college ! Sad result of the situation to which the church of France has been reduced—sad result, that of no longer having learned teachers ! It has a clergy that admirably, often heroically, discharge their active duties—they preach, they catechise, they confess ; but it has not a clergy who know how to either contend for the faith, or teach it systematically.'[g]

In the days of its strength the Catholic church of France had preachers who wrote their names in the annals of the world. If now we ask where are the successors of Bossuet, Massillon, and

---

[g] 'Annales de la Philosophie Chrétienne,' April, 1850.

Bourdaloue? Echo answers, Where? The greatest preacher of
the present day, M. Lacordaire, is little more than a distinguished
petit maître in the pulpit. Greatness is gone with the cause and
source of greatness. The flattery which has always dishonoured
the highest efforts of French pulpit oratory, when the great had to
be addressed, adapting itself in his mouth to republican tastes, has
gone so far as to declare that in Paris M. Lacordaire saw *a new
Zion.* Take as a specimen of his Christian truth and pure eloquence (!) the following :—

'Jesus Christ well said *There are few that be saved;* but this was
a speech made for his own time, for there are many classes of humanity
that are in the condition of safety. Thus, 1. infants who in great
numbers die at the age of innocence : 2. Women ; God gave two gifts
to women, the gift of faith and the gift of charity. Every woman
without exception when going down to the tomb hears in her right ear,
" I salute you, full of grace, the Lord is with you !" or in her left ear,
" Many sins will be pardoned because she has loved much !" And how
many of that sex are there that are saved? The half of the human
race : 3. the poor in a mass : 4. nearly all the rich.'

Unmeaning talk like this may well be terminated by bathos
such as the following :—

'Tares of despair, separate yourselves from God's wheat ! O thou
demon, where are thy elect, and what remains as thy share ?'

Not better is the condition of the Ultramontane controversial
theology. We give as an instance the 'Table of Contents' of a
book approved by a bishop, and distributed among the young of
his diocese :—

First Question ;—' What ought you to think of a religion which had
its origin in libertinism ?'

Second Question ;—' What ought you to think of a religion which
has spread and strengthened itself by plunder and violence ?'

Third Question ;—' What ought you to think of a religion which
still supports itself by the aid of violence ?'

Fourth Question ;—' What ought you to think of a religion which
depends on falsehood and calumny ?'

Fifth Question ;—' What ought you to think of a religion which
allows its professors to believe and do whatever they like ?'[h]

Such barefaced misrepresentations, such gross caricatures, could
not be offered as a picture of Protestantism unless to a people
already prepared by a series of falsehoods and even burlesques to
believe the most outrageous untruths. This state of the popular
mind has been produced by the popular religious (irreligious) lite-

[h] 'La Bonne Année, 1848, Catéchisme Protestant, à l'usage des hommes de bonne
foi, par L.B., avec approbation de l'Evêque.'

rature of Romanism in France. The general tendency of that literature is to befool its readers, and prepare them for any statements the priests may make. Chiefly does it consist of the *Lives of Saints* crammed with prodigies. These books seem no less fitted than intended to occupy in the people's imagination the histories of enchanters current in the middle ages. 'The Life of Sainte Rose de Lima' is a specimen. The author shows how in her infancy Sainte Rose of Lima endeavoured to imitate Catherine of Sienna, 'that seraphic lover of the Saviour;' by what series of miracles she healed a tumour in her head; how with a view to self-mortification she stuck and fixed a needle in the sore; how celestial fire came forth from the gloves which she was forced to wear in spite of God; how she disfigured her face in order that she might not inspire any one with the sentiment of love; and how all *that* caused her to receive the gift of prophecy, and the power of controlling angels as she pleased; so that she sent her guardian spirit to do her errands. Those who may wish to study a history of the same sort from the pen of an eminent writer, may procure 'Sainte Elizabeth de Hongrie,' by M. de Montalembert.[i]

Devotional books, or books intended for religious edification, are overrun with the prevalent Marian superstition. 'The Rosary of Mary,' or 'The Garland of Mary,' by A. Constant, is a kind of Prayer-book for 'Mary's month,' that is, the month of May. For every day in the month there is a prayer and a legend in honour of 'the Virgin Mother of God.' In one instance we have two little children who, every time they recite the *Ave Maria*, feel a rose bud forth on their lips. In another, a lily suddenly grows up out of the sand to prove to a learned man the spotless purity of Mary. In another, a Madonna is exhibited as weeping before the whole church.

'The pretended wise men,' says the author, 'will not believe these things. Over this infidelity God mourns. The heaven is pictured to the reader, and in heaven the angels are heard to cry, "There is no longer any faith on earth." Then God covered himself with darkness; but in that night Mary still shone like the moon when the sun is gone down. A great cry arose in heaven; God withdrew his hand; the earth sank; then Mary rushed from her seat, stretched out her arms *and saved the world* a second time.' (p. 5.)

Did not these books bear evidence of being meant as manuals of devotion, some of them might be taken to have a very different

---

[i] A biographical work of similar tendency may be found in 'Les Mémoires d'un Ange Gardien.'

For religious Novels read the following: 'Eloi l'Organiste;' 'Elise, ou les Suites d'un mariage d'inclination,' by d'Exauvillez; also 'Les deux Athées,' by Mademoiselle E. Brun.

object ; nor are we sure that their tendency is not impure.   In reading passages in the work entitled 'A Marie, Gloire et Amour' ('To Mary, Glory and Love,' by Couvelaire), the uninitiated might doubt whether some passages were not an offering to Venus :—

'Mary—how sweet is that name ! my charmed ear delights to hear it ; my eager mouth takes pleasure in uttering it, and my heart—it swoons at thy name, O Mary !   Sweet is honey to the parched lips ; sweeter is thy name, O Mary !   Sweet is the murmur of the brook ; sweeter is thy name, O Mary !'

From amorous ecstacies the writer passes to blasphemy, applying to a dead woman language used in Holy Scripture of the Creator of the universe :—

'Mary so loved the world that she gave her only begotten Son. (John iii. 16.)   What can separate me from the love of my mother? Nothing, neither persecution, nor raillery, nor seduction, nor any other creature.'   (Rom. viii. 38.)

Enough has been said to exhibit the poverty of the French Catholic literature.   It is poor in theology ; it is poor in the pulpit ; it is feeble in controversy, if only by its violence ; and in its practical works it is superstitious, nay, grossly idolatrous.   A church whose foundations are so weak cannot stand.   Sustained for a time by the political adventurer into whose arms she has thrown herself, and enabled out of his spoils to make a show and a parade which win the hearts of the French populace by dazzling their eyes and gratifying their vanity, this branch of the Jesuitism which is now labouring to become universal, possesses no vital power, has none of the guarantees of life ; but having shot up like a gourd, will perish at the very dawn of day.   O P

HADES AND HEAVEN.

1. *The Many Mansions of the House of my Father.* By G. S. FABER, B.D., Master of Sherburne Hospital, and Prebendary of Salisbury. London. Royston and Brown. 1851.[a]
2. *The Future Human Kingdom of Christ, or Man's Heaven to be this Earth.* By D. J. HEATH, M.A., Vicar of Brading, and late Fellow of Trinity College, Cambridge. London. J. W. Parker. 1852.
3. *The State of the Departed, and the Time of the Reward of Glory.* By ALEX. YOUNG, M.A., Mochrum, Wigtownshire. Glasgow. Maurice Ogle and Son. 1851.

BISHOP BUTLER remarks that the full meaning of the Bible may yet have to be learned; that the inspired documents intrusted to men are such that their whole purport can only appear by continuous study; and that, therefore, as we advance in ability to interpret the book, so we may arrive at better knowledge of God's ways, perhaps even at different views of our present position and future destiny.

We imagine that a feeling of this kind has originated, among Roman Catholics, what is called *the doctrine of development*, or a belief that the Scriptures do not give us a *finished* revelation; but that the church is privileged to repeat and extend that revelation from time to time. We say that this doctrine arose—like the other falsehoods of the Latin Church—upon a veritable basis; when men experienced how faulty was the popular apprehension of Christianity, and desired the presence of a power that might (without pronouncing popular Christianity to be wrong) supply what would adapt it to the growing wants of society.

The feeling of deficiency was a very genuine one; but the fault lay not in the book of God's revelation. Man's faculties were, at a season of much darkness, unequal to the task of investigation, and were to be improved and strengthened, so as to read anew the already uttered manifestation of God's will.

The latter position is that of Bishop Butler, and, in the present day, there is an increasing desire on the part of many Protestant Christians to prove the correctness of his opinion, by teaching lessons from the Bible which oppose our traditionally received theology.

---

[a] There was a short notice of this work in the January number of this Journal but not such as to anticipate or interfere with the further investigation contained in this article, from the pen of another writer, whose views, as here set forth, will, it is hoped, excite a discussion of the whole subject in these pages.— ED. J. S. L.

It is, indeed, a thing to be expected that, during the long period of ignorance when the original language of the Scriptures was almost forgotten—when the science of interpretation was erroneous—when the current philosophy was absurd—and when many social rules, now abhorred, were embraced as certainly true —much of the sense of the book lay hidden; and even when it began to be studied with more extensive knowledge and upon sounder principles, its complete meaning would not, perhaps, immediately appear.

Hence, many writers among ourselves affirm that the first generations of the reformed church had not sufficiently advanced in Biblical acquirements to escape from all the traditional doctrines in which they had been educated.

It is moreover asserted that there were some opinions, universally received in the apostolical times, which have faded altogether from modern theology, or have been handed down, only in a distorted form, with the dogmas of the Roman see, and that Protestants fell into error, because, while shrinking from the exposed falsehoods of the church they had abandoned, they oftentimes neglected what that church had partially and confusedly preserved from primitive ages.

These observations will prepare us for considering the opinions, now extensively prevailing, that at death the immaterial part of man is reserved in *Hades*, while his judgment and final position are postponed until the body is resuscitated on the great day; and we may have to wonder whence arose the customary phraseology that the soul, when it quits the body, goes at once either to heaven or to hell.

Such phraseology seems to be modern and unscriptural. The disciples of Paul and of John were taught to believe, not that their material bodies were essentially vicious, and that the deliverance effected by Christ was to be a separation from the body, and an immaterial existence in some fancied heaven, but that the *corruption* of their bodies would be removed by their passing through the condition of death, (which the Lord's work had rendered sanative,) and by their resurrection, *in the body*, to meet Christ, and be with him on this earth. They looked upon the present life, therefore, with feelings very different from those either of the Epicurean or the Gnostic. They acknowledged, equally with the former, how good and desirable was the material creation; but they saw, as the latter had seen, that much evil had been allowed to stain it. They did not shut their eyes to this corruption, but were glad to learn that the event of death, regarded by the world as an unmitigated curse, was really the wholesome, though bitter, medicine presented to them by God for the destruction of the evil which was really foreign to their natures, and for raising up, from the dissolution of the material elements, a more glorious body, free from imperfection of every kind.   It is plain that this belief had nothing in common with that which was the product of paganism, and which represented the body as lost at death, and the immortality of the soul as an unintelligible spiritual existence, with no happiness that can be appreciated or even conceived by beings with faculties such as ours.

On the contrary, with the early Christians, the bliss of the resurrection was precisely what they felt the want of, and, with this hope firmly and constantly in view, there is no wonder that they deemed their sufferings and afflictions of no account : being, in fact, a part of the death to which they were subjected, and which was to be the passage to every joy they could anticipate. It might furnish us with useful matter of reflection how far the loss of this belief, or its feeble hold upon the public mind, is responsible for the want of interest with which the majority of mankind treat the Gospel.   At any rate, it seems that the notion of departure from all which humanity counts as most dear (and this is the general idea of heaven) must exercise a pernicious influence upon the religion of the world ; for there are few who can contemplate a vague promise of ethereal felicity, with hopes sufficiently strong to bias their lives.

As soon, however, as we come to look stedfastly on the doctrine of our all rising, with material bodies, to meet the Lord on this earth at the great day of His appearing, we cannot but inquire into the state of the departed during the interval that elapses between death and resurrection ;—a question of no interest to those who are accustomed to speak of going to heaven as soon as the soul leaves the body. This question has, moreover, been avoided by Protestant divines, from a fear that it might lead to the popish fancy of a purgatorial fire during the period alluded to. But it is manifest that if the constant expressions in the New Testament of a great day of judgment be not the most figurative possible, we must make some account of the intermediate state of the dead,—whether we believe it to be a conscious or an unconscious existence.

The connection is so intimate between these two doctrines, which Mr. Young appropriately calls the state of the departed, and the time of the reward of glory, that we shall endeavour to make our article turn upon them both ; and, without venturing to lay down any system of our own upon the circumstance of Hades and of Heaven, to point out what we believe to be faulty in the books we are about to notice.   These doctrines we have no intention formally to deny or to disprove ; but, since they are in a great measure novelties to many Christians, we ought not to dogmatize too hastily upon them, but content ourselves with passing them in review, and carefully weighing the most obvious difficulties in them, until they have received a more thorough sifting than has yet been applied to them.

We would seriously recommend the three books of which we are speaking to those who have never yet sufficiently thought of either of these doctrines. The little work of Mr. Young, remarkable for its Christian tone, may be usefully read as an introduction to the subject—a kind of preliminary statement by the junior counsel of the great cause to be handled at length and in detail by his senior Mr. Faber. And Mr. Heath, though not exactly the counsel for the opposite side, yet advocates views so striking and often so different from those of Mr. Faber, that we ought not to adopt any opinions on the correctness of the cause until his arguments have been duly considered, and, if not answered, yet accounted for.

Mr. Faber, the veteran theologian, whose work we criticise with hesitation, on account of his high standing, but which we must review as the most important and decided treatise upon eschatology, divides his subject into two principal portions. In the one he advocates the existence of a Limbus or Hades wherein the dead are perfectly conscious, and await either in suffering or in bliss the day of judgment when they shall be consigned to their proper and ultimate destinations. In the other, which is the chief part of his book, he insists on the prediction of an approaching millennium, ushered in by the conversion and restoration of Israel, in which (such is his opinion) Christ will not be personally present, but at the close of which, after a fearful apostasy and outburst of wickedness under Satan's leadership, a universal conflagration will take place, the righteous being ' caught up to meet the Lord in the air,' and so escaping that great burning. Then will occur the second advent, the judgment of the human race, the imprisonment of the condemned along with Satan and his hosts in a literal lake of fire inside this earth, and the renovation of its surface for the habitation of the glorified righteous.

This is the substance of the *Theology* of Mr. Faber's work ; but the title he has given to it arises from a poetical idea (beautiful, indeed, whether well or ill founded) that, in the beginning, this world was one of the many mansions of God's house : this, as well as the other mansions, that is the other planets, being the abode of a host of angels, subordinated to some chief angel. On this earth Satan had been the viceroy. He rebelled against Christ, who, Mr. Faber thinks, was the only archangel, and identical with Michael. In consequence, the earth was reduced to the chaotic state described at Genesis i. 2 ; and it was then, in the course of

the six days' creation, refitted for a new being, man, whom Satan
began immediately to envy and to persecute, as an interloper in
his own former dominions.   The tempter succeeded, and from
that time kept up a contest with Christ or Michael, that will be
eventually concluded at the restitution of all things, when regenerated man, under Christ, will occupy the position formerly held by
Satan and his angels; while the archfiend and his adherents will
be confined for ever within the very world he once ruled, and had
sought to ruin.

Now we say again, that with one of Mr. Faber's attainments
and rank we would express our disagreement in the most modest
terms possible.   But we cannot help thinking that he has drawn
too largely upon his imagination, and has often assumed as demonstrated, on one page, what he only *supposed* on the page preceding.   Indeed it is tolerably certain that he has adhered to the
kind of divinity contained in the 'Paradise Lost,' which he frequently quotes with unfeigned admiration.   For our part, we have
always held that this master-poem has inflicted an almost irre-
parable injury upon the popular views of Scripture, not only in
spite of the majesty of its imagery and music of its verse, but
even in consequence of them; just as historical romances destroy
history, by sacrificing homely and unpoetical truths, for the sake
of the picture or the story.

Upon the *poetry* of the 'Many Mansions' we shall offer no
remark; but wherever it appears to us that there are objections,
either scriptural or metaphysical, in the way of some of the author's
positions, we shall content ourselves with stating them, and leaving
to the reader the task of forming his own judgment.

The work of Mr. Heath is entirely different.   Although he
agrees with other restorationists, and with Mr. Faber, that the
time of the reward will be postponed until the Last Day, and that
man's heaven will be on the face of the renewed earth; he insists
on the perfect humanity of the inhabitants of that heaven, and on
the truth that, while the surface of our globe will be only slightly
changed (except in the absence of sea, in order to make room for
the past generations of men), men themselves will be much the
same as now; being only freed from temptation : that is, there
will be all shades of goodness, from the glorified saints in
Christ's presence, to the utterly outcast, living still on this earth,
at a great distance from Jerusalem, the metropolis of the kingdom
of heaven.   He excludes altogether any actual hell from his
theory; supposing that men will, in the next life, take up and
continue their position in this.   He draws a distinctly marked
line between the glorified saints, who will rise at the beginning
of the millennium to reign *along with* Christ, and who are not to

be judged ; and the saved nations, whom Christ and the saints will judge at the end of the millennium, and who, still more or less imperfect, will be rewarded according to their works. A remarkable feature in the book is, that he takes the so-called Calvinistic texts as absolutely as the most determined supra-lapsarian would do ; but as he confines their application to the glorified saints only, he does not think he injures the non-elect, by making them, not reprobated to misery, but called to be governed by the saints.

It is to be regretted that Mr. Heath, handling a most delicate subject, with talents every way fitted for the work, should have written so hastily and often carelessly, especially as his method of interpretation, founded upon a literal acceptation of the words of Scripture, is always entitled to respect, even when wrong ; and might have appeared to much more advantage, had he taken a little additional pains to arrange his arguments in a systematic shape, and a little longer time to re-write what he should have considered as only the author's private notes.[b]

We regret this the more, as he lays himself open to the criticism of those who have not fairness enough to discriminate between the goodness of a cause and an error committed by an advocate of that cause ; or who cannot see that a writer's arguments are quite unaffected, if we cast out one page or two from his otherwise valuable book. Indeed we are inclined to believe that his arguments are oftentimes sound, and that, in spite of some oversights, few would hesitate in giving at least a qualified assent to his theory ; though we are sorry that Mr. Heath, like nearly all propounders of novelties, has turned some passages away from their natural sense, to support his views ;—a labour which is always a vain one, inasmuch as there will be, of necessity, many expressions in a book like the Bible (composed by such different men) seeming to oppose even the most solidly established

---

[b] Mr. Heath makes an unfortunate mistake at pp. 335, 336, in interpreting Heb. xi. 16. In his anxiety to prove that the patriarchs were looking to no other locality than this present earth, he finds fault with our English translation, for having made *Heavenly* (ἐπουρανίου) agree with *country* (πατρίδος), because, he affirms, they cannot be of the same gender. 'They desired,' he says, ' Heavenly citizenship, Heavenly institutions, Heavenly communion, a Heavenly King, or, in fact, as St. Paul says himself, Heavenly promises ; but *not* a Heavenly *country ;* for Heavenly is masculine or neuter, and country is feminine.' Now, independently of the general rule that a compound word like ἐπουρανιος is masculine *or* feminine, it is singular that, in the very next quotation made by Mr. Heath (Heb. xii. 22), this very word (ἐπουρανίῳ), is made to agree with a feminine substantive ('Ιερουσαλήμ. See Matt. xxiii. 37). And this grievous mistake is also quite unnecessary ; since it might easily have been argued that the Heavenly country need not be *in* Heaven when men inhabit it, St. John having expressly said that he saw, at the close of all things, the new Jerusalem coming down *from* Heaven (Rev. xxi. 2).

doctrines. And truth, in Scripture as elsewhere, is determined rather by balancing probabilities, than by rigid unexceptional proof. At the same time we offer our unfeigned admiration of Mr. Heath's boldness, and of his very charitable and candid tone, joined to the patience with which he has pursued his object.

But, being thus introduced to our authors, let us proceed to the cause they advance; and first we have to consider how far Mr. Faber's notion (which is certainly very ancient, if it be not apostolical) of a Hades, inhabited by sentient dead men awaiting the judgment, can be supported by the Bible.

The main Scriptural proofs of this notion seem to be, 1st. The occasional invocation of the dead back to life; as of Samuel in the Old, and of Moses in the New Testament. 2ndly. The parable of Lazarus and Dives. And, 3rdly. The words of our Saviour to the thief on the cross.

Mr. Faber, while treating, at great length, the account of Samuel's resuscitation at the house of the witch of En-Dor, has not mentioned the most probable explanation of the matter, viz., as the work of a *clairvoyante;* and, whether we regard Mesmerism as an imposition or a reality, the consultation of Samuel's spirit by the wretched king of Israel bears so striking a resemblance to the modern performances of animal magnetism, that, if these are false, then the witch was an impostor also; and, if these are genuine, then (as Dr. Maitland argues) the transaction at En-Dor was also a real invoking of the dead prophet by the mesmeric powers of the woman. And it must be acknowledged, in spite of Mr. Faber's arguments to the contrary, that the king does not appear to have *seen* Samuel at all, but to have consulted him through the intervention of the Baalath-Oboth, or the dealer in familiar spirits.

And, whatever opinions we be disposed to form, yet the calling back the dead to life in no way implies that they were conscious *while dead*, unless they report what happened to them during their absence. Indeed, from the Scriptural mention of other resurrections, such as those effected by Elisha, and by our Lord himself, there seems every reason for concluding that those raised from death had no news to tell of the world they had just left. They came back as though awakened from a deep sleep or a trance.

Under this aspect, we may see immediately that such reanimations as these did in no way interfere with the inspired assertion that Christ was the *first-fruits* from the dead. Because the men did not rise with renewed, glorified bodies, as did our blessed Lord, and as we shall also do at the last great day, but returned to the same bodies they had left; and such instances were no more resurrections (regard'd as victory over the grave) than recovery from a state of coma or from the influence of chloroform would be. They were, to be sure, *miracles*, inasmuch as a real death had preceded; but there was no change from corruptible to incorruptible, which took place in Christ's resurrection, and which shall constitute ours likewise, when we hear the last trumpet.

The parable of Lazarus and Dives is constantly referred to, both by Mr. Faber and Mr. Young, as decisive on the point—as teaching beyond all controversy the conscious existence of the dead in two compartments of a great receptacle called Hades. But it appears to us, on the contrary, that this parable has been one of the presumed Scriptural grounds for the prevailing vulgar belief, that the good and the bad proceed *immediately* to their final destinies; for, beyond all doubt, there are no expressions referring to a future change from the condition mentioned in the parable. It is clearly implied that there could be no communication between Dives and those not along with him. This narrative, moreover, being in the parabolic form; we must, as usual in such cases, extract the point or moral from what is mere drapery, and therefore not intended to be taken literally. Our Saviour uttered this parable chiefly for the illustration of his preceding lesson concerning the unjust steward; to show that those who, like the rich man, had not made friends of their unrighteous mammon, to receive them into *everlasting* habitations, were consigned to misery. We must be cautious, therefore, not to take too literally the story in which this lesson was conveyed; more especially if it be true that (from the expressions employed) the story was a Rabbinical one, applied, according to our Saviour's custom, to his own instructive purposes.

Unless we receive the parable as figurative, we are startled by there being so detailed a description of the state of the dead; quite opposed to the rest of Scripture, which maintains a marked reserve on the subject, revealing little more than that the good are to be rewarded and the wicked punished. But, if we are obliged to understand the parable *literally*, it certainly may be appealed to by those who believe an *immediate* transition to the ultimate state, rather than by those who hold an *intermediate* consciousness in Hades.

The words of our blessed Redeemer to the thief on the cross are, for the same reason, applicable at least as well to the belief in an immediate fruition of Heaven as to the belief in the state of Hades; although it must be confessed that we cannot interpret these words of comfort to a dying penitent in the same figurative way as the *parable* of Lazarus in Abraham's bosom. But, while we acknowledge the great difficulty that lies in this expression, we do not feel ourselves justified in accepting an unqualified sense of it, so long as the unusual word *Paradise*, into which the malefactor was promised an entrance, remains so undetermined as it is at present. And we do not quite understand how the assurance of being in the better half of Hades (supposing Paradise to mean this), from which a future judgment was to be expected, could really be a direct answer to the dying man's prayer, ' Lord, remember me when thou comest into thy kingdom,' unless Christ's kingdom, *which was to come*, comprehended Hades, as well as earth or heaven.

Still less do we understand how Mr. Faber can appeal to St. Paul's desire to be with Christ at his death (Phil. i. 23), as illustrative of his position that at death St. Paul expected to be conscious *in Hades*. For we are expressly assured that Christ was not left in *Hades*, but ascended to *Heaven;* and therefore the apostle, in his expectation of being with Christ, could assuredly not have been hoping for a transmission into Hades.

We have thus mentioned what we sincerely think to be the only tangible grounds for the belief in question. There are, it is true, other texts which are considered to teach a conscious existence between death and resurrection ; but we believe we have mentioned the most important, and we have given to them all the force they can have. And, while we do not pretend to have answered the difficulties contained in them, we are confident that there are reasons against Mr. Faber's opinion, which, if not insurmountable, ought at least to be explained, before we can agree to the theory of a Limbus.

And, first, we would notice, what has already been referred to ; the evidently implied ignorance on the part of those who came back from the dead, of anything that had occurred to them since they died. It is not imaginable how the Scriptures could have passed over in silence the knowledge acquired by Lazarus, or by the saints raised on the day of crucifixion, if they *had* acquired any. Can we understand the absence even of inquiries put to these visitants of Hades by their former friends? Could any preacher of the Gospel have been so effective as one of these men would have been, had they been able to tell us, from their own actual experience, that believers in Christ were then happy, and disbelievers wretched? We deem it almost beyond contradiction that the Scriptures imply an entire ignorance on the part of these men concerning the world of shades.

It is worth observing also that there are some expressions in the Old Testament respecting the nothingness of the grave (*i. e.* of Hades), which are not only inexplicable on the hypothesis of the dead being conscious, but certainly contradict it, so far as the words go. Take, for instance, the following passage from Ecclesiastes (ix. 4, 5): 'A living dog is better than a dead lion: for the living know that they shall die, but the dead know not anything.'[c] Is it possible to reconcile this declaration with the opinion that the good are comforted and the wicked tormented *during death?* If this theory be true, are not the above words untrue?

Moreover, the allusions in the New Testament to the speedy advent of Christ are quite unintelligible, if those who die in the Lord take any note of time during their repose in the grave; whereas, on the supposition of the absolute unconsciousness of the dead, then Christ might be said *to come quickly* as well to those who lived 1800 years ago, as to ourselves who are in the later times of this dispensation. Upon this supposition, also, we understand how we can (for practical purposes) identify the death of each one of us with the coming of Christ; for, as we measure time only by the succession of ideas, then, if we have no ideas whatever during our absence from the body, the moment of the resurrection will appear to follow immediately the moment of death.[d] And we can thus receive the warning of our Lord, addressed to *us all*, to watch for his coming *to us;* which would have no meaning, if we did not believe that (practically) this must imply preparation for death, because the inhabitants of Hades cannot watch for the advent *to them*, and prepare themselves for it, if it be true that the coming is to be to *this earth*, and if those in Hades cannot change their condition. Let us add the consideration that the watching for the reward, through an indefinitely prolonged period, would be a sore trial to the faith of the righteous, who are always exhorted to patience and perseverance, because they have but a short time to await the coming of their Lord. And if we believe the perfect unconsciousness of the departed, we can then reconcile the manifestly revealed doctrine of a universal resurrection to judgment, with the prevailing opinions (appearing to be justified by some Scriptural phrases) that we pass immediately from this life to the next.

There is, besides, another serious difficulty in the way of the doctrine in question. If it be true that the righteous, at death, are transferred to a region where they can enjoy, by actual possession, as well as by anticipation, the reward which the Lord is to bring with him on the great day, and that the unholy are to be tormented, like Dives in the parable, as an earnest of the greater torments they shall assuredly hereafter experience;—then, we ask, would not such a consignment to the two provinces of Hades be, in

[c] See also Psalm vi. 5: 'In death there is no remembrance of thee: in the grave, who shall give thee thanks?'

[d] This statement is not contravened by the admitted fact that, in sleep, or even during the operation of chloroform, the notion of time is not entirely lost. For a consciousness and a succession of ideas still subsist more or less imperfectly.

effect, a judgment *never to be reversed ;* the consequences of which would be only *augmented,* not *changed,* at the day of judgment? And what would be the meaning of such a day, where we are certified that some of the wicked will be surprised at the doom they shall receive? (Matt. vii. 22, 23 ; xxv. 41-46.)   Is it possible that the wicked could expect praise and reward from Christ, if they had just come from a place of torment such as the rich man had tenanted, and which was understood to be anticipatory of the damnation at the last day?

We feel persuaded that this objection is so important and so palpable, that there is but one resource left for those who acknowledge a limbus or Hades of consciousness : — viz., that the condition of man is *not determined* when he enters Hades, but that the probation and preparation of *this* life have to be continued in *that.* It has been from a feeling of this kind,—from the difficulty of otherwise believing both a universal judgment and an intermediate life, that the Romish doctrine of purgatory has arisen.   Indeed, we have grounds for knowing that there are some who, while they reject the idea of purification by *fire* in Hades, yet hold to the opinion that Christ's moral work may be applied to men there, and that those who die unsaved, may embrace the offer of mercy during the supplemental life below.   With these opinions, either of the Romanist or the Protestant, we are not now concerned, because they are not put forth in the books we have undertaken to review. But we call the attention of Messrs. Faber and Young to them, and desire their solution of this question : ' How can we avoid regarding the intermediate state as one of trial and probation, if it be succeeded by a judgment unexpected by some in Hades ?'

There is, besides, an objection of a metaphysical, rather than of a biblical nature, which we have reserved to the last, because in one sense, there is greater force in it than in those we have already mentioned.   For, had it been originally weighed and determined, it is likely that the supposition of Hades would never have existed. Is it *possible* for a disembodied spirit to be conscious of anything exterior to itself ? or, in the language of modern philosophy, can an entity, deprived of the organs of communication, receive *objective* knowledge ?   We have no intention of denying the *existence* of disembodied spirits, though we may observe that the scriptures say nothing about them.   Man is spoken of as *consisting* of body, soul, and spirit, but not of being *divisible* into body and soul ; still less is the soul ever mentioned as performing the functions properly belonging to the body, of which the chief is the possession of organs through which one man can communicate with another.

We cannot conceive any definition whatever of a material body, which shall not involve this function, even though we imagine it to be ætherialised and attenuated to the merest vapour, such as angels' bodies may be; or, though we attribute to it the absence, or the modification of laws which affect it now, so that it may have a glorified form, independent of gravity, and with vastly increased powers of locomotion, or capable of unlimited extension and compression. In short, we may believe our material bodies, after the resurrection, to be very different in many respects from what they are at present, while we must still believe in the main attribute of all material organs, viz., as forming the means of intercourse between one spirit and another.

It seems to follow, as a necessary consequence, that a disembodied spirit *cannot* perceive *objects;* cannot acquire knowledge from without itself; can do nothing but feed upon what it has already gained;—perhaps exercise memory and reflection, but not perception or communication. We affirm that we might, from purely metaphysical reasons, concede such a life as this to a disembodied spirit; but from scriptural reasons, or from actual experience (as far as it goes), we are led to deny even this. At any rate, there seems to be an inherent absurdity of allowing any *outward* knowledge to what has lost the means of receiving it.

Mr. Faber has felt this difficulty, and has sought to obviate it by a theory (advocated by Mr. Isaac Taylor), that there is a *material* germ in man,—a subtle vehicle (he calls it), which death does not destroy, but only deprives of its covering of flesh, and bones, and sinews, and organs;—that this germ of matter is always united to the spirit, and that, at the resurrection, it will be reclothed with its glorious outer body. This theory is entirely gratuitous, and introduced only for the purpose of evading the manifest difficulty of conceiving how any mere spirit (except the one pervading Great Spirit, who may create matter for this very purpose), can act on others, or be acted on by them. It involves us also in the necessity of supposing that this germ can be recognized as the body which *had existed;* nor can we understand what great boon the resurrection of the outer body would be, if the germinal body (in Mr. Faber's hypothesis) could perform all the functions of intellectual and moral existence without it.

We know, indeed, it is said that the ghost of Samuel *appeared,* if not to Saul, yet at least to the woman of En-Dor. But, avoiding all abstruse explanation of this event, we may content ourselves with affirming that, while we are far from denying God's power to reinvest Samuel's spirit with some kind of corporeal clothing, sufficient to give it the means of communication with the denizens of earth, we are not nearer to a proof that the ghost, *before its appearance upon earth,* had a material body, or even a conscious existence.

And, it is worthy of notice, that the transfiguration, whereat Moses and Elijah were made to appear before the eyes of the three disciples, in no way destroys our argument, that, when the body is separated from the spirit, the spirit cannot perceive, or be perceived; because we have in one of these cases, proof; and in the other, a strong presumption, that the body was *not* separated from the spirit. We are informed of Elijah, that he did not die. And although Moses died, there was something very unusual about the circumstances of his burial, in that no man assisted at it (Deut. xxxiv. 6). In the valuable epistle of Jude, we are told that Michael and the devil disputed about the body of Moses; and, if we think Michael succeeded, we must then also conclude that Moses escaped the power of Satan, and the corruption to which he subjects other men. So that the bodies of these two great prophets were preserved, uncorrupted, in some locality, and might, of course, be reproduced, as at the transfiguration.

We are aware, moreover, that some persons will think of the phænomena of Mesmerisim, as contradicting our assertion that spirit must communicate with spirit, through the intervention of matter. Of these phænomena (whether real or not), we know but little. Nevertheless, if our opinion be correct, that they are not supposed, even by Mesmerists, to be independent of all material media, but only of our usual organs of sense, they do not (though they be real) contravene our argument; especially as we believe that the more scientific advocates of animal magnetism are so impressed with the need of *material* intercourse, that they assume the existence of a subtle fluid, called Odyle, along which the magnetic influence is conveyed. And Somnambulism, or what is called *divided consciousness*, instead of proving a conscious existence, while the operation of the body is removed, does rather prove the direct contrary. Because, however we account for the sleeping man *seeming* to have a different consciousness from the waking man, yet the waking man preserves no recollection of his state during his absence from the body.

Now, while we may not obtain any definite ideas of the state of death, and of the mode of resurrection, there are certain reflections which may remove a part of the difficulties. It would appear from the constant language of scripture, that man consists of body, soul, and spirit. The body and the spirit being brought together, do not constitute a living creature until the soul (ψυχή, or principle of life) is breathed in by God's direct action.[e] At death, this soul, or ψυχή, is recalled by God; the connection between body and spirit is then severed; the body corrupts and dissolves, and leaves

---

[e] See Gen. ii. 7; Job xxxiii. 4; Isaiah ii. 22; and 1 Cor. xv. 45.

the spirit, not only without clothing, but without organs, until, by reason of the victory which our Lord has obtained over Satan, the body (the same body of the same spirit) has the ψυχή again breathed into it, and the spirit becomes again a sentient, and intelligent, and perceptive being. From whatever source the material atoms (composing the restored body) be gathered, the presence of the former spirit will make it identical with the former body ; for it is not the conformation of the very same particles of matter that constitutes identity ; as we know that not one of us has the same particles in his body now as he had a few years ago, and yet he is identical with his former self, and is recognized as such.

It might be supposed from 1 Cor. xv. 44 and 45, that the ψυχή in the regenerated man is no longer to be the principle of life, because St. Paul says that the body is sown a σῶμα ψυχικόν, but *raised* a σῶμα πνευματικόν, and that the one of these bodies is not the same as the other. He says moreover in allusion to Gen. ii. 7, the first Adam became a living ψυχή, but the last Adam a life-producing spirit, and that the spiritual was to *succeed* the ψυχικόν. We know also that in other places (as at 1 Cor. ii. 14; James iii. 15 ; Jude 19), these two descriptions of men denote respectively the religious and the irreligious. So that the future glorified body may possibly have no ψυχή (or soul), but the regenerated spirit be to it the immortal principle of life.

However, without pronouncing upon this abstruse question, we may see clearly enough that in no place of scripture is either of these immaterial *portions* of man put for the man himself. He is never mentioned as the object of God's dealings, unless his body be supposed to be joined with his spirit. At the same time, if the identity of the future body must be established by its junction with the former spirit, then this spirit has some intermediate existence, which cannot be, properly speaking, sentient, and may be purely quiescent.

Modern medical experiments have shown that *we* can detach the immaterial part of man entirely from his body, and may do anything with this isolated body, without creating any perception in the man. We might cut away and mutilate the body until we destroyed (or removed) the ψυχή, and then, no art of ours could reconnect the body with the spirit. The body, having lost the principle of life, would dissolve and disappear. At the resurrection, God will recall the identical body (identical, we repeat, not because it possesses the same atoms, but because it belongs to the same spirit), and will give life to it, either by again breathing the ψυχή into it, or by giving to the spirit its acquired life-producing qualities.

In the striking phænomena of chloroform, it is certain that man has the ability to take the spirit from the body, and also to restore it; but he may not trifle with the ψυχή; he may not take that away, without consigning the body to corruption, never to be recovered, except by God's immediate agency. Perhaps the only difference between restoration from the effects of chloroform and from the effects of death, may be, that in the former case, the spirit returns, unchanged, to the body unimproved; whereas, in the resurrection, the spirit, having become a life-giving spirit, comes back to a better and more glorious body.

We cannot help thinking that the notion of a Hades, full of sentient, but incorporeal beings, is of Pagan growth;—that when the resurrection of the *body* had been forgotten, the belief in the immortality of the man remained. The Magian and Gnostic philosophy, which depreciated the body, and represented it as incapable of amelioration (when joined to the strong impression that man was fit for a more extended life than he enjoyed in his *first* body), gave rise to the fable of Hades, of Elysium, and of Tartarus, which passed into the Jewish, as well as, subsequently, into the Christian creed, from the close contact and influence of Persia.

However, while thus offering some suggestions for the re-consideration of the Intermediate State, we have no hesitation in agreeing with the doctrine advocated by the three authors we are now reviewing;—viz., that the final reward is not conferred at the instant of death, but is reserved until Christ shall come in power and great glory. Indeed, we suspect that the vulgar phraseology of going *at once* to bliss, comes only from forgetting the great revelation of the Bible,—the destiny of man's body to be the tabernacle of the Holy Ghost.

And this phraseology—the expression of 'going to Heaven'—is held by many to be not only unscriptural in its application to the moment of death, but to be altogether an error, for which there is no foundation. It is urged that Christ promised to return *to us*, and that he said nothing about our going to heaven to meet *Him*. It is affirmed that the Bible is silent on the subject of the end of the world (κόσμος), that it speaks merely of the termination of the age (αἰών). St. Peter does, it is true, predict that the heavens and the earth which are now, are reserved unto fire, and that the heavens shall pass away with a great noise, and the elements melt with fervent heat. But there appears an obvious answer to all this, in that the perishing by fire may only imply a change of form, as did the perishing by water (with which St. Peter compares it), and that the apostle himself says, that after this great fire we may look for a new heaven and a new earth, wherein dwelleth righteousness.

And Mr. Heath aptly quotes a distinction made by Joseph

Mede between *mundus continens*, or κόσμος, the world, and *mundus contentus*, or the inhabitants of the world, and points out the strong reasons there are for supposing that the predicted destruction is only applicable to the latter. Nay, we may find many expressions, not only in this very chapter of St. Peter (iii. 7, 11), but in other parts of scripture (Zech. xii. 6; Malachi iv. 1, 2; 2 Thes. ii. 8; Rev. xiv. 9-11), where the burning seems evidently to be confined to those who *resist* the power of Christ. Moreover, if Christ's work on earth be to overthrow Satan and to recover the world from the evil to which the Great Enemy has subjected it, the victory will appear incomplete and slight, when the frame-work of the world is annihilated, and the unsaved left in Satan's grasp.

But among those who believe in our future heaven being placed upon this renovated earth, there is an important difference of opinion. Some, like Mr. Faber, hold that the conflagration will be not only literal, but universal also, utterly changing both the form and constitution of the earth, accompanied by the real second coming of the Lord, and immediately preceded by the great outburst of wickedness, spoken of in the book of Revelation as the unchaining of Satan for a season; the holy being snatched up into the air, to meet the Lord (1 Thes. iv. 17), and so to escape the suffering of that fire. This scheme, which we think is scarcely distinguishable from the popular opinion, is, however, objected to for two principal reasons. 1st. It is affirmed by chemists that the bulk of this earth's matter has already been oxidized, and is therefore incapable of burning, in the sense of Mr. Faber's hypothesis. 2nd. By taking this conflagration to be contemporary with Christ's coming, no interpretation can be given to our Lord's promise that his advent should be unexpected by the wicked, who would be pursuing their ordinary avocations, and that he would call *all* his servants, good and bad, and reckon with them according to what they had done. It is hardly to be understood how this prediction can be reconciled with the theory that his good servants are first to be removed from the presence of his coming.

Let us add, that St. Peter's account of the final conflagration, unless it be understood figuratively, stands by itself. Our Saviour, with all the apostles and the prophets, never speaks of the *world*, but only of Christ's *enemies*, being destroyed. The analogy from the rest of the Bible would lead us rather to expect a terrible judgment upon the adherents of Satan, purifying the earth from them, as similar judgments removed the wicked from the old world, and the polluted city of Sodom from the land of Canaan. Especially does the prophecy of Zechariah look like a decided contradiction of the theory of a universal destruction happening to all who are not carried off into the upper regions of the heavens. The prophet, in speaking of the *last* siege of Jerusalem, says expressly that only half of the people should go into captivity, and that the residue should *not be cut off from the city* (xiv. 2), but that they should be helped by the overthrow of the enemy, and so Jerusalem made safely habitable. This chapter seems not to harmonize with the expectation that Christ will first carry his saints from the earth, and then burn up and remodel the earth for them to inhabit; while the wicked, together with the hosts of Satan, shall, *after* the conflagration, be confined within the bowels of this same earth, in a huge and secure dungeon, called Gehenna in the Gospel, and the fiery lake in the Apocalypse.

Now, Mr. Heath's view is entirely different. He lays great stress upon the implied doctrine of Scripture, that Christ is always supposed to restore mankind to the condition they would have occupied if Adam had not fallen, viz., a sinless condition in a terrestrial locality. He believes that, at the great day and final overthrow of Satan, man will be put into much the same position as he occupies now; excepting that all *external* temptation will be removed, and that he will be rendered capable of a continually increasing goodness and happiness by the unimpeded influence of Christ and his atonement. He expects, equally with other restorationists, a great confederacy of godlessness at the end of the millennium, which Christ will overthrow and for ever render powerless. This overthrow may be effected by a terrible volcanic eruption, that shall not only destroy the enemies that are beleaguering Christ's servants, but very materially change the surface of the globe, and perhaps literally remove the sea (Rev. xxi. 1); thus affording room for all the generations of men that have ever lived, raised to judgment at that time; and placed nearer to Jerusalem (the city of the great king), or farther from it, according to the issue of that judgment.

It will doubtless be alleged that the records of the early Christian church show that this expectation was present in the minds of those who were nearest to the original propagators of the Gospel; and that it was the reason why they could leave all things for the coming reward, the nature of which, while entirely terrestrial, they could understand and appreciate. It may be also said that, to arrive at a consistent view of Christ's mission, we ought to suppose that he will eventually introduce the same kind of happiness as he would have given to the world, if they had not been sinful and ignorant enough to reject him. If, then, his first invitation to mankind was that they should be terrestrially happy under his sovereignty, why should we invent another species of happiness altogether, on his return to do what the sin of men has so long interrupted?

Let the reader well observe that we are pronouncing no opinion upon this subject; we are merely placing before him the reasoning of restorationists, and the difficulties in the way of receiving their theories. We must say, however, speaking for ourselves, that the most decided objection to Mr. Heath's views, concerning the close similarity between our actual condition and our future destiny, arises from the very plain declaration of our Lord, that in the resurrection men neither marry nor are given in marriage, but are as the angels in heaven. One can scarcely understand much analogy between such a state of things and our present society. Mr. Heath says that the cessation of the marriage relation is revealed as the only apparently needful distinction between *now* and *then*, inasmuch as, according to his scheme, the hundred thousand million men, supposed to be either then alive or raised from the dead, will have just enough room, and none to spare, on this globe (giving about five hundred to the square mile); and that, therefore, they may not be *increased*. How far this population, the density of which would be nearly double that of England, and almost eight times the average density of Europe, would be possible in the earth (two-thirds of which would be recovered from the sea), unless there were some much greater change in either earth or man than Mr. Heath supposes, we beg to leave for consideration.

The most startling part of Mr. Heath's view is the distinction he draws between the Saints and the Saved. He holds that the former only are the perfect, who have been judged already in this life, and are prepared for perfection. They are the few *elect*, absolutely predestined to the position they shall occupy as assessors along with Christ in the judgment of the world, and partners of his throne. Reference of course is made to the prophecy of Daniel (vii. 22), of 'judgment being given to the saints of the Most High;' and of the time coming that ' the saints should possess the kingdom;' to the promise made by our Saviour to his apostles that they should sit on thrones, *judging* the tribes of Israel (Matt. xix. 28, Luke xxii. 29, 30); to St. Paul's affirmation that the saints should judge the world (1 Cor. vi. 2, 3); to the prophecy of Enoch, preserved in the Epistle of St. Jude, that ' the Lord will come with ten thousands of his saints to execute judgment upon all' (ver. 14, 15); and to many similar expressions in the Apocalypse (i. 6; ii. 26; iii. 21; iv. 4; xx. 4-6, etc.). It is singular that this theory almost coincides with that of the Church of Rome, which also distinguishes between saints and disciples. But it is certain that we find no such distinction in St. Paul's epistles, which use the word saint as a common designation of Christian. The theory itself is so novel, and has so many attendant difficulties, that we scarcely know how to speak of it; although we are ready to acknowledge that there is something in it very pleasing to the moral sense, and very likely to put aside many obstacles frequently encountered by students of theology.

We cannot, however, but think that Mr. Heath may have appropriated to his heaven many things which belong properly to the millennium, or the reign of peace and goodness which we are certified will prevail upon this earth before the end of all things. We conceive that there are many misapprehensions afloat respecting this period. At the same time it is a period which is not only predicted very distinctly in the book of Revelation, but seems necessary, in order to account for the tone of Christ's own ministry.

Was not the offer made by the Redeemer to his own nation of Israel, that if they would receive him, and acknowledge him as Jehovah their king, he would institute the kingdom of heaven, and through the instrumentality of the Jews, his chief subjects, bring all mankind to the Light of Israel, and destroy Satan's work among them? It does not affect the nature of this offer, that men were in such a state of sinfulness that they *could* not accept it, because they *could* not recognize the incarnation of Jehovah. Their very refusal to receive the Lord established the chief truth which men must feel before they can become perfect, viz., their own actual alienation from the source of good. Because throughout the Bible this great principle stands forth, that man lost the power of beholding God as an object, when the inner spiritual perception of God had been forfeited. Saints only, or perfected spiritual men, could *see* a *glorious* incarnation; and the *sin* of Adam must be obviated before his privilege could be restored.

We leave it to the reader to consult the following passages, and to discover how palpable is the doctrine of Scripture, that only the pure in heart can *see* God:—Gen. xxxii. 30; Exod. xxxiii. 9-23; Judg. xiii. 22; Isa. vi.; Matt. v. 8; 1 Cor. xiii. 12; Heb.. xii. 14; 1 John iii. 2, 3.

The Jews, forgetting this important truth, rejected and crucified the Lord of Life, who did not come in a form such as saints only could witness; thus, by their crime, producing that remedy which was eventually to cure the sin. And then our Saviour declared that, in consequence of this rejection, the covenant with Israel (which was to endure only as long as they should obey Jehovah) was terminated; that their house should be left desolate, and they subjected to tribulation. Nor should the Jews again see him, until they should say, Blessed is he that cometh in the name of the Lord. When we know that this was the cry with which his disciples had recently hailed him, when they called him King of Israel (Matt. xxi. 9, and John xii. 13), and with which the Jews found fault, this expression seems equivalent to saying that the Jews should not again behold him until they should become his disciples.

The curse went forth from his lips, even though he wept while he uttered it,—that Jerusalem was forsaken, and the reign of goodness postponed. The disciples, by way of deprecating this curse, called his attention to the stately grandeur of the temple, as though they would say, 'These piles of Israel's glory, beloved by Jehovah, cannot surely be doomed to so dreadful an end.' But he answered that not one stone should be left upon another.

The disciples thereupon, understanding that allusion was made to two events—first, the destruction of Israel's polity ; and, secondly, the end of the present age (*i. e.* of course, the commencement of the age to come)—asked him to give them clearer intimations whereby they might know more of these things.

He told them, in reply, that the overthrow of Jerusalem was to happen within that generation, and that certain determinate signs would precede the catastrophe (Matt. xxiv. 4-28 ; Mark xiii. 5-23 ; Luke xxi. 5-24). Then an indefinite, or rather an unknown period (unknown even by the angels) was to elapse, called by St. Matthew the *tribulation of those days* (xxiv. 29), and by St. Luke (xxi. 24) and St. John (Rev. xi. 2) *the treading down of Jerusalem by the Gentiles*, until the times of the Gentiles should be fulfilled. The end of that tribulation was asserted by our Lord to be the end of the age concerning which his disciples asked him ; and it must also be coincident with the restoration of the Jews to their own land—their willingness to say ' Blessed is he that cometh in the name of the Lord,' and the reappearance of Christ. We fancy that few restorationists disapprove of this view of the matter.

We would, however, observe that much obscurity is thrown over the manifest implication from Christ's curse, no less than from the original covenant recorded at the end of the book of Deuteronomy (which unquestionably speaks of Israel not being restored until they should acknowledge Jehovah, *i. e.* Christ), by the apparent meaning contained in the 12th chapter of Zechariah, where the looking upon Christ is made to *follow* the restoration to the land. Now the *looking* upon Christ here spoken of, and the particular spirit of grace and supplication which was to bring that vision to them, do not of necessity mean conversion to Christianity *merely*, because we who are Christians are not on that account so favoured. There is no reason, in reality, from this passage, why we should not still retain the belief so evidently deducible from the rest of the Bible, that *when* the Jews shall have been converted, *then* they shall be restored ; and after the restoration the actual display of Christ's bodily presence may occur.

But, furthermore, we cannot help thinking that there may be

some mistake in referring this portion of Zechariah's prophecy to the second coming at all. It is true that in the Revelation (i. 7) this vision of Christ appears to refer to the second coming;[f] but St. John in his Gospel (xix. 37) as evidently illustrates the first advent by it. And does not the prophet allude (from xii. 1, to xiv. 2) to what really did occur either at or after the *first* siege of the holy city? The mourning for the Lord (at Zech. xii. 10) looks like that predicted by the Redeemer himself (Luke xxiii. 28-31); and can scarcely be made to synchronize with any part of St. John's millennium, or we should assuredly find it in the 20th chapter of the Apocalypse, where mention is made of the misery of the *wicked only.* And the curious expression (at ver. 12-14) of the land mourning *apart,* seems to imply the dispersion and separation of Judah, and not the *union* of the tribes in Palestine during Christ's reign.

The opening of the fountain for sin and uncleanness (xiii. 1) cannot surely mean anything but the atonement once offered for all. The cessation of prophecy, of idolatry, and of possession by unclean spirits, has, we know, followed the first coming. We are not able to explain the similarity between Zech. xiii. 4, 5, and Amos vii. 14; neither can we say with certainty that the reference at ver. 6 is to the piercing of *Christ's* hands; but we find that the following verse is by our Saviour quoted (Matt. xxvi. 31) as predictive of what would happen to his flock after his death; and the 9th verse is mentioned in the Epistle to the Hebrews (viii. 10) as peculiarly significant of the New Covenant.

It is possible that commentators may have been deceived by the announcement of the overthrow of those nations which should be gathered together against Jerusalem. But our present inquiry will not be thus put aside, if we be careful to remember that the day of the Lord, in which this overthrow is to happen, does not mean the actual *presence* of the Lord upon the earth, but that presence, together with its consequences. The day of the Lord is thus identical with the whole period called by St. Matthew the tribulation of those days, which we have said is the same as St. Luke's treading down of the holy city by the Gentiles, *i. e.* of course, the dispersion and trouble of Israel. Under this aspect, the day of the Lord is lasting now, and its termination will be *the end of the age,* and the commencement of the millennium. And if this view be correct, we may have a ready answer to the question, How did the Lord seek to destroy the nations that compassed Jerusalem? by merely considering the destiny of the Roman

[f] Which appearance, nevertheless, in great part vanishes, if it be true, as some modern scholars aver, that the Apocalypse was written before the destruction of Jerusalem by Titus.

power which destroyed it, and the position of the empire which now holds it.

Whenever the new age shall commence, which it is customary to denominate the millennium, it is believed by all restorationists that the external hindrances to Christ's work will be abolished, or, in the language of the Apocalypse, Satan will be chained; and much of the state of things which Mr. Heath attributes to his heaven will then have place on the earth. Jerusalem will then be the foremost church in the world, capable of giving laws to the kingdom of Christ, because possessing inspired authority, on account of Christ's presence with it.

There are signs given us in the book of Revelation, which, if we were able to interpret, would directly indicate when and how the kingdom of Christ will commence. The most remarkable of these signs is the prophesying of the two witnesses in sackcloth for 1260 days. Much ingenuity has been exercised in endeavouring to determine who these two witnesses are. The English and Greek churches—the two volumes of the Bible—the Waldenses and Albigenses—Luther and Calvin—are some of the favourite interpretations among Protestants. But has it never struck commentators that perhaps the predictions in the Apocalypse may be no metaphors after all? What if these two witnesses should be really two living men, whose office it will be to inaugurate the reign of Christ? What if the days of their ministry, and of their lying unburied, may mean so many days as are mentioned, and nothing more?

In this case we cannot help thinking of Moses and Elijah; for, independently of the prominent character given to these two seers, and of its being Elijah's office, according to our Lord's and Malachi's predictions, to herald His advent, we must not forget that the particular province of Elijah will be to recal his countrymen to the law of Moses, as he formerly did in Ahab's time, and as Malachi intimates he will also do in the great day of Jehovah. These two witnesses are said to be the same as the two olive-trees and the two candlesticks *standing by the Lord of the whole earth* (mentioned in Zech. iv.). And it is singular that these two prophets (the one certainly, and the other probably) have their bodies up in heaven, and therefore may be said to be constantly standing by the Lord ; they were His witnesses, not only during their lives, but when they re-appeared at the Transfiguration. The signs to accompany them (Rev. xi. 5, 6) are strikingly those which accompanied Moses and Elijah. The lack of burial also points to the circumstance of neither of these men having seen corruption.

If this be so, then of course the two witnesses will labour to convert their own countrymen in the head-quarters of Judaism, Jerusalem itself (Rev. xi. 8), and shall succeed so far as to arouse the persecuting enmity of some great power called ' the beast that ascendeth out of the bottomless pit.' This is evidently not an *ecclesiastical* power, because it makes war with the whore or false church, as well as with the bride or true church (Rev. xvii.). It will be, probably, a powerful temporal government, either actually possessing, or greatly influencing, Jerusalem.

This government, it would seem, will be offended by the successful preaching of the witnesses, and will kill them, leaving their dead bodies unburied and exposed to public view, for the purpose, as will be thought, of convincing the Jews that their testimony was valueless. This plan will defeat itself. After three days and a half, they shall, in the presence of the city, relive, and ascend up into heaven. Then (following the literal meaning of this part of the Apocalypse) shall the kingdoms of this world become the kingdoms of the Lord; which event it does not seem possible to regard but as the end of the Tribulation, and the restoration of the Jews to be again the Theocratic nation.

Then shall commence the kingdom of Christ *with* His Saints, who are to rise at that time in order to partake of His throne. Peace and virtue shall prevail over the earth. But only the saints will be perfect during this preliminary season. They only will *see* Christ; they will be His vicegerents, and rule in His name. The metropolitan church of Jerusalem will be the organ through which the world will be governed, and gradually made happy, much in the same kind of way as good Roman Catholics believe it may become by submitting cordially to the one true church.

It is natural to expect that this reign will meet with much opposition. The dreadful punishments inflicted upon the beast, to be closed by the battle of Armageddon, indicate the gradual extinction of all enemies. But while the powers of the earth will thus in time become subjects of the King of Jerusalem, receiving their authority from Him or from the Saints, His nuncios,—one power remains, called the Whore, or Babylon. It is not conceivable how this can be other than a false church, because the very name of *Whore* and her connection with the *beast* are evidently contrasted with the *Bride* who is awaiting the *Lamb*. And the name of Babylon also seems easily applicable to the false church, because it was, in Biblical usage, the proper antithesis of Jerusalem, the true church;[g] still more remarkably, she is represented as saying (xviii. 7), ' I sit a queen, and am no widow,

[g] We may observe that this interchange of the names of places is of Rabbinical origin, and that the Talmudical writers do not speak of *temporal* Rome as Babylon, but as *Edom.*

and shall see no sorrow,'—a striking expression, which leads us to think of the church of Jerusalem as *mourning* during the absence of the bridegroom, and especially as being (according to Isaiah, chap. liv.) reproached for her widowhood. If the church of Rome be not this power—utterly opposed to the return of Christ to Jerusalem—and having long aped the privileges of the Bride—it will be some church yet to arise. This church must clearly be destroyed before its rival in Jerusalem, where Christ will be, can become omnipotent. There are very fearful announcements of her burning to be found in the book of Revelation, and men point with awful curiosity to the volcanic, sulphureous nature of the Italian territory, containing materials for the conflagration. We may readily imagine that this catastrophe, however much of sorrow and of surprise it would at first excite in the kings of the earth, and the shipmen and merchants of the Mediterranean, would not only prepare men's minds for the reception of the truth, but would, more particularly, make way for them to bow before the church of Jerusalem, when she who had lived deliciously with the kings of the earth, and had reigned over them, shall have ceased to exist.

Thus far Millennarians are in agreement. But there are some who believe in Christ's actual presence during this period, while others think that He will not come until the *close* of the millennium. Mr. Faber, who is one of the latter class, asks how it is possible for the great outburst of wickedness to take place at the *end* of this reign, if Christ in person is actually presiding upon the earth. He forgets that at that season the world will not be perfectly pure in heart, and therefore cannot *see* His glory. None but the saints will possess that ability. It seems also that this reign of one thousand years is a *progressive* growth of goodness and truth, and that the end of it, the final victory over Satan and Gog and Magog, denotes the putting down of all rule and authority and power. For this one thousand years, as we have said, is only preliminary; Christ's work is not completed until all the dead rise again to judgment.

This sitting in judgment Mr. Faber believes to be the real second coming; and so undoubtedly it is, if regarded as Christ's manifestation to *all men*. Then will occur the great burning mentioned by St. Peter, which may be considered as at first issuing from the earth to destroy the Lord's enemies, and so continuing, that it may either entirely change the globe and turn it into the abode fit for such æthereal beings as Mr. Faber supposes we shall be; or, as Mr. Heath thinks, only so far modify it as to make room for the resuscitated of all generations to inhabit, and be placed in good or bad positions according to the result of the judgment.

As we said before, we are not desirous of proffering an opinion of our own upon these subjects; we are only making the reader acquainted with them. But we would, nevertheless, propose a suggestion that may tend to reconcile these conflicting theories. Restorationists are agreed in the reign of happiness here on earth before the end of all things. May there not be an error in those who confine this reign to the thousand years? Would it not be more in accordance with Scripture to look upon that millennium as the *commencement* of Christ's kingdom, during which his principles have to grow and gather strength unimpeded by Satan's temptations, and fostered by His own communion with the Saints who shall rule mankind, and at last put down for ever all opponents, when the great confederacy of Gog and Magog shall be overthrown and the wicked destroyed?

At the close of this period, the time may have arrived for the full benefit of Christ's work to be applied; men may be entirely recovered from the effect of Adam's fall, and placed in the same circumstances as they would have occupied had our first father remained upright. They may, therefore, continue on this earth, as Mr. Heath imagines, and yet not have attained their final position. They may be subjects of the kingdom of heaven, and yet there may be another heaven reserved for them.

We may certainly concede that this next habitation, this world ($\varkappa \acute{o} \sigma \mu o s$) to come after the present, is not revealed; because the proper object of the Bible is to tell us merely how Adam's fall shall be rectified. But when this shall have been done, we have to consider what would have been the ultimate destiny of man had he retained his purity, and never become subject to death. Whatever it may be thought that destiny would have been, ought also to be deemed still the destiny, or else Christ will not have undone Adam's deed.

If it was intended for man to be removed from *this* earth to another stage of existence in a still better world, without the *sting* of death, as Enoch was (and Christ himself when he had overcome the grave), why may we not believe this progression in glory and order still to be ours, when we shall have completed, during the life after our resurrection, our apportioned tasks here?

The stagnation in our acquired intelligence, such as Mr. Heath supposes, seems contrary to the analogy of the universe: one rather loves to think of progress, of advancement up the never-ending series of ranks between us and God; and so we may look upon eternity, not as a dreary monotony without care and without interest, but in the way that the gifted author of 'The Physical Theory of another Life' regards it, a state of growing and learning. And this state, which we may imagine, but may not put into our creeds (because it does not form a part of the scriptural revelation), in no way interferes with the great doctrine of the Bible, that our actual condition of death now is only an entrance and vestibule to the real mansion Christ will prepare for us on this earth; and that when we shall be thus free from sorrow and sin, and shall be guided by Christ's own human self—in this then lovely world—lovely as well by its moral as its material constitution—we shall be the objects of God's free and unchecked solicitude, so that He will raise us still nearer to Himself than a terrestrial creature can be—even to the dignities of archangels or of cherubim.

W. H. J.

THE HARMONY OF THE GOSPELS.

The Elements of the Gospel Harmony. By B. F. Westcott, M.A., Fellow of Trinity College, Cambridge. Cambridge. Macmillan and Co. 1851.

The Four Witnesses: being a Harmony of the Gospels on a new Principle. By Isaac da Costa, of Amsterdam. Translated by D. D. Scott, Esq. London. Nisbet and Co. 1851.

It has always been a question of much interest and some difficulty, how the complete inspiration of a writer may be reconciled with the exhibition of personal characteristics in the writing. Many of those who have given their attention to the subject have been too eager to separate the two, to distinguish between the divine message and the human messenger, and imply that the one is transmitted to us tinged as it were with the gratuitous additions of the other. Hence arises the theory of an inspiration varying in kind and degree. The ten commandments, it would be alleged, afford the highest example of a Divine word. They were written on stone by the finger of God himself. The human medium was not permitted to intervene. God authoritatively speaks, and the word is addressed at once to the ear of those who are called upon to obey. An inspiration second only to this would be observed in the prophets who spake by immediate revelation. Prophecies there are which are distinctly observable as not being of any private interpretation, or coming by the will of man. The will of Balaam, for example, ran in a current directly opposed to the words which he uttered; nor could he have given any private interpretation of his message of 'the star that should come out of Jacob,' or 'the sceptre that should rise out of Israel.' When the prophet prefaces his revelation with 'Thus saith the Lord,' he is recognized as speaking words of inspiration. The same may be remarked of visions. The Apocalypse of John is felt to be an inspired production, equally with the chapters in which Ezekiel and Daniel describe the scenes that passed before them in sublime magnificence. But when we descend to the exhortations of prophets and the pastoral letters of evangelists and apostles, it is pretended that a mixed inspiration is discernible. Many of the statements are of the nature of a message from Heaven; others again are no more than comments on the Divine word, or directions for daily conduct, plain rules for church guidance, or perhaps allusions to personal feelings and experience. These writers, we shall be told, were infallibly versed in the matters with which they were commissioned to instruct the church of God; but they were perfectly at liberty to choose their own mode of statement, and could introduce, if they pleased, matters for which divine inspiration would have been superfluous. In the authoritative announcements of divine truth we discern the agency of the Holy Spirit; in the greater or less sublimity of style, in the modes of thought and reasoning, in the characteristics of schools of learning, whether of Athens or Alexandria—in the tenderness of one writer, the ardent zeal of another, the glowing devotion of a third, we recognise Moses or Isaiah, John, Peter, or Paul.

When these reasoners pass from prophecies or epistles to histories, and examine the records of facts and the reports of colloquies or discourses, it would seem to them again as if a yet lower degree of inspiration would suffice. St. Luke, for example, gives in the closing chapters of the Acts a glowing account of St. Paul's last voyage, his shipwreck, his reception at Melita, and his journey to Rome. Localities are described, and allusions to the manners and customs of the times introduced, which give us vivid conceptions of the scenes in which the holy apostle took a part; but it will be suggested that Herodotus has in like manner placed on record descriptions of scenes and localities—that Pliny and Strabo have done the same—and that as each of these writers has his own definite style, so also has St. Luke; that the human features of the writing are so strongly developed, that a high degree of inspiration is scarcely recognized—at least such a one as would absorb individual peculiarities. This perplexity is yet further increased when the Gospels are passed under review. Let it be assumed that inspiration implies divine dictation, in which case the mental state of the writer has no influence on the writing, and the report given, though transcribed by various persons, has only one origin, then our four Gospels will be four coincident records, or will differ from one another as separate paragraphs of the same history; where different facts are related there will be the same style; where the same facts are described there will be the same words. Now our Gospels do not coincide; they do not exhibit the same style; they

do not adhere to the same chronological order ; they do not exhibit
the same phases of the life of Jesus ; and when the same facts are
reported they do not place them in exactly the same aspect.
Moreover, there is occasionally an actual divergence of detail, of
which the enemies of truth have eagerly availed themselves to
attack the credibility of the witnesses. The four Gospels do not
coincide ; but they do that which Infinite Wisdom has ordained as
a more precious result—they *harmonize.* The differences in their
structure are not simply verbal, but organic. Four musical notes,
which differ by slight shades of sound, would produce a single tone
of a somewhat discordant nature ; but if they differ according to
prescribed and measured intervals, a chord is the result which
satisfies the ear by its complete harmony.

We have ever been anxious to account for the differences observable between the evangelical records, on a principle which shall
establish their complete inspiration. We willingly accept Gaussen's
definition, as 'that mysterious power once exerted by the Divine
Spirit on the authors of Holy Writ, to guide them even to the
selection of the words of which they have made use, and to guard
them alike from all error and from all omission.'[a] Now it is to
be noticed that inspiration, considered objectively in God as its
prime cause, is not all that we have now to consider. There are
those who regard it as a mechanical power acting on man. How
often does the infidel demand that the truth of God should be
written as with a sunbeam on the broad expanse of the heavens !
In fact, he would ask for a communicated intuition, that, without
any intervening medium of prophet or prophetical writing, the
truth should be engraven on the human mind. Now it is difficult
to conceive of inspiration without supposing a medium by which
it shall be conveyed. How do we transfer our thoughts to each
other ? Do we by a mere volition awaken in another mind the
precise impressions and reflections which have existed in our own ?
No ; we make use of a medium, and that is *expression.* We make
use of this term as the most general that we can adopt, for it may
include various modes—language, for example, or gesture. But
if we confine our attention to language, and that in its spoken form,
we again find a variety of media. Language is itself a combination
of articulate sounds arbitrarily arranged, each nation and tribe of
the human family having its own peculiar dialect. If therefore we
wish to convey our thoughts, we give them expression by means of
language ; we convey language by articulate sounds framed by our
vocal organs ; those sounds play upon the ear of the person whom
we address, and we hope to awaken in his mind the same thought
to which we had given utterance. We *hope* that this will be the

---

[a] Théopneustie, ou Inspiration plénière des Saintes Ecritures. Par L. Gaussen.
Paris, 1842. P. 43.

case, for after all we have but used imperfect media. There are many steps in the process, at each of which there may be a failure; for we know full well that where the ideas are in any degree complicated which we desire to convey, the difficulty may be great in expressing them even to our own minds; may be increased when we attempt to clothe them in language; the words employed may be associated with different ideas in the mind of the person whom we address; and the train of thought awakened may widely diverge from that which we desired to convey. Such being the complexity of the process by which man communicates with man, shall we expect God to communicate with man by a method more simple or less so? We admit of course that He might, had He so willed it, have dispensed with these media; in other words, He might have wrought without means. But He chooses that means shall be employed; and what is more, He uses existing means to accomplish His purpose. Heavenly truth is to be conveyed to man. Human ideas are the medium by which God chooses to convey it, human language embodies it; the human understanding receives it; and the human soul is influenced by it. In this consists the anthropomorphism of divine inspiration. Nay, we may trace this organic principle further. As sounds must be adapted to the ear on which they are intended to strike, so must ideas be clothed according to the nature of the mind which is expected to recognize them; as every voice has its own distinguishing tone, so also every mind has its own modes of expression. When a man addresses another, he adopts his habitual tones of voice and his ordinary forms of speech. If his address assumes the form of argument, he employs the illustrations with which he is most familiar, and the sequence of ideas to which he is habituated. As his argument rises in intensity, and his desire of securing the conviction of his listener gathers strength, the individuality of his character is more strongly developed, the entire man is revealed, and all that distinguishes him from other men may be observed. Moreover, it is this intense exhibition of individuality which in general moves and influences mankind. By the force of sympathy it brings into play corresponding emotions, and in this way minds are assailed at every point.

Now when a divine revelation was to be made, we recognize at once as consistent with our ideas of inspiration that man should be addressed in his own language. Whether it be in Greek or Hebrew or Chaldee that the heavenly truth finds an utterance, we see that God may make use of one or the other. Further, let the words be oral, as when a voice said at the baptism of our Lord ' Here is my beloved Son '—or written, as when a mysterious hand wrote ' Mene, Tekel, Upharsin,' on the wall, before the eyes of the astonished Belshazzar—we still admit that it is God who makes use of human voice or written characters. But to rise to another step. Let the voice be that of a man—a prophet, habited in the garb of men—or let the writing be that of an apostle or an evangelist—we may still recognize the inspiration. God can and does make use of the voice of the prophet and the pen of the evangelist. And if we arrive at this point, we have only one more admission to request. The prophet or the evangelist has a heart and an understanding, as well as a voice and a pen; an inspired writer has all the attributes of a man—affections, tastes, and all the shades of human character; nay, he may have his own habits of thought, his own modes of observation, his own peculiarities of training and education; and God may make use of all these, and give them full exercise, in order to convey his own inspired infallible word.[b]

We may readily perceive that this non-extinction of the personal attributes of the inspired writer serves a merciful purpose with regard to the recipient of the message. It was not essential to the inspiration of any prophecy that the prophet should understand that which was uttered, that he should believe it, or even that he should be a man of holy life, for the example of Balaam establishes as much. But the sacred writings which edify us came from ' *holy* men of old.' They were men who deeply felt an interest in heavenly things; though we may admit that they had not sounded the depths of every mystery which they were made to convey. And if each writer had personally his own features of character as well as his own besetting infirmities—if there was a point of view from which he loved more than any other to contemplate divine truth—it follows that in their aggregate they supplied that which should commend itself to all orders and conditions of men. The Bible has thereby been constituted a book of universal sympathy—coming from God, but speaking in all varieties of tone and expression the language of men.

Having made these remarks preliminary to our main discussion, by way of avowing our distinct belief that plenary inspiration is perfectly compatible with the manifestation of individual characteristics, we proceed to introduce to our readers two works, one

---

[b] On this point Gaussen's remarks are valuable. ' So far are we from disavowing this human individuality, every where stamped on our sacred books, that, on the contrary, it is with the deepest gratitude and an ever-growing admiration that we reflect on that living, real, human dramatic character, extending with so powerful a charm throughout every portion of the word of God. "Yes," we can rejoice in saying, in the very language of our opponents, " here is the phrase, the tone, the accent of a Moses; there, of a St. John; in the one place of an Isaiah, in the other of an Amos; here, of a Daniel or a St. Peter; there, of a Nehemiah or a St. Paul. They can be recognized, they can be heard, they can be seen; it is as it were impossible to mistake them." We admit the fact; we delight in studying it; we deeply admire it; and we see in it a proof of that divine wisdom which has dictated the Scriptures.'—*Théopneustie*, p. 54.

of which may serve to pave the way for the other.   Mr. Westcott's 'Elements of Gospel Harmony' may be regarded as a suggestive sketch of what the learned Dr. Isaac da Costa of Amsterdam has elaborately developed in his larger work, 'The Four Witnesses.' In each of these writers we are glad to recognize that full and devout belief in Divine inspiration, without which the evangelic histories could do little more than take a place among the fallible productions of man.

Mr. Westcott is a young writer, but his mind has obviously been well trained into habits of careful thought.   Indeed he is occasionally betrayed into the error of over-refinement, and investing a subject with a scholastic obscurity that is not always calculated to work any good end.   There is an unquestionable charm in the discovery that matters long familiar may be subtilized by the intellectual alembic; but obscurity is sometimes only a mock substitute for depth, and truths which might be presented in an obvious form are only

'*Sicklied* o'er by the pale cast of thought.'

The present essay, he tells us, in its original form obtained the Norrisian prize for the year 1850 (in the University of Cambridge), when the following subject was proposed : 'The plenary Inspiration of the Four Gospels is not invalidated by the alleged discrepancies which are objected against them.'   'My chief object,' he adds, ' has been to show a true mean between the idea of a formal harmonization of the Gospels and the abandonment of their absolute truth.   It was certainly an error of the earlier Harmonists that they endeavoured to fit together the mere facts of the Gospels by mechanical ingenuity ; but it is surely no less an error in modern critics, that they hold the perfect truthfulness of Scripture as a matter of secondary moment.   The more carefully we study the details of the Bible, the more fully shall we realize their importance ; and daily experience can furnish parallels to the most intricate conjectures of commentators, who were wrong only so far as they attempted to determine the exact solution of a difficulty, when they should have been contented to wait in patience for a fuller knowledge.'[c]

Many *à priori* arguments might be adduced to prove that a multiform Gospel was needed, from the nature of the subject, as well as from the diversity of those to whom it is addressed.   The entire Bible, as respects the mode in which it has been written, supplies us with a case in point.   Its subject is the unity and perfection of Deity ; and it is addressed to the whole family of man, inclusive of every class of mind, Jewish and Grecian, Barbarian,

---

[c] Preface, p. viii.

Scythian, bond and free. The more exalted a subject is, the more diversity does it require in its treatment. The volume must resolve itself into many sections, the sections into chapters, the chapters into paragraphs. Its index will exhibit a complicated analysis; its table of contents will necessarily lengthen itself out. But how is the need for diverse treatment increased when the minds addressed, and to be enlightened, convinced, and persuaded, are of all degrees of intelligence, and influenced by all phases of circumstance! Let a Newton communicate to a Leibnitz his system of the universe, and he will know what reasoning will be admitted, what terms will be understood—he will know, in short, how far the mind of his illustrious correspondent has been habituated to the investigations which are being brought to bear; but if, after composing a treatise of which Leibnitz is to be reader, his task is to make the celestial movements intelligible to a child, how widely different must be the method he adopts—how much of his subject must of necessity be suppressed! In either case he places himself in imagination on the stand-point of the person to be instructed, and uses terms and methods which shall be intelligible. Now the Scriptures have a far higher topic than the system of the universe or the works of nature; their theme is the God of nature in relation to a fallen world. It is a theme exalted beyond the ken of angelic intelligences; and yet the most debased of mankind are interested in becoming acquainted with it. Philosophers stand in need of the message; but the world has few philosophers amongst its inhabitants. Plato addressed himself to this class, and little more than his name is known to the great majority. The Bible addresses itself to all; and whilst the learned and the wise marvel at the depths of the revelation, the mouths of babes and sucklings are made to perfect God's praise. The explanation of this wondrous spiritual result is, that the varied multitude has been addressed through selected writers, which in their aggregate comprise all their variety; and the multitude, consequently, is made acquainted with the mystery.

The theme of the Gospels is the life of the Redeemer. It had previously been handled by psalmists and prophets. All the Old Testament books had each in its own manner and degree testified of it; but now his earthly sojourn was matter of history. By the providence of God it was ordained, as we might have anticipated, that a single historian should not suffice. We do not say that conflicting biographers were made to occupy themselves with the portraiture, as will be found necessary in the case of those prominent individuals who became identified for a space with the world's history, and have gathered to themselves as many foes as friends. We speak of One who, though he had many enemies, had none who could disprove his words or impugn his actions. We have not therefore the compositions of rival biographers from whose jarring statements we derive a resultant truth, but harmonizing narrators from whose varied but not divergent testimony we draw the richness and fulness of the Saviour's person and work. Neither have we the testimony of four men who have been selected without regard to any previously existing conformity or diversity; their testimony is not valuable simply because it is multiplied. Had the four been of the same nation—had they spoken the same vernacular tongue—had they been equally companions of the Lord Jesus, and much thrown into each other's society—had they been engaged in the same occupations before their conversion, and shared the same office in the Church of God subsequently—as witnesses they would not have had the same weight. It would appear that among the four there were as many Gentiles as Jews; an equal number of apostles and of those who were not so. Moreover these Gospels do not bear the same date. One was written long subsequently to the rest by him whose peculiar office it was to close the inspired canon. The testimony of two or three is true, said the law. How much more then of four; and these in a degree independent—varying at least in nation, in language, in previous habits and education, in the modes by which they would be disposed to contemplate the character of Messiah? Is it not possible that the four writers, thus differing from one another, will accommodate themselves to as many classes of the human family, or to as many phases of the human mind? If in the great community there are some who are warmly attached to ancient institutions, and would reconcile themselves to change only as a gradual development of that which already exists—if the traditions of the past are their law and the universal test by which every new principle is to be tried; if, on the other hand, there is a division consisting of those who are severed from the past—to whom all things wear a new aspect—who have been habituated to institutions which are now beyond their reach, and have no choice but to conform to a new system on its own inherent merits; if to these classes we add the lovers of abstract truth, to whose minds perfection has been portrayed in speculative forms, and the class (which is its antithesis) attached to the objective and the real, preferring detail to idealism; if, we say, these four classes are selected from a community, we shall have nearly all the phases of mind to which a history of any social movement could be submitted; and a quadriform narrative, addressing itself respectively to the four classes, yet adhering with strict truth to the facts described, would give a perfect picture, and one which must needs realize that which is portrayed. We shall yet see whether our four Gospels accomplish a result analogous to that which we have supposed. Before referring to Mr. Westcott's remarks on the several objects of the Gospel

writers, which constitute, as we think, the highest claim to originality in this admirable essay, and give to the writer no mean
claim to a place among the most thoughtful and original of our
rising theologians, we may remark that many of our readers, to
whom the coincidences of the evangelic narratives are more familiar
than the differences, will impute exaggeration to any attempt to
class any of the evangelists (the three synoptists especially) in
different ranks of writers. Let it be remembered, however, that
the more nearly any two of these narratives correspond, the more
significance will attach to the clauses or words in which a difference
may be discovered.

In speaking of the multiformity existing in the subject of the
Gospels, Mr. Westcott remarks acutely, that 'the fulness of Christian
truth will appear clearly if we consider the mode in which it was
set forth by the first circle of its human teachers;' that is
to say, in the epistles addressed to the early church. We may
observe that, omitting that of St. Jude, we find the Epistles, like
the Gospels, to be the work of four pens. Peter, John, and James
the son of Alphæus, three of the disciples, and the great apostle to
the Gentiles, are the four to whom we allude. Now, suggesting
that one of the epistle writers was the fourth evangelist—that
St. Peter had the second evangelist as his companion—let us quote
Mr. Westcott's remarks on St. James and St. Paul :—

' With some,' he says, ' the mysterious glories of the ancient creed
were mingled with the purer light of Christianity; and they transferred
the majesty of the Mosaic law, which they had observed with reverent
or even ascetic devotion, to the new and spiritual faith. St. James sets
before us this form of Christianity; he contemplates it from this side
of Judaism, as the final end and aim of the earlier training. His language must be taken in an objective sense; so that "faith" is almost
equivalent to "profession," while "works" are the only outward proof
of true vitality. From this position he proves that the historic belief of
the sons of Abraham is not enough to secure their spiritual acceptance,
and unfolds the real essence of that external religion (θρησκεία) which
the ritual service regarded.[d] With him Christianity was like a flower,
which is fuller, indeed, and more perfect than the bud from which it
opens, while still it rests on the same support, and is confined within
the same circle.

' The true antithesis to this view we find in one who was called to

---

[d] Coleridge, in his 'Aids to Reflection' (Aphorism xxiii. p. 14), gives an admirable comment on St. James's use of the word θρησκεία (James i. 26, 27), which
corresponds with Mr. Westcott's view. The outward service (θρησκεία) of ancient
religion, the rites, ceremonies, and ceremonial vestments of the old law, had morality for their substance. They were the letter of which morality was the spirit;
the enigma of which morality was the meaning. But morality itself is the service
and ceremonial (*cultus exterior*, θρησκεία) of the Christian religion. The scheme
of grace and truth that became (ἐγένετο) through Jesus Christ the faith that looks
down into the perfect law of liberty, has light for its garment; its very robe is
righteousness.

believe in a glorified Lord, and not to follow a suffering teacher. With St. Paul, Christianity is a new creation; it appeared before him in its power and independence, and, recognizing there the source of spiritual life, he regarded it wholly from within—subjectively—and then "faith" alone is its test, since works may be wrought through a servile obedience. We must, however, gladly receive both this inner and that outer view; the teaching of the apostles must be combined and not identified, for we lose the fulness of the truth if we attempt to make out their literal accordance; they wrought differently for the establishment of the Christian society, and they wrote differently for its edification.'[e]

It may be readily admitted that St. James has the same resemblance to St. Matthew that St. Paul has to St. Luke. The two former were companion apostles; the two latter were fellow-travellers and preachers of the word. St. James writes, as does St. Matthew, to Hebrews; St. Paul and St. Luke alike address themselves to Gentiles. St. Mark is well known to have been the companion and disciple of St. Peter—that his history may almost be called the Gospel according to St. Peter, whilst that of Luke is the Gospel according to St. Paul. When, therefore, we have admitted an identity of aim between James and Matthew, we may have the names of Matthew, Mark, Luke, and John, corresponding to James, Peter, Paul, and John, the four evangelists to the four who have (if we except the epistle of St. Jude) completed the New Testament canon. This correspondence is something more than accidental; for it shows that the same multiformity was necessary for the exhibition of doctrine to the church as was made use of in portraying the life of Christ. Doctrine is abstract history, as history is concrete doctrine; and though the one is delivered in a dogmatical, the other in a narrative form, the essence of each will correspond, and the methods needful for their development have strong features in common.

Mr. Westcott traces with considerable ingenuity the principle of quadriformity as existing in the aspect of the Roman world, in the requirements of spiritual teaching, and even in the chief forms of doctrinal error. If we have in the Evangelists the Jew resident in Judea, the Roman proselyte, the Hellenist proselyte, and the Jew resident in Patmos, and made familiar with the Grecian schools of philosophy, so in the Roman world the Gospel had to find acceptance with the devout Israelite, the hardy son of Rome, the Areopagite, and the cultivated Alexandrine.

The fourfold spiritual problem will best be described in Mr. Westcott's own words:

'The Apostles had to unfold and declare the significance of the *past;* they had to point out the substance of Christianity, as shadowed forth in the earlier dispensation; they had to make known the mighty

[e] Elements of the Gospel Harmony, p. 30.

Lawgiver of a new covenant—the divine King of a spiritual Israel—the Prophet of a universal Church. They had to connect Christianity with Judaism.

'Yet more; they had to vindicate the reality of the *present*; they had to set forth the activity and energy of our Lord's life, apart from the traditions of Moriah and Sinai; to exhibit the Gospel as a simple revelation from heaven, with all the vividness and life of those who had witnessed its first promulgation. They had to connect Christianity with history.

'Again, they had to declare the hopefulness of the *future*; they had to show that the Gospel fully satisfies the inmost wants of our nature; that it not only removes "the leprosy of castes, and the blindness of pagan sensuality," but gives life and strength to the helpless sufferer, who has no one to put him in the healing waters. They had to connect Christianity with man.

'Nor was this all; many there were whom their deep searching of the human heart had taught to feel the want of a present God; these longed to see their ardent aspirations realized in the life of the Saviour whom they had embraced, and to find their hopes confirmed and directed by his own words. For such, a spiritual history was needed, and the Christian teachers had to exhibit our Lord in His eternal relations to the Father, alike manifested in the past, the present, and the future—as the Creator, the Redeemer, and the Judge. They had to connect Christianity with God.'[f]

We will not dwell at present upon the exact correspondence of this quadriformity with that of the Gospel writers, for to our own minds the distinction between the second and third Evangelists is not so obvious as that we can style the one the Evangelist of the present, the other the Evangelist of the future. In our own view St. Matthew's Gospel is Messianic, St. Luke's historical, St. John's prophetical. We think it enough to add that St. Mark's is a transition Gospel between the first and second. We can more readily agree with Mr. Westcott's remarks on the difference of the Gospels as indicated by the four classes of heretics who distracted the early Church. He quotes (1 Cor. i. 12) 'One said, I am of Paul; and another, I am of Apollos; and another, I am of Cephas; and another, I am of Christ.' If the last mentioned party professed to be of *Matthew,* as the Evangelist apostle who aimed most to establish Christ as the Messiah of Israel, the remaining three names comprise Cephas, the friend of St. Mark; Paul, the companion of St. Luke; and the Alexandrine Apollos, who drew his knowledge from the same fountains as St. John.

Let us, however, listen to Mr. Westcott's comment.

'The rational exhibition of Christianity, its mystic depths, its outward and ritual aspect, and its historic power were thus separated and substituted for its complex essence; just as the Sadducee, the Essene,

---

[f] Elements of Gospel Harmony, p. 34.

the Pharisee, and the Herodian, had already found in the law a basis for their discordant systems. In later times these fundamental differences were clearly and boldly defined. Some were not content to cherish the ancient law with natural reverence and pride, but insisted on the universal reception of the Mosaic ritual; they saw in Jesus nothing but the human Messiah, and in the Christian faith nothing but the perfection of Judaism; they rejected St. Paul as an apostate, and retained only the Hebrew Gospel of St. Matthew—the life of the second lawgiver modified and interpolated to suit their peculiar views.

'Again; others there were who dwelt only on the works of Messiah's power, and not on the mysteries of His Incarnation and human sufferings—who separated Jesus from Christ—and thus distinguishing between the divine power and the human instrument, found their Gospel in the recital of miracles and mighty acts, which bore the impress of God, rather than in words and discourses, which might seem like those of man. These preferred the Gospel of St. Mark.

'Such were the results of a purely outward view of Christianity, according as men saw in it a fixed form of religion or a specific manifestation of God; others, however, regarded it in its logical or mystical aspect. The principles of St. Paul were soon carried out to the rejection of the ancient covenant; a son of a Christian bishop, ... Marcion, found in Christianity a new and spiritual religion, framed to defeat the earthly kingdom which had been promised to the people of Israel. He endeavoured to construct systematically a universal faith, and placed its historic basis on the Pauline Gospel of St. Luke.

'Lastly, some of the mystic schools of the Gnostics found a support for their doctrines in the Gospel of St. John. The deep significance of his language, the symbolic use of the words "Light" and "Darkness," "Life" and "Death," "the World," "the Word," and "the Truth"—furnished the Eastern speculator with an occasion for his favourite theories.'[g]

We have thus far given *à priori* arguments for a quadriform or multiform Gospel, and the general features by which we infer that the Evangelical narratives which we possess correspond to the previously existing want. It will be evident, however, to any reader, that no satisfactory appropriation of the Evangelists can be made to the respective classes of mankind and modes of thought, until their distinguishing peculiarities have been pointed out by a minute criticism. The old fathers were in the habit of following the example of Jerome and Augustine in adapting the cherubic symbol to the four Gospel writers. A theory was admitted throughout the Christian world by which the 'man' was assigned to St. Matthew, the 'lion' to St. Mark, the 'ox' to St. Luke, and the 'eagle' to St. John. Doubtless it would be equally easy to

---

[g] Elements of Gospel Harmony, p. 49.

find in the four winds, in the four quarters of the globe, in the four seasons, in the four elements, or in any other quadrilateral combination in the world of nature, symbols that would answer the same purpose. Mr. Westcott's essay shows that he is fully competent to substantiate his theories by an examination of the Gospel-text, and in many of the leading features he has succeeded in doing so. It was not, however, possible to complete an investigation of such magnitude within the limits of an essay, and this has sometimes given an appearance of unauthorized assumption or hasty hypothesis where greater space would have advantageously permitted him to draw the different shades of difference with stricter accuracy. We would be careful not to lay these charges too heavily upon Mr. Westcott, as we gladly discern in his method that which would tend to yet deeper discovery, and in the knowledge he has at his command the result of patient and laborious research.

We now beg to introduce to our readers the more important work of Dr. da Costa, entitled 'The Four Witnesses,' with which Mr. David Dundas Scott has by his translational labours enriched our theological literature. We have read this work with unqualified satisfaction. The line of reasoning adopted by this great Dutch theologian is in the highest degree accurate and safe. If the true principles of inductive philosophy can be applied to theology, the present work is an example. Everything is made to proceed from rigid experiment. Four Gospels are in our possession, which we take for granted are the inspired productions of the men whose names they bear, and of whose personal history we have incidental notice. Each of the four is a record of the life of Jesus, and three confine themselves so much to the same class of events and discourses as to be termed ' synoptical ;' but no two are exactly alike. Each Gospel has portions which are peculiar to itself ; some passages there are which belong to two Gospels, some to three ; whilst a limited number of transactions of a more important character, as the miracle of the loaves and the sufferings and death of Christ, are treated of by the whole diatessaron. We have, as it were, four planetary orbits described about the same central sun, evincing a general resemblance, but differing in their elements. To ascertain these elements a series of observations must be accurately made and tabulated, and from these the respective ellipticities, inclinations, and nodal longitudes will be deduced. Thus do we illustrate the task which Dr. da Costa has most conscientiously performed without hasty generalisations, without an ill-regulated desire to substantiate a theory, but with a scrupulous care to discover from the differences of detail, style, and subject-matter what were the leading aims of the Gospel writers.

The investigation of which we should desire to give some faint sketch to our readers is one that relates to the internal structure of the Gospels. It is well, however, to premise that enough is known of the Evangelists, their respective countries, the language in which they wrote, the persons to whom they addressed themselves, and the immediate objects which they had each of them in view, to give a key to those differences in detail which we find by accurate inquiry. A preliminary hypothesis approximating to the truth is an advantageous, if not a necessary, aid to researches of this kind. Let us therefore glance first at the better understood facts relating to the Evangelists, from whatever source they may be derived.

Matthew, surnamed Levi, the son of Alphæus, was a native of Galilee, though of what city we are not informed. Before his conversion to Christianity, he was a τελώνης, or tax-gatherer, under the Romans, collected the customs of all goods exported or imported at Capernaum, and received the toll paid by all passengers who went by water from that place. While employed at the receipt of custom Jesus called him to be his disciple, and, subsequently, commissioned him to be an Apostle and preacher of the everlasting Gospel. Thus was he qualified for that task by which he was the instrument of so much blessing to the Church of God, for he was an eye-witness of those transactions which his pen has described as well as a hearer of the discourses which his pen has recorded. To assign a date to St. Matthew's Gospel would only be to attempt a balancing of the arguments of many learned men who vary in their conclusions from 38 A.D. to 63 A.D.; but it is clear that it took precedence of the other Gospels in order of time, and was published whilst the temple was standing, and the Jewish ordinances observed by all believers who were of Hebrew origin. It is more than probable that this Gospel was in the first instance written in the language of Judea, and afterwards translated by the Apostle into the Hellenistic form, in which it has been transmitted to us. If the earlier date is admitted, for which such writers as Owen, Tomline, and Townson have contended; there was, according to Greswell's computation,[h] no Gentile Apostolate when this Gospel was promulgated, and the Christian Church was strictly confined to the Jewish nation, and even to the territory of Palestine; consequently, this Jewish Apostle may well be expected to have addressed 'his own kinsmen according to the flesh.' The voice of antiquity accords with Irenæus, Origen, and Eusebius in testifying that Matthew wrote his Gospel in Judea, for the Jewish nation, while the Church consisted wholly of the circum-

---

[h] Harmony of the Evangelists, vol. ii.

cision, that is of Jewish and Samaritan believers. From the Jewish Apostle and companion of our Lord we turn to one who was not so honoured, and who may have been no more than a Gentile proselyte to the Jewish religion. That he was the friend and companion of Peter is universally reported, and the person alluded to by that Apostle (1 Pet. v. 13) as Marcus my *son*, by which we understand a son in the faith. He may or may not have been the John surnamed Mark, the son of Mary, a pious woman at Jerusalem, and sister's son to Barnabas (Col. iv. 10). This supposition, which we must admit is most commonly received, would at once establish Mark as a Jew by birth, and one of those friends of St. Paul whom, in the Epistle to the Colossians, he styles ' of the circumcision.' The external evidence does no more than leave it an open question whether there were two Marks or one ; whether the same individual was intimate alike with St. Paul and St. Peter ; whether the tradition that the Gospel was written from Rome tends to strengthen the argument that Peter resided for a portion of his life in that city. What St. Mark's Gospel is, and to whom it is addressed, must be determined mainly from its internal features.

The author of the third Gospel was, according to Eusebius, a native of Antioch, that centre of heathenism in which Christians first received that name as a reproach in which they glory. It seems most probable that he was descended from a Gentile stock, while in his youth he had embraced Judaism. His profession was that of a physician ; his superior education as such is discernible not only in the elegant Greek which he employs, but also in the scientific terms in which he refers to various diseases. At the same time we observe a tinge of Hebraistic phraseology combined with an accurate knowledge of the Jewish religion, its traditions, rites, ceremonies, and usages, which indicate his having sat at the feet of some Jewish instructor. In these particulars he was well qualified to be the companion of the great Gentile Apostle, a circumstance which is made apparent in several passages of his own history of the Acts of that Apostle, as well as in incidental allusions in St. Paul's Epistles. From the unanimous voice of antiquity, we have the testimony that this Gospel, which was probably written A.D. 64, after the word of truth had been widely preached to the Gentiles, was written for the benefit of Gentile converts, and with a view to win to Christ's religion those who had been trained as ' aliens from the commonwealth of Israel.'

Of St. John we seem to know much more than of either of the synoptists. He was the beloved disciple, one who had in early years followed his Master, and from his lips received the promise that ' he should tarry till he came.' He lived to see the destruction of Jerusalem, and it was most probably about the year 97 that this Apostle wrote his Gospel, selecting Ephesus as the place of his residence. Though John was the son of Zebedee, a Galilean fisherman, though (Acts iv. 13) he is ranked among the ἀγράμματοι and ἰδιῶται, in our version rendered *unlearned* and *ignorant* men, but which would with greater correctness be translated *unskilled in Jewish law* and *uninvested with official dignity*, it is evident that he was well instructed in the Hebrew Scriptures and not unacquainted with the philosophy of the Alexandrine schools.

The object of this Evangelist in writing his Gospel may be expressed most forcibly in his own words : 'These are written that ye might believe that Jesus is the Christ, the Son of God, and that believing ye might have life through his name.'—John xx. 31.

We do not regard it as superfluous to refer to these well-known features of the personal history of the Gospel-writers, because we are thereby prepared to anticipate in some degree a divergence in style, though modified by an identity of subject and controlled by the guidance of the Holy Ghost. They wrote in different countries, they addressed themselves to distinct classes of readers, they had each their own view of our Lord and his mediatorial work. Their harmonizing though non-coincident narratives have been appointed by the Superintending Providence of God as the revelation of the life of Jesus, and in them we have all that can settle the faith of the inquirer, and edify the heart of the believing disciple.

We have already noticed that St. Matthew was a Jew by birth, a publican by occupation, and an Apostle by the appointment of his Divine Master. In the details and style of his Gospel this may readily be traced. He does not conceal his Apostleship, though with characteristic humility he differs from the other Evangelists in styling himself Matthew the *Publican* (Matt. x. 3). His humility in not suppressing the nature of his original employment, disreputable though it was in the eyes of those whom he addressed, may be more strikingly observed by a comparison of three accounts of his calling as a disciple and servant of the Lord.

MATT. ix. 9, 10.	MARK ii. 14, 15.	LUKE v. 27-29.
9 And as Jesus passed forth from thence, he saw *a man*, named Matthew, sitting at the receipt of custom: and he saith unto him, Follow me. And he arose, and followed him. 10 And it came to pass, as Jesus sat at meat *in the* house, many publicans and sinners came and sat down with him and his disciples.	14 And as he passed by, he saw Levi the son of Alphæus sitting at the receipt of custom, and he said unto him, Follow me. And he arose and followed him. 15 And it came to pass, that, as Jesus sat at meat in *his* house, many publicans and sinners sat also together with Jesus and his disciples: for there were many, and they followed him.	27 And after these things he went forth, and saw a publican, named Levi, sitting at the receipt of custom: and he said unto him, Follow me. 28 And *he left all*, rose up, and followed him. 29 And Levi *made him a great feast in his own house:* and there was a great company of publicans and of others that sat down with them.

On this narrative, as given by the three Evangelists, Dr. da Costa makes the following comment—

'Speaking of himself, the first Evangelist calls the publican who was called to the Apostleship, *a man* (ἄνθρωπον, an expression no wise honourable in this sense), *a man named Matthew.* The second and the third Evangelists give him his own proper Jewish name; one of them adds, by way of honourable distinction, the name of his father, *Levi, the son of Alphæus.* There is, also, a particular circumstance which we find noted, not by himself, but by another Evangelist (St. Luke)—that he *left all* to follow Jesus. There have been doubts, however, as to the identity of the person, on account of the names of Levi and Matthew; and particularly because, in the first of the Gospels, we are not expressly told that the feast was held in Matthew's house. But it is precisely this omission of the *feast* in the Gospel of St. Matthew, and still more the omission of the name of the owner of the house in which the feast was held, that clearly shows that here he was speaking of his own proper self—a personality which the authors of these writings are accustomed to put forward as little as possible wherever anything praiseworthy or honourable happens to have to be mentioned. The mention of Matthew's *leaving all* to follow the Lord, is not to be found in his Gospel, but only in St. Luke.'[i]

The same humility in the publican-apostle may be observed throughout his Gospel, in the readiness with which he seizes any point in the characters of those whom he portrays, which may embody this grace. He alone records the expostulation of John the Baptist, addressed to our Lord, 'Comest thou to me?' (iii. 14). He alone supplies the quotation from the prophecy with reference to the humiliation of Jesus, 'He shall be called a Nazarene' (ii. 23). But the Apostle, as we have suggested, does not suppress his high calling in the Church of God. It is he who relates the promise of the Kingdom to the twelve expressed in its richest plenitude (xix. 28), 'And Jesus said unto them, Verily I say unto you, that ye which have followed me, in the regeneration when the Son of man shall sit on the throne of his glory, ye also shall sit upon twelve thrones, judging the twelve tribes of Israel.' It is he, too, who gives the solemn institution of the baptismal rite in connection with the apostolic commission (xxviii. 19), 'Go ye therefore and teach all nations, baptizing them in the name of the Father, and of the Son, and of the Holy Ghost : teaching them to observe all things whatsoever I have commanded you;' and he adds the emphatic words which are recorded by no other Evangelist, 'Lo, I am with you alway, even unto the end of the world' (ver. 20).

St. Matthew may always be recognized as the Apostle Evan-

---

[i] Da Costa, p. 13.

gelist of ignoble origin, but humbly rejoicing to be the inspired chronicler of the life of Jesus. It is yet more evident from the internal structure of his Gospel that he was the Hebrew Apostle writing for the Hebrew nation. The language appears throughout clothed in an Old Testament garb. In the very first verse he styles his history ' the book of the generation of Jesus Christ, the son of David, the son of Abraham,' as though he would proclaim the 'second Adam' in the very words of Gen. v. 1 : 'This is the book of the generations of Adam.' So, also, he quotes more than his brother Evangelists from the prophecies, and refers to their fulfilment in the various incidents of the Saviour's life. They make many references, it is true, but in a manner subordinate to their own history; St. Matthew deals with the fulfilment of prophecy as though it were his main object. Moreover, he does not confine himself to express and direct citation from the Old Testament. Mr. Hartwell Horne's valuable analysis of the quotations from the Hebrew Scriptures in the New Testament shows that in those which differ slightly from the original, and in those which agree in sense but not in words, St. Matthew is more abundant than the remaining three combined. But St. Matthew seems to *think* in Old Testament language, and even to bear the Lord's words in remembrance in association with the words of ancient in spiration. Dr. da Costa argues that this peculiarity of St. Matthew need not militate against our belief of his being absolutely inspired. We subjoin his remarks :—

' St. Matthew throws in such allusions (or rather they come of themselves) in his exhibition of the works, the sayings, and the parables of our Lord, in the way either of paraphrase, or of development, or of explanation. For it pertains to the high authority of the sacred writers not always to render *literally* their Master's words, but, as it were, to identify these with their own inspired conceptions and expositions of them, in such sort that one cannot make, and that there is no need of making a distinction. Here we may apply our Lord's saying, "He that heareth you, heareth me." ' [k]

A careful attention to this principle adopted by the first Evangelist of clothing his subject in a Hebrew dress will go far to explain many alleged discrepancies in his Gospel. He speaks of the fulfilment of prophecies, as, for example, that which we have quoted, ' He shall be called a Nazarene,' where we cannot specify the *prophet* from whose pages they are taken. He disregards chronological sequence in his record of Jesus Christ's acts and discourses, his object being to group them according to their connection with prophecy rather than in the historic order under which

---

[k] Da Costa, p. 18.

a writer would arrange them who did not participate in that aim. So also he shows a disregard to number, not unlike that with which he deals with historical dates; he frequently uses the *plural* where his brother Evangelists adopt the *singular*, speaking of the blind, the lame, the paralytics, where another Evangelist might, with greater attention to detail, specify the individual, or even supply his name and that of his family.

In the internal structure of St. Matthew's Gospel we discover evident traces of the Hebrew Apostle as the writer. We find as the great subject, Jesus the Messiah, King over Sion, Prince and Saviour of Israel and of all nations. The opening chapter contains the *legal* genealogy of Christ, connecting him with kings and patriarchs, to whom the promises had been given, showing thereby that of them 'as concerning the flesh He came who is God over all, blessed for ever.' As the genealogy given by St. Matthew connects Messiah's person with the progenitors of the race of Israel, so also the sermon on the Mount connects his teaching with the law, and exhibits him as the prophet like unto Moses, and yet as much greater than Moses as the son is than the servant. Here we find Jesus speaking by authority and not as the scribes, not as a mere interpreter of the law, but as one from whom the first lawgiver derived his commission. The prophet predicted by Moses had arisen, and the Hebrew evangelist is careful to record the title applied to him by the multitudes at the time of his solemn entry into Jerusalem—a title omitted by the other Gospel-writers : 'This is Jesus the Prophet of Nazareth of Galilee.' (xxi. 11.)

From the Gospel of Matthew, the Hebrew apostle, we pass to that of Mark, the Gentile convert. Admitting that it may be left as an open question whether the evangelist Mark and the John Mark who was sister's son to Barnabas be identical, we cannot but lean to the supposition that they were distinct. All writers are agreed that the Gospel was written under the inspection of St. Peter ; and if so, we have at the outset a strong presumption against the writer having been the companion of St. Paul, as we know John Mark to have been ; St. Peter and St. Paul having apostolic commissions of so different a character, the one being sent to the Jews, the other to the Gentiles. The most satisfactory solution of this question, so far as it admits of being solved, will be derived from the internal evidence of the writing ; and here we think strong traces may be discerned of a Gentile cast of thought, contrasting with the Hebrew tone of the preceding Gospel. True, it will be remarked that this evangelist wrote to instruct and edify Gentiles or Romans :—

' But why not,' asks Dr. da Costa, ' prefer this simple explanation, that he, the son of St. Peter in the faith, was in point of fact born himself among the heathen—nay, was himself a Roman? And why should not the friend and fellow-labourer of St. Peter have been a Gentile by birth, as well as St. Luke, the friend and companion of St. Paul? Yes; how striking, if the fact be once admitted, that our four Gospels should thus have had for authors, not only two apostles of Israel, but two evangelists also, one Greek and one Roman, from the nations that were admitted to the fellowship of the Gospel! How striking that thus, from the very first among the historical witnesses of the Gospel of Jesus Christ, the middle wall of partition is seen to be taken away!'

The probability of St. Mark's Roman origin is confirmed by his use of Latin words in a Greek form, in a manner quite distinct from his fellow-evangelists. It is true that Latinisms are employed even by St. Matthew, as, for examples, the words ἀσσάριον (Matt. x. 29), κῆνσὸς (Matt. xvii. 25); but it is evident that these words had been imported into Judæa, and their usage enforced by their Roman conquerors. St. Mark, on the other hand, uses similar terms, as if from long habit. He alone terms a military executioner σπεκουλάτωρ, speculator (Mark vi. 27); and where St. Matthew and St. Luke translate the term centurion into pure Greek, ἑκατοντάρχης, he uses Latin-Greek, κεντυρίων.

An indication yet more recondite of St. Mark's Roman origin, and possibly of the military training which Dr. da Costa is inclined to attribute to him, may be traced in his reference to the Roman *watches*, as compared with parallel passages of the first and third evangelists :—

MATT. xxiv. 42-44.	MARK xiii. 33-37.	LUKE xii. 35-38.
42 *Watch* therefore: for ye know not what hour your Lord doth come.	33 Take ye heed, *watch and pray:* for ye know not when the time is.	35 Let your loins be girded about, and your lights burning;
43 But know this, that if the goodman of the house had known in *what watch* the thief would come, he would have watched, and would not have suffered his house to be broken up.	34 For the Son of man is as a man taking a far journey, who left his house, and gave authority to his servants, and to every man his work, and commanded the porter *to watch.*	36 And ye yourselves like unto men that wait for their lord, when he will return from the wedding; that when he cometh and knocketh, they may open unto him immediately.
44 Therefore *be ye also ready:* for in such an hour as ye think not the Son of man cometh.	35 *Watch ye therefore:* for ye know not when the master of the house cometh, at EVEN, or at MIDNIGHT, or at the COCK-CROWING, or in the MORNING:	37 Blessed are those servants whom the lord when he cometh shall find watching: verily I say unto you, that he shall gird himself, and make them sit down to meat, and will come forth and serve them.
	36 Lest coming suddenly he find you sleeping.	38 And if he shall come in the SECOND WATCH, or come in the THIRD WATCH, and find them so, blessed are those servants.
	37 And what I say unto you I say unto all, *Watch.*	

St. Mark's enumeration of the Roman vigiliæ by the terms which would be employed by soldiers of that nation contrasts remarkably with St. Luke's reference to three watches only, the division of the night originally used by the Hebrews.

We find a further trace of the Gentile in St. Mark, in the explanations which he gives of Jewish customs as one who had observed them from without. Compare the following parallel passages :—

Matt. xv. 1, 2.	Mark vii. 1–5.
1 Then came to Jesus scribes and Pharisees, which were of Jerusalem, saying,	1 Then came together unto him the Pharisees, and certain of the scribes, which came from Jerusalem.
2 Why do thy disciples transgress the tradition of the elders? for they wash not their hands when they eat bread.	2 And when they saw some of his disciples eat bread with defiled (*that is to say, with unwashen*) hands, they found fault.
	3 For the Pharisees, and *all the Jews*, except they wash their hands oft, eat not, holding the tradition of the elders.
	4 And when they come from the market, except they wash they eat not. And many other things there be which they have received to hold, as the washing of cups, and pots, brazen vessels, and of tables.
	5 Then the Pharisees and scribes asked him, Why walk not thy disciples according to the tradition of the elders?

' This explanatory statement,' remarks Dr. da Costa, ' is not given by our author as one of Jewish birth would have given it to a foreigner, but manifestly in the tone and with the words to be expected from a well-informed narrator, who nevertheless was just as much a foreigner and a Gentile as those whom he addressed. The more we reflect on the expression *all the Jews*, the more we feel convinced that he who wrote thus was not himself a *Jew by birth;* and consequently, that whatever in this Gospel is written from a non-Israelite point of view must be explained not only by the position of those to whom this Gospel was addressed, but also by the national origin and national peculiarities of the person by whom it was written.' [m]

The style of this evangelist is peculiarly his own, and by its striking characteristics indicates what was his peculiar object. Not being so much the historian as the biographer, he has not aimed at introducing into his narrative every incident that admitted of record, so much as selecting those more prominent facts which would reveal the Divine Person who is his great theme. Hence he abridges the history, whilst he enlarges many of the details. Conversations, addresses, and discussions are omitted, whilst minute descriptions of particulars which other evangelists have passed over in silence are carefully noted down. St. Mark becomes what we should term a spirited writer. He is always graphic, flowing, and eminently realizes to our imagination the scenes which are portrayed. Witness his unique description of the Gadarene demoniac (Mark v. 5), ' Who had his dwelling among the tombs ; and no man could bind him, no, not with chains ; because

---

[m] Da Costa, p. 108.

that he had been often bound with fetters and chains, and the chains had been plucked asunder by him, and the fetters broken in pieces; neither could any man tame him. And always, night and day, he was in the mountains, and in the tombs, crying and cutting himself with stones.' A similar pictorial eloquence may be observed in the description of the child possessed by a dumb spirit, whom our Lord cured on his descent from the Mount of Transfiguration (see Mark ix. 14-28). The foul spirit *tears* (ῥήσσει) the unhappy victim, who thereupon *foams* (ἀφρίζει) and *gnasheth with his teeth* (τρίζει τοὺς ὀδόντας), and *pineth away* (ξηραίνεται); anon the spirit *teareth* him (σπαράσσει), and the possessed person *falls on the ground*, and *wallows, foaming* (κυλίεται ἀφρίζων). He afterwards reiterates this tearing of the child (ver. 26); the spirit cried, and rent him sore (κρᾶξαν καὶ σπαράξαν), and came out of him.

This eloquent style of writing harmonizes, as we have suggested, with St. Mark's great object of presenting to our view the Blessed Saviour as perfect man. In the outset of his Gospel he styles him Jesus Christ the Son of God, while St. Matthew calls him the Son of David; but this is consistent with the general mode adopted by the inspired writers in portraying the twofold nature, the less obvious title being given as an antithesis to the circumstances under which he is represented. It is 'Jesus of Nazareth' who appears to the persecutor Saul, speaking from the clouds of heaven; it is the 'Son of God' whom the wonder-stricken centurion recognizes as he hangs upon the cross. Having announced this divine title of Jesus, St. Mark applies the eloquence of his language to represent him in all the different phases of his human nature. Not only are the earthly scenes in which he takes a part brought before us with peculiar vividness, but the emotions which exhibited a condescension to our infirmity carefully noted down. We read of his sighs when he cured a deaf man; his anguish of soul at the malice of the Pharisees, for he *sighed deeply* (ἀναστενάξας), viii. 12. He looked round on the Scribes and Pharisees on another occasion with anger, 'being *grieved* for the hardness of their hearts.' In like manner, it is St. Mark who records how much displeased Jesus was (ἠγανάκτησε) at the disciples for preventing children being brought to him (x. 14); and how, on the other hand, he *loved* (x. 21) with a kindly feeling the rich young man on account of his natural amiability. Do these marks of a nature condescending to human weakness suggest a doubt of the Saviour's proper deity? No; we are made ever to bear in mind by the evangelist's opening phrase that he is 'Son of God.' Hence we may go yet further, and find no hindrance to this belief in the words of our Lord, recorded *only* by St. Mark (xiii. 32): 'But of that day and that hour knoweth no man; no, not the angels which are in heaven, *neither the Son*, but the Father.' The scope of the evangelist, his style, and the relation which he bears to the other three, combine in making clear to our minds that special aspect of the grand truth which he laboured to establish.

Passing from the second to the third evangelist, we come to the writings of one whom we are better able to identify. In St. Luke we have the beloved physician, the companion of St. Paul—one who is mentioned in the Epistle to the Colossians in a category distinct from those who were of the circumcision. Consequently, we are led to believe that he was a Gentile by birth, as we know that to the Gentiles his Gospel was addressed. At the same time it is evident, from many passages, that he was closely acquainted with Jewish usages. Though less Hebraistic than Matthew, he is obviously more so than St. Mark; and this consideration would suggest that he may have been in the first instance a Jewish proselyte, and one who was trained in medicine and Grecian literature in one of those towns of Syria or Asia Minor where society assumed something of a transition state between the Jewish and the Grecian. The art of medicine was at that time very much in the hands of the Greeks, and particularly of slaves and freedmen—a sort of people who were often discovered to be at that era highly gifted, and in many respects in advance of their social and political superiors. The termination of the Greek name Λουκᾶς was common to the name of many freedmen of that period. St. Luke, therefore, may have been one who attained to social liberty, ere he received the higher liberty wherewith Christ made him free. Do we trace the ' beloved physician' in the style of his writings? We may in many cases observe the technical accuracy with which diseases are referred to, as the ' great fever' of Peter's wife's mother, the obscured vision of Elymas, the fever and dysentery of Publius at Malta, and the dreadful malady which cut short the career of Herod Agrippa. If the terms used by St. Luke denote his medical education, no less do we observe a quick discernment of facts, or even of rhetorical figures which are in any way associated with his early studies. It is he alone of the four evangelists by whom the healing of Malchus' ear is mentioned (Luke xxii. 51). He alone accounts for the sleep of the disciples in the garden of Gethsemane during the agony of their Master, as traceable to their depression of mind (xxii. 45). In the commissions given by our Lord to the twelve, and again to the seventy, he is most careful to observe the clause, ' Heal the sick' (ix. 2 ; x. 9). In this Gospel, moreover, we see Jesus more prominently than in the others as ' forgiving our iniquities and healing our diseases.' We may mention also that by St. Luke alone is the proverb placed on record, ' Physician, heal thyself' (iv. 23).

We have said that in St. Luke we recognize one who was familiar with Jewish laws and customs. Whilst, however, St. Matthew views the subject in hand more exclusively through a Jewish medium, watching everywhere for the fulfilment of the prophecies, especially as they related to the Jewish people, St. Luke, without disparaging the claims of the Jew, connects his fall with the bringing in of the Gentile. His Gospel appears to illustrate the argument, ' If the fall of them be the riches of the world, and the diminishing of them the riches of the Gentiles, how much more their fulness? For *I speak to you Gentiles*, inasmuch as I am the apostle of the Gentiles, I magnify mine office' (Rom. xi. 12, 13). Jewish privileges and Jewish woes are alternately set before us. See the exclamation of Zacharias (v. 68): ' Blessed be the Lord God of *Israel.*' See also the annunciation to Mary of the kingdom of Jesus (v. 32, 33): ' The Lord God shall give unto him the *throne of his father David*; and he shall reign over the *house of Jacob* for ever.' On the other hand, where do we find so copiously as in this Gospel the woes pronounced against the Scribe, the Pharisee, and the entire city and polity? Our remarks concerning the connection of Jewish fall with Gentile privilege will find the most direct illustration in that striking prophecy (xxi. 24): ' And they shall fall by the edge of the sword, and shall be led away captive into all nations; and Jerusalem shall be trodden down of the Gentiles, *until the times of the Gentiles be fulfilled.*'

In suggesting a correspondence between the entire scope of St. Luke's Gospel and a particular passage quoted from the Epistle to the Romans, we touch upon a principle which admits of much wider exemplification :—

' The epistles of St. Paul,' says Dr. da Costa, ' and the two books left to us by St. Luke, when placed together, are often found the readiest helps for mutually explaining, elucidating, and confirming each other. We meet with, or recognize in both, the same fundamental ideas, the same points of view, the same representations of the highest doctrines of the Gospel; and so much is this the case, that from the most remote times the Gospel of St. Luke has been thought a Pauline Gospel; and that, following out this idea, the Marcionites (the adherents of a false doctrine, who owned no authority except that of St. Paul, understood in their own way) admitted none of the Gospels but that of St. Luke exclusively.'[n]

It is remarkable that in one of St. Paul's Epistles we have a distinct portion of evangelic history which admits of verbal collation with the records of the three synoptists. We allude to the narrative of the Last Supper. Their comparison is the more im-

[n] Da Costa, p. 167.

portant, as it is seen that St. Luke and St. Paul more nearly correspond than do either of them with St. Matthew or St. Mark :—

MATT. XXVI. 26-28.

26 And as they were eating, Jesus took bread, and blessed it, and brake it, and gave it to the disciples, and said, Take, eat; this is my body.

27 And he took the cup, and gave thanks, and gave it to them, saying, Drink ye all of it;

28 For this is my blood of the new testament, which is shed for many for the remission of sins.

MARK XIV. 22-24.

22 And as they did eat, Jesus took bread, and blessed, and brake it, and gave to them, and said, Take, eat: this is my body.

23 And he took the cup, and when he had given thanks, he gave it to them: and they all drank of it.

24 And he said unto them, This is my blood of the new testament, which is shed for many.

LUKE XXII. 19, 20.

19 And he took bread, and gave thanks, and brake it, and gave unto them, saying, This is my body which is given for you: *This do in remembrance of me.*

20 Likewise also the cup *after supper*, saying, *This cup is the new testament in my blood*, which is shed for you.

1 COR. XI. 24, 25.

24 And when he had given thanks, he brake it, and said, Take, eat: this is my body, which is broken for you; *this do in remembrance of me.*

25 After the same manner also he took the cup, *when he had supped*, saying, *This cup is the new testament in my blood:* this do ye, as oft as ye drink it, in remembrance of me.

St. Luke, we may observe, is pre-eminently the historian. If St. Matthew's object was to render his narrative a continuous comment on the Messianic prophecies—if St. Mark is careful to give a series of lively pictures—St. Luke aims at writing *in order* (καθεξῆς), having examined the things which he had undertaken to set forth from the very first (ἄνωθεν), desirous that his friend Theophilus might know the certainty of those things wherein he had been instructed. Consistently with this declaration, we find a strict sequence of events according to chronological order ; a due connection is noted with incidents of contemporary history ; and all the references to place or family are made with an accuracy which is only rendered more apparent by the most searching investigation. Such are the means employed by this third evangelist for establishing the truth of his grand theme, Jesus the anointed One ; for such we may regard as the peculiar phase in which he undertook the sacred portraiture. It is in this Gospel that we learn in every chapter how God *anointed* Jesus of Nazareth with the Holy Ghost and with power. ' In St. Matthew we behold Jesus more on the side of his prophetic royal grandeur ; in St. Luke, more on that of his unction as high-priest ; while in St. Mark the reality of his human nature stands most prominently forward.'

In passing from the Gospels of the synoptists to that of St. John we enter upon a new line of investigation. We have at once brought before us a Gospel whose distinctive features are manifest and of universal recognition. The first three so closely resemble each other, that our labour would be applied to finding their points of mutual difference; whilst in examining St. John's Gospel, our object would be to discover its relation to the other three. We are reminded at the outset that it was composed long after those which had preceded it. A vast change had passed over the face of the moral world, and the Church of Christ had now become something more than the mustard-seed; it was already the wide-spreading tree. It is more than probable, too, that Jerusalem had fallen before the armies of Titus; and the people who had crucified the Lord of glory were drinking to the dregs the cup of woe. The sacrifices had now ceased to be offered. Israel was 'scattered and peeled,' without an altar, without a home. At such a time did the disciple whom Jesus loved take up his pen to give, at the Lord's directions, the last revelation to the Church of God. And he took up his pen more than once. His first writing was a history; then came certain letters addressed to the churches and to particular believers; and, lastly, the setting sun of Revelation shed its prophetic beams in glorious effulgence as the canon was closed in the Apocalypse. The shadows lengthened, and the valleys grew dark and hazy, whilst the mountain-tops caught the gilded ray; meet picture of the Church in her hour of tribulation, as she was bidden to offer the prayer, 'Lord Jesus, come quickly.'

We derive no unimportant comment on the scope and style of the fourth Gospel, from the consideration that he who wrote it was also commissioned to close the inspired Word of God. There is an elevation of style, a glow of heavenly love, a depth of prophetic insight, and, above all, a devout adoration of the Saviour's person, which we should expect from one writing under the circumstances to which we allude. He writes from the height and from the depth—he carries us back to the eternal Past, and onward to the eternal Future. In the *beginning* was the Word. The Word was made *flesh*. I am the *First* and the *Last*.

'We must at once be sensible,' says Da Costa, 'that our fourth Gospel has something in it powerfully distinctive, something profoundly illustrative, something that takes a strong hold of our minds. There are here, as in the other Gospel writings, historical incidents taken from the life, and sufferings, and resurrection of Jesus Christ. But no sooner do we enter upon it than we find something more than the artless and childlike simplicity of St. Matthew's narrative—more than the rapidity and terseness of St. Mark's record—more than the calm and flowing historical style of St. Luke. With that artlessness, and that terseness, and that calmness, there is here mingled a higher and more elevated tone—a tone derived from the monuments of the remotest sacred antiquity, as well as from the hidden depths of the most profound theology; a tone, reminding us sometimes of the Mosaic account of the Creation, sometimes of the wise sayings of Solomon, sometimes akin even to the later theology of Jewish-Alexandrine philosophers.'°

This Gospel is chiefly remarkable as recording the words in preference to the works of Jesus. Every where the Saviour himself speaks; and even in the six miracles which are recorded (a number very small in comparison of the 'many other signs' to which St. John alludes), the facts mentioned are eminently illustrative of the truths conveyed. Moreover, they are carefully selected as most calculated to 'set forth the Saviour's glory;' the healing of a long-standing infirmity; the cure of a man that had been *born blind;* the restoration of a dead man, not from the couch or the bier, but from the grave.

St. John quotes much from the prophets, and shows how in the various incidents which he records, the ancient predictions were fulfilled; but not only so, he makes it his special vocation to point attention to what was prophetical in our Lord's own words (ii. 22; xviii. 31, 32), and in the words even of those who were bitterly hostile to him (xi. 49, 50). Like the Apocalypse, the Gospel is prophetical; like the same divine book, it is eminently mystical and abounding in symbol; and we may add that in every chapter of this evangelist-apostle we discern a direct aim to exalt the great name of Jesus as the only begotten Son of God.

Thus have we endeavoured to give a faint sketch of a principle that we cannot but feel to admit of deep application—that the differences observable in the evangelical records suggest the respective phases in which the writers were inspired to view their great theme, and in the development of which they have given us a whole truth. Let the devout Christian study the Scriptures as a whole; let him, for the especial purpose of ascertaining the mind of the Holy Ghost in the revelation made of the person and work of Christ, study the Gospels in their quadriform but harmonious testimony. We are persuaded that in the existence of *four* Gospels we have a fact of deep significance; we are equally persuaded that from the combined study of the four Gospels the deepest views of truth will be obtained.

C. D.

° Da Costa, 233.

THE REPHAIM, AND THEIR CONNECTION WITH EGYPTIAN HISTORY.*

CHAPTER XVI.

Religious System and Pantheon of the Rephaim.

IN endeavouring to bring under a systematic arrangement the few fragments of half-obliterated record that we may yet be able to render available in illustrating the religious forms and ideas of the Rephaim, it will be best to abstain from conjectures on their system of theogony and symbolism. Whatever is conjectural is unprofitable to our purpose. We are not framing a theory, but seeking to recover a lost history. All details connected with the worship of this people, which illustrate Scripture or receive illustration from it—all those which assist in confirming their identity with the subjects of the Egyptian monumental records—and all those which tend to exhibit the original connection of their system with the oldest forms of the Egyptians, and thereby to indicate the common origin of the two contending powers,—such are the points to be as prominently brought out as the limits of the materials at hand will allow. The more recondite meaning of the sacred emblems which constitute the image-gods of antiquity, and of their attributes, would only lead to speculations on a floating basis, and to conclusions incapable of tangible demonstration. If we find substantial grounds to establish that the fundamental Osiris and Isis of the Mizraimite pantheon were also the basis of that of the Rephaim, while their secondary forms only are peculiar, an important fact will have been elicited; and the religious monuments of Egypt will as clearly point out the beginning of that nation, as her historical monuments reveal their end.

The sources from which we may gather all particulars of the worship of the Rephaim that are susceptible of recovery are :—

1. Their religious symbols, and the effigies and names of their gods, on Egyptian monuments, occurring either on detached commemorative tablets, or in historical subjects and inscriptions.

2. Proper names peculiar to the lands we have identified as their lands; referable to and manifestly derived from the same gods.

3. Occasional allusions in the Bible to the same gods, and to the religious practices of the people.

4. Similar allusions in ancient profane writers.

---

* Continued from the July Number of the *J. S. L.*

These data are of no interest, and are often unintelligible, when viewed separately. They are all complementary to one another. It is only by bringing the facts obtained from one source to bear upon those gathered from another, comparing those that are analogous, and reuniting those that are obviously connected in their origin, that we can obtain a whole sufficiently complete to be accepted in illustration of history.

Certain votive tablets are occasionally found in Egypt, chiefly in tombs, bearing figures and names of gods different from those of the Egyptian pantheon, and obviously of foreign origin, but of Egyptian workmanship, as, for instance, the tablet of Kaha in the British Museum. The great number of noble captives brought to Egypt during the Theban wars will account for the occurrence of those monuments. Such captives were not always prisoners taken in battle; these, after being dragged in triumph, chained together and handcuffed, behind the conqueror's car, were presented to the Theban gods, and then consigned to the task-master, to expiate, by a degrading servitude, the crime of having lifted their hand against the majesty of Pharaoh. Instances occur, however, when the chiefs of the invaded lands offered no resistance, but disarmed the conqueror's wrath by offering themselves up voluntarily, ' to be presented in their captivity to Amun-Ra,' like the Ekronites and Philistines to Rameses III. Such captives were of course very differently treated. Their forts were indeed laid low, and their cities subjected to tribute; the proffered submission of the chiefs to the form of following the royal train and appearing before the gods of Thebes, was accepted, and the ceremony fulfilled, but under circumstances of great leniency, and involving no personal discomfort or degradation. When they reached Egypt, they were honourably treated; the parallel cases of Daniel, Haman and Mordecai, and Nehemiah, in the Jewish captivity, even show that it was not unusual for such strangers to be invested with offices of distinction in the royal service. And this service did not necessarily entail any interference with the private devotion of these exiles.

As the Rephaim were the object of the whole long series of Egyptian wars, we might have expected, *à priori*, to find their gods occupying a conspicuous place among these mysterious memorials of an unknown worship found in Egypt. We will give a separate account of all those which can be thus recognized by their names.

ASTR·TA, *Astarte,* or *Ashtaroth.*

The tablets in the Louvre and British Museum, representing this goddess under the secondary names and attributes of AT·SH okgo.

and KEN, are the most ancient delineations of her extant in the world: they belong to the period of Rameses II.

They are only provincial forms of Ashtaroth; and, even at that early age, they exhibit a marked departure from her primeval type, in depicting her with a human countenance; for the original Astarte, the 'two-horned Ashtaroth' of the Rephaim, was figured with the head of a cow, with a globe between her horns. In this form, we find her graven image among the effigies of various gods surmounting the gold and silver vessels consecrated to their worship, which the Egyptian conquerors, according to custom, carried away from the sanctuaries of the Rephaim with other spoils, and presented to the temple-gods of Thebes. Sanchoniatho assigns as the reason for her being delineated under this form, that it was emblematical of her supremacy.[a]

Sacred symbols are the written language of ancient religions, which invest its forms of outward expression with a permanent character, both in virtue of their consecration to ritual uses in the sanctuary, as exponents of the abstract ideas they were framed to embody; and also, through a commendable veneration on the part of later generations, for the ancestral teachers who first instructed them through the medium of such emblems.

Accordingly, when we find the Ashtaroth of the Shethite tribes bearing, on private memorials, attributes different from those consecrated in their sanctuaries, we cannot but ascribe to the latter representations priority in antiquity over the former. We understand the variations presented in the more recent forms as intentional departures from the primitive type, introduced either from a desire to give more explicitness to the attributes they symbolize, or in order to superadd, either by appropriate emblems, or by a different descriptive name, the notion of new attributes ascribed to the divinity they represent. To the same cause, also, we may easily trace that progressive departure from their prototype, which is rendered so evident in the Egyptian gods by the manner in which one divinity is found gradually sliding into another, dropping first its own attributes, and then its name, till its original character is completely superseded. This sort of gradation is exemplified in a very interesting manner by the history of Ashtaroth, whose transformations, by the gradual development of one fundamental idea into a connected series of typical forms, may be systematically traced to their respective periods in their respective lands, through-

---

[a] Cory, *Ancient Fragments.* Ex. Eusebius, *Præp. Ev.*, l. 1, c. 10. For the identity of the cow-headed type throughout the nation, compare, in Rosellini's *Mon. Storici*, the spoils of the SHAS'U, or Chief Rephaim, pl. 52; those of the Anakim of TAHI, pl. 56; those of the Emim, or SHET'TA, pl. 59; and those of the Elathites, or LT'N, pl. 48.

out the wide geographical range over which the influence of her peculiar people extended, not only in the days of their dominion, but even of their dispersion.

We found the normal type of Ashtaroth to be, *a cow-headed female figure bearing a globe between her horns.* Its design is immediately brought under our view, in the Egyptian representations of the spoils taken from the Rapha nation; for these are undoubtedly matter of fact copies from the original sacred utensils themselves. Nothing, therefore, can be more satisfactorily authenticated than the *genuineness* of this type. The *sacredness* of the type, and its consequent *antiquity*, are thereby attested; and also its *universality*, by its identity in the sanctuaries of the whole nation. A corresponding testimony to its universality at a later period, and to its being of old the time-honoured form under which the worship of the goddess had been introduced into the land of Canaan, is further afforded by the allusion to her in the book of Tobit (i. 5) as τῇ Βάαλ τῇ δαμάλει, *Baal the heifer*, to whom all the tribes of Israel who had apostatized offered sacrifices; and, finally, similar representations of her, on Phœnician coins of a much later date, testify to its persistency. From all this, it appears that the national goddess of the Rapha race—the patroness of their first settlement, and especially (by name) of its metropolis, Ashtaroth-karnaïm, or *the two-horned*—was, in the origin, no other than the particular form of the Mizraimite Isis known in the Egyptian pantheon as Athor, 'the abode' (or mother) of Horus.[b] The most ancient representations of Athor are those with a cow's head, enclosing the disk between its horns, precisely like the emblem among the spoils of the Rephaim. She was also represented with a human head bearing the horns and disk; in this resembling the Shethite Astarte, Atesh.

Isis herself, in her own name, is often found bearing the emblem of Athor, either with or without the cow's head. Of the very few things certain in Egyptian mythology, none are more so than the sameness of these two impersonations. So obvious a derivation of Ashtaroth from Isis in the form of Athor is therefore an incident of great importance, as pointing out a period, however remote in the world's history, when the religious systems of the Rephaim and of the Egyptians met in one; before those changes had been wrought in either system by the several foreign influences which superimposed astronomical associations and animal-worship on the Egyptian system; and which degraded the simple cosmogonic idea

---

[b] Plutarch gives this as the signification of her name (*De Is.* s. 56), which its hieroglyph explains: a hawk (emb. of Horus) *within* a square, emb. of a house or abode, ht or eiʼt; whence ht-hor, or eiʼtʼhor, the abode, receptacle, of Horus. (Vide Wilkinson, *Anc. Egyptians*, vol. iv. p. 387.)

embodied in Athor by attributes and rites of unspeakable depravity in the other.

In the absence of any equally ancient full-length representation of the primitive Ashtaroth of Bashan, we must remain content to accept the well-known figure of the cow-headed Athor as the nearest approach to her emblem; since we have at least a satisfactory verification of its authenticity, both in the effigies of Astarte which occur on the spoils of the SHAS·U people identified by so many tokens with the Zuzim of Scripture, and in the recurrence of the same emblem on their helmets, as a religious and national token.[c]

We are more fortunate in possessing the contemporaneous image of the very ÂSTR·TA, goddess of the SHET·TA, who is mentioned with SUTH, or SUTH·SH, as ratifying the treaty between that people and Rameses II. It is the middle figure of the triad sculptured in relief on the upper part of the tablet of Kaha. The Shethite tribe, whose tutelar goddess she was, bore her name, KEN קין, as the senior and metropolitan tribe bore that of their tutelar god Sheth, שת, or SUTH.

The proper name of this goddess is equivalent to a Hebrew translation of the Egyptian component HT or AIT, in the Mizraimite proper name Athor, the abode, receptacle, container, of life. קין is derived from קן, a primary root which, under the forms קנה and קנן, covers all the compound acceptations of our simple verb *to hold*, viz., obtain, contain, retain. The power of the play of words on this proper name, in Balaam's denunciation, is rendered doubly impressive by its evident allusion to the patron goddess and city of the nation :—

Thou settest בַּסֶּלַע {in the Rock, קִנֶּךָ {thy nest, in Sela, Petra {thy ken,
Nevertheless, Ken shall be devoured!

As patroness of a junior tribe, Ken has not the horns and globe worn by Atesh. Moreover, her signature by proxy, in the treaty, exhibits her punctilious regard for the etiquette of precedence, by coming after the SUTH or SUTH·SH of the senior tribe. Her hair is dressed like that of the statues of Athor; but she is naked. She stands on a lion, holding in her left hand two serpents tied together, and in her right, a circle formed by the curved stems of a lotus-flower and two buds, which she presents to her consort, Khem, or Chemosh.

---

[c] Four plates, illustrating the consecrated symbols and the costumes of the Rephaim, will appear in the next number of this journal, with the concluding part of the present series. The reader will be referred to these plates for figures of all the gods described in this chapter.

All these emblems are so different from the primeval type of
Athor, that we would not have recognized her relation to that
goddess without the connecting link afforded by the additional
globe and horns of her counterpart AT·SH in the Louvre tablet.
This evidence, however, is decisive ; were it less so, it would be
confirmed by the name of the goddess.

The title of Ashtaroth on the Louvre tablet is ' ATSH, goddess,
lady of heaven, queen of gods.' This legend explains her title,
' the queen of heaven,' in Sacred Writ, and the epithet Urania,
or Aphrodite-Urania, by which the Greek writers distinguish her
from their own Aphrodite. Her territorial appellation, as Ken,
makes her out especially as the Urania called Alilat and Alitta by
the Arabians ; and as the Babylonian Mylitta, whose worship was
introduced into Chaldea by the Arabians and Assyrians.[d]

Some sculptured figures of gods, found at Khorsabad, and given
in Mr. Layard's great work on Nineveh, very distinctly establish
the derivation of the Assyrian Astarte from the Shethite AT·SH and
KEN. In one of these subjects, she sits on a throne, holding the
mystic circle. Like AT·SH, she has two horns. She wears the
Assyrian costume and crown, surmounted by a round ornament,
equivalent to the globe. Another form of the goddess is more like
AT·SH and KEN ; she stands on a lion, holding the circle, and also
has two horns, and a star within the disk on the crown of her cap.
These representations are much more recent than the Egyptian
tablet that gives us her prototype, Ken.

The account given by Herodotus of the profane customs by
which the Babylonian Mylitta was honoured, loses much of its
incredible character, when, even at so early a period as the residence of Israel in Shittim (Num. xxv.), we can already trace analogous customs prevailing in a land under the particular tutelage
of the same goddess Astarta, who, under the secondary forms of
Atesh, Ken, Alilat, or Alitta, was protectress of the four Shethite
provinces, Shittim, Ken, Amalek, and Elath. The catastrophe of
the Midianite war proves that the people so called were deemed
the principal agents in working out the scheme of corruption
suggested by Balaam. The daughters of Moab were only put
forward on the occasion as the tools of a political movement.
From their kindred origin, and the brotherly feeling the Moabite
tribe had manifested towards Israel on their passage through Ar,[e]
they were judged more likely to succeed in alluring the children
of Israel to break down the bar of religious separation that kept
them aloof from the indigenous population.

It may be deemed no small addition to the antiquarian value of

---

[d] Herodotus, *Clio*, 131.   [e] Deut. ii. 29.

our Museum-tablet, that the goddess who appears upon it should thus prove to be the heroine of two transactions so memorable in antiquity as those in which she figures as the imaginary witness to the most ancient international treaty in the world, and as the stumbling-block of Israel in Shittim.[f] But any shade of incredulity that might still remain as to this most interesting coincidence, must give way before the actual admission by Josephus—already referred to—that the idolatrous Midianites were the people one of whose five kings, Rekem, was the king of the city of Arekem, afterwards called Petra ; when, on the other hand, we had already ascertained, from Scriptural references, that this very city, Petra or Arekem, was the stronghold of the Kenites, and that the Kenites themselves were subjects of the ruler of the metropolitan province, Heshbon in Shittim.

The degraded attributes of the southern Astarte, combined with the fact well known to antiquity that Athor was her primary form, may explain the selection of their Aphrodite by the Greeks, as the conventional synonym for the Egyptian Athor, although these two impersonations have not a discernible attribute in common. Some connection is indeed traceable between those of Astarte and the Grecian Aphrodite ; even though the latter has been veiled under a garb of imaginative grace and poetic beauty totally alien to the primitive framers of her Eastern prototype.

We have no direct proof in Scripture that the more corrupted worship of Ashtaroth had gained a footing among the Rephaim beyond the domains of the Shethite tribes ; unless the local names of Kinah and Ken in southern Judea (Josh. xv. 22, 57), and Kenath in Bashan (Num. xxxii. 42), are to be taken as indications that she had some votaries in those quarters. The very little we know of the primary Phœnician Astarte rather shows that, while her original form of Athor was never materially changed, the incidents of her mythical history draw her still nearer to the primeval source, by their close approximation to those of the bereaved Isis

---

[f] Our common version of Amos v. 26, 27, gives the noun כִּיּוּן *Chiun*, as if it were a proper name ; and from the resemblance of this to the name of Ken, it has been conjectured that Ken was the Midianite goddess alluded to. It is rather curious that a conjecture founded on an etymological error should turn out true in the fact ; for Ken *is* the Midianite goddess, but on other grounds. Even if כִּיּוּן were here a proper name, it would not apply to this goddess, whose name is written with different letters ; neither would it suit her as an epithet, 'the burning object,' the incandescent, implied by its root, כוה, to burn = κα-ω (see Isa. iii. 24 ; Exod. xxi. 25). The application of this epithet will be shewn in its place ; here, I will only remark that the Scriptural name corresponding to the monumental KN, קֵין, which gives its etymology, and the land and history of the goddess, is written with a ק, and the final ן is radical ; whereas in the epithet *Chiun* the initial is כ, and the ן final is a formative.

of Mizraim mourning the untimely death of her lord. Indeed the Greek fable of Venus and Adonis was so evidently derived from the Phœnician version of the Isidian myth, that it has retained the title of the god אדון, Adon, *the Ruler,* as a proper name, though his original relation of husband is changed to that of a lover. The proto-Phœnician Osiris in this peculiar character bore the name of Thamus ; and according to Gesenius, the mournful rites by which his supposed decease was celebrated are alluded to by Ezekiel : ' He brought me to the entrance of the northern gate of the Lord's house ; and lo ! there sat the women weeping for Thammuz ' (viii. 14). The reference in Ps. cvi. 28, to the backslidings of Israel in Shittim, apparently relates to the same subject :—

' They became united to Baal-Peor,
And ate the sacrifices of the dead,'

inasmuch as the Syrian Belphegor, the local Baal of Peor in Shittim, exhibits many attributes of Osiris in the Plutonic character the latter assumes after his death.[g]

However slight such passing allusions may appear, they assume a deep significance, considered in connection with the Mizraimite origin of the goddess to whose mythical story the allusions apply ; and with the local character of the fabulous beings themselves, who figure in it as home-gods, not as importations ; as absolutely identified by their names with the oldest and chief settlements of the land in which they appear as subjects of the allusions. But this argument must be reserved as a separate topic, to be resumed when the whole of the pantheon has been disposed of. Then only can its force be appreciated.

KHEM. *Chemosh. Khammon.*

Chemosh next claims our attention, as he is not the special patron of one tribe of Rephaim, but the great god of the whole nation. The Scriptural references to his name represent him as the Dispenser of Good, both to the Ammonites in virtue of their incorporation with the residue of the Zuzim, and to the Moabites amalgamated with the small remnant of the Shethite tribe.

The character and attributes assigned to this god may be seen by the tablet of Kaha, in which he appears as the consort of Astarte-Ken. They in no wise differ from those of the Egyptian Khem of the Mizraimite pantheon, whose name was afterwards changed to Amun-Ra. A little allowance must of course be made for some mannerisms in the treatment of the costume, which is wholly Egyptian ; ascribing them to the conventional rules imposed by custom upon the artists who executed these subjects. But

[g] Selden, *Syr. Syntag.* i. c. 5.

characteristic attributes cannot be brought within the pale of such
allowance. Those of the god's companions, Ken and Renpu, are
so *un*-Egyptian, that the sculptor's total departure from the formulæ
prescribed in Egypt strongly argues that he wrought from a description, following no familiar exemplar at home; and that,
consequently, had the fundamental attributes of Chemosh been
different from those of the Egyptian Khem, he would have been
obliged to make them different, since he has made those of Astarte
so different from their prototype, the Egyptian Athor. As on the
contrary a figure of Khem of the most orthodox Egyptian construction was chosen by the artist, and accepted by the devotee
Kaha, as a representation of his god Chemosh, it must be because,
in their significant emblems, their identity was obvious to and
admitted by both.

The variation between the typical name KHEM, and the Chemosh
of the Rephaim, may be thus explained :—As the tutelar god of
the Shethites is styled indifferently SUTH or SUTH·SH on the same
monument, and their city on the Arnon, AT·SH, named from the
goddess, is often written ATI, or AT·T,[h] it thereby is demonstrated
by two authentic precedents found in the same land, and referable
to the same dialectic principle, that the final ש in these names is
no part of them, but only a mutable suffix or enclitic, whose
grammatical or etymological power is unknown; and the emblematical hieroglyphic of the Egyptian Khem being here used
for the name of Chemosh (כְּמוֹשׁ) in this tablet, shows that it sufficed
to express it.

Towards the close of the 18th dynasty, the phonetic name of
Khem was systematically erased from every inscription in which
it occurred, and the characters for AMN were substituted. Sir
Gardner Wilkinson limits the date of this change to the reign
of Amenoph III. ;[i] and Chevalier Bunsen has further noticed that
where the compound form AMN-RA is found, the former name only

---

[h] By the elision of the mutable ש from this name, the radical remains AT, or
AI·T, which is the first component of Athor (vide note [b]) אי, with the fem. particle,
and exactly equivalent in sense to קין, the *abode* or *receptacle*, but expressed in a
term common to the Shethite and Egyptian dialects; whereas קין is not Egyptian.
If it be not irrelevant for a suggestion to occupy the place of an illustration, may
not the Phœnician form Tham·us itself be a similar compound? By dropping the
enclitic ש, it leaves חם, the Complete, Perfection, Integrity, root of the Egyptian
god ATHUM, or THUM, a title of Osiris after his death, as judge of the lower world.
Chevalier Bunsen quotes the following remarkable passage concerning him from
Lepsius' *Book of the Dead:* ' I am ATUM, making the heaven, creating beings,
going into the world, creating all generations which produced the gods, self-created,
lord of life, renewing the other gods.' The very same enclitic letter recurs in
Baal·is, name of an Ammonite king, Jer. xl. 14. A fabulous king Tham·us also
appears in the primeval legends of Egypt.
[i] Wilkinson, *Anc. Egyp.*, vol. iv. p. 243.

is over the erasure, and RA is unaltered. The suffix RA, the sun, is the addition peculiar to the Egyptian system, in which cosmogonic and astronomical elements are blended in one impersonation, a mixture totally unknown to the Rapha pantheon. We find among them nothing but the Mizraimite forms of the cosmogonic ideas. Their Khem-osh is like the Egyptian Khem, the primeval Osiris, as the Universal Parent of all created nature, manifested in the generative power by which the existence of the animate and inanimate is continued. It is an extension of the creative idea embodied in the primary PTAH (פתח) of the Mizraimite system, he who causes the opening or entering-in of existence, the active principle of original creation, who was therefore regarded in the proto-Phœnician mythology as the Father of all the other Cabiric theophanies.

In the old Egyptian pantheon, Khem was the consort of Maut, *the mother*. In the tablet of Kaha, Chemosh appears in an analogous relation to Isis-Athor in the character of Ken, the dwelling or receptacle of the power typified by the god. Their offspring, RNPU, forms the third member of this very remarkable group, remarkable from its being obviously composed on the genuine Mizraimite principle of the Egyptian local triads, in which the third or junior member embodies the development of the agency typified by the other two; the combination of two harmonious principles producing an effect; the active and passive agencies of nature guided by a Supreme Intelligence, and their result.

In the proper name of Khem we cannot fail to recognize the Ham (חָם) of sacred tradition, progenitor of the Mizraimite race. Wherefore, this venerated ancestral name may have been purposely selected by his descendants, to distinguish the particular impersonation of divine power represented by that god,—Osiris, considered as dispenser of existence to all animated nature. Not that they worshipped their ancestor under the name or form of a god, but rather a sensible manifestation of divine power rendered intelligible by an emblematical representation, upon which, for distinction's sake, they conferred the name of their ancestor.

Chemosh is doubtless a form, or the proper name of מוֹלֶךְ, Molech, he who reigns, '*the king.*' His Egyptian correspondent, or rather substitute, Amun, or Amun-Ra, is generally entitled 'the king of the gods.' This identification of the god by his attributes appears to explain the origin of the custom so often alluded to in Scripture, of 'passing children through a fire unto Molech.' It was originally a symbolical rite by which the people who owned him as their 'king of gods' solemnly dedicated their offspring to the giver of increase, in grateful acknowledgment of the gift. The offering of cakes and incense to the 'queen of heaven' (Jer. xliv. 17),

Ashtaroth, feminine principle of the same divine power, appears grounded on the same idea that the fruits of the earth, in Egypt, were offered to Khem, these two deities being regarded as joint givers of the earth's increase. Accordingly, the Jews in Egypt attribute the scarcity they complain of in their exile, to having left off their propitiatory offerings to the feminine giver of abundance, worshipped by their apostate fathers, kings and princes, in the cities of Judah, and in the streets of Jerusalem. The spoils of the Rephaim (vide the plates referred to in note ª) present us with the very pattern of the vessels used in pouring out these libations. From their shape, they were evidently made of a cow's horn, emblem of the goddess; and the tip is finished with her head, in a human form. She wears a crown of lotus flowers and buds, and a long curl hanging down the side of her face. The offering was poured out from the broad end of the horn.

The figure of Khem generally has an altar beside it, bearing the offerings of fruit and corn claimed by that god.

There are strong grounds for believing that groups of Khem and Ashtaroth, similar to our tablet, are implied by the obscure references in Isaiah (xvii. 8; xxvii. 9) to הַחַמָּנִים, the Khammanim, and הָאֲשֵׁרִים, the Asherim, which occur together, and are rendered in our common translation *images* and *groves*. The names of Baal and Asherah are found similarly connected (Judg. iii. 7; and 2 Kings xxiii. 4). Gesenius has established that in such instances 'the Asherah' (אֲשֵׁרָה) is not *a grove*, as it is commonly translated, but the proper name of a goddess, a synonym of Astarte.[k] In Hebrew it has a meaning, 'the giver of prosperity,' and was probably her Canaanite name; it is easily recognized in another well-known synonym of that goddess (Hellenice), Beltishera, *i. e.* Baalath-Asherah, or Asherah, consort of Baal; the very name thus associated with Asherah in the Bible. חמן Kham·n, is found compounded with the epithet Baal, in the following interesting Punic inscription on a votive tablet found by Chevalier Scheel near the site of ancient Carthage, and deposited in the museum of Copenhagen :—

לרבת · לתנת · ולבע	'To the Great One, to Thanath (THNTH)
ל · כל · אדן · לבעל · חמן	and to the Lord of all lords, to Baal-
אשנדר · עבד · מלקר	Hamon (KHMN) devotes himself, the
ת · השוטי · בן · ברמל	servant of Melkarth, Hashoti, son of
קרת · בן · חנא	Bar-Melkarth, son of Hana.'

---

[k] Vide particularly 1 Kings xv. 23: *groves* cannot well be said to be *built* under a high tree. Also 2 Kings xxi. 7, where the qualifying term פֶּסֶל decidedly implies *an object hewn in stone*, which cannot apply to *a grove*, but may mean a statue or a relievo figure of the Asherah.

This form, KHM·N, is obviously the Canaanite augmentative of Khem ; and Bâl-Khm·n is the name and title corresponding to the Molech-Khem·sh of the unknown dialect of the Rephaim, and to the 'Amun-Ra, king of gods,' of the Thebaid ; consequently, the same god is meant, whether the compound be used, or either of its separate constituents ; Baal or Molech, the epithets ; or Kham·n, Khem·ush, or Khem, the specific name. From the distinction suggested by 1 Kings xi. 7, we may perhaps infer that the royal tribe of the Rephaim, territorial predecessors of the Ammonites, had preferably called him by the epithet Molech, the *royal* god ; while the southern branch, represented by the Moabites, had retained the proper name of the same deity.

A lion's head, crowned, appears to have been the emblem of the 'king of gods' on the consecrated utensils of his sanctuary. This form occurs on an urn among the spoils of the SHAS·U of the Upper MNA region, or Rephaim of Jerusalem. There is a similar urn, with the lion's head uncrowned, among the spoils of the TAHI (Anakim), and of the SHET·TA (Emim). In the latter, the lion is placed between two geese. This may be an intimation of the god's parentage ; as a goose is the hieroglyphic figure employed to write ideagraphically the name of Seb, father of Osiris and Sheth.[m] A lotus-crowned patera, supported by two geese, occurs among the TAHI symbols ; and the same bird surmounts an urn belonging to the SHET·TA : so that the goose is evidently a sacred symbol common to the Rapha nations.

SUTH, SUTH·SH, or *Sheth.*

In the historical notice of the children of Sheth, I partly anticipated on the account of their tutelar god ; especially on his unquestionable Egyptian character and pedigree, granted by the Egyptians themselves. He was the third son of Seb and Netpe ; and consequently, brother of Osiris, Harœris or Horus the elder, Isis, and Nephthys ; patron gods, with Sheth, of the five days over the year.

On Egyptian monuments, he is represented under several names, as a figure with the head of a fabulous long-snouted animal whose ears are square at the top. One of these gives the phonetic name ST. When he bears the name of BARO—Baal—he has the same head on an equally imaginary animal's body, sitting like a dog, with an upright tufted tail.

Sir Gardner Wilkinson gives a copy of a most interesting seal in the possession of Chevalier Kestner, in which the figure with the characteristic square ears and pointed snout stands for the third

---

m Wilkinson, *Anc. Egyp.*, vol. iv. p. 311, pl. 31, fig. 1.

name of the five patrons of the epact; and this third day was the day dedicated to Sheth.   He also refers to the occurrence of the same five names with those of the parent gods, Seb and Netpe, on the wooden cubits found at Memphis.ⁿ   The same figure forms the name of the king whom Manetho calls Sethos; it also determines the god's name, when written phonetically sᴛ, and the corresponding form sᴜᴛʜ or sᴜᴛʜ·sʜ of the god who signs the treaty with Rameses II. on behalf of his children.   It therefore appears that Plutarch was correct in giving Sᴇᴛʜ as the name of the brother of Osiris whom the Greeks called Typhon; and the appropriation of that proper name to the square-eared god is verified beyond a doubt.

Sheth is represented on the sculptures of Rameses II. with the title of ɴᴜʙ·ᴛᴛ, with Horus, putting the double crown on the king's head,ᵒ and in another subject, pouring life and power upon him; at Karnak, he is pictured teaching Thothmes III. the use of the bow.   Several variants of the square-eared god's figure are given in Burton's Excerpta (pl. 37); but all these subjects are purely Egyptian. If the form and emblems under which the Shethite Rephaim represented their tutelar genius under his proper name differed in any essential point, they must remain unknown.

The metaphysical functions of Sheth among his mythical brethren may be deduced with certainty from what is well known of theirs, by their attributes on Egyptian monuments.   Osiris was the Divine Agency dispensing good to man; Horus and Sheth protected him from evil; the former, by watching over him; the latter, by enduing him with the power to withstand it.ᵖ   Sᴇᴛʜ may be regarded as a personification of the *Divine Helper*.   I own I cannot assent to the prevalent opinion that this impersonation was primarily meant to embody an evil power or being, under any qualification of terms.   He who assists Horus in crowning the king—he who with Horus sheds life and power upon him—he who teaches him *how to use his weapons against his enemies*, a most significant suggestion—he who is called 'Suth·esh the son of Netpe, the great disturber Baal *who smites his enemies*,' and to whom Egyptian hierogrammatists are proud to compare their royal heroes in their character of avengers of their land by the destruction of its foes,—surely *he* cannot, at that time, have been regarded as an *evil* being, in any sense!   Such an idea appears to involve an

---

ⁿ Wilkinson, *Anc. Egyp.*, vol. iv. p. 415, and pl. 38, part 2, where his name was given Ombo, the force of the characters which compose it being then considered doubtful.

ᵒ Ibid., vol. v. pl. 78, and iv. pl. 39.

ᵖ Plutarch thus gives the etymology of the Egyptian name: 'Σηθ φράζει μὲν τὸ καταδυναστεῦον καὶ καταβιαζόμενον,' what *exercises power over* . . . and *overpowers* or *restrains by force.*

absolute inversion of his attributes. So far from representing the abstract Power of Evil acting in opposition to Good, even to produce good, he seems, both by his primary name and secondary forms, to embody that Good Agency that encourages and empowers frail humanity to act in opposition to evil, under whatever form it may present itself. This view of his character explains his constant association with his brother Horus, who embodied the Divine Guardian, the Superintending Providence.[q] In the picture of the young Thothmes III. learning the use of his weapons, the king holds the bow and arrows, but Sheth *teaches him*—he guides his hands : the king darts the javelin into a target, but Horus *loves him*, for the god's arms are most affectionately—though rather awkwardly—entwined round the neck of his youthful charge. Indeed the functions of the two *forms* assumed by the protecting power are so nearly allied, that in one very curious representation of Sheth they are found united in a double-headed body, the square-eared Sheth looking one way, and the hawk-faced Horus the other.

It is not until a much later epoch than that of the above designs that Sheth, under his own name, became unpopular in Egypt. The change of feeling towards him was gradually wrought out by circumstances. As tutelar god of the fiercest enemies the Egyptians ever had to encounter, he first came to be regarded from a *political* point of view as the foe of Osiris their benefactor, and of Horus their protector ; his more abstract character being partially lost sight of. Popular legends now took up this view ; the heroic compositions of a secondary age adapted the political similitude to the primeval religious mystery ; and so, by grafting one myth on another, transmitted his name to future generations as the betrayer and murderer of his brother Osiris the good. Thus, little by little, the national mind became so familiarized with the tangible idea of his *antagonism to Osiris*, that this character ended in superseding the metaphysical conception of which Sheth had originally been the type. The Beneficent Antagonist of evil actually ended in becoming so obnoxious to popular prejudice as the Malevolent Antagonist of good, that his very figure became an object of aversion, and every opportunity was sought of erasing or defacing it on the sacred edifices its presence was thought to profane.

The representations of Sheth under the title of NUB-TET are important, as intimating that he and the Egyptian TET (Thoth) are

---

[q] The well known *winged-globe* emblem is one of the secondary forms of Horus ; HOR-HT, or HT, *the shelter.* Hence Egypt is described as 'the land of the overshadowing wings,' b. xviii. 1. The 'shadow of thy wings' is a frequent metaphor in poetic Scripture for the providential care of Jehovah.

only considered as various forms of the same emblematical being,[r] TET the *teacher* in general, NUB·TET or Nebo-Thoth, the *lord-teacher* in particular. So that the Egyptian factotum, Thoth, is merely one among several secondary manifestations of the prime exemplar Sheth, brother of Osiris, helper of man, viz., his helper in understanding. According to Sanchoniatho, the Phœnicians professed to have been instructed in letters and all useful things by one called Thautus, just like the Egyptians by their Thoth. And this derivation of Thoth from Sheth seems to illustrate the ancient tradition of the ' pillars of Seth,' on which the elements of their learning were inscribed and preserved.

The identity of Thoth with Sheth in a special character is admitted by the Egyptians themselves. One of the names of Sheth given by Plutarch, is SMU ; whereupon, in his chapter on Sheth, Chev. Bunsen remarks, ' it reminds us of Thoth's title Lord of Eshmunein, derived from *Shmun*, the eighth. In a passage of the Book of the Dead noticed to us by Birch, we read " *Tet, otherwise Set.*" This intimates that Thoth inherited many of the attributes of Seth.' And in his chapter on Thoth, the same distinguished author observes on the titles of Thoth, ' Lord of Shmun—Hermopolis—literally, *lord of the Eighth region ;* this reminds us of the well known Cabir Esmun of Phœnicia and Samothrace.' (P. 427 and 393.) To these suggestions, I will only add ; put them together, and they confirm each other. SMU, given by Plutarch as a title of SETH, is simply ESHMUN, a little mangled by the Greek interpreter ; the Phœnician אשמן, derived from שמן, *eight ;* for the title of Thoth in his legends, Lord of SHMUN-NU, is written with *eight strokes ;* which proves both the orthography and the etymology of the name : ' Lord of the region of Eshmun, ' or ' *the Eighth ;*' and in so doing, establishes the Phœnician character of the original possessor and patronym of the region appropriated to Thoth. This region is still called Oshmounein: the Greeks called it Hermopolis, *the city of Hermes,* because they *identified* their Ἑρμῆς, the Interpreter, with Thoth, ' *otherwise Sheth,*' though they *derived* him from the Pelasgic or Proto-Phœnician Cabir Eshmun ' *the eighth,*' who is SMU the synonym of Sheth. The conclusion arising out of these considerations, is therefore clearly this :

---

[r] The ancient Egyptian radical *tt* is exactly equivalent in all its derivations to those of the Hebrew דבר and the Greek λεγ, ' to say,' or speak, whence λογος. The Egyptian Greeks, therefore, made out Thoth to be Hermes, ' the interpreter.'

The Egyptian form of NUB·TT consists of the gold bowl (syllabically read NUB in the title of Amenemha II. on the tablets of Abydos and Karnak), N, and the complementary leg, B, followed by the name of Thoth phonetically written, T and the s. of duplication = TT. The gold vessel seems to have been chosen for its sound rather than the common vessel NEB, because of its greater resemblance to NBU, נבו ; but the radical sense of the epithet remains the same, ' lord-teacher.'

Sheth or SUTH is the proper name, the *character-name*, and represents the primary form of the divine impersonation it denotes ; while the other character-names are qualifications of that primary, and therefore secondaries to it.

Sheth, which means ' what exercises power over . . . and over-powers,' is that emanation of the Primeval Osiris, the overcomer of Evil, which is *the Helper*. Hence he is mythically regarded as *brother* to the same Osiris, considered in a more exclusive light as *the Giver*, whether of life or of all other good things. And under that, his primitive and proper name, we find Sheth established in a territorial character also, as the tutelar god of the Emim, and patronym of their land and tribe, Shittim or SHET·TA·N, the ' land of SHET.'

Baal or ' BARO, who smites his enemies,' is a title applied to him as *Helper of the nation :* whether in Egypt or in Phœnicia.

Thoth or TT, the speaker and teacher, or interpreter, is the *Helper in Wisdom*, and likewise a character common to Egypt and Phœnicia.

Nebo-Thoth, or NUB·TT, is a more exclusive form of the same, peculiar to Egypt, the imparter of knowledge and power to kings.

Eshmun, Shmun or SMU, *the Eighth*, is simply his ordinal designation in the primeval Cabiric scheme ; for originally, according to Herodotus, the Cabiri had *no names*.

It is under the latter designation that Sheth was revered by the Canaanites, his proper name being regarded as the privilege and heritage of his children. In this way, the synonym Eshmun became known to the garbled traditions of the post-Phœnician period, ascribed to Sanchoniatho by his copyists ; but this period only *begins* with the Hebrew conquest. The name Eshmun occurs on Punic inscriptions ; an ancient tombstone discovered near the site of ancient Carthage presents it as the name of a deity patronym of a man.

קברי הובס עבד חוא בן עבד-אשמן

Grave of Hobas, servant of Hava, son of Abd-Eshmun.[s]

The scriptural form corresponding to NUB נְבוֹ, Nebo, is found as a local name in the domains of the children of Sheth. Mount Nebo was the most elevated part of the Abarim or Moabite moun-tains, in which that tribe pastured their flocks. Its being charac-terized as the summit of the high-land, רֹאשׁ הַפִּסְגָּה, suggests the most probable situation of the height called Mount Nebo, as the watershed which separates the valley of the Zurka from that of the Arnon, and where the latter and its tributaries take their rise.

---

[s] Falbe, *Carthage.* Hava, *Life*, is a synonym of Astarte.

From this high ground, the vapoury vale of the Jordan might be just discernible, the mountains of Judea looming in the far distance above it.   It is a strange coincidence and worthy of a passing notice, that there, on a mountain dedicated by name to the primeval mythical embodiment of the Fountain of Religion and Knowledge, that great lawgiver died, whose books are *our* foundation of religion—*our* treasury of all knowledge in History and Antiquity;—though no man knoweth his grave to this day.

Renpu. *Remphan.*

From his attributes, Renpu was undoubtedly a secondary form of Sheth, the Helper as the Avenger, the warrior-god fighting for his children.   His figure, in Egypt, is only found on tablets, and does not belong to the Pantheon of that land.   It corresponds to the Egyptian Baro or Baal.   His characteristic emblem is the head of an oryx or a mountain gazelle, which appears projecting from his forehead.   This same head is a very prominent emblem among the sacred vessels of the Rephaim; quite as much so as that of the cow-headed Ashtaroth.   In the origin, he was very probably represented with the head of that animal.

In Sir Gardner Wilkinson's illustrations of the Egyptian Pantheon, two single representations of this god are given, which differ very slightly in their accessories.   Their Egyptian costume (for they wear the crown of the Upper country) shows that they must have been executed for a devotee residing in the Thebaïd. In the first figure, Renpu is in a walking attitude, armed to the teeth; he brandishes a battle-axe over his head with his right hand, while his left grasps a shield and spear; a quiver is slung to his back.   The other figure is seated, and has the battle-axe and shield, but neither spear nor quiver.[t]

In the triad of the tablet of Kaha, Renpu stands on a pedestal on the left of Astarta-Ken.   His right hand holds the long spear, his left the emblem of life.   He has no crown, but only the simple fillet and tie round his hair, like that of the Horite chiefs; and the distinctive oryx's head projecting in front.   But what is most worthy of attention in this representation, is the *form* and *cut of his beard.*   Nothing can be more un-Egyptian.   It is the peculiar angular clipped beard characteristic of those among the Rephaim race who wear any beard.   We need not ask why they affected that particular fashion: *their god was shaved so!*

One of the Khorsabad sculptures given in Mr. Layard's work on Nineveh contains the figure of Baal, in an attitude and with emblems as evidently copied from the attributes of Sheth the war-

---

[t] Wilkinson, *Anc. Egyp.*, vol. v. pl. 69.

rior, as those of the Assyrian Astarte were from the Atesh of Shittim. The god is walking; he has an axe in his right hand, and in his left a bundle of either arrows or thunderbolts. He wears, of course, the Assyrian costume, and his head is adorned with a double pair of horns, but the oryx-emblem is absent. However, as we know from the Egyptian monumental notices that Sheth, and Baal or 'Baro who smites his enemies,' are the same god, the one in his proper local name, the other in a special character, his identity with the Egyptianized Renpu is substantiated by the Assyrian copy of the latter bearing the name of the one with the form of the other. By tracing this god to his original form and home, we obtain another interesting elucidation of a very obscure passage of Scripture: the much-commented and never-explained Amos v. 26, 27. I have already remarked on the misappropriation of the epithet כִּיּוּן to the goddess Ken; I have therefore only to follow up the clue to its right appropriation. This is suggested, and as we shall find, correctly, by the Septuagint substitute 'Ραιφαν, or according to the quotation in Acts vii. 'Ρεμφαν. These translators, residing in Egypt at a period when its hieroglyphic writing and mythological system were known matters of every-day teaching, appear to have availed themselves of the knowledge that the tutelar god Sheth of the Midianite region was SUTH·SH or Sothis, patronymic of the brilliant dog-star,[u] and that Renpu or Remphan was particularly his local character in Ken, to point out the ultimate application of the vague epithet כִּיּוּן, 'the Incandescent,' to the god it meant, by substituting *his name*, and thus rendering it perfectly clear *who* was the 'star-god' in the explanatory verse that follows.

> 'The sacrifices, and the offering,
> Did ye present them unto Me
> In the desert, forty years, O ye sons of Israel?'

Heb.	Sept.
Ye bore the shrine of *your* 'Molech,' And the Burning-object (chiun) of *your* images, The Star of your god Which ye made for yourselves.[x]	Ye bore the shrine of Molech, And the star of your god *Raiphan* (for chiun), *their* images Which ye made for yourselves.

We need not inquire which of these various distributions is the most likely to be the authentic reading: that is a question of verbal criticism foreign to the present subject. All that concerns us is the fact that SUTH·SH or Sothis was the patron of the dog-star, the Chiun, כִּיּוּן, or 'Incandescent;' and that he was also Renpu, Raiphan, or Remphan; and that this identity, notorious

---

[u] Bunsen, *Egypt's Place*, vol. i. p. 429.
[x] This may be translated 'Your images of the Incandescent,' 'Your Star-god.'

in Egypt, and well known to the Greek interpreters, dictated their substitution of the *name* Renpu for the *epithet* Chiun (כִּיּוּן).

The *crux ansata* held by Renpu in the tablet group deserves a remark. As it is the well known hieroglyphic emblem of life, generally put into the hands of Egyptian divinities, it might here be taken for an Egyptian conventionality. But the spoils of the Rephaim in the triumphs of Seti-Menephtah shut out this supposition, for among these, that very emblem forms a conspicuous object, beautifully ornamented. A vessel among the LT-N (Elathite) spoils is formed by the cross; two kneeling figures of men support the arms, and the effigies of two gods, Ashtaroth and Renpu, surmount the circular upper limb. In another, among the spoils of the SHET'TA (Emim), the cross is supported by the oryx-head of Renpu, but the effigy over the top is obliterated. The specimen among the spoils of the TAHI Anakim is not ornamented with any effigies of gods.[y]

ANK. *Anak, Onka.*

Onka is well known to antiquity as a great Phœnician goddess. Pausanias regards her as the Athene of Thebes in Bœotia, where, like the Egyptian prototype of Athene, NEITH, she was worshipped in a temple without a roof; and her establishment there is quite in harmony with the tradition that ascribes the foundation of Thebes to Cadmus the Phœnician. From what we have seen of the children of Anak, it is manifest that she was the tutelar genius and patronymic of their nation, which by its name עֲנָקִים, Onkites, justly claims to be the original people from whom the appellation Phœnicians was derived, though we find it applied in after-times to a different people.

The costume of the gods is generally borrowed from that of the people. I have already had occasion to notice the identity of the head attire of the Philistians, and that of the Egyptian goddess ANK; the resemblance is not only in the circular crown of upright feathers which crests the cap, but in the form of the cap itself.[z] This indicates a particular locality—Southern Palestine—as the original seat of a divine impersonation, which we nevertheless find extending at the earliest period of Egyptian history to beyond the cataracts of the Nile; since ANK is found there as a member of the northern Ethiopian triad. She was honoured as a contemplar deity throughout all Egypt, though we must go out of Egypt to find her territorial and primary seat. The only Egyptian goddess

---

[y] See note [a] for references.

[z] Compare the goddess ANK nursing the king, Rosel., *Mon. Stor.*, pl. 62, s. 4, with the battle-scene (127 and 131) of Medinet Abou, and the figure of ANK in Wilkinson's *Anc. Egyp.*, vol. v. pl. 48, part 2.

besides ANK, who wears the same head-dress, is PE or TPE, the personification of the celestial firmament on monuments of the remotest antiquity.

On an inscription of the Ptolemaic period, in the island of Sehayl, immediately below the first cataract, the Greek form of her name is given as ''Ανουχη, called also Εστια.'[a] As the Grecian Aphrodite, in her attributes, was connected with the Athor of the Rephaim, though she had nothing in common with that of the Egyptians—so we shall find the Grecian Hestia (Vesta) connected in hers only with the ANK of the Rephaim, having nothing in common with the Egyptian goddess. Sir Gardner Wilkinson gives a copy of a triad in the temple of Denderah, composed of Isis, Horus, and Nephthys, in which the latter is styled ' NEB·TEI, the Saviour-sister, ANK.'[b] Here, the Egyptians themselves, in an orthodox temple-representation, admit that the mythical Nephthys, sister of Osiris, Horus, and Sheth, and wife of the latter, is one and the same with her who in her territorial character is called ANK. Now, in this identity alone can we understand her being identified with the Grecian Hestia or Vesta. The *name* of Nephthys, which gives *her character*, is in its Egyptian etymology, ' The lady over the abode.'[c] This ascribes the very same character to her, as the Greek 'Εστια, the goddess guardian of the household and domestic hearth. The Greeks recognized this character in ANK, and yet it could only suit *her*, from her being *also* ' NEB·T·EI, the Saviour sister.' The Greek parentage of Hestia also agrees with that of Nephthys, as Seb and Netpe are the Egyptian correspondents of Chronos and Rhea, parents of Vesta.

'Nephthys, the Saviour-sister,' was the consort of Sheth. It was a beautiful idea, thus to subdivide the *Power that averts Evil* into a masculine and a feminine impersonation ; the former, as teaching man to defend his person and father-land,—the latter, as presiding over his hearth and home !

Nephthys, the Saviour-sister, ANK, has also another character, in which she assumes a more active office as protectress of her children. This form is also common to the Egyptian and proto-Phœnician goddesses ; for Onka was regarded as the Athene of Bœotia, Pallas the warrior, the shield and champion of her votaries ; and Neith, the territorial divinity of Saïs in Lower Egypt—Neith, the prototype of Athene, and patronym of Athens, which was founded by a colony of emigrants from Saïs,—even Neith herself was only regarded *in Egypt* as a derivative form of ANK, ANK as

---

[a] Wilkinson, *Anc. Egyp.*, vol. v. p. 26.

[b] Ibid., vol. iv. p. 438.

[c] ' Her name consists of a bowl, called *neb*, placed upon a house, answering to EI or TEI.'—Ibid.

the warrior goddess. A very important representation of her in that character, at Thebes, is given in Sir Gardner Wilkinson's valuable collection of Egyptian divinities,[d] where she is figured with a bow and arrows in her hand; the name on her legend is TH·NTH-ANK. And an equally explicit admission of the identity of Neith with Onka in her warlike character, on the part of her children in Palestine, will be found on the person of the chief of the Anakim who represents the TEMAHU race (or Rephaim) in the tomb of Seti-Mcnephtah;[e] but if we would feel the full value of its testimony, we must recur to the mysterious prohibition in Lev. xix. 27, which has already received, in part, so striking an illustration in the monumental representations of some branches of that extraordinary people.

' Ye shall not round off the extremity (of the hair on) your heads, neither shalt thou destroy the extremity of thy beard : Ye shall not make incisions in your flesh for a corpse, nor put upon yourselves כְּתֹבֶת קַעֲקַע the writing (or impression) of a token-mark : I am JEHOVAH ! '

We know that the *first* of these prohibitions aimed at a religious demonstration we have traced home to the Amalekites : the *second* at the national token of the whole Rapha race without exception. The *third* was probably one of their customs, since it is alluded to as a rite of the priests of Baal in cases of peculiar solemnity.[f] But at what people and at what religious custom did the *fourth* specially point ?

The son of Anak, in the Theban tomb painting, bears the answer *on his person*. Details of costume are here given, which would be superfluous, confusing, and irrelevant in an historical subject ; but in a representation intended to exhibit the characteristic customs of the races whom the great Theban king claimed as his subjects, it was indispensable to express them. All the minutiæ of his costume are therefore given with scrupulous precision ; and, among other things, we observe certain marks conspicuously painted or tattooed on the fore part of the bare arm and leg of this Anakite chief—an unknown object of a very peculiar form, and certainly not put there for ornament, for it is not a flower, nor an animal, nor any natural object that might be regarded as ornamental. It is simply the well-known figure conventionally called

---

[d] Wilkinson, *Anc. Egyp.*, vol. iv. pl. 28, fig. 1. I understand from Sir Gardner Wilkinson that this interesting representation is of Pharaonic age.

[e] Vide Rosellini, *Mon. Storici*, pl. 155.

[f] Compare 1 Kings xviii. 28. Herodotus relates a practice of the Arabians of Jenysus, analogous to this, when they make a solemn pledge. A man, who stands between the contracting parties, grazes the skin of the hand of each with a sharp stone, and with a shred of their garment dipped in the blood he anoints seven stones lying between them, invoking Orotal and Alilat. Thalia, 8.

a *shuttle* by hieroglyphists (though it rather resembles a *bracelet*), which is employed in Egyptian inscriptions to write the name of Neith, or as the determinative of the name when written phonetically, NTH. It is the goddess's *primeval symbol*, and it is the religious and national token-mark of a son of ANK, imprinted on his person.

This fact speaks for itself; it needs no comment. On the walls of their sanctuaries, the Egyptians admit that their great local goddess Neith is only a form of ANK; and the children of Anak boast of their allegiance to her as the patroness of their homestead by bearing upon their flesh before the face of their enemies the protecting name of Neith! [g]

The statement of Pausanias that Onka *in the character of Athene* was the deity honoured by the Thebans and Gephyreans of Bœotia, is thus doubly verified. The exile Phœnician chief introduced the tutelar genius of his father-land under the form that had been most honoured by his people—their defender in danger. But that, as in Egypt, was only a *secondary* character of ' the Lady over the home, the Saviour-sister, ANK.' She is also to be met with by name in this secondary character on her own soil, under the corresponding forms of ANATH and THANATH, and is figured by that name, ANTA, in Egypt; so that we can place side by side and compare the NEITH-ANK of the Egyptians with her not less ancient counterpart, the Anath-Onka of the Rephaim.

ANTA. ANATH. Th·anath.

ANTA is thus a deity analogous to RENPU; a modified form of the Averter of Evil. She bears the same relation to NEB·T·EI ANK, *Protectress of the Homes* of the children of Anak, that RENPU does to SUTH, protector of the children of Sheth; being the patronym of their land in the special character of *Protectress of the national Homestead.* She then bears warlike attributes corresponding to those of the Egyptian Neith-Ank.

ANTA is not a member of the Egyptian pantheon, and is not found in any temple.[h] She is depicted in the lower compartment

---

[g] Since the above was written, Sir Gardner Wilkinson has mentioned to me two other instances he has met with in Egypt of ANK and NETH being identified with each other. I quote from his own communication on the subject:—' That this goddess (ANK), the Egyptian Vesta, was a character of Neith is evident, as we find her on an ancient tablet in the island of Sehayl, as well as in the Temple of Philæ; the former of Pharaonic, the latter of Ptolemaic time. She is called ANK, lady of the land of Neith.'

These two instances are very valuable; 1stly, as corroborating the view I expressed above, that Neith and Ank are only two forms of the same primary character, Nephthys, guardian of the house, wife of the defender of the land; 2ndly, as showing, by the dates of the two representations referred to, the antiquity and persistency of that opinion in Egypt; 3rdly, as proving the orthodoxy of that opinion, by the fact of its being confessed in a templar representation.

[h] Vide also Wilkinson, *Anc. Egyp.*, vol. v. pl. 70, part 1.

of the tablet of Kaha in our Museum, receiving offerings from the wife and family of that functionary; the upper compartment being occupied by the great national triad. She sits on a throne, brandishing the same battle-axe as Renpu, with one hand, and holding a shield and lance in the other. She wears the crown of Upper Egypt, like the single figures of Renpu, and for the same reason, her devotees being residents in that country; but with this difference, that it is decorated with *two feathers.* A crest of two feathers we know to be a characteristic point of costume among some Anakim tribes; they are a very conspicuous ornament on the figure who bears the hieroglyph of Neith on his limbs. This being a national peculiarity, it was necessary to introduce it in the costume of the goddess of the nation. Consequently, the Egyptian artisan who executed the figure has rather awkwardly tried to combine it with the conical cap of the Upper country, which custom required she should wear in Egypt, by fixing the two feathers up the side of the cap.

This distinctive feature of costume suggests, that in order to distinguish their tribe by some outward token, the Philistine children of Onka had adopted the badge of the goddess of the land in her domestic character, the simple Onka-Nephthys, the *Guardian;* whereas the mountain-tribe, who garrisoned the fortresses, had given the preference to that which indicated her bellicose attributes, Onka-Anath the Defender.

Among the mutilated sculptures of Beit-el-Wally,[i] illustrating the early campaigns of Rameses II., there occurs a subject which enables us to identify the emblem of Anath among the sacred symbols of the Rephaim. The king is engaged in single combat with a chief whose imperfect costume makes it uncertain whether he be one of the Anakim, or of the SHAS·U of the Upper MNA, or Jerusalem region; the head-dress square-cut behind and short kilt being common to both. Rameses of course is giving his enemy the *coup de grâce;* and, as if to show that even the tutelar goddess of his enemies had forsaken them, she is introduced joining the king in his attack, under the form of *a dog,* a domestic dog with a collar on: over its head is the name ' Anta the Goddess.'

Now, among the spoils of Seti-Menephtah there is a vase crowned with lotuses and buds, in three rows, of a beautiful form, apparently representing the land and the river; and on the foot of the vase, supporting it like the other sacred emblems we know to be gods, are *two dogs.* It is the only instance of this animal's being found among these objects, and it occurs among the spoils of the LT·N, dependency of the children of Sheth. The faithful

---

[i] Rosellini, *Mon. Storici,* pl. 66.

and watchful house-dog is a very appropriate emblem to typify the Protectress of the Homestead.

The name of Anath occurs in the geographical notices of Scripture ; there was a Beth-Anath, בֵּית־עֲנָת, in northern Canaan, Anathoth, עֲנָתוֹת, near Jerusalem, and Beth-Anoth in southern Judea.

The form Thanath, TH·NTH, in which the feminine particle appears combined with the name, is of frequent occurrence on Phœnician inscriptions. It is found on the Punic tablet quoted above ; and shows that the goddess was greatly venerated by the Tyrian colony of Carthage. As Anata and Anaïtis, she was also extensively honoured in the land northward of Phœnicia, even to the confines of Armenia.

HOR. HAROERI. *Horus.*

It hitherto appears that four out of the five gods to whom the five supernumerary days of the year were dedicated by the Egyptians, are the types into which the chief and tutelar gods of the Rephaim are ultimately resolvable : Osiris and Isis as the givers of life—Sheth and Nephthys as the Averters of Evil. This leaves a reasonable probability that the fifth member of this mythical family—Horus the Protector—was not unrepresented in the pantheon of the Rephaim.

Hor, or Haroeri, brother of Osiris, is also called HT, 'the Shelter,' and HOR-HT, under which names he is figured either with a hawk's head, or as the well known *winged globe*, the Agathodæmon of Egypt. Now, according to Eusebius, the Agathodæmon of the Phœnicians also had a hawk's head ;[k] and this statement is not inconsistent with the fact that among the spoils of their precursors, the Rephaim, there occurs a sacred vessel with the head of a hawk, eagle, or rapacious bird of some kind, on its cover.

Certain local names in their land, by their repetition, would also testify to the worship of Horus. There was a Beth-Horon in Judea, and another in Shittim, and also Horon-aïm, the double-city of Hor. On the frontier of southern Judea we find the fortress of Aroër ; another Aroër on the Arnon, on the frontier of Moab ; a third 'before Rabbah,' on the frontier of the Zuzim ; as if frontier cities were specially committed to his guardianship. Whether this form of the Divine Protector was selected by the Amalekites as the watchers of the nation, is a question which may be further suggested by the name they gave to the form of the Universal Osiris they especially reverenced—Oro-tal. The syllable TAR or TAL occurs so often as a mere *addition to the name,*

---

[k] Eusebius, *Præp. Ev.* l. 10. Vide Rosellini, *Mon. Storici,* pl. 48.

among those of the Shcthite chiefs drowned before Atesh,[m] that it appears very probable it was only a title or compound, of which the power is not known; and that HOR is the radical name of the god referred to by Herodotus in his account of the Arabians of Jenysus.

Aon. *Oannes. Dagon.*

The figure of the Chaldean Oannes, discovered on the sculptured remains of ancient Nineveh, is valuable in two respects; firstly, in that it enables us to reunite him by name to the Mizraimite On, his original; and by his form, to the particular portion of the Mizraimite people inhabiting Pelesheth and its dependencies. Secondly, in that the mythical account by Berosus,[n] of the manner in which Oannes first made himself known on the shores of the Persian Gulf, by rising from the sea to instruct the Chaldeans in all religious and useful knowledge, implies that a certain learned and civilised people, who navigated those seas, were the medium of those communications, and taught in his name; whence the great probability that the other gods of the same people, found in company with Oannes, were also introduced by that people.

Herodotus says that the early maritime settlements of the Phœnicians were on the Erythrean Sea. Under that name he of course could not mean the Canaanites, who never extended beyond the Jordan. Neither must we apply this statement to the nation who more strictly claim the name of Phœnicians—the children of Onka—since they were an *inland* tribe of the great parent nation, extending by the Philistine branch to the Mediterranean in quite another direction. These, however, were only part of a whole; a member of that great body whose wealthiest commercial establishments were on the Elanitic Gulf, and whose ships had navigated the Erythrean Sea to the south, while their caravans brought merchandise across the Arabian desert from the north, for many ages before the wilds of Greece had received from their western colonies the elements of her arts, letters, and civilization. Although Herodotus has evidently put one part of the nation for another, his statement is based on a truth; for the 'Phœnicians' read the 'Rephaim,' and it becomes strictly correct. As early as the period of Thothmes III.—while Joseph was living in Egypt—when the great nation, her rival, was beginning to decline, and its emigrant

---

[m] Out of *twelve* legible names, in the legends over their floating bodies, *four* present this compound: TAR-KANUNASA, TAR-KATI, TEKA-TAR, and SAP-TAR, besides beginning another mutilated name. The reader will bear in mind that L and R are represented in Egyptian by the same character. Rosellini, *Mon. Storici*, pl. 109, 110.

[n] Cory's *Ancient Fragments*, p. 28.

kindred from Lower Egypt were founding settlements in the Peloponnesus, while those of Palestine were concentrating all their forces from far and near to resist the Egyptian invading power; even so early do we find the name of the Horite city Elath, LT·N·NU, bringing to the treasury of the conqueror the tribute of the wealth she had amassed in her traffic with the Euphratesian regions of SAENKAR (Shinâr, שִׁנְעָר) and BBL (Babel, בָּבֶל).[o]

Oannes, Ωανν-ης, thus introduced into the East, is merely the Hebrew Aon, און, with a Greek case-termination; and the Hebrew form is only a transcript of an ancient Coptic word which, according to Champollion, signifies 'to enlighten.'

Aon was the original name of the god worshipped in the great sanctuary of Heliopolis, which is called in Scripture by its name, Beth-Aon, the 'house of On,' as well as by its translation, Beth-Shemesh, the 'house of the sun.' The language that explains a local god's name, surely points out the nation who first worshipped him under that name. The primitive Aon was therefore the 'enlightener of man,' to a people speaking the primitive language, out of which the Coptic sprang; and such a people were the Caphtorim of Lower Egypt, whom we afterwards find established among the Philistines in Palestine. Under this pure spiritual attribute, the Supreme God was known to the ancient Heliopolitans, and continued to be an object of secret adoration by the religious conservatives of the land, its priests, who veiled under the garb of mysteries and initiations the purer Mizraimite worship of their ancestors, long after the subjection of Lower Egypt to the Thebans; long after the dominant race had identified this god with their Ra or Sun, which appeared his most fitting emblem. Nevertheless, in the popular religion—that of the rulers, who commanded, and of the people, who must obey—Aon gradually glided into the mixed Sun-god Râ, of the Egyptian astro-mythological system; in the same way that Thoth, the early instructor of the Mizraim in letters, arts, science, and the division of time, according to their ancestral traditions, had the moon, the natural divider of time, placed under his care.

The ancient Mizraimite name Aon is never mentioned as a synonym of Râ by the Egyptians themselves. Except in the name of their month Paôni, we only meet with the primeval name among the kindred races out of Egypt, as that of a contemplar god worshipped under the same attributes; or learn its former existence in Egypt obliquely, from extra-Egyptian sources. As under the prescribed form of the state religion, he was named Râ,

---

[o] Birch on the Statistical Tablet of Karnak, *Trans. R. S. of Literature,* vol. ii. New Series.

and identified with the sun, the physical light,—the sanctuary of Heliopolis, in Scripture is alluded to either as Beth-Aon, the House of Aon, or as Beth-Shemesh, the House of the Sun. And the Egyptian name of the city in the Mosaic period, when the Delta was annexed to Egypt, is accordingly found as רע־מסם Ra-meses, the birth-place of Râ, rendered by the Greeks Heliopolis, city of the Sun. An explanatory gloss of the Septuagint translators, subsequently copied into the text, and thus most fortunately preserved, intimates their knowledge that the Aon of which Joseph's father-in-law was priest was the same as Heliopolis, and their accuracy as to that reference is proved by the priest's official name, פּוֹטִיפֶרַע Pet-Ph-Râ, dedicated to Râ.[p]

Aon, the divine enlightener of men, was therefore the patronymic god of ' the land of Rameses' or ' Goshen.' His outward symbol was a young bull. In the ancient Egyptian language the same hieroglyphic denotes a *bull* and a *chief*.[q] In the Hebrew, likewise, the name of a bull (שׁוֹר) is derived from the root שׂר, to rule. Such is the simple origin of all sacred symbols. It is only our ignorance of an ancient people's language that leaves the import of their emblems a mystery. In Egypt a live animal was substituted for the ideagraph, in after-times: Manetho gives the reign of Kaiechos, second king of the Thinite dynasty, a descendant of Menes, as the era of the innovation that brought in the worship of a living animal-symbol. It formed no part of the original Mizraimite system.

The worship of Aon under the tauriform emblem is also clearly traceable in the land of the Rephaim; Beth-El is called Beth-Aon in Josh. vii. 2, and 1 Sa. xiii. 5. Hosea also alludes to ' the calves of Beth-Aon,' Ch. iv. 15; v. 8; x. 5. The name, as *Beit-In*, is still extant. It was the antiquity of this symbol of local worship at Beth-El which induced Jeroboam to select the spot for its restoration. We now refer to the Egyptian monuments. After the defeat of the SHAS·U in the upper MNA or Shepherd region, Seti Menephtah presents their spoils to Amun;[r] among them is conspicuous a beautiful vase, on the cover of which the emblematical bull is represented, leaping among the water-plants. Another bull, standing on a pedestal, forms the cover of a tall urn among

---

[p] Wilkinson, *Anc. Egyp.*, vol. iv. p. 301.

[q] The root *ka* in Egyptian is *a bull;* and also *to set up;* corresponding to the Hebrew נשׂא, from which נְשִׂיא, *a prince*, literally *a superior.*

[r] Rosellini, *Mon. Storici,* pl. 52. There is also a bull-headed urn among the spoils of the Anakim of TAHI, pl. 56, and of the SHET·TA, pl. 59. These are known from the Ashtaroth urns by the absence of the disk, and the head being in profile. The entire figure of a bull on the top of a beautiful lotus-plant vase also occurs among the SHET·TA symbols.

the same spoils, similar to those crowned with the emblems of Ashtaroth and Renpu. This bull of Aon was the golden calf of the Exodus—the consecrated emblem of the ruler of Goshen; its living exemplar was called Mnevis at Heliopolis, and Apis at Memphis.

The maritime Aon, or Phœnician and Chaldean Oannes, is a symbolical form peculiar to the people of the sea-coast, Pelesheth. It is the Dag-on or Fish-on of Scripture, compounded of דג, fish, and ן, contracted form of the name of the god. I have a copy of an ancient coin in the British Museum, which represents Dagon on one side, and a ship on the other. The god has a human head and arms, and the tail of a dolphin. In his right hand he holds a fish with its head upwards, in his left another with its head downwards. This ingenious hieroglyphic signifies that in the land over which Aon, the enlightener of men, ruled and guided the sun, it began its course on land, in the east (*the front*), figured by the human fore-part; and ended it in the sea in the west (*the back*), figured by the hind part of a maritime creature. It reached its greatest elevation at the *right hand* of the god, *i. e.* the south,—this is implied by the fish looking upward; and it sank below the horizon at *his left*, the north; this is expressed by the fish going down. Such an emblem must have been designed in a country of which it accurately described the geographical bearings;—one with the continent eastward, and a western sea; and, moreover, for the emblem to be intelligible, it requires that the mode of orientation which refers the east to the *front*, the west to the *back*, &c. should be customary in the language of the country. These conditions are fulfilled in Palestine alone,—in the region of the maritime proto-Phœnicians, where we find the Scriptural Philistines, worshippers of Dagon. And they must have introduced it into Babylonia, for there the emblem loses all its descriptive significance, and consequently it never could have been framed in that country.

The Oannes of Chaldea, by the internal evidence of his representation and his Coptic name, confirms the admission of Berosus that he was introduced into that country by foreigners. His figure in the Khorsabad sculptures only differs from the original type in that it wears the Assyrian costume. He has a double pair of horns; his geographical emblems, the human fore part and fish's tail, the right hand pointing upwards and the left downwards, are preserved; but the accessory fishes are absent.

The form of Dagon in both representations illustrates with a singularly circumstantial precision the allusion to the catastrophe of his fall, in 1 Sa. v. 4, 'Behold, Dagon was prostrate with his face to the ground before the ark of the Lord; the head of Dagon and both the palms of his hands being cut off upon the threshold:

only the dagon of him (*i. e.* the fish part) remained.' If such a figure as the Khorsabad subject were cut in stone, and its upper part happened to separate from the stump at the waist, the weight of the two projecting arms would inevitably bring the trunk down on its face; the two hands first, and then the head, being broken off by the fall.

There are two sites extant by name as Beth-Dagon, in Palestine; one near the coast near Ekron, and one east of Shechem.

The Philistine form of Ashtaroth was a feminine Dagon; the Greek equivalents only of her name are known as Atargatis[s] or Derketo. The Atargateum at Karnion is referred to in 2 Macc. xii. 21-26, as a place difficult to besiege or even to approach, taken by Judas. It thus appears that the maritime Aphrodite was a contemplar deity with that of the inland Rephaim, or rather was considered as a local form of the same impersonation. In referring to her temple at Ashkalon,[t] plundered by the Scythians, Herodotus calls her Aphrodite-Urania, without distinction as to her fishy attribute.

PTHAH.

Although Memphis, the capital of Middle Egypt, was the central locality from whence the particular impersonation of the creative power called Pthah first emanated and was accepted by the Mizraimite nation, this god claims a place in the pantheon of the Rephaim as a contemplar deity. It is interesting to find by the geographical reference of Josh. xv. 9, to the 'Waters of Nephtoah,' near the entrance of the valley of the Rephaim, that the primitive Pthah, parent of the Cabiri or great gods of the Pelasgic or proto-Phœnician races, had a temple within a few miles of Jerusalem, prior in antiquity perhaps to the metropolis of Middle Egypt; for נֶפְתּוֹחַ, Nephtoah (read without the points), is letter for letter the same name as that by which Moses designates the Memphite family נַפְתֻּחִים, Naphtuhim, and means 'the abode of Pthah.'[u]

Two forms of Pthah were reverenced in Egypt. Of the Thebanized form we need not speak; that which concerns us is the primeval god, the entrance, opening, or cause of the entering-in of existence, פתח. Under the Theban system of modifying without abolishing the existing state of things in Mizraim, the name of

---

[s] These two corrupted and incomplete forms may perhaps correct one another, and reveal the primitive etymon of the name, Der=Atar, AT-HOR; and γατ=גֹ, *the fish*, reversed, translated by κητος, a marine animal; the maritime Athor, or 'abode of Horus.'

[t] Herod., *Clio*, 105.

[u] Na or No, an Egyptian formative of locality; No-Amun, נֹא אָמוֹן, Thebes (Nahum iii. 8); apparently akin to the Hebrew נוה, and the Greek ναι-ω, to dwell.

Pthah was not changed, though it has no known sense in the language of Egypt; but it was given to a new form of the same god, an upright mummy-shaped figure; and the more ancient character was then distinguished by a qualifying name, Pthah-Sokar-Osiri. The monumental effigies of the god bearing this name[x] shew him to be the Great Lord of the mysterious rites, referred to by Herodotus, whose time-honoured and most sacred effigy was in the form of a pigmy man like the figures called by the Phœnicians Pataikos (likeness of Ptah), which they fixed to the prows of their vessels. If an emblem is understood, its object is fulfilled; but to us it seems a strange expedient to suggest so abstruse and majestic an idea as that of the Δημιουργός, 'maker of the people' at the entering in of its existence on earth, through so contemptible a medium as an unperfected representation of his own work—an undeveloped human being—a stunted and deformed little pigmy!

The Theban form of Pthah varied the expression of the same conception by a figure wrapped up in bandages—undisclosed; and Sir Gardner Wilkinson mentions a very curious illustration of the notion embodied in this impersonation—the door or opening of the creative act—the Creator designing his work by a representation of Pthah tracing with a reed the outline of a human figure.[y]—F. C.

ON THE GREEK VULGATE.[a]

ALL who possess any acquaintance with the Greek scriptures of the New Testament are aware that, during the last fifty years, several editions of that inspired book have issued from the press, differing, in some places greatly, from the *textus receptus*. The illustrious individuals, to whose exertions we are indebted for these works, are confessedly entitled to our highest praise for their unwearied zeal, vast erudition, and extensive research. It remains, however, to be inquired—how far the text which they have published is to be preferred to that which we previously possessed? And, if we are not mistaken, the result of a really independent and thorough examination of the subject would be—with all intelligent and devout men—the rejection of the corrected text of Griesbach, Lachmann, and Tischendorf, and the adoption of the common Stephanic and Elzevir text, of which our English Testament is a version. It must not be inferred, from what we have

---

[x] Wilkinson, *Anc. Egyp.*, vol. iv. p. 253, pl. 24, fig. 2.　　[y] Ibid., p. 253, pl. 23.
[a] This article is inserted in the hope and expectation that it will excite a full discussion in this Journal of the important subject of which it treats. ED. *J. S. L.*

said, that we regard the received text as in all particulars a correct one. Indeed, it would have been little less than miraculous if the first editors of the New Testament, with the small number of manuscripts which they possessed, had given us an immaculate edition. Still, whilst admitting that there are many passages which might be corrected, by the careful collation of the many manuscripts which have since come to light, we believe that the corruptions of the so-called corrected text of Griesbach and Tischendorf, very far exceed the comparatively trifling errors of the *textus receptus.*

Instead of occupying the reader's time needlessly in discussing the new-exploded theories of Griesbach and his immediate successors, we propose to direct our attention to the more recent systems of Drs. Tischendorf and Tregelles ; the former of whom has lately published a fresh edition of his New Testament (Lipsiæ, 1849) ; the latter, the book of the Revelation, and a prospectus of the whole Greek Testament.

The principle adopted by both of these distinguished scholars is substantially the same,—that of relying chiefly on the *most* ancient Greek manuscripts in the formation of a text, to the entire neglect of the more modern or cursive manuscripts. Dr. Tischendorf includes *codices* from the fourth to the ninth century in his list of *most ancient* authorities. Dr. Tregelles restricts this appellation, as regards Greek manuscripts, to those written during the first half of this period.[b]

At first sight this principle appears so plausible, that most persons we think would be disposed to give it their assent. The more ancient a manuscript is, the less must have been—it is natural to suppose—its chances of corruption. But though specious in theory, it is unsafe and dangerous in practice, and will altogether fail to furnish us, we think, with any fair idea of the state in which the text existed at the time to which the manuscripts referred to are assigned. The following are some of the reasons on which this opinion rests :—

1. The *fewness* of the manuscripts which have come down to us from the first six centuries—which is the period embraced by Dr. Tregelles' plan—forms, we consider, a very strong argument against the supposition that they afford a fair idea of the Greek Vulgate as it then existed. It is well known to all who are con-

---

[b] ' Textus petendus est unice ex antiquis testibus, et potissimum e Græcis codicibus, sed interpretationum patrumque testimoniis minime neglectis.'—Tischendorf, Proleg. ad Nov. Test. Gr., p. xii. Lipsiæ, 1849.

' The text is formed on the authority of the oldest Greek manuscripts and versions (aided by early citations), so as to present, as far as practicable, the readings which were commonly received at the earliest period to which we can revert to obtain critical evidence.'—Dr. Tregelles' Prospectus.

versant with the textual criticism of the New Testament, that the number of *most ancient* manuscripts is very small; whilst the number of those which were written since the tenth century is very considerable. If we except the mere fragments, whether we look at the Gospels, the Acts, or the Epistles, we have scarcely half a dozen that date back so early as the sixth century; and in the book of Revelation still less. On the other hand, the number of manuscripts of later date, written from the tenth to the fifteenth century, is very considerable—amounting, we believe, to four or five hundred in the Gospels, and more than half that number in the Epistles. It is manifest, then, that so small a proportion of copies as that of the Uncials of the first six centuries, is quite insufficient to afford any just or fair idea of the actual text of the New Testament in that age.

This statement is founded upon the plain fact that, with the exception of the Alexandrine manuscript, which constantly differs from the others, we are wholly ignorant of the real character of these *Codices Antiquissimi.* That they are very ancient is allowed by all. But if we ask the learned men whose labours have brought them to our knowledge, are they genuine copies of the Greek Testament?—do these most ancient manuscripts contain, substantially at least, the text in use amongst the faithful, at the periods to which critics assign them?—no answer can be given. That there were many hundreds of copies in circulation at the time referred to will be granted by all. The majority of these, we suppose, were good copies, but others were, in various ways, corrupt. Many were in the hands of heretics, and moulded in accordance with their views. Out of all this vast number—with the exception of a few fragments—scarcely half a dozen manuscripts in the Gospels, the same number in the Acts and Epistles, and still less in the Revelation, have reached our age. That these few copies present a fair idea of the Greek Vulgate of the early Church, is, then, we hold, an assumption which no critic is justified in making.

2. The great diversity of reading discoverable in these *most ancient* codices affords further evidence, we consider, that, taken as a whole, they do not represent the actual state of the *textus receptus,* in the age to which they are assigned. It is more than probable that, when all books were written, no copy of the Scriptures of the New Testament existed without verbal inaccuracies. But the discrepancies to which we refer are not mere verbal errors, but variations of the most serious nature—affecting faith and practice. We lately had occasion to examine all the more important passages in the Gospels where the Greek codices contain various readings, and found that, of manuscripts of the

sixth and previous centuries, B, C, D generally differed from A. On referring, however, to the manuscripts of the next three centuries, we found that the testimony of A, the celebrated Alexandrine manuscript, was confirmed. The great body of these codices, E, G, H, K, M, and some others, usually reading with that venerable codex, in opposition to B, C, D, and L.[c] Now that variations on important points should be found in the very few *most* ancient manuscripts which we possess, does certainly afford a strong presumption that there are corrupt copies amongst them—whose evidence for or against a reading is of no worth. Instead, then, of blindly following the majority of the manuscripts of the sixth and previous centuries, as undoubtedly containing the received text of the early Church, the plain course would be, we conceive, to use all practicable means to determine which of these codices are best entitled to the praise of accuracy and truth.

3. As matter of fact it may be added, that some of these very manuscripts, on the testimony of which Dr. Tischendorf and—so far as we can judge from his Prospectus—Dr. Tregelles, cancel whole passages of the Greek Vulgate, are admitted to contain manifold corruptions. The *Codex Bezæ* (D) abounds not only with orthographical errors, but with alterations and interpolations of various kinds. The *Codex Ephræmi Rescriptus* (C) is said to be disfigured by similar errors. The *Codex Regius* (L in the Gospels), the text of which agrees with the Uncial manuscripts, B, C, and D, in a remarkable manner, though of a later date, is thought to have been written by a transcriber of extreme ignorance, who probably introduced readings from various copies, or from the margin of the manuscript from which he copied. Some of these readings even make absolute nonsense of the passages where they occur. Griesbach himself makes the following candid admission of the corruptions of these highly lauded Uncials. ' Nullius codicis vitia de consulto me celasse aut dissimulasse ; satis inde patet quod *innumeros gravissimosque errores* in iis commissos codicibus, quos cæteroque magni facio, velut B, C, D, L, 33, 124, &c., ingenue indicavi.'[d] Such is the character given by this celebrated critic of his favourite codices, yet a number of readings which rest, almost exclusively, on the testimony of these very manuscripts (B, C, D, and L) have been inserted by him and Tischendorf, and—we have reason to believe—by Dr. Tregelles also, into their respective editions. And we can assure our readers that

<hr>

[c] It is a significant fact, that the ancient Peshito, which Tischendorf, with many others, assigns to the second century, mostly contained in such passages the readings of A. In some cases the other two Syriac versions agreed with the Peshito.

[d] Præf. in Nov. Test., § ii. p. 1.

they constitute the most exceptionable of all the alterations which the so-called corrected text exhibits.

We submit, then, that the attempts already made, or at present making, to furnish us with the text prevalent in the time of Chrysostom, or of Gregory the Great, by adhering to the testimony of the codices termed *most ancient*, cannot be sufficient. We are not in a position to do this. The materials necessary for the work are wanting. We must therefore be content to go back to that period in which the vast number of manuscripts written and still extant enable us with positive certainty to ascertain the state of the text then in use ; believing, in accordance with his word, that the Most High would in his Providence so order things, that the writings of the New Testament would be indubitably preserved down to that time from all material corruption. Indeed, the hypothesis on which the system of those critics rests, who rely chiefly upon the testimony of *ancient* authority in the formation of a text, lies open to this fatal objection — that it throws the greatest doubt upon the integrity of the text of the New Testament, by supposing that for a period of nearly a thousand years it has existed in a state of grievous corruption.

In the system adopted by the most recent editors of the Greek Testament, considerable importance is attached to the citations from the New Testament on the writings of the early fathers, especially of Origen, whose works it is said contain about two-thirds of that inspired volume.

If these fathers coincided with each other in their quotations, and if their works had descended to our time substantially correct, there would be considerable force in the argument drawn from that source. But the fact is that, in both particulars, the very reverse is the case. The fathers do not generally agree with one another except to a certain extent. And so far as they do coincide in their testimony, the fact that their writings have been grievously corrupted destroys, in a great degree, the value of their evidence. The manuscripts from which Tertullian's works were printed are said to be extremely faulty.[e] The copies of Clement and Origen were corrupted even in their lifetime.[f] The copies of Cyprian demonstrate their own corruption, by their want of agreement among themselves. It is admitted, too, that the fathers in many cases quoted *memoriter ;* in others they adopted the arguments and the citations of each other — occasionally even quoting from the Heretics themselves.[g] Griesbach, whose system rested

[e] Rigalt de Tert., præf. p. 2.

[f] See the controversy between Rufinus and Jerome, on the corruption of Origen's works.—Rufin. de Adult. librorum Orig., p. 50 ; and Hier. Apol. adv. Ruf., lib. ii. c. 4, 5, p. 244.

[g] See, for instance, Tertullian de Carne Christi, cap. xix. p. 30-8.

upon the quotations of Origen, has conceded so much against the accuracy both of his writings and of the editions of his works, that we wonder at the place which they still occupy in the system of recent editors. ' Librarii etiam,' says the learned critic, ' qui Origenis opera transcribendo propagarunt, et editores qui typis excudi ea curarunt, sæpenumero, justo negligentiores fuerunt, in describendis aut recensendis locis e Sacr. Scrip. citatis ; eosque e codicibus junioribus aut editionibus bibliorum Græcorum quibus assueti ipsi erant, interpolarunt.' In a previous passage Griesbach admits, too, that, in quoting Scripture, Origen frequently deserted his written authorities,—'immutato uno et altero vocabulo, aut constructionis ordine.' [h]

As to the cursive MSS., it is admitted that a remarkable uniformity exists in their readings. When we consider that they amount to several hundred, and have been written in various nations and ages, this is certainly no mean argument in favour of their genuineness. And though it is asserted that they have been altered for ecclesiastical purposes, we are not aware that any proof of this statement has ever been produced. Were it true, the admitted remarkable coincidence in the readings of these manuscripts and the Peshito version—a document which dates from the second century—is quite unaccountable.

It is worthy of notice, that out of the five Uncial manuscripts of the sixth and previous centuries, in the gospels—two are what are termed palimpsest manuscripts—that is, manuscripts from which the text has been erased, and other writing substituted in its place. These are the *Codex Ephræmi Rescriptus* (C), and the *Dublin Rescriptus* (Z). We know not whether we are justified in hazarding such an opinion, but it appears by no means improbable, that the cause of their being thus treated was the circumstance of their containing a corrupt text. When we remember the statement of Griesbach respecting one of these manuscripts, the suspicion seems somewhat strengthened. [i]

And really the very circumstance of the continued preservation of the most ancient of the Uncial manuscripts during a period of fifteen centuries, affords some ground for the supposition that, being corrupt copies, they were long laid aside, and thus escaped the wear and tear under which genuine copies of the same date have long since perished. It is obvious, however, that the Alexandrine manuscript is above the reach of such suspicion—the history of it having been handed down to us from immemorial tradition. [k]

---

[h] Symb. Crit., tom. 1, pp. cix. and cviii.
[i] Griesbach, Præf. in N. T., sec. ii. p. i.
[k] Woide, Præf. in Cod. Alex., p. ix, sec. xl.

In illustration of the above remarks in defence of the Greek Vulgate, we proceed to a critical examination of a few of the more important of those passages which have been expunged from the Gospels, by the German Editors of the Greek Testament, on the ground that they are omitted in certain of the *most ancient* codices.

MATT. VI. 13.

'For thine is the kingdom, and the power, and the glory, for ever. Amen.'

The doxology at the end of the Lord's prayer is omitted, not merely by Griesbach and Tischendorf, but likewise by most other editors of the Greek Testament. We have given our best attention to the subject, and cannot but think that the evidence in its favour outweighs all that has been adduced against it.

As regards manuscript authority, it is wanting, according to Tischendorf, in B, D, and Z, three of the most ancient Uncial manuscripts, which are known to us, also in the cursive codices, 1, 17, 118, 130, 209. On the other hand, it is found in Δ, and, according to Scholz, *in all the manuscripts* which he inspected and collated (except those just mentioned), and these include the Uncial manuscripts, E, K, L, M, S.

The versions in which the clause is wanting are, according to Tischendorf, the Vulgate, most manuscripts of the Italic, the Coptic, the Arabic of the Polyglot, and some manuscripts; the Persian according to one text, and the Anglo-Saxon. On referring to Scholz for the versions in which it is found—Tischendorf usually gives only the testimony *against* the readings rejected by him—we find they are the following:—the ancient Syriac, the Jerusalem Syriac Lectionary, and the Philoxenian Syriac; the Arabic according to the edition of Erpenius, the Persian according to one text; the Æthiopic, the Armenian, the Georgian, the Gothic, the Slavonic, a very few manuscripts of the Coptic, the Sahidic, and *some* Latin manuscripts.

To sum up the evidence for and against this passage, it appears that we have three Uncial manuscripts against its authenticity, in opposition to six in favour of it. The greater *antiquity* of the former *three*, however, which range from the fourth to the sixth century, must be set against the greater *number* of the latter, which reach from the eighth to the tenth century. In cursive manuscripts, however, the authorities may almost be said to be all on the side of the genuineness of the clause; only five codices being known which omit it, against the numerous copies which contain it. These five codices too, except one, which is of the tenth century, are comparatively modern; whilst of the vast number which contain the passage, many are of the tenth century, many more of the eleventh, and a vast number of the twelfth.

The majority of ancient versions, we have seen, contain the clause. This is a circumstance of great weight—the ancient versions being uniformly regarded by critics as most important witnesses in the case of passages and clauses. In the number of those versions in which it occurs, we find the Peshito, or ancient Syriac, a document, as is generally agreed, of the second century. We infer, then, that, at that early period, it formed a part of the Gospel by Matthew.

The passage is found in some of the Fathers of the early Church, the Apost. Constitt., Chrysostom several times, and Isidore of Pelusium. In the case of some of those who are referred to as omitting it, we think some mistake has arisen. They are said to have been ignorant of the clause, because they do not include it in their exposition of the Lord's prayer. This, however, is a most unwarrantable inference, as may be proved from the case of Isidore of Pelusium. This Father passes it by altogether in his exposition, but frequently quotes it in other parts of his writings.

On the whole, then, we submit that, whilst there is sufficient critical testimony to cast a measure of doubt upon the passage, the course adopted by the critical Editors of the Greek Testament, in entirely expunging it from the Word of God, is altogether indefensible, when the number and respectability of the witnesses in its favour are taken into account.

MATT. XIX. 17.

In this place the common text reads,—'*And he said unto him, Why callest thou me good? There is none good but one (that is) God.*' The recent Editors of the Greek Testament, Griesbach, Tischendorf, and Tregelles, give it thus:—'*Why speakest thou to me of good? He that is good is one.*'

The authorities for the new reading are as follows:—the Uncial manuscripts, B, D, and L, and the cursive manuscripts, Nos. 1, 22, 251. It is supported by the Vulgate, Italic, Sahidic, Coptic, and Armenian versions; as also by the citations of several of the Fathers—Origen, Eusebius, Cyril, Dionysius, Antiochus, Novatian, Jerome, Augustine, and Juvencus.

On the other hand, we find in favour of the received reading, the Uncial manuscripts, C, E, K, S, V, Δ, together with, as Scholz affirms, all the cursive manuscripts of the Constantinopolitan recension. It is also found in the ancient Peshito, as well as the Philoxenian Syriac; and in the Persic, the Slavonic, the Arabic versions, and in one very ancient manuscript of the Italic, the

Codex Brixianus. The passage is also quoted according to the common text by the following Fathers—Justin, Cyril, Chrysostom, Theophylact, and Hilary.

When it is considered that the Evangelists Mark and Luke give the passage according to the received reading here, it must surely require some very preponderating evidence to lead any who reverence the Word of God to substitute for it the absurd and unmeaning sentence found in the text of recent editors. Instead of this conclusive testimony, we have only three Uncial manuscripts against six, of which one is of the fifth century, and a very few cursive codices against some hundreds on the other side. It appears to us, therefore, that there exists but little doubt as to the true reading of the passage.

The only principle on which the corrected lection can be defended is that of sacrificing all other evidence, whether internal or external, to what we cannot but denominate an accidental circumstance, the majority of ancient manuscript testimony. Hence we find that Griesbach, Lachmann, Tischendorf, and Tregelles, the avowed advocates of ancient testimony, are the only editors, we believe, by whom it is adopted.

MATT. xx. 22, 23.

' Are ye able to drink of the cup that I shall drink of, [and to be baptized with the baptism that I am baptized with?] They say unto him, We are able. And he saith unto them, Ye shall drink, indeed, of my cup, [and be baptized with the baptism that I am baptized with,] but to sit on my right hand and on my left,' &c.

The words enclosed in brackets are omitted by Griesbach, Lachmann, and Tischendorf, on the following grounds. They are absent in the Greek Uncial manuscripts, B, D, L, and Z, and the cursive manuscripts, 1, 22. The Vulgate, Italic, Coptic, Æthiopic, and Sahidic versions want them; and the following fathers appear to have been ignorant of them—Origen, Epiphanius, Hilary, Ambrose, Jerome, and Juvencus.

In favour of the authenticity of the clauses, we have the following evidence. They occur, if we understand aright the statement of Scholz, in the Greek Uncials, C, F, G, H, K, M, X, V, and in the cursive codices, 4, 6, 18, 28, 122, 124, 127, 142, 148, 167, 209, 234, 235, 262, 299, and very many others of all the recensions. The *Evangelistarium*, 63, an Uncial manuscript of the ninth century, contains the disputed clauses, as do many others of the same class, according to Scholz. The versions which contain these passages are, the ancient Peshito, and the Philoxenian Syriac, the Armenian, the Persic, the Slavonic, and some very ancient codices of the Italic.

It appears to us, then, that there is no sufficient evidence for the rejection of these clauses from the Word of God. Four Uncials are against its genuineness, and eight in favour of it. And although the four are of greater antiquity than the eight, it will probably be thought by most that the superior age of the former is balanced by the superior number of the latter. And when to these are added the vast numbers of cursive manuscripts in which the clauses are found, written, many of them, in the tenth, eleventh, and twelfth centuries, and belonging not to one family but to all —Western, Constantinopolitan, and Palestine—we think there remains scarcely a doubt that the received reading here forms an actual part of the inspired Scriptures.

MARK xvi. 9, 20.

This passage, which constitutes the close of Mark's Gospel, is marked by Griesbach as probably spurious, and is totally omitted by Tischendorf.

The passage is omitted in only one manuscript, B, the celebrated *Codex Vaticanus.*[m] It occurs in all the other manuscripts of the Gospels, which are unmutilated here, including the following, A, C, D, E, F, G, H, K, L, M, S, U, V, Δ, besides upwards of two hundred cursive manuscripts, written from the tenth century downwards. It was cited by Irenæus, and Clemens Alexandrinus, in the second century, by Cyril of Jerusalem, Nestorius, Athanasius, Ambrose, Augustine, and others, in the fourth and beginning of the fifth centuries. It is found, moreover, in all the ancient versions which contain the chapter, without a single exception.

We think it needless, in so plain a case, to waste words in attempting to vindicate the genuineness of the section. Dr. Tregelles himself, we believe, acknowledges it, nor can we think that any who entertain any real veneration for the inspired writings will unite with Dr. Tischendorf in expunging this passage from the Word of God.

LUKE ii. 33.

The common text reads here, ' And Joseph and his Mother marvelled at those things which were said of him.' But the revised text of Griesbach and Tischendorf gives ' And his *Father* and his Mother,' etc.

The passage is found according to the corrected reading of modern editors in very few manuscripts. The following are all

---

[m] This circumstance appears to us sufficient to stamp the character of this highly lauded codex as unworthy of trust, although the most ancient, it is thought, in existence.

that are enumerated—B, D, L, 1, 130, 131. It is supported by the Coptic, Sahidic, Armenian, and Vulgate versions, and also by the Philoxenian Syriac. Many of the fathers too appear to have read the passage thus.

On the other hand, the reading of the common text occurs in the Uncials A, K, M, and all the codices which follow the Constantinopolitan recension. The ancient Peshito Syriac, the Arabic, the Persic, the Gothic, and the Italic versions confirm the *textus receptus* here. Some of the fathers also appear to have read it as we have it now. It appears too, from the evidence of Jerome, that so early as the fourth century it was alleged by Helvidius that the true reading, '*And Joseph and his Mother*,' had been corrupted as we find it in Griesbach and Tischendorf.[n]

The statement contained in the reading adopted by the German critics is so opposed to the doctrine of the supernatural procreation of our Lord's humanity, and the phraseology of the passage is so unlike what we find elsewhere in scripture, that we think few will be disposed, on the slight preponderance of ancient authority, to reject the lection of the Greek Vulgate here—supported as it is by the ancient Syriac, and the vast majority of cursive manuscripts.

Luke xi. 2.

'*When ye pray say, Our Father,* [*which art in heaven,*] *hallowed be thy name, thy kingdom come,* [*thy will be done, as in heaven, so in earth.*']

The words enclosed in brackets are rejected as spurious, both by Griesbach and Tischendorf, on the ground that they are wanting in the manuscripts B, L, and in several cursive codices.

According to Scholz, they are found in the most ancient manuscripts, A, C, D, and indeed in all the other Greek codices, both Uncial and cursive, which contain the chapter. All the versions too support the common text here, except the Vulgate, the Armenian, and the Persic according to one text. The citations of the fathers are also decidedly in favour of its genuineness; all of whom, except four, are said to have recognized it.

It appears then, that their favourite plea of *testes antiquissimi* fails the German editors in this passage; nor can we account for the fact of their rejection of the common reading here, unless we attribute it to a latent desire of forming a text differing as much as possible from the Greek Vulgate.

---

[n] ' Et erant pater illius et mater admirantes super his quæ dicebantur de eo.'— Licet tu mira impudentia hæc in Græcis codicibus falsata contendas. Hier. advers. Helvid.

John i. 27.

'For he was before me.'

This important clause is omitted both by Griesbach and Tischendorf, and is placed in brackets by Lachmann. The testimony against its genuineness appears to us inadequate to account for its rejection.

It is absent, says Scholz, from the Uncial codices B, C (a primâ manu), L, and from the cursive manuscripts 1, 13, 22, 33; as well as the Evangelistaria 19 and 20. The versions which omit it are the Coptic, Armenian, Æthiopic, and Slavonic.

In favour of the claims of the passage, we infer from Scholz that it is found in all the Greek Uncials which contain the chapter, viz. A, E, F, G, H, K, L, M, S, V, X. The Codex Sangallensis, Δ, was not collated by Scholz, but, as it is not cited by Tischendorf against it, we presume that it contains the clause. We find it in the ancient Syriac and Vulgate, and the Italic in some manuscripts. From the silence of the critical editors of the New Testament, it may also be inferred that it occurs in all the other ancient versions, except the four already specified as omitting it.

The preponderance of critical authority is clearly, then, in favour of the passage. We feel it due therefore to the cause of truth, to enter our protest against those critics, who, on such comparatively slender grounds, have not hesitated to expunge from the Scriptures so important a testimony to the pre-existence of the Son of God.

John v. 2, 4.

'Now there is at Jerusalem by the sheep-market a pool which is called in the Hebrew tongue Bethesda, having five porches. In these lay a great multitude of impotent folk, of blind, halt, withered, [waiting for the moving of the water. For an angel went down at a certain season into the pool, and troubled the water; whosoever then first, after the troubling of the water, stepped in, was made whole of whatsoever disease he had.']

The words enclosed in brackets are marked as probably spurious by Griesbach, and are altogether rejected by Tischen·dorf. We entertain little doubt that it is the supernatural character of the facts related in it which has led those German critics to expunge this passage from the word of God—the external evidence against its genuineness being wholly insufficient.

According to Tischendorf, it is wanting in B, C, but has been subsequently placed in the margin of the latter codex by a less ancient hand. The cursive manuscripts 157, 314, too, omit it.

The passage is also absent from the Sahidic version, and from many manuscripts of the Coptic. The codices D, 33, contain the clause—'waiting for the troubling of the water;' but omit the fourth verse, which describes the descent of the angel and the effects which ensued. This verse is also marked with obeli in S, and upwards of fourteen cursive manuscripts.

With these exceptions the passage is found in *all the manuscripts both uncial and cursive so far as is known.* Among these are A, E, G, H, K, L, M, V, and Δ. All three of the Syriac versions contain it, as do the Italic, the Vulgate, the Æthiopic, the Gothic, and the Slavonic. Tischendorf adds, that Tertullian, Cyril, Euthymius, Ambrose, and Chrysostom cite these verses.

It thus appears that nearly all the critical documents which we possess acknowledge the passage as genuine. There can be no question, we think, that the German critics have been influenced by their known repugnance to the miraculous events of the Scripture in their rejection of this passage. To us, however, who feel nothing of this kind, the internal evidence would add weight, were any needed, to the external testimony, since we feel assured that the simplicity and conciseness which adorn the narrative would never have been found had it been the interpolation of a scribe.

John vii. 53—viii. 11.

The narrative of the adulterous woman is altogether rejected as an interpolation by Griesbach, Tischendorf, and Tregelles.[o] Let the reader judge whether on sufficient grounds.

The passage is omitted by the codices B, T, X, and 51 cursive manuscripts. A and C are mutilated here, but from a careful computation it is inferred that these manuscripts could not have contained it. The Sahidic, Gothic, and Armenian versions omit the section, as does the Philoxenian Syriac, executed in the sixth century. The scholia to many Greek codices also state that it is wanting in many manuscripts.

On the other hand, it is found, according to Tischendorf, in the following Uncials—D, E,* F, G, H, K, M,* S,* V. Besides which the transcribers of L and Δ have left a space here for the insertion of the passage, which proves, as Dr. Davidson justly observes, that they 'were acquainted with the passage, and found it in some manuscripts, but thought fit to reject it.' Besides these it is found, according to Scholz, in most of the cursive manuscripts which have been inspected—except the 51 mentioned above—amounting to 277. The Vulgate, the Italic, the Jerusalem Syriac,

---

o Journal of Sacred Literature, No. ix. p. 54.
* In these manuscripts it is marked with obeli.

the Slavonic versions contain it, as do the Arabic of the Polyglot, and, according to Scholz, some manuscripts and editions of the Peshito. Augustine, too, at the commencement of the fifth century, informs us that it was found in his time in many copies both of the Greek and Latin, although absent from many others.

On the whole we think it plain that the passage has far too many witnesses, some of them, too, of the very highest character, to be rejected as spurious. And in fact the absence of the section from the comparatively few which omit it is amply accounted for by the statement of Augustine, that 'some men of weak faith, or rather enemies of the true faith, fearing lest impunity in sin might be granted to their own wives, took away from their manuscripts the act of our Lord in forgiving the adulteress, as if he had given them free licence to sin in saying, " Go, sin no more." '[p]

The result of our examination of these disputed passages of the Word of God—the length of which has very far exceeded our original intention—has been, we think, to prove that the principle of adhering implicitly to the testimony of the *most ancient* manuscript witnesses in deciding for or against the genuineness of a reading, will lead to the rejection of passages which can be undeniably proved to have belonged to Holy Writ in the second and subsequent centuries. It has also brought before our notice evident proofs, we submit, that some of the recent editors of the Greek Testament have been guilty of a capriciousness and inconsistency most reprehensible in those who undertake a work of such vast responsibility. And, unless we are mistaken, they have also appeared, at times, to be greatly wanting in due reverence for the Word of God, in wholly rejecting passages, of which, to say the least, the evidence of their spurious character was far from decisive.

W. E. T.

CLEMENS ALEXANDRINUS,

HIS WRITINGS AND HIS PRINCIPLES.

De Clemente, Presbytero Alexandrino, — Homine, Scriptore, Philosopho, Theologo, Liber; quem scripsit HUB. JOS. REINKENS, Presbyter Vratislaviensis, S.S. Theol. Dr. Vratislaviæ (*i.e.* Breslau), Apud G. Ph. Aderholz, 1851.

BY the close of the second century Christianity had already won many peaceful victories, and carried off many bloodless trophies from the camp, the senate-house, and the forum, from the walks of private life, the mart of commerce, and the idol temple. 'We

---

[p] De Conj. Adult., cap. ii. sec. 2.

are but of yesterday,' said Tertullian, ' and we have filled your cities, islands, towns, and boroughs, the camp, the senate, and the forum. They lament that every sex, age, and condition, and persons of every rank, are converts to that name.'[a] Elsewhere he says, ' Moors and Getulians of Africa, the borders of Spain, several nations of France, and parts of Britain, inaccessible to the Romans, the Sarmatians, Dacians, Germans, and Scythians,'[b] had listened to the Gospel. The fiat of Cæsar could not prevent the disciples of the Lord from fulfilling his decree, ' Go ye into all the world and preach the gospel to every creature.' (Mar. xvi. 15.) The sword of Rome contended in vain against ' the sword of the spirit.' The priests of paganism could not keep up their altar-fires amid the splendours of the sun of righteousness. But there was one place where but a few enemies had been overcome, and, of the little progress which had been made in it, the greater part was of an uncertain character. That place was the School of Philosophy. Was Christianity to fail there? No. How then must it act? Some said, ' Let us attack and destroy it as our most dangerous foe :' —others, ' Let us ally ourselves to it and agree to baptize it into Christ :'—but others, ' Let us pursue a middle course ; admitting all that is good in it and true, let us reject all which we cannot harmonize with Christian doctrine. Let us not extinguish this lamp, but trim it, and feed it with the pure oil of the gospel—for it is a lamp.' Thus reasoned the bold, the timid, and the prudent. We cannot but feel that the latter was the most plausible principle, though we may often doubt the wisdom shown in its application. The extremes of mysticism, allegorizing, Gnosticism, and so forth, would be not heeded by many who heard the fame of Justin Martyr. The errors of Tatian would not prove a beacon of warning, for Athenagoras, a philosopher, had become a convert. If, as Philip Sidetes says, Athenagoras was the first teacher of the school at Alexandria, his influence would be very widely felt. Pantænus, his probable successor, who, Fabricius tells us, had been a stoic philosopher, would give fresh impulse to the movement. This impulse Clement of Alexandria received and transmitted—Origen was his pupil.

Believing that the attempt to philosophize Christianity was with a view to christianize philosophy in many instances, and bearing it in mind in the inquiries which follow, we shall freely confess that Clement of Alexandria was one of the most illustrious Christian philosophers of the early Church.

The plan we propose is—to give an outline of the life of Clement ;—to enumerate and characterize his extant works ;— to call

---

[a] Apol. c. 37.　　　　　　　　[b] Ad. Judæos. c. 7.

attention to his philosophical principles;—and lastly, to exhibit some of his doctrinal views. The man, the author, the philosopher, and the divine, will successively claim our attention.

Titus Flavius Clemens, whom we call Alexandrinus, was born near the middle of the second century; in all probability, between 150 and 160 after Christ. There is some dispute as to the place of his birth, though it is now generally believed to have been Athens. Epiphanius in his work on Heresies, names 'Clement, whom some call an Alexandrian, but others an Athenian.'[c] Whether, as Reinkens maintains,[d] '*some*' here denotes *the few*, and '*others*' *the many*, is, we think, a question which cannot be decided by the mere form of speech. At the same time the evidence from his writings favours the opinion that he was a Greek, and not an Egyptian, as Brucker[e] and others have supposed. He is called Alexandrinus, because at Alexandria he spent the prime of his life, filled the offices to which he was called, and wrote the works by which he is known. His parents, according to the testimony of Eusebius,[f] were heathen, and this is confirmed by expressions in his works. Clement's early training must have been of a superior kind, as he was familiar with all the learning of the age. Eusebius describes his attainments as universal; and his knowledge must have been very great, as attested by his works. 'The *penchant* for studies, which is generally attended with the mental conformation best adapted to their acquisition, led him in early youth to devote himself wholly to them. His labours and writings prove the ardour with which he loved them. For study was not then, as now, a tranquil and sedentary occupation. Books had not yet brought civilized nations into ready communion with erudition; and to obtain instruction, one must go far to seek the learned, and even their writings.[g] Upon his conversion, or, as he himself says, 'when he believed in Christ,'[h] he seems, like many since, to have received a new impulse. Already acquainted with Greek and general literature and philosophy, and with religion even to its mysteries, he began to desire a fuller knowledge of Christ and the Gospel. In pursuance of this object he entered upon a course of travel. The first Christian teacher whom he seems to have heard was in Greece, and is called by him Ionicus.[i] It has been doubted whether this was a proper name, an epithet applied to him from his native country, or the name of a sect. The last is very improbable, though maintained by Le Clerc in

---

[c] Κλήμης τε, ὃν φασί τινες Ἀλεξανδρέα, ἕτεροι δὲ Ἀθηναῖον, Hær. 32, 6.
[d] P. 1.   [e] Hist. Crit. Phil. a Christo nato, tom. iii. 415.
[f] Prep. Evang., lib. 2, cap. 2.
[g] Houtteville, Discours Historique et Critique, p. 41.
[h] Pædag. ii. p. 205, Potter's edition.
[i] Strom. i. p. 322. Ὁ μὲν ἐπὶ τῆς Ἑλλάδος, ὁ Ἰωνικός.

Clement's life.[k] Cave defends the first opinion, and says that Ionicus was a native of Cœle-Syria.[l] Brucker thinks Ionicus is here equivalent to *Græcus*, but Reinkens understands by it an Ionian.[m] If so, what was his name? Athenagoras, Dionysius Corinthius, and Caius, have been mentioned, but with no satisfactory support. Whoever his teacher was, Clement left him, proceeding first to Magna Græcia, by what route we know not. There he met with two Christian teachers, one a Cœle-Syrian, the other an Egyptian. After a time he journeyed eastward. In the east he heard two other teachers, an Assyrian and a Hebrew. He next directed his steps to Egypt, and at Alexandria found the 'Sicilian bee' as he calls him, whom he felt to be the man for whom he had hitherto sought in vain. Henceforth Alexandria was to be his chosen home.

Pantænus, who was now his master, presided over the old Catechetical School; he was a man of rare learning, and of a philosophical cast of mind. Of all Clement's teachers this influenced him most, and the grateful scholar in his Hypotyposes recorded and expounded the doctrine of his master.

At Alexandria, Clement was created a presbyter of the Church, about the year 195. Demetrius was at that time bishop there. Of Clement's conduct in this office we know little. He was next summoned to succeed Pantænus in the School, but whether because of the president's death, or of a commission to visit India to promote the claims of the Gospel, is disputed. Jerome makes Clement president of the school after the death of Pantænus,[n] while ' Ph. Sidetes makes Pantænus succeed Clement at his death.'[o] Cave, Dodwell, and Fabricius endeavour to harmonize the two accounts. The case was probably this: Pantænus, on his departure for India, left Clement to conduct the school in his stead. When he returned, Clement held it conjointly with him, till the persecution of Severus, which drove Clement from Alexandria. He retired from those flames of martyrdom which Origen his young disciple was so willing to brave. (On this, see Reinkens, pp. 12-14.)

Dr. Reinkens[p] gives a glowing description of Clement's attainments. He describes him as a citizen of the world—a gentleman: his knowledge of the arts of domestic life—of universal history—of the principles and history of philosophy—of poetry, music, physiology, and medicine, is carefully set forth; and above all, his acquaintance with Christian doctrine. This mass was no rude and unformed heap; the true was separated from the false, and by his great genius it was all reduced into one coherent and harmonious system. He had a quick and ready mind, subtle, but

---

[k] In Bibl. Univers., tom. x. p. 76.   [l] Antiq. P.P. et eccles.   [m] P. 7.
[n] De vir. illust., cap. 38.   [o] P. 11.   [p] Cap. 1, sec. 8.

redundant and exuberant thought, a power of arranging with logical precision, and of representing with surprising accuracy, while his manners and course of life prove him to have been exemplary in the offices to which he was called. 'We are shepherds,' said he, 'the leaders of the Church after the pattern of the good shepherd.'

Parted from with grief, and remembered with regret, Clement early in 203 left Alexandria, as already said, and proceeded to Cappadocia, where Alexander, who had been once his pupil, but now a bishop,[q] received him. Certainly in 211, when Alexander sent a letter of congratulation to Antioch by Clement, he had been some time there. Möhler[r] incorrectly refers this mission to the time when Alexander was bishop of Jerusalem. It is probable that Clement had visited Antioch before this, but of his subsequent movements nothing is known. Reinkens is very persuaded that he never returned to Alexandria.[s] Guerike maintains that he did return, and presided over the school there, in the reign of Caracalla,[t] but this is not only not supported, the facts of Origen's life disprove it. The last earthly home of this great man is unknown. His grave is even more obscure than his cradle, and the year of his death as much so as that of his birth; he most likely did not survive A.D. 217.[u]

Alexander and Origen have been named as his pupils, and, if he had no other glory, this alone would be great. Eusebius calls him 'admirable' (θαυμάσιος), Theodoret 'a holy man,' the Chronicon Paschale 'most holy,' John of Damascus 'blessed,' and 'Usuard reckons him among the saints.' 'On all these accounts,' says Reinkens (p. 21), 'and because his writings prove his integrity, sincerity, sanctity, and most tender love to God and men (although his festival has not been observed since Bened. xiv [1740-1758], owing to the proofs of his life not being sufficiently explicit), I regard him as a saint,' *eum duco Sanctum.* On the question of his saintship we confess to less anxiety, and shall therefore turn from this meagre outline of Clement's life to the consideration of his works.

The testimonies of the ancients to Clement as an author are numerous and emphatic. Eusebius calls him 'the best teacher of the Christian philosophy.' Cyril of Alexandria says, 'Clement follows the holy apostles everywhere, and attained the most comprehensive knowledge of Grecian history.' Jerome calls his works 'rare volumes and full of erudition and eloquence, both scriptural

---

[q] Vid. Euseb., Hist. Eccl., vi. 14.   [r] Patrolog., i. p. 432.   [s] P. 19.
[t] De Schol. Alex., p. 35.
[u] P. 21; and Jerome, as quoted there, Cat. 38: 'Floruit autem Severi et Antonini filii ejus temporibus.'

and secular.' Socrates describes him as 'skilled in all wisdom.'
Sozomen accounts him as one of the 'wisest men.' Theodoret
terms him 'a holy man, who left all men behind in variety of
attainments.' St. Maximus names him 'the philosopher of philosophers.' And Georg. Syncellus repeats the sentiment of Eusebius, that he was 'the best teacher of the Christian philosophy.'
—Reinkens cheerfully subscribes to these praises, and gives all the
references to the authorities, and most of the original passages.
Vid. cap. 2, sec. 3.

Manuscripts of Clement are few, and those which exist need
considerable revision. Future editors will perform a useful task,
who give heed to this. Fragments and quotations are numerous,
and would, if collected, not only correct many imperfections in his
existing works, but add much to our knowledge of those which are
lost.[x]

The works of Clement which remain are principally four :—

1. The λόγος προτρεπτικὸς πρὸς ῞Ελληνας or *Hortatory Discourse
to the Greeks,* belongs to the class of Apologies, which distinguished
the early Church writers. It was probably written about 190-191.
Some translate the title, ' to the Gentiles,' or '*Adversus Gentes,*'
as Jerome renders it, and even Eusebius seems to have understood
it. The structure, design, and argument, however, indicate that
though it may be applicable to the Gentiles universally, it is
addressed to the Greeks in particular.[y]

Amid the talent, erudition, polish, and urbanity of Athens, all
steeped in heathenism as it was, Clement had heard a 'new thing ;'
he had learned a higher wisdom than Athens taught, and had left
her attractions to follow Christ. He became more and more convinced that he was right, and anxious to show the infinite advantage
of the exchange he had made. This book is Clement 'speaking
for himself.' But while it is *his* apology, it is that of Christianity,
and an attack on all false systems, with an earnest endeavour to
bring their adherents to Christ. It is a defence, a refutation,
and an exhortation.[z]

Many Greek fables are enumerated, and, recognizing the latent
truths they contained, the author points to Christ for a clear, full
and salutary exposition of them. The earlier portions contain
sentences, and many ideas and arguments, such as are to be found
in most of the early apologists. Various great principles are
enounced, and from an investigation of the mysteries, worship, and
images of the gods, and a comparison of these and of the pagan
philosophies with Scripture, he argues their inferiority, and exhorts
to the reception of Christ, and the abandonment of every form,

---

[x] Reink., cap. 2, sec. 1, 2, pp. 23-32.   [y] Id., cap. 3. 1, sec. 1, 2.
[z] Id., sec. 3.

doctrine, and habit of error, for the principles and glorious doctrines of the Gospel.

In this, as in all Clement's works, there is much to interest and instruct. While we think he often admits too much to belong to the Greek philosophies and superstitions, we do not forget that he always turns to Christ as setting forth purer worship—a divine philosophy—and the only plain way of salvation.

2. His next great work, the παιδαγωγός—*Pædagogus*, or *School-master*—was written probably about 192-194.

The design of this—which consists of three books—is to direct us how to conform our conduct to the rule of Christ's law : to use his own words, 'it is practical, not theoretical (πρακτικὸς οὐ μεθοδικός), for its aim is to make the soul better, not to teach, and to furnish a guide to a temperate and not an intellectual life.' (σώφρονος οὐκ ἐπιστημονικοῦ—βίου.) He invites to duty by the presentation of precepts, and by exhibiting to posterity the example of those who before went astray. He aims to teach ' a good life, which is begun in catechizing, and is strengthened by faith,' and this prepares the mind to receive the higher or *gnostic* wisdom, of which more anon.

The 1st book is chiefly preliminary, explaining who the School-master is, viz. Christ ; and who the children that he teaches, viz. simple-hearted believers. The 2nd book is occupied with an infinite variety of details relating to conduct in ordinary life. Food, drink, furniture, entertainments, pleasures, conversation, good-manners, sleep, marriage, dress, and ornaments, all pass under review. The 3rd book continues the consideration of the things to which a Christian should attend, and in which there is temptation either to luxury, pride, excess, frivolity, neglect, or sin. The whole concludes with a hymn or prayer to Christ in figurative terms, but sufficiently indicative of the author's belief in the doctrine of the divinity of the Son of God.

3. The στρωματεῖς, *Stromata, i.e. Miscellanies,* or *Patchwork,* was most likely written after the two already named, and published at intervals—Reinkens[a] believes, between 193-203. The title of the book has been often animadverted upon, but, although Dr. Adam Clarke calls it ' a silly ██,' we must remember that strange titles have characterized works in all ages, and that one of such varied texture and plan as this is as well described by such a word as by any other.[b]

The difficulty of fully understanding many passages in Clement's writings, and particularly in the Stromata, has led some to term him *the Obscure*[c] (ὁ σκοτεινός). If the charge of obscurity be true,

---

[a] Cap. 3, 3, sec. 1.   [b] Vid. 3, 3, sec. 2.

[c] Heraclitus was called the ' *Obscure Philosopher ;*' hence Clement has been called the ' Christian Heraclitus.'

it is worthy of remark that Clement says he wrote this book with a personal reference; 'neither is it a writing artistically disposed for display, but there are records laid up in it, like treasures, for my old age. It is an antidote against oblivion, a true image and shadowing forth of those clear and vivid words which I was privileged to hear, and of those praiseworthy men.' This suggests that he composed the work in order the better to remember and understand, and to perpetuate the memory of the opinions and sayings, of those to whom he alludes. We need not regard the 'blessed tradition' to which he refers, as such in the Romanist sense, and, indeed, it is doubtful if we can. However, to subserve the interests of religion may have been a powerful motive to the publication of the Stromata. To maintain that it was the preservation of Church tradition[d] is a hazardous opinion. He wished to exhibit the views of doctrine which he regarded as apostolical. He does speak of disseminating 'the true tradition of blessed doctrine which had been received immediately from Peter, James, John, and Paul,' and had come to him; but what is this more than we mean when we speak of the orthodox faith, meaning thereby the faith held by our Reformers, to whom so many love to trace it? Clement, doubtless, believed his views to be Scripture theology—nay, the very doctrine and teaching of the Apostles in their ordinary ministry.

Be it so. *We* have no evidence that anything which cannot be deduced from the Scriptures was taught by the Apostles; but we have evidence that what does not agree with Scriptures was *not* taught by them. Whatever is in harmony with the word of God we accept, not as tradition, but as Scripture doctrine. Now, if Clement really asserts that he gives the Apostles' own view of disputed doctrines, we must ask—1. Who are his authorities? 2. Did he accurately understand them? 3. Did he fairly represent them? 4. Did they really deliver what they professed? 5. Can we know what portions of Clement's book are tradition and what are not? 6. If we can, do they accord with the Scriptures, or throw light upon them? There are some things which are omitted through forgetfulness, and others from design, and therefore we have, we can have, but a part of what Clement received.[e] Again, some things were regarded by him as mysteries, and 'mysteries,' he says, 'are mystically taught.' We fear that they are also mystically understood, and that, when we think we attach his own ideas to his writings, such an author may be least understood.

---

[d] Reink., p. 90 et seq.

[e] We admit that Clement's views on this subject of tradition are unsatisfactory and confused, but cannot admit that to record 'Church tradition' was his object in this book. The whole contexture of the work forbids such an idea.

No regular order and plan has been followed in this work: Its books, he himself says, are not like gardens in which everything is arranged and planted by art, but like a thickly wooded hill in which all kinds of trees are found, but intermingled — the cypress and the plane, the laurel and the ivy, the apple, the olive, and the fig. The materials of a garden are here, if the rules of art are applied, and the various trees are transplanted and trained; but 'the Stromata pay regard neither to order nor diction.' Hence there can be no regular dependence or connexion between the several books, which are eight in number. Doubtless, there is such a relation among them that it is undesirable to invert or transpose them, and they are the development of one general idea. More than this we should not like to say.

There is a more evident relation between the *three* works we have named, and each is in advance of the other. In each of them Clement assumes a different character. In the Exhortation he is the *Evangelist*, and addresses those who have not yet received the Christian doctrine. In the Pedagogue he is the *Catechist*, and addresses those who have received the truth, whom he instructs and qualifies for active life. In the Stromata he is the experienced and the wise *Philosopher*, seeking to make the mere believer a true gnostic, *i. e. wise man*, who *knows* the hidden principles and secret operations of religion, or, who knows the truth experimentally, and by the perceptions of the spiritual faculty of insight with which he is endowed by the grace of God. But in all it is the Logos, the Word made flesh, who really exhorts, trains, and teaches—it is not Clement, who is the instrument calling attention to the actual speaker.

In the Stromata, as in the Pedagogue, a vast variety of subjects are treated. As in the one he has in a manner ransacked ordinary life, so in the other he animadverts upon the philosophy and religious principles, doubts, questions, doctrines, theories, and hypotheses with which he was conversant. It is the *table-talk* of his soul, the *colloquies* of his intellectual nature, his *thoughts* on all themes. Here are philosophy, chronology, divinity, casuistry, experience, religion, faith, unbelief, controversy, and logic.

The glowing eulogies which have been pronounced upon this work by many able men in all ages are sufficient evidence of the importance and value which attach to it.[f]

4. The only other extant work by Clement is entitled τίς ὁ σωζόμενος πλούσιος, *Who is the rich man that is saved?* This was first

---

[f] For a full account of this and the other works of Clement we may refer either to Reinkens, pp. 38 to 270, or to Lumper, in vol. iv. of his 'Hist. Theol. Crit. SS. Patrum,' &c. A short and useful one is in Dr. A. Clarke's 'Success. Sac. Lit.,' vol. i. 116-127.

printed in the middle of the seventeenth century, having been discovered by Matthew Caryophilus among the Greek MSS. in the Vatican, in the same volume with some Homilies by Origen, to whom some have ascribed it. But Eusebius, Jerome, and Photius all testify to its being Clement's, and a separate work. It is uncertain when it was written, but probably late in the author's life. He shows in it that salvation is possible to the rich, and that riches may be rendered conducive to the interests of the soul. It seems intended to check presumption and despair in the rich; hence its aim is practical. Some of its principles may be considered too rigid, especially for a relaxed and self-indulgent age.

Of the works of Clement which are lost, or exist but in fragments, we may first mention his *Hypotyposes,* or *Institutions,* which comprised eight books. Both Eusebius and Jerome praise this work very highly, but the language of Photius is strongly condemnatory: he says, 'The Hypotyposes discusses certain passages of the Old and New Testaments, of which the writer gives a summary exposition and interpretation. In some places he speaks correctly, but in others utters fabulous and impious sayings. For he thinks matter is eternal, and that ideas are produced as it were by certain divine decrees. He degrades the Son to a mere creature. Moreover, he supposes the transmigration of souls, and fictitious worlds before Adam. He says Eve was not of Adam, as the Scriptures tell us, but in an obscene and impious manner. He dreams of angels becoming the parents of children by human mothers; that the Word was not made flesh, but only *seemed* to be; that there are *two* Words of the Father, miraculously formed, of whom the lesser appeared to men. "Yea," he writes, "the Son is also called the Logos, by the same name (ὁμωνύμως) as the Word of the Father; but neither the one nor the other was truly made flesh, but a certain influence from God, flowing as it were from Him, was made mind, and pervaded the hearts of men." All this he attempts to confirm by Scripture testimony. There are many other blasphemies in which he indulges—*if not himself, some other who assumed his character.* And these monstrous blasphemies fill the eight books. He refers to them often, and speaks as if struck with a species of stupor. The plan of the entire work appears to have included Genesis, Exodus, the Psalms, the epistles of Paul, the general Epistles, and Ecclesiastical interpretations. Now he was, he says, the disciple of Pantænus.'

Upon this important passage Reinkens[g] says, 'Since neither

---

[g] Vid. cap. 3, 4, sec. 5, where the passage from Photius is given.

Jerome nor Eusebius make mention of these blasphemous fancies, it is not only very likely, but most manifest, that the book read by Photius had been interpolated. For doubtless Eusebius and Jerome were more skilled in Christian doctrine than not to recognise errors so gross.' But Photius's suspicion that some other person had assumed the character of Clement would suggest that the entire work was a forgery. We cannot but believe that, if Clement had departed so lamentably from the faith, some record of it would remain.

When Clement wrote the genuine Hypotyposes cannot be ascertained, nor can we say in what precise relation they stand to his other productions. They appear to have been expositions of Scripture on the principles of Pantænus, and were probably published after the Stromata.

Jerome tells us that Clement also wrote ' *De Pascha*, lib. i.' One book upon the *Passover*. Of his discourses upon *Slander*, and upon *Fasting*, both Jerome and Eusebius make mention : they also name his *Exhortation to the Newly-baptized*, and his *Ecclesiastical Canon*, or *Against those who Judaize*. Besides these he wrote upon *Continency*, upon *Marriage*, upon *Providence*, and an *Exposition of First Principles* (αρχῶν) *and Theology*. Lastly, Reinkens (p. 269) gives the titles of twelve treatises of which Clement speaks in his writings, as *to be* written. Some of these were probably never produced, but none of them are known to exist. The following are the subjects : *The Resurrection ; Prophecy ; The Soul ; First Principles ; The Origin of Man ; Metempsychosis ; The Devil ; That there is One God, proclaimed by the Law, the Prophets, and the Gospel ; Against Heresies ; Prayer ; The Origin of the World ;* and *The Theory of Dogmas.*

There are three works improperly assigned to him : *Summaries from Theodotus, and the Oriental Doctrine, in the times of Valentinus ; Selections from the Prophets ; and Notes (Adumbrationes) upon the General Epistles.* There is no proof whatever that Clement wrote any of these.[h]

But it is time to turn to the consideration of the *opinions* of Clement, and we shall therefore proceed to regard him as a Philosopher.

It is presumed no one will dispute his right to this title. We have less difficulty in deciding the character of a man's claims to the name of philosopher, than we have in defining the limits of philosophy, and explaining why philosophers arrive at so different

---

[h] The edition of Clement by Potter, 2 vols. fol. 1715, with Latin translation, still keeps its place. There was an edition at Würtzburg, 3 vols. 8vo. 1780. And there is a portable edition in the 'Biblioth. Pat. Eccl. Gr.,' Lipsiæ, 1830-34, 4 vols. 12mo.

results.   Truth is one, but its relations are various and manifest.
The feebleness and imperfection of the mental powers, the education we receive, the school to which we attach ourselves, our
friendships and associations, all combine to lead us to conclusions
which, with perfect faculties and pure truth before us, we should
have never reached.   It is owing to these things that, even with
the same fundamental principles, philosophers differ.   Those who
occupy common ground may assume a different stand-point,
i. e. the point mentally chosen by the philosopher, in order
to obtain his view of the subject.   The philosopher, like the
painter, selects his own point of observation, and philosophy, like
painting, will present different views of the same object, for the
same reason,—a different stand-point has been occupied.

Reinkens[i] says that in order to describe Clement as a philosopher we must inquire—1st, What are his views of human nature?   2ndly, What power of acquiring knowledge he assigns to
man?   and 3rdly, What (on Clement's principles) is the relation
of this power to essences.[k]   But before these questions are entered
upon there remain two other points for consideration : 1. That
all who have hitherto written of Clement as a philosopher have
treated of the *results* of the Clementine philosophy, which any-
body would regard as legitimate, if a few extracts were given in
support of them : they have proved *nothing* respecting the real
principle and nature of his philosophy.   The second point is, To
ask if Clement decides whether anything can be certainly known
or not ; for if he thinks man cannot certainly know anything,
the three questions previously indicated will be superfluous.

1. The errors of previous writers.   Very many have written of
Clement as a philosopher, but it would be a wearisome task to
transcribe their opinions.   With one exception, to be named below (says Reinkens), all who say anything definite of Clement as
a philosopher do measure his character not by the *principle* of his
philosophy, but by its *fruit.*

There are many who, not without an invidious reference, call
him an Eclectic.   Now, those who term the method and principle
of his philosophy eclectic, both wrong him, for his principle was
definite and fixed, and contend for what seems to be an absurdity.
True, many believe in the existence of an eclectic philosophy : but
what is it?   Perhaps, that one should employ the principle of
Protagoras for the discovery of this truth, Plato's for that, Aristotle's for another, Epicurus's for a fourth, and so on.   Inconsistent in itself, it is by no means the rule of Clement.   Is the

---

[i] P. 274.

[k] Philosophers are thus defined : 'Philosophi, *i. e.* qui essentiarum cognitionem
quærunt,' p. 272.

Eclectic the man who selects what he believes to be true from any and every school? But this is not philosophizing at all. It is true that all must have some principle of philosophy, or they would cease to be men. The philosophy of most, however, is rather in action than in wise doctrines systematically arranged. He who has neither eyes nor hands must test the quality of all fruit by tasting it; and he who has no principles of philosophy must test the qualities of things by experience: under such circumstances alike, the preservation even of life would be difficult if not impossible.

But you remind us that Clement, in his Stromata,[m] says, 'Now, I mean by philosophy not the Stoical, nor the Platonic, nor the Epicurean, nor the Aristotelian, but whatever is spoken well by each of these systems, and teaches righteousness with holy wisdom,—all this when selected I call philosophy,' &c. True, and what does it amount to? Simply this—'I choose nothing from the dogmas of any sect, because they are such, but I select whatever I find true in any, even the most corrupt, because it is *true*.' In order to do this, the stand-point of Clement must be apart from each of these sects. Where then does he stand? This is a question which no one has answered. In the passage just quoted two adversaries appear to be in view, one who embraces all that may be taught by a particular sect, *because* that sect teaches it; the other rejects all for the same reason. Both these are shown to be wrong by Clement, but he certainly does not prove himself an Eclectic.

Some have called him a Stoic, others a Pythagorean, others a Neo-Platonist, &c. Reinkens wonders no one has made him an Epicurean! [n]

But how prove him a Stoic, &c.? Very easily (*i. e. sine multo labore!*).[o] They have only to compare detached passages, which may resemble, or *seem* to resemble, the doctrines of these philosophers, it is not of much importance which,—they compare them. Le Clerc, for instance, who calls Clement an Eclectic, but leaning most towards the Stoics, seems to have proved it by comparing these two sentences: one, Clement's, 'The Christian alone is rich;' the other, the Stoic's, 'That the wise man alone is rich.' No doubt Clement contrasts the appearance of virtue with virtue itself, but Le Clerc sees in opposites the closest resemblances. The fact is, the words do not set forth philosophical dogmas, and, if they did, they have no reference to Clement; and if they had, they would not prove what his philosophy is. Other writers have advanced more proofs, but have left the great question untouched on several accounts: the quotations are common property, and not

---

[m] Strom., lib. i. p. 338.   [n] P. 276.   [o] Ibid.

peculiar to the parties who furnish them; and if they were peculiar they prove nothing, because they do not reach the *principle* of
Clement's philosophy.

The only exception is A. F. Dähne,[p] whose work Reinkens says
he read with pleasure, but laments that he cannot admit his conclusion. Dähne makes Clement a Neo-Platonic, but differs himself
from many in his views of Neo-Platonism. If space permitted, we
should have liked to follow our author through the examination
and refutation of the views of Dähne, which we regard as ingenious and satisfactory as any portion of the book. See pp.
276-283.

2. Clement clearly holds that man can acquire certain knowledge, on principles which are distinctive and established. But it
may be asked, How can man attain to the knowledge of the truth?
This suggests several inquiries.—What is the nature of man?
Man is compounded of a rational and irrational part, of soul and
body. These, though different, are not contrary, and together
constitute human nature. The soul includes the intellectual or
rational and the emotional, as anger or desire. The supreme
authority is the rational, to which belongs also the power of
knowing (γνῶσις, *i. e.* as a principle). To this also belongs the
power of choosing. The soul, properly speaking, is the reason,
the faculty which thinks and reasons; but in a secondary sense
the term is applied to the faculties by which we are subject to
emotions and passions—this is the ψυχὴ σωματική. Nay, in a
third sense the word soul is used to denote the whole man.
But this is common to writers of all ages, and is customary
among us.[q]

The soul of man tends towards God, and is made in his image
and likeness. In respect to the rational soul (ψυχη ἡ λογικη),
Clement believed it to be breathed into the nostrils from above by
the Creator, and this opinion he supports by reference to Gen. ii. 7.
But the body, which is earthly, tends towards the earth, is not
made for itself, and is merely the instrument which the soul employs. It follows, however, from Clement's view of the twofold
character of the soul as *rational* and *corporeal,* that the ability to
acquire knowledge belongs to the bodily as well as intellectual nature properly so called. This difficulty is met by supporting the
idea that irrational animals have the power of acquiring knowledge,
and man has all the faculties with which they are endowed; the
difference is, they cannot reason nor acquire the knowledge of any

---

[p] De γνῶσει Clem. Alex., A. F. Dähne. Lipsiæ, 1831.

[q] See the words נֶפֶשׁ, نفس and ܢܦܫ in Heb., Arab., and Syriac, and ψυχή
in Greek Lexicons, &c., in confirmation of this remark: 'Not a soul was there.'
vid Sophocles Antig 1069 ψυχην τ᾽ ατιμως &c.

but *sensible* objects, while man can apprehend and appreciate *spiritual* truths.

What is truth? Truth, Clement answers, is the knowledge of the true.[r] We at once ask, what is knowledge? and, what is the true? He tells us that the true involves sensation, thought, knowledge, and opinion. But this only describes what is true between man and man. Let us moreover remember that knowledge and opinion (ἐπιστήμη and ὑπόληψις) have not the same relation to the true as sensation and thought (αἴσθησις and νοῦς). These last are very distinct; things which are cognisable by the senses are the province of the one (αἰσθητά), and those beyond their province, but which can be the objects of thought, are the province of the other (νοητά). Now, as the true may include one or both of these (the αἰσθητά and νοητά), knowledge will be twofold, a higher and a lower; the one will be traceable to no particular cause, and capable of no special proof; the other may be accounted for and attested: the one relates to things which *happen* (*fiunt*), the other to things which *are* (*sunt*); the one to circumstances, the other to essences: and this higher knowledge is the truth.

No truth can be acquired by the corporeal nature,—mere perception is, *per se*, no apprehension of the truth. Hence brutes, which have no contemplative faculty (νοερά), cannot arrive at truth. If man know, therefore, *i. e.* know the truth, it must be by his nobler nature—the rational τὸ λόγικον.

There is no room for pyrrhonism in the doctrine of Clement. The dogma which says you must assent to nothing, forbids assent to itself. If *anything* be true, however small, it refutes itself: if *nothing* be true, it is not true itself. It either speaks truly or not; if truly, *some* truth may be found; if not, the same, viz. the *truth* that it is false. Clement assigns to man the power to know the truth, but it is to man as part partaker of reason, and part not. There is no *tertium quid*, and therefore τα νοητα, the knowable, are γυμνάσια τῷ νῷ—exercises for the mind, or objects upon which it may and should exercise itself. Indeed God created the mind —the *nous* or rational soul—for knowledge.[s]

How does Clement recommend us to pursue this object, Truth? What is his *via philosophandi?* He admits that there are essences and appearances (τὰ ὄντα and φαινόμενα), as also our power to know them. In what relation does this power stand to these things? He is here in agreement with Aristotle, *i. e. Clement as a philosopher is an Aristotelian.*

Having discovered what philosophy Clement approved in theory, let us see how he applied it to human life. His principle is this:

---

[r] τὸ ἀληθές.   [s] Strom., viii. p. 880.

—We first feel surprise, then become conscious of our ignorance. The knowledge or consciousness of our ignorance is the first lesson we learn; we then desire to know; this is followed by the wise and earnest search after truth. The surprise we feel is owing to our ignorance of the causes of a thing. Our desire to know the truth is a natural endowment of man. When we become conscious of ignorance, this desire is awakened. Hence it appears that not only is the mind excited to action by the senses, but they forthwith furnish it with the steps whereby it may ascend to the truth.

This was also the principle of Aristotle.

It would not be difficult to trace, in many respects, an identity, or close analogy, between the principles of philosophy of Aristotle and of Clement. Aristotle, for instance, divides human nature into two parts, one with, and one without, reason: each of these again is twofold,—one irrational, the vital principle; the other, by which we long for or desire a thing, and which is subject to reason. The irrational nature of man cannot attain to the understanding of things. The rational in man is also twofold; one is called the intellectual, and the other the logical, faculty. The former of these contemplates actual realities, the other, things which may or can be: everything is either αἰσθητὸν or ἀναίσθητον—to be, or not to be, perceived by the senses: the higher faculty is conversant with the latter. We may be said to know the truth when we know the reasons or causes of a thing. The demonstration which leads to knowledge is ratiocination—(συλλογισμὸν ἐπιστημονικόν). We must reason from premisses, which must be admitted: we argue from known to unknown—not from those things which are truly more real to those which are truly less so. If the premisses are necessary, so will the conclusion be; if probable, so also the conclusion. Knowledge is acquired by the understanding—opinion (δόξα) by the logical faculty. Now men are led and inclined to philosophize naturally. He shows that surprise is the first step, and doubting is the second—not doubting of the reality of what we see, but of our acquaintance with it: then follows the desire to escape from ignorance—and in order to escape from ignorance men philosophize.[t]

Such are some of Aristotle's principles, and 'if,' says Reinkens, 'it be admitted that I have properly expounded the principles of both Clement and Aristotle, then Clement was an Aristotelian. But while I think him an Aristotelian, I do not affirm that he chose that system because it seemed the best when compared with others; nor am I prepared to say how he was moved to select it.' p. 309.

It will not be necessary to pursue further an inquiry which to

---

[t] The principle of doubting, which Clement recognized with Aristotle, after Socrates, Plato, &c., must be carefully distinguished from ancient and modern scepticism. They doubted in order to find reasons to believe.

many will be dry and uninteresting. We shall only add, there-fore, that we regard a thorough investigation of the philosophical principles of Clement as necessary to those who would understand even his theology. At the same time we admit the difficulty of always arriving at a satisfactory conclusion. Words are used in various senses, and with more or less restriction. In some instances the expression is confused and obscure. In other cases sentiments are advanced which appear to conflict with what one finds else-where. But by a broad and comprehensive survey of what bears upon the subject, we may reach a satisfactory conclusion—the know-ledge of his main philosophical principles, which have been shown to accord with those of Aristotle.

Clement was a Divine as well as a philosopher, and to his consi-deration in that character we must now turn.

Theologians are distinguished from one another by some mark or *characteristic*. It may be assumed to be their view of the rela-tion between God as revealing himself, and the human faculty of knowing that fact:—the fact of revelation, and the proof of revela-tion (*Offenbarungsthatsache*, and *Offenbarungsinhalt*). We may regard both creation and redemption as facts of revelation, but could either be known on the principle of Clement? and, how far is the argument of revelation perceptible by the human mind? To the first of these questions Clement answers, Certainly. In his Exhortation, after naming the false gods of the Greeks, he says, 'But I desire the Lord of spirits, the Lord of fire, the maker of the world: it is God I seek, who gives light to the sun, not the works of God. Which of you can aid me in this investigation? Plato, indeed, if you will, is not wholly rejected by us. How, then, O Plato, is God to be sought? He answers, " It is difficult to dis-cover the father and maker of this universe, and, when you have found him, it cannot be that you should directly declare him." But can he reveal himself? " He can be in no manner made known." Well done! O Plato, thou hast attained the truth; do not there-fore weary thyself, but with me enter upon the search for what is good! For in all men there is instilled a certain divine influence, especially in the learned. Wherefore, even if unwillingly, all con-cede that there is one God, without beginning or end, who some-where above, in his own proper place of observation, truly abides for ever.'[u] Refuting Menander, who thought we should give thanks to the sun for making God known to us, he says, 'It is not the sun which will reveal the true God to you, but it is the saving Word, the sun of the soul, by whom alone, when risen within the soul's depths, the eye of the mind itself is enlightened.'[x] Reinkens

---

[u] Exhort., p. 59.   [x] Ibid.

regards this inward light as the *prevenient grace* in which his church believes, and of which we have ourselves often heard in these last days.[y]

The knowledge of God which philosophy attains, is of him as a Creator rather than as a Father, in which latter character the Son manifests him to those who believe.[z]

To the question, By means of which faculty (the αἰσθητὸν, or the νοητόν) can we know God? Clement answers, By both. By the *senses* we may know God. Thus Pythagoras, Socrates, and Plato knew him, for they tell us that they *heard* the *voice* of God. What is the voice of God? Let Moses answer: 'He spake and it was done' (*dixit et factum est*). His voice is his work; and by contemplation of the creation and preservation of the world they knew God.[a] Whether Clement interprets their doctrine aright or not does not concern us, his own doctrine is what we seek; and he thus declares it, 'God can be known by the contemplation of nature. Abraham passed from the contemplation of the heavens to faith in God (Gen. xv. 5, 6); and the same way is open to all.'[b]

God can also be known by the contemplation of mind: 'from the divine in us we ascend to the view of the efficient cause, as far as may be.' This is meant to explain 1 Cor. xiii. 12, 'By a glass we see reflected what is in it.' What is the glass? the divine (τὸ θεῖον), *i. e. animus*, or the mind, in which we see God, *i. e.* his reflection, for we are made after the image of God. In this way the Greeks saw God; and whoever knows himself therein knows God, and he who knows him will become like him. Now, if the Creator could thus be known, the fact of creation, *i. e.* a revelation, could also be known by man.

To the second question, respecting a supernatural revelation, we now proceed. Some have falsely asserted that Clement would supersede the necessity of a divine revelation. The fact is, he makes the greatest difference between a natural and a supernatural revelation. He believed a supernatural revelation to be most necessary. Without it men *generally* are ignorant of God, for they do not know the true God, and those which are not gods except in name they have believed in. Only the few attained the truth in this matter, and they only in part. Hence the Christian philosophy is distinguished from the Greek, in regard to its extent, its certainty, divine power, and so forth. Human philosophy is ignorant of the greatest truths, *e. g.* of the Son of God, and divine Providence: it scarcely saves its followers, for it is all too weak to give divine precepts; therefore, when that fails us, 'let us bring the truth down from above, out of heaven.'—*Exhort.* p. 3.

---

[y] P. 312.   [z] Strom., lib. v. p. 731.   [a] Ibid., lib. v. p. 707.
[b] Cf. Strom., lib. i. p. 334.

Clement believed that the revelation which was so necessary actually existed. It names God directly and immediately: philosophy shows him indirectly and mediately through the creatures. Of this revelation God is the cause, as of all good things—of some *primarily*, as of Scripture; of others *by consequence*, as of philosophy.

Clement further believed that the fact of such a revelation having been given could be proved. The Exhortation sufficiently indicates his desire to show to all nations, to Greeks in particular, that their gods were false, either demons, or creatures, or mere fancies of philosophy; but that the true God, who is REVEALED *by his Son*, had made the heavens. He shows them that they ought to have believed the prophets, that the Word speaks plainly to shame their unbelief. He held that the revelation could be known by every man, and charges with greater sin every one who has heard the Word without believing, though others have the excuse of ignorance. The proofs of revelation must be such only as no man of sound mind would reject—not demonstration. In order to faith, two things are required—the things which are heard, and the persuasion that only God's words are spoken; 'faith is by hearing, and by the preaching of the apostles.' Those who were dead, by hearing the Gospel have lived anew. Christ, therefore, came as a teacher, and we are 'taught of God' (θεοδίδακτοι). 'The truth is not taught by imitation (μίμησις) but by instruction.' 'Catechizing leads to faith.' Catechizing adorns and enters the ears: 'but when the eyes are anointed and the ears are bored by the Word of God, one is made a hearer of divine, and a seer of holy things.' Sight, hearing, and voice contribute to the attainment of the truth, but it is the mind which discerns it. 'They who hear, *and* believe, shall be saved.'[c] If there must be faith as well as hearing, still divine grace is necessary. This grace is a certain enlightening, (φώτισμα) before alluded to. But faith in its highest form will not even thus be attained. What is still needed? That we prove and examine, select or reject what we hear. We must 'prove all things—prove whether they are the Word of God.' 'We do not seek the testimony of men, but prove this point by the Word of the Lord, which is more worthy of faith than all demonstrations, or rather it is itself the sole demonstration.' The 'Word of the Lord' in this last passage Reinkens very coolly assumes to be 'sacred Scripture and *our tradition*.'

Clement teaches that Christ is God, which he goes on to prove by various arguments. Believing that Christ is God, how do we know that what we have as his words truly proceeded from him? Who

---

[c] Strom., lib. vi. 765.

first received the treasure of the World?   We answer with him,
'Those who first constituted the church.'   But what is the church?
which is the true church?   Many are called churches of Christ;
if all cannot bear that appellation, which really deserve it?   The
testimony of Scripture will describe them, and the history of heresies, which sooner or later perish, will prove the truth.   'In the
truth alone (*i. e.* in Scripture), and in the ancient church, is the
most exact *gnosis*, and the most excellent *heresy*' (αἵρεσις).[d]

Surely the fact of a revelation in redemption may be known.
This knowledge begins by hearing, is assisted by divine grace exciting and helping, and is made perfect by demonstration; demonstration admits us to real faith—it recognises Christ as God, and
the church as existing and as a true church.

But how does the mind apprehend the arguments for the twofold
revelation?   In two ways—by faith and by knowledge (πίστει and
γνώσει).   What is *faith?*   Faith implies partial knowledge.   'Whatever is held for argument must be sought where we believe all
revelation is still preserved, *i. e.* in the true church,' says Reinkens
in the true spirit of his system;[e] and asserts that ecclesiastical tradition, in the sense in which Catholics receive it, is not only the rule
for the interpretation of Scripture, but the *fountain* and *proof* of
such doctrines as are scarcely mentioned in Scripture, or not found
there at all.   These, he says, are also the opinions of Clement, but
does not adduce a single passage in proof.[f]

Truth must furnish its own criterion; if we derive one from any
other source we are in danger at every step.   But 'he who is
endowed with knowledge (γνῶσις), who has grown old in the study
of the Scriptures themselves, who keeps to the apostolical and church
rule of doctrine (ὀρθοτομία τῶν δογμάτων), and strictly conforms his
life to the Gospel, is sent by the Lord to find out the demonstrations which he seeks from the law and the prophets.'[g]   The voice
of Christ must be ever heard, but it must also be proved to be his
voice.   (See Luke xxiv. 44.)   Not to prove it is heretical, idle,
and vainglorious.   The Christian defends the truth, he employs
logic, he does not fear philosophy, he compares, selects, judges,
and discerns, and is always ready to answer for himself.   Philosophy and reason therefore have their use and value, within proper
limits, in relation to the explanation of divine truth.   Indeed,
philosophy is a kind of preparatory instruction (προπαιδεία) for
those who desire to reach faith by demonstration.[h]   Thus it neither
supersedes nor supplements a divine revelation.

'God does not compel to faith, but persuades to it.'   Faith

[d] Strom., lib. vii. p. 888.   [e] P. 328.
[f] On the meaning of παράδοσις, see Van Hengel, in 1 Cor. xv. pp. 25-27.   1851.
[g] Strom., vii. 896.   [h] Ibid.., i. 331.

comes by free assent to certain knowledge—it is the rational assent of a free mind (ψυχης αυτεξουσίου). 'He who accords with that which he is most persuaded is taught him—on the authority of God, and affirms it to be true apart from all doubt—is, in Clement's opinion, a believer.'[i]

The knowledge which faith requires is twofold; one, which in part at least perceives and understands what is believed; the other, which is very clear, comes by demonstration, and refers to the reasons of belief. But neither is a blind faith in authority, for without some understanding, and some proof, faith cannot be. Reinkens maintains that the 'Reformation' did nothing towards giving clearer views of faith, but only robbed man of his free will, the lamentable consequences of which we see abundantly in our own day! and denies that, although good works do *not* necessarily follow faith (as Clement admits), that therefore he defends an inactive and inanimate faith. When good works do follow faith, which they do when faith is real and complete, the believer becomes assimilated to God, and a partaker of the divine nature. Redepenning[k] and Neander[m] have ascribed to Clement the opinion that men are led to faith by a natural sense of the truth—'*Vermöge des der menschlichen Natureingepflanzten Wahrheitsgefühles*' (the implanted truth-feeling power of human nature). But such a sense of truth is not needed, for certain knowledge followed by the decision of the judgment produces faith: the will bows to the decision thus authoritatively pronounced upon clear evidence, and not because it has any presentiment of the nature of truth. When belief follows either feeble reasons, or strong reasons insufficiently understood, it is rather mere opinion which feebly 'imitates faith as a flatterer his friend, or as a wolf a dog.' Still, we remember that saying, 'Blessed are they who believe and have not seen,' but we are cautious in its application to those things which can be proved to be, but the reason for which cannot be apprehended. The authority of God is the demonstration of faith. Faith depends, as we have said, upon free will, and the truth we know *can* be denied: and if so, it depends upon our voluntary choice whether good works shall follow our faith. The province of faith is 'to know God, to believe the Saviour's doctrine, and to live to God.'[n] Clearly, then, good works do not precede persuasion, and good works constitute likeness to God. Nay, in one sense a believer is a god;[o] he resembles God, and his communion with him is of the most perfect character.

---

[i] P. 332.   [k] Redep. Origen. p. 153.
[m] Gesch. der Christl. Kirche, vol. i. pp. 3, 153.
[n] Strom., vii. 831. πίστις οὖν τὸ εἰδέναι τὸν Θεὸν ἡ πρώτη, κ.τ.λ.
[o] Pedag., lib. iii. 251, where he quotes with approval the saying of Heraclitus, ἄνθρωποι θεοί: θεοί ἄνθρωποι.

Hence the Christian *gnosis*. As the eye to the body, this is to the soul. But Clement was not a gnostic in any other sense than an honourable one. Thus, when he describes 'Agar as secular Philosophy, Sarah is the celestial Wisdom, restoring it to its right mind.' This Wisdom is Christian doctrine. Christ is truth itself. Philosophy is but part partaker of it. True, like the Gnostics, he held a secret tradition, or mysterious doctrine, to be mystically· conveyed; but it was not what they held, nor was it derived from the same source. To those whom God deigns to choose as teachers he gives a greater understanding of his mysteries; which Clement supports by Eph. iv. 11, and 2 Tim. ii. 2. His principles of interpretation were quite opposed to the gnostic. They (generally) allegorized, but, while he occasionally gave allegorical interpretations, he maintained a rational exegesis, and demanded a learned exposition, and the application of *the church canon.*[p] The Gnostics said their secrets could be apprehended by a few naturally spiritual men, but the gnosis of Clement is only ascribed to few, because few are really renewed in heart. The Gnosis of Clement is not a kind of speculative theology. It is not the reward of learning and of learned disquisitions, but the prize and crown of a life in harmony with the word of God. When Neander ascribes to it the power of clearly proving, and of reducing precepts to scientific form, he is in error. It is rather the result of proof, and the harmony of a man's spiritual nature and religious principles. It is neither a process, nor the faculties necessary in order to one: it is the state in which he is who has personal experience of the power and truth of religion—'*thätsachlichen Beweis:* in a word, the Clementine gnostic is not another person than the mere believer, though he is more than he—he is an enlightened believer. See Neander's Kirschengesch. vol. 1, 3, 907, 908, 910, 927, &c.

Gnosis is to be traced to the grace of God. The divine operation is felt upon the new heart, infusing into it fresh light. (See 1 Cor. ii. 9.) They receive as it were a new eye, ear, and heart, by which they henceforth see, hear, and act spiritually. But this grace is ever accompanied by the truth. Christ, who is truth itself, bestows upon them this mark of distinction   Hence it cannot come from demonstration and the reading of Scripture without personal virtue and divine grace. The true gnostic already knows the doctrine of God—he hears *what* God says, and *as* he says it— the Scripture produces fruit in him, but is barren in heretics —and he has attained that which human science never could (Matt. xvi.

---

[p] What this can be but the harmony and analogy of Scripture with Scripture we cannot divine; certes, it is not that indefinable, though convenient, 'nothing contrary to the received doctrine,' *nihil nisi conforme doctrinæ ac fidei Catholicæ.*

17), for it is by the power of the Father alone that we know the Son of the Almighty.

This gnosis cannot exist without a life in agreement with a sound faith, and which springs from love of the commandments of God. Love in its turn leads to nobler contemplation, and to larger acquisitions, if God enlightens our eyes and is present with us. This sublime conception and perception of truth is the only true gnosis. The truth is attained and discerned by the truth : it is not self-consciousness (*Selbstbewusstsein*), but from truth imparted. 'The Lord says, " He that hath ears to hear, let him hear," that he who believes may understand *what* he says, *as* he says it.' New evidences are not given to faith, but higher degrees of power to contemplate. 'It is the soul's vision of things which are.' The influence of love and a holy life upon the true gnostic is most salutary; but the influence of gnosis is to purify and refine the faculties and powers of the Christian : gradually shall the mists and prejudices of ignorance vanish before it, till the gnostic knows as he is known; and at length the glorious end shall be reached, when the soul shall be made perfect in love, for a sublime and spiritual love is the proper object and consummation of the evangelical gnosis.

Here we must pause and draw to a conclusion, considering it undesirable to enlarge, but refer those who desire a fuller view of the subject to the work of Reinkens, pp. 337-358 ; or to Clement himself in the Stromata *passim.* We would therefore in general remark, that what remains of Clement proves him to have been a close observer, a diligent reader, a man of great and varied attainments, with keen and active faculties, amazing energy and industry. Destitute of the transparency and beauty of style which some of the Fathers claim, he is yet sometimes eloquent, and there is a solid stratum of thought which invites industry and rewards research. Others may be the flowery fields which gladden and allure; he is the mine, in which with much refuse there is much genuine ore. With more on the surface they have less beneath ; but Clement with little often on the surface has much beneath. Some of these wrote for readers, he for thinkers : they were more for practical men, he for students : they are Christians, or Christian divines; he is a Christian, a divine, and a philosopher. While we speak thus, we can deplore his errors, when he departs from the gospel truth.[q] But then we carry the true test of all doctrine with us, we have the word of God, and to apply this wisely is to free ourselves from all danger.

Those who venerate antiquity because it is ancient egregiously

---

[q] This especially refers to the Stromata.

err, for this claim is shared equally by Menu, Mahomet, Zoroaster, and Confucius, and the Greek mythology as well. We must never forget that truth is not such because it is old. The word of the Lord never, and that word only, never becomes effete. It may become old, but not antiquated—ancient, but not imbecile. We may say of it as of its author,—

'*Jam senior; sed cruda Deo viridisque senectus.*'

A recent American writer says, 'the grass of human doctrine withereth, the flower of human wisdom fadeth, but the word of the Lord endureth for ever.'[r] To those who can separate the grass of human doctrine and the flower of human wisdom from the word of the Lord, the writings of Clement are of much value. But let others beware. We almost lament that he does not yet speak in our own tongue. For, while we cannot admit many of his views, of tradition, baptism, the church, and the operations of divine grace upon the soul, and of other points, we remember that not all who speak English are sound in the faith: nay, that he may be sound where they are not, and they where he is not, and so corrective of each other. Why should we fear who have sound principles of exegesis and a more refined philosophy, *free-will*,[s] free thought, and free action, and the word of God?

Clement is not answerable for all the views he expounds, any more than he is for all which are ascribed to him. Besides, we are ever to remember the influence of the age in which a man may live upon modes of thought and forms of expression. In Clement's time various forms of error already existed in the church, and passed current for truth: and an alliance had been formed between profane philosophy and Christian theology, while the influence of mysticism and spiritual pride were very great. He found the age, he did not make it, and he found these things in it. The covenant between human wisdom and divine revelation he neither ended nor wished to make an end of, but he desired and strove to make it subserve the all-important end—glory to God, and salvation to man. Ever subordinating the human to the divine—the natural to the supernatural—reason to faith—and faith itself to charity, he strove to exhibit Christianity as the true philosophy—the divinely appointed remedy for the woes of man, and the best gift of heaven. He recognised God as a Creator, Preserver, and King—he admitted the doctrine of the Holy Spirit and of grace—and he owned Christ as man's deliverer, but rather from the slavery of falsehood and error than of sin and death, not that these are overlooked. Christ the Saviour was to him the

---

[r] Prof. Packard, in Am. Bibl. Sac., Jan. 1851, p. 73.
[s] Vid. Reink., p. 335, n. 2, and p. 20, lin. 30, *supra.*

Word, the incarnate Logos, the reason and the wisdom of God—man's teacher and guide. Clement's views of sin seem rather those of sin in acts and opinions, than of principle; rather those of sin as bringing evils to man than as abominable to God. And yet there are particular expressions which declare universal obligation, and an intense aversion from sin.

Whatever errors he held, however, in regard to tradition, baptism, and free-will especially, the defender of Romanism will find no universal precept of clerical celibacy, for Peter and Philip were both married, he says, and had children: and he maintains unbroken silence upon Mariolatry, invocation of saints, the use of images in Christian worship, and the pope; upon purgatory, penance, and the mass.[t] His negative evidence on these points is valuable—he knows nothing of them, for he never heard of them.

In respect to some of Clement's opinions, they are not all we take them to be; our modern phraseology often ill interprets the old church phraseology of that day, and it requires nice discrimination, and good knowledge of the age, its philosophy, its characteristics, and its forms of speech, always to expound aright the strange speech of its philosophical Christian writers.

The influence which Clement received he transmitted, and it was felt for many years. But great as were his name and influence, he was not alone. There was Justin the Martyr, there was Tertullian, and there was Athenagoras: there were also Pantænus and Origen, who clustered around Clement, before him and after him. They were stars of different magnitude; but while one of them, Origen, eclipsed all who had preceded him, he was the pupil of Clement, and the glory of the pupil the master shares. In regard to the philosophy, especially, there was error in their systems, and the ignorant and designing alike perverted it to bad uses, while they too often overlooked the truth they contained. As already suggested, Christianity had made noble progress: the Jew had trembled, for the star of Moses was lost amid the brightness of the Day-spring from on high—the idolater had trembled, for Dagon had fallen again before the ark of the Lord—the hand of the persecutor trembled, for the blood it had shed was the seed of the church. But philosophy still remained, and the question was how to snatch its laurels and entwine them in the wreath they wove for the Prince of Peace. We honour their aim, though we lament many of their measures. After all, however, we may say of Clement,—' Happy these later ages if the mystics they have produced had all, and always, drawn from a source as pure. The

---

[t] His calling the Lord's Supper the *Eucharist* is only what all did; and his saying that Melchisedec gave *bread and wine to Abraham as a type of the eucharist* proves nothing. Vid. Strom., lib. iv.

gifts of God would not so often be exposed to the raillery of the profane, nor the unveiled glories of the church turned to blasphemy and scandal by impious lips.'[u]

The work of Reinkens, in which many of the views here presented are embodied, will take its place among the best sketches of the life and writings of Clement. For though, as an avowed Romanist, the author writes under an influence which he rather owns than denies, yet he is the safer as a guide, inasmuch as he declares his principles. His zeal in defending the views which he believes to be those of Clement, his diligence in producing proofs, and the ingenuity of their application, are sure to command attention. The labour bestowed upon the analyses of Clement's works has been great, though we confess that we think him sometimes partial. To those who are debarred from larger works, or who cannot find time to read the original productions of Clement, and to others, this work will be valuable. The activity of our friends on the continent in producing works on church history and patriotic literature we often commend. It is acceptable to us whose practical turn induces us to shun the labour of such tasks : most of us are content to know the results of the investigations of our neighbours. Be it so : still, here, where the details of the life of Clement are few and meagre, we may obtain a good knowledge of *the man*, from the copiousness, variety, interest, learning, acuteness, and intelligence which are so abundant in all his works. Certainly we would rather canonize him for his writings than many a one who has been made a saint for his actions : nay, we would believe that among the stars which excel in glory above (as well as here below), not the least glorious is Titus Flavius Clemens, presbyter of Alexandria.

B. H. C.

THE ORIGIN OF THE CHERUBIC FORMS MENTIONED IN THE HOLY SCRIPTURES,

CONSIDERED IN CONNECTION WITH SOME OF THE DISCOVERIES OF LAYARD AT NINEVEH.

THE discoveries of Layard form an era in literature. The startling ideas they have given birth to, the historical associations they have formed, and the solutions of numerous enigmas which they afford, will be appreciated with increasing interest, as they are more earnestly studied and their various bearings more accurately deciphered. The symbols which lie scattered amongst the

---

[u] L'Abbé Houtteville, p. 47, lib. cit.

other remnants of ancient literature, or seem to be scattered from our imperfect knowledge, are shown in a collective form; and although their explications are even yet obscure, still their concentration furnishes us with a more original source than any we had before possessed.

It is asserted by an ancient author that the Ninevites had obtained their polished manners from an anterior race; and without any such authority it is a matter even of itself of the highest probability. But however they may have borrowed from others, they themselves were evidently the originators of powerful influences upon other portions of the globe. Passing by other points, they evidently possessed symbolical emblemry in a more connected system than the nations which afterwards separated and remodelled the very same emblemry according to the caprices of their different superstitions. To the moderns it appears very strange that men in the ancient world should have been so guided by type and symbol; and consequently the expression of their sentiments in this manner wears even a grotesque appearance. For instance, the frequent occurrence amid the ruins of ancient nations of monstrous unions between figures not only of every species of bird and beast, but also of man. Again, when the utter folly of mankind led them so far to abuse this mode of representation as to worship the symbols themselves, we wonder at our fellow mortals having fallen down to worship an ox, an eagle, and animals of still lower grade; and our wonder increases at their veneration for images, the absurdity of whose composition remains still for modern inspection. But, on the other hand, if these representations had been restrained within the bounds of hieroglyphical instruction, such mode would not only appear natural and interesting, but, while it was inferior in many respects to alphabetical writing, it contained some points of marked superiority; for example, it is more calculated to arouse the faculties of reasoning, by filling the mind with images and by exciting comparison, illation, and deduction. Such training would also strengthen the memory and stimulate the imagination. To men accustomed to such modes of communication, the solution of enigmas and parabolic illustration would not only be suitable, but far more congenial than any other method. Plutarch, in his very interesting history of Isis and Osiris, amongst others furnishes the following examples. The Egyptians affirmed that the sun and moon pursued their courses, not as the Greeks described in chariots, but in ships, to betoken that all nature was sustained by the genial influences of these luminaries upon the collection of waters. That Sirius, the dog-star, was so named because at its rising was the time also for the rising of the Nile; the star thus giving timely notice, just as the useful domestic animal gives notice of the approach of any novel visitor. Osiris, the great Lord, is depicted by an *eye* and a *sceptre*, to express omnipresence and omnipotence. Heaven, on account of its activity and eternity, is depicted by a *heart*, whose pulsations are kept up perpetually by a hearth containing a glowing fire. At Thebes, images of Judges were represented without hands, and with their eyes fixed on the ground, to show that those who administer justice should not have hands which will receive bribes, or eyes which will be allured from the truth. Beetles represent soldiers, because the Egyptians believed that females were not to be found among that species of insect. The symbolical figures discovered at Nineveh were prior to most of the representations of the same class in other countries; and if not to be considered as originals, were assuredly nearly the common sources of all. The whole routine of circumstances connected with the representations of fire-worship, the human-headed bulls and lions, the eagle-headed characters displayed in the sculptures of Nineveh, reveal a centre whence has flowed the main emblemry of all known mythologies. The symbol of the ox was universal, which is thus given in a very startling generalization by Fred. von Schlegel:—'The Indian and Persian word *gau*, with which the German *kuh* (cow) perfectly coincides, quite agrees with the Greek word for earth in the old Doric form of $\gamma\tilde{a}$; the Latin bos (ox), in its inflections bovis or bove, belongs to a whole family of Sanscrit words, such as *bhu*, *bhuva*, *bhumi*, which signify the earth, earthy, or whatever is remotely connected therewith. So originally in this language, one and the same word served to denote the earth and the bull. Comparisons of this sort, when not strained by etymological subtlety, but founded on matter of fact and clear self-evident deductions, may offer much curious illustration of the state of opinion and the nature and connexion of ideas in the primitive and mythic ages, or may serve at least to give us a clearer and more lively insight into the secret operations of the human mind, and into the modes of thinking prevalent among ancient nations.'

This proves the universal prevalency of the veneration for the ox throughout India, Egypt, and indeed the whole ancient world. The Indians conceived the bull the best representative of creative energy, and described Siva riding on the bull Nandi. The Apis of the Egyptians received divine honours for the same reason. Through all Pagan mythology the lion and the bull are the emblems respectively of royalty and power; and these animals are consequently of frequent occurrence, either singly or conjointly, among almost all the ancient structures of Persia. India, along the whole course of her extended history to the present day, displays her unwavering reverence for the ox as one of her principal symbols. The next great scene in which the world's civilization was advanced, namely, from the banks of the Euphrates to the Ægean Sea, revealed as ardent a devotion to the same symbol. Baal, the chief deity of this mythology, was represented under the ox-form partially or wholly. Nimrod, who either was Baal or his prototype, has firmly established his name and pretensions throughout this part of the East; and its writers, according to the authors of the 'Universal History,' make him not only the first king of Babylon, but of all the world; and they affirm that he was the first who wore a crown, the model of which he took from one he had seen in the sky; for being pleased with the appearance, he immediately sent for an artist and had a crown of gold cast in the same form, which he placed upon his head, whence his subjects took occasion to say that it came down to him from Heaven. The Orientals make Nimrod the author of the sect of the Magi, or worshippers of fire. They tell us that, accidentally seeing fire rise out of the earth at a distance from him in the east, he worshipped it, and appointed one Andeshan to attend the fire and throw frankincense upon it. 'There is a pretty constant tradition extant (says Vaux) that Nimrod taught the adoration of fire as one of the simple elements, or as the symbol of the Divine Majesty, a faith we have abundant proof was from very early times common in many parts of the East, and is even now, after the lapse of 4000 years, not altogether extinct.' His name, arising from a consideration of his deity, was *Bel, Pul,* or *Baal,* words of different sound but the same in sense, signifying Lord or Chief, and as such was acknowledged very generally through the Semitic and Celtic races. Tyre, Sidon, and Carthage, although their own records have perished, have yet left indelible proofs of their intimate adherence to the religion of their Eastern progenitors in the names of their greatest worthies, Ethbaal, Annibal, Asdrubal, Amilcar. Nay, at the very present time, in the middle of the nineteenth century, Ireland retains customs and names plainly showing that some of her ancestors at least must have come from the land of the 'mighty hunter.' O'Halloran affords one remarkable instance of the knowledge possessed by the ancient Irish in astronomy, shown by the Druidical name for the year in the Celtic language; and a more scientific one could not be found, since it is elegantly expressive of the course of the sun through the astronomical course of the zodiac: the word is *Bliaghan,* from Baal the sun, and *ain* a circle.

Another talented Irishman, Dr. John England, R.C. Bishop of Charleston, in a speech delivered in an American society for the relief of Irish orphans in that country, thus refers to the primitive history of his native country :—' Rome never gave her deities to Ireland ; but while that proud people dictated to a subject world, Ireland preserved even her idolatry unchanged. Her deities were of Eastern origin, and her rites of worship were of Asiatic institution ; not those of the Brahmin, but those of the Phœnician. Baal was her chief deity, and he was worshipped by fire. We need not the Sacred volume for the Asiatic facts and customs : they are too plain to be questioned. And which of us could not testify to the fires of May-eve[a] in this island of our nativity? The custom still continues, though Christianity has purified the observance by stripping it of the criminality of the object. So interwoven with the fibres of his heart are the usages of his fathers to a child of Erin, that they are to be eradicated only by a dreadful pang after it has been found absolutely necessary. Our earliest writers inform us that the fires of Baal, whose worship was always known amongst the Milesian settlers, were lighted with great solemnity on that day, which now corresponds to May-eve. We have ourselves seen the fires, and passed through them with sportive thoughtlessness of youth to avoid some indefinable evil which we dreaded from spirits. We know that the month of May is still called, in the language which some of us have lisped in childhood, *Baal-thinne*, or the fires of Baal. How many other facts which our historians testify, which our eyes and our ears have known, are totally inexplicable without the mythology of Phœnicia !' That the mythology of Egypt equally partook of reverence for the same symbols is evident. Pomponius Mela assures us that ' Apis was the god of the whole Egyptian nation, of the shape of a black ox, but spotted or pied with several other colours; his tongue and tail were quite different from other oxen. They affirm also that his birth was caused by lightning from Heaven (hence, probably, his name from Aph, fire). His birthday was celebrated throughout the whole kingdom by a solemn feast. Pliny gives a more ample description of this animal. The ox Apis is worshipped as a god in Egypt. It was required he should have a peculiar mark on his left side, namely, a crescent, white at both the extremities, and upon his tongue he was to have a node, called cantharus. The period of his life was limited to a certain number of years, which being expired, he was drowned in a spring, called the Spring of the Priests ; which done, they looked out for another to be put in his place. They appeared in mourning, and shaved their hair until they found another, which they were not long in accomplishing, and then he was conducted by the priests to Memphis. Here were two temples, intended for the prediction of future

---

[a] We think the gentleman has here mistaken the day ; what he here describes takes place at present in Ireland on the eve of St. John's day, the 24th of June.

events. If he went of his own accord into one of these halls it was a good omen, if into the other an evil one. To private persons he delivered his answers by taking or refusing the food which they offered. He would not take what was offered by Germanicus, and it was remarked how shortly the latter died after this circumstance. Long before either of these authors, Herodotus wrote,—'This ox, Apis, is the same with Epaphus, conceived by lightning. He must be black, with a square spot in the forehead, a figure of an eagle on the back, and a node or cantharus on the palate.' Jamblichus emphatically affirms Assyria to be one of the *sacred countries* whence emanated to all parts of the world the original rites and ceremonies of deep antiquity. There were two countries through which Greece chiefly received her religion, and these were Thrace and the island of Crete; and through both it would be difficult to distinguish what Assyria afforded as distinct from Egypt's additions. Perhaps upon close examination it would be found that in the Cretan supply the Assyrian element exceeded, while in the Thracian ritual the Egyptian mythology predominated. Diodorus Siculus declares, 'The Cretans boasted that they were the originators of all the mysteries and religious rites; nay, that most of the gods themselves were born among them. And this claim, as far as Greece was concerned, is nearly true, their chief god, Zeus, himself being an importation from Crete; while many learned men suppose him, prior to his Cretan transmutation, to have been the Bel of the East. And by this means we are enabled to trace the systems of the Western world to their origin in the East. The most casual glance at the map of the south of Europe displays the position of Crete as exactly the land whence communication would be introduced to Europe from Asia; in familiar language it might be styled the great stepping-stone of civilization from the one division of the world to the other; and the grand mythic symbol of Cretan antiquity, the Minotaur, is identically the winged human-headed bull of Nineveh.

'Semibovemque virum semivirumque bovem.'

The Cretan institutions and religion formed the groundwork of the Lacedemonian polity; and Athens borrowed much, very much of her early constitution in the intercommunication of commerce which marked the original union of these states. The myth of Theseus appears to me to have been founded partly upon the fact that the Hellenistic genius moulded the stern mysteries of deep antiquity into the brilliant representations of Grecian imagination. This tendency of the human intellect to change antique ideas for others more suited, or supposed more suited, to modern modes of thought, is observable in all ages and in all religions,

particularly in the Western world. Another symbolism modified
from the same source was the Sphinx, which, as a learned writer[b]
remarks, appears to have been a sort of hieroglyphic symbol
common to all the nations of antiquity. It expresses the difficulty
and danger of attempting to compass the distant and the forbidden but tempting object of human ambition. The gold-
defending gryphons of the Indians (Herod. iii. 116); Cerberus,
who blocked the access to Hades; the fire-breathing dragon
which guarded the apples of the Hesperides and the golden fleece
in Colchis; the Simurg and Rok of the Persians and Arabs, are
but so many expressions of the same notion. The gryphon, the
dragon, and the Greek sphinx generally had wings; the Egyptian
sphinx was generally without them. But there was no other
essential difference between them; for the head of the Egyptian
sphinx was not always human, and the gryphons, as they were
depicted upon the monuments, were merely sphinxes with eagles'
heads. M. Bunsen asserts her right,—'she is the enigma of
history.' We believe we have the Egyptian name of sphinx in
the word כְּרוּב *krûb*. That the Hebrews employed the Egyptian
word to denote even their religious symbols is clear from the Urim
and Thummim;[c] and the word כְּרוּב, which is not explicable from
the Hebrew language alone, has every appearance of being connected with the Sanscrit *grabh*, Gothic griepan, and the Greek
γρυπή and κέρβερος.' The veriest tyro in literature recognises the
sphinx as a leading emblem in Egyptian mythology; and the
Grecian legend of Thebes proves the widely-spread adoption of
the symbol. In the description of Euripides we have proofs of
the deeply graven traditional description of her more original
type :—

> ' Would that the Sphinx, in part a virgin form,
> But still a full-wing'd mountain monster,
> Had never come to be the plague of this
> Our land, with her discordant strains, as when
> Heretofore hovering near our walls she bore,
> Clutch'd within the gripe of her four-footed claws,
> The fated race of Cadmus to the light
> Inaccessible of the pure heaven.'

If the name of Thebes and the dwelling of the Sphinx point to
Egypt as their origin, the name of the surrounding country, Bœotia,
the land of the ox, points as strongly to the East, as it were to
corroborate a certain amount of truth as belonging to the myth of
Cadmus and his heaven-directed ox.

The lion and the eagle are also found very prominent in every

---

[b] In the Edinburgh Review.   [c] Wilkinson's Ancient Egypt.

mythology. The former of these predominated in the old Persian polity ; and as to the eagle, it is a well-ascertained fact, that all the primitive temples of Greece had sculptured on them, in various parts, the spread eagle, emblematic of the Cretan Jupiter. 'Let a man,' says Pierius, ' peruse the histories of the Assyrians, Medes, or Persians, or the records and glorious achievements of the Greeks and Macedonians, or of the Romans, who afterwards eclipsed them all—what will he meet with among them more frequently than the eagle, what more honoured, what more sacred ? To this bird alone, by the consent of all ages and augurs, is the honour given of always portending prosperous events.' Few need be reminded that the very principal emblem of the Grecian Zeus and of the Roman Jove was this bird, thus identifying their emblemry with that of Nineveh and Egypt. The universality of fire as an emblem is equally remarkable. The ancient Persians, although they did not worship it as a god, venerated it as the purest representation of the deity's glory. Zerdusht or Zoroaster in the time of Darius Hystaspes improved or remodelled the great eastern system introduced by Nimrod or Bel. He maintained the existence of a kingdom of light, in which Ormuzd, the author of all good, resided, and a kingdom of darkness, in which Ahriman, the source of all evil, moral as well as physical, had his dwelling. Thus runs their apology for the devotion to their favourite emblem. ' Forasmuch as fire was delivered to Zerdusht by the Almighty as the symbol of his majesty, wherefore it was required that we should esteem it holy and respect it as an emanation from the fountain of light, and that we should love all things that resemble it, especially the sun and the moon, the two great witnesses of God, and the sight of which should put us in mind of his omniscience ; therefore let us without superstition keep the command given us, evermore praising God for the great usefulness of this element, and beseeching him to make us always bear in mind the obligations we are under to do our duty towards him, which is as necessary to the health and happiness of the mind, as light and fire are to the ease and welfare of the body.'[d] This beautiful emblem was adopted into all the religions of the ancient world, in one form or another. Vesta, the goddess of fire, was worshipped all over Greece, where, says the Universal History (vol. v.), 'there was not one city but could show a temple dedicated to this goddess, with a lamp always burning in honour to her ; which has made some think that the rites and ceremonies of Vesta were introduced into Italy by the Greeks, and not by the Trojans.' It is worth while to mention here, that in the celebrated temple of Apollo, at Delphi, a fire was

---

[d] Univer. His., vol. iv. 514.

kept constantly burning. The worship of Vesta was the most solemn among the Romans, her priestesses, the Vestal virgins, the most sacred of her sacerdotal order. Should by any means the consecrated fire be extinguished, the whole city was thrown into consternation; and if it had happened through negligence, the severest inquiry was instituted to discover the delinquent, and the fire was again kindled, not from ordinary fire, but from the rays of the sun. Every year, as mentioned by Plutarch, they renewed it in the same manner, whether it went out or not. If Layard's discoveries did no more than show us a locality where these emblems of the early religions of our race were more concentrated than in any of these nations with whom we have been more acquainted, his labours would have been of considerable importance to theology. The histories of Egypt, Greece, Rome, and India, abound with allusions to those subjects; but these allusions are disunited and fragmentary by the loss of old traditions, and by the innovations of increasing knowledge, which introduced new ideas and new opinions. The student therefore had often to wonder at the frequent occurrence of similar emblems in various liturgies, without being able to discover a root whence they emanated as a whole. The excavations of Nineveh have supplied the desideratum. Covered by the débris of centuries, the prototypes of all the mythologies have been displayed to the wondering gaze of the 19th century, and we are furnished with an infallible clue to guide us to a still more profound original, whose interpretation, whilst it throws a splendour about what would otherwise surprise, at the same time offers an easy solution to what would otherwise remain obscure. When we contemplate the lion, the man, the ox, and the eagle joined together in the human-headed lions and oxen in the spacious mansions of the successors of Nimrod, we contemplate figures containing a junction of the emblemry of other races, and we are brought in direct connexion with the evident fountain whence they themselves emanated, and all the imitations of them, however distant or imperfect. Layard was so struck with the resemblance between these gigantic forms and the cherubic representations mentioned in the prophet Ezekiel, that he pronounced at once with the utmost confidence that the Jewish prophet must have borrowed his imagery from the palaces of Nineveh. But that an inspired Jewish prophet would have borrowed any imagery from what he utterly abhorred as the very height of profane abomination, is the most improbable supposition possible. Besides, the prophet uses not imagery of his own imagination. The representations were portrayed before him in visions from God himself, and these glorious revelations were assuredly not sent through the portals of the proud and sinful monarch of Assyria. Isaiah and Ezekiel both prophesied in the decline and fall of the Jewish church in the time of the Assyrian and Babylonian ascendancy; both were inspired, not only with the commission from the Lord God of Israel, but with the spirit of poetry of the very highest order. Isaiah's writings abound with specimens of every species of poetry, from the simple elegance of the pastoral to the loftiest flight of the epic. Ezekiel, too much absorbed in the lowly state of his commonwealth, describes the glorious visions sent to instruct and invigorate the church, in strains of sublimity necessarily arising from the influence of such transcendent visitations. This was much required at the particular time in which he lived. The power of the Jewish nation was prostrated, the temple had been utterly destroyed, not a rite or a ceremony could be attended to, and the customary responses of God were silent. When thus the ordinary means had been withdrawn, the Lord revealed himself in a way as glorious as it was extraordinary.

The prophet, as he stood upon the banks of the Chebar, saw a mighty wind bearing from the north, wafting along a thick collection of clouds, enveloping a mass of fire, whose splendour continually scintillated around the whole spectacle, whilst in the midst of the fire was the appearance of amber, rather of electrum, a metal much prized by the ancients, composed of four parts of gold and one of silver. When the stupendous congeries opened there was revealed to the astonished gaze of the prophet 'the likeness of four living creatures.' Each had four faces and four wings, and their feet resembled those of an ox. They had the hands of a man under their wings on their four sides, and their wings were joined to one another; they turned not when they went, they went every one straight forward. As for the likeness of their faces, they four had the face of a man and the face of a lion on the right side, and they four had the face of an ox on the left side: they four also had the face of an eagle. Beryl-coloured wheels studded round with eyes attended the living creatures, and followed all their movements. Who does not perceive at a glance in this 'living machinery,' as it has been most happily styled, the very types of all the leading emblemry of Nineveh? But this magnificent grouping was but secondary in its office; the heads of the cherubim supported a firmament of terrible crystal, that is diamond, and upon this diamond pavement was a sapphire throne, whereon was seated a man whose dazzling appearance was far beyond the power of language fully to convey, but, enshrined in all the brilliancy of light, was as it were encased amid the glory of the rainbow. We are emphatically told that 'this was the likeness of the glory of the Lord.' In plain terms, the cherubim and wheels form the emblematical chariot of the providence of 'God in Christ.' And here I cannot resist quoting a coincidence of sentiment on this point from the 'Journal of Sacred Literature.' 'We remember the magnificent description given by the prophet (Ezek. i.) of the wondrous chariot of the Lord. When the living creatures went, and the high and dreadful wheels went by them, the noise of their wings was like great waters; they moved like a flash of lightning, they were controlled by one spirit, they went every one straight forward. And when rest succeeded the irresistible might of their action, no tremor vibrated through the complex living machinery; nothing betokened that a great effort had been made; the pause is sudden, absolute, perfect, the wheels are motionless, the cherubim let down their wings, and amidst the solemn stillness that ensues the voice of the Almighty alone is heard from the firmament of the terrible crystal over their heads.' An attentive reader of Scripture will find a vast deal throughout its pages indicative of the fact that similar visions to this of Ezekiel had been seen by the earlier worthies of the Jewish polity, although not fully described by them, and very many passages, otherwise obscure, will be rendered perfectly plain by applying the key of this explanation. David evidently beheld a similar vision to that of the prophet of the captivity, the description of which was considered important enough not only to be preserved in 2 Sam. xxii., but also to be repeated in Psalm xviii. Dr. Watts observes, that many learned men suppose that this very vision appeared to the elders of Israel, when with Moses they were summoned by the Lord, as described Exod. xxiv. 10. It is evident also, as he says, that the form of a cherub was well known to the Jews of that age, since Moses gives no description of them to instruct the artificers; they were known of old, probably to the patriarchs and to mankind, as emblems of divine majesty and terror, guarding the way to the tree of life. Gen. iii. 24. The glorious vision of Deity to John, as described in the Apocalypse, is in every point identical with that of Ezekiel, and I feel great pleasure in being able to adopt the description of another writer who was not in the least influenced towards the views advocated in the present essay. 'Let us turn to the principal visions of the book (the Apocalypse), and first we have the glorious theophany which was presented to the eye of the seer when he entered by the door opened in heaven,' and which we hold to have been a preface to the whole of the subsequent visions, and not, as our author represents it, only an introduction to the seven seals. A throne appears before the apostle, and one sitting on it. He was like a jasper and a sardine stone. The jasper clear as crystal (see ch. xxi. 2), the sardine stone of a flesh colour, setting forth, according to Hengstenberg, the fire of the divine anger, along with the radiating light of the divine holiness. Around the throne sat four-and-twenty elders, crowned, and with white robes. These are the symbols of the church, of which the number twelve is the signature, doubled, here as in ch. xxi., to take in the twelve patriarchs and the twelve apostles. Their crowns and raiment proclaim them to be 'kings and priests.' In the midst of the throne and round about, *i.e.* beneath it, and yet visible on every side, were four living ones, the cherubim not representing angelic beings, for the angels (see ch. vii. 2) form a circle around the elders, nor yet the symbol of the church, which is represented by the elders, but the emblem of creation bearing up the throne of the God of the whole earth. The number four is, according to our author, the signature of the earth. Their likenesses represent the whole visible creation, for the man is first among the creatures, the eagle among birds, the ox among cattle, and the lion among beasts. Beautifully does our author explain their 'resting not day nor night,' by referring to Psalm xix. 3. 'Day unto day uttereth speech, and night unto night shows knowledge.' As the heavens without ceasing declare the glory of God, the God of Hosts, so also do the cherubim or the creatures upon earth.

The rainbow also round about the throne, the pledge of the covenant with Noah for the preservation of the earth, teaches us that the vision has respect unto the earth; grace returning after wrath is predicted; a new heaven and a new earth after the deluge of fire. The thunders, and lightnings, and voices, testify of approaching judgment, and the seven torches of fire burning before the throne symbolize the operations of God's spirit upon the earth, especially as bringing chastisement and destruction. The sea of glass, like unto crystal, which appeared before the throne, is identified by Hengstenberg with the sea of glass, mingled with fire, which is mentioned in ch. xv. 2. It seems to be identical in this place with the firmament which Ezekiel saw beneath the throne, and with the pavement of sapphire, as it were the body of heaven in clearness, which Moses saw under the feet of Jehovah.

Dr. Watts and the authors of the 'Universal History' agree with Grotius, Bochart, Spencer, Le Clerc, Mede, &c., in deriving the word cherub from Charab, which in the Syriac, Chaldee, and Arabic, means to plough; therefore these authors believe that the cherubim resembled oxen, if not in the whole, at least in the face, and some other parts of the body. To this we may add the authority of an ancient Father (Clemens Alexandrinus), who believed that the Egyptian Sphinx and other hieroglyphical beasts were borrowed from those of Moses and Ezekiel. Nothing could be more sublimely descriptive of Christ's guidance of universal providence, borne on the wings of intellect, power, and rapidity; for, to use the words of Layard, 'no better type of intellect and knowledge could be found than the head of the man, of strength than that of the lion, and of ubiquity than that of the eagle!'

Dr. Watts uses nearly the same words in reference to these symbols. 'The understanding and beauty of the man, the obedience and labour or diligence of the ox, the courage and strength of the lion, together with the sharp sight and swiftness of the eagle, in fulfilling the commands of God and in administering his providence.' And here a most important and astonishing parallel is established between these visions and the cherubim in the tabernacle of Moses, and in the temple of Solomon; and surely a sublimer lesson could not be established amongst any people than such a stationary remembrancer of a doctrine, the most important to keep steadily in man's heart, namely, the universal providence of God the Redeemer. There was one difference in respect to the artificial cherubim, for, although they had their wings always raised to support the visible glory of the Lord, it was only occasionally that the glorious visitor 'shined forth' from between them. It is to be noted also, that sometimes this brilliant manifestation appeared without its cherubim-chariot, and was recognised by the Jews by two names declarative of its great importance; the one was the *shechinah*, that is, 'the dwelling;' the other *Kisse hachabod*, 'the throne of glory,' one of the seven things which the Jews believed were created before the world.

This divine appearance is referred to in many passages both in the Od and New Testaments. One of the last records of its manifestations is by an eye-witness, the destiny of whose existence was for ever altered by its appearance, and than whom there never was mortal better calculated to describe it with accuracy and power. I allude to the appearance of glory to St. Paul in his memorable journey to Damascus. What can surpass the brilliancy he describes? (Acts xxvi. 13). 'At midday, O King, I saw in the way a light from Heaven above the brightness of the sun shining round about me, and them which journeyed with me.' Let us for a moment consider the splendour of a midday sun in an Eastern sky, and then attempt the contemplation of an effulgence which threw that midday sun into shade.

The reason that this divine mode of communication was so well known to the patriarchs and ancient Jews was, that it was a regularly established institution of the Deity from the time that man was banished from Eden. This is distinctly revealed to us in Gen. iii. 24, which is thus translated in our version—'And he placed at the east of the garden of Eden cherubim and a flaming sword, which turned every way to keep the way of the tree of life.' A very current idea among the religious world from this translation is, that herein is described the presence of an angel with a flaming sword in his hand ; than which nothing can be more erroneous. In no passage of Scripture does the word 'cherubim' mean an angel or angels ; and the word translated sword, by the construction of the sentence in the original, may be totally independent of any connection with the cherubim. 'The words commonly rendered "flaming sword,"' say the authors of the Universal History, 'are in the original the *flame of cutting*, or *division*, or a *dividing flame*, for the same word which signifies a sword signifies also division, and is translated both ways.' This is simply, in other words, a description of the original institution of the grand primeval prototype of the cherubim-chariot and brilliantly revolving flame which occasionally appeared to patriarchs, prophets, and apostles, and the stationary artificial model of which was placed in the tabernacle of Moses, and in the temples which succeeded in its place. But the influence of this grand prototype (Gen. iii. 24) spread far and wide in all the tribes of mankind, as has been shown in the notices of the fire-worship, and the emblemry of the ancient world.

J. H. C.

THE ACTS OF ANDREW AND MATTHIAS IN THE CITY OF THE MEN-EATERS.

OF all the stories contained in Tischendorf's collection of apocryphal Acts of Apostles, this is one of the most remarkable, both on account of its contents and from its wide circulation in early times.

In the following pages we give an epitome of the book, so as to exhibit a pretty full idea of its contents. In some copies the name of the Apostle associated with Andrew is *Matthias*, and in others *Matthew ;* we have retained the former as being that which Tischendorf has adopted in his text. In other versions of the legend *Matthew the tax-collector* is expressly mentioned as the one who went to the city of the men-eaters.

In 'The Acts and Martyrdom of Matthew,' also published by Tischendorf, we see that the legend of the visit of that Apostle and Andrew to the city of the men-eaters was the basis of many narrations, all embodying the same general notion ; though the particulars in the several narrations are utterly contradictory.

'The Acts of Andrew and Matthias' commence thus :—'At that time all the Apostles were gathered together, and they distributed the countries to themselves, casting lots, that each one might go to the part which fell to him. It fell, therefore, to

Matthias by lot that he should go to the land of the men-eaters. Now the men of that city neither ate bread nor drank wine, but they were accustomed to eat the flesh of men, and to drink their blood. Every man, therefore, who arrived in their city they seized him, and put out his eyes, and gave him to drink an enchanted potion prepared by magic and enchantment; and when they drank the enchanted potion, their hearts were changed, and their mind altered.

'When, therefore, Matthias entered into the gate of their city, the men of that city seized him and put out his eyes; and, after having put them out, they gave him to drink the enchanted potion of their magic deceit; and they took him away to prison, and gave him grass to eat, and he ate it not. For when he partook of their enchanted potion his heart was not changed nor was his mind altered.'

This story then goes on to describe Matthias as praying to Christ on account of the treatment which he had received, and entreating that he might not become the food of the men-eaters, and that his sight might be restored to him. Thereupon a light shone in the prison, and Matthias was addressed by a voice, 'Matthias, beloved, receive thy sight:' and his sight was at once restored. He is then told not to be cast down, for he should be delivered out of every peril, together with all his brethren that were with him. He was to wait twenty-seven days, and then Andrew should be sent to bring him out of prison, together with all the auditors (whether of Matthias or of Andrew is not said). Matthias recognizes the voice as being that of Christ.

In the morning, the people of the city came to take out of the prison the men whom they would eat; Matthias shuts his eyes that they may not perceive that his sight had been restored. Each of the captives is represented as having a label to signify the day on which he should be taken out to be eaten. That of Matthias signified that he was to be taken out on the thirtieth day.

The scene next changes to the country where Andrew was teaching; to whom the Lord appears when the twenty-seven days were expired, and charges him to go with his disciples to the land of the men-eaters, and deliver Matthias from that place: for it was but three days before they were going to slaughter him for food. Andrew answers that he cannot get thither within three days, and he proposes that an angel should be sent swiftly, but that as he was himself flesh he could not make such speed. Andrew, however, was commanded to obey his Maker, who could treat the city as he pleased; and he was told to go early to the sea with his disciples, where he would find a ship to take him to the place. He does this, and accordingly finds the ship with three men in it. The Lord himself, concealed as a man, was the helmsman of the vessel. Andrew rejoiced, and inquired whither the ship was bound; to this, reply was made, To the land of the men-eaters. Andrew then says that he too was going thither; and the helmsman bade him embark. However, he first states that he has no money to pay his fare, and no provision for the voyage. He then goes into a theological discussion as to why, as a disciple of Christ, he carries neither food nor money. They are received on board cheerfully, and furnished with bread.

The helmsman asks Andrew to narrate some of the miracles of Christ, to occupy the attention of his disciples and to keep them from the fear of the sea; for they were at once to move off from the shore. Andrew then narrates how Christ was with his disciples in the vessel asleep during the storm; and he bade his companions to be of good cheer, because they were under the same care: and he prayed that they might go to sleep, and accordingly they went to sleep.

Andrew's own attention was then taken up with the remarkable manner in which the ship sailed, differing from anything that he had seen in sixteen voyages that he had made. On asking the helmsman for an explanation, he is told that the sea knew him as a disciple of Christ, and therefore the vessel passed through it steadily as if on dry land.

The helmsman then asks Andrew why the Jews did not believe in Jesus; to this the Apostle is made to reply by narrating a strange story.

'Truly, brother, he manifested to us that he is God. Do not, then, suppose that he is man; for he himself made the heaven and the earth, and the sea, and all things that are in them.' After some further conversation, in which Andrew mentions some of Christ's *Scripture* miracles, he proceeds to tell the strange account of what Christ did *in secret*.

'It came to pass when we, the twelve disciples, went with our Lord into a temple of the Gentiles, that he might show us the ignorance of the devil; and the chief priests seeing us following Jesus, said to us, O wretches, how is it that ye walk with him who says, I am the Son of God? Has God a son? . . . Is not this the son of Joseph the carpenter? . . . Now when we heard these words our hearts turned into weakness. But Jesus, knowing that our hearts were cast down, took us to a desert place, and wrought great miracles in our presence, and showed us all his Godhead. But we said to the chief priests, Come you also, and see; for behold he has persuaded us.

'And the chief priests came and went with us, and they entered into the temple of the Gentiles. . . . And there entered with us thirty men of the people and four chief priests. And Jesus, looking on the right and left of the temple, saw two carved sphinxes; and he turned to us and said, " Behold the sign of the Cross; for these are like the Cherubim and Seraphim which are in heaven." Then Jesus looking on the right where the sphinx was, said to it, " I say unto thee, thou likeness of what is in heaven, which the hands of craftsmen have sculptured, be thou severed from thy place and come down, and answer and rebuke the chief priests, and show them whether I am God or man."

'And immediately, in that hour, the sphinx came down, and receiving a human voice said, " O the foolish children of Israel! the blindness of their hearts alone is not sufficient, but they wish others to be blind like themselves, saying that God is a man."' The sphinx goes on with much more in the same strain, saying that Christ was he who had called Abraham, charging the Jews with unbelief, with desecrating their synagogues, &c. Then Andrew continues: ' And we said to the chief priests, " It is now right that you should believe us, for even the stones have rebuked you." And the Jews answered and said, " These stones speak through magic; and do not ye suppose that he is God. For if ye test the things spoken by the stone, ye know his deceit. For where did he find Abraham, or where did he see him? For Abraham was dead many years before he was born, and how did he know him?"

' But Jesus, turning again to the figure, said to it, " Because these disbelieve that I talked with Abraham, go into the land of the Canaanites, and go to the double cave [the cave of Machpelah] in the field of Mamre, where the body of Abraham is, and call it out of the sepulchre, saying, Abraham, Abraham, whose body is in the sepulchre, but whose soul is in paradise, thus saith he that formed man, who made thee his friend from the beginning: Arise thou, and Isaac thy son, and Jacob thy son's son, and go unto the sanctuary of the Jebusites, that we may rebuke the chief priests, that they may know that I know thee and thou me." And when the sphinx heard these words, immediately it walked before us all, and went into the land of the Canaanites to the field of Mamre, and called out of the sepulchre, as God commanded it. And immediately the twelve patriarchs came forth alive out of the sepulchre; and they answered and said to it, " To which of us art thou sent?" And the sphinx answered and said, " I am sent to the three patriarchs for a witness; but go you and rest until the time of the resurrection." And when they heard this, they went into the sepulchre and fell asleep. And the three patriarchs went with the sphinx unto Jesus, and rebuked the chief priests. And Jesus said to them, " Go away to your places;" and they went; and he said to the figure, " Go up to thy place;" and immediately it went up and stood in its place.'

When Andrew had given this narration, and after some further conversation had taken place, the vessel had approached the land, and Andrew fell asleep.   Jesus commands the angels to bear Andrew and his companions on shore, and to lay them on the ground outside the city of the men-eaters.

In the morning Andrew wakes and sees that he is on the land, and that his companions are sleeping by him : he wakes them, and tells them that the Lord had been with them in the vessel, though they knew him not.   His companions tell him that while they were overcome with sleep *eagles* from heaven had carried their souls to the heavenly paradise, where they saw Jesus on his throne of glory with the angels, and with Abraham, Isaac, and Jacob, and David praising with his harp, and the twelve Apostles, each accompanied by an angel in the likeness of himself; and they heard the Lord command the angels to hear the Apostles in every thing that they asked.

After Andrew had prayed, Jesus appears to him as a child, and tells him that he had been brought to the end of his voyage by a miracle, although he had said that it was impossible to get thither in three days.   He then tells him to go into the city to Matthias and to bring him out of prison, together with all the strangers that were with him.   Andrew is then told that he will have to suffer much in the city, that his flesh will be strewed through the streets, and his blood flow upon the earth ; but that they will not be able to kill him, and that the city contained those who should believe.

Andrew and his companions enter the city invisibly, and go to the prison ; the guards fall down dead at his prayer ; and at the sign of the cross the doors open.   After some conversation with Matthias, whom he seems to reprove for not having freed himself by miracle, he looks up and sees certain captives,[a] eating grass naked ; and after bewailing their condition and giving vent to his feelings in a pretty long rebuke addressed to Satan, he and Matthias pray, and restore first the sight and then the reason of the unhappy captives.

Andrew then bids them go to the lower parts of the city, where they would find a fig-tree under which they should sit, and of the fruit of which they might eat until he came, however long he tarried.   They ask Andrew to accompany them as a guard and protection, lest the wicked men of the city should see them and treat them worse than before ; the Apostle, however, assures them that they shall be safe, and they all go to the fig-tree.

---

[a] τρεῖς ἄνδρας is the reading of the text; but as they are afterwards said to be 270 men and 49 women, in all 319, the numeral τρεῖς may be copied by mistake for τιθ′ (319).

Andrew then commands a *cloud* to bear away Matthias and the disciples who had accompanied him; which it does accordingly, and carries them to the mountain where Peter was teaching. So that the whole journey of Matthias to the city of the men-eaters results in nothing as far as his preaching is concerned; the distribution by lot appears to be no good guide.

Andrew goes forth from the prison, and walking into the city sees a pedestal of a statue, behind which he sits down to see what would take place. The people go to the prison to take out the men who were to be eaten, but they find the prison open and empty, and the keepers dead. They report this to the governors of the city, who are filled with wonder at what has happened; but to provide food they command that the dead keepers shall be brought to be eaten for the food of that day, and that for the morrow they shall gather together all the old men of the city, and take seven of them by lot for food, until they should be able to send out marauding bands to bring in prisoners to be eaten.

They bring the seven dead keepers of the prison to the middle of the city, where there was a furnace and a wine press, for cooking the victims and for squeezing out their blood for drink. When they bring the keepers to the wine-press, a voice from heaven comes to Andrew, 'See, O Andrew, what is done in this city!' The Apostle prays that no evil may be allowed to happen, and the swords fall out of the hands of the executioners. (The victims, however, were already *dead*.) The rulers seeing this exclaim that the escaped prisoners must be magicians, and that as they cannot eat the dead keepers, they must collect the old men and cast lots, because they are very hungry.

They gather together 217 old men and select seven by lot; one of these begs that they will spare him and take his son instead; the officers employed consult the rulers of the city, who consent to the substitution. The old man then (*why*, it is not at all apparent) offers them his daughter to be eaten as well as his son. The children lament their doom, and entreat that they may be spared to become of full stature before they were slain; the officers show them no pity, but take them off to the wine-press. Andrew weeps at the sight, and prays that the victims may be delivered; whereupon the swords fall from the hands of the slaughterers, which causes great fear amongst the people.

The rulers weep, and know not what to do; and the devil comes amongst them in the form of an old man, and says, 'Woe unto you! for you will now die for want of food; what will the sheep and oxen do for you? They will not suffice for you. But now rise and search here for a stranger named Andrew and kill him; for if not, he will not suffer you to carry out your custom any more ; for it was he who freed the men from the prison, and he is in this city, and you know him not : now, therefore, arise and seek for him, that henceforth you may be able to partake of your food.'

Andrew was all the while unseen by the devil, but he replied, 'O most hostile Belial, enemy of the whole creation ; my Lord Jesus Christ will humble thee down to the abyss.' The devil replies, 'I hear thy voice, and I know thy voice, but where thou standest I know not.' Andrew answers, 'Wherefore then wast thou called *Amael*—was it not because thou art blind, not seeing all the saints ? ' The devil then tells the people to search for him who thus was talking with him, for he was the person. They shut the city gates, and look for the saint, but they see him not. The Lord commands him to show himself to the people, that they might learn *His* power, and the impotence of the devil who energized *them*.

Andrew then stands forth and says, 'Behold, I am Andrew whom ye seek.' They run on him, saying, 'As thou hast done to us, so will we do to thee ;' and they take counsel how to treat him. They think that if his head were cut off it would be a death without torture, and if they burned him they would not have him to eat. At length one into whom the devil had entered, proposed that a rope should be tied round his neck, and that he should be dragged through the streets and lanes of the city, and when he died he should be divided into shares.[b]

Accordingly, they thus treat Andrew, dragging him by the rope round his neck, so that pieces of his flesh clave to the earth, and his blood flowed on the ground like water. In the evening they put him in prison and tie his hands behind him, 'and he was exceedingly weary.'

The next day they drag him in the same manner ; and when he prayed, the devil came behind and said to the multitude, 'Strike him on the mouth that he may not speak.' In the evening they put him in prison as before ; and the devil comes, bringing with him seven demons which the saint had cast out in the circumjacent countries ; and the demons stand before Andrew, seeking to kill him. After they had upbraidingly addressed him, they sought to accomplish this, 'but when they saw the seal on his forehead, which the Lord had given to him, they were afraid, and instead of drawing near to him they fled. And the devil said to them, " Why do ye flee from him, my children, and have not slain him ? " The demons answer and say to the devil, " We are not able to kill him ; but if *thou* art able, kill him, for *we* knew him before he

---

[b] This is just the way in which Romanists treat the real or reputed bodies of their saints when long dead ; the portions are sometimes very minute.

came into the tribulation of his humiliation." ' On this the demons resolve to *mock* Andrew, as they could not kill him; this causes him to weep; and a voice comes to him saying, " Andrew, why weepest thou ? " But it was the voice of the devil disguised.

' And Andrew answered and said, " I weep because God commanded me, saying, Be long suffering towards them." The devil said, " If thou canst do anything, do it." Andrew replied, " Why then do ye treat me thus? but far be it from me to disobey the commandment of my Lord; for if the Lord should visit me in this city, I will chastise you as ye deserve." And when they heard this, they fled.'

In the morning the people drag him through the street in the same manner; he prays, saying that in three days he had suffered enough, and asking what had become of his *hairs*. He receives an answer, and he is shown fruit-bearing trees growing where his hairs had fallen.

In the evening they again put him in prison, thinking that he might die of exhaustion and suffering in the night; but the Lord comes to him and heals him. He sees in the prison a pedestal, and on it a statue of alabaster, to which he approaches, and clapping his hands seven times, he says to the statue, ' Fear the sign of the cross, at which heaven and earth tremble; and let the statue on the pedestal pour forth much water from its mouth, until all those in the city are chastised: and say not, I am a stone and am not meet to praise the Lord; for the Lord formed *us* of earth, but *you* are pure, wherefore He gave the tables of the law from you.'

A mighty stream of water accordingly flows from the mouth of the statue, and in the morning the people of the city are afraid and begin to flee. The water slays their cattle and their children; and Andrew prays that Michael the Archangel may be sent with a cloud of fire so as to surround the city that no one may flee. This takes place, and the people are all hemmed in with water up to their necks. They lament and say, that all this has happened because of Andrew, whom they now propose to let go; and they cry, ' Oh God of the stranger, take away this water from us.' The Apostle on this says to the statue, ' Let the water cease, for they have repented; and I say to thee, that if the citizens of this city are persuaded, I will build a church, and set thee in it, because thou hast done me this service.' The water then ceases, and the people come to the prison praying for mercy. Andrew comes forth and the water withdraws from his feet. The people when they see him, all cry, ' Have mercy on us.'

The old man who had given his children to be slain in his stead then comes to Andrew's feet crying, ' Have mercy on me ! ' The holy Andrew answered and said to the old man, 'I wonder how thou sayest, Have mercy on me, when thou hadst no mercy on thy children, but gavest them up to be slain in thy stead: I say, therefore, to thee that at what hour this water departs, thou shalt go into the abyss, with the fourteen who slay the men daily!' Andrew then goes on to where the wine-press stood and prays; the earth opens and drinks down the water with the old man and the other fourteen. The rest of the people cry out for fear, expecting that they too will be destroyed; Andrew, however, bids them not to fear, for those who had gone down to Hades had been so punished that the rest might believe on the Lord Jesus Christ.

Andrew then commands that all who had perished by the water should be brought, who were a vast multitude; and at his prayer they were all restored to life. He then caused a church to be built, and baptized the people and gave them the commandments of Christ. They beseech him to remain some days with them to instruct them, since they were neophytes. He refused to remain, and says that he must go to his disciples. The little children follow him weeping, but he departs, promising however to return. Jesus comes to him in the form of a little child, and reproves him for thus departing, and commands him to return to the city for seven days, and that afterwards he should go with his disciples to the country of the barbarians: and that on entering into the city he should preach and bring up the men again from the abyss, and do whatever he was commanded.

He accordingly returns and remains there the seven days.

Such is the purport of this strange invention; a story which in early times obtained a wide circulation in various forms, all of which, however, were the same in their general idea.

There can be no doubt that the tale as it stands amongst these apocryphal acts has been embellished from time to time, and that the original story can only be sought by looking at the general outline apart from the episodes.

These narrations have one important use, they show how narrations *grow*, and what we might expect the New Testament to have become, had it been (as the adherents of the mythic theory tell us) composed after the middle of the second century.

It is remarkable how early this tale was known in England; it forms the subject of an early Anglo-Saxon poem.

Did the writers of such narratives *believe* the marvels of which they give such profuse pictures? This is a question of some importance; if they did, then it shows how strong must their *credulity* have been, for them to believe such stories without evidence:—if they did *not believe* them, it shows how utterly weakened all right principle must have been, for it to be thought justifiable on any account to put forth such feigned tales, which would impose on the credulous.

Whoever upholds fictitious miracles does what is calculated to weaken the force of all Scripture miracles; for in this way an endeavour is made to put both classes on the same level, and thus to bring down Scripture miracles from the high ground on which they stand, to the mere level of feigned tales. In this manner apocryphal legends of saints have done much harm in weakening the force of Christian evidence; while if they are *rightly* understood they have their value, as showing the real historic character of Scripture narrations, so utterly different from what they would have been, had they presented merely a fictitious narrative drawn from man's own fancy, instead of being a relation of facts.

L. M.

THE ESSENES.

BEFORE the advent of the Messiah, the Jewish people are generally considered by ecclesiastical historians as divided into three separate sects; viz. the Pharisees, the Sadducees, and the Essenes. The last of these, however, cannot be classed, as they have hitherto been, among the Jewish sects, if the hypothesis which identifies the Christians with the Essenes be correct. We are aware that several writers have maintained that there is *a resemblance* between Essenism and Christianity; but none of them have gone so far as to consider the Essenes to be actually Christians. This has been done by the Church of Rome in order to support the antiquity of the Monastic institution;[a] but with her it is a dogma, as no proof is given. A writer in one of our popular periodicals, supposed to be Thomas De Quincey,[b] gives what he considers satisfactory arguments to show that 'in this particular instance the dogmatism of Rome rests upon a sense of transcendent truth—of truth compulsory to the Christian conscience.' Now, seeing that this is the first attempt in our country to defend this dogma of the Romish Church, we intend to prove in the present article that the arguments brought forward by this writer (which we believe have not been answered), although certainly very ingenious, are anything but convincing, and that the hy-

---

[a] See the works of Baronius, &c. There are, however, some writers of the Romish Church,—for instance, Valesius (Not. in Euseb., lib. ii. c. 17) and Pag (Critic. in Baron. An., 62. 4),—who admit that the monastic system did not begin till the close of the third century.

[b] In Blackwood's Magazine for the year 1840, vol. xlvii.

pothesis which they defend is untenable. The writer alluded to begins with maintaining two propositions—1st. No 'such philosophical sect as the Essenes ever existed amongst the Jews.' 2ndly, 'In the Judæan history of Josephus there is no notice taken of the new-born brotherhood of Christians;' this he considers so very remarkable as to entitle him to conclude that Josephus, in describing the Essenes, describes the primitive Christians. 1st, His 'objections to the Essenes, as any permanent or known sect amongst the Jews,' are as follows :—1st obj. Because, 'whilst all other sorts and orders of men converse with Christ during his ministry in Palestine, never do we hear of any interview between him and the Essenes.' To this objection we give the answer, that, as the Essenes did not visit the temple,—for, although they sent gifts,[c] yet they offered no sacrifice in that place,—how could our Saviour, who 'ever taught in the synagogue and the temple,' converse with members of a sect who seldom went abroad, and who secluded themselves from places of public resort? And how could 'a body of men so truly spiritual in the externals of their creed' win a word of praise from Christ, or 'a word of reproach for that by which they might happen to fall short of their own professions,' seeing the rumour of the Saviour's doings—his discourses the most sublime and his miracles the most astonishing— could not make them leave their solitary abodes on the mountains or their dwellings in the villages and towns? Could He, whose every word and whose every action was said and done in the market-places and public highways, so far forget the eternal interests of more than three millions[d] of Jews, as to leave them in order to converse with a sect who would not come to him, and who would in all probability reject his counsels with scorn, as it was one of their rules not to admit a man of another sect into the apartments in which they lived?[e] We, however, do not think with some writers that the Essenes were, unlike the cotemporary sects of the Pharisees and Sadducees, uncondemned by our Saviour ; for in Matthew xix. 11 and 12, Christ, in answer to an inquiry of his disciples, says, 'All men cannot receive this saying,[f] save *they* to whom it is given. For there are some eunuchs (*i. e.* such as lived in voluntary abstinence) which were so from their mother's womb ; and there are some eunuchs which were made eunuchs of men ; and there be eunuchs which have

---

[c] Joseph., Ant., xviii. c. 1, s. 4.

[d] We take only the population of Galilee, as our Saviour chiefly preached in that part of Palestine. From Josephus and other writers we learn that the population of Palestine, during the time of Christ, was ten millions.

[e] Joseph., De Bell., lib. ii. c. 8.

[f] Or, as it is rendered by Bloomfield, 'All are not capable of practising this thing,' viz. οὐ γαμῆσαι.

made themselves eunuchs for the kingdom of heaven's sake.'
From this description of an existing state of things we learn that
three classes of individuals abstained from marriage, viz. those
who were physically unable 'from their mother's womb;' and
those who were, under the command of others, 'made eunuchs of
men;' and lastly, those who abstained for the sake of the kingdom. All the best commentators are of opinion that the contemplative Essenes are here alluded to, because they abstained from
the society of women, in order to be (as they thought) better fitted
for heaven. Now, in the above passage, does our Lord reprehend celibacy *for the sake of religion*, or does he not? If he does
not, then the Essenes are to be considered as uncondemned; if,
however, we answer the question in the affirmative, then one at
least of the doctrines of the Essenes must be considered as condemned by the only infallible authority, Jesus Christ. That the
question must be answered in the affirmative is evident, when we
consider that, if our Saviour did regard celibacy in itself as pre-
eminently excellent, then he would have said, as was his custom
on other occasions (*e. g.* the sermon on the mount), 'Blessed are
those who abstain from marriage for the kingdom of heaven's
sake;' and the reason why he did not thus express himself was
just because the motive ('for the kingdom of heaven's sake') was
selfish, and not such as 'implies the sacrifice of human feelings
from love to the kingdom of God, and for the sake of rendering
it more efficient service. This decision, therefore, was opposed
not only to the old Hebrew notion that celibacy was *per se* igno-
minious, but also to the ascetic doctrine which made it *per se* a
superior condition of life.' [g] Let us now consider the 2nd objection,
which is, that 'the death-like silence of *all the evangelists*, and *all
the apostles*, makes it a mere impossibility to suppose the existence
of such a sect as the Essenes in the time of Christ.' We do not
see how 'no one of the four Gospels' alluding to the Essenes is a
proof of their non-existence as a Jewish sect; for, as it was their
design to write only the history of our Saviour's ministry, and nothing more, we must consider any particular notice of such a sect,
when there was no necessity, no particular occasion for so doing
(as they never, like the Pharisees, Sadducees, Herodians, and Samaritans, conversed with Christ), not only as uncalled for, but as
being very remarkable, seeing that the history of the Jewish sects
had nothing to do with their histories. To conclude, therefore,
that the obscure Jewish sect called the Essenes never existed, because the Evangelists do not notice them, is not only very bad
reasoning, but very unbecoming a candid inquirer after truth.

[g] Neander, Life of Christ, Bohn's translation, p. 363. This edition of Neander's
works is the one always referred to in the text.

For what would we think of a French writer if he should maintain that no such religious sect as the Society of Friends existed in Great Britain, because there is no allusion to them in Grimshaw's Life of Legh Richmond? Now this reasoning is just the same as that which we are at present considering—the objector maintains that no such sect as the Essenes existed in the time of Christ, because there is no notice taken of them in the Life of Jesus Christ by the Evangelists! But how could the disciples, who seldom left our Lord, know (even if they had been willing) anything about a society of men who, secluding themselves from public life, passed their days in humble abodes and lived as they died—unhonoured and unsung? The secrecy of this Jewish sect has been sufficiently described by Sir John Marsham.[h] With regard, however, to 'the death-like silence of all the Apostles,' we are of opinion that there is not sufficient evidence to prove such an assertion. Not only do we agree with all the best commentators in maintaining that there is a reference to the Essenes in the 2nd chapter of St. Paul's Epistle to the Colossians, but we believe also that there is *a complete condemnation of their errors and dogmas.* As this has not been sufficiently noticed by the commentators, we will at once proceed to prove the above proposition. In the 8th verse Paul warns the Christians at Colossæ to 'Beware lest any man spoil you through philosophy and vain deceit, after the tradition of men, after the rudiments (or elements) of the world, and not after Christ.' Now read what Josephus says: 'They also take great pains in studying the writings of the ancients, and choose out of them what is most for the advantage of the soul and body.'[i] From this passage we see, as Neander says,[k] that the Essenes 'sought to explore the powers of nature,' and that 'connected with their secret doctrines was a traditional knowledge.' In the 16th verse Paul goes on to say, 'Let no man therefore judge you in meat, or in drink, or in respect of an holiday, or of the new moon, or of the sabbath-days.' Not only had the Essenes an overrated esteem for the outward practices of religion, but in the strict observance of institutions, &c., received from their fathers, they would yield to no living Jew; especially in the superstitious observance of the sabbath, for on that day 'they would not,' says Dr. Beard,[m] 'remove a vessel from its place, even for the most pressing wants of nature.' What the Apostle says regarding meat applies, we are of opinion, only to the Essenes, for, according to Josephus, they were bound

---

[h] Can. Chr. Sæc., ix.
[i] Bell. Jud., ii. c. 8, s. 6. Whiston's translation.
[k] Church Hist., vol. i.
[m] Kitto's Biblical Cyclopædia, art. ' Essenes.'

by oath to avoid all food which had not been prepared by their own sect, and some, he says,[n] suffered death rather than partake of any other. But it is in the 18th verse that we have the strongest condemnation of the dogmas of Essenism; 'Let no man beguile you of your reward in a *voluntary humility* (or, as it may be rendered, *by humility*) and *worshipping of angels*, intruding into those things which he *hath not seen*, vainly puffed up by his fleshly mind;' with this verse the 23rd should be taken in connexion. Now, the candidates for admission into the sect were bound by an oath never to reveal to any mortal the names of the angels which were communicated to them. And there is no proof that the angels here mentioned had the same duties, &c., as those named in Revel. i. 20, although maintained by the writer whose opinion we are considering. 'There are,' says Josephus, 'also those among them who undertake to foretel things to come (*i. e.* intruding into those things which they have not seen), by reading the holy books, and using several sorts of purifications (or, as Neander says, "a particular method of ascetical preparation "), and being perpetually conversant in the discourses of the prophets.'[o]

From these considerations we therefore deny that 'St. Paul, the learned and philosophic apostle, bred up in all the learning of the most orthodox amongst the Jews, gives no sign that he had ever heard of such people' as the Essenes. Having satisfactorily, we think, answered all the objections brought forward against the commonly-received opinion that the Essenes are a Jewish sect, we will now proceed to consider the second proposition, viz. 'In the Judæan history of Josephus there is no notice taken of the new-born brotherhood of Christians.' This is a bold assertion, and one which should not have been so confidently made, seeing that scholars of no mean standing have maintained a different opinion; for it is wrong to say that the celebrated passage in the Antiquities of Josephus (xviii. c. 3, s. 3) 'has long been given up as a forgery by all scholars.' The passage is as follows: 'Now, there was about this time Jesus, a wise man (if it be lawful to call him a man), for he was a doer of wonderful works (a teacher of such men as receive the truth with pleasure). He drew over to him both many of the Jews and many of the Gentiles. (He was Christ, ῾Ο Χριστὸς οὗτος ἦν.) And when Pilate, at the suggestion of the principal men amongst us, had condemned him to the cross, those that loved him did not forsake him (for he appeared to them alive again the third day, as the divine prophets foretold these and ten thousand other wonderful things concerning him); and the tribe of Christians, so named from him, are not extinct at this day.'[p] The existence of this passage in Josephus is not denied by our opponent, for he says, 'True it is, *that an interpolated passage*, found in all the printed editions of Josephus, makes him take a special and a respectful notice of our Saviour.' To consider the whole passage as interpolated is to deny facts, for all the MSS. and Hebrew translations of Josephus possess it, and Baronius relates[q] that a MS. of the Antiquities was found in the Vatican library, translated into Hebrew, in which this passage 'was marked with an obelus,'[r] a thing no one would have done but a Jew. That Josephus knew of such a person as Jesus Christ is evident from the allusion to James, 'the brother of Jesus, who was called Christ' (τὸν ἀδελφὸν Ἰησοῦ τοῦ λεγομένου Χριστοῦ).[s] Eusebius was the first of the fathers who quoted the passage, and it was unchallenged till the 16th century. The majority of critics, however, support its authority as a whole, but differ in its extent; in Germany the great difficulty (the silence of Origen) is got over by considering the words which we include in brackets as interpolated. 'To me,' says Milner, in his History of the Church, 'Josephus seems to say just so much and no more of Christ as might be expected from a learned sceptic of remarkable good sense and supreme love of worldly things.' But although we should admit that the whole passage is interpolated, still we would not be justified in concluding that Josephus never alludes to the Christians; for, in the account already alluded to, of the martyrdom of James, we read that the high priest delivered (A.D. 62) James, the brother of Jesus called Christ, *and some others*, to be stoned; or, according to Neander, 'he caused James, with *some other Christians*, to be condemned to death by the Sanhedrim.'[t] It is, therefore, wrong to maintain, after reading this, that 'in the compass of 854 pages we do not find one passage, line, or fragment of a line, by which it can be known that Josephus ever heard of such a body as the Christians.' Of a truth such a sen-

---

[p] Whiston's translation.

Γίνεται δὲ κατὰ τοῦτον τὸν χρόνον Ἰησοῦς, σοφὸς ἀνήρ (εἴγε ἄνδρα αὐτὸν λέγειν χρή), ἦν γὰρ παραδόξων ἔργων ποιητής (διδάσκαλος ἀνθρώπων τῶν σὺν ἡδονῇ τἀληθῆ δεχομένων). Καὶ πολλοὺς μὲν Ἰουδαίων, πολλοὺς δὲ καὶ ἀπὸ τοῦ Ἑλληνικοῦ ἐπηγάγετο. (Ὁ Χριστὸς οὗτος ἦν.) Καὶ αὐτὸν ἐνδείξει τῶν πρώτων ἀνδρῶν παρ' ἡμῖν σταυρῷ ἐπιτετιμηκότος Πιλάτου οὐκ ἐξεπαύσαντο οἱ τὸ πρῶτον αὐτὸν ἀγαπήσαντες. (Ἐφάνη γὰρ αὐτοῖς τρίτην ἔχων ἡμέραν πάλιν ζῶν, τῶν θείων προφητῶν ταῦτά τε παὶ ἄλλα μυρία περὶ αὐτοῦ θαυμάσια εἰρηκότων). Εἰσέτι τε νῦν τῶν Χριστιανῶν ἀπὸ το δε ὠνομασμένων οὐκ ἐπέλιπε τὸ φῦλον.—Arch., lib. xviii.

[q] Ann. Eccles., an. 134.

[r] See Lardner's Works, vol. i., Appendix ix. and x. to his Life.

[s] Arch. xx. c. 9. This passage, like the former, has also been called in question; but Neander has shown, in his 'Planting of the Christian Church' (vol. i. note p. 367), that it is absurd to consider it as interpolated.

[t] Planting of the Christian Church.

tence would never have been written, if this advocate of a favourite theory had taken the advice of the poet,—

> Lock up thy senses, let no passion stir;
> Wake all to Reason—let her reign alone.

Now to explain this supposed omission of any allusion to 'a growing sect transcendently interesting,' in the writings of one who passed his infancy, youth, and manhood in the very midst of it, we have seventeen features of agreement, says the writer we review, taken from Josephus' description of the Essenes, which identifies them with the Christians of Palestine. As the most of these apparent religious similarities have been alluded to by several writers, and seeing Neander has fully answered them in his 'Life of Christ,' we will not go over the same ground, for, as that profound historian has remarked, 'This argument, by proving too much, proves nothing; on the same principle we might show a connexion between Christianity and every form under which mysticism has appeared and reappeared in the history of religion.' We will, therefore, at once proceed to consider the arguments brought forward to prove that the Essenes arose 'in the necessities of the epichristian generation.' This proposition is thought to be undeniable, from, first, the origin of the name; and, second, from their constitution as a society.

First. The origin of the name. To the question, 'who were the Sicarii and the Galileans?' our opponent gives the answer, 'they were semi-Christians.' His words are, 'We have little doubt that the Sicarii and the Zealots were both offsets from the same great sect of the Galileans, and that, in an imperfect sense, *all were Christians;* but also we believe that this very political leaven led to the projection from the main body of a new order called the Essenes,' because, he goes on to say, 'by tolerating the belief that they countenanced the Galileans or Sicarii, the primitive church felt that she would be making herself a party to their actions.' Now, to say that the Primitive Church had any connexion with the Galileans, Sicarii, and Zealots, is to contradict not only historical facts, but also the evidence of Scripture. We do not deny that the Galileans and Zealots were followers of Judas the Galilean, but we deny that they, along with the Sicarii, were followers, in any sense of the term, of Jesus Christ. For if we admitted this, then we must admit that 'the man Jesus' taught his disciples never to obey civil authority, and never to spread the Gospel by any other means than that of arms; that rapine, plunder, and murder are lawful; and that to kill and privately stab your enemy becomes a follower of 'the meek and lowly Jesus.' That these attacks upon the usages of society were made by the Jewish sects already mentioned, is evident from Josephus' Antiquities and Wars of the Jews. The Galileans taught that tribute ought not to be paid to

the Romans, and that the laws of Moses were to be defended by
the force of arms.   The Zealots are, it is true, alluded to in Scripture (Acts xxi. 20; xxii. 3; John xvi. 2); but they are not to be
confounded with those of that name who were followers of Judas,
and who perpetrated the greatest enormities, for they 'merely insisted,' says Horne, 'on the fulfilment of the Mosaic law, and by no
means went so far as those persons, termed Zealots, of whom we
read in Josephus.'   The Sicarii were so called from their using
the *sica*, a short cutlass, which they carried under the arm, as the
Italians do the *stiletto*, and privately stabbed in the daytime the
object of their hatred.[u]   It is said, we admit, that the description
given of these sects by Josephus is greatly exaggerated, and that
his statements must be qualified, as he is anything but trustworthy.
Since, however, scholars of the greatest erudition, from Baronius
down to Neander, have thought otherwise, the fidelity and veracity
of this faithful historian cannot suffer by being questioned by an
anonymous writer.   He goes on to state that this secret society of
the Essenes arose from the persecution which took place at Jerusalem, 'and its organization was most artful.'   They could not
call themselves 'the brethren,' as such a name 'had been too dangerous;' for to try by any means to stay the fiery persecution 'was
to solicit and tempt destruction, which could not be right.   What,
then, did the fathers of the church do?'   We read, 'that, during
a part of this epichristian age, "the churches had peace;"' and
why? just because they proceeded 'to hide themselves effectually.'
They said, 'Let there be darkness, let us muffle ourselves in thick
clouds which no human eye can penetrate.   And towards this
purpose let us take a symbolic name.'   In order that this name
might disarm the suspicion of the bloody Sanhedrim, it was 'derived from the very costume of the Jewish high priest.   This great
officer wore a breastplate, containing twelve stones representing
the twelve tribes; *and this was called the Essen.*   Consequently,
to announce themselves as the society of the Essen, was to express
a peculiar solicitude for the children of Israel.'   The persecution
at Jerusalem here alluded to occurred immediately after the death
of Stephen, and was chiefly caused by the Sanhedrim, who employed
Saul of Tarsus, a firm believer in the intolerant principles of the
Pharisaic system, to search out and imprison all those of the new
sect who, dwelling at Jerusalem, endeavoured to overthrow the
religion of his fathers.   The time, long and anxiously wished for,
at last arrived when 'the churches had rest throughout all Judea,
and Galilee, and Samaria.'   And why were the churches left unmolested?   There are two opinions as to the answer we should

---

[u] *Sicarii* literally means cutthroats.   Lardner calls them, 'Villains that went
with short swords concealed under their clothes.' — *Works*, vol. i.

give to this question: 1st, The sufferings undergone by the Jews
at Alexandria from the Egyptians, and the attempt of Petronius
(A. D. 39 or 40) to set up Caligula's statue in the temple at Jerusalem, completely engaged the Jews, so that they took no notice
of anything else; Philo and Josephus agree in representing the
concern of the Jews as very great and general. 2nd. The conversion of the chief persecutor, Saul, who, from being a demon in
human form, became, by the grace of God, one of the most learned
and courageous champions of the Christian church. The majority
of commentators are of this opinion, which is objected to chiefly
because St. Paul was then a young man (Acts vii. 58), and, though
active and intelligent, 'yet,' says Lardner, 'he could be no more
than an instrument in the persecution.' Either of these opinions
will hold good in point of fact; we are, however, inclined to agree
with Lardner, who says, 'I had no sooner read the account which
Philo and Josephus have given of the sufferings of the Jews in
Alexandria, and the imminent danger of ruin which that whole
people in Judea and other places were in, in the reign of Caligula,
but I concluded that this state of their affairs brought on the rest
of the Christian churches which St. Luke speaks of, and which
certainly happened about this time.'[x]

Seeing then that history, sacred as well as profane, gives us no
other reason than the cessation of the persecution by the Jews for
the churches having peace at this time, we must regard what is
said about the primitive Christians hiding or muffling themselves
in thick clouds which no human eye could penetrate as the pure
invention of a fertile imagination; and what is asserted regarding
the derivation of the name Essenes, we consider as just another
conjecture, which must be added to the number that have already
been given, for it is the general opinion that the origin and etymology of the word cannot now be clearly made out. Philo de-
duces it from ὅσιος, 'holy;' Salmasius says, they were named from
the town Essa; Calmet considers the Chasidim of the Psalms, and
the Assideans in the Maccabees, to be their true source; De
Wette says the name is from the Syriac word signifying 'pious;'
and Serrarius gives no less than twelve opinions concerning the
origin of their name. These different opinions show how absurd
it is to fancy that we can obtain anything even like an approximation to the true solution of this difficulty. But it signifies little,
even allowing that the name Essen is derived from חשׁן (as the
breastplate of the high-priest was called), for such a derivation
proves the Jewish, and not the Christian origin of the sect.

Secondly.—The constitution of the Society. It was thus constituted :—' By *arranging four concentric circles* about one mysterious centre, the Christian fathers were enabled to lead men onwards insensibly from intense Judaic bigotry to the purest form of Christianity. The outermost circle received those only whose zeal for Judaism argued a hatred of pagan corruptions, and therefore gave pledge for religious fervour. In this rank *all was Judaic*, and the whole Mosaic theology was cultivated.' In the second rank ' the eye was familiarized with the prophecies respecting the Messiah.' In the third, ' the attention was trained to the general characters of the Messiah, as likely to be realized in some personal manifestation :' and in what degree these characters met and were exemplified in Jesus Christ they were required to consider, and if the disciple retained his bigotry ' he is excluded from the inner ranks,' in which were ' placed, no doubt, all those only who were throughly Christians. The danger was from Christianity; and this danger was made operative only by associating with the mature and perfect Christian any false brother, any half Christian, or any hypocritical Christian. To meet this danger, oaths, pledges to God as well as to man, must be exacted. All this the apostles did.' Now this description of the Primitive Church is evidently maintained in order to show that it agrees with what Josephus says of the Essenes; ' they are parted *into four classes.*' We admit that the description may apply to the state of the Church *before the death of Stephen*, when the Gospel was preached to the Jews only, and when the Jewish converts generally conformed to the Mosaic ritual; but we cannot, however, maintain, without denying historical evidence, that it is at all suitable to any other period. For we know that after Stephen's martyrdom the persecution which ensued dispersed the Christians through all Judea, and through all Samaria. Then, and not till then, was the Gospel preached to the devout and idolatrous Gentiles. If we admit this, the description cannot apply to the Essenes, as it is asserted that they arose *during*, and not *after*, the persecution which arose at Jerusalem. Should it be said that the description can apply to the Christian church after this period, then how does it happen that there is not the remotest allusion to ' the four concentric circles about one mysterious centre' in the account which we have in the Acts of the conversion of Cornelius and his household? We might also ask why no ' oaths, pledges to God as well as to man,' were exacted by the apostle Peter on the day of Pentecost, when three thousand individuals were converted and baptized, being thereby admitted to the communion of the church : but as this event happened A.D. 33, the year in which Stephen died, according to Usher, we will not consider it as an illustration suitable for our present argument. But if ever there was a time for exercising 'the simple precaution of graduation,' it was when the great apostle of the Gentiles explained the Christian system to the philosophers of Athens from the Hill of Mars. Instead however of doing so, he spoke of the most mysterious—at least to them—of the Christian doctrines, viz. the resurrection from the dead, and the life to come. Thus it is evident that this hypothesis is entirely gratuitous and unworthy of further consideration. The strongest argument against the opinion that the Essenes arose 'in the epichristian generation' is the fact that the elder Pliny maintains that they existed long before even the name of Christ was known among men; he says they had been many thousand years in existence, living without marriage, and without the other sex: his words are, '*Ita per sæculorum millia, incredibile dictu, gens æterna est, in qua nemo nascitur.*'[y] It is said, however, that this is to be considered as a 'hyperbolical fairy tale.' But surely we are not justified in maintaining that Pliny's testimony is unworthy of notice, seeing that in the fourth book of Maccabees we find them mentioned as being established into a society before Hircanus was high-priest, about A.M. 3894, B.C. 110. From these considerations we are of opinion that ecclesiastical historians are perfectly right in classifying the Essenes among the Jewish sects. How presumptuous then to assert that, 'if the Essenes were not the early Christians in disguise, then was Christianity, as a knowledge, taught independent of Christ!' Is it Christianity never to change our garments till they are entirely worn out by time, and to think it the greatest sin to kindle a fire on the sabbath?[z] Is it Christianity to believe that fate governs all things, and that nothing befals men but what is according to its determination?[a] Is it Christianity to remain year after year excluded from the society of our fellowbeings? 'The first Christians formed themselves,' says Neander, 'into no monkish fraternities, nor lived as hermits, secluded from the rest of the world, but, as history shows us, continued in the same civil relations as before their conversion.'[b] Reasoning therefore from historical evidence, we are certainly entitled to conclude with Dr. Prideaux, 'that almost all that is peculiar to this sect is condemned by Christ and his apostles.'[c]

P. S.

---

[y] Nat. Hist., lib. 5, c. 17.

[z] Joseph., Bell., ii. c. 8, s. 9. Those of our readers who will take the trouble to read this section will see why we refrain quoting largely from it.

[a] Joseph., Ant., xiii. c. 5, s. 9.

[b] Planting of the Christian Church, vol. i.

[c] Connect., p. 2, b. 5.

MEN OR GOD?'—GAL. I. 8-12.

A CRITICISM.

' But though we or an angel from heaven preach any other gospel unto you than that which we have preached unto you, let him be accursed.

' As we said before so say I now again, If any man preach any other gospel unto you than that ye have received, let him be accursed.

' *For do I now persuade men or God?* ('Αρτι γὰρ ἀνθρώπους πείθω ἢ τὸν Θεόν;) or do I seek to please men? for if I yet pleased men, I should not be the servant of Christ.

' But I certify you, brethren, that the gospel which was preached of me is not after man;

' For I neither received it of man, neither was I taught it but by the revelation of Jesus Christ.'

THE above, the common translation of the words "Αρτι γὰρ ἀνθρώπους πείθω ἢ τὸν Θεόν (*Do I now persuade men or God?*), is strictly literal, and thoroughly correct. It is not possible, however, that the Apostle can mean to assert, or to imply, that he persuaded not men but God, in the common acceptation of the word *to persuade*, i. e. in the sense of *to induce, to prevail upon, or to seek to do so*; for in this, its ordinary sense, he did persuade men, and did not persuade God, and could not. Indeed, to persuade men, as he himself elsewhere asserts, was the very end and object of all his preaching. 'Knowing the terror of the Lord,' he says, '*we persuade men;* for we must all appear before the judgment-seat of Christ, that every one may receive the things done in the body according to that he hath done, whether it be good or bad.' How, then, are we to understand the demand here made, seeing that that demand implies that he did *not* persuade men, and that God he *did* persuade?

Commentators for the most part endeavour to avoid the difficulty that appears, at first sight, to be inseparable from a fair and literal translation of the words, by boldly telling us that the word πείθειν (*to persuade*) is sometimes employed in the sense of *to conciliate, to please,* or *to seek the favour of.*

' The sense of these words,' says Bloomfield, ' has been not a little controverted; and no wonder, considering their obscurity. Many eminent modern commentators, as *Luther, Erasmus, Vatablus, Crellius, L'Enfant,* and others mentioned by *Borger,* render them " Divinè suadeo, an humanè?" Not very different from this, is the interpretation of *Theophylact,* from *Chrysostom.* But I greatly prefer that of *Œcumenius, Theodoret,* and of the moderns, *Grotius, Hammond, Elsner, Wolf, Krebs, Wetstein, Koppe, Rosenmüller, Schleusner, Borger,* and others, who assign the following sense: Do I *seek to conciliate the favour of* men? or of God?'

' What πείθειν ἀνθρώπους ἢ τὸν Θεόν (*to persuade men* or *God*) means, must, says *Hammond*, be taken from the like phrase in the Old Testament, 1 Sam. xxiv., where the Greek hath these words: Ἔπεισε Δαβὶδ τοὺς ἄνδρας αὐτοῦ ἐν λόγοις, "David persuaded his men with words." The men that were with David were very eager to have him take the advantage against Saul, and kill him (ver. 4), and were ready to rise up against him to kill him (ver. 7); and David's speech to them took them off from this bloody purpose, and that is expressed by ἔπεισε—he *persuaded, appeased, pacified* them. Thus is it the office of a Rhetor, or advocate, πείθειν, to *persuade, i.e.* to *appease* the judge to the client whose cause is pleaded—*to propitiate* him.

' So also Matt. xxviii. 14. " If the Governor hear of it, *i.e.* of the soldiers being so negligent as to let Christ be stolen out of the grave which they were set to watch, πείσομεν αὐτὸν, we will *persuade* him," *i.e.* *appease* him, obtain his pardon for you, and (as it follows) will free you from all solicitude of securing yourselves from that heavy punishment that by the Roman laws was due to the watchman that fell asleep. By which it is clear that πείθειν is *to propitiate,* or *gain one's favour, to appease wrath* or *punishment, to avert displeasure.*

' And so here. *To persuade men,* is to say or teach those doctrines which will avert the displeasure of the persecuting Jews, which the Gnostic teachers did; and *to persuade God,* is to endeavour to say and preach that which may avert God's wrath, be acceptable to him, obtain and secure his favour.'

' The word which is here rendered *to persuade,*' says *Barnes,* ' has been very variously interpreted.' *Tindal* renders it, Do I now *seek the favour* of men or of God? And so *Doddridge*—Do I now *solicit the favour* of men or of God? This also is the interpretation of *Grotius, Hammond, Elsner, Koppe, Rosenmüller, Bloomfield,* &c.; and is undoubtedly the true interpretation.

' The word properly means to persuade or to convince, Acts xviii. 4, xxviii. 23; 2 Cor. v. 11. But it also means *to bring over to kind feelings, to conciliate, to pacify, to quiet;* as in 1 Sam. xxiv. 8; 2 Mac. iv. 25; Acts xii. 20; 1 Joh. iii. 19.'

Whether this be the true interpretation or not, it is unquestionably the most extensively adopted. But the passages that are usually produced in support of the same, are far, very far, from proving the admissibility of any such interpretation of the word, in the passage before us. None, perhaps, are more frequently insisted on in its support, than those referred to in the last of the above quotations; but in every one of these passages it is clear that the strict and proper meaning of the word is simply *to persuade,* in the ordinary acceptation of the word, viz. *to persuade* in the sense of *to prevail upon.* If these passages be quoted in full, this will, we trust, be manifest.

Acts xii. 20. And having made Blastus, the king's chamberlain, their friend; *i.e.* And having *persuaded* Blastus; viz. to befriend them.

Acts xiv. 19.   And there came thither certain Jews who *persuaded* the people, and, having stoned Paul, drew him out of the city, supposing he had been dead.

—— xix. 26.   Not alone at Ephesus, but almost throughout all Asia, this Paul hath *persuaded* and turned away much people.

1 John iii. 19.   Hereby we know that we are of the truth and shall *assure* our hearts before him.

1 Sam. xxiv. 8. (lxx.)   So David *stayed* (or *persuaded*) his servants with these words.

2 Mac. iv. 45.   But Menelaus, being now convicted, promised Ptolemy, the son of Dorymenes, to give him much money, if he would *pacify* (*i. e. persuade*) the king.

The strongest of these texts, and the one most frequently referred to, in support of the common interpretation, is the one first quoted.   There the translation, *to seek the favour of*, or *to make a friend of*, though not strictly literal, is admissible—the party persuaded being a *man*, a fellow-man, who is won over by persuasion to do a friendly action.   But it will by no means follow that the word will admit of such translation, or of such an interpretation, when used in reference to *God*.   It is not by persuasion that God's favour is secured.   The Apostle, in telling us that he persuaded not men but God, cannot, therefore, be supposed to have meant— that, as by persuasion one man prevails upon another—as by persuasion the men of Tyre and Sidon, for instance, made Blastus, the king's chamberlain, their friend, so by persuasion did he obtain, or seek to obtain, God's favour rather than man's.   Whatever may be the meaning of his words, this *cannot* be their meaning.

But there are others, who, understanding the word πείθειν (*to persuade*) in the sense of *to inculcate*, or *to preach*, have suggested that the demand, 'Do I now persuade men or God?' is simply tantamount to a declaration on the part of the Apostle that the doctrine taught by him was not of human origin—that his announcements were not the deductions of human reason, nor the dogmas of human authority, nor the inventions of human superstition; that, as he had already said in a verse preceding, he was an apostle not of men, neither by man, but that he spoke by revelation; or (if the term 'by inspiration' be preferred) by inspiration.[a]

There were other respects, indeed, in which he may be said to have preached or persuaded 'not men but God.'   Thus, he preached not human worthiness, but God's free grace; not the strength of

---

[a] Adversarii mei homines prædicant, ipsisque unice se approbare student; ego Deum. (*Beza.*)   Non de personis quibus suadetur, sed de rebus ipsis quæ suadentur hic agit; q. d.   Vos testes esse potestis me non humana sed mere divina suadere ac docere; nec humanum aliquid spectare, sed solam Dei gloriam (*Gomarus, Erasmus, Vatablus, Vorstius*).   Poli Synops. *in loc.*

Thus explained, the words *men or God?* are, of course, an *accusativus rei.*

human ability, but the Gospel *of God*, and the promises *of God*; but (judging from the context) the idea principally intended, may, we think, be presumed to have been as already stated, viz. that he spake *by revelation*.

This latter interpretation, however, has never been very generally received; partly, it would seem, because this usage of the word πείθειν, though not wholly without precedent (see, for instance, Acts xix. 8[b]), is unusual; and partly, perhaps chiefly, because of the apparent harshness of the supposition, that by the expression 'men or God' is meant, not the parties persuaded, but the doctrines taught.

If that interpretation be correct, it must be granted, indeed, that the sentiment supposed might have been more clearly expressed. If, for instance, the apostle, instead of asking, 'Do I now *persuade?*' had said, 'Do I now *preach* men or God?' or if, in the place of the expression 'men or God?' some other less metaphorical expression, some more common, some more hackneyed phrase had been employed—such, for instance, as, 'The doctrines of men or the truth of God,' 'Human traditions, or that which I am divinely commissioned to proclaim'—these, or equivalent expressions, would have been more conventional, and therefore less obscure. But the words actually employed, though somewhat obscure, are not so obscure as to render the interpretation proposed improbable; nor so obscure as to compel us to believe that πείθειν means *to conciliate*, or *seek the favour of*. If obscure, the obscurity is the same, let the interpretation be what it may; if obscure, it is simply needful that we understand the words 'men or God' as above suggested, and the obscurity is gone; if obscure, the expressiveness and the appropriateness of the phrase is its sufficient vindication.

If, then, the above, the less common interpretation, be not on other accounts improbable, there seems to be no reason for rejecting it upon the ground that the sentiment which it was intended to convey is expressed obscurely. The phraseology of St. Paul is often obscure—extremely obscure. Like any other man, he had his own peculiarities of thought and style. He never seems to cast about for 'clearer expressions' or for 'better words.' The words to his mind were, or seem to have been, the first (suited to his purpose) that presented themselves; and these, though it is not to be doubted that they were always, in some respect, per-

---

[b] 'Disputing and *persuading* the things concerning the·kingdom of God.' See also Thucyd. iii. 43: Δεινότατα πεῖσαι (to *persuade* things most mischievous);' and Soph. Œdip. Colon. 1442: Μὴ πεῖθ' ἃ μὴ δεῖ. '*Persuade* not that which is not right.'

ceived or unperceived, the most appropriate, were not always the most perspicuous. We may, if we will, wonder that, in a revelation intended for our guidance, every expression is not so clear as to be incapable of misapprehension, by at least the honest and sincere; and that every point, whether of doctrine or of practice, or of Church discipline and government, is not so distinctly laid down as to render a difference of belief impossible. But (as has often been remarked) the obscurities and uncertainties of Scripture have an obvious moral use, and are in strict analogy with the whole course of God's dealings with mankind.[c] God, had he seen fit, or had it (all things considered) been desirable, could doubtless have so moulded and controlled every expression, every word, therein contained, that nothing should have been uncertain, nothing obscure. But unless, upon the ground of its obscurities, we are prepared to reject Scripture altogether, we must take it as we find it. We may captiously wonder, or captiously object, not in reference to it only, but in reference to everything which we have from God; for, says Paley, 'it is seldom or never that we are able to make out a system of strict optimism—there being few cases in which, if we permit ourselves to range in possibilities, we cannot suppose something more perfect, something less objectionable, than what we have. The rain which falls from heaven—how partially and irregularly it is supplied—how much of it falls upon the sea, where it can be of no use—how often it is wanted where its use would be of the greatest! We could imagine, if to imagine were our business, the matter to be otherwise regulated. We could imagine showers to fall just where and when they would do good; always seasonable, everywhere sufficient; so distributed as not to leave a field upon the face of the globe scorched by drought, or a plant withering for lack of moisture. But does the difference between the real and the imagined case, or the seeming inferiority of the one to the other, authorise us to say that the present disposition of the atmosphere is not a production of the Deity?'

In the present instance, however, so slight is the obscurity of the words made use of, that it is almost an abuse of terms to speak of their obscurity at all. They are clearly susceptible of the interpretation which we have been attempting to defend; there is in that interpretation no violence offered to the signification of any one single word; whilst the sentiment which they are supposed to express is in thorough harmony with the context with which they stand connected, and in thorough harmony also with St. Paul's character of thought and of expression. The words themselves, notwithstanding their very slight obscurity, if

---

[c] Upon this point see also some most appropriate and very excellent remarks by he Rev. A. J. Morris of Holloway, in 'The Homilist' for May, pp. 54-56.

obscurity there be, are moreover most appropriate; for what possible substitute could so briefly and yet at the same time so forcibly express the importance attached by the Apostle to the reception of his doctrine as the word '*persuade?*' 'Do I now *preach?*' though more intelligible, would have been tame in comparison. 'Do I now *persuade?*' tells us more than that he preached. It brings him before us as one who was in earnest; as one who cared for the results of his preachings; as one who, knowing the truth and the vast importance of that which he was commissioned to proclaim, was anxious to impress upon others that conviction of their importance which he so felt himself. And then, with reference to the expression '*men or God,*' how could the fact that his sole criterion of truth was the revealed will and word of God—that he recognised in matters of religion no merely human authority, no merely human wisdom—be in so few words so forcibly or so impressively expressed?				J. C. K.

British Museum.

CORRESPONDENCE.

COULD THE APOSTLES FORGIVE SINS?

[Answers to Query of 'A Sincere Inquirer' in the last Number.]

Amongst the many disputed questions between the Latin Church and her opponents the above has appeared to many sincere inquirers as clothed with peculiar difficulties. In what way the question would be entertained by candid and impartial inquirers, were it to come before us totally new, is now perhaps impossible to say; but in the present state of the question the Latin Church has the advantage of it having appeared in her harness for ages. Whenever, therefore, the subject of remission of sins comes to be exactly inquired into, unavoidably the dogma so firmly established in the Church of Rome advances its pretensions in the mind, and the idea of a clerical absolution of individuals struggles for predominance. The Protestant yields imperceptibly to a certain extent to effrontery of assertion and established custom, and before he rallies to defend himself he has already to struggle with a puzzling plausibility. The entire question is one of a numerous class wherein modern habits and feelings have been so grafted by gradual changes upon supposed similar ancient ones that the dissimilarity strikes but comparatively few inquirers, while the cheat runs current through the multitude. On the other hand, the weakest reader of the word of God must feel convinced that the tenor of its teaching, doctrinal, historical, and experimental, establishes the fact that God alone can forgive sins, and that he will not forgive sin unless the sinner truly repent. To render, then, the power of forgiving individuals effectual to the apostles, they must have been granted the equally sublime power of searching the hearts of the applicants, and this surely none will be hardy enough to ascribe to them. The commission, therefore, to the apostles, although it included the remission and retaining of sin, yet by no means clothed them with authority to pronounce on the sins of individuals who may have had recourse to them for such purpose. And upon this point we have so clear a testimony in Holy Writ that I cannot imagine what objection can possibly be offered to it by any person admitting the validity of the New Testament. I refer to the history of Simon Magus as related in the eighth chapter of the Acts. When Philip the evangelist preached and performed miracles in Samaria, Simon became one of the congregation which rallied round him, and it is emphatically recorded that ' Simon himself believed also,' and in consequence was baptized. The Church at Jerusalem sent Peter and John to edify and establish the growing Church in Samaria, and by these of course Simon was recognised as a Christian brother; nor did the hollowness of his profession appear even to him styled the prince of the apostles until by ' his fruits' he proved that he had ' neither part nor lot in this matter' (ver. 21). Now this is a case exactly in point, and the mode of the apostle in treating it should be considered as absolutely decisive. Suppose an objector to observe that Peter could not absolve him because Simon did not repent; this objection is perfectly abortive, because the apostle most appropriately makes supposition concerning the reality of repentance, and the consequence immediately resulting. ' Repent, therefore, of this thy wickedness, and'—here, if ever, should we meet with the dogma of the Latin Church, but Peter dreamed of no such power in after years to be attributed to him, and which power would have authorised him to adopt the language of the priests of the Roman Church—' and I will give you absolution.' But far otherwise, the apostle's declaration is in the fullest sense protestant in its principle, and perfectly accordant with the testimony of Holy Writ in every other passage where the subject is treated of or alluded to: ' Pray God if perhaps the thought of thine heart may be forgiven thee.' The commissions, then, to the apostles then mentioned (Matt. xvi. 18, 19, and John xx. 23) were not by any means believed by the apostles themselves as bestowing on them the power of specifically absolving from sin any individual presenting himself for that purpose, nor was such a doctrine hinted at even among the early Christians. In the present instance, among all his errors, Simon himself never thought of such a refuge. The power of the keys bestowed upon Peter and the other apostles perfectly agrees with the previous simile of a magnificent building to which Christ in Matt. xvi. 18 compares his Church. They were to go forth into the whole world with the power of opening this glorious temple for the reception of believers, and of course remission and retaining of sin, loosing and binding, attended every delivery of their commission to the sons of men. To this inference we possess the inspired ratification of St. Luke, who sums up the whole commission in one verse (xxiv. 47), ' that repentance and remission of sins should be preached in his name among all nations, beginning at Jerusalem.' But what is still more coincident and remarkable, Peter himself, who was favoured by the first use of the spiritual keys both to Jews and Gentiles, in his very first public proclamation of his master's doctrine explains it identically in the same way (Acts ii. 37, 38) : ' Now when they heard this, they were pricked in their hearts, and said unto Peter and to the rest of the apostles, Men and brethren, what shall we do ? Then said Peter unto them, Repent and be baptized, every one of you, in the name of Jesus Christ, for the remission of sins.'

Like many other customs of the Latin Church, the present mode of confession adopted by her is, to use a homely phrase, at the best but the mere ghost of a primitive custom. Whenever a member of any of the churches had so acted as to be debarred from communion, upon repentance such member expressed in the public assembly sorrow for the past conduct, and hope that by God's grace his or her future course might be truly consistent. As long as the churches retained the vivid feelings of their primitive devotedness this apologetic expression of feeling was gladly given and as considerately received, not as a matter of prying curiosity or of satirical comment, but as a subject to be rejoiced in by all parties. But when the numbers of Christians began far to exceed their amount of fervent feeling, worldly sentiments, envyings, and indifference all but transmuted the spiritual congregation to a worldly assembly. Henceforward the idea of standing up before such a meeting to acknowledge any transgression or number of transgressions was so irksome that a more than ordinary amount of assurance was required to perform the task. If the male portion of the community felt the growing evil, to the female portion it became all but insuperable, and therefore we have on record that in the church of Constantinople a particular case was met by a new contrivance. A rich and influential matron was placed in this disagreeable predicament, and could not or would not meet the ordeal. A medium course was adopted. One of the deacons was authorised to wait upon the nervous lady to receive the confession, which was thus delivered by proxy, and the expedient was found so happy that it very probably became an established custom very rapidly, forming a precedent to be universally adopted, though of course, as similar causes produce similar effects, this custom may have been adopted in other churches independently. The Magister Sententiarum mentions distinctly that it was introduced into the Latin Church by a pope whom he calls Leo, and who, as he affirms, alleged as a reason for such a change the impropriety of requiring men to discover their secrets and crimes before their enemies and others who would be on the watch to take advantage of them. The ecclesiastics, soon discovering the immense treasury which the arrangement rolled into their finances, took care to modify the system until it finally embraced all the disgusting monstrosities of auricular confession as disgraceful to those who submit to it as it is derogatory to their allegiance to God.

C. H. I.

To 'A Sincere Inquirer.'

Sir,—In reading the Bible we meet with several passages which are difficult to be explained. Some have an inherent difficulty, others a connectional, and others a conventional difficulty. By inherent difficulty I mean that which arises from the nature of the subject treated, such as, for instance, when an attempt is made to present spiritual ideas in human language, or to clothe infinite subjects in a finite form. By connectional difficulty I mean that which arises from the connection in which the passage stands, or from the fact of an allusion being made to some person, place, thing, or event, with the history of which we are at present unacquainted. By conventional difficulty I mean that which we find in certain passages which have been from time to time abused and misquoted by writers and speakers, darkening counsel by words without knowledge. Many such passages unfortunately are to be found in the Bible, and it seems to me that the greatest part of the difficulty attaching to such passages as do apparently imply that Christ did bestow the power of forgiving sins on the apostles, arises from the fact that some men have claimed this power for themselves, or for a certain class of persons in the Church. It is well known that the Church of Rome claims this prerogative for its officers, and that Protestants deny their claim to any such prerogative. However, it seems to me that your question aims at the root of the controversy— Had the apostles power to forgive sins? for, if it can be proved that they had not, then neither can their successors have any such power; therefore I shall confine myself to examine what answer the New Testament will give to this question. I shall, therefore, in the first place examine those passages which seem to imply that Christ did confer the power of forgiving sins upon his apostles; and, secondly, what may be gathered from the general conduct and conversation of the apostles themselves on this point. The passages most in point are Matt. xvi. 19, xviii. 18, and John xx. 23. I think that, in order to expound these fairly, we must not confound them as meaning the same thing, but as referring to different conceptions. Every passage discloses a new element, and admits of a new idea. For instance, in Matt. xvi. 19, we have the idea of the keys and of binding and loosing connected with one person; in ch. xviii. 18, we have the idea of binding and loosing, but without the keys, joined with all the apostles; and in John xx. 23, we have the idea of binding and loosing *sin* connected with all the apostles. Thus, though we have some new elements added to the original idea, yet others are dropped, so that we are obliged rather to regard these passages as containing different conceptions rather than a development of one and the same truth. In Matt. xvi. 19, we find our Lord addressing Peter alone, and presenting him with the keys of the kingdom of heaven as well as the power to bind and loose. The occasion of these words was that Peter had uttered a full and free confession of his faith in the divinity of our Lord Jesus Christ; in which confession Jesus recognises the elements of divine revelation, which was to him a proof that the spiritual nature of Peter was more fully developed than that of any of his fellow disciples; and that it had pleased the Father to reveal unto him first the great mystery and the fundamental truth of the kingdom of heaven. Therefore, since Peter was thus well fitted, both by natural temperament as well as early spiritual acquaintance with divine truth, to be an active agent in setting up the kingdom of heaven, Christ is pleased to confer upon him the power of opening the door of the Church to its widest extent both for Jews and Gentiles. This he did effectually by his sermon on the day of Pentecost, and that at the house of Cornelius. What I judge, therefore, as you will perceive, to be the meaning of the keys of the kingdom of heaven is the power, or rather the honour, of being the first to show forth the plan of salvation in its adaptedness to the world at large; to proclaim that Jews and Gentiles were fully welcome into the kingdom of heaven. We find that the power of binding and loosing, which is here conferred on Peter alone, is in ch. xviii. 18 extended likewise to all the other apostles. The connection of that verse proves that it entirely relates to church government and discipline. The meaning seems to me to be, that whatever you as my inspired apostles shall ordain for the future conduct of the churches which shall be planted by you, the same shall stand as of divine appointment (Acts xv. 28, 29); and whenever the churches shall put in execution those rules which you shall give them in order to exclude their unruly members, those members shall be fully excluded; and in conformity with these rules, the Church will have the power to revoke its sentence, and receive again into its communion the member or members which it formerly excluded (1 Cor. v. 3–5, and 2 Cor. ii. 6–8). We must bear in mind here that Christ spoke to the apostles as inspired persons, and of churches conforming entirely to the rules laid down by them.

We now pass on to John xx. 23. Here we are presented with a new idea altogether. This passage refers to something different from the others; the other passages, as we have shown, relate to the preaching of the gospel and governing the Church. But this verse treats of remitting and retaining sins; it must, therefore, refer to some personal transactions which were to take place between the apostles and their fellow-men. It seems to me, therefore, that these words imply the healing power which was given to the apostles. The Greek verb, which is here translated *remit*, is used in Matt. ix. 2–6 and Mark ii. 5–9, in order to denote the act of healing. Christ here confers upon them the power of freeing men from bodily diseases which sin had brought upon them, in order that they might be more easily persuaded to believe the gospel preached by the apostles, which showed them the way to Jesus Christ, who was able to deliver the soul from sin and its spiritual consequences. The latter part of the verse seems to refer to the authority which was given to the apostles to punish certain offenders in a miraculous manner. Such was the dealing of Peter with Ananias and Sapphira, and Paul with Elymas the sorcerer. Thus far we have found nothing in these passages analogous to the conception the phrase 'pardoning sins' gives us; their real meaning, if I have succeeded in bringing it forth, seems to be very different from that: it remains for us, therefore, just to inquire whether the apostles in their conduct or conversation ever manifested any consciousness of such an authority to pardon sins being conferred upon them; for if they did show at any time that they believed themselves to have this power, then our conclusion must be false; but, on the other hand, if they never acted as those who had any such authority, it is a strong presumptive evidence that they understood these commissions something similar to the manner in which we have explained them. As cases in point I shall cite Acts ii. 38 and viii. 22, where Peter directs his hearers to God as the only one who can forgive sins. Even so early as the day of Pentecost we find that the apostles felt themselves incapable of forgiving sins; all they could do was to direct their inquiring and penitent hearers to God. Peter, in addressing Simon Magus, speaks as having himself no power to pardon the sins of one individual. The same thing we gather from the Epistles of Paul and John, viz. that it is God alone can forgive sins, and that all the power which the apostles ever had was that they were authorized to set forth the gospel as the plan which God had wrought out and revealed for the salvation of all men, and to accompany their preaching with signs and wonders.

Hoping that the above remarks will help you towards a satisfactory solution of your difficulties,

Rhayader.

I remain yours obediently,
RHYS GWESYN JONES.

SIR,—I beg to suggest to 'A Sincere Inquirer' that there surely is not even the semblance of contrariety between the truth that 'God alone can forgive sins,' and the clearly revealed fact that Christ committed to His Apostles and their true successors in the ministry, power, not merely to 'declare,' but even to 'pronounce,' *i. e.* to deliver the judicial sentence of, the 'absolution and remission of their sins' to all who 'truly repent and unfeignedly believe.' The terms of the commission received by the Apostles, 'As my Father hath sent me, even so send I you,' 'Whosoever sins ye remit, they are remitted unto them,' 'I appoint unto you a kingdom as my Father has appointed unto me,' 'Lo, I am with you always, even unto the end of the world,' clearly imply that they, and in them their true successors, 'received the Holy Ghost,' in order that their acts might serve, *ministerially,* to convey the free grace of forgiveness, of which God alone is the *origin,* to all who should not, through the want of the requisite qualifications, oppose any obstacle to the operation of that grace.

That such is the teaching of the Church of England is clear, from her service for the Ordination of Priests, to each of whom the ordaining bishop applies the words of Christ to the Apostles; and from the form of absolution prescribed in the Visitation of the Sick. The following comment from Bishop Sparrow's *Rationale,* on the form of 'Absolution or Remission of Sins, to be pronounced by the Priest alone standing,' is to the point:—'If our confession be serious and hearty, this absolution is effectual as if God did pronounce it from heaven; so says the Confession of Saxony and Bohemia, and the Augsburg Confession (xi., xii., xiii.), and so says St. Chrysostom in his fifth homily or essay, "Heaven waits and expects the priest's sentence here on earth; and what the servant rightly binds or looses on earth, that the Lord confirms in heaven;" St. Augustin, and St. Cyprian, and general antiquity say the same.' It might be added that Cranmer, Jewell, and a continuous series of standard writers, from the Reformation downwards, concur in bearing the same testimony to the truth of this branch of that article of our Christian faith which relates to the 'forgiveness of sins.' Bishop Pearson observes that to 'deny the Church this power of absolution is the heresy of Novatian.' *

I am, Sir, your obedient servant,
CLERICUS.

INTERPRETATION OF ACTS vii. 18.

Whether ἄχρις οὗ ἀνέστη κ.τ.λ. is properly translated in the common English Version?

[Answers to Query of R. B. B. in the last Number.]

Sir,—The Syriac, Vulgate, and all the modern versions which I have consulted, translate ἄχρις οὗ by *until* or its equivalents. It is surely wrong to say that the Eng. Vers. 'does not truly state the historical fact,' for the idiom here employed is common to all languages, and founded in nature. The writer has not said that they *did not* increase after the βασιλεὺς ἕτερος arose any more than that they *did* increase, both being foreign from his intention, which is to state the fact of their increase *until* the period introduced by the 20th verse.

Again, it is erroneous to say ' neither does our version translate οὗ,' for ἄχρις οὗ = *until*; and, as in many other languages, is an expression composed of an adverb or preposition and relative pronoun. Thus, Heb. עַד אֲשֶׁר; Chal. עַד דִּי; Syr. ܟ݂ܡܳܐ; Lat. *quo usque;* Fr. *jusqu'à ce que;* Germ. *bis dass;* Gr. μέχρι οὗ; Eng. (full form), *till that,* &c. How then can οὗ be untranslated?

But suppose οὗ = *when* (or *what time,* Ps. lvi. 3, Dan. iii. 5, Eng. Vers.), our conclusion must be the same, for *till when* = until.

The truth is that ἄχρις here is a preposition governing the genitive, as in Luke xvii. 27, ἄχρι ἧς ἡμέρας = till what day, *i. e.* the day on which; the expression, too, is the same, except that there the noun ἡμέρα is supplied, and here χρόνος is understood.

There is no difference in meaning between ἄχρι and ἄχρις. The form in ι is more common before consonants, and that in ς before

---

* On the Creed (Burton's edition), p. 436.

vowels; both forms occur before aspirated vowels. In 2 Macc. xiv. 15, we have ἄχρι αἰῶνος, but it is not common. The use of the words in the classics is similar to that in the New Testament. Two other words which have the same variety of form are αμφι and μεχρι— αμφίς, μέχρις, under the same circumstances and with no change of sense.

ἄχρις οὗ does sometimes mean *while* in the New Testament, which can in every case be accounted for. In Acts vii. 18, however, that sense is neither necessary nor proper. From what I first said it is not necessary; neither is it proper, because the expression ' the people increased and multiplied in Egypt, during which (time) another king arose,' is unintelligible; and instead of regarding the accession of the king or dynasty as a single definite act, would treat it as occupying a continued period. This is the whole difference between *till* and *while*. *Till* or *until* implies a previous period and its transactions, but fixes attention upon their end; *while* describes the period itself, with little reference to its end.

In conclusion, I cannot admit that ἄχρις οὗ takes its meaning from what precedes in ver. 17, but from what follows in ver. 18, and therefore accept the present translation.

I am, Sir, yours, &c.

London, July 21, 1852.   B. H. C.

Sir,—Your correspondent R. B. B. is mistaken in his proposed emendation of the Authorized Version in Acts vii. 18: ἄχρι, μέχρι, ἀμφί, οὕτω, and other words are written with or without a final ς, without any difference of signification. The ς is purely euphonic, and a matter of taste, though it is often found before a vowel; ἄχρις οὗ, like ἕως οὗ, can only be rendered *till*. Nor is the historical fact misstated. The following remarks from Gesenius on the usage of the Hebrew particle עַד, *until*, will, I think, satisfy your correspondent :—' It has been often observed . . . . . that the particle עַד sometimes also includes the times *beyond* the stated limit; but this is manifestly false, so far as this is supposed to lie in the power of this particle from any singular usage of the Hebrew language. But, on the other hand, it is not less certain that the sacred writers have not stated the extreme limit in places of this kind, but have mentioned a nearer limit without excluding the time beyond. When any one, setting out on a journey, says to a friend, Farewell *till* we meet again ! he is *now* indeed resting on this nearer limit, although wishing well to his friend after his return as well. In the same manner are we to judge of the passages in Ps. cxii. 8; Dan. i. 21; Gen. xxviii. 15; 1 Tim. iv. 13.'

Whether *until* marks rigorously a *terminus ad quem*, as it is called, or is to be taken in the looser way, as exemplified in the above passages, may at times have to be decided by other than grammatical principles. In Matt. i. 25, for instance, the sense of ἕως οὗ is connected with a controversy to which a very undue importance has been attached by many. Professor Campbell remarks on the passage, ' In regard to the preceding clause, Joseph knew her not until, ἕως οὗ, all we can say is, that it does not necessarily imply his knowledge of her afterwards. That the expression suggests the affirmative rather than the negative can hardly be denied by any candid critic.' On this point the opinion of Neander was quoted in the January Number of the ' Journal of Sacred Literature,' p. 463. It has long appeared to me that Ps. lxix. 8 alone is decisive of the question.

As to the question proposed by ' A Sincere Inquirer,' I think there can be no doubt that the absolute forgiveness of sins is a power that never was or could be delegated to any creature. The apostles in no instance claimed it. But prophets are not uncommonly said to do that which, in fact, God alone does, when they declare the divine will (see *e. g.* Jer. i. 7, 10; Ezek. ix. 1, 5; xliii. 3). Mr. Seymour, in his interesting volume, ' Mornings among the Jesuits at Rome,' pp. 64, 65, on the subject of binding and loosing, very aptly illustrates the point by a reference to Lev. xiii. The priest declared or pronounced the man unclean (LXX. μιανεῖ, shall *defile* him) when he was already, in fact, unclean: so again, the priest (καθαριεῖ) shall *cleanse* him, when he was already free from leprosy. In either case the priest is said to do that which he only declared and pronounced to be already done by God. So the apostles, in binding or loosing the sinners, were to declare, like the Jewish priest, forgiveness, or the reverse. See also verses 3, 6, 11, 13, &c., of the chapter above quoted.

Even in the Papacy itself there have been found those who have opposed the doctrine of absolute and unlimited absolution. ' John of Salisbury, that zealous champion of the hierarchy, wrote thus to Pope Alexander the Third, in the name of the Archbishop of Canterbury (Ep. 193), "Undoubtedly, to the Pope all things are allowable—that is, all things that belong by divine right to ecclesiastical authority. He is free to make new laws, and to do away the old ones; only it is not in his power to change anything which, by the word of God, has eternal validity." I might venture to assert that not even Peter himself can absolve any one from his guilt who perseveres in sin or in the will to sin; that even he has received no such key as gives him power to open the door of the kingdom of heaven for an impenitent person.'— Neander's *Church History,* vol. vii. p. 269 (Bohn's ed.).

' Peter Lombard declared that the power to bind and to loose bestowed on the priest did not consist in this, that he actually had it in his power to forgive sins and confer justification, which was the work of God alone. The priest could only declare the judgment of God (*ostendere hominem ligatum vel solutum*), and the priestly sentence was valid only when it agreed with the divine. He distinguished, therefore, between absolution in the sight of God and in the view of the Church,' &c.—*Id.* p. 482.

Faithfully yours,

Teignmouth.   G. J. W.

JUDICIAL ASTROLOGY BASED ON THE ' YEAR-DAY ' PRINCIPLE.

DEAR SIR,—I believe the students of prophecy are not in general aware of the fact that the ' year-day' principle forms the basis of judicial astrology; at least, I have never met any one who knew it, and I do not recollect ever seeing the fact alluded to in any commentary, treatise, or dissertation on the subject, although I have been a student of prophecy for thirty years.

Some years ago I felt a desire to know the elements of astrology, and this was one of the first peculiarities of that interesting remnant of antiquity that attracted my notice, and the conviction was as sudden as it has been permanent that the language of prophecy in respect to numbers was the language of astrology—a language familiar with all the inhabitants of the ancient world, as, according to Herodotus, every Babylonian wore a signet, and that signet, as we know from the specimens lately dug up in the ruins of Babylon, usually bore an astrological device. Daniel and Ezekiel both lived in Babylonia when they employed the ' year-day' type, and Moses was just coming out of Egypt, another astrological country, when he employed it; besides, the year of 360 days is the old astrological year—in fact, it still is the astrological year.

But let us observe the ' year-day' principle as employed by astrology.

An arc of direction is the distance of a planet from a point in which it will make a configuration with another planet—say, a square, a trine, a conjunction, or opposition; and whatever be the amount of that arc of direction in degrees, these degrees are converted into time by allowing, according to Ptolemy, *a year for every degree* and *a month for every five minutes of a degree.* This proceeds upon the principle of the old and venerable division of the year, like the circle, into 360 parts. But later and more mathematical astrologers have changed this system, and they measure or equate their time by observing in the almanac how long the sun would take to travel from the beginning of the arc to the end of it; and if he take 15 or any other number of days, they call *these days years*, and say the event will take place in 15 years—that is, a year for a day. Two hours are equal in equation to one month.

This analogical or typical theory is the very foundation of astrology. It could have no existence without it, and therefore it (*i. e.* the ' year-day' theory) must be of immemorial antiquity. This accounts for the familiarity of Moses with the ' year-day' language, learned as he was in all the Egyptian lore; and it may equally account for the use of the same language by the prophetic speech of Daniel and Ezekiel during their residence in the astrological region of Chaldea.

But the ' year-day' principle goes a little farther; for if a day represents a year, four minutes must also represent a year, for the sun moves round the heavens in 24 hours, and therefore he moves through one degree of the circle in four minutes. But this one degree represents a year; therefore the four minutes represent a year also, for they represent a degree; and this also is a fundamental principle of astrology. Supposing you are born when the moon is within 15° of the midheaven, then, in astrological language, your moon comes to its meridian when you are 15 years of age (I speak in round numbers merely to illustrate the subject in outline); but it passes through these 15 degrees in one hour, and therefore a movement of one hour represents a period of life equal to 15 years, or four minutes to one year. In astrology, therefore, one year, one day, and four minutes, are synonymous, and without this astrological triplicity the science must perish, for each is indispensable to the other.

Nor is it at all derogatory to the spirit of prophecy to use astrological language any more than to indulge the wise men of the East with an astrological direction on the Star of Bethlehem. Besides, the prophetic numbers themselves are cycles; 1260, 2300, and their difference, 1040, are all cycles, and the 2520 is a double cycle; and there is a beautiful propriety in making use of the language of astrology in sacred numerical prophecy; for of all the ancient sciences, astrology is the one which most distinctly and reverently maintains by professing to demonstrate the doctrine of a particular providence. Its corruption is one thing, and its fundamental principle is another. It may be false with a remnant or a germ of truth in it, and it may be corrupt with a most religious and divine origin, or divine indulgence, for God has spoken to men by dreams and visions, and by teraphim, and Urim and Thummim, and many other ways of the gentiles, and, for aught we know, by astrology too: at all events, here is the language of astrology employed as a vehicle for the most magnificent prophecies that have been recorded in the pages of revelation.

Yours, &c.

J. S.

HEROD AND HERODIAS.

A CORRESPONDENT has called our attention to a statement made by the Bishop of Exeter, in a speech delivered in the House of Lords (Feb. 25, 1851), on a motion for the second reading of 'a Bill to make lawful marriages within certain prohibited degrees of affinity,' and has expressed a wish that we should submit it to the investigation of our readers. It may be remembered that the object of the bill was to legalize marriage with a deceased wife's sister, and that it was rejected, being strongly opposed by the Bishop of Exeter and others. Referring to the case of Herod Antipas, who 'had taken his brother Philip's wife,' and who imprisoned John the Baptist because he had rebuked this iniquity, and declared 'it is not lawful for thee to have her,' the Bishop declares that the former husband of Herodias was then dead, and that consequently the offence reprobated by the

Baptist was not, as usually supposed, adultery, in taking the wife of his living brother, but incest in marrying the wife of his deceased brother. As a point involving the correct interpretation of a transaction recorded in the Gospels, this becomes a question of some biblical interest; and we therefore request such of our readers as may be inclined to investigate this question to favour us with their views upon it as a matter of fact and criticism, without regard to the special interests involved in it.

To render the points intelligible, we subjoin the Note, as appended to his published speech, in which the Bishop of Exeter explains and vindicates the view he has taken.

' Josephus' account corresponds with that of the sacred writers, except that he calls Herodias' former husband by the family name of Herod, it being common, in those times, to use either the individual or family name. Thus Dio Cassius (1. 55) calls Herod the Great's eldest son, Archelaus, simply " Herod of Palestine." " Herod Agrippa is called by St. Luke (Acts xii.) five times Herod; by Josephus, repeatedly Agrippa."—(Noldius de Vita et Gestis Herodum, n. 209, who gives many other instances, n. 207–217.) Hudson also (on Josephus, Ant. 18, 15, 1) mentions that there is nothing more remarkable, that, of Herod's nine sons, one should be called Philip, another Herod Philip, than that one should be called Antipater, another Antipas, being the same name. He had two sons, whom Josephus calls Herod without any further distinction than their mother's name (De Bello Judaico, 1, 18, 4).

' To the account of the Evangelists Josephus adds the fact that the former husband was dead. His account is, " Herodias their sister [*i. e.* sister of Agrippa and Aristobulus] marries Herod, the son of Herod the Great by Mariamne, daughter of Simon the High Priest, and they had a daughter called Salome, *after whose birth* Herodias, being minded to break her country's laws, marries Herod, brother, on the father's side, to her husband, having parted from him *while yet living*."—(Antiq. l. 18, c. 5, § 4.) By "the laws of her country," Josephus, writing for the Romans, means the laws of Moses, *i. e.* the law of God. He speaks in exactly the same way, of the same incest, in the case of Archelaus, who had married his brother's wife, after the brother had been put to death by his father. In both cases Josephus lays the stress upon its being against " the country's laws," and, in both, notices that the brother had left children, which took away the only exception allowed by the Levitical law. " Transgressing *the law of his country*, he (Archelaus, the Ethnarch] married Glaphyra, the daughter of [king] Archelaus, *having been* the wife of his brother Alexander, *by whom also she had children*, it being a thing strictly forbidden (ἀπώμοτον) to the Jews to marry brothers' wives."—(Ant. 17, 13, 1.)

' Now, 1st. Adultery is not simply against the Levitical law; it is against all law—the Roman also. 2nd. Josephus himself explains that by " the law of the country" he means the law by which it was strictly forbidden to the Jews to marry brothers' wives. 3rd. All three Evangelists (Matt. xiv. 3; Mark vi. 17; Luke iii. 19) dwell on the fact that he had " his brother Philip's wife." St. Mark uses the same word as Josephus, that he had " married" her. None of the Evangelists, nor Josephus, say that it was adultery. 4th. Josephus expressly says that she had " left him when alive," which he could not have said, had not the husband been then dead. He adds, as an addition to her guilt, that she " had quitted him when living" (ἀποστᾶσα ζῶντος).

' The origin of the supposition of Baronius and others, that Philip was alive when St. John Baptist rebuked Herod, was that they assumed that " Philip" was " Philip the Tetrarch." Whereas Josephus expressly says that " Philip the Tetrarch married (—not Herodias, but—) Salome, the daughter of this Herodias, and that, he dying childless, Aristobulus, son of Herod, the brother of Agrippa, married her." Josephus also mentions that Herod the Great had made this " Herod, his son by the daughter of the high-priest," his successor, in case of the death of Antipater (Ant. 17, 3, 3); but that he struck him out of his will on discovering that his mother Mariamne had known and concealed his son Antipater's design to poison him (ib., c. 4, n. 2). This Herod Philip, then, being in a private station, is the less spoken of; and his wife Herodias, being (Josephus relates, Ant. 18, 7, 1) an ambitious woman, was probably, therefore, the more tempted to desert her husband. There is then no ground to set Josephus at variance with the Evangelists; the more, since Josephus' account of the family of Herod is so minute, and his history was authenticated by King Agrippa. So far from being at variance with one another (as Baronius has assumed), the Evangelists and Josephus remarkably agree with one another, with the slight difference that one gives the family, the other the personal, name. The well-known fact that one person bore two names (as Matthew and Levi), which is plain from the Gospels themselves, removes the only semblance of difference between the Evangelists and Josephus (Vita Josephi, § 65, p. 33, ed. Huds.). Tertullian, an early authority, assumes that Philip was dead when St. John Baptist rebuked Herod. (Adv. Marc. iv. 34.) "John, rebuking Herod, because against the law he had married the wife of his *deceased* brother, he having a daughter by her (the law no otherwise permitting this—nay, enjoining it, unless the brother died childless, that so seed should be raised up to him by his brother and his wife), had been cast into prison, and afterwards slain by the same Herod."

'Since the above was written I have seen that the same line of argument is adopted by Lardner (Credibility of the Gospels, p. 1, b. 1, c. 5) " on the different names given to Herodias' first husband by the Evangelists and Josephus." Lardner observes moreover that the title "Tetrarch," "King," &c., is uniformly added in Holy Scripture, so that the fact that the three Evangelists speak of Philip in this place, without any addition, is in itself a presumption that he was not the Tetrarch. In a word, it is a mere assumption that Philip, whose wife Herod married, was Philip the Tetrarch. The Evangelists say nothing to identify them, but rather distinguish them in that the Tetrarchs have their title added, this Philip has not. Josephus clearly and repeatedly distinguishes them.

' I may add that even Bellarmine (De Matrim. Sacr. i. 27, col. 1394) allows that it was forbidden in the time of Herod, not as adultery, but because marriage with the brother's wife was then forbidden by the law of God. "Toto tempore Joannis lex Mosis vigebat, et tenebatur Herodes, qui eam legem profitebatur, observare. Non licebat autem ei, secundum legem, habere uxorem fratris sui, sive is viveret, sive mortuus esset, quia proles ex illo matrimonio jam nata erat, nimirum filia illa Herodiadis."

' To us, surely, this is conceding the whole question. We shall hardly be brought to think that what three Evangelists have recorded as the only cause of the martyrdom of the forerunner of our Lord, was part of the carnal ordinances which were done away by his coming.'

NOTICES OF BOOKS.

Karl Lachmann, eine Biographie von Martin Hertz.
Berlin, 1851.

The late Professor Charles Conrad Frederick William Lachmann of Berlin is so intimately connected with modern textual criticism of the New Testament, that students of sacred literature can do no other than feel under obligation to Martin Hertz for thus presenting them with the particulars of his life.

Lachmann was born at Brunswick. March 4, 1793; and in that city he received his early education. In 1809 he became a student at Leipsic, and even then he was interested in the subject of New Testament Criticism. His stay at Leipsic was but short; for in the same year he removed to Göttingen, where he continued his studies until 1813. That university at that time was included in the ephemeral kingdom of Westphalia (whose only sovereign, Jerome Buonaparte, is the sole survivor not only of Napoleon's brothers, but also of all who then in Europe bore the regal title); and thus, after the battle of Leipsic, the University of Göttingen was involved in the resulting changes in common with all that depended on Jerome's government at Cassel; and in consequence of this condition of things Lachmann returned for some months to his father's house at Brunswick. In 1814 he obtained the degree of Doctor of Philosophy from the University of Halle; and in the following year we find him turning from studies to arms. He was busily occupied at Göttingen with the preparation of an edition of Propertius, with the text based on MS. authority, when the return of Napoleon from Elba excited all Europe; no land seems to have felt the need of repressing the power of that man who had so long trampled on the liberties of Europe, more fully than Germany, which had suffered so deeply during ten years of military oppression. To take a part, if needful, in the struggle of Germany *pro aris et focis*, was, in Lachmann's eyes, *a duty*; and no consideration, therefore, could restrain him—not even his father's entreaties; it was one of his characteristics to take up as *a duty* whatever object he had before him, and to carry it out at all hazards. 'Propertius' was sent in haste to the press, and Lachmann left Göttingen to join a corps of volunteer infantry at Duderstadt; his feeling seems to have been that of the inhabitants of the duchy of Brunswick in general, whose resolution was strong at all cost to resist the French domination, remembering how their sovereign, when mortally wounded at Jena, had been compelled to seek a refuge on Danish territory to die unmolested, and how they had themselves suffered the miseries and oppressions of military occupation.

But it was not Lachmann's lot to take a part in the dangers of that short and memorable campaign. At Duderstadt he heard of the battle-field of Quatrebras (June 16, 1815) and of the fall of his sovereign, 'Brunswick's fated chieftain,' to whose memory he poured forth his tributary lay: and so, too, did he celebrate the decisive victory of Waterloo (or, as he terms it, *La Belle Alliance*), fought two days after.

Shortly subsequent to that event Lachmann's corps moved towards the Rhine (marching from Duderstadt July 7), to form part of the army of occupation of Paris. In that city he arrived Aug. 15; the actual location of his corps, however, was Nogent-le-Rotrou, near Chartres. On his march in returning to Germany in the following October he had a brief opportunity of seeing Paris.

He soon returned to the pursuits of a man of letters; and after a short residence at Berlin he received an appointment to a Professorship at Königsberg in 1816, where he continued until 1824. In 1825 he was removed to Berlin, where he remained until his death.

The variety of his literary studies, and the extent of his labours in various departments, are detailed in Hertz's 'Biographie;' to give any account of them here in detail would be to transcribe whole sections of the book. At Berlin he seems to have found the literary society, the want of which he had greatly felt at Königsberg; and there, too, his varied erudition as a literary antiquary was better understood and prized.

Lachmann's philological labours in connection with the text of various profane authors had an important bearing on his work as to that of the Greek New Testament. His small edition of the sacred text appeared in 1831, after a labour of five years; it was without any preface or statement of the critical principles on which it was formed; hence it is not remarkable that in the 'Edinburgh Review' and other publications its plan and principles were but little understood. All the explanation given by Lachmann himself was in a note of fifteen lines, prefixed to the synopsis of the passages in which the common text differed from his (p. 461). In this note he said that it was sufficient in that place to say that he had never followed his own judgment, but the accustomed reading of the ancient churches of the East; and that, where this was uncertain, he had adopted such eastern readings as were confirmed by the combination of Italian and African authority; that where all was doubtful, he had indicated the uncertainty by putting sometimes the readings in the margin, and sometimes by enclosing words in brackets, according to the nature of the case. For further information he referred to a paper in the 'Studien und Kritiken' for 1850, pp. 817-845. But as many into whose hands this manual edition came were unacquainted with German, or had no access to the periodical work in question, whose existence was but recent, it is not surprising that it was but little understood in general what Lachmann proposed, what means he took to carry out his plan, what critical authorities he admitted, what the indications of his nomenclature were, and how far he himself considered that he had presented the genuine text of the sacred volume. The absence of all citation of authorities prevented most from readily forming a correct judgment as to the grounds on which his text rested. Lachmann, however, knew what he had himself intended, and that was for the time enough for him. But had he been more explicit, it would have hindered others from making many mistakes, and, in the end, it would have saved him from much vexation.

There were, however, those who wished Lachmann to prepare an edition with critical apparatus; and after some time he engaged in 1837 the aid of Philip Buttmann the younger, whose part of the labour was the arrangement of the authorities for the *Greek text only*. This occupied him for *seven years*, part of which time was of course after the publication of the first volume of this edition.

In 1839 Buttmann accompanied Lachmann to Fulda, that they might together examine and copy for the forthcoming edition the readings of the 'Codex Fuldensis.' In this ancient Latin MS. the *Gospels* are thrown into a sort of combined narrative; the object kept in view being *not to omit* any part of any narrative ; the consequence of this procedure is that a Diatessaron is formed, always tautological, and often contradictory.   As an authority for the Latin *text*, however, the ' Codex Fuldensis' has a peculiar value.

For this edition Lachmann carefully arranged the Latin readings of the more important MSS. of Antehieronymian texts ; those only being selected which he considered to be *unaltered*, and which had been *published entire*, namely, the Codices Vercellensis, Veronensis, and Colbertinus (and occasionally the Latin of the ' Codex Cantabrigiensis') of the Gospels ; besides these MSS. he used the citations found in the Latin fathers, Cyprian, Hilary, and Lucifer, as well as the Latin version in which Irenæus has been transmitted to us.

Buttmann's work was to arrange the readings of the Greek MSS. A, B, C, D, and the fragments, P, Q, T, and Z, and those found in Origen.

These two associates in labour had so far advanced in 1842 as to publish the first volume, containing the four Gospels.   The Greek text (again revised) occupies the upper part of each page ; then the Critical apparatus of Greek and Latin authorities (in which the text is referred to merely by *lines*) ; and at the bottom of the page is the version of Jerome, edited in accordance with the ' Codex Fuldensis' and other ancient authorities.

Lachmann's Prolegomena to this volume explain--but only, however, in partial measure—the plan and object of his recension of the sacred text.   An attentive reader may gather the principles substantially, but still they were not distinctly enunciated, so as to be intelligible to readers in general.   His notion stated broadly was this,—to give the text best attested in the fourth century, so far as it might be gathered from Greek and Latin sources ; in this he did not propose to go beyond what was commonly known as to the readings of the cited authorities, and thus the *re-collation* of the Greek MSS. used formed no part of Buttmann's seven years' toil.   Lachmann seemed simply to say, on such and such data we ought to come to such and such conclusions. If, then, the reading of any MS. were more correctly known, it would affect such conclusions only so far as that particular reading was concerned.   Did Lachmann, then, suppose that by this means he arrived at the genuine text, as it proceeded from the sacred writers?   Those who have criticised his text seem to have assumed that he so thought, whereas his real opinion was that he arrived at a text that might be made the *basis of criticism*; so that we might proceed from the readings of the *fourth* century, and not those of the *sixteenth*.

It will be obvious to most readers who are acquainted with critical subjects that the limits of evidence within which Lachmann confined himself were needlessly narrow ; for instance, some of the other ancient versions possessed claims quite as good as the Latin to be heard in evidence ; and also it would have been far better to use all care in obtaining the readings of the Greek authorities as accurately as possible, instead of going no farther than using collations of some which were known to be incomplete.

But let all drawbacks be made, and still Lachmann stands forth as the first editor who gave forth a text founded solely on ancient authorities, and who in this entered into the domain of Textual Criticism, the direction of which and the channel of entrance to which had been pointed out by Bentley 120 years previously.

One effect of Lachmann's limited range of critical evidence is, that he sometimes gives readings in his text which are not supported by his Greek authorities. He drew this contrast between his own critical proceedings and those of Griesbach; Griesbach's inquiry was (he said), ' Is there any necessity to depart from the common reading?' His own was, ' Is there any necessity to depart from the best attested reading?' And thus he very rarely upheld a reading which was not found in some, at least, of the oldest copies.

The publication of this first volume of his larger edition was followed by new criticisms, not only from those who were acquainted with the subject, but also from those who were *not*. Some (such as Tholuck) seemed completely to misconceive what Lachmann proposed, and what he had done. But the criticisms which he felt the most were those of his friend De Wette, who, as a pupil of Griesbach, was attached to a very different school of textual revision, but who would in all probability have spoken of Lachmann's labours in a very different manner had the ' ratio et consilium' been properly explained to him. Lachmann was so affected by De Wette's want of apprehension of his labours, that his second volume, though ready in 1845, did not appear till 1850.

It is on the same plan as the first, containing the critical authorities which in age and character answer to those given in that part of the New Testament.

Lachmann's last literary work (besides the editing of some ancient German remains, completed by other hands after his death) was his edition of Lucretius, from critical authorities, followed by a Commentary. These appeared in the latter part of 1850. Towards the end of January, 1851, he suddenly felt great pain in his left ankle when going out, so that he returned into his apartment. Two days afterwards he obtained medical advice: the disorder in the ankle increased, so that amputation was considered, in a few weeks, to be absolutely needful. Two hours after this was announced to him as being requisite, the amputation took place, and afterwards there were hopes of his recovery; these, however, were fallacious. He breathed his last the morning of March 13, 1851.

But a few months before he had deeply lamented the death of Neander as a *personal* loss to his friends, but a *public* loss to the University of Berlin; and now that same University was similarly deprived of another of its most distinguished and honoured professors.

India in Greece ; or, Truth in Mythology : containing the Sources of the Hellenic Race, the Colonisation of Egypt and Palestine, the Wars of the Grand Lama, and the Bud'histic Propaganda in Greece. By E. POCOCKE, Esq. Illustrated by Maps of the Punjab, Cashmir, and Northern Greece. London: 1852.

THAT the early history of the people of Egypt, of Greece, and indeed of Europe in general, is closely connected with that of India is, we imagine, at present admitted by almost all inquirers into antiquity. Not only do the mythologies of these various lands and their early modes of worship point to a common origin, but their languages give unequivocal witness of a very close and intimate relation. No philologist doubts that the ancient language of India is very nearly related to the Greek, the Latin, and the Teutonic, and all, with scarcely an exception, are agreed that in many respects the Sanscrit presents the language in its fullest and most ancient form. On such evidence it has come to be a settled point amongst ethnographers that the people of India are as a race closely related to the European nations, and that, if they cannot lay claim to be the parent stock, they may at least be regarded as one of the oldest branches of the great Indo-European family of mankind.

So far the work before us does but re-affirm what is generally admitted. But Mr. Pococke takes higher ground than this, and, as will be seen from the title of his book and much more from the work itself, claims to have *demonstrated* the origin of the more western nations of antiquity from the tribes of India, and in doing this to have removed the veil of fable that rested on the earliest annals of Greece, and to have converted the legends of mythology into genuine and sober history. The principle on which Mr. Pococke relies is briefly this :—he finds that the Greeks who lived within the period of history were unacquainted with the more ancient inhabitants of the country except through legends, which, as they have given them to us, cannot be received as historical accounts ; the names by which they designated their legendary heroes, as well as those of the regions which they inhabited, he finds had no significance in their own language. He concludes therefore that these names were imposed on persons, tribes, and localities by some other race, in whose language the terms were significant, and his object is to show that their meaning is to be found in the language of ancient India. Having thus laid down the foundation of his argument, not without some considerable, though perhaps excusable, eulogy of its strength and completeness, our author proceeds to apply his principle to the names of towns, rivers, mountains, tribes, districts, heroes, and gods. The transmutations which are effected by this application of the Sanscrit are indeed very surprising. The most refractory vocable is decompounded with perfect ease. Even where the word, in consequence of its resemblance to some term or terms which to a Greek ear were significant, had been, as Mr. P. conceives, tortured from its true meaning and made to wear a Grecian dress, and to speak with a Grecian voice, one touch of this magician's wand strips it of its disguise, places it before us in its true form, and scatters into thin air the spurious meaning which the Greeks in their ignorance had imposed upon it. Thus not only does Attica derive its name from the Indian Attac, which 'is at present a fort and small town on the east bank of the Indus, 942 miles from the sea, and close below the place where it receives the waters of the Cabul river and first becomes navigable' (p. 58), but the term by which the Athenians so proudly distinguish themselves as indigenous to the soil, and which they believed, and taught us to believe, was genuine Greek, with a meaning of course distinctly known to them, proves to be nothing more than an Indian compound which in reality they did not understand. 'They were, then, not AUTO-CHTHŌNS, "sprung from the same earth," but ATTAC-THĀNS, *i. e.* the people of "THE ATTAC-LAND."' (p. 60.) And again, 'The source of the *grasshopper* symbol of the children of Attica is, by the plain and very unpoetical aid of geography, as clearly developed as their *autochthonous* origin. This ingenious people, who compared themselves to TETTIGES or GRASSHOPPERS, could they have referred to the original cradle of their race, would have discovered that, while the northern section of their tribe dwelt on the ATTAC adjoining the magnificent valley of Cashmir, with whose princes their tribe was connected by policy and domestic alliances, and whose lineage long ruled over the brilliant Athenians, by far the greater part of that primitive community whose descendants raised the glory of the Attic flag above all the maritime powers of Hellas, dwelt in a position eminently fitting their subsequent naval renown. They were the " PEOPLE OF TATTA," or " TETTAIKES."' (pp. 61, 62.)

So also by the HYPERBOREANS we are to understand not the far-north people but 'the " KHYBER-POOREANS," or the " people of KHYBER-POOR," *i. e.* the city or district of Khyber.' (p. 129.)

It is not to be expected that names in other lands should be more intractable under this philological alchemy than those in Greece : Egypt, Italy, Britain, Palestine, Peru, must all submit the names of their peoples and their localities to the same process, and in all the same transmutations may be effected.

We give one example in reference to Rome. Mr. Pococke states that ' Ravana, the rival lord paramount of India, was expelled by Rama, the sovereign of Oude, his warlike opponent,' and that a large body of his people, the Lancas, eventually settled in Italy ; hence ' PATAVI-UM ' or ' BUD'HA'S TOWN,' PADUS or BUD'HA'S river, and the ' LINGONES, that is, in plain terms, the LANC-GŎNĔS or LANCA TRIBES.' He then proceeds thus :—' And now we are about to arrive at the crowning certificate of history. Behold the memory of their chief, RAVANA, still preserved in the city of RAVENNA, and see on the western coast of Italia its great rival RĀMA or ROMA. How that great city of the Solar Rajpoots, the " GENA TAGA-TA" or " GENS TOGA-TA," that is the TAG RACE, gradually reduced by the combined powers of policy and war, the once mighty 'TOROOSHCAS and HOOSCAS (E'TRUSCA'S and OSCANS), a people of Cashmirian origin, is well known to the student of history. He may not however as clearly understand the internal structure of the society of Rome and her domestic policy ; for this he must exercise independent and energetic research. That city had its CURULE, chair of *ivory*, from the royal chair of the CURUS, the opponents of the Pandus (Pandusia); its tribe of "PLEB's" (PLEBE-IANS), from the Soodras of India, and its "SEN-ATORS," more correctly "SEN-NĀT-WARS" or WAR-CHIEFS, from the same land. The reader will perceive that the knowledge of the Romans relative to the sources of their own language was about as correct as that of the Greeks, when speaking the old Hellenic tongue. The office of the "Sen-nath-war" had nothing to do with a *Senex.*' (pp. 172, 173.)

In the first instance of derivation which we have adduced, Mr. Pococke is careful to give, as his principle requires, a meaning to the Indian word; Attac he informs us means *obstacle*, and is therefore applied to a town situated at the highest point up a navigable river: but in many of the other instances cited he is contented with having reduced the Greek or Latin word to an Indian name, without the slightest intimation that that Indian name has a meaning of its own. This is strikingly shown in his derivation of *Togata*. *Toga* considered as a Latin word has a significant derivation: of the Tag-race we are merely informed that 'the Tag is a renowned Rajpoot tribe.'

We must hasten however to speak of what more immediately concerns us now. Greece and Rome are not the only people that are to be traced back to India—thence also, according to Mr. Pococke, are we to derive the ancient inhabitants of Canaan. 'The most ancient name of that renowned region, so early the seat of civilization, is CANYA, a name received by us as CANAA, through the Hebrew form, and by them [it does not clearly appear by whom] applied as to a nation of CANAANITES or Traders. The appellation, however, is that of Canya, classically called Apollo. Its other name, *Palæstine*, is derived from the term "PALI STAN," or the LAND OF SHEPHERDS, those very HYCSOS or OXUS tribes who have been lately noticed as overpowering, and for a long time holding in bondage, the Egyptians.' (p. 214.)

The land of Palestine, moreover, did but exchange one tribe of Indians for another when the Canaanites were expelled. The Hebrews had the same origin as those whom they dispossessed. 'We have,' says Mr. P., 'in the Cabeiri, the representatives of a form of Bud'histic worship and Bud'histic chiefs, extending from the Logurh district (Locri) to Cashmir, the object of worship of the Hya and the Phœnician race, for they are but one. There is yet another most important point in which the KHAIBERI are to be considered. They are the KHEBREW-I, or Hebrews. The name A-BRAHAM (properly "BRAHM" in the Indian dialects) is considered by some Hebrew antiquarians to be derived from "HAIBRI," signifying "passenger," in allusion to his emigrating from Mesopotamia. The tribe of YUDAH is in fact the very YADU of which considerable notice has been taken in my previous remarks. The people of God, therefore, were literally taken out from amongst the other tribes, to be especially sanctified for the important work of the moral and religious regeneration of mankind. Hence it is that among the Greek writers of antiquity, such a stress is always laid on the piety of the "HYPERBOREANS," that is, the people of KHAIBER, or the

HEBREWS. . . . The Afghans have claimed descent from the Jews or IOUDAIOI (YOUDAI-OI); the reverse is the case. The HAIBREWS, or KHAIBREWS, are descended from the YADOOS. In that very land of the Yadoos, or Afghans—DAN and GAD still remain as the feeble remnants of Jewish antiquity.' (pp. 221-222.)

Here are assertions made certainly with sufficient confidence, but where is the proof of them? As far as we can understand, we are to accept the simple fact of the similarity of names as the sole and self-convincing proof that the Jews are the descendants of the Afghans.

On the whole we cannot but feel, both that Mr. Pococke attempts to prove too much, and that he mistakes assertion for proof. No one, we presume, will deny the ingenuity of the transmutations which he effects. But most sober-minded philologists will pause before they receive all this as a *demonstration* of the origin of nations. There is throughout the treatise far too much dependence on mere similarity of sound, to gain the confidence of those who require evidence for their belief. That which the author regards as the strength of his argument, seems to us, we must confess, to be its weakness; we mean the astonishing ease with which all names become Indian. There is no endeavour to gather up any hints of the actual migration of these tribes, no investigation even of the changes which the names have undergone, but, as the few specimens we have given will serve to show, the two names, the Indian and the Western, whether Greek, or Latin, or Hebrew, are set side by side, they are asserted to be one and the same, they are used interchangeably, and then we are told that we have an irrefragable geographical proof of identity. The whole process continually reminds us of the unexpected results of sleight of hand. We admire the cleverness of the operator, while we feel sure that some delusion has been practised upon us.

Let us not be understood, however, to depreciate the value of philological evidence in matters of history. We doubt not that much, very much, may be done in determining the grand outlines of the early history of the world by means of philology, but it is on this very account that we are anxious, even in this hasty notice, to state what we think are the fatal defects of the work before us. There is need of a far more severe and cautious method to arrive at safe conclusions, and when all is done the result will be very far indeed from demonstration.

———

The Free Church of ancient Christendom, and its Subjugation under Constantine. By BASIL H. COOPER, B.A. London : Albert Cockshaw.

THE author of this work informs us that it makes no pretensions to rank as a Church history. It simply aims to present, in a series of rapid historical sketches, a general view of the process through which the Christian Church passed from the day of her espousals to Christ till she was brought to hail what a living Roman Catholic historian (Dr. Ritter) complacently calls 'her *emancipation* by Constantine.' This emancipation the author regards as her 'subjugation.' The animus of the work is as against any connection of the Church with governments, against established churches, against episcopal institutions. These matters lie out of our range; but, apart from these more special objects, we may observe that the writer divides his 'sketches' into generations of three to a century, and that the substance of the book is good historical matter, produced in a sufficiently attractive shape by a writer of competent learning, and embodying considerable research, furnishing the reader with a clearer idea of the important period of which it treats than could easily be found in an equal compass. Special objects furnish inducements for writing to many who would not have written without them, and to this powerful influence we owe many works which have greatly enriched our literature. Still there is no department in which impartiality is so much important as in history, and, above all, in Church history; and as one whose impulse to write is derived from the desire to support or to overthrow particular views is not and cannot be impartial, we regard, not indeed with disfavour but with caution, surveys of historical periods taken, whether avowedly or not, under such influences. This of course applies not merely to the work before us, but to *all* works the authors of which take up the treatment of history for the advocacy or subversion of *any* particular views, religious or political, and the demand necessarily made in the perusal of works of this class for the exercise of the critical judgment renders the reading of them a less pleasant matter than those written by authors whose object is simply to describe and to relate, and the absence of any perceptible bias in whom to influence their judgments, enables one to accept their guidance without reserve. But for sturdy readers there is no better exercise than the survey of the same period of time, or the same series of events, in the company of writers of different views and under opposing influences, and amidst all the disagreements of men, essential truth is never difficult to find to him who diligently seeks it.

We recommend to special attention the introductory dissertation comprised in the two first chapters of this work, 'On the state of the World at the Advent,' first of the heathen and then of the Jews and Samaritans. The views of the writer as to the comparative ripeness of the Samaritans, notwithstanding some heathenish tendencies and their rejection of the prophets, are especially interesting.

Cyclopædia Bibliographica; a Library Manual of Theological and General Literature, and Guide for Authors, Preachers, and Literary Men; Analytical, Bibliographical, and Biographical. London: James Darling, 1851. Part I.

This is the first portion of an undertaking, the preparatory progress of which we have more than once announced to our readers, and the appearance of which we hail with the liveliest satisfaction. The aid which a work like this will afford to theological students and writers, by at once enabling them to find what has already been produced on any subject to which their attention may be turned, cannot be too highly estimated; and those who have ever felt the need of such assistance will do great wrong to themselves if they fail to afford this very arduous enterprise the encouragement to which it is so abundantly entitled.

The First Volume, which the present Part commences, and which will be complete in itself, will contain the authors and their Works in alphabetical arrangement. In the second volume the whole of the matter contained in the first will be arranged under heads or common-places in scientific order, with an alphabetical index, by which the subject can be easily referred to. To many it will appear that the second volume should be more essentially useful and valuable than the first. But whatever may be the *relative* importance of the two volumes, a slight inspection of the present specimen will suffice to evince the *absolute* utility and high value of the first or alphabetical catalogue. The name of each author is accompanied by a short biographical and characteristic notice, so far as can be ascertained from authentic sources. These notices have, though concise, been evidently prepared with the most conscientious care. The *full* titles of the works are then given; and in all cases where more than one subject is treated of in a volume, the whole are enumerated. Critical notices of the works are sometimes furnished. The variation of editions is noticed, and those considered the best are indicated.

It is difficult to give *adequate* specimens of this work within our limits, the best examples being of necessity the most copious: thus five closely-printed columns are given to the contents of the ' Acta Sanctorum,' five to the works of Arnauld, four to those of Dr. Arnold, four to those of St. Athanasius, ten to those of St. Augustine. The following short specimen will serve, however, to illustrate the method, though not the rich fulness, of this excellent catalogue.

' ABUL-PHARAGIUS, Gregory, [or, Bar-Hebræus.]

' Born at Malatia, in Asia Minor, 1226. Consecrated Bishop of Guba at the age of twenty. Soon after translated to Aleppo; at the age of forty became primate of the Eastern Jacobites. Died 1286. His great work on universal history he wrote in Syriac, and translated it into Arabic. Gibbon speaks of this author in high terms of praise.

' Historia compendiosa dynastiarum [orientalium], historiam complectens univer-salem, à mundo condito usque ad tempora authoris. Arabice edita et Latine versa, ab Ed. Pocockio, cum supplemento Latine conscripto. 2 vol. 4º.
                                                                      Oxon. 1663*

> Vol. 1. Arabice.   Vol. 2. Latine.

' Specimen historiæ Arabum, auctore Ed. Pocockio; accessit historia veterum Arabum, ex Abul-Feda, cura Ant. Is. Silvestre de Sacy. Edidit Josephus White. 4º.   *Oxon.* 1806*

' The " Specimen" is a short extract from the preceding work, and was origin-ally published 1650.

' Chronicon Syriacum, è codd. Bodleianis descripsit, maximam partem vertit, notisque illustravit Paul Iac. Bruns; edidit, ex parte vertit, notasque adjecit G. G. Kirsch. 2 vol. 4º.   *Lips.* 1789*

' This work contains the first part of the Syriac text of Abul-Pharagius's his-tory. No more has been published. One volume contains the Syriac text, the other the Latin translation.

' Nomocanon ecclesiæ Antiochenæ Syrorum, Latine, interprete Aloysio Assemano.
                                                   Mai Script. Vet. 10, p. 2. 1–268.'

' ADAMS, Thomas.

' A pious and excellent divine, and a writer of great animation of style, full of bold metaphor and striking allusions. In 1614 he was " preacher of God's word at Willington, in Bedfordshire." He afterwards became Rector of St. Bennet's, Paul's Wharf, London, from which he was sequestered for his loyalty in the grand Rebellion, and died before the Restoration. Dr. Southey, with whom he was a favourite author, said that he had " all the oddity and the felicity of Fuller's manner."

' An exposition of the second Epistle general of St. Peter. Imp. 8⁰. *Lond.* 1839

' Originally published in folio, London, 1633. Pp. 1634. Dedication and index. A hiatus occurs on the paging between pp. 764 and 801.

' Workes, being the summe of his sermons, meditations, and other divine and moral discourses. Collected and published in one entire volume, with additions of some new and emendations of the old. Folio.   *Lond.* 1630

' The white devil; the two sons; the leaven; the black devil; the wolf worrying the lambs; the spiritual navigator. 4⁰.   *Lond.* 1615.'

' AINSWORTH, Henry.

' An eminent Nonconformist divine. Died 1622. In 1590 he went to Amsterdam, and became one of the ministers of the English sect of Brownists there. He was profoundly learned in Hebrew and Rabbinical literature, and on that account his annotations have always been held in great esteem.

' Annotations upon the five bookes of Moses, the Booke of Psalmes, and the Song of Songs: wherein the Hebrew words and sentences are compared with and explained by the Greeke and Chaldee versions, but chiefly by conferring with the Holy Scripture. Folio. *Lond.* 1627.

' Including a new translation of these books of Scripture.

· This work was reprinted in 1843 in 2 vol. 8°.

' A preface concerning Moses' writings and these annotations upon them.

' The five books of Moses [translated with annotations].

' Index.

' Advertisement touching some objections made against the sincerity of the Hebrew text, and allegations of the Rabbins in these former annotations.

' Of the interpretation of the stone Jahalom in Ex. 28. 18.

' The book of Psalms [translated with annotations, and preface concerning David, his life and acts].

' Index.

' Solomon's Song of Songs [translated, and] in English metre, with annotations and references to other Scriptures.

' The communion of saints; a treatise of the fellowship that the faithful have with God and his angels, and one with another, in this present life. Gathered out of the Holy Scriptures by H[enry] A[insworth]. Sm. 8°. *s. l.* 1628.

' An arrow against idolatry. Taken out of the quiver of the Lord of Hosts. Pp. 121. 18°. *Nova Belgia,* 1640.'

An Analysis and Summary of Old Testament History and the Laws of Moses. With an introductory Outline of the Geography, Political History, &c.; the Prophecies, Types, and Intimations of the Messiah; Jewish History from Nehemiah to A.D. 70; Examination Questions, &c. Oxford: J. L. Wheeler. 1850.

An Analysis and Summary of New Testament History, including the Four Gospels harmonised into one continuous Narrative; the Acts of the Apostles and continuous History of St. Paul; an Analysis of the Epistles and Book of Revelations; with copious Notes, Historical, Geographical, and Antiquarian. Oxford: J. L. Wheeler. 1852.

THESE two works are by the author of the well-known ' Analysis and Summary of Herodotus,' who now, in the second of the volumes above specified, avows himself as ' J. Talboys Wheeler,' the bookseller at Cambridge. The object of this set of ably digested volumes seems to be to put young students, and especially university students, into the easiest possible possession of the contents of works on which they are founded, without exacting that deep study of the originals which would be necessary to secure the same information at the first hand. In realising this object the author has rendered a service to the real student, by furnishing what may be of material aid to him in directing his own researches and in fixing their results.

The two volumes before us are well described in their titles. The first is the most simple in its plan, but, simple as the plan seems, its execution must have been a work of time and labour, and the author has lost sight of nothing that might conduce to the object in view.

The summary and analysis of the text, which is of itself a work of no small difficulty, is cleverly done, especially in the Mosaic laws and ordinances; and the author generally endeavours to explain or illustrate any obscure points in Jewish history, 'particularly,' as he frankly remarks, ' those portions which are most frequently the subjects of college examinations.' The 'cramming' purpose, thus acknowledged, further appears in the Examination Questions, which are drawn from the Cambridge examination papers, in Old Testament history, for a series of years; and, if these be fair specimens of such questions, we may felicitate the young gentlemen at Cambridge on the ease with which they are let through this examination.

The other volume is a more elaborate, and it seems to us greatly more useful, performance for the general public. It differs so much from the former that, but for the desirableness of maintaining uniformity of title in the series, this should be rather named an Analysis and *Paraphrase* than an Analysis and *Summary*, the narrative having been often expanded for the fuller development of the meaning rather than condensed. It is a thoroughly good and useful book, and one of the best, if not the very best, companions we have met with for a young person undertaking the thorough study of the New Testament history. The four evangelical accounts are digested on the basis of Mr. Greswell's *Harmonia Evangelica;* the Gospel and Acts are reproduced under remarkably distinctive typographical arrangements, well suited to aid the memory; a good deal of information is incorporated in the narrative itself, and such as demanded more detailed explanation is given in footnotes, which, taken collectively, form a considerable mass of very useful and interesting explanatory materials, judiciously selected and well condensed.

Notes and Reflections on the Psalms. By Arthur Pridham. Bath: Binns and Goodwin. 1852.

In the last Number we had occasion to notice favourably this author's analogous works on the Epistles to the Romans and to the Hebrews. This one is of the same class. It is a practical work; and of the various works on the Psalms which have passed under our notice this is, for *practical* purposes, by much the most satisfactory; and we cannot but regard with especial favour any well-considered attempt to deepen to the Christian mind the vital importance and influence of a portion of sacred Scripture so peculiarly practical as the Psalms. The spirituality of the author's mind, as evinced in all his writings, is for him a precious gift, which well qualifies him for the task he has undertaken. He informs us that he has had a twofold aim in the preparation of the volume—' of ministering to the refreshment of the lovers of sound doctrine, and of affording assistance to the inexperienced but godly inquirer after truth. With this desire an attempt has been made to present a faithful though general outline of the Book of Psalms, and also its immediate application to the Christian as a partaker of the heavenly calling.'

The work takes the aspect of reflections upon the general scope and prominent topics of each Psalm, with occasional textual criticisms in foot-notes. ' The longest articles have been devoted to those Psalms which relate immediately to the person and work of our Blessed Lord, or in which some great doctrinal principles are affirmed. Those which illustrate the dispensational government of God have in general been treated more or less fully. *All* have been examined under the liveliest and most thankful consciousness of the thoroughly practical bearing of the varied utterances of the Spirit of Christ upon the experiences of this people in their day of wearying yet hopeful conflict.' In regard to the first of these classes we should say that the author assigns a Messianic character to more of the Psalms than are usually supposed to bear it, or than will in all instances be generally allowed. This is a natural result of the craving of the spiritual mind to find Christ everywhere in Scripture. Thus the first Psalm is, in our author's view, Messianic. ' The outline which the Psalm presents is such as can be filled up worthily by the person of the Christ alone. It is a sketch, if one may so speak, drawn clearly and distinctly by the Holy Ghost, as the spirit of prophecy, of Jesus in his character of Jehovah's perfect servant (Isa. xlii.). The Just One, found in fashion as a man (Phil. ii. 7, 8), is before us in this portrait.' Mr. Pridham considers also that ' very frequently particular expressions, which can only apply in truth to Jesus, occur in Psalms, the general subject of which is widely different.'

Apart from all question as to these matters, and as to some special views which the author introduces, and which indicate the school to which he belongs, this volume will long be valued for the deep and varied spiritual experience and the vitally important truths which it embodies as connected with and evolved from the Psalms of David.

The Saints' Rapture to the Presence of the Lord Jesus ; with Appendix in refutation of Dr. Cumming's Tract entitled ' The Pope the Man of Sin.' By R. GOVETT. London : James Nisbet and Co. 1852.

WE are pleased to see any new emanation from the pen of Mr. Govett. We are familiar with his ' Isaiah Unfulfilled,' and often consult it with advantage. Moreover, his tracts and smaller works, which are rapidly multiplying, have attracted many readers, and Mr. G.'s pulpit at Norwich becomes the centre of a holy influence. We are not, however, prepared to say that the views of this excellent man are always clear. They are more often characterised by originality and enterprise than by that patient spirit of investigation which avails itself of the labours of those who have gone before, that spirit which elucidates as well as confirms.

We were familiar with the tract ' The Pope the Man of Sin,' and were therefore anxious to listen to Mr. Govett's refutation of some of its positions. In that tract Mr. Cumming sets forth in his usual clear and eloquent style the Protestant view of 2 Thess. ii. 1-12, in accordance with the invariable mode adopted by our own Wickliff and the

Reformers generally, subsequently by Bishop Jewell, in modern times by Scott and other evangelical commentators, and in our own day by Elliott and the generality of anti-papal advocates. Mr. Govett hates Popery as much as we do; this we admit. We recognise therefore in him an impartial defender of an interpretation which the Romanists would only be too glad to establish. Much of Mr. G.'s 'refutation' turns upon the critical meaning of ἀποστασία, the falling away or apostacy, and he would, in accordance with his view, make the man of sin an individual who is hereafter to rise as an enemy to God's Church, and his apostacy a complete surrender of Christianity for the most absolute atheism. Of this word, to use the language of Schleusner, we could say, Bis tantum legitur in Novo Testamento; but though it occurs only in one other place, a reference to that passage will materially aid us—᾿Αποστασίαν διδάσκεις ἀπὸ Μωσέως, Acts xxi. 21, translated in the English version, Thou teachest .... to *forsake* Moses. In the absence of much scriptural employment of the word Mr. Govett consults *Johnson's Dictionary*, and is told by the great lexicographer that 'apostate' is generally applied to one that has left his religion, and argues therefrom that the apostacy cannot include those who professedly hold the doctrines of the Christian faith as do the popes. But Schrevelius, a better authority than Johnson, tells us that in its primary meaning the word signifies a defection or revolt. It is, in fact, the casting off an authority and substituting another in its place. Let any impartial mind, capable of judging of all that has been advanced by Rome on the subject of the Rule of Faith, judge whether this does not exactly describe the Jeroboam-like position of the popes whom Paul characterises under the prophetic title The Man of Sin.

Ireland's Miseries; the grand Cause and Cure. By Rev. Edward Marcus Dill, A.M., M.D., Missionary Agent to the Irish Presbyterian Church. Edinburgh: Johnstone and Hunter, 1852.

Ireland has always been a mystery alike to the statesman and to the Christian philanthropist. The one has directed all the resources of political science, the other all the efforts of patient benevolence, to the cure of its manifold evils, and both have found it a deep, unfathomable slough of despond, into which their injected measures have brought no solidity. The last few years have, as our readers well know, witnessed events which seem to be on the one hand the terrible climax of Ireland's despair, and on the other, as we trust, the turning-point in her hitherto wretched career. Has a brighter sun beamed on that unhappy land? Is the horizon tinged with streaks of the coming dawn? Shall her once Eden-like pastures always be a wilderness? Shall her sons be Cain-like wanderers on the face of the earth? Shall she be a focus of sedition and the hot-bed of a degrading superstition? Dr. Dill examines the country at this turning-point. From amid the desolate potato-fields of Connaught he surveys the woes, from the evangelised districts of Connemara he welcomes the coming blessings.

In plain truth, we never saw so powerful a portrait of Ireland in its social, political, and moral condition as Dr. Dill has given us in the early portion of his work. By undeniable facts and figures he reveals the results of the recent famine, in the tide of emigration, the growth of pauperism, and the diminution of wealth among the higher classes. No one can deny the facts which are brought forward. Imagine two hundred and seventy thousand dwellings swept away from the depopulated districts. Conceive nearly 300,000 persons emigrating in the year 1851 alone. Realise the fact that there are in America three millions of native Irish, and four millions and a half of Irish descent, whilst the whole population of Ireland is only six millions and a half. These are features of the case that are patent to all. But what cause can be assigned for evils so gigantic? Is it the physical condition of the land or of the race? No! answers Dr. Dill in a masterly chapter. Are unequal laws the explanation? The laws are unequal, replies Dr. Dill, but the inequality consists in England bearing the burden which Ireland imposes. The grand cause is shown to be the papal system, which lies as an incubus upon the people, shutting out the light of truth, eclipsing the mind, corrupting the conscience, destroying the heart, debasing the whole nature, blasting man's prospects for time and for eternity. We do not hesitate to predict that this small volume, in which these topics are so powerfully set forth, will excite wide attention, and open the eyes of thousands to the fearful yet hopeful state of the 'Isle of Saints.'

God in Disease; or, the Manifestations of Design in Morbid Phenomena. By James F. Duncan, M.D. London: Nisbet and Co. 1851.

This is a really valuable little work, for if it has a fault it is in being too much compressed. The subject is one so little investigated hitherto, at least by students of theology, and the author is so thoroughly qualified to treat upon it, that we only regret he has not expanded it to the dimensions of a Bridgewater Treatise. He takes a principle which is universally to be discovered in the field of nature, to which we may apply the term *norma abnormium*, the law which regulates that which is irregular—a law of necessity more recondite and requiring more acute powers of observation than that which is written on the harmonies and analogies of created things. Physiology is always engaging to the attention, that of the human frame more especially so, as it awakens the response in each one *Ego sum proximus mihi*. To know our own frames, their liability to disease, the uses of the different functions, the exquisite simplicity of means accomplishing the most elaborate complexity of results,—to know this will be the ambition of any inquiring mind. But Dr. Duncan carries physiological research to a point yet more deserving of notice, as it helps to solve a great moral problem— the nature, the modifications, and the object of suffering reconciling the existence of physical evil with the wisdom and goodness of God.

'When we examine the details of sickness,' he says, 'we discover special provisions for allaying pain, for restoring health, and for rendering ailments, which are necessarily incurable, to a certain degree more compatible with the comfort and activity of the invalid. Is not this mercy properly so called? Is it not discriminating in its compassion, and does it not adapt the peculiar benefits it dispenses to the exact necessities of the object it designs to relieve? The provisions of which we speak do not exist except where their assistance is required; but no sooner do the circumstances occur which render them desirable than we find them developed; proving beyond all question the reality of the existence of this attribute, and of its active exercise.'

Many persons are aware of some of the more obvious examples of the vis medicatrix naturæ, of the use of pain as a warning against injury, of the power inherent in the body of adapting itself to altered circumstances; but for an extension of these ideas in amount as well as in accuracy, and the sublime lessons of our divine relations to be taught thereby, we refer our readers to this admirable work, which we have perused with unqualified satisfaction.

Devotions for the Daughters of Israel. Translated and adapted from a Prayer-Book in general use throughout Germany, by M. H. Bresslau. London.

This is, as the title further expresses, 'a collection of concise prayers for Jewish females, for week-days, sabbath, new moons, festivals, and fasts; also prayers suitable for various occasions.' The preface has something like an apology for allowing the use of the vernacular to females in their private devotions: 'The imperative necessity of retaining in any authorized form of prayers the original and sacred language, the Hebrew, has been too strongly pronounced to allow infringement on its sanctity; yet in the case of females a slight relaxation of that rule, in so far as regards private devotions, cannot but be productive of beneficial effects.'

These prayers read strangely to us, from the absence of the usual topics of Christian prayer, and still more from the style and sentiments being by no means framed on Old Testament models. There is want of that simplicity of thought and language we should have expected, and a show of fine writing and of poetical conceptions, which we certainly did not expect. There seems also such a pervading tone of self-righteousness, and assertion of the sufficiency of the human will, as grate harshly on the ear; and in this and other respects we are painfully reminded that there are many doctrines of the Old Testament, clear to us by the light of the later revelation, to which the Jewish people are still blind.

Apart from the exceptions we have taken, these prayers present many striking expressions and many tender and beautiful thoughts. Nothing, for example, can be finer of its kind than the 'Prayer of an Orphan.'

'Heavenly Father! Thy inscrutable justice has willed it that my dear parent should be taken away from me, and that with this loss I should be deprived of my greatest happiness. Alas, Father! how heavy and afflicting was this punishment for a weak heart, which—now already weighed down by intense grief—would lie in the dust had not the religion of my fathers taught me that Thou art called

"Father of Orphans." I am now Thy child, Thy heir; Thou wilt be my parent unto eternity; Thou the mightiest Father in heaven or earth. Thou wilt hear me as often as I call upon Thee; Thou wilt protect me when I walk in Thy ways. To Thy paternal hand I now commit my spiritual weal. I trust in Thy fatherly love, and exclaim with the Psalmist, "For Thou wilt light my lamp; the Lord my God will enlighten my darkness."—Amen.'

The Twin Pupils; or, Education at Home. A Tale addressed to Young Persons. By ANN THOMSON GRAY. London: T. Hatchard, 1852.

STRUCK by the piety and vigorous sense of the passages that met the eye in opening up the pages of this thick volume, we have been induced to read it through with attention. Of this we found no reason to repent, and believe that the work will be highly interesting, and will offer many valuable suggestions to those who, whether as parents or guardians, have the solemn responsibility of deciding upon the education for time and for eternity of children intrusted to their care. The writer has a deep sense of the defects and inconsideration of the existing modes of education, especially for females; and in this work she very forcibly sets forth her views, and illustrates them in an account of the parents and children of three families, whose different characters, training, and results, are set forth more in conversations than in recitals. There is not much story, but as much perhaps as is needed for the purpose in view. The characters are skilfully discriminated and graphically described; and a pervading interest grows out of the fact that one of the 'twin pupils' (sisters) is afflicted with congenital and incurable blindness. The father of this the central family of the tale is the organ of the author's sentiments, and her model of a Christian father, deeply alive to the responsibilities which God has laid him under. His words are thoughtful and weighty, and his conduct full of strength and wisdom. The real object of the work is to enforce the moral, 'Train up a child in the way that he should go, and when he is old he will not depart from it;' and although this moral is less forcibly wrought out *in the story* (which shows some deficiency in constructive skill), and although the volume is in a few places needlessly encumbered with lessons to the pupils—good, but out of place—the work must be pronounced a very superior one of its kind, calculated to be of essential service to both parents and children.

History of the Council of Trent. From the French of L. F. BUNGENER. Edinburgh: Thomas Constable and Co. 1852.

LOOKING at the revived pretensions and convulsive energies of the Church of Rome, it has become of essential importance that there should be some better and easier means than the works of Sarpi and Pallavicini offer, for becoming acquainted with 'what took place and what was done in the assembly at which Roman Catholicism was finally constituted.' The opposite errors of the histories by the two authors named, with their dreary and unmethodical treatment of the subject, and the absence in both of the qualities now looked for in an historian, rendered such a work as that which M. Bungener has produced a great desideratum, which, if not before very strongly felt, will be generally acknowledged now that it is supplied. Aware of this, the translator, Mr. David D. Scott, of St. Andrew's, had himself meditated the production of some such work, when the performance of M. Bungener was put into his hands. 'It came highly recommended,' says Mr. Scott, 'and at once recommended itself by a clearness, truthfulness, and vigour in the narrative, an acuteness and terseness in the reasoning, and a spirit of true fidelity and charity which I am sure my countrymen will appreciate, if I have at all succeeded in doing it justice in the translation.' This he has, we think, very fairly done, and we subscribe with little reserve to his estimate of this interesting, readable, and trustworthy book, the author of which has manifestly taken due pains in comparing and sifting the original authorities, and in gathering from every source whatever bore upon his subject. It may be added that the author, hearing how the translator was engaged, wrote to him expressing his satisfaction, and offering his last notes and additions, so that the translation is in some respects more complete than the original. Altogether, a history of the Council of Trent so well prepared and so clearly written, so comprehensive and yet so compendious, will be a valuable acquisition to the theological and ecclesiastical student, and will claim a place among the select books of his library.

The Curse of Christendom; or, the System of Popery Exhibited and Exposed. By the Rev. J. B. PIKE. London: Ward and Co. 1852.

IT is not easy to say anything new on the subject of popery in these days, because for three centuries it has been analysed, exposed, and inveighed against in every possible way. And yet a clear exposé of it, a fresh analysis, an additional invective is no unwelcome thing, not only because readers in general love new books, but because a system, however old, nay, however unvarying, has new relations to society in its incessant developments. Mr. Pike's work has great merits. He has made himself well acquainted with ecclesiastical history, and quotes most appropriately from the old ecclesiastical writers. He is himself deeply imbued with a love of evangelical truth, and is always prepared with comments equally clear and satisfactory on those occasionally obscure passages of Scripture from which popish writers love to deduce the arrogant claims of their church. Added to this, Mr. Pike is remarkably systematic, and his chapters are linked together according to a well-arranged sequence that enchains the interest. Beginning with the foundation of the system in its hostility to the Bible and substitution of *church*-teaching, he shows how the supremacy of the pope has been reared thereupon, and proceeds to the description of the idolatrous practices and superstitious tenets that lay the mind of man prostrate at the feet of an unscrupulous priesthood. We know not to what denomination Mr. Pike belongs, but we rejoice that in every denomination of Protestant Christians right-minded and competent men like himself should spring up to teach their especial disciples the nature of that controversy which is daily pressing more closely upon us all. Protestants have a common bond of union in ' the faith which was once delivered to the saints;' they have a common enemy in that anti-Christian power which travesties the great truths of religion, and speaks blasphemous words against the Most High.

Calvin's Tracts. Translated from the original Latin and French by HENRY BEVERIDGE. Vol. the Third. Edinburgh : Printed for the Calvin Translation Society.

THIS volume comprises some of the anti-papal treatises of Calvin, and is brought forward somewhat out of its place to meet the want which the invidious encroachments of the Church of Rome have created. The tracts comprised in the volume are An Antidote to the Council of Trent ; German Interim, with Refutation, and True Method of Reforming the Church ; and The Sinfulness of Outward Conformity to Roman Rites. The last treatise is not, however, of this class, being Psychopannychia, or the Soul's Imaginary Sleep between Death and Judgment. This is not the least valuable of the many volumes the English reader owes to the Calvin Translation Society, whose operations we have watched with interest and satisfaction. It is needless to characterise the treatises comprised in the volume ; but as the last of them touches on a subject to which an article in the present number of this Journal is devoted, we may state that Calvin maintains the view that the souls of departed saints remain in a state of *rest* in heaven until the resurrection and the judgment, when the soul, re-united to the body, is admitted to *glory.* He opposes the idea of the intermediate sleep of the soul ; indeed, the tract is wholly levelled against it. He says, ' *First,* we give the name of " rest " to that which our opponents call " sleep." We have no aversion indeed to the term *sleep,* were it not corrupted and almost polluted by their falsehoods. *Secondly,* by " rest " we understand not sloth, or lethargy, or anything like the drowsiness of ebriety which they attribute to the soul, but tranquillity of conscience and serenity, which always accompanies faith, but is never complete in all its parts till after death.'

Popular Scripture Zoology, containing a Familiar History of the Animals mentioned in the Bible : by MARIA E. CATLOW. London : Reeve and Co., 1852.

THE distinguishing feature of this handsome book is formed by the engravings, in which the examples, given on a somewhat large scale, are drawn with spirit and coloured with tolerable care. There are, however, some mistakes. Thus, that which is given as the ' Syrian Bear ' is the common brown bear, and not the true *Ursus Syriacus*, as figured in Ehrenberg's *Symbolæa Physicæa*, and in the Pictorial Bible, which is the main source from which the materials of this book are derived. A more careful examination of the *last* (the standard) edition of that work, in which the zoological notes have been greatly amended and altered, would have spared the authoress some mistakes and oversights. Indeed it may appear that the edition of fifteen years ago was mainly used, and the one of 1848 only referred to afterwards. It is surely the duty of an author to acquaint himself with the *latest* sources of information on the subjects of which he treats, and we therefore venture to notice this, as well as point out the present writer's evident unacquaintance with the Cyclopædia of Biblical Literature, in which the zoology of the Bible has been examined, and in some measure readjusted, by a naturalist of eminence. Still, this kind of work is, in general, so carelessly done, that Miss Catlow is entitled to the praise of comparative care and judgment; and although the work admits of some improvement and revision, it is about the best of the kind we have met with, and the one best suited to interest young persons in the study of Scripture zoology.

Morisonianism Refuted; a Review of the Rev. James Morison's Exposition of Romans IX. By the author of 'A Defence of Infant Baptism.' Paisley: Alex. Gardner, 1852.

THIS is an able and searching analysis of Mr. Morison's Exposition, and the work of a mind deeply attached to Scripture truth, and showing that disposition 'earnestly to contend for the faith' which is in a degree characteristic of our northern fellow-Christians. To *review* a review would involve an equal amount of writing with that which we discuss; we cannot therefore in a short notice do more than express a general concurrence in the views of the analyst in preference to those of the expositor. Our author remarks that 'the ninth of Romans has formed the battle-field of many a hard-fought polemico-theological contest.' The consciousness of this might almost suggest a method of treatment consistent with such a fact, not to descend into the arena of combatants and repeat the old strategetical evolutions, but view the contest from a neighbouring eminence, and discover the rationale of the whole controversy. Does any one ask where our atmosphere has its boundary-surface, at which shall begin that impalpable luminiferous ether which is said to pervade all space? We are content to breathe this atmosphere, and receive the light which the ether by its undulations transmits to us from the great central orb, though we cannot point out where the rays pass from the rarer into the denser medium. So in spiritual things we live in an atmosphere of free will, and yet the light of grace and truth which comes to us traverses the mysterious illimitable ocean of the divine sovereignty. 'It is God that worketh in us to will and to do of his good pleasure.'

Premillennialism a Delusion. By a Member of the Presbytery of Northumberland. Edinburgh and London: Johnstone and Hunter. 1851.

WE have no doubt that the anonymous author of the essay which bears this startling title is possessed of some theological learning, more especially of the German school, to judge by his orthography of the words 'dogmatik' and 'hermeneutik.' We have been accustomed to regard premillennialism not as a delusion, but as a subject on which the opinions of Christian men are to be formed according to the relative weight of argument on either side. It would be far safer to divide the formula, placing the first word as the actual title and the last at the climax of the argument. The leading fallacy of our friend's method is assuming the exact nature of the subject, as if the reasoning could be based on a series of ultimate truths as fixed as Euclid's definitions and postulates. It is after all a matter of delicate criticism in which much room is left for divergency of opinion, and more than all for the exercise of charity. The author talks much of 'Cæsarianism.' We never heard this term anywhere but in surgery; to our ears it is equally strange and harsh. If allusion is intended to the well-known text 'Render unto Cæsar the things which are Cæsar's,' we would in interpreting that passage include the privilege and duty of every Christian Cæsar to take care that his subjects 'render unto God the things that are God's.' Is this what is meant by Cæsarianism?

The Tried Christian; a Book of Consolation for the Afflicted. By the Rev. WM. LEASK. London: John Snow. 1851.

IT is often remarked that young ministers are given to preach upon affliction, therein selecting a subject in which it is presumed they would have but slender personal experience. An explanation of this may be found in the prevalent impression upon their minds caused by their introduction to so many scenes of distress which they had hitherto seldom witnessed. Their sensibilities are therefore in full action, whilst the powers of the mind are on the stretch to acquire the means of evincing sympathy with the mourner and conveying the consolations of the Gospel. The theme is, as a natural result, carried into the pulpit, and hence the cause of the observation being made. At the same time the mourner will rather turn for sympathy to the more advanced man of God. Now such we believe Mr. Leask to be. He has treated this subject with tenderness, and with the hand of one who testifies to that which he has seen and known. Moreover he is no mere sentimentalist, he encourages no delusive errors, he is no flatterer to the sorrowful one 'of this world,' but sets God's dealings with his people in a true, a sober, a practical light, tracing their effects in maturing the believing soul for a heavenly inheritance, whilst Jesus alone is looked to as giving a title to future blessedness. The style is simple, the flow of language characterised by ease and elegance.

The Titles and Similitudes of the Lord Jesus Christ. A Handbook for Sunday-School Teachers. By JAMES LARGE. 2 vols. London, 1852.

WE have here a series of thirty-six short and familiar lectures on the titles of Christ; the number of titles considered in each chapter varying, with their pre-eminence and importance, from two to ten. Some readers will regard the list of titles and similitudes as redundant, and as including many of doubtful or remotely mystical application; while others may deem it defective, as they will find several titles wanting which they have seen included in popular lists. This diversity of opinion will probably suffice to indicate that Mr. Large has exercised a sound discretion in a matter where, as he complains, there was no unanimity of interpreters for his guidance. We think he has done so; though there are a few titles which we should scarcely have included in such a list. The titles chosen are treated by the author in a manner well calculated to engage the attention of young people while conveying to them much solid religious information and suggestions. This is a difficult task, especially upon subjects of this description; but the author has certainly succeeded, by means of an animated style, lively illustration, and apt anecdotes, in making an interesting and useful contribution to a branch of religious literature, the importance of which cannot be too highly estimated.

The Analysis of Sentences explained and systematised. By J. D. MORELL, A.M. London: Theobald, 1852.

IF language is the vehicle of thought, grammar assuredly supplies the wheels, axles, and springs. It is well that the springs should be now and then examined lest the heavy loads of thought may have started a rivet, and the axles should in like manner be oiled lest the velocity of a winged Pegasus should bring about too great a friction, and cause heat or unpleasant noise. Welcome then the coachbuilder who will introduce some new adaptations suggested by this locomotive age of ours, and for a while let us turn from the pleasures of the journey to the practical necessities of the vehicle :—

'The method of analysis I have adopted,' says Mr. Morell, 'is that which has been applied to the German language with so much advantage by Dr. Becker. Since the publication of his celebrated grammar in Germany, every enlightened teacher in that country has seen the advantage of proceeding upon the principles there inculcated.

'The chief advantage I look for is to show the folly of putting etymology over syntax, and of inculcating the mere study of individual words, and their structure, in preference to the investigation of language, as the great complex organ of human thought.'

Precious Stones; being an Account of the Stones mentioned in the Sacred Scriptures. By ROBERT HINDMARSH. London: Hodson.

THIS is a curious and eccentric performance of a deceased author. It treats not only of precious stones but of all sorts of stones mentioned in

Scripture, as for altars, pillars, memorials, and the like; and also respecting the mode of obtaining responses by Urim and Thummim, with suggestions respecting the formation and use of a Christian breast-plate, like that of Aaron, only composed of texts of Scripture instead of precious stones, for the solution of all difficulties. The material information on the subjects treated of is derived from the common sources, and is not always accurate, while the interpretations and applications of a mystical character are founded on the views and mainly derived from the writings of Emanuel Swedenborg.

A Textual Commentary on the Book of Psalms. By H. N. CHAMPNEY. London: Bagster and Sons. 1852.

THIS little work simply consists of the parallel passages printed *in extenso* which are indicated in the marginal references of the larger Bibles. A small addition to the compiler's plan would have given it a utility of which we fear it falls short: we mean, the insertion of the text with marks of reference. It would then be a useful and portable manual of devotion. At present it is difficult to discover to what clause of any verse particular texts refer. Moreover, as this textual commentary cannot be used without a Bible, it follows that a single volume, though it might involve the search for references, would give less trouble than Mr. Champney's, and the saving of trouble is the sole end that he has in view.

The Bible Unveiled. London: Sampson Low. 1851.

A BOOK without the author's name or preface stating his object. The title is ambiguous, we should say unfortunate, as it might at first sight be supposed to imply a hostile unveiling, the term being more often used for the manifestation of evil than for the exhibition of the truth. But the author appears to be a right-minded Christian person, though not a scientific theologian, and has used the title in the sense of an 'apocalypse,' the development of Bible truth, or the clearing up of Bible mystery. We are presented by him (or her?) with a series of essays on the Papacy, the Millennium, Original Sin, Baptism and the Lord's Supper, the Trinity, the Atonement, Predestination and Free Will, and Apostolical Succession.

The Future; or, the Science of Politics. By A. ALISON, Esq. London: J. Rowsell. 1852.

AN elaborate essay on questions of the deepest importance. The author embraces in his scope a large field of inquiry. The papal aggression, the currency, free trade, electoral reform, church reform, civilisation, past, present, and future, the present state of Europe, and the right of private judgment are just a few of the topics which are comprised in this small volume. We do not know whether he is destined to realise his theories, or whether his labours only add one more offering to the infinite, profound vortex of human speculation. We recommend to Mr. Alison the study of the book of Ecclesiastes.

Scripture Teacher's Assistant, with Explanations and Lessons, designed for Sunday Schools and Families. By HENRY ALTHANS. London, 1852.

THIS little work embodies what seems to us a well-considered and good plan for exercising the thoughts, the understandings, and the feelings of children upon the contents of such portions of Scripture as may be read to them or by them. This is its object, and that object has been carried out with judgment and skill. The use of this plan, or one based upon it, in schools and families could not fail to be beneficial.

INTELLIGENCE.

BIBLICAL.

The Editor of the *Chronological New Testament* has in preparation, and intends publishing in January, Part I. (containing Genesis) of the *Chronological Old Testament*. The work will be framed on the model of that of the New Testament; but as the Old requires and admits of more extensive improvement, so it has received at the hands of the Editor many helps to its elucidation which the New was not capable of receiving.

I. It has been attempted to supplement the unsystematic simplicity of the historical portions of the Old Testament by full chronological and geographical notes.

II. A translation is given in the margin of every passage in the Septuagint cited in the New Testament, from which it will be seen that, though it is sometimes the case that the writers of the New Testament take their citations from the Septuagint, yet that it is not generally true, for in some instances they differ from both the Hebrew text and the Greek version.

III. Parallel passages, affecting the sense and throwing light upon the text, are printed in full, instead of being simply referred to.

IV. At the end of each book is given a series of critical notes on the original Hebrew, with a collation of the various readings in all the ancient versions in Walton's Polyglot Bible, viz. the Samaritan text and version, Chaldee Targums of Onkelos, Jonathan Ben Uziel, and Jerusalem, Syriac, Arabic, Septuagint, and Vulgate.

The design of this part of the work is two-fold:—First, to compare the authorised English version with the original text, with the view of rendering the translation more strictly conformable to the Hebrew, and more uniform in its renderings. Secondly, to compare all the versions above named, noting down the variations in order to enable the English reader to judge of the meaning attached to Scripture by the ancient interpreters. If this part of the work is well done, as we doubt not it will be, from the specimens which we have seen, it will be worth the price charged, whatever that may be, for the whole Part, for it will to a great extent supersede the necessity of acquiring a knowledge of the originals at all.

Besides these main features, there are given several minor helps, viz. an entire re-division of the Bible into paragraphs and sections, instead of, but still retaining, the chapters and verses; references to the parallel histories of the Kings of Judah and Israel, and to the sections of prophecy delivered during each reign, with a re-division of the prophecies, putting each section of prophecy by itself, with its date and an analysis of its contents.

To a limited extent instances of mis-translation have been noticed, and a more correct rendering offered. In fine, the Editor of the Chronological Bible aims at presenting an interesting edition of the Scriptures, retaining the authorised version, but extending its usefulness by giving such helps as the age demands and the state of Biblical science admits of. In common with the voice of the whole of the contemporary press, we have more than once expressed our admiration of the taste and skill displayed by the Editor of the *Chronological New Testament*, and we have no doubt that the same sound judgment, aided as that is by experience, will carry him safely through his more difficult task.

A careful examination of the different periods during which the missionaries of the different societies have laboured in India, will at once explode a fallacy, widely circulated among the friends of missions, in relation to the length of missionary service. It is generally believed that in India, owing to the deadly climate, the average duration of missionary life is seven years; and many have come out as missionaries under the idea that they would be certain to meet with a premature death; but this is a great mistake. From a careful induction of the lives or services of 250 missionaries, we have found that hitherto the average duration of missionary labour in India has been 16 years and 9 months each. It was doubtless much less at first, and numerous cases can be adduced in which young missionaries were cut off after a very short term of labour. But a better knowledge of the climate, and of the precautions to be used against it, the use of airy dwelling-houses and light dress, with other circumstances, have tended very much to reduce the influence of the climate and preserve health; so that the average duration of life and labour is improving every year. As an illustration of this fact, we may state that, out of the 147 missionaries labouring in India and Ceylon in 1830, 50 (we can give their names) are still labouring in health and usefulness; while of the 97 others who have since died or retired, 20 laboured more than 20 years each. Several living missionaries have been in India more than 30 years. It is a remarkable fact that the average missionary life of 47 of the Zanguebar missionaries last century was 22 years each.—*Calcutta Review.*

The American National Intelligence contains the following. 'By the politeness of Colonel Lea, Commissioner of Indian Affairs, we have seen a curiosity of great rarity and interest, left for a few days at the Bureau. It was brought from the Pottawatomie Reservation on the Kansas river, by Dr. Lykins, who has been residing there nearly 20 years.

' It consists of four small rolls or strips of parchment, closely packed in the small compartment of a little box or locket, of about an inch cubical content. On these parchments are written, in a style of unsurpassed excellence, and far more beautiful than print, portions of the Pentateuch, to be worn as frontlets. Dr. Lykins obtained it from Pategwe Pottawatomie, who got it from his grandmother, a very old woman. It has been in this particular family about 50 years. They had originally two of them, but one was accidentally lost in crossing a rapid. The one lost was believed by the Indians to contain an account of the creation of the world. It has been kept for a very long period in the medicine-bag of the tribe. Pategwe had it in his possession many years before his curiosity prompted him to cut the stitches of the cover and disclose the contents. Dr. Lykins came to a knowledge of it from a half-breed. The wonder is how this singular article came into their possession. When asked how long they can trace back its history, they reply they cannot tell when they had it not. The question occurs here, does not this circumstance give some colour to the idea, long and extensively entertained, that the Indians of our continent are more or less of Jewish origin?'

At a meeting of the Society of Antiquaries of Scotland a communication was read by Mr. Alexander Christie, entitled ' Remarks on the occurrence of ornamentation of a Byzantine character on weapons and carved wooden implements, made by the natives of an African tribe on the coast of the Red Sea.' Various specimens of native workmanship, including weapons and domestic implements recently brought from Aden, were exhibited. The most beautiful were a set of large wooden spoons, decorated with the same interlaced ornaments as are familiar to us on the sculptured Scottish standing stones, and on ecclesiastical relics of native workmanship, both in Scotland and Ireland, previous to the 12th century. Mr. Christie also read an account of this African tribe from notices of a recent traveller, shewing that they still retain among them the traces of a corrupt Christian creed, and expressed his belief that in the remarkable correspondence of the style of art still preserved and practised among them we have evidence of their descent from a branch of the ancient African Church planted by some of the early Christian fathers in Abyssinia and along the coast of the Red Sea.

It appears from a paper recently read in the Academy of Archæology, at Rome, that Father Secchi has found a new interpretation of the Egyptian hieroglyphics, which enables him to declare that most of them are not mere tombstone inscriptions as is generally assumed, but poems. He has given several of his readings, which display great ingenuity, and he professes to be able to decipher the inscriptions on the obelisk of Luxor at Paris.

The Minister of the Interior, Paris, has received further accounts of the explorations which are being carried on by M. Place, Consul of France at Mossul, in the ruins of Nineveh. In addition to large statues, bas-reliefs in marble, pottery, and articles of jewellery, which throw light on the habits and customs of the inhabitants of the ancient city, he has been able to examine the whole of the palace of Khorsabad and its dependencies, and in so doing has elucidated some doubtful points, and obtained proof that the Assyrians were not ignorant of any of the resources of architecture. He has also discovered a large gate, twelve feet high, which appears to have been one of the entrances to the city, several constructions in marble, two rows of columns, apparently extending a considerable distance, the cellar of the palace, still containing regular rows of jars, which had evidently been filled with wine, and at the bottom of which jars there is still a sort of deposit of a violet colour. M. Place has, moreover, discovered the storehouse of pottery, containing various articles. In addition to all this, he has caused excavations to be made in the hills of Baashiekhah, Karamles, Teu Leuben, Mattai, Kerkúk, Digan, &c., on the left hand of the Tigris, within ten leagues from Khorsabad. In them he has found monuments, tombs, jewellery, and some articles in gold and other metal and stone. At Dziziran there is a monument, which, it is supposed, may turn out to be as large as that of Khorsabad.

At Mattai, and at a place called Barrian, M. Place has found bas-reliefs cut in the solid rock; they consist of a number of colossal figures, and of a series of full-length portraits of the Kings of Assyria.

M. Place has taken copies of his discoveries by means of the photographic process; and he announces that Colonel Rawlinson has authorised him to make diggings near the places which the English are engaged in examining.—*Morning Herald*, Aug. 4th.

From the Report of the Foreign Translation Committee of the Society for Promoting Christian Knowledge, for 1852, we learn that two editions of the Scriptures in French have been published, a 4to. edition printed at Paris, and an 8vo. edition printed in London. The work is not an entirely new translation, but a revision of Martin's, under the superintendence of Dr. Matter. A smaller edition in 16mo. is nearly completed.

The report states that 'The version of Martin was carefully corrected, by comparing it with the original Hebrew and Greek, obsolete words and expressions were replaced by those more in accordance with modern usage, and the language in general was rendered more perspicuous, without altogether robbing it of its venerable air of antiquity.'

The fourth and concluding volume of the Septuagint, printed at Athens for the use of the Greek Church, having been completed last autumn, there is now printing an edition of the Greek New Testament, to form a uniform fifth volume. The Septuagint is printed from the authorised Moscow text, which appears on examination to follow the 'Codex Alexandrinus,' and not, as is the case with editions in popular use in this country, the 'Codex Vaticanus.'

A translation of the Old Testament into Spanish is progressing satisfactorily. Arrangements have been made for a new and complete revision of Diodati's Italian Bible. Existing circumstances render this at once a most important and also a most delicate undertaking, but the Committee indulge the hope that they have come to a wise decision as to the principle on which the revision should be conducted.

A new edition of 5000 copies of the Book of Common Prayer, in the Maori or New Zealand language, will soon be completed. The Committee have been able to take advantage of Archdeacon Williams's visit to England, to correct this version where necessary, throughout, and to supply, in full, the Epistles and Gospels, which were only referred to, in the former editions, by their chapters and verses.

It was one of the objects of the Archdeacon's visit to London to carry through the press a corrected version of the New Testament in the Maori language; and this task accomplished, the completion of the Prayer Book was an easy work.

The Committee have also undertaken translations, in Italian, of Jewel's 'Apology,' and of Bishop Bull's 'Treatise on the Corruptions of the Church of Rome:' they have published an edition of Archbishop Whately's tract on the Christian Evidences, in Polish; and they have made arrangements for the translation of the same useful little treatise into the Bohemian language. Very recently also, in consequence of important and interesting information received from the East, measures have been adopted for the translation of Professor Blunt's 'History of the Reformation in England' into Arabic.

LITERARY AND EDUCATIONAL.

Mr. Talmage, of the American Mission, whom we mentioned in our April No. as engaged in an experiment in the hope of giving to the Chinese, by the use of the Roman alphabet, a literature in their spoken language, writes thus, 22nd January, 1852. 'This experiment promises well, but it necessarily advances very slowly. We have no printing-press at Amoy: and at Canton and Hong-kong, where they have printing-presses, there is no one thoroughly acquainted with the Amoy dialect, to correct the proof-sheets. The only part of the Bible yet printed in the Amoy colloquial is a small tract, called the 'History of Joseph.' This was printed by Mr. Williams of Canton. In consequence of his general knowledge of the Chinese language, he has been able to give it to us with very few typographical errors. The gospel of St. John is now nearly ready for the press; and Mr. Williams has kindly offered to print this and other parts of the Scriptures for us.'— *American Missionary Herald*, May, 1852.

At the Asiatic Society, July 3, Mr. Norris read a paper ' On the so-called Median inscription of Behistun,' which he trusted he could shew to be in a Scythic dialect, analogous in many of its forms, and most of its grammatical structure, to the language called Ugrian, including the Magyar and Ostiak, and the several tongues still spoken on the banks of the Volga, more especially the Volga Finnish. In concluding the reading, he said that the only names of a people found on the rock, not immediately taken from the Persian original, was one that might be read Amardi or Avardi, and he thought that this was one of the tribes who spoke the language which he was engaged in investigating. He suggested also that the Avars, who were found upon the Volga, towards the decline of the Roman empire, might have been allied to the same race.—*Literary Gazette*, Aug. 7.

The Theological Prize Essays at Oxford, for the present year, have been thus adjudged :—

Ellerton Essay.—'The Effects of the Captivity on the Jewish People.' Daniel Trinder, Esq.

Mrs. Denyer's.—'The Justification of Man before God, only by the Merits of our Lord Jesus Christ.' The Rev. James Leycester Balfour, B.A.

'The Duties of Christianity incumbent on individuals as members of a private family.' The Rev. T. E. Espin.

The electors for the Kennicott and Pusey and Ellerton Hebrew Scholarships, have elected James D. Kelly, B.A., to the Kennicott Scholarship; and Thomas H. Thornton to the Pusey and Ellerton Scholarship.

At the University of Cambridge, the Norrisian Prize, for the best prose essay 'On the Analogy between the Miracles and the Doctrines of Scripture,' has been adjudged to F. J. Jameson, B.A., of Caius College.

Mr. Kennet Loftus, the first European who has visited the ancient ruins of Warka in Mesopotamia, and who is attached to the surveying staff of Colonel Williams, appointed to settle the question of the boundary-line of Turkey and Persia, writes thus:—'Warka is no doubt the Erech of Scripture, the second city of Nimrod, and it is the Orchoe of the Chaldees.

'The mounds within the walls afford subjects of high interest to the historian and antiquarian: they are filled, nay, I may say they are literally composed of coffins piled upon each other to the height of 45 feet. It has evidently been the great burial-place of the Chaldeans, as Meshed Ali and Kerbela, at the present day, are of the Persians. The coffins are very strange affairs: they are in general form like a slipper-bath, but more depressed and symmetrical, with a large oval aperture to admit the body, which is closed with a lid of earthenware.

'The coffins themselves are also of baked clay, covered with green glaze, and embossed with figures of warriors, with strange and enormous coiffures, dressed in a short tunic and long under-garments, a sword by the side, the arms resting on the hips, the legs apart. Great quantities of pottery, and also clay figures, some most delicately modelled, are found around them; and ornaments of gold, silver, iron, copper, glass, &c., within.'—*Art Journal.*

At the Asiatic Society, June 19th, General Briggs delivered a lecture in continuation of one given by him on the 8th of May, 'On the Aboriginal Race of India.' The hypothesis which the General desired to establish is one that has for the last six years been discussed in the Ethnological Society, and was brought before the section of that society, at the meeting of the British Association in Edinburgh. Every day, however, seems to throw some new light on this interesting but hitherto obscure subject, and to afford evidence that the Aborigines of India belong to a distinct race from the Hindu and Caucasian bands which invaded their country more than 32 centuries ago, enslaving the Indigenes, whom in many parts they still hold in bondage, but many of whom still retain a precarious independence in the several mountain ridges of the continent of India, where they adhere to their ancient and barbarous usages. The historical facts mainly relied on are that the Vedas state distinctly that the Asians, whom the lecturer called Hindus, in distinction from the Aborigines, came from a region north and west of India; that they were a fair race, and that they distributed themselves about the lands of those whom they subdued. 2nd. Menu describes the limits of the Hindus, but alludes also to other races. Herodotus (Thalia, c. 2) speaks of Indians living on the rivers, and of another race more remote whose habits were civilized.

The former are yet to be seen, subsisting on fish caught from boats made of bamboos covered with leather, and themselves without any covering than a rough mat.

There are also many tribes scattered over the country, on the sea-coast, in the villages, and especially on the mountain ridges. The physiognomy of the latter, and also their habits, are Scythian. They have nothing in common with the Hindus, by whom they are held in abomination. Their customs have a close affinity to the nation inhabiting Lower Thibet; and, finally, all the vernacular dialects of India have a uniform grammatical structure totally different from the Sanskrit.

The hypothesis then is, that Ancient India was inhabited by two races, and that these Aborigines are the remnant of a Scythian race in a state of barbarism, and in which they now are, and who were subdued by the Hindus, a civilized race, coming from the West.

In a religious point of view these Aborigines are in the happiest condition to receive the Gospel. Their minds are a mere blank, without any pre-conceived notions of a revealed religion, and scarcely acknowledging a God. On what portion of the Indian population could the efforts of the missionary be more usefully and successfully employed than in the conversion to Christianity of the benighted Aborigines, who have, as subjects, proved themselves the best police in the world, and the earliest and best portion of our native troops, and who have, on all occasions, been willing to hear and accept the blessings which a revealed religion offers to them in a future state ?—*Literary Gazette.*

As a supplement to the above Report of General Briggs' *Lecture,* we give the following extract from an Address by the Rev. H. R. Hoisington, of Ceylon, delivered before the Society of Inquiry at Andover, U. S., 1st September, 1851. 'The Hindus were not the first inhabitants of India. Remnants of the aborigines of the country are still to be traced in various tribes inhabiting the fastnesses of the hills and forests. They are known under different names. Their several dialects, in most cases allied to each other, have no affinity to the Sanskrit. Never incorporated with their victors, they have maintained their simplicity of manners and a rude religious creed which bears no resemblance to Hindûism. As successive conquerors poured into the country, these aborigines betook themselves to the protection of the less accessible regions, where they still exist.'

In further elucidation of the subject of the aboriginal races of India, we add the following from Dr. Wilson's work on the Evangelization of India, p. 320:—' They are to be found in all the recesses and table-land of Sahyádri range and its adjoining districts, to its termination near Cornerin. Amongst them are to be ranked the well-known Shanars, and the slave and degraded population of Canara, Malabar, and Travancore. They abound in the ceded territories on the banks of the Nirmadá, and are the principal inhabitants of the province of Gondwáná. They extend eastward to the Gangetic provinces; and on the line of the Mahámadí they approach Kattak. They cover the sides and flanks of the Himalayan range, and are the principal inhabitants of the provinces east of Bengal. In short, there is not a district in India, of any considerable extent, of the population of which they do not form a considerable part.'

To the prosecution of missionary labour amongst these tribes there are peculiar encouragements. ' No venerated literature records the deeds or characters of their deities, no powerful and sagacious priesthood holds them in a state of mental or moral vassalage ; but, led simply by feelings of mysterious awe and dread, which sin has given as our heritage, to deprecate by sacrifices and mystic ceremonies the supposed wrath of an unknown God, they have ever evinced a disposition to listen to the soothing assurances of the gospel, to be charmed by the beauties of knowledge and truth, as it is unfolded to them, and to return the most ardent gratitude to those who have turned with Christian affection to raise them in the scale of being.'—*Dr. F. M'Leod, of the Bengal Civil Service.*

' The results of our own labours,' says the *Church Missionary Intelligencer,* ' amongst the Shanar population of the Tinnevelly province, sustain such observations, and encourage us to attempt more in the same direction. The hills and mountain valleys, and dense jungles of India, contain tribes and races well worthy of being sought out—remnants of nations who have secluded themselves from intercourse with their fellow-men, because the traditions of the past testified of no deeds of love, but only of cruelty and oppression experienced at their hands; who found themselves weak, and, fearing power because they never found it combined with mercy, interposed the impervious forest or the precipitous mountain range between themselves and man, their greatest enemy, in comparison with whom the wild elephant and tiger ceased to be formidable.'

The subject of the Newdigate prize poem for next year is the 'Ruins of Egyptian Thebes.' That of Dr. Ellerton's theological prize for the ensuing year is 'The legitimate use of the Apocrypha;' and those of Mrs. Denyer's theological prizes are, 'The influence of practical piety in promoting the temporal happiness of mankind;' and, 'In the unity of the Godhead there are three persons, of one substance, power, and eternity.'

Bishop Payne, of the American Church Missions, was to sail at the beginning of May for Cape Palmas, with several missionaries. The Bishop of Shanghai has set about making a selection (out of the 40,000 characters which are said to be comprised in the Chinese language) of about 4000 which are most commonly in use, or most needed for religious teaching.

At the Asiatic Society, July 3rd, there was a letter read from Dr. Royle, relative to internal evidence in the Vedas, derivable from natural history, which might bear on the locality of their origin. He stated that he had found none which was not Indian. The most curious of the substances he had looked at was the *soma* plant, which played so important a part in the religious ceremonies of the ancient Hindus.

From several data which he gave, Dr. Royle inferred that the early Hindus could have found it only in the west of India in the abundance necessary for their daily sacrifices. He was also of opinion that there only could they have known the sea and made laws relative to marine insurances, and that it was there that the Hindus attained to such a point of civilization that the Arabians and the Phœnicians coveted their manufactures, and carried their spices and productions through the Red Sea and the Persian Gulf to all the nations of antiquity.

The notice of a comparative vocabulary of the Sghā and Pgho dialects of the Karens was then submitted to the Meeting, and some interesting remarks were read relative to the connection between the Indo-Chinese monosyllabic dialects and the Indo-Germanic tongues, by J. W. Laidly, Esq. The tribes who spoke these dialects are an immigrant people, but they have preserved uncontaminated their nationality and their peculiar religious tenets. The remarks of Mr. Laidly tended to shew the mode, or one of the modes, in which the polysyllabic languages have been formed. A paper was laid before the meeting, written by Captain Chapman, purporting to shew that Asoka, the great Buddhist monarch of India, was identical with the Sandracottus of Megasthenes.

An extract of a letter from Colonel Rawlinson was also read, in which the Colonel made three rectifications, which, since his paper on 'The outline of the Assyrian Empire,' he had found it necessary to make.—*Literary Gazette*, Aug. 7.

At the Royal Society of Literature, July 7th, there was a letter read from Charles Newton, Esq., giving an account of the objects which he saw still preserved in Athens, and chiefly of the numerous fragments of the ancient Greek art contemporary with and posterior to the time of Phidias, with lists of these fragments, and notices of the places in which they are at present preserved. Mr. Newton remarked that it would be difficult, without actually visiting the Acropolis, to form any idea of the interest and value of these fragments as a further illustration of the sculptures in the Elgin room, to which they are as essential as leaves torn out of a MS. are to the book itself.—*Literary Gazette*, July 24th.

Clot Bey, a French physician of Cairo, converted to the Mussulman religion, has resolved to present his valuable collection of Egyptian antiquities, consisting of bronzes, sculptured wood, figures of divinities, mummies, &c., to the Louvre at Paris. Some of these things date from the oldest Egyptian dynasties.—*Literary Gazette*, Aug. 14th.

At the Royal Society of Literature, July 21st, Mr. George Scharf jun. read a paper 'On the ancient portraits of Menander and Demosthenes.' Mr. Scharf observed that, after long familiarity with the thoughts and actions of a great man, one naturally forms some idea of his personal appearance, rarely however finding this preconceived notion realised. Of Menander, who is known to us by his excellent comedies (and who is quoted by St. Paul), we cannot speak with certainty which of two or more is the real portrait.

With regard to Demosthenes it is very different: the portraits are very numerous, and the similarity in the likeness in all of them is very striking. A bronze bust, with the name inscribed in silver letters, found at Herculaneum, determined the identity. Another bust has also been found, with the name written in the field in a kind of open tablet. But busts of Demosthenes are too numerous to be even specified. There exist also some noble life-size statues of him—one in the Louvre, and formerly in the Vatican, which is seated; one at Rome, standing perfectly erect; and the finest of all, a full-length figure, the size of life, which is preserved at Knowle Park, Kent, the seat of Lord Amherst. It exactly resembles the figure in the Vatican; its material is a fine highly crystallized marble. The surface is in the genuine condition in which it was found. It was discovered in Campania and brought to England by the Marquis of Dorset.—*Literary Gazette*, Aug. 14th.

For philologists and archæologists an interesting book has been published lately, by Dr. Lachs, of Berlin, under the title *Contributions to Philology and Archæology.* Though the sources from which the author derives his observations are principally the two Talmuds and the Midraschim, yet not only the oriental student, but, students of the Latin and Greek languages, and historians also can gain much information from these investigations.—*Norton's (American) Literary Gazette*, July, 1852.

From Italy we learn that the Princess of Canino has resolved on setting on foot fresh excavations in the country lying between the Tiber and Garigliano, where already so many treasures of art and antiquity have been discovered. The direction of the works will be given to M. Alessandro François, who has the reputation of being an eminent archæologist.—*Literary Gazette*, Aug. 28th.

We beg to direct the attention of our readers to the efforts made by Mr. Peter Drummond of Stirling, by the circulation of short printed tracts, to awaken the masses of his countrymen to a sense of the importance of the concerns of the soul. In pursuance of this object Mr. Drummond since 1848, mainly at his own expense, has printed fully 4½ millions, and the series is now about 90, including 18 Prize essays, written in a fresh, vigorous, earnest style, well fitted to arrest attention. As literary efforts the Essays are highly creditable to their authors, and these Stirling Tracts generally are well fitted to promote living religion amongst professors. We cannot but wish the scheme abundant success.

ANNOUNCEMENTS AND MISCELLANEOUS.

An official notice from Bombay has been circulated far and wide through Asia, in several native languages, establishing two commercial fairs in Scinde—one at Kurachie, to commence on December 1st, and last 60 days; the other at Sukhur, about 200 miles inland, to commence January 1st, and last 45 days—the East India Company arranging for the preservation of order and the prevention of crime when the traders meet. Steamers ply regularly up the Indus as far as Hyderabad. An increasing communication with the western provinces of Persia, now admitting an annual import of 1,500,000*l.* worth of British cotton goods, has for some years been established at Trebizonde, on the Black Sea; and in the opinion of Sir H. Willock, Vice-Chairman of the Hon. East India Company, and of various eminent Manchester merchants, these proposed commercial fairs will supply a similar inlet to the almost unknown nations of Central Asia.—*Church Missionary Intelligencer*, August.

The following is interesting if the statement can be relied on:—

America is the great point of attraction to all Europe, and not more so to any people than the Jews. In her at length, after wandering for 20 centuries, they have found a resting-place. In her they meet the warm embraces of an affectionate foster-mother. She restores to them civil liberty, religious toleration, and intellectual freedom. Here the Jewish mind, if it will, may shew its greatness and pristine splendour. This it is beginning to do.

But the immigrants have left numerous friends behind· with whom they hold correspondence. America to them is portrayed as a second Canaan, and the consequence is, the constant influx of Jews by thousands. The number of Israelites in America cannot be far from 100,000; and the probability is, that in the course of ten years there will be five or ten times that number.—*American Jewish Chronicle, July,* 1852.

M. B. St. Hilaire has been appointed one of the twelve editors of the Journal des Savans, in the room of the late Burnouf, the Oriental scholar. The salary is 240*l.* per annum.—*Literary Gazette,* July 31st.

In the Episcopal Convention of Pennsylvania, held at Philadelphia, a resolution for the admission of white delegates representing the coloured church of the Crucifixion was, after a protracted debate, and an appeal by Bishop Potter in favour of the resolution, negatived. The vote was—clergy 39 ayes to 35 nays; laity 23 ayes to 27 nays.

The Rev. Jacob Abbott is preparing a series of papers for early publication, under the general title of *Memoirs of the Holy Land,* illustrated by maps, sketches of scenery, and personal incident, &c.

Memorials of Early Christianity; presenting, in a graphic, compact, and popular form, some of the Memorable Events of Early Ecclesiastical History, by the Rev. J. G. Miall, Author of 'Footsteps of our Forefathers,' with illustrations.

Geography of Herodotus Analysed and Arranged; illustrated by a digested Commentary, compiled from the Researches of Ritter, Rennel, Niebuhr, Humboldt, Bredow, Heeren, Baehr, Forbiger, &c.; and the works of Layard and other Modern Travellers, with numerous maps.

Locke's Essay on the Human Understanding, abridged for Collegiate and General Use, by John Murray, A.M., LL.D., including Copious Exercises, compiled chiefly from the Researches of Reid, Stewart, Brown, Kant, Cousin, Whewell, &c. &c.

An Elementary Treatise on the Differential and Integral Calculus, with numerous Examples; for the Use of Schools and Students in the Universities, by I. Todhunter, M.A., Fellow of St. John's College, Cambridge.

Historical Geography of the Old and New Testaments, comprising a Geographical Account of each Nation according to Periods, with an Analysis of the Political History, with numerous maps.

A Critical History of the Language and Literature of Ancient Greece, by William Mure of Caldwell, Vol. 4, comprising Historical Literature from the Rise of Prose Composition to the Death of Herodotus.

Modern Romanism, by B. B. Woodward, B.A.

The Times of the Gentiles, as revealed in the Apocalypse, by Dominick M'Causland, Esq., Author of 'The Latter Days of the Jewish Church and Nation.'

The twelfth part of *Meyer's Commentary* (Kritisch exegetischer Kommentar über das Neue Testament) has made its appearance. It contains the Epistles of Peter and Jude. From the pressure of very numerous duties, and the necessity of re-editing the former portions of his work, Dr. Meyer has engaged the services of Dr. Lünemann, of Gottingen, and Dr. Huther, of Schwerin, to finish the Commentary. The tenth part (1850), containing Thessalonians, is the production of the former of these scholars; the eleventh (1850) and twelfth (1852), on Timothy and Titus, and on Peter and Jude, are written by the latter.

Huther notices, at considerable length, the remarkable agreement between the first epistle of Peter and the Pauline epistles. He regards the epistle as having been written to Gentiles, and therefore considers that Peter, the Apostle of the Circumcision, uses the word διασπορά of Gentile churches, looking upon Jerusalem as the centre of Christianity, since it was the scene of the Saviour's death, and of the first publication of the Gospel. On the difficult passage, ch. iii. 19, 20, Huther gives a good abstract of the opinions which have been held, and concludes his own investigation by saying,—'The meaning of the Apostle in this passage is this, that Christ in the spirit, after his death . . . went to Hades, and there became a preacher of salvation (ein κῆρυξ des Heils) to the souls of those who had perished in the deluge. Herein must the Exegete take his stand, for this—no less—no more —do the words of the Apostle teach.'

Philippi has just published the third part of his valuable *Commentary on the Romans.* The first part contains chapters 1– 6, the second 7—11, the third 12—16.

Dr. Michael Sachs, the erudite author of *Die religiöse Poesie der Juden in Spanien,* has recently issued the first part of a useful and learned work entitled, *Beiträge zur Sprach und Alterthumsforschung,* derived from Jewish sources. This part treats, among other things, on the Greek and Latin words in the Mishna; the connection between the Midrash and the Byzantine Church literature; Greek and Latin words of Semitish origin; and on the meaning of some obscure words. Among others, he notices the word carat, a jeweller's weight of four grains, and derives it through the Syriac from the Latin 'quarta.'

A most beautifully printed and valuable edition of the *Agricola* of Tacitus has just been issued from the Brunswick press. We should not notice it here, were it not for some remarks which its editor, F. C. Wix, makes on the slightly latinized colouring of the Apostle Paul's Greek. On the expression ἐπὶ στόματος δύο μαρτύρων καὶ τριῶν, 2 Cor. xiii. 1, he says—'Cum dicit ἐπὶ, &c., jure quaeris, cur ille dicat δύο καὶ τριῶν, praesertim quum eadem illa lex apud Matthaeum, c. xviii. 16, sic pronuntietur: ἐπὶ στόματος δύο μαρτύρων ἢ τριῶν, itemque in primo fonte legis Deut. xix. 15, aut (אוֹ) scriptum legatur. Quid igitur est, cur Paulus dicat καὶ τριῶν? Paulus quia in imperii Romani finibus linguam graecam didicit, inde factum est, ut graeca ejus dictio latino colore tincta sit. Ille igitur quoniam dicit δύο καὶ τρεῖς, inde conjicio eum ex Romanorum ore saepi audivisse *duo tresque.* Conclamabunt multi, non latinizat hoc loco Paulus, sed vere ex Graecorum consuetudine ita loquitur, nam Graecos notum est δύο καὶ τρεῖς dicere pro δύο ἢ τρεῖς. Hunc igitur inveteratum errorem (non licuit legere, quae de hac re scripsit Schoemannus ad Isaeum, p. 307) refutare studebo.'

Again, in 1 Cor. xiv. 14. he writes,—'Satis habeo ad unum particulae ἵνα usum animos advertisse; ad 1 Cor. xiv. 14, διόπερ ὁ λαλῶν γλώσσῃ, προσευχέσθω, ἵνα διερμενεύῃ, *i. e.* precetur *ita, ut* interpretetur (unter der bedingung, &c., cf. v. 5. ἐκτὸς εἰ μὴ διερμενεύῃ) c. ix. 16, ἵνα τὶς κενώσῃ, *mihi moriendum potius videtur, quam ut,* &c., c. iv. 3, ἵνα ὑφ' ὑμῶν ἀνακριθῶ, *parvi illud facio ut,'* &c.

An enlarged edition of Dr. Wette's *Commentary on John* has been published, under the care of Dr. B. B. Brückner.

A second edition of Hitzig *On the Minor Prophets,* and Hirzel's *Job,* by Dr. J. Olshausen, has been called for.

The third part of the *Catalogus codicum manuscriptorum bibliothecæ palatinæ Vindobonensis* is out. It is edited by J. Goldenthal, and contains the list of Hebrew manuscripts.

Dr. Hilgenfeld has published a *Commentary on Galatians,* with a treatise on the Chronology of the Apostolic Ministry of St. Paul.

Hengstenberg comes out with two small works,—*Die Opfer der heiligen Schrift, Ein Vortrag,* and a treatise *Über den Tag des Herrn.*

The *Monatschrift für Geschichte u. Wissenschaft d. Judenthums*, edited by Dr. Frankel, still continues to be published. Our Biblical scholars would do well to see this learned Jewish periodical.

Dr. Rudolf Stier is bringing out a new edition of his admirable work, *Die Reden des Herrn Jesu.* We are glad to learn that many copies of the first edition have been sold in England. Alford in his New Testament has made great use of it, while Archdeacon Hare styles it 'one of the most precious books for the spiritual interpretation of the Gospels.' The first volume of the new edition is published. It will be more fully noticed in our next number.

The following works are noticed in the German periodicals and book catalogues. Others will be found in our usual List.

Hupfeld's (Prof. H.) 'Commentatio de primitiva et vera festorum apud Hebræos ratione ex legum Mosaicarum varietate eruenda.'

Räbiger (Dr.) 'De Christologia Paulina contra Baurium commentatio.'

Rauwenhoff, 'Disquisitio de loco Paulino, qui est de δικαιώσει.'

Rudow (T.) 'Dissertatio de Argumentis historicis, quibus recentu epistolarum pastoralium origo Paulina impugnata est.'

Schumann (A.) 'Christus, od. die Lehre d. Alten u. Neuen Test. v. du Person d. Erlösers—biblisch-dogmatisch entwickelt.'

Kaerle (Prof. Dr. J.) 'Chrestomathia targumico-chaldaica ex Onkelosi, Jonathanis, aliorumque targumistarum paraphrasibus collecta—addito lexico.'

Lowistz (Dr.) 'Aus der hebräischen Grammatik,' &c.

Loch, 'Ubersetzungsbuch aus dem Hebraische in das Deutsche.'

Rabbinowicz (Dr. In.) 'Hebräische Grammatik.'

Dillman (Dr A.) 'Liber Henoch, Æthiopice, ad quinque codd. fidem editus, cum variis lectionibus.'

Ritter (Carl), 'Ein Blick auf Palästina u. seine christliche Bevölkerung. Ein Vortrag auf Veranstaltg. d. Evangel. Vereins. kirchl. Zwecke am. 19 Jan. 1852, gehalten.'

Hupfeld (Dr. Guil.), 'Exercitationum Herodotearum specimen III. sive rerum Lydiarum particula I. cum epimetro de Chaldaeis.'

A Paris bookseller advertises a production of the National printing office at Vienna, 'The Antiquities of Peru' (in Spanish), by de Rivere and de Iscudi, Directors of the National Museum of Lima. It is a quarto, with a folio atlas of 58 coloured plates.

The work exhibits the archæological treasures of the ancient empire of the Incas.

There is also advertised an 'Essay on the Foundations of Human Knowledge, and the Characteristics of Critical Philosophy,' by M. Cournot, an eminent geometrician and Inspector-General of Public Instruction; also a treatise 'On the Faculties of the Soul,' comprising a history of the principal psychological theories, by M. Adolphe Garnier, Professor of Philosophy in the Paris Faculty of Letters.

Also a new edition of the translation of the Koran, from the Arab text, by Kasimetski, interpreter of the French Legation in Persia, and two volumes of the 'History of Christian Theology in the Apostolical Age,' by R. Reuss, Professor in the faculty of Theology, and at the Protestant Seminary, in Strasburg.

A new monthly periodical has commenced, entitled 'The Scottish Educational and Literary Journal,' especially in connection with the Educational Institute of Scotland.

Mr. John Russell Smith announces 'The Retrospective Review,' a new literary journal, to be published quarterly. The design is, to seek, from the literature of the past, subjects most likely to interest modern readers—accounts of rare and curious books; essays on various branches of the literature of former days, English and foreign; and the contents of old books critically analyzed: one division of each part will be devoted to the printing of short manuscripts in Anglo-Saxon, Norman, and English, preserved in our public libraries, and another division to correspondence on literary subjects; the works of living authors will not come within the scope of the journal.

Amongst new publications at Paris there is a translation of the tragedy of Gregory of Nazianzum 'On the Passion and the Resurrection of Jesus Christ.' It is in three acts.   The first represents the Saviour's sufferings—the second, his burial—the third, his rising from the dead.   The Virgin Mary figures in all three, and is made to bewail the woes of her blessed Son, in the most eloquent and affecting language.   She and the other characters are responded to by choruses in the style of the ancient Greek dramas.

There are now in the press a 'Series of Letters from Florence,' giving an account of the arrest, imprisonment, and trial of Francesco and Rosa Madiai, edited, with an Introduction, by Dr. Tregelles.   It is thought that the character of this persecution will be more fully brought before Christians in England by means of extracts from letters *written at the time,* than in any other manner.   Such selections have therefore been made; and in the same volume will appear large extracts from official documents relating to the case, translated from the Italian.   The systematic character of the persecuting policy of the Romish authorities is thus plainly exhibited as being directed against all open profession of the Gospel.

CONTEMPORARY PERIODICAL LITERATURE.

JULY.

The CHURCH OF ENGLAND QUARTERLY REVIEW for July has for its first article a paper entitled *Popular Interpretations of the Apocalypse.* The writer says, 'It appears to us that so large a portion of the Apocalypse has now been fulfilled, and there are so many points in which the majority of interpreters are agreed, that it would not be difficult, by combining these points of agreement, and arranging the remainder of the book in conformity with these general principles, to produce an interpretation of the whole on one uniform plan, so as to become both intelligible and satisfactory to the great body of Christians.'   This all will admit, and the paper is occupied with endeavouring to shew in what manner such an arrangement may be effected.

The second article, on *Immortality,* suggested by the perusal of some essays by M. Guizot, will be found interesting by the students of mental science; and students of the matters of fact and criticism, in which our Journal is most conversant, would perhaps do themselves a benefit, intellectually, by an occasional excursion into the field of metaphysics.   The writer says in summing up, 'Such then is the true character of the spontaneous and primitive beliefs of man.   They give no reply to doubts, they solve none of those problems which are raised by science, they exist, they inspire, they affirm; but they have no further power, and they pretend to nothing further.   In respect for the dead there is evidently contained the belief—first, in the immortality of the soul; secondly, a belief in the individuality of the immortal being; and thirdly, a belief in the perpetuation of a certain bond, or of a certain kind of society, between those who have gone from the actual world and those who continue in it.   An instinctive faith, the basis of a universal and invincible sentiment—a sentiment which could not exist if there were no faith—attests from the bottom of the soul these three facts, nothing less and nothing more; but no further demands must be made upon it to explain and systematize them. Beyond the simple affirmative of the simple fact, it has nothing to say: at once sublime and modest, it *reveals* the future, but does not attempt to *unveil* it.'   We are not satisfied with the proof offered of its being able to do even so much as is here affirmed, but we commend the article to the notice of our readers.

The CHRISTIAN REMEMBRANCER for July is a good and interesting number, but not theologically. The first article is devoted to an examination, or rather an acquiescing report, of Mr. Herbert's theory of Stonehenge, which he believes to have been of much later origin than is usually supposed—namely, in the fifth century, after the retirement of the Romans, when there arose a convulsion of national feeling in Britain, connected with, if not greatly dependent on, an attempt to restore the old Druidic system, to which the Church, too weak to resist, submitted on terms of compromise. Under these circumstances, it was not likely that men would be satisfied without a visible and striking image of their new common faith. The demand for the marvellous and gigantic was not to be contented with any existing form, whether Christian or Druidic, but by common consent they adopted one which they found traditionally connected with the family of nations to which the mass of the people belonged.

The paper in favour of *Open Seats in Churches* is interesting from the facts it produces. In a short article Lord Shaftesbury is censured for the assertion, in his speech at the Meeting of the Bible Society, that tractarianism looks with tenderness on infidelity, which is retorted by the charge that 'he himself is acting publicly in company and concert with a very distinguished and accomplished sceptic.' That Chevalier Bunsen's very lax views of the authority and inspiration of Scripture lay him open to this designation we do not deny; but to argue, or even to put hypothetically, that Lord Shaftesbury sympathised with, or countenanced, such views from the accident that he and Chevalier Bunsen were both present, and made speeches at the same great public meeting, is not only unfair but absurd. It must on the other hand be allowed that Lord Shaftesbury's charge which produced this attack is unjust and incapable of proof. A grave and thoughtful article upon Miss Sellon is followed by one of 67 pages on Pascal and Ultramontanism, founded upon the edition of *Les Provinciales* which has lately been issued by the Abbé Maynard, with a running commentary of *intended* refutation, the inadequacy of which is in the review very satisfactorily shewn by an evidently able hand.

The QUARTERLY JOURNAL OF PROPHECY—consisting of about 100 pages—is too short to comprise an adequate variety of thorough articles. They are, however, interesting contributions to prophetical literature. The first article is *On the New Heavens and the New Earth*, the writer of which argues that the *astral* heavens are not intended to be involved in the earth's dissolution. We did not imagine that any one supposed they were. It therefore follows that, 'The stars continue during the millennium, and will not literally fall from heaven at its commencement. Their falling will be merely *optical* is apparent,' &c. The question *Is Rome the Babylon of the Apocalypse*, is scarcely yet brought to an issue, in the continuation article this Number contains; we therefore pass on to *The Age to Come*, which takes the aspect of 'an appeal to those who love the Lord.' It is designed to reassure those who shrink from the idea of our Lord's speedy premillennial advent (which this publication warmly advocates) under the idea of its being 'a day of wrath, which shall involve in its sweep the *entire* earth, laying waste all regions and kingdoms *alike*.' The writer argues that the vast millions of Heathendom will *not* then be visited with a 'penal infliction of wrath, similar to those penal and exterminating inflictions which shall then overtake nominal Christians as the righteous award of a just God for their wilful rejection of the Gospel.' This involves a disquisition on 'the first resurrection,' advocating the literal resurrection of the righteous dead at the beginning of the millennium. This is followed by a continuation article, being a sort of expository discourse upon that portion of the third chapter of Genesis which contains the history of the fall; and the body of the number is wound up with some notes on Scripture—mostly on the Psalms.

The (American) BIBLIOTHECA SACRA for July contains a continuation of Moses Stuart's *Observations on Matt.* **xxiv.** 29—31, and the conclusion of Professor Robbins's *Life of Zuingli.* The fresh subjects are, a clever article in advocacy of *Classical Studies*, as a means of general culture; followed by one on the *Castes of Ancient Egypt*, from the French of J. J. Ampère. The next article, on the *Conservative Element of Christianity*, by President White, is devoted to the illustration of the point that 'Christianity is no less remarkable as a cautious guide, an efficient conservator, than as an aggressor and transformer.' The *System of the Jewish Cabbalah, as developed in the Zohar*, by Dr. Theoph. Rubinsohn, is a curious and instructive paper, but which does not admit of or need analysis. A translation of the first portion of the *Prolegomena to Tischendorf's new edition of the Greek Septuagint* is then given; and we then reach, under the title of *Messianic Prophecies*, a popular and instructive lecture on the 110th Psalm, from the pen of the late Professor Edwards.

The PRINCETON REVIEW for July is remarkably deficient of articles in sacred literature. There is, however, an able paper on the *Origin of Language*, the writer of which examines the various theories on the subject—particularly the current one, which is that of Humboldt—that language was 'not *made* at all, but burst forth from the breast of man, as necessarily and as easily as her warbling notes from that of the nightingale.' This of course supersedes the divine origin of language, which old-fashioned and undoubtedly true belief, the Princeton reviewer does not fear to re-assert.

The METHODIST QUARTERLY REVIEW also gives us a singularly untheological Number. After passing articles on *Comte's Positive Philosophy*, on *Colonization*, on *Plutarch's Theology*, (an excellent paper), and on *Birds*, we come to one on *Methodist Preaching*, comprising characteristic sketches of some eminent American Methodist preachers—Summerfield, Cookman, Bascom, Fisk, and Olin. With the last of these names the English reader is most familiar, and he is here spoken of in most exalted language—'The original powers of his mind were his great distinction, and these, like his person, were all colossal—grasp, strength, with the dignity which usually attends it, a comprehensive faculty of generalization, which felt independent of details, and presented in overwhelming logic, grand summaries of thought.'—'Dr. Olin was gigantic in person. His chest would have befitted a Hercules; his head was one of those which suggest to us superhuman capacity, and by which the classic sculptors symbolized the majesty of their gods.' The substantial matter concludes with a review of M'Cosh, on the *Divine Government*—a work on which our own opinion has already been given.

The ENGLISH REVIEW for July has no *prominent* article of a Biblical or theological character. There is a paper reviewing the *Eclipse of Faith*, and in the course of his review the writer suggests some points of an interesting parallel which might be shewn between the two brothers John Henry and Francis William Newman. The estimate given of this remarkable book is very favourable, and though we ought not to repeat the opinions of other reviewers upon books that may very possibly appear before our own tribunal, yet we cannot withhold the closing paragraph. The writer ' has discharged a very noble office with great ability. His book is replete with acute reasoning, and studded with powerful bursts of eloquence; many passages possess a calm and sacred beauty, which must delight the taste and conciliate the affections of the reader; and, last not least, wit and humour abound, and ridicule is most felicitously employed for the signal discomfiture of mischievous neology. We wish the author God speed, and congratulate him on the successful achievement of his work.' The same remark applies to the review of the Rev. A. Litton's *Church of Christ*, the author of which is treated with a good deal of candour, notwithstanding he is suspected to be ' an ultra low churchman,' whose views as such the writer of the article combats, while claiming for him a fair hearing upon matters he has obviously studied well, and in many points acquiescing with him, even somewhat more than we should have been prepared to expect from the *English Review*. We give the following as a specimen, and as being in itself just and beautiful. ' The value of his work appears to us to lie in its tendency to raise the mind above the merely external and formal aspect of the Church of Christ to its more immediate relations with its Divine Head. It directs us to the vital essence of the Church, to the idea and reality of that Divine institution as pervaded and influenced by the spirit of God, as the primary idea, and to the outward manifestations of that spiritual commonwealth as a secondary and subordinate feature. It connects with the highest scriptural promises and characteristics of the Christian community that inner body of Christ on earth which is justified and sanctified, and redeemed and animated by a common faith, subject to a common Head, and inspired by a common charity.   And it teaches us to look for an imperfect realization, nay possibly for no realization at times, of the characteristics of this spiritual body in the outward Church.   We hold this to be in general a view which is calculated to spiritualize the mind, and to open larger and more philosophical as well as more scriptural views than any exclusive dwelling on the Church in its more external form can ever lead to.'   The longest article is a vigorous one upon *Mr. Gladstone, the Church Press, and Religious Liberty*—the writer of which contrasts the present opinions of Mr. Gladstone with those which he formerly held, and while believing that this gentleman and many of his followers have no deliberate *wish* to dissolve the alliance of Church and State, yet firmly believes, and believing deplores, 'that the *principles* Mr. Gladstone now advocates do tend directly to such a consummation.'   The question is not one that comes within our sphere; but the article will be of interest to those who wish to understand the position which this eminent person now holds in the estimation of the very persons by whom he was ' once universally regarded, except by a discerning few, as emphatically the champion of *the* English Church.'

The JOURNAL OF PSYCHOLOGICAL MEDICINE AND MENTAL PHYSIOLOGY, edited by Forbes Winslow, M.D., comes more within our range than the title might suggest.   The leading article, on *The over-worked Mind*, is of the deepest interest, and full of awful warning to brain-workers and to their friends.   In previous numbers there have been other articles bearing more or less directly on the same subject—·all of deep and often pathetic interest.   The article on *Magic, Witchcraft, and Animal Magnetism*, is another article possessed of general interest from its facts, as well as from the conclusions to which it leads.   In fact, we know not of any medical publication containing so much matter generally readable, or so much suited to the literary and theological student, while the serious, and even at times religious tone of the writers, bears gratifying evidence of the fact stated in the article last named : ' All the eminent physicians of the present age have avowed their adherence to the faith of Christianity, and recognised to the fullest extent the spiritual ascendancy of man.   The late Sir Henry Halford, Mason Good, Abercrombie, Charles Bell, Monro, Cooper; and among our living physicians, Chambers, Holland, and hundreds of others who hold a distinguished position in the profession—in fact all the members of the medical profession—are thus far spiritualists in the discharge of their professional duties.'

The ECCLESIASTIC AND THEOLOGIAN has articles on such matters as *Ought the Laity to sit in Convocation?*—unfinished, but apparently adverse; and on *The Law of Marriage, Ecclesiastical and Civil*, in which it is argued that Registrars' certificates are inadmissible by the clergy; and stating that the clause in the Marriage Act which directs the clergyman to solemnize marriage on the production of the Registrar's certificate, in like manner as after the publication of banns, 'was introduced, how, why, by whom, no one can discover;' in fact, that it was foisted in surreptitiously, at the latest possible stage, and in such a manner that it never came under the cognizance of those who would have given it the most vigorous opposition.   If this be so, it is assuredly a very curious incident in the history of law-making.

The BIBLE AND THE PEOPLE for July contains, first, an able examination of Theodore's *Theory of Natural Inspiration*.   There is so much infidelity in the country under the mild name of rationalism, that our clerical and ministerial readers will do well to make themselves acquainted with the weapons with which modern unbelievers seek to overthrow the Scriptures or nullify their contents. We say this more for the sake of their usefulness among their flocks than their own satisfaction, for it will not need much argument to shew with the writer (the Rev. B. Grant) that ' This invidious form of infidelity must deny its own theory, or submit to the Saviour, for it says that every man must be inspired, but confesses that none have been so much so as Christ, who will judge them out of their own mouths, for the inspiration they applaud in Him is either a delusion in Him, or their denial of His universal authority is blasphemy against the Son of God.'

'*The Danger of the Soul*' is the conclusion of some very impressively written papers. We wish to draw attention to these as good models of the style of thought and address likely to be useful from the pulpit: high-toned, searching and affectionate.

The only article in the ECLECTIC REVIEW bearing on theology is a paper entitled *Modern Depreciation of the Bible*, the causes of which the writer, under ten heads, endeavours to point out. Nine of these heads resolve themselves virtually into the natural aversion of the corrupt heart; if that were removed, these symptoms of the disease would be cured or at least alleviated. The third head is, that 'The vast multiplication of other books has been prejudicial to the power of the Bible. The mass of periodicals, pamphlets, and fictions pouring from the press in our day, has too often acted as a gravestone upon the word of God. Formerly the Book had no competition to encounter. In many houses it was *alone*, in others it was flanked by volumes which were expressly founded on, and which sought to illustrate or to defend it;' and concluding with—'a thing of Heaven, it has yet unquestionably suffered from the competition of earth.'

We are inclined to think that this is not so wholly an evil as to merit unmitigated censure: the thing is, in our judgment, inevitable from the advanced state of the human mind; men may love the Bible who cannot sit down restricted to the perusal of the *Pilgrim's Progress*, and a few simple books and tracts. We should like to see this matter fully discussed.

The miscellaneous articles in the CHRISTIAN OBSERVER for July are five in number, but all of them under the usual standard of excellence. *The Puritans and George Fox* is a subject unexhausted in its interest, but is not suited for our pages. The review of Olshausen's *Commentary on the Gospels* has much pleased us. 'Germany,' the writer says, 'can still boast emphatically of some great and good men, who stand in the forefront of the Christian host; men whose highest strain of learning and most matured powers of intellect have been ceaselessly devoted to the labour of wiping away the stains from their fatherland.' And again the writer says—

'Wherever Dr. Olshausen's exposition is such as to awaken any feelings of distrust in the healthy-minded English reader—and we fear this will occasionally happen—it must always be remembered with whom he was conflicting, what prejudices (in spite of its vaunted philosophy) he had to allow for in the Hegelian factions, what a cool eclectic spirit he had to assume towards his rationalizing contemporaries. It cannot be denied that he at times handles facts and introduces inferences, in the apologetic portion of his commentaries, in a manner which startles the reader; that he uses too much the language of his adversaries, and seems to consider questions still open for discussion which we should regard as having been finally closed. Still, on the great and fundamental doctrines of Christianity, Olshausen is as fixed and as stable as the rock on which the Church is built. The consciousness of sin is, as his translator well remarks, the pivot in Olshausen's mind round which moves all the rest: deep inward experiences, and the pressing need of a Redeemer, make him ever feel and ever avow that we are not following cunningly devised fables, but real substantive and vital truths, which breathe and burn through every page of the blessed Gospels.' We quote these sentences, not altogether for our readers, who do not need to be convinced that 'modern commentaries cannot be wisely or profitably disregarded,' but mainly for the purpose of expressing our satisfaction at such sentiments in the pages of our excellent contemporary, who adds, 'we cannot question the duty, especially of students in theology, availing themselves of the new light shed upon Scripture by the laborious and learned critical scrutinies of Olshausen, and what are called the orthodox German school.'

In reference to this matter we may remark, that in the *Journal of Sacred Literature* we have endeavoured to make use of German criticism and erudition, but to look at things from a truly English point of view—to present, in our contemporary's words, 'a body of sound, sure, *dependable* interpretation:' and though we may not always have succeeded to our own satisfaction, yet we have to some extent succeeded, and our hopes of final success are greater than ever; and our daily increasing circulation is both the element of our future success and proof of an approximate attainment.

The UNITED PRESBYTERIAN MAGAZINE for July contains a paper entitled *The Rainbow round about the Throne*, which the writer conceives is evidently 'designed to set forth spiritual truth.' We notice the paper for the sake of the following paragraph, which we extract as a something for our readers to investigate :—'Even in expounding the Divine word there is a legitimate field for the exercise of a Christian imagination. Leaving first principles and advancing to truths, the knowledge of which is designed for rewarding patient thought, cheering and animating the heart, and enlarging and maturing the character, it is reasonable to expect that the mind of the Spirit should be couched in terms that address themselves to all the powers—the imagination among the rest—with which our minds have been endowed. This mode of treatment may be allowed to be specially suitable for conveying truth respecting the glory of the Church in a future world.'

AUGUST.

The NORTH BRITISH REVIEW for August is an interesting and valuable Number. There are two articles of a theological tendency, and seeing that this is the quarterly organ of a non-liturgical Church (the Free Church of Scotland), we turned with some curiosity and interest to an article on *Liturgical Reform in the Church of England*. It opens with a warm eulogium upon the Liturgy—'The exquisite beauty and majesty of its language, the simplicity and dignity of its ritual, the richness and sweetness of its melody, the touching harmony of its cadences, the depth, warmth, and elevation of its devotional spirit, have for ages soothed the feelings, stimulated the piety, and earned the reverence of a great and religious people. The Liturgy is the precious tradition of the religious feeling and most exalted aspirations of many centuries of Christianity. All that the most saintly men, under every circumstance of human life and human emotion, have felt in depth of their souls and poured forth to the God of their adoration—all that the bitterness of the keenest penitence, or the resignation of the profoundest suffering, or the fervour of Christian hope, or the exultation of triumphant faith, or the submission of the sincerest humility, or the intensity of the most earnest prayer has conceived and uttered, is here treasured up for the sustaining of Christian life and perpetuating of Christian feeling during unnumbered generations.' After more in the same strain, the writer proceeds to examine the objections to which, as still a 'work of mortal origin,' and as such bearing 'the impress of human frailty,' it has been considered open. Respecting the Athanasian Creed, he admits that in it the theory of the incarnation is developed to an extent consistent neither with man's real ignorance of this deep mystery, nor with a due reverence for the God-Man himself. 'But, on the other hand, it appears to us that nowhere is the cardinal doctrine of the Trinity expounded with greater felicity and greater power than in the Athanasian Creed.' The presumption of the damnatory clauses is strongly condemned. We guess that the writer is rather in favour of the omission or softening of certain clauses, than for the exclusion of this creed altogether. The 'sure and certain hope' clause in the burial service is next examined. The writer urges that, although it were desirable that such an alteration should be made as might limit the declaration to a general statement of a belief in the blessed resurrection of the faithful, yet that there is no fault to be found with the religious *general* doctrine of the service; it is in the application to individuals only that the difficulty lies. It is however clear 'that the Church of England has constructed her services in the supposition that the rite was complete in all its parts, that the necessary qualifications on every side were present, and that, consequently, full scope might be given to the free utterance of the natural feeling connected with each office, unchecked by any reserve founded on the possible failure of any of the required conditions.' The writer does not find 'any formidable difficulty in the absolution in the service for the visitation of the sick. It does not assert the power of the keys. That the penitent sinner is authorised to gather from Scripture an assurance of forgiveness, 'provided his repentance and faith be sincere, no one will dispute; and if the Church deems it proper to impart greater support to a soul trembling under a sense of guilt, by a solemn declaration of the pardon whose sole warrant is the word of God, then we do not see why a Presbyterian or any other minister may not use this formula as fitly and as naturally as an Episcopal clergyman.' The ordination service is, on the other hand, encumbered with a real though not insuperable difficulty. The imperative mood in the formula of ordination, 'Receive the Holy Ghost,' is objectionable as open to misconstruction, but contains no untruth. 'If the Church chooses to frame her services on the presumption that, man performing his part, God will perform his, then the assertion that along with the office the grace needed for its discharge is imparted, has nothing that ought to wound a Protestant conscience.' The words, 'whose sins thou dost forgive, they are forgiven; and whose sins thou dost retain, they are retained,' are not so easy of explanation. It is regarded as an authority delegated by the Church to its minister ' to pronounce in the name of Christ an assurance of forgiveness, or to withhold it, according as the disposition of mind required for the receiving of pardon is present or not in the sinner.' 'No intelligent Protestant can wish to see this formula retained; but even here we may fearlessly maintain that no anti-Protestant doctrine is asserted.' There only remains the service for Infant Baptism, and here the writer takes somewhat peculiar ground. Without questioning ' the legitimacy and importance of infant baptism,' he contends it is not the baptism to which the Scriptural terms are applicable. While, therefore, 'the Church can and does uphold infant baptism as a truly Christian and most precious institution, it ought not to speak of it as a full sacrament until the understanding of the baptized has conscientiously accepted the Christian faith, and ratified the baptismal covenant. Then, and not till then, may the words of Scripture regarding baptism be applied; for then only will the sacrament be such as Scripture in these words supposes it to be.'

Article V. is an interesting memoir of Niebuhr. The writer, at the close, justly says that Niebuhr's great merit consists in his being ' in some sense the author of that new conception of history which regards the whole life of a people in its social and constitutional development. This conception was no doubt rising upon the age, and making itself therefore more or less consciously intelligible to many minds; but there were none who as yet had so clearly grasped and applied it as Niebuhr did in relation to the Roman people. The man to whom it is given first clearly to express or render intelligible such an idea is a master man in his time, and even by those who may least acknowledge his teaching, his influence must be felt through many generations.' We strongly recommend this article to our readers, hoping that it may lead to a study of the character of Niebuhr, and an imitation on the part of English students of his noble and engaging qualities. 'A rare simplicity and conscientiousness, a tender and beautiful affectionateness, united with an exquisite polish and culture of understanding, are the characteristics that shine out upon us from the whole course of his career. There is, above all, a thoroughness about him, a genuine frankness and honesty which will brook no disguise.' It is with exceeding pleasure that we further learn from the writer that Niebuhr ' was far from the desolating naturalism that still holds so many minds in Germany. The Christian convictions of Niebuhr seem to have gathered strength and clearness as his mind continued to dwell on the facts of the Christian history. "In my opinion," he says, "he is not a Protestant Christian who does not receive the historical facts of Christ's earthly life in their literal acceptation, with all its miracles, as equally authentic with any event recorded in history, and whose belief in them is not as firm and tranquil as his belief in the latter; who has not the most absolute faith in the articles of the Apostles' Creed, taken in their grammatical sense; who does not consider every doctrine and every precept of the New Testament as undoubted divine revelation in the sense of the Christians of the first century, who knew nothing of a theopneustia. Moreover, a Christianity after the fashion of the modern philosophers and Pantheists, without a personal God, without immortality, without human individuality, without historical faith, is no Christianity at all to me, though it may be a very intellectual, very ingenious philosophy. I have often said that I do not know what to do with a metaphysical God, and that I will have none but the God of the Bible, who is heart to heart with us." '

Article VII. is especially deserving of perusal. It is devoted to an exposition of Dr. Whately's (the present Archbishop of Dublin) publications on the Errors of Romanism. His Grace's former work, of which a 2nd edition was published in 1837, ought to be in the library of every Christian minister, especially in the present day, and we venture to hope that this article, and our own necessarily brief notice of it, will be the means of introducing into greater publicity his Grace's *Cautions for the Times, addressed to the Parishioners of a Parish in England by their former Rector.* 'These Cautions have been published occasionally for about a year and a half past, and now amount to seventeen. They profess to be the production of several persons, but it is understood that they are composed principally by Dr. Whately, and that they have all been published under his superintendence. As a whole they are quite worthy of his high standing and distinguished reputation. They contain much important matter deserving of a wide circulation, because fitted to be eminently useful. The first eight Cautions treat of topics connected with the Romish controversy, and the remainder present a very valuable exposure of the tendencies of Tractarianism and of the conduct of its advocates.'

The BRITISH QUARTERLY REVIEW for August contains an article which will be perused with interest by many of our readers. Among the productions which Athanasius, the renowned Bishop of Alexandria, was known to have given to the world, history has recorded some pastoral letters which he sent to give notice to all the towns under his episcopal jurisdiction of the day on which Lent should commence as well as the feast of Easter. Notices of these letters and also some slight remains of them are found in ecclesiastical writers, but until now they were thought to have perished. In a collection of manuscripts brought by Dr. Tattam from Egypt in 1842, Mr. Cureton, of the British Museum, found a portion of the Festal Letters of Athanasius; and in another collection, procured by M. Auguste Pacho, Mr. Cureton, to his great delight, found another large portion of the Festal Letters, which he transcribed, and gave the whole work to the learned world, the volume being printed at the expense of ' the Society for the publication of Oriental Texts. Great praise is due to Mr. Cureton for this and his many other labours in the department of Eastern learning. A translation of the Letters into English has recently been completed by the Rev. Henry Burgess, of Blackburn, under the editorial superintendence of the Rev. Henry G. Williams, Fellow of Emmanuel College, Cambridge.' We commend the whole article to our readers, in which they will find an account of the MS. and of the printed copy, and some exposition, which they will find nowhere else, of the literary contents of the Letters of Athanasius thus unexpectedly brought to light.

The ECLECTIC REVIEW contains this month only one article suited to our special field, viz., an analysis of Mr. Pococke's work, *India in Greece, or Truth in Mythology;* but as our own opinion of that work is given in the present Number, we need not repeat that of our contemporary.

In the EVANGELICAL MAGAZINE for August will be found a judicious paper on Work,—'the work which lies immediately before us—the work for which we are not only qualified by the laws of our creation and the gifts of His grace; but the work which God in His providence has brought near to us.' There are also two good reviews, one on the Eclipse of Faith, another on Weiss' work on the Psalms. The tone and spirit of the *Evangelical Magazine* are admirable ; and we have long admired the talent with which it is edited.

The BIBLE AND THE PEOPLE for August contains an able article, entitled *The Importance of Fixed Principles of Religious Belief.* The writer says, ' In reference to religious doctrines there are three positions taken by existing parties: I. *Inde-*

finiteness, no settled Faith. Indefiniteness, or mysticism, is the grand enemy of human progress and liberty, because so many things may be wrapped up in it; and nothing is a greater asylum for mysticism than a general and indefinite style of expression.—II. *Verbally expressed Creeds.* In the language of Dr. Whately, "these leave no room for doubt, no call for vigilant attention in the investigation of truth,—none of that effort of mind which is now requisite in comparing one passage with another, and collecting instruction from the scattered, oblique, and incidental references to various doctrines in the existing Scriptures; and consequently none of that excitement of the best feelings, and that improvement of the heart, which are the natural, and doubtless the designed result of an humble, diligent, and sincere study of the Christian Scriptures."—III. *Living Truths,* expressed in the words of conviction and judged of the Living Conscience of the Church, and becoming our ruling opinions, abiding convictions, and master-thoughts, dealing in living shoots, grafted in our souls, bearing fruit unto eternal life.'

The CHURCH OF ENGLAND MAGAZINE realizes nearly our ideal of a religious Magazine. Its sermons and sketches, its extracts and its poetry, are selected and arranged with much taste, and furnish food for profitable meditation.

The CHRISTIAN SPECTATOR for August contains a good paper on 'Inasmuch as not everything either wonderful or inexplicable is necessarily miraculous, the profession of having wrought an attesting miracle, itself requires to be subjected to a test,' viz., an investigation of its reality; and having stood this well, next, to an examination of its practical tendency.
The third paper, on the Canon of the Old Testament, is not to our taste.

From the SCOTTISH CONGREGATIONAL MAGAZINE, a well-conducted monthly Journal, we extract the following description of articles in a good Magazine. 'They illustrate or confirm our views of truth; they enforce obedience to the dictates of conscience; they inculcate the value of *principle*, and recommend adherence to it through evil report and good report; they expatiate on the vitality of *truth*; they expose the deformity of error; they recommend sincerity, earnestness, zeal, love, peace, purity; they denounce hypocrisy, strife, error, and every evil work.'

SEPTEMBER.

The EVANGELICAL MAGAZINE is so much, doubtless, in the hands of our readers as scarcely to need our pointing out anything in it. The September No. continues an animating paper on the *Results of Christian Missions;* one of these is the number of translations of the Scriptures, either in whole or in part. It may, perhaps, stimulate some of us at home to greater efforts to ponder the fact that ' these translations, in numerous cases, have been effected from the original tongues, with continuous and immense labour in collating versions, and after the most minute and extended reading in the sacred writings of the natives to collect lucid and suitable words, and to correct idioms, that the whole translation might be marked by extreme care and precision; several of these versions, too, have been printed in succeeding editions, and each has been revised with attention and labour almost equal to those which the translations demanded; and it is important to observe, that in many cases distinct and independent translations have been executed in the same language. These versions embrace the languages of more than one-half of the human family, and some of them confessedly among the most intricate and difficult in the world.'

The BIBLE AND THE PEOPLE, for September, has for its first paper *The Relation of Christianity to other Systems in the Age in which it originated.* The paper is suggested by *Neander's History of the Christian Church.* Perhaps our readers, after the perusal of the article, will procure Neander's work. They will find i interesting ' historically to trace, that when the old superstitions were dying out, and the little morality they supported giving way—when, accordingly, the nations were entering upon a decline, which was vainly attempted to be arrested by an artificial faith in the philosophers, and a blind faith in the people—that Christianity appeared in the fulness of time, at the right moment, to unite intellect and devotion, and thus to secure morality, together with national and social progress, and the perpetuation of all the improvements of society.'

The ECLECTIC REVIEW, for September, contains an abstract of a remarkable book, entitled *The Christian Robinson*, by a Madame Le Prince, published at Paris. It is intended to illustrate the wretched character of infidelity. Its form of a story will gain a hearing for its argument, which, in the words of the reviewer, may be stated as follows:—' That the soul of man, in its passage through this transitory state, requires a resting-place on which to repose its weakness. It refuses to be content with pleasures which result from the mere indulgence of earthly appetites and passions. It shrinks, as the sensitive plant recoils from the touch of man, each time that we are led into forgetfulness of the spiritual and divine portion of our nature. The God that called all things into existence, implanted in our hearts a yearning for something purer than the delights of this world to distinguish and elevate us above other portions of the creation: this is the hope of immortality—the very essence of religion—without which the most glorious efforts of human genius have perished, and the expansions of the finest intellects have been dimmed without its presence.'

The UNITED PRESBYTERIAN MAGAZINE for September has some judicious preliminary remarks on the Number of the Beast, 666 ; the solution which the author ventures to propose is to be given in the October Number.

The CHRISTIAN OBSERVER for September contains two useful papers: the first entitled *On the Degree and Manner in which young Ministers may profit from other Men's Labours.* The following is the closing paragraph :—' Above all things prayer must blend itself with all ministerial labours. Nothing, indeed, makes a thought derived from others more certainly our own than the attempt to make it a subject of serious and earnest petition. This gives a new and a somewhat original cast to the thought itself, and it flows from the mind and from the tongue with a mild yet winning force which few hearts are able to resist. To a preacher who thus combines study and devotion, though he may give no signs of extraordinary genius, the hearers listen—they know not why—and are impressed by his preaching in a manner they can scarcely understand. The secret of his influence is, that God is with him, and makes whatsoever he does to prosper.' The second paper is, *A few Words for Country Clergymen* on keeping up the habit of mental exertion. ' The duties (of his position) cannot be efficiently discharged without real exertion and energetic application of mind—in one word, without *pains;* cannot be adequately filled but by a man who has exercised and improved himself to the utmost. I am not urging upon myself and my brethren that we ought to be clever, but I am urging that we ought to be conscientious, and the conscientious man, who knows himself to be employed in the Lord's service, will desire to do what he does in the best manner that he can.'
The review of *Trench on the Study of Words* presents the cream of a highly valuable book which all our readers should possess ; and the review of the Bishop of Ossory's Charge, delivered September, 1851, on *Papal Encroachments,* will repay perusal :—' To a perceptive faculty unusually clear, Dr. O'Brien adds a judgment unusually profound, and clothes the most original thoughts in language at once intelligible, impressive, and classical: around a subject which many may begin to think is worn threadbare he throws a light which invests it with renewed interest.'

The THEOLOGICAL CRITIC for September commences with a reply by Mr. Scudamore to an article on his *Letters to a Seceder,* which appeared in the *Dublin Review.* Thiersch's *Church in the Apostolic Age* supplies a long extract, forming the second article, on the authorship of the Epistle to the Hebrews. A translation of the work from which this is taken has just appeared, and will engage our attention in the next number of the Journal, so that we may pass by the specimen which our contemporary offers. The author of *Israel after the Flesh* commences, in the fifth article, *An Essay on the Life of Christ*, 'exhibiting his divinity, his love, and the sins of men; tracing all our evils, and the reason of the atonement, to the absence of God's Spirit from human hearts.' The present portion is occupied with the nature of God as manifested in the Three Persons of the Godhead. This is written in Mr. Johnstone's usual forcible and suggestive manner, and appears to intimate, as does the title, that the essay is to be mainly doctrinal and practical. We expect much advantage from it; but it seems already clear that it should have taken the shape of a book, instead of a series of articles in a Magazine. We have next an article on the *Ignatian Controversy*, being a condensed report of some papers on the subject that appeared in a German periodical, the writer of which defends the integrity and genuineness of the seven Ignatian Epistles, according to the Medicean text, against the claims put forth on behalf of the Syriac version by Mr. Cureton and the Chevalier Bunsen. We then come to a letter from an American lawyer to the Rev. A. W. Haddan, upon *The working of the lay element in the convention of the American [Episcopal] Church;* the conclusion of which is that 'the effect of the presence of the laity in our conventions has been to give an additional security against change, a more practical character to our legislation, and greater confidence in the action of the synodical bodies to the laity of the Church at large.' The continuation of the Rev. Henry Browne's article *On the Cycles of Egyptian Chronology*, closes a variously interesting number of a valuable periodical.

LIST OF PUBLICATIONS.

ENGLISH.

Aguilar (Grace)—The Women of Israel. 2 vols. Fcp. 8vo.

Aiton (John), D.D.—The Lands of the Messiah, Mahomet, and the Pope, as visited in 1851. 15 Engravings and Map. 8vo.

Analysis and Summary of New Testament History. 12mo.

Assembly's (The) Shorter Catechism, in Samaritan. 12mo.

Atlas (An) of Scripture Geography, adapted for Pupil Teachers and the Upper Classes in Elementary Schools. 10 Maps, with Letterpress. By Walter M'Leod and Edward Weller. Medium 8vo.

Balfour (J. L.)—The Justification of Man before God, only by the Merits of our Lord Jesus Christ. A Theological Prize Essay. 8vo. pp. 68.

Baylee (Dr.)—The Mysteries of the Kingdom. Fcp. 8vo.

Bellairs (Rev. H. W.), A.M.—Work: the Law of God—the Lot of Man. With an Appendix on Manual Industry, Graduated School Payments, &c.

Benisch (Dr. A.)—Hebrew Primer and Progressive Reading Book, preparatory to the Study of the Hebrew Scriptures. 16mo.

Benson (Christopher)—Sermon on Christian Education. 8vo., sewed.

Bertie (Hon. and Rev. H. W.)—Historical and Illustrated Chart, exhibiting in one view a Record of the Several Ages of the World.

Bevan (Rev. W. L.), M.A.—A Manual of Ancient Geography for the Use of Schools. Fcp. 8vo.

Binney (Rev. Thomas)—Formation of Character, a Book for Young Men. 18mo.

Blomfield (Bishop)—The Church in Africa. Preached in the Chapel of Lambeth Palace on Whitsunday, 1852. 8vo. pp. 30.

Bouchier (Rev. Barton)—Manna in the House; or, Daily Expositions of the Gospels. 2 vols. Fcp. 8vo.

Browne (R. W.)—A History of Rome from the Earliest Times to the Death of Domitian. Post 8vo. pp. 396.

Campbell (Rev. J.), D.D.—Popery and Puseyism Illustrated. A Series of Essays.

Caughey's Helps to a Life of Holiness (American).

Champney (H. N.)—A Textual Commentary on the Book of Psalms.

Chrysostom (S.)—On the Acts of the Apostles. Part II. 8vo.

——————————— On St. John. Part II. 8vo.

Cooley (W. D.)—Inner Africa Laid Open, and the Communications Traced between the East and West Coasts; with the Discoveries of the Missionaries in Eastern Africa.

Coquerel (A.)—Treatise on the Christian Religion. 18mo. pp. 150.

Curtis (T. F.)—Communion:—the Distinction between Christian and Church Fellowship and between Communion and its Symbols. 12mo. pp. 310. (Philadelphia.)

D'Aubigné (Dr. Merle)—The Reformation in England. 8vo.

Dowding (Rev. W. C.)—Africa in the West:—its State, Prospects, and Educational Needs. 8vo. pp. 32.

Epistles of the New Testament, A General Introduction to; with a Table of St. Paul's Travels. By a Bishop's Chaplain. 8vo., sewed.

Evans (Rev. John), M.A.—Origin and Progress of Mariolatry. 8vo. pp. 38.

Evans (J.)—The Doctrine of the Ever Blessed Trinity of Three Persons in one God, Scripturally proved. 12mo., sewed.

Forster (Rev. Charles)—Primeval Language. Part II.:—Monuments of Egypt and their Vestiges. 8vo.

Forbes (Bishop A. P.)—A Short Explanation of the Nicene Creed. Fcp. 8vo.

Genesis, Chap. XLIX. v. 10, Remarks on. 12mo.

Gorham (G. M.)—Essay on Eternal Duration of Future Punishments. 8vo. pp. 78.

Gosse (P. H.)—Assyria: her Manners and Customs, Arts and Arms, restored from her Monuments. Post 8vo. pp. 660.

Goyder (G. D.)—Spiritual Reflections. Vol. 3. 32mo.

Gunnison (J. W.)—The Mormons, or Latter-Day Saints, in the Valley of the Great Salt Lake: a History of their Rise and Progress, peculiar Doctrines, present Condition and Prospects, derived from Personal Observation during a Residence among them. 12mo. pp. 168. (Philadelphia.)

Guiana (Diocese of)—A Journal of the Bishop's Visitation in 1851. 12mo. pp. 82, sewed.

Hamilton (W. T., D.D., New York)—The Friend of Moses; or, a Defence of the Pentateuch as the production of Moses and an inspired Document against the Objections of Modern Scepticism.

Hare (Julius C.)—The Contest with Rome. A Charge to the Clergy of the Archdeaconry of Lewes in 1851. 8vo. pp. 350.

Hengstenberg (E. W.)—Commentary on the Book of Revelations. Vol. 2. 8vo. (completing the work).

Hind (Bishop)—Charge, 1852.

Hitchcock (E.)—Religious Lectures on Peculiar Phenomena in the Four Seasons. 12mo. pp. 154. (New York.)

Hope (J.)—Brittany and the Bible; with Remarks on the French People and their Affairs. Sq. pp. 140.

Home Friend (The), in Weekly Numbers. (Society for Promoting Christian Knowledge.)

Hughes (Rev. Henry)—The Portraiture of a Christian Young Man. 18mo.

India, The Urgent Claims of, for more Christian Missions. 8vo. pp. 60.

Jameson (F. J.)—Analogy between Scripture Miracles and Doctrines. 12mo.

Jervis (Rev. J. J. W.)—Genesis Elucidated. A New Translation from the Hebrew, compared with the Samaritan Text and the Septuagint and Syriac Versions. With copious Critical Notes. 8vo.

Kirby, Life of the Rev. W., M.A., Rector of Barham. By John Freeman. 8vo.

Leask (Rev. W.)—The Closet Book. 12mo. pp. 106.

——————— Moral Portraits; or, Tests of Character. 12mo. pp. 106.

Legge (Rev. James), D.D.—The Notions of the Chinese concerning God and Spirits; with an Examination of the Defence of an Essay on the proper rendering of the words Elohim and Theos into the Chinese Language by Bishop Boone. 8vo.

Lepsius (Dr. Richard)—Letters from Egypt, Ethiopia, and the Peninsula of Sinai. From the German. 8vo.

Looking unto Jesus; a Narrative of the Brief Race of a Young Disciple. By her Mother, J. T. G. Fcp. 8vo.

Lothrop (Amy)—Glen Luna. An American Tale. Crown 8vo.

Macfarlane, C.—An Account of Japan, Geographical and Historical. 8vo. pp. 456.

Manly (J. G.)—Ecclesiography; or, the Biblical Church Analytically Delineated. Post 8vo. pp. 414.

Mason (W.)—The Passion on the Cross; including an Explanation of the Import of the Blood of Christ as mentioned in the Holy Scriptures. 8vo. pp. 60.

Molyneux (Rev. Capel)—ISRAEL'S FUTURE. Crown 8vo.

Muston (Alexis)—The Israel of the Alps; a History of the Persecutions of the Waldenses. 8vo.

Neander's Church History. Vol. 7.

Nihill (Rev. D.)—The Angels: an Investigation of what is taught in Scripture concerning them. Fcp. 8vo.

Noel (Rev. B. W.)—Letters to Dr. Farant on the Church of Rome. 12mo.

Olin (Dr. Stephen)—Works. 2 vols. Post 8vo.

Pike (Rev. J. Baxter)—The Curse of Christendom ; or, the System of Popery Exhibited and Exposed.

Pitman (Rev. J. R.)—A Practical Commentary on Our Blessed Lord's Sermon on the Mount, &c. 8vo. pp. 450.

Pridham (A.)—Notes and Reflections on the Psalms. 12mo. pp. 636.

Romanism an Apostate Church. By Non-Clericus. 12mo. pp. 453.

Randall (J.)—Twelve Lectures on the History of Joseph during Lent, 1852. 12mo. pp. 140.

Rawlinson (Lieut.-Col.)—Outline of the History of Assyria, as collected from the Inscriptions discovered by Austen H. Layard in the Ruins of Nineveh. 8vo. pp. 32.

Reuss (E., of Strasburg)—History of the Christian Theology in the Apostolic Age. 2 vols. 8vo.

Sandford (Rev. G. B.)—An Attempt to Illustrate the Chronology of the Old Testament by a Reference to the Year of Jubilee. 12mo. pp. 122.

Sierra Leone (Bp. of)—Parish Sermons. 12mo. pp. 390.

Simon (T. C.)—The Mission and Martyrdom of St. Peter, containing the Original Text of all the Passages in Ancient Writers supposed to imply a Journey from the East. 8vo. pp. 392.

Solly (H.)—The Development of Religious Life in the Modern Christian Church. 12mo.

State of Man subsequent to the Promulgation of Christianity. Part III.

Strife for the Mastery, The : 1. Church Militant ; 2. The Wild Beasts. Two Allegories. Crown 8vo.

St. John (Bayle)—Village Life in Egypt. 2 vols.

Suckling (R. A.)—Memoir, Correspondence, and Sermons. By Williams. 12mo.

Theodoret (Bishop)—Commentarius Gr. in omnes Pauli Epistolas. 8vo.

The Tree of Life bearing Twelve manner of Fruits, and yielding its Fruit every Month. Sewed.

Thiersch (H. W.)—History of the Christian Church. Translated by Carlyle. Vol. 1. Post 8vo.

Thomson (T.), M.D.—Western Himalaya and Tibet. 8vo.

Thorn (J. H.)—St. Paul's Epistles to the Corinthians ; an Attempt to convey their Spirit and Significance. 8vo. pp. 460.

Tregelles (S. P.)—Heads of Hebrew Grammar ; containing all the Principles needed by a Learner. 12mo. pp. 126.

Trevilian (M. C.)—An Examination of the Sign of the Beast, Rev. XIII. 18. 8vo. pp. 29.

Troup (G.)—Art and Faith ; or, the Harmony of Science and Scripture. 12mo. pp. 416.

Tytler (C. E. F.)—A New View of the Apocalypse ; or, the Plagues of Egypt and of Europe identical. Part I. 8vo. pp. 98.

Vinet (Professor A.)—Pastoral Theology ; or, the Theory of a Gospel Ministry. Royal 12mo.

Whately (Richard), D.D., Abp.—The Claims of Truth and of Unity considered, in a Charge to the Clergy of Dublin, &c., delivered July, 1852. 8vo., sewed.

——————————————————— Elements of Logic, Questions on, by the Rev. J. Forsyth. 12mo., sewed.

Woodman (W.)—Baptism: its True Nature, Object, Necessity, and Uses. 8vo. pp. 96.

Wordsworth (C.)—Occasional Sermons, preached in Westminster Abbey. 8vo. pp. 296.

FOREIGN.

Avesta Die heil. Schriften der Parser, übers. von Fr. Spiegel. Band 1. (Versidad.) 8vo. Leipzig.

Baumgarten (M.)—Die Apostelgeschichte oder der Entwicklungsgang der Kirche von Jerusalem bis Rom. Ein biblisch-historischer Versuch. 1, 2 Theil, 1 Abth. (Von Antiochia bis Korinth.) 8vo. Halle.

Bernhard (T. J.)—Biblische Concordanz. Complete. 4to. Leipzig.

Codex Claromontanus, sive Epistolae omnes Pauli Graece et Latine. Ex cod. Parisiensi celeberr. nomine Claromonti dicto eo. C. Tischendorf. Imp. 4to. Lipsiae.

Corpus Reformatorum ed. Bretschneider. Vos. 18. (Melanchthonis Opera, Vos. 18.) 4to.

Delitzsch (F.)—Die Genesis ausgelegt. 8vo. Leipzig.

Düsterdieck (F.)—De rei propheticae in Vet. Test. quum universae tum messianae natura ethica. 8vo. Göttingae.

Ebrard (J. H. A.)—Christliche Dogmatik. Band 2. 8vo. Königsberg. (Complete.)

Eusebii Pamph. Historia ecclesiastica ed. Schwegler. 8vo. Tubingae.

Ewald (H.)—Geschichte des Volkes Israel, bis Christus, Bd. 3. Halfte 2. (Now complete in 5 Vos.) 8vo. Göttingen.

Hengstenberg—Uber den Tag des Herrn. 8vo. Berlin.

——————— Die Opfer der heiligen Schrift. 8vo. Berlin.

Hilgenfeld (A.)—Der Galaterbrief, ubersetzt, in seinen geschichtlichen Beziehungen untersucht und erklärt. 8vo. Leipzig.

Hoffmann (J. Ch. K.)—Der Schriftbeweiss. Ein theolog. Versuch. Hälfte 1. 8vo.

Huther (J. E.)—Kritisch-exegetisches Handbuch über den 1 Brief des Petrus, den Brief des Judas und den 2 Brief des Petrus. 8vo. Göttingen. (Meyer's Krit.-exeget. Commentar zum N. T. Band 12.)

Jacobi (J. L.)—Basilidis philosophi gnostici sententias illustratae. 8vo. Berolini.

Jonas (E.)—Die Kanzelberedsamkeit Luthers nach ihrer Genesis, ihrern Character, Inhalt und ihrer Form. 8vo. Berlin.

Justini (Phil. et Mart.)—Epistola ad Diognotum graece et lat. prolegomenis et annotatt. ornavit indices adjecit J. C. Th. Otto. 2nd Edition. 8vo. Lipsiae.

Luther's Sämmtliche Werke, herausg. von J. K. Irmischer. Band 48, 49.
Erlangen.

Lutterbeck,—Die neutestamentlichen Lehrbegriffe oder Untersuchungen über
das Zeitalter der Religionswende. Band 2. 8vo.

Pitra—Spicilegium Solesmense complectens Sanctorum Patrum scriptorumque
ecclesiasticorum anecdota hactenus opera, selecta e graecis orientalibusque et latinis codicibus.
Vos. 1.—Imp. 8vo. Paris.

Ritter (H.)—Geschichte der Philosophie. Band 11. (Christl. Philosophie,
Bd. 7.) 8vo. Hamburg.

Schleiermacher's (Fr.)—Briefwechsel mit J. Chr. Gass. Mit einer biograph.
Vorrede, herausg. von W. Gass. 8vo. Berlin.

Taute (G. T.)—Religionsphilosophie.   (Vom Standpunkte der Philosophie
Herbarts.) 2 Vols. 3. 8vo. Leipzig.

Tertulliani quae supersunt omnia ed. Fr. Oehler. Vos. 1 et 3. 8vo. Lips.

Testamentum Novum, Graece et Germanice, ed. C. G. G. Theile. 8vo.
Lipsiae.

Thiele (H.)—Kurze Geschichte der Christlichen Kirche. 8vo. 2nd Edition.
Zurich.

Tholuck (Dr. A.)—Der Geist der Lutherischen Theologer Wittenbergs im
Verlaufe des 17 Jahrhunderts. 8vo. Hamburg.

Thiersch (H. W. J.)—Geschichte der Christlichen Kirche im Alterthum.
Theil 1. 8vo. Frankfurt.

Uhlhorn (G.)—Fundamenta chronolog. Tertullianae. 8vo. Göttingae.

Volckmar (G.)—Das Evangelium Marcions.   Text und Kritik mit Ruck-
sicht auf die Evangelien des Märt. Justin, der Clementinen und der apostol. Vater. 8vo.
Leipzig.

Wette (W. M. L. de)—Kurze Erklärung des Evangeliums und der Briefe
Johannis. 4to. Ausg. bearb. von B. B. Brückner. (Handbuch zum N. T. Band 1, Theil 3.)
Leipzig.

——————————— Lehrbuch der historisch-kritischer Einleitung in die Bibel
Alten und Neuen Testaments. 2 Vols. 7th Edition. 8vo. Berlin.

OBITUARY.

May 4th. At Wymondham, Norfolk, the Rev. Theyre T. Smith, M.A. Mr. Smith was for more than ten years assistant preacher at the Temple, where his sermons were very admirable. His collation to the vicarage of Wymondham, a preferment entirely unexpected and unsolicited, was made in consequence of the Bishop of Ely's (Dr. Turton) admiration of Mr. Smith's discourses as Hulsean lecturer at Cambridge. His published works were, 1. 'Sermons preached at the Temple Church, and before the University of Cambridge, during January, 1838.' 8vo. 2. 'Hulsean Lectures for the year 1839 : Man's responsibility in reference to his religious belief explained and applied.' 8vo. 3. 'Hulsean Lectures for the year 1840.' 4. ' Remarks on the influence of Tractarianism, or Church Principles, so called, in promoting secessions to the Church of Rome,' 1851. 8vo.—*Gentleman's Magazine*, July.

On July 1st, in his 54th year, the Rev. Edward Murray, Vicar of Northolt. He was a member of Trinity College, Cambridge, and took his B.A. degree in 1820. Mr. Murray was a good Hebrew scholar. He was the author of ' Enoch Restitutus ;' of a work on the Apocalypse ; and of a compilation of Calvin's Prayers. —*Gentleman's Magazine*, Sept.

Count Pompeo Litta, a well-known Italian author, died on the 17th of August, at Milan, his native place, at the age of 72.
His principal work is a ' History of celebrated Italian Families,' in which, in addition to much literary merit, a good deal of patriotic spirit is displayed. The deceased was at one time a soldier, and took part in some of the celebrated battles of Napoleon.—*Literary Gazette*, Aug. 28th.

On the 15th of August, died at Bad-Weilbach, on the Rhine, Dr. Herbert Mayo, F.R.S.
He was a man of much professional ability and of varied accomplishments. His published works are numerous, the earlier ones chiefly on practical subjects and on physiology, which was the department of medical science most congenial to him. The latest of his works, and those most interesting to the general reader, are, ' Letters on the Truths contained in popular Superstitions,' and ' On the Philosophy of Living.' In the former of these works he traces, with much ingenuity, the physiological causes of various illusions, admitting a real foundation for many of these popular beliefs. The other work contains precepts on diet, exercise, bathing, regimen, and other points of the philosophy of living, in language adapted to popular use.—*Literary Gazette*, Aug. 28th.

May 3rd, 1852, at 10, Chester Place, Regent's Park, Sara Coleridge, aged 49, only daughter of S. T. Coleridge, and widow of H. N. Coleridge, Esq. The deceased lady was the inheritrix of her father's genius, and almost rival of his attainments ; but her high intellectual powers were held in harmony with feminine delicacy and gentleness. Her first publication was a translation from the Latin in three 8vo. volumes, when she was just 20 ; then ' Pretty Lessons for Little Children ;' and in 1837, a fairy tale, ' Phantasmion.'
During the remainder of her life she was employed in collecting and arranging for publication the scattered remains of her great father, and during the decline of her husband's health she was his amanuensis in copying papers for him as a Chancery barrister, exhibiting the spectacle of a pen, fit as it was for creative or poetic service, ready to do the mechanical drudgery of the most technical and unattractive copying.

Plate 1.

THE REPHAIM.

Plate 11.

Pantheon.

THE REPHAIM.

PANTHEON OF THE REPHAIM.

DESCRIPTION OF PLATES.

PLATE I.

Fig. 1. The Shethite Ashtaroth AT·SH; from a tablet in the Louvre.
2. The Phœnician Pataïkos, or PTHAH.
3. Sheth as RENPU; from a tablet in the British Museum.
4. Onka as Anath or ANTA, the Neith of the Anakim.
5. Dagon, the Philistine form of Oannes or AON, from a Punic coin in the British Museum.

Consecrated vessels from the spoils of the Rephaim, exhibiting a selection of their most remarkable forms and symbols :—

Fig. 6. Patera, with the emblem of AON, the sacred bull Mnevis.
7. Vase, with a crowned lion, emblem of the king of gods, KHEM, Chemosh-Molech or Baal-Khammon. 8. Patera, with sphinx-figure of Ashtaroth. 9. Vase, with the emblem of Renpu. 10. Patera supported by the emblem of Anath.

PLATE II.

Fig. 1. The Egyptian AT·HOR, with a cow's head and globe and horns; counterpart of the Ashtaroth of Bashan.
2. The Egyptian SET, son of NU·T·PE. 3, 4. Names of SUT and SUT·SH in the treaty with Rameses II. 5. Name and figure of Baal, BARO, from inscriptions of the same period. 6. Heads of Sheth and Horus united in one body.
7. The Egyptian ANK lady of the land of NTH, counterpart of the Phœnician Onka. 8. Name of T·NTH ANK. 9. Phonetic name of NTH, with her symbol as determinative. 10. Head of Neith bearing her symbol. 11. TEMAHU chief of the children of Anak, TAHI tribe, bearing the same on his limbs.

Sacred symbols :—

Fig. 12. Crux-ansata, surmounted by emblems of Ashtaroth and Renpu. 13. Vase, with head of unknown bird. 14. Crux-ansata vase supported by emblem of Renpu. 15. Horn for pouring out libations to the Queen of Heaven. 16. Patera supported by the emblem of SEB or Chronus, father of the gods. 17. Ashtaroth-headed vase. 18. Crux-ansata without figures.

THE

JOURNAL

OF

SACRED LITERATURE.

New Series.

No. VI.—JANUARY, 1853.

WHY HAVE THE GREEK AND ROMAN WRITERS SO RARELY ALLUDED TO CHRISTIANITY?

TRANSLATED FROM THE LATIN OF H. T. TZSCHIRNER.[a]

THAT those Greek and Roman authors who were contemporary with the apostles should have recorded nothing either of the birth and actions of our Lord, or of the history of the primitive church, can appear strange to no one; for the Greeks and Romans were not in the habit of visiting Jerusalem in the same way as the former resorted to Rome and the latter to Athens. Into Palestine, the remotest quarter of the empire, and destitute of everything attractive to men either of learning or of leisure, very few travelled except the military, magistrates, and tax-gatherers; and though a report may have been made to Tiberius by Pontius Pilate of the crucifixion of Jesus Christ under his authority, it was probably known to few, and by them regarded as in no way extraordinary or worthy of notice.[b] The Greeks and Romans despised the Jews as a superstitious, illiterate people, and consequently had neither read their sacred books, written in a language

[a] Græci et Romani Scriptores cur Rerum Christianarum raro meminerint; the ninth Dissertation in H. T. Tzschirneri Opuscula Academica, Lipsiæ, 1829.

[b] The books now circulated under the title of *The Acts of Pilate* are clearly spurious; nor will any one readily believe that Pilate would write to the Emperor such things as Tertullian ascribes to him. But that Pilate did report the case of Jesus Christ to Tiberius is quite credible, since it was the duty of the procurators to send information of such matters.

unknown to them, nor did they take much interest in their history. It is not therefore to be wondered at that they were either ignorant of the early Christians, or passed them over in silence.

But how is it that the writers who flourished in the reigns of Domitian, Trajan, Hadrian, and the Antonines, when the Christians were widely spread over the Roman empire, so very rarely allude to them? Were the Christian churches for a whole century (for Domitian began to reign A.D. 81, and M. Aurelius died A.D. 180) hid in such obscure corners as not to be observed? Might it not have been expected that a class of persons who were exposed, now to the censure of the magistrate, now to popular violence, as revilers of the gods, would be objects of public notice? Was it from ignorance, or from what other cause, that under such circumstances so little is said of the Christians? The subject deserves inquiry; and as the question has been recently started and judged worthy of a more minute examination, by a person to whom we have been accustomed to listen, we have been induced to pay a little attention to a point not foreign to those pursuits in which we are chiefly engaged.[c]

The question we have undertaken to solve relates to those Greek and Latin writers only who flourished from the time of Domitian to the end of the period of the Antonines; for after that time the Christians, brought as it were out of the shade into public view, attracted much attention both from friends and foes; and in the third century, the most celebrated of the Neo-Platonic school, almost the only cultivators of philosophy and of Greek literature, not only noticed them, but formally attacked their cause and their doctrines. But from those who lived in the times of Domitian, &c., the allusions to the Christians are very rare; the greater number are altogether silent, while some have noticed them very slightly, and as it were in passing, and a few have entered the lists against them.[d]

The Greek writers who have passed over the Christians in utter silence are Dio Chrysostom, Plutarch, Œnomaus (who in

---

[c] The learned person referred to is Eichstadt, who, in a discourse on the question 'Whether Lucian had any intention to promote the cause of Christianity,' tells us that he had long wished that this subject might be more accurately examined.

[d] It seems, however, not very improbable that in various works no longer extant mention of them may have been made. Nor shall we strongly contest it if any one should be of opinion that superstitious narrow-minded persons may have erased from MSS., or have omitted in their transcripts, such things as appeared to be said reproachfully against the Christians. That this has sometimes been done may be collected with some appearance of probability from hence, that in many MSS. Lucian's dialogue on the death of Peregrinus, in which he attacks the Christians, is not found; and in one MS. there is written, ἐνταῦθα παρείθη ἑκοντὶ ὅπερ ἐστὶ Περεγρίνου τελευτῆς λόγου, διὰ τὸ ἐν τούτῳ ἀποσκώπτειν εἰς τὸν χριστιανισμόν.

Hadrian's time set the example to Lucian of turning the gods into ridicule), Maximus Tyrius, and Pausanias. In Plutarch, indeed, some have fancied they found an allusion to the Christians in that passage of his Convivial Disputations where he speaks of certain philosophers who taught that the happiness of life was as it were comprised in *hope*, without which it would be tasteless and intolerable, and whom he therefore calls ἐλπιστικοί. But as there is nothing here which refers to that heavenly hope which the Christians cherished, and as the Christians in Plutarch's time neither called themselves philosophers, nor were so styled by others, it is quite incredible that they should lie hid here under this title.[e] We therefore include Plutarch with the other writers above mentioned who are altogether silent on the subject, which is certainly remarkable in the case of one who accounted nothing human unworthy of his regard, who paid particular attention to religious affairs, who taught many things not unlike the precepts of Christianity, and who had some knowledge of the Jews.[f] After Plutarch we might chiefly look for a knowledge of the Christians in Œnomaus, who wrote a treatise entitled φώρα γοήτων, on the falsehood of oracles; for if his object was to overthrow superstition, it would have been to his purpose to notice the Christians, who also rejected the oracles and opposed the tricks of the soothsayers; but if he proposed, in ridiculing the gods, to decry religion altogether, the same motive would have led him to notice and ridicule those by whom new forms and objects of worship were introduced. But Œnomaus is entirely silent concerning the Christians, a fact which we collect not merely from the small remaining fragments of his book, but from the circumstance that Eusebius does not mention him, either with praise for speaking favourably of the Christians, or with censure for calumniating them.[g]

The same silence on this subject prevails in the great majority of the Latin writers. It is true that Lucan, Silius Italicus, Quintilian, Martial, Florus, and Curtius Rufus, poets, rhetoricians, and historians of more ancient times, may have found no convenient opportunity for speaking of the Christians; but that the same remark should apply to Juvenal, who is wholly occupied in

---

[e] This passage occurs, L. iv. Quæst. iv. c. 3, p. 503, tom. iii. edit. Wyttenbach. Heumann, in 'Actis Philos.,' vol. iii. p. 911, *et seq.*, thinks the Elpistici were Christians; but Brucker, in his 'Critical Hist. of Philosophy,' denies that he had any sufficient reason for thinking so.

[f] As may be inferred from the 'Convivial Disputations,' L. iv. Quæst. iv. p. 507, and Quæst. vi. p. 512.

[g] The Fragments of Œnomaus (concerning whom see Fabricius, Bibl. Græc., vol. iii. p 522) may be found in Eusebius, 'Præparatio Evangelica,' L. v., c. 18; L. vi. c. 6, 7.

satirising the manners of his own age, and also to Gellius and
Apuleius, must appear strange.   To Juvenal[h] especially very frequent occasions for this purpose must have presented themselves,
as when he condemns those who, despising the Roman laws, —

> Judaicum ediscunt, et servant ac metuunt jus
> Tradidit arcano quodcunque volumine Moses ;[i]—

how could he help going on to blame the Christians, who in like
manner rejected the Roman usages and embraced a foreign religion?   Aulus Gellius, in his Noctes Atticæ, has heaped together
things worthy of notice from all quarters, but has entirely omitted
Christianity; and in the same manner Apuleius has made no
mention of the Christians either in his Metamorphoses, where he
treats of the sacred mysteries of his own time, or in his treatise
on the dæmon of Socrates and ' de mundo,' in which he discusses
the theological opinions of the Platonists.

   Thus are the great majority entirely silent on this subject.
Others have alluded to the Christians, but for the most part
briefly, not of set purpose, but as it were by chance.   Before the
time of Trajan not one allusion to them occurs; but of those who
wrote during the reign of this emperor, they are mentioned by
Tacitus, Suetonius, and Pliny the younger.   Tacitus, having related that the city was burnt, as was believed by command of
Nero, and that the emperor to get rid of this rumour laid the
blame on the Christians, many of whom he put to death in horrible torments, takes this opportunity of explaining the origin of
the name, which they received, he says, from Christ, who suffered
under Pontius Pilate in the reign of Tiberius, and speaks of their
execrable superstition and the universal hatred of which they were
the objects.[k]   The same sufferings of the Christians, whom he describes as a race of men of a new and pernicious superstition, are
spoken of by Suetonius in his Life of Nero ;[m] and the same writer
also informs us, in his Life of Claudius, that the Jews, having
raised a tumult, at the instigation of Chrestus (*impulsore Chresto*),
were by this emperor expelled from Rome.[n]   By Chrestus some
have thought was meant not Christ, but an unknown proselyte of
Greek origin; because Suetonius, though very ignorant on all
points relating to the Christians, could not have supposed that
Christ was at Rome to raise a riot there in the time of Claudius.[o]

---

[h] Satyra xiv. 1. 100 *seq.*

[i]   ' That worship only they in reverence have
           Which in dark volumes their great Moses gave.'—DRYDEN.

[k] This well-known passage occurs, Annal. lxv., c. 44.   [m] C. 16.   [n] C. 25.
[o] This was the opinion of Hilscherus, in his ' Dissertation on the Chrestus
spoken of by Suetonius.' But we have not had an opportunity of seeing either this
Dissertation, or those of Heumann and Wirthius on the same subject.

But what the learned men who have made this suggestion object to is not found in this passage. Suetonius tells us that Claudius expelled the Jews from Rome as being hateful to him on account of their continual tumults, of which he conceives that Christ must have been the author, because he had heard that this man, though he had been put to death for aiming to be king of the Jews, had yet obtained many followers, who still continued to call themselves by his name; but that the Jews had raised a tumult at Rome, and that Christ was at Rome in the reign of Claudius exciting them thereto, is not stated by him. So that nothing hinders our supposing that Suetonius may have meant Christ, who, as we learn from Lactantius, was also called, with the change of one letter, Chrestus.[p] Nor is it an objection, as Ernesti has remarked, that the word '*impulsore*' implies a person present; for as the Jews are said to have been *constantly* (assidue) tumultuous, the person stimulating cannot have been seen always on the spot. Suetonius therefore has twice mentioned the Christians, but more briefly than Tacitus, and so superficially as to show that he knew very little about them.

In the well-known letter of Pliny the younger, in which, when Proprætor of Bithynia (about A.D. 104), he applied to the emperor Trajan on the subject of the Christians, we find both more copious and more exact information. The Christians, as we learn from this epistle, were extensively spread through Bithynia, insomuch that in some places the temples were deserted and the sacred solemnities discontinued. On this account they were brought before the governor, who considered it to be his duty to examine and sit in judgment on those who contemned the established public rites. In what manner he had acted he relates at length to the emperor, and informs him of what he had further ascertained concerning the Christians—that they were accustomed on a stated day to assemble before the dawn and recite a hymn to Christ as to a god; that they bound themselves by an oath, not to any kind of wickedness, but not to be guilty of theft, robbery, or adultery, not to break their word or withhold a deposit when demanded. He adds, that the contagion of this superstition (in such terms he describes the Christian religion), previous to his endeavours to suppress it, had pervaded not only the cities but the villages and fields. Such things as it was necessary for the Proprætor to report of the Christians in his appeal to the emperor Pliny had ascertained; but he had no more accurate knowledge of their religious doctrines, nor had he examined their sacred books; he commits to writing what he had collected, not

---

[p] Instit. div., L. iv. c. 7.

with a view to its being handed down to future ages, but merely that the emperor might be acquainted with what had been done, and decide what else he thought right to have done.[q]

The same paucity of writers making mention of the Christians which we have seen in the time of Trajan extends also to that of Hadrian. For besides Hadrian himself, properly numbered among Roman writers (he is said by Spartian to have been very studious of poetry and of all kinds of literature),[r] Arrian is the only one who has named them. Of Hadrian's writings all have perished except one epistle to Servianus, which Vopiscus has extracted from the books of Phlegon, Hadrian's freedman, and inserted in his Life of Saturninus.[s] In this epistle the emperor finds fault with the manners of the Egyptians, that is of the Alexandrians, calling them a most seditious, vain, injurious race, and in this connection speaks of the Alexandrian Christians in the following terms: 'They who worship Serapis are Christians, and there are devotees of Serapis who call themselves Christian bishops. There is no ruler of the Jewish synagogue there, no Samaritan, no Christian presbyter, who is not an astrologer, a soothsayer, or a diviner. The patriarch himself, when he comes to Egypt, would be compelled by some to worship Serapis, by others Christ.' At Alexandria, where there was a concourse of persons of every race, he had heard some particulars of various classes of religionists, among the rest of the Christians, even the titles of presbyter and bishop. But stimulated by curiosity rather than by a genuine desire of knowledge, and precipitate in forming his judgments, he neglected to examine what he heard, and so confounded the Christians with the worshippers of Serapis, who were very numerous at Alexandria; and those arts of divination which were often practised by the votaries of other new and foreign superstitions, detested indeed and punished in the magician, but always sought after by the emperors themselves, he supposed to be in use among the Christians. Hence it has happened that what he has written concerning them in the above extract is plainly false and absurd. There is nothing in Hadrian which can throw the smallest light on Christian history. Neither are we in the least indebted to Arrian, who flourished in his reign; for from

---

[q] Every one knows that this epistle is the ninety-sixth of the tenth book of Pliny's 'Epistles,' and its authenticity is well defended by the latest editor, Gierigius, against the objections of Semler. This epistle, which is found in all the MSS., is perfectly suited to the characters both of Pliny and of Trajan, corresponds with all we learn from other quarters of the affairs of the Christians, has no internal mark of suspicion, and is cited by Tertullian, Eusebius, and Jerome—this epistle, I say, with Trajan's answer, must be received as genuine, unless we would reject as spurious all the monuments of antiquity, and take away the credit of all history.

[r] Life of Hadrian, c. 13.   [s] C. 8.

the passage in which he appeals to the example of the Galileans, nothing more can be collected than that the Christians were regarded by Arrian or by Epictetus (if these are the words of the master, not of the disciple) as a set of men who were led by fanaticism and mechanical habit to the same results which right reason taught the wise man in despising pain and death.[t]

Such, as far as we know, is all that can be found in the Greek and Roman writers relating to the Christians, previous to the time of the Antonines. In that period, having at length obtained learned and eloquent advocates of their cause, they come forward more into public view and general notice. Still, however, the eyes of men were not universally turned upon them; many were either ignorant or regardless of their proceedings, and the ruin which they were destined to bring on the religious establishments of the state no one as yet foresaw. But in this age, especially towards the close of it, a greater number than before directed their eyes and attention upon the Christians, some of whom have alluded to them in a few words, while others have attacked and opposed them at greater length.

They are briefly noticed and censured by Galen, a very celebrated physician of that age, and by M. Antoninus. Galen has made mention of them in two places. In one of these, speaking of those physicians and philosophers who adhered obstinately to their opinions, so that he who would dispute with them gains nothing for his pains but silly trifling, and comparing them with twisted timbers which cannot be straightened, and with old trees, which, though grafted on another stock, produce no fruit, he adds, that it would be easier to convince the disciples of Moses and of Christ than such physicians and philosophers;[u] thus stigmatizing the Christians as a pertinacious and obstinate set of men, whom he who attempted to move to a change of opinion, would labour in vain. In another place he is disputing against one Archigenes, who had maintained that there were eight quantities of the pulse, 'octo esse pulsus quantitates defenderat,' and tells him that he ought to adduce, if not a certain demonstration, at least a suitable ground of argument, so that no one, as though he had visited the schools of Moses or of Christ, might listen to precepts established by no reasons;[x] thus condemning the Christians equally

---

[t] This passage occurs in the 'Dissertations of Epictetus,' L. iv. c. 7. Of another passage, L. ii. c. 2, it may not be easily decided whether it refers to the Jews or the Christians The *Jews* here mentioned are indeed called βαπτισται, which seems to point at the Christians. But it may apply also to the Jews, either on account of their frequent ablutions, or of the baptism by which they were accustomed to introduce proselytes to their religious profession.

[u] This passage is found in his book 'De Pulsuum Differentiis,' L. iii. c. 3.

[x] L. ii. c. 4.

with the Jews, as men who rashly followed precepts not demonstrated, and devoid of all rational proof.

In a similar style the Christians are introduced by M. Antoninus in the Commentaries (or Meditations) which he wrote to himself concerning himself. The imperial philosopher, in that well-known passage in which their name occurs, inquires whence arises that affection of the soul when about to quit the body, by which, whether it survive the change or perish, it is ready and prepared for the issue which awaits it; and he answers that this preparation ought to spring from its own judgment,—that is, the judgment of a wise man, not from mere obstinacy, as is the case with the Christians. He adds, that it becomes a man to depart out of this life with consideration and gravity, and so as to persuade others to this constancy of mind by his example, not in a tragic or theatrical manner; which words seem to refer to the fact that the Christians, when led to execution, often boasted of their hope and the joyfulness of their spirit, or sang a hymn to Christ, or exhorted their brethren to constancy and contempt of death. In the judgment, therefore, of M. Antoninus, the Christians, of whom many were put to death during his reign, were men whose contempt of death, which some of them are said to have even courted, in their desire to reap the honours of martyrdom, proceeded not from wisdom but from a perverse obstinacy, departing out of life as from a stage, like ranting players.[y]

In this place only has M. Antoninus mentioned the Christians, nor have we anything further to produce which would give a more precise view of his sentiments concerning them. For the two epistles written in his name, one of which is said to have been addressed to the Senate of Rome, the other to the General Council of the cities of Asia, we conceive to be spurious, and think that they were forged by some Christians, with the design of recommending to the emperors of their times a lenient policy towards themselves, from the example of the most admired princes of the preceding age. As to the first of these epistles, in which Marcus announces to the Senate of Rome his wonderful victory over the Marcomanni near the river Granua, through the prayers of the 'thundering legion,' the thing admits of no dispute. For the authenticity of the other some things not unplausible have been alleged, both formerly and of late years.[z] But there are still many reasons for doubting it. For, to say nothing of what we read near

---

[y] This passage is found in the 'Commentaries' which M. Antoninus addressed to himself, L. xi. c. 3.

[z] By Kæstner, in a work entitled 'Die Agape oder der geheime Weltbund der Christen,' p. 399, against which Eichstadt, in the fourth of his 'Exercitationes Antoninianæ,' has so argued as to give us additional confidence in our opinion.

the beginning, ' that it is the business of the gods themselves, not of man, to punish the contemners of their divinity,' a sentiment not very suitable to the character of the emperor, who, as Pontifex Maximus, presided over the public religious solemnities, it must surely appear to every critic a just cause of suspicion that neither by Athenagoras, who addressed his ' *Presbeia* ' to this same emperor, and who has omitted nothing which might either redound to his credit, or persuade him to indulgence towards the Christians, nor by Melito, in that passage of his Apology addressed to the same prince, in which he reminds him of the edicts in favour of the Christians published by Hadrian and Antoninus Pius, is this epistle mentioned.[a] For sufficient reasons, therefore, we have passed over these two epistles ascribed to M. Antoninus, and have cited only that single place in his Meditations in which the Christians are indeed noticed, but so that the author would seem to have introduced the mention of them rather incidentally than by design.

Those writers, however, in addition to Galen and M. Antoninus himself, who in this period have spoken of the Christians, have not noticed them in the same brief manner, but have formally argued and disputed against them at great length. For that reason they have been called, and not improperly, the earliest adversaries of the Christians; among whom may be enumerated Crescens the Cynic, Fronto, a very celebrated rhetorician and one of the preceptors of M. Antoninus, Lucian of Samosata, and lastly Celsus, a philosopher of the Epicurean or Platonic school.

Crescens, the first in this list, lived at Rome in the reign of Antoninus Pius, and there publicly accused the Christians. He had a controversy with Justin, called the Martyr, and opposed and laid snares for him on account of his vehement attacks on the philosophers. These things are related by Justin, and his disciple Tatian, to whom Eusebius owes all he has on the subject of Crescens.[b] Justin does not say in plain terms that he wrote against the Christians, nor can it be collected from what he says that Crescens denounced the Christians as atheists and impious publicly, and in order to please and gain favour with the multitude. He may have done it in discourses delivered in the school, or other appointed places. But when Justin in the same place speaks of questions proposed by himself, and answers given to them by Crescens, of which he says he knows not whether they were laid before the emperors or not, we infer that Crescens had

[a] See the fragment of Melito's ' Apology ' in Eusebius, ' Hist. Eccles.,' L. iv. c. 26.

[b] See Justin's ' Apology,' ii. c. 3; Tatian's ' Oration against the Greeks,' c. 3; Eusebius, ' Hist. Eccles.,' L. iv. c. 16.

contended against the Christians, not only verbally but in writing.
He was, however, an obscure man of mean abilities, and that his
book came into very few hands, may probably be collected from
the silence of all heathen writers, and the small number of Christian writers who have mentioned it.

To Crescens succeeds Fronto, of Cirta, a celebrated rhetorician
of this period, the author of orations and epistles which were
highly admired, some fragments of which have been recently discovered by Angelo Maii. Antoninus Pius appointed him to
instruct the royal youths, M. Aurelius and L. Verus, in Roman
eloquence, and conferred on him the honours of the consulship;
so that he appears to have been a man of high fame and repute.
Of this man, flourishing in literary reputation and high station,
his contemporary Minucius Felix, in his 'Octavius,' (a book in
which he ably pleads the Christians' cause,) informs us that he
wrote against the Christians, accusing them of incestuous banquets. Minucius has nothing further on the subject; for the
notion that the arguments urged against Christianity by Cæcilius
(the speaker in the Octavius who advocates the cause of heathenism) are those of Fronto, is a mere conjecture adopted by
some because it is believed that Minucius was an imitator of
Fronto's style. On what occasion Fronto wrote, or what object
he thought to gain by this gross abuse, we learn neither from
Minucius nor any other writer. As history is silent, we may arrive
perhaps at no improbable conjecture, if we suppose that a rhetorician residing in the palace of M. Antoninus, in whose reign not
a few Christians were put to death under the charges of homicide
and nefarious lusts, might write against them for the purpose of
justifying the emperor in his severe judgments, by alleging (what
appears to have been a prevailing belief) that it was for no fictitious crimes that they were punished. It is but very little that
we have ascertained concerning Fronto; but that little deserves to
be known, because we may learn from it that there had arisen
adversaries of the Christians in the imperial palace itself, and
that the Apologists had sufficient reasons for protesting against
the infamous charges brought against them.[c]

Of Lucian of Samosata we have more to say than of Fronto.
In two places only he has mentioned the Christians by name; for
the Philopatris, in which many things are alleged against them,
is not Lucian's, but was written as late as the time of Julian.[d]

---

[c] The passages of Minucius Felix referring to Fronto are found in his 'Octavius,'
c. 9 and c. 31. Of the life and writings of Fronto see a learned account by Angelo
Maii in the Introduction to his recently discovered Epistles.

[d] This is well proved by Gesner in his 'Dissertation on the Age and Author of
the Dialogue ascribed to Lucian, entitled Philopatris.'

One of these places occurs in the book entitled Alexander, or Pseudomantis, where it is said that this Alexander, a fabricator of new religious rites and a cunning impostor, was wont to exclude from his mysteries the Christians and the Epicureans, imitating in this respect the conductors of the Eleusinian mysteries.[e] The other, from which Lucian's opinion of the Christians may be collected, is in the book on the death of Peregrinus, the famous Cynic, who, after having committed (if Lucian is to be believed) many base and wicked actions, burnt himself in the presence of a great multitude at Olympia, in the year 166. Among other things, Lucian tells us that this Peregrinus, who chose to be called Proteus, had learnt the marvellous wisdom of the Christians, and, having become a prophet and leader among them, was worshipped by them like a god ; thus designating the Christians as credulous men easily deceived by any impostor. He says much also of the solicitude of the Christians when Peregrinus was imprisoned on account of his profession of Christianity, assembling from all quarters, and seeking by all possible means to effect his liberation, and, when in confinement, cheering and consoling him like another Socrates; with the view (if we mistake not) of representing them as factious men, ready to dare anything in support of their cause. He also calls them miserable men, who, hoping for immortality in soul and body, had a foolish contempt of death, and suffered themselves to be persuaded that they were brethren, because, having abandoned the gods of the Greeks, they worshipped that crucified sophist, living according to his laws, and rashly believing these and other things, so that it was not to be wondered at that any clever and cunning impostor might easily grow rich among them and delude their unskilfulness.[f] Thus does Lucian condemn the Christians as unexperienced, credulous, and superstitious men. But he nowhere impugns their opinions, or enters the lists against the Apologists, either because he knew nothing of them, or, as is more probable, because he wished to assume the appearance of contempt for those against whom he was incensed as the authors of a new religion. For that Lucian, well versed, above any man of his age, both in public and private affairs, and intimately connected, both by travel and correspondence, with men of every race and country, should know nothing of the writings of Justin Martyr, Athenagoras, and even Tatian, his countryman (for Tatian was a Syrian by birth), we think quite incredible.

While Lucian here abuses the Christians in set terms, in his

---

[e] C. 38, p. 244, tom. ii. edit. Reig.
[f] See this passage in the book before cited, ' De morte Peregrini,' c. 11--14.

books in the proper mode of writing history he is thought in many places to glance at them obliquely. But we apprehend that this is done only in a few instances, as we no longer agree to what Krebsius has advanced on this subject, notwithstanding that Eichstadt has sanctioned it by his assent.[g] For all those passages which are supposed to relate either to Jonah, the prophet, remaining three days in the whale's belly, or to Jesus walking on the sea, or to the battle of the archangel Michael with Satan, as described in the Apocalypse, are so expressed that they might have been written either in jest, or to ridicule the Greek credulity and superstition, by a man even altogether ignorant of Christianity. The story which Lucian gives at great length of the sailors who entered with their ship into a whale, fifteen hundred stadia in magnitude, touching at islands and cities in its belly, where they find plants and animals of all sorts, and after the lapse of a year and eight months emerging from the beast's belly, and finding themselves again upon the sea, is widely different from what is read in the Bible concerning the prophet Jonah.[h] In like manner the story of the battle of Endymion and the Selenites, or inhabitants of the moon, with Phaëthon and the Heliots, or inhabitants of the sun, has little resemblance to the battle between Michael and Satan. For if Lucian meant to imitate the account of the battle related in the 12th chapter of the Apocalypse, he ought to have introduced into his narrative either what relates to the character of the accuser, represented by Satan, or to the blood of the lamb by which he was vanquished.[i] Besides, the contest between Endymion and Phaëthon is terminated by a peace convenient to both parties; but the battle of Michael and Satan ends with the victory of Michael expelling the adversary from heaven. These things are improperly thought to have any reference to Christianity, yet some things which have such a reference may, we think, be found in Lucian's writings. Such are what he says of the city in the islands of the blessed, all of gold, and the walls covered with emeralds.[k] For whereas nothing is found of such a city in any Greek writer, the heavenly Jerusalem, destined, according to the millenarians, shortly to descend upon the earth, which the author of the Apocalypse describes as shining with the splendour of precious stones, seems to have been in Lucian's mind.

[g] See the Dissertation of Krebsius, 'On the malicious Design of Lucian to render the Christian Religion absurd and ridiculous by his scurrilous drollery;' Eichstadt, in his Dissertation on the question, 'Whether Lucian proposed to serve the cause of Christianity by his writings:' Jena, 1820. In a work entitled 'Historiæ Apologeticæ,' Lips. 1805, we adopted the opinion of Krebsius. At present many of the places cited by this learned man appear to us in a different light.
[h] See this story in the book 'De vera Historia,' L. i. c. 30-40.
[i] Ibid., c. 10-21.   [k] Ibid., L. ii. c. 11.

In like manner, what he says of fountains full of honey, and rivers of milk ;[m] and also what is said of the dying Peregrinus, that he left his followers orphans, which seems to be imitated from the words of our Lord (John xiv. 18), may be thought to have a similar reference.[n]

But these things are all, as Eichstadt has remarked, matters of feeling, rather than of proof. Learned men will always differ as to the interpretation of passages of this kind. But from those adduced in the book on the death of Peregrinus, it may easily be gathered that Lucian thought very injuriously of the Christians, and no one who reads them can ever be persuaded that he had any wish to favour them or to promote their cause.[o] Such an idea is altogether vain and absurd. Lucian certainly ridicules the gods of the Greeks, and impugns their religious tenets, but he might laugh at what was ridiculous, and hold up to contempt what he despised, without any view of making way for Christianity ; which if he was instrumental in promoting, it certainly was not intentionally. For he held all sacred things in contempt, and sought to overthrow and drive out of men's minds, not only superstition but religion.

If there is enough in Lucian to show that he noticed and decried the Christians, Celsus, his contemporary (for it is highly probable that the Celsus refuted by Origen was the same to whom Lucian has dedicated his Pseudomantis [p]), towards the end of this period wrote against them expressly for the purpose of defending the national religion, which he perceived was threatened by them with ruin, of opposing their doctrines, and branding them as factious innovators, and dangerous to the state. His book, entitled λόγος φιλαλήθης, has not come down to us entire. But from the not inconsiderable remains of it preserved in the author's own words in the eight books which Origen wrote in reply, we may sufficiently perceive that he was well acquainted with Christianity, a subtle and agreeable disputant, mixing pleasantry with more serious arguments, and omitting nothing which could either overthrow the doctrine of his opponents, or bring upon them public odium. In this book Celsus is the forerunner of the Neo-Platonic school of the succeeding period, who were also defenders of their national rites, and enemies of the Christians ; though he himself was, we appre-

---

[m] Ibid., L. ii. c. 13.   [n] De morte Peregrini, c. 6.

[o] The arguments deserve to be read which Eichstadt, in the Dissertation already cited, has brought forward in reply to Kæstner.

[p] It is inferred from hence that Lucian, in his book entitled ' Pseudomantis,' mentions certain books on magic by Celsus, to whom his own work is inscribed ; and that Origen, in his reply to Celsus, speaks of it as very probable that his opponent was the same Celsus under whose name certain books on magic were circulated.

hend, not a Platonist but an Epicurean, who was induced to defend the religion of the state, not through piety towards the gods,
but because he thought it becoming in the opponent of new and
strange doctrines (for this was what he chiefly objected to in
the Christians, that they followed βάρβαρον δόγμα and νομοθεσίαν
καινήν) to vindicate what was received by general usage, and sanctioned by the law.

With Celsus the series of writers who have noticed the Christians
from the time of Domitian to the end of the age of the Antonines
is brought to a close.   Everything, therefore, which relates to the
subject, having been produced, it remains that we endeavour to
explain why the Greek and Roman writers have so rarely alluded
to Christianity.   Certainly, whether we count them or weigh them,
the notices of Christianity in heathen writers, down to the year
180, appear few and slight.   The greater part of these writers, as
we have already seen, are altogether silent on the subject; some
notice the Christians briefly, and censure them in a few incidental
words (unless it be thought that Lucian has more frequently spoken
of them); and under the Antonines, Crescens, Fronto, and Celsus
took up the pen expressly to oppose them.   It may therefore be reasonably asked why the Greek and Roman writers have so rarely
adverted to the subject, and the question well deserves an accurate
consideration.

Now, in solving this question, we are above all things carefully
to distinguish the periods of time.   For what could not have taken
place in the Antonine period, we believe to have happened in the
time of Domitian, Trajan, and Hadrian,—that great numbers were
either totally ignorant of the Christians, or had heard nothing of
them but the name.   For the Christians, down to the time of
Trajan, were regarded merely as a Jewish sect or family, and
found shelter for the most part, as Tertullian informs us,[q] under
that shadow of the tolerated religion of the Jews.   Nor will this
appear strange, when it is considered that at this time many
Christians were of Jewish extraction, and that the Church, whether
you consider its constitution or its form of worship, differed little
from the synagogue.   As with the Jews, so with the Christians,
it was the custom to assemble every seventh day, for prayer, for
reading the scriptures, for singing sacred hymns;—as the Jews
had rulers and elders, so the Christians had presbyters and bishops
set over their religious affairs; the one as much as the other repudiated the gentile gods, refused to undertake public offices or
receive salaries, and avoided the theatres, processions, and public
festivals.   It is true that not a few native Syrians at Antioch, of

---

[q] Apology, c. 21.

Egyptians at Alexandria, of Greeks at Corinth and at Athens, of
Romans at Rome, united themselves to the Christian Church, and,
by slow degrees, those of the uncircumcision were so increased, that
in many cases they equalled, or even exceeded, in number those of
the circumcision.   But this did not hinder the Christians from
being considered as a Jewish party.   For it was no new or unheard-
of thing, that native Egyptians, or Greeks, or Romans, having
become proselytes to the synagogue, should pass over to the
observance of the Jewish religion, and live according to the Jewish
law.   Nor were the discords between the Jews and the Christians
any obstacle to their being thus confounded.   For those who had
any cognizance of these bickerings easily ascribed them to the
domestic feuds and contentions of the various parties into which
the Jews were divided ; and of this opinion were those Roman
magistrates who, when the Jews accused the apostle Paul of breaking the law, replied that these things were 'questions of words
and names, and of their law,'—or 'questions of their own superstition.'[r]

Moreover, there were not among the Christians of that period
many conspicuous for rank or family, or flourishing in literary
fame, on whom the eyes of men might be fixed.   Those indeed
are in error who fancy that they were *all* collected from the lowest
dregs of the people, relying perhaps more than is fit on the
disparaging statements put into the mouth of Cæcilius, the accuser
of the Christians in Minucius Felix's 'Octavius.'   It cannot be
doubted that from the earliest times there were not a few in good
circumstances, and not devoid of literary culture, who became
votaries of Christ.   For what did Paul and Peter intend, when
they advised the Christian women, that they should not place their
true adorning in plaited hair, or gold, or pearls, or costly array,[s]
unless there were in the churches some who could procure for
themselves such precious ornaments?   And could Lucian, in the
place above cited, where he says that any impostor joining himself to the Christians could easily enrich himself, be speaking of
a herd of paupers and mendicants?   Nor were all the Christians
rude or unlearned ; for there were always found among them those
who, not only by speech but in writing, could explain their tenets
and plead their cause, and in the churches, if not as orators,
trained in the art of speech, could yet discourse on divine things
and comment on their sacred books.   And sometimes one or two
even of noble rank and station seem to have joined the churches.
For that Flavius Clemens, who was consul and cousin to the
emperor Domitian, with his wife Domititta, were Christians is

[r] Acts xviii. 15 ; xxiii. 29 ; xxv. 19.   [s] 1 Tim. ii. 9 ; 1 Pet. iii. 3.

very probable. For τὰ ἤθη τῶν Ἰουδαίων, the customs of the Jews, to which Dio Cassius says they had strayed, may be understood just as well to mean the Christian as the Jewish faith ; and what is said of their being accused τῆς ἀθεότητος, of atheism, leads us to think of the former more than of the latter, as this charge was often brought against the Christians, but could not so easily be brought against the Jews.[t]

Still it must certainly be admitted that the great majority of the Christians were of inferior condition, and not versed in Greek or Latin literature. For otherwise Cæcilius, in Minucius Felix, though as an accuser we may suppose him to have exaggerated, could not have spoken of them as gathered from the lowest refuse ; nor could he have said to them, 'Behold, the greater and better part of you, as ye say, are in want and cold, oppressed with hunger.'[u] Similarly, Celsus could not have said that those who sought to entice boys and weak women into the Christian party were weavers, cobblers, and fullers—uneducated and rustic men.[x] And if under the Antonines that could be said which Cæcilius and Celsus have said of them, no one will suppose that in the churches of preceding times there could be found many of high reputation for Greek learning, or conspicuous for family and station. The churches of the primitive age would seem to have resembled the meetings of the Mennonites and Quakers, to which resorted for the most part working men, artificers, and tradesmen, respectable and honest men, many of them not uncultivated, and sufficiently prosperous, but not really learned men, or men of rank and opulence. The first churches, it should be remembered, were small, and composed of men lying hid in the shades of private life, concealing rather than displaying their peculiarities, in perpetual fear of danger (on which account the Christians are styled by Cæcilius a skulking tribe, avoiding the light, mutes towards the public),[y] and these collected, not in country towns and villages, where all private matters are commonly made known, but in large and crowded cities, where those things which shun public view are easily concealed. It is easy to conceive that the Christians, under such circumstances, may have been utterly unknown to multitudes of their contemporaries. We have no doubt that many persons now live in London who know nothing either of Quakers or Baptists, and we have found many of our own fellow-citizens who have no idea that there are men in Leipsic who conduct their private worship after the usages of the Bohemian brethren. In like manner we imagine that there were many citizens of Antioch, Alexandria, Rome, Athens, Thessalonica,

---

[t] Dio Cassius, L. lxvii. c. 11.　　[u] C. 8, c. 12.
[x] Origen against Celsus, L. iii.　　[y] Minucius Felix, 'Octavius,' c. 8.

who were either totally ignorant of the Christians, or knew nothing but the name of Galilean, indicating their Jewish origin. Such things as neither dazzle men's eyes by their splendour, nor raise a strong emotion by their magnitude or their atrocity, nor attract and allure them by the hope of gain or the enticements of pleasure, may long remain in concealment.

But in the age of the Antonines, the Christians, distinguished from the Jews since that of Trajan, were no longer hidden, but came forward to the view and knowledge of all. All those who paid attention to public affairs could not but know that the church differed from the synagogue, that a peculiar religion was professed by the Christians, that they rejected the gods of the popular worship, that they were held together by a close bond of union, and that they had been repeatedly punished by the magistrates, and treated with indignity and violence by the multitude, enraged at the contemners of their gods. But very many who knew these and other circumstances relating to them saw nothing remarkable in them, and therefore had no sufficient reason either for examining or recording them. For at that period, when in all the large cities, particularly at Rome and Alexandria, not only foreign rites of worship, brought from all parts of the world, like those in honour of Isis and Mithra, were from time to time making their appearance, but frequently new ceremonies (like those of the Alexander whom Lucian assailed under the name of Pseudomantis) were instituted, the mere novelty of the Christian rites would excite little notice. Nor would it seem strange that the Christians worshipped the Divine being without temples, altars, or images. For the Jews, scattered over the Roman empire, had for a long time celebrated their worship in the same manner wherever they pleased. In like manner the invectives of the Christians against the gods of the public worship would not be much thought of. For in the same way the gods were contemned and laughed at by very many of the philosophers. Nor would it be thought a very memorable thing, that sometimes the magistrates took cognizance of the Christians, at others the mob was excited against them. For neither the populace tumultuously demanding the death of the Christians, nor the sentence of the judges condemning them to death, disturbed the state, and those who perished in this manner were obscure men, whose fate it did not seem worth while to hand down to posterity.

In addition to this, many of the Greeks and Romans both despised the Christians as professors of the Jewish religion, and were irritated against them as well for the crimes of which they were suspected as for their pursuit of new institutions. It is well known that the Greeks and Romans despised the Jews as a people barbarous, superstitious, and averse from literary culture, and consequently neglected what related to them. This was a reason with many for contemning the Christians also, who, as they derived their origin from the Jews, were votaries of Jesus Christ, a Jew by birth, and looked up to the Jewish prophets as messengers of God, were supposed to profess the Jewish religion, and to imitate the Jewish customs. To contempt were speedily added hatred and indignation. For it was likely that those would be exasperated against the Christians who suspected them of infamous feasts and incestuous lusts, a suspicion which took strong hold of the minds of many, as we may learn from the Apologists leaving no stone unturned to do away these charges (Θυέστεια δεῖπνα, and Οἰδιπόδειοι μίξεις, they were called by the Greeks) which were objected to their party. But even those who laid no stress on uncertain popular rumour, or were aware that these charges were unfounded, could ill endure that obscure and unlearned men like the Christians should seek to be wise beyond the vulgar, and set at nought the commands of the law. For persons in eminent stations are wont to disapprove of whatever is contrary to law and received usage, and to deny to others the privilege of neglecting and repudiating this usage which they assume to themselves. Thus it happened that many who were very sparing in their own worship of the gods, took offence at the Christians for their contempt of the state religion, and taxed them with mere obstinacy, because they steadily refused to burn incense on the altars of the gods, or to swear by the genius of the emperor.

Thus we think it has happened that even in the age of the Antonines most of the Greek and Roman writers were either entirely silent on the subject of the Christians, or mentioned them only incidentally and in few words. They seemed to themselves to have remarked nothing particularly deserving of notice or record on these matters, and when they either despised them as disciples of the Jews, or were inflamed against them as suspected of heinous crimes, and as promoters of religious novelties, they could not but be hostile to their cause.

But it was not all the Greek and Roman writers who thought thus of the Christians, or neglected to acquire a more accurate knowledge of their affairs. Those who either read the Apologies written by Justin, Melito, Athenagoras, and others (and that such books, widely dispersed by the Christians, and sufficiently well written, would be read who can doubt?), or who had personal intercourse with the Christians, would not only hold them guiltless of the crimes laid to their charge, but must have known that maxims and moral precepts were received by them agreeing with the doctrines of the philosophers in highest repute. Therefore it may be further asked, why among the philosophers, wise beyond the vulgar, and more learned in religious matters, the Christians found none to speak well of them.

But the truth is, that many of those who rejected the national religion as mere superstition, and sought to worship the Deity and nourish the piety of their own minds by religious exercises, became not only commenders of the Christians, but Christians themselves. Of this number were Quadratus, Aristides, Melito, Justin, Tatian, Athenagoras, Theophilus, Minucius Felix, and many others, who, by birth Syrians or Greeks, or Ægyptians or Africans, became converts to the Christian faith, and transferred into the Church the literature of Greece and Rome, and, especially under the Antonines, pleaded the Christian cause. All these men, revolting from the established heathenism, but possessing minds bent on religious meditation, joined the Christian Church for this reason, that a religious dispensation harmonizing with their own views, and a sacred history, the witness as it were and messenger of God, were there presented to them, and divine worship, well fitted to nourish the piety of the soul, was celebrated by men united together in the bond of a common faith and mutual love. Thus no small number of those who were led by the Greek philosophy to feel themselves wiser than the vulgar superstitions, openly approved and embraced the Christian faith. But philosophers turned Christians are no longer reckoned among the Greek and Roman writers of whom we now speak, but among Christian writers, to whom our present argument does not apply.

Others, however, and those the majority of this class, thought differently, disapproving and keeping aloof from the Christian worship, either because they wished the public solemnities to be retained as long as they were established by law and custom, though containing many things which they disliked, or because they made no account of sacred rites of any kind.

Of this class were the Stoics and Platonists, the forerunners of those who were called, by way of distinction, Neo-Platonists. The Platonists of these times, as Plutarch, Alcinous, Apuleius,— and the Stoics, as Arrian and M. Antoninus,—having formed, under the guidance of philosophy, more correct notions of theology, and perceiving that there were many absurdities in their myths equally unworthy of gods and men, chose rather to worship the Deity in the mind than by sacrifices, and carefully distinguished between εὐσέβεια and δεισιδαιμονία. In Plutarch there are many things admirably argued on religious matters, showing that he and others like him had a wisdom far superior to the popular superstition, and taught not a few tenets closely resembling the doctrines of Christianity. But to abolish the public rites, and substitute others in their place, the greater part of these philosophers by no means desired. For they reverenced them as sanctioned by law and usage, and feared lest, if domestic were to give way to foreign, and ancient to recent institutions, great disturbance might ensue. For this reason they either thought it the part of a wise man to follow the guidance of philosophy in private, but in public to conform to the law and practise the rites established by ancient usage, or took pains that, whether by an allegorical interpretation translating their mythology into a physical and moral meaning, or, by distinguishing the *dæmons* from the gods, and transferring to the former what appeared unworthy of the latter, they might mend the popular religion, and bring it into a consistency with philosophy. But those who thought and acted thus could neither espouse Christianity nor commend its votaries, who despised, vilified, ridiculed, and were aiming at the downfall of the public rites. Many of the Christian doctrines they doubtless approved as conformable to right reason. But in their opinion it was not from the Christians, but from their philosophers at home, in subtilty and eloquence far exceeding the Jewish prophets or the apostolic founders of the Christian churches, that a knowledge of divine and human things was to be sought for. Thus the Christian cause was not patronized even by those philosophers to whose doctrines those of the Gospel made the nearest approach.

But there were those who had other reasons for either neglecting or vilifying the Christians, by whom all sacred things whatever were held in contempt, and who regarded all religion as superstition. Of this class were the Epicureans and the Cynics; which is not only learnt from the testimony of Plutarch, who often taxes the Epicureans with atheism, and rebukes their profane jests and scoffings,[z] but is shown by the example of Lucian, a follower of the Epicurean philosophy. For Lucian not only attacks the Grecian mythology, laughs at the gods, and exposes to ridicule the public religion, but also, especially in those pieces of which one is entitled Ζεὺς ἐλεγχόμενος, the other Ζεὺς τραγῳδός, he argues against religion itself, and seeks to overturn the idea of a divine superintendence over the affairs of men.[a] But those philosophers who rejected the belief in a Deity could not but despise the Christian religion along with all others, and keep aloof from those whom they regarded as the authors or patrons of a new superstition. Nor were the arguments of the Christians against the received religion particularly alluring to them. For, in their own opinion, they themselves, excelling Evemerus and other philosophers of former times, had perceived and demonstrated the vanity, folly, and absurdity of the received mythology.

[z] See his book on the Cessation of Oracles, c. 19.
[a] See especially Zeus Tragœdus, c. 47–49.

It is, therefore, sufficiently evident how it was that the Christians, even after the time when they came into general notice, obtained, among the philosophers, a few adherents, but none besides to praise or patronize them.

But of these philosophers, they who stood aloof from the Christians because they did not wish the public religion, established by law and custom, to be disturbed and overthrown, seem to have had sufficient reasons not for silence, but for open opposition. For certainly the Christians laboured to destroy the public religion; it was the theme of the Christian poets, known by the name of Sibyllistæ, following the example of the author of the Apocalypse; and the Apologists, impugning the popular superstitions in every possible way, did not conceal their wish, their earnest desire and endeavour, that all men, deserting the temples and altars of false deities, should turn to the worship of the true God. It may, therefore, be rightly asked, why none except Celsus (for Crescens and Fronto seem merely to have assumed the character of reprobaters and accusers) should have sought to refute the Christian doctrine, and defend the public religion. Those who might have done this seem to have omitted it because they imagined that there was little ground of apprehension from the Christians. Foreign rites had often been imported, and for a long period the Jewish worship had been celebrated without any danger to the public religion. The Christians, few in number, suspected by the magistrate, hated by the populace, and not even secure from the fear of capital punishment from the law, did not seem to be the parties destined to destroy institutions received from their fathers, strengthened by the law, and sanctified by the authority of antiquity. No one at that time could readily foresee that domestic institutions were to give place to foreign ones, ancient things to novelties, Greek and Roman to a system originating in Judæa; and that by the labours of the Christians the opinions of men, the laws of the empire, the sacred solemnities of the Roman world, were about to undergo an entire change. The beginnings of Christianity were on a small scale, and even in the time of the Antonines the Christians were not yet so strong, either in number or literary reputation, that, whatever they might intend, they could threaten any serious danger to the public establishments. The sword being drawn against them, the pen seemed not to be called for. Few possessed the sagacity which led Celsus to discern, in the efforts of the Christians, the causes of mighty revolutions; deceived by outward appearances, it was imagined that their small and slender churches would speedily be put down. For mankind are then most easily deceived when they attempt to estimate by number and weight that which belongs to the mind and will.

Besides, even they who were unwilling that the public institutions should be disturbed or overturned were not so earnestly bent upon this object that they could endure nothing that was said on the opposite side. Neither against Œnomaus, the Epicurean or Cynic, who in the time of Hadrian exposed the pretended art of divination,[b] nor against Lucian, who in the period of the Antonines traduced the gods and turned them into ridicule, did these defenders of their country's rites bestir themselves. It was also no easy matter to recall the long-neglected Greek theology, and to bring a religion proceeding from the senses, and in many respects plainly opposed to right reason, into conformity with philosophy. It may not, therefore, appear wonderful, that in this period no one except Celsus undertook to maintain the cause of heathenism by opposing in argument the doctrines of Christianity. For though Platonists were never wanting, the Neo-Platonic philosophy, which supplied the defenders of received institutions with arms best adapted for their purpose, did not begin its reign till the third century.

By the observations which have now been made we think a sufficient answer has been given to the question proposed, which we have chiefly discussed in order that it might be perceived that the grounds of our faith in Christianity are in no degree affected by the scanty notices of the subject in Greek and Roman writers. This object, we flatter ourselves, has been attained. For that the writers of whom we have spoken had either no reason at all, or very slight ones, for mentioning the Christians is, we think, abundantly evident from what has been said.

The less we can learn relating to Christian affairs from these writers, the greater reason we have to rejoice that so many writings of Apostles, Apostolic Fathers, and Apologists have been preserved to our times. For by the study of these monuments of Christian antiquity we have sufficient means of acquainting ourselves with the origin and progress of our religion, and nothing more excites the mind to a meditation on divine things than the contemplation of the ancient Church.

---

[b] His book, of which considerable fragments are preserved by Eusebius, 'Præparatio Evangelica,' L. v. c. 18, L. vi. c. 6, is entitled φώρα γοήτων, a detection of sorcerers.

THE REPHAIM, AND THEIR CONNECTION WITH EGYPTIAN HISTORY.[a]

CHAPTER XVII.

THE Divine forms reverenced by the Rephaim being thus found identical in name and office with those of Mizraim, the common origin of the respective systems proves itself. The Creator manifest in His works was the object of their worship. To obtain a distinct view of the Divine attributes, the Mizraim separated these into so many figurative impersonations, distinguished by appropriate names. In this, they did not differ from the Hebrews, who knew the true God under various names. Their JEHOVAH is the Eternal; their ELOHIM is the fountain of Power manifest in creation; their SHADDAI, the Power exercised over all creation; their ADONAI, the Governor of the world; their ZEBAOTH, the Spiritual Defender of their Theocratic polity. By these various epithets, a Hebrew no more understood five Gods, than a primitive Mizraimite when he distinguished his primeval Osiris, or *maker of being*, from Isis, *the receptacle of being;* and expressed by various appropriate emblems his idea of God the Creator of the world, called Pthah, as distinguished from God the Enlightener of the world, called Aon; from God the all-pervading Spirit animating the world, called Neph;[b] or from God the Sustainer, renewing the world, called Khem. These names did not designate a variety of gods, but the same Divine Being considered as the subject of a different attribute expressed in the name.

We need not digress to trace how these purely abstract impersonations, on becoming multiplied, degenerated into polytheism; or how the use of mnemonic symbols to suggest the attribute they personified, degenerated into idolatry. This is a secondary point, in which the Rephaim erred in common with all heathen antiquity; and beyond our present purpose, which is rather to distinguish the origin and connection of their system with that of Egypt, from the internal evidence of the system itself; to confirm their ethnographical position in the primeval civilized world, as a branch of the great Mizraimite family.

The four manifestations of the primeval Osiris, that are called Pthah, Aon, Neph, and Khem, with their consorts Pasht, Neith,

[a] Concluded from the October number of the *J. S. L.*
[b] Otherwise Num, p and m being interchangeable. The resemblance of this name to the Greek πνευμα, *wind, spirit*, is remarkable.

Sati, and Maut, constitute the eight great gods of the *first order*, in the Egyptian system. Whereas, their exemplars, Osiris and Isis, under these their own primary names, and considered as belonging to the system of five manifestations known as the family of Seb and Nutpe, are only ranked in the *third order* of precedence; the *second order* being filled by twelve divinities whose various characters show that they arose out of subdivisions—particularizing developments as it were—of those primary generalizations that form the third order. Such is the principle on which the Egyptian pantheon was framed. All we have to show, by adducing a few cases in point, is, that the national deities of the Rephaim are those primary and generalizing forms of the Mizraimite theogony, out of which the Egyptian system itself was elaborated; and consequently that the criterion of rank assigned to a deified form is not its *antiquity*, but its *nationality*; precedence, in Egypt, being given to the patron-gods of Egyptian lands, over those whose domains were extra-Egyptian.

Osiris, who under that popular name only ranks in the third order, is nevertheless the great god worshipped over all Egypt alike; the mysterious being whose real name it was not lawful to utter. Osiris unmanifested, is Amun (*the concealed*), an expletive for that sacred name. In this character, he ranks in order 1, as god of Thebes. Osiris manifested is Khem, the Pan of Thebes, consort of Maut (*the mother*). In this character, his name in Egypt was cancelled; its equivalent, Amun, being substituted. But under that obliterated name we find him the king of gods, in Palestine.

Isis, though only ranked in order 3, is found under that name, with all its appropriate titles, bearing the form and emblems of the great goddesses; the graceful vulture head-dress, symbol of maternity, characteristic of Maut, goddess of Thebes;—or the cat's head, globe, and uræus of Pasht, goddess of Bubastis—both o' order 1;—or the globe and horns of Athor, of order 2; she is even found combining the latter emblem with the bowl and house of her own sister, Nephthys, of order 3. All these emblematical beings are therefore Egyptian forms of Isis, though unacknowledged in Palestine. There, her original name is merged into those of her characters, like in Egypt; but, as the great Ashtaroth, *producer of abundance*, she is the primitive Isis herself, antitype of the Greek Demeter or Ceres; and as Ate·sh and Ken, she is equivalent, both in name and office, to Maut and Athor, in Egypt.

Thoth, god of letters, is ranked in order 2; yet we found him to be a secondary form of Sheth the Helper, who only ranks in order 3.

Ank, ranked in order 2, where she is not related to Thoth, we

Plate III.

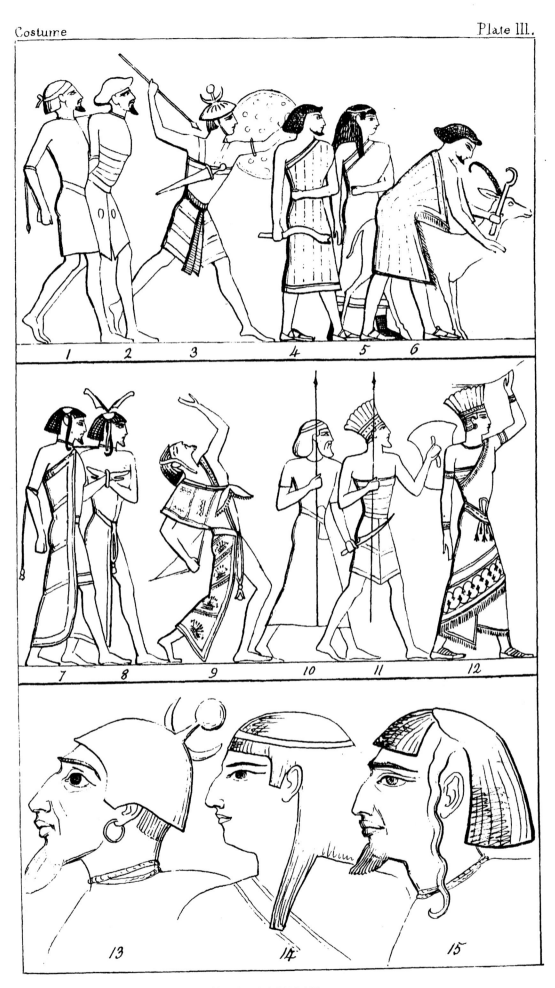

THE REPHAIM.

THE REPHAIM

found to be a local name and form of Nephthys, wife and sister of Sheth, and like him ranked in order 3. This same Ank, localized in Egypt as Neith, is then placed among the eight great gods of order 1.

Osiris, Isis, Sheth, and Nephthys, the primary forms, must be more ancient, as divine impersonations, than their derivatives. The mythical family of Seb (*adoration*) and Nut·pe (*the celestial abode*), must therefore exhibit a more ancient phase of the Mizraimite theogony, than that which includes the territorial gods of Egypt proper. Yet the five deities constituting this family *form the whole national pantheon of the Rephaim;* for Pthah and Aon do not appear as patronyms in their land, although these forms received divine honours. Their position in Palestine seems analogous to that occupied by the family of Seb in Egypt.

From this comparison of the leading divine characters reverenced by the Egyptians and by the Rephaim, it is manifest that the latter nation did not borrow their system at second-hand from Egypt, nor Egypt from them; but that the two are parts of a whole framed on a common principle of national agreement, which had become firmly grounded among them before the tribes were divided, and each separated people began to follow up a principle of development—peculiar to itself—from the common exemplar; the Egyptians, by increasing the number of divine functionaries with every shade of distinction in their offices, so that Isis, Maut, and Athor, become different goddesses of different ranks, as also Nephthys, Ank, and Neith; whereas the Rephaim distinguished the secondary shades of difference in the attributes of each primitive cosmogonic form without increasing the original number of five; so that with them, Chemosh, or Khem, is Osiris: Ashtaroth, Atergatis, Ken, are equally Isis; Renpu, Baal, Nebo, are equally Sheth; Anath, and Onka, are equally Nephthys. And this original unity seems to bear out a proposition which, on other grounds of inference (see ante, Ch. IV.), we might have held as doubtful—the common origin of the Rephaim and Egyptians.

The absolute separation between the Palestine branch of Mizraim (including the Delta) and that established on the Nile, must date as far back *at least* as the empire of Menes and the amalgamation of the Sabean element with the Mizraimite cosmogony. Not a trace of this mixture is to be found in the system of the Rephaim; not an indication of it either in their sacred symbols, or in their local names. Whatever corruptions of idea and form their system may subsequently have undergone, they are totally distinct from those by which the Egyptian system is overlaid. Its elements were strangely perverted,—its pure intellectuality became grossly brutalised,—but it exhibits no admixture of foreign elements,

The absence of every vestige of astral worship in the religion of the Rephaim is a fact the more remarkable, that Scripture contains very decisive evidence of its having constituted the idolatry of the Canaanites before they fell under the influence, or power, of their eastern neighbours. In Canaan proper, we still find a few names alluding to that worship. Nor was it altogether eradicated when the Canaanites consented to the divine forms of the Rephaim as superior objects of reverence. But what remained of it was not, like in Egypt, wrapped up in a complicated garb of cosmogonic similitudes; it remained plain, unqualified adoration of the sun and moon. Both forms are found subsisting separately, long after the Hebrew conquest. The children of Israel are not only enticed to the worship of Baal-Hamon and Asherah, but also to that of the 'Host of Heaven.' The kings of Judah burn incense to Baal; and also to 'the sun, moon, and planets.' They give chariots and horses to the sun, at the same time that they make their children 'pass through fire to Molech;' and pour out libations to his consort, 'the Queen of Heaven.' Ezekiel, in particular, brings out the various corrupt practices of the apostatizing Israelites, with a marked distinction in their *kind* as in their *degree*. Even so late as this, though still co-existent, they remained unblended. The idolatrous elders offering incense in their own image-chambers, before the symbols of a degraded worship, is indeed qualified as 'an evil abomination;'—but the prophet regards it as 'a greater abomination than this,' to find the women sitting in the house of Jehovah, not worshipping Him, but 'weeping for Thammuz.' Yet even this profanation of the holy temple is not the consummation of idolatry :—

'Hast thou seen, son of man? thou shalt see *still greater abominations than these!* And he brought me to the inner court of the House of Jehovah; and lo! at the entrance of the Temple of Jehovah, between the porch and the altar, about five and twenty men, with their backs to the altar and their faces to the east, were bowing themselves before the sun, towards the east!' (Ez. viii. 9-16.)

The allusion to the ode of Deborah is also decisive evidence that this was especially the idolatry of Canaan. The pictorial sarcasm that introduces the defender of Anak under the form of her Phœnician emblem, a dog, dragging the chief of her people down by tugging at his garment behind, while the king of Egypt knocks him on the head,—is not more intense in its power of expressing how utterly the gods of the Anakim have forsaken them, than the daring poetic image :—

'Even from the heavens, they fought—
The stars in their orbits fought against Sisera '—

is in declaring how powerless were those objects of an idolatrous worship to save their infatuated votaries, the Canaanite host of Jabin. But, indeed, the Canaanite nomenclature of the four quarters, based on the posture of a worshipper of the rising sun, is as strong an indication as we could desire, that sun-worship was the pristine idolatry of the people in whose language those terms have that significance.

This point being clear, and the distinctness of the co-existent systems equally so, some idea may be formed of the influence the Rephaim must have obtained over the whole land of Canaan, by the fact that their local gods became the gods of Canaan; and even, in some influential states, quite superseded the astral worship. But though Ashtoreth is 'the abomination of the Zidonians,' as well as of Ken, we do not find her the patronym of the Canaanite foundation city, as in Bashan. Though Sheth, as Thautus or Eshmun, and Onka, as Thanath, are reverenced by the Tyrians up to the very destruction of their Carthaginian colony, we do not find those divine forms patronyms of a single tribe or metropolitan city, like Sheth among the Shittim, Onka among the Anakim, Pthah in No·pth (Noph, Memphis), by the Naphtuhim, and Athor in Pathyris or Pathros, by the Pathrusim.

In the remote East, the same phenomenon meets us. The local gods of Shittim are established in Babylon, but they are neither patronyms of the city, nor of the land, nor of the people. Their Baal is not Baal-Kham·n, the universal progenitor, but Seth-Baal or Renpu with axe and thunder in hand, 'BARO *who smites his enemies:*' the god who 'exercises power and overpowers.' Their Hermes bears the surname of Nebo, the assistant of *lords*, not Thoth or Thautus, the popular teacher. Their Astarte is not AT·SH the abode of being, but Mulitta, openly confessing the Arabian origin we could have ascribed to her from her name. All this speaks as distinctly of conquest, as the fable of Oannes teaching and civilizing the brutal savages of the 'desert of the sea' spoke of colonization.[c] When, therefore, we find the dim and confused traditions of Berosus, which do not gain in clearness by being transmitted through the sieves of several intermediate theorists, declaring the intelligible fact that a primeval dynasty of mythical Chaldean kings was succeeded by *an Arabian dynasty*, we only require the concurrent testimony of Scripture, to see through a whole series of changes in that primeval empire, though

---

[c] Whether we take the Assyrian queen-consort, Semiramis, for a genuine or only for a mythical personage, we must not lose sight of the historical indications contained in the tradition that assigns as her birthplace the Philistine city Ashkalon, and gives her pedigree as the daughter of Derketo or Atergatis, the Ashtaroth of Pelesheth.

we cannot retrace its details, or assign the period of the changes. And the Scripture record is not silent. Its testimony is strangely significant, as well as definite. It opens with the notice of the Rephaim, yet in their greatness, though verging towards decline. A chief of Shinar has joined a powerful combination of Assyrians, rivals of the Shepherd race, against the whole body of that race; but the object of hostility is manifestly the Emim—the Terrible people—that one tribe which stands out from the rest, branded as an exception of depravity in religion and morality from the very day of its introduction to our notice. And thus, the united evidence of sacred and classical tradition enables us distinctly to trace the primary source of their perversion to that great city which sacred revelation has marked out as the typical centre of every religious and moral corruption, 'Babylon, the mother of all the abominations of the earth.'

This hints at the beginning of that subversion, both of principle and practice, which the Mizraimite cosmogonic system underwent while transplanted in Chaldea by the tribe which established its dominion there so long. Success, by increasing riches, and engendering luxury, tempts to the misuse of power. To conciliate the population of the wealthy region they had acquired, the children of Sheth may have consented to bring down their religious formulæ to its level, instead of rather exalting and refining those of the people as they found them. Israel and Judah, in Canaan, fell in the same way!

When the power of the Rephaim in the East was broken, they brought back to their native homestead the taint in all its fundamental principles with which they infected their brethren of Palestine; but which they perhaps had not originated:

' Behold,' says Ezekiel, addressing Judah, ' This was the iniquity (עון perversion) of thy sister Sodom : pride, fulness of bread, and prosperity undisturbed, were hers and her daughters', yet she strengthened not the hand of the humble and needy. They became haughty, and committed abomination before me—and I removed them, because I saw it !' (Ez. xvi. 49, 50.)

Fearful indeed must the social condition of a people have become, in whose city ten righteous men could not be found, to incline the scale of judgment on the side of mercy! And terrible indeed was that ' *removal of them,*' to become from thenceforth in every prophetic denunciation, the crowning comparison for the deepest abyss of desolation; so that terms more emphatic cannot be found to express the fall of Babylon herself, the arch-corrupter, than that even she 'shall become as the overthrow of Sodom and Gomorrah,' and that the only possible aggravation to her degradation, is to be taunted in her perdition by those whose ruin she wrought :—

> ' Art *thou, too*, enfeebled, as we ? art *thou* become like ourselves . . .
> The couch beneath thee, worms—the grub, thy covering !'

While the awful visitation was impending which blotted out from the face of nature the beautiful vale of Shiddim, its cities and its degraded population, as corrupt beyond the power of any ordinance, human or divine, to reclaim—the contrast presented by the religious and moral condition of the elder branch of the nation, and its Philistine offset, is interesting to observe. Here, indeed, we find ample proof that there was nothing in the creed of Mizraim derogatory to the majesty of a God whose glorious attributes they reverenced according to the best of their understandings ;— nothing debasing to humanity in the outward forms by which they sought to do Him honour. The great chief of the Rephaim dwelling in Shalem is the head of his people as administrator both of religious and social order, according to the primitive patriarchal appointment. He invokes the same 'Supreme God, possessor of heaven and earth,' as Abraham himself. He considers it a sacred duty to acknowledge, in a public ceremony of thanksgiving, his gratitude to that Supreme God for the deliverance of his people ; and to bless Abraham for the service his interposition has rendered to the nation. This ceremony is accompanied by an Eucharistic rite, which most certainly existed as an ordinance of the true patriarchal church before the Mosaic dispensation. For in an instance of equal solemnity, that of the great national deliverance, as soon as the children of Israel have reached the holy mountain in safety, after the difficulties and dangers of their departure from Egypt and desert route, Jethro the priest comes forth to meet his long expected guests ; like Melchizedek, he blesses God for their preservation, and he, with the elders of Israel, Aaron, the elder of his family among them, go up into the mount to offer sacrifices and to eat bread before God (Exod v. 12.). The sacred historian is careful to indicate both the orthodoxy of the rite performed on the parallel occasion by Melchizedek, and the lawfulness of his ministry thereof. 'Melchizedek brought forth bread and wine : (he was priest of the Supreme God) and blessed Abram,' saying :—

> ' Blessed be Abram of the Supreme God, Possessor of Heaven and Earth ; and Blessed be the Supreme God, who hath delivered thine enemies into thine hand.'

Equally unequivocal is the testimony borne in the same holy page to the piety and integrity of the contemporaneous Philistine chieftain. God appears to the Royal Father of this tribe, in the visions of the night, as to the Hebrew patriarchs ; not to warn him of any great impending national calamity, but simply to caution him against the unconscious commission of a crime in appropriating to himself the wife of another man. And Abimelech fears not to address the Almighty with an appeal which speaks as highly for the moral character of his people as for his own. ' Adonai ! wilt thou slay also a righteous nation ? Said he not unto me, " she is my sister ?" and she, even she herself, said, " he is my brother." In the integrity of my heart and innocency of my hands have I done this.' And God said to him in the dream, ' Yea, I know that thou didst this in the integrity of thine heart, and I have accordingly withheld thee from sinning against me.' (Gen. xx.)

Manetho's account of the behaviour of the Shepherd rulers in Egypt is perfectly in keeping with the state of religion in Palestine at that time, if we consider that account as emanating from an Egyptian priest deeply imbued with reverence for the most corrupt superstitions to which the primitive Egyptian religion had become degraded at the latter period. The very acts he denounces as sacrilege are precisely those from which we should argue favourably of their religious practices. They did what the Hebrew conquerors of Palestine were expressly commanded to do for the extirpation of idolatry in Canaan. They closed the temples of the false gods, defiled and pulled down their images, sacrificed, and even ate without scruple the sacred animals adored by the Egyptians. They doubtless deemed the religious customs of Egypt idolatrous and debased ; and endeavoured, while they were in power, to suppress them. They thereby incurred the odium of the priesthood, and of the people governed by the priests. As this preceded by four centuries Abraham's arrival in Egypt, it is tolerably certain that the tendency to harmonise with his own religious feelings, which existed among the Shepherd people, and so strangely contrasted with the surrounding corruption, was rather the motive that induced him to settle among them, than the consequence altogether of his example and teaching. Nevertheless, the beneficial effects of these, in purifying and exalting the religious ideas of a nation originally so well disposed, by drawing them even nearer to the primitive standard of the patriarchal faith than he found them, may safely be presumed.

Neither do the Canaanites of Judea show any traces of demoralization in the days of Abraham. We are indeed expressly told that the יוע perversion of the Amorites was not then accomplished. Abraham resides among them in the suburbs of the metropolis of Anak. Three of their chiefs are under a special

contract of amity with him, and aid him in pursuing the captors
of Lot. In the day of his bereavement, his acknowledged character of a religious teacher, נְשִׂיא, 'superior-one of God,' is
urged by the children of Heth as giving him a special claim on
their good will and liberality. The choicest family sepulchres are
placed at his disposal; the one he offers to purchase is pressed
upon him as a gift by the owner. Everything in that land speaks
of a social condition orderly, virtuous, and prosperous, at the time
of Abraham's residence there.

The degradation of the race who ruled over that land is thus
almost as incomprehensible for its rapidity as for its enormity.
Soon after Abraham's death, the Shepherd power in Egypt was
finally broken. Then began the great war of the races. It must
have been during the interval of Israel's sojourn in Egypt that
the work of depravation was consummated; but had the body of
the nation maintained the high moral and religious ground it held
when Abraham dwelt in its land, the sceptre might not have departed from their ruler; that war might never have begun; the
Rephaim would not have been cast out of their heritage that it
might be given to another.

After the outbreak of the contest with Egypt, the common cause
of the tribes brought them into closer contact. They became fami-
liarised with each other's ideas and forms: the evil race corrupted
the good. The taint spread with fearful rapidity, especially among
that tribe which we find so constantly associated with the children
of Sheth, the Anakim; for these are marked out by name, in Scripture, among the evil-doers cast out by the decree of the Almighty.

'Thou hast heard: who can stand before the children of Anak?—
Understand therefore this day, that the Lord thy God Himself passeth
over before thee: as a consuming fire He will destroy them, He will
bow them down before thee; so wilt thou drive them out and destroy
them quickly. . . . Say not in thine heart: "For my righteousness the
Lord hath brought me in to inherit this land;" but for the wickedness
of these nations the Lord doth drive them out from thy presence. Not
for thy righteousness, nor for the uprightness of thine heart, goest thou
to succeed to their land: but for the wickedness of those nations doth
the Lord thy God drive them out from thy presence!' (Deut. ix. 3-5.)

It is as painful to trace the degradation of principle and feeling
thus wrought in a people whose beginning was so great and pure,
as it is difficult to seize on the particular processes by which it
may have been wrought; the particular point in which the debasement of abstract conceptions began, which started by substituting
impure ideas and forms, as representations of actual divinities, for
those simple emblems of names originally conferred on attributes
of Deity; and which ended by investing the most cruel and im-

moral practices with the notion of doing homage to those divinities! Among the medley of Phœnician traditions ascribed to Sancho- niatho, there occurs a very remarkable one, which, from the illus- tration of Scripture it both receives and gives, will serve our purpose better than any other, as a means of tracing a primitive institution through several successive stages of corruption.

When the nation was in imminent danger from war, a solemn and painful ceremony was enacted to avert the calamity impending over the land. The king brought forth his son, his heir, attired in all the insignia of royalty, and in the presence of all the assembled chiefs he offered him up in sacrifice in front of the city walls, to appease the wrath of the offended Deity.

Some commentators have looked on this tradition as originating an obscure and disfigured reminiscence of Abraham's sacrifice; but we have positive evidence in the Bible itself that such a custom really did exist among the Rephaim, by the incident related in 2 Kings, 26, 27, which occurred in the days of Jehoshaphat, at the siege of Kir-Harasheth. 'When the king of Moab saw that the battle was too sore for him, he took with him seven hundred men with drawn swords, to break through unto the king of Edom, but they could not. Then he took his eldest son, who was to reign after him, and offered him for a burnt offering upon the wall.' Seeing that the Moabites, by their intimate amalgamation with the remnant of the Emim, cannot fail to have inherited most of their usages as well as their lands, we here obtain a circumstantial verification of Sanchoniatho's story, that this painful scene was sanctioned by custom as the last resource of despair, by the whole body of the nation to whom the Emim appertained, and thus it came to be perpetuated among the later inhabitants of Phœnicia, in the same way as among the Moabites.

It would therefore appear that the presumed connection between the ordeal of Abraham and this Phœnician tradition has been interpreted backwards, and that we should be much nearer the truth if we were to regard the previous existence of such a custom, sanctioned by a fierce but generous fanaticism, in the land where Abraham was settled, as the fact which gave occasion to the *special form* it pleased the Almighty to ordain for the trial whereby the stedfastness of the Patriarch's faith was to be manifested as a glorious example to all future generations.

'There was a great indignation against Israel; and they de- parted from it, and returned to the land,' adds the sacred chro- nicle. Certainly the sudden outbreak of religious excitement, produced on a brave and enthusiastic people, at such a manifesta- tion of devotion to the national cause, both on the part of the royal parent who gave his son, and of the son who thus consented

' to die for the people, that the whole nation perish not,' might very well have the effect of stimulating the disheartened people themselves to almost superhuman efforts; and the success achieved by the wild energy of despair would not fail to be regarded as a token that the Divine displeasure had been appeased by the sacrifice, and confirm the faith of the people in its efficacy.

Once a fatal aberration of judgment has let in the false principle of an inherently meritorious or expiatory efficacy in any sacrificial act, we can trace step by step the processes of degradation by which this one, at first perfectly voluntary on the part of its victim, having begun by assuming a right to dispose of human life, ended by degenerating into the barbarous practice of infanticide which the Israelite kings are reproached with having imitated from their predecessors in dominion. When the war-cry of all the tribes was raised against invading Egypt—when, year after year, army after army poured in upon the devoted race, until their land was ' a conflagration before and behind '—its fields devastated, its women and children massacred, its cattle carried off as booty, and its warriors as slaves—when a savage despair had taken hold of a people forsaken of the God whose attributes they had corrupted and forgotten—we can understand how the simple form of consecrating their offspring to its Giver by an emblematical rite of purification, having degenerated into the notion that the God *individually* had *appropriated* the dedicated offspring, ended in the persuasion that he claimed their blood to appease his wrath in the season of national visitation. Thus a form of sacrifice, originally ordained under the pressure of an exceptional public calamity, and required only of the chief ruler of the land, came at first to be regarded as insufficient, and instances were multiplied in the hope of ensuring its efficacy, firstly by the chiefs, and finally by the whole population.

The perversion of this rite suffices to illustrate the march of every other depravation which stains the memory of the Rephaim at the close of their national career. Scripture history is utterly silent concerning them during an interval of four centuries. After placing before our eyes the glaring contrast of their pristine moral condition, as presented by the majestic piety of the King-Priest Melchizedek and the single-hearted purity of his Philistine vassal, side by side with the terrific catastrophe of the Pentapolis, it leaves them to work out their own destiny. It leaves them, neither unwarned nor uncared for, with the virtuous Abraham and his increasing family circle among them on one side, to point out the way of holiness, and exhibit in their own persons the blessings of peace and prosperity that crown those who choose to walk in it; and with the example and admonition of Lot and his sons in the midst of them on the other side, to point out the application of the awful warning against national iniquity, vouchsafed even in the great judgment which rained down fire and brimstone out of Heaven upon their metropolitan cities! How far these means may have been effectual in bettering the moral condition of the race for a season, and drawing them back a little way from the verge of the precipice, we cannot exactly know; neither how far and how long the descendants of Lot themselves escaped the general contamination by keeping aloof from them, as industrious nomads tending their flocks in the mountains during the grazing season, and dwelling apart in their own tribe communities when they returned to winter at home. Neither warning nor example ultimately availed: the whole mass of the people became corrupt, and the whole were abandoned to themselves, to perish!

For our admonition, the sacred history relates their original condition and their final doom; but it does not say *how* they perished. This we have learnt from the monumental history of Egypt. But what matters the *how*, in a religious history that regards God himself as the guide of all sublunary transactions, and all human determinations only as secondary means? The Scripture history is very explicit in informing us *why* they perished; for that is the momentous lesson it behoves man individually, and nations collectively, to lay to heart: 'FOR THE WICKEDNESS OF THOSE NATIONS, DOTH THE LORD DRIVE THEM OUT.' It recounts, under the doubly solemn form of a Divine prohibition addressed to Israel, every abomination that the most depraved humanity can possibly imagine to commit, as actually committed by that people, in idolatry, superstition, cruelty, and impurity. 'Defile not yourselves in any of these things,' concludes the warning Oracle; 'for in all these, the nations are defiled which I cast out before you, and the land is defiled! Therefore I do visit the iniquity thereof upon it, and the land herself vomiteth out her inhabitants! Keep ye then my statutes and my ordinances, and commit none of these abominations, neither your own nation, nor the stranger who sojourneth among you (for all these abominations did the men of the land commit, who preceded you, and the land was defiled), that the land spue you not out also, for defiling her, as she spued out the nations who preceded you!'

CHAPTER XVIII.

Costumes of the Rephaim.

The slight outlines given in plates III. and IV. are only *a selection* of the most striking forms characterising the national costume of the Rapha tribes. They are intended to appeal to the mind through the eye, inasmuch as a verbal description, however accurate and elaborate, would still fail to convey a distinct idea of form : but they are rather calculated to assist those readers who have not time to consult the voluminous illustrations of Egyptian antiquity from which the materials of the foregoing pages were gathered, than to supersede a reference to the original works themselves. This reference is so important, that in describing the costumes of the tribes, my principal aim will be directed to furnishing the reader with a classified index to the original subjects ; so that any student, however unversed hitherto in that class of research, may at once find himself furnished with all the necessary materials to judge for himself whether the generic resemblances of costume which distinguish and connect the national groups whose history we have now gone through, and the specific differences which separate one tribe from another, have been correctly indicated, and sufficiently bear out the ethnographical classification they are called upon to sustain.

So long as we knew nothing of the people figured in these monumental illustrations beyond the bare fact that they had been conquered by the ancient Egyptians, we turned over the pages with very little interest. We might perhaps indulge in a laugh over the quaint and distorted attitudes of the combatants, the wry faces of the chained captives, and the ludicrous expedients to indicate the relative personal consequence of the actors in the scene by their size, with an utter disregard of proportion as well as of perspective ; but the subjects told us no story we cared about, for the actors were nothing to us but abstractions without either 'a local habitation or a name,' and as soon as the book was closed, the passing impression they made had vanished from our minds.

But the case is widely altered when we have learnt that the personages in these strange old pictured memorials are a people consecrated in our memory by their intimate association with Scripture history ; that those Philistines, whose name and deeds are familiar to our ears as household words, even from the earliest teaching of our childhood, are the very people who figure in one picture, and that their fellow captives in another are the formidable children of Anak; that on looking at another, we may actually realise the presence of Og king of Bashan as he marched out to encounter the children of Israel; or call up a correct and unquestionably authentic presentation of the redoubtable Goliath of Gath hurling a boastful defiance in the teeth of Saul's warriors; while another presents us with a warlike array like that with which the king of Sodom went forth to meet Abraham; or that of Balak the son of Zippor, as he stood on the high place of Baal, bribing the Eberite prophet to curse the conquerors of the land of his fathers. Such associations impart a strange and thrilling interest to these hitherto unintelligible forms, as the barbaric abstractions they presented are replaced by definite ideas of national personality, and our knowledge of these mysterious people's names and history suddenly places them before our eyes in the new light of old and familiar acquaintances.

In the *onomasticon* which gave the Egyptian forms of their names I divided them into five geographical groups. Three belong to the Rephaim, one to their Aramite subordinates, and one to the only Canaanite tribe casually associated with them. Leaving out this solitary case as exceptional, all the rest resolve themselves into two ethnographical groups, totally distinct in origin— the Rephaim, children of Ham, and the Aramites, children of Shem. Our plates, III. and IV., exhibit the monumental representations of these nations in their peculiar costumes, from which it will be evident at a glance that if these groups had been classified according to their *costumes* instead of their *names*, they would have fallen into precisely the same two ethnographical groups, the members of each group being characterised by similar generic peculiarities, and differing only in those secondary details wherein a difference is to be expected in different provinces of the same land, or in different tribes of the same people.

The plates in Rosellini's great work on Egyptian monuments will be found the best to refer to. Although most of its subjects are repeated in Champollion's more voluminous publication, the former is more convenient; firstly, because the religious and the historical monuments are in separate volumes; secondly, because the illustrations are arranged according to the chronological succession of the Pharaohs to whose reigns they belong, two highly judicious examples of arrangement entirely disregarded in Champollion's work, where subjects of all kinds and all periods are indiscriminately mixed up together. I would not so strongly recommend a reference to the descriptive volumes of Rosellini's work, in connection with the present subject, as it would rather confuse than assist its understanding, partly because Rosellini has not identified or even read off many of the proper names; partly because his ventures at identifying a few of those he has read have no foundation but a deceptive verbal resemblance, and some of his random guesses are singularly infelicitous; partly because he followed a now obsolete system of dynastic classification; and partly because of the very erroneous series of dates, founded on Champollion's chronology, which he assigns to his reigns and dynasties.[d] We must set aside, in fact, all that was *speculative* in this work, and look at nothing beyond its *graphic* portion. This, whether ill or well interpreted, always remains the same—a faithful transcript of those vast sculptured designs which constitute the body of the ancient Egyptian annals.

In describing the characteristic costumes and properties of the three Rapha nations, it will be desirable to reverse the order I adopted for the historical arrangement, beginning with the Anakim and ending with the elder tribe. The fact that the costume of the children of Anak was selected by the Egyptians to impersonate the whole TEMAH'U nation, in the typical representations of the subjects of Thebes in the royal tombs, added to the general points of resemblance between the attire of this tribe and that of the children of Sheth, both argue that if we would obtain what is original and peculiar to the Rapha nation in these respects, we must look to those two branches of it that were least mixed up with Egypt and her population, who retained their national characteristics the most tenaciously, and who contended the most resolutely for their national independence. The Zuzim and the mixed Philistines of the latter monumental period became half Egyptianised in their costumes and national predilections. What we have seen of their history sufficiently explains these later deviations from the original national type, which we must look to much more ancient representations to recover.

§ A. THE ANAKIM.

The monumental illustrations referring to the Anakim are all included in the following plates of Rosellini's work, *I monumenti dell' Egitto e la Nubia*, Mon. Storici.

Ros. Mon. St.

1. Impersonation of the Rephaim nations, or TEMAH'U, in the tomb of Seti-Menephtah, at Biban el Moluk (*Thebes*) . . . . Pl. 155
2. Ditto, in the tomb of Rameses III. . . . . Pl. 158[e]
3. Battle-scene (*from Karnak*)—Seti-Menephtah defeating the TAHI . . . . Pl. 54

---

[d] The origin of this chronological error has been ably pointed out in Chev. Bunsen's 'Egypt's Place in Universal History,' B. 1.

[e] In the plates illustrating this tomb, the copyist has misapplied the epithets, giving that of SHEM'U to the TEMAH'U people.

The costume of the Anakim was remarkably picturesque. The figures 7, 8, 9, of our plate III., and the heads, fig. 15, and plate II., fig. 11, will convey a correct idea of its leading forms. Their limbs were generally bare; for an under garment, they wore a short narrow kilt, fastened round the loins by a rich girdle, often with long ends hanging down in front, and finished with a tassel. Over this they threw a very peculiar kind of mantle, which, in its general form, may be considered as the characteristic garment of the Rapha people. It was narrow, hanging straight down without folds, and open at the side; it was most generally worn by simply passing it under one arm, and fastening it over the shoulder on the other side; but the figure 9 of the TAHI tribe in pl. III., and the TEMAH'U chief of pl. II. fig. 11, present a slight variation from this make. This garment was of gay colours, and richly ornamented, either with stripes elaborately figured, or fancy patterns. That of the chief of TAHI (Ros. pl. 83) is yellow, and is divided by broad diagonal stripes with water-plants between. Those of the TEMAH'U (Ros. pl. 155) are figured, some with palm-leaves laid horizontally across, with a row of spots between each, some covered all over with marks in imitation of a leopard's skin. From these figures, which are on a sufficiently large scale to render details omitted in ordinary monumental illustrations, we further learn that the Anakim printed or tattooed token-marks on their arms and legs; the object thus impressed on the TEMAH'U typical figure is, as we have seen, the characteristic emblem of his national goddess, Onka-Athene: compare this figure in our plate II. with the head of an ancient Egyptian Neith bearing her name, fig. 10, and the names in the legends NT, fig. 9, and T-NT-ANK, fig. 8. The Anakim sometimes shaved their face entirely, but more generally they wore a very small pointed beard, only on the chin. In this respect their practice was common to them and to the other Rapha nations. Their head-dress is peculiarly their own. It consists of a long braided lock of hair hanging down the side of the face, and a helmet in form very different from those worn by the Rephaim of Bashan. The top sits close to the head, the front falls partly over the forehead, and forms a sort of squared flap, from the side being scooped away in order to exhibit not only the ear and the characteristic pendant lock, but a rather unsightly square-shaped patch of the shaved temple above it. The back of the helmet was also cut square, just low enough to leave the neck free. The details in the helmets of the TAHI chiefs (Ros. pl. 54) show how it fastened on by a leather strap passing under the chin; but most of the historical representations omit these minutiæ, giving only the general forms. Not a vestige of hair ever appears from under the helmet except the side lock. This, and the round bare skulls of the CHERBU prisoners in pl. 93, who have lost their head-pieces in the fight, encourages a suspicion that this people shaved their heads, and that in their civilian costume, apparently that given in the TEMAH'U tomb-figures, they wore, not their own hair, but a kind of wig-like head-gear, which the helmets replaced in battle, and were intended to imitate in form. This head-gear (see pl. II., fig. 11) seems made of small plates or beads strung together so as to look like ringlets falling from a common centre: the metal helmets were grooved in a corresponding form. The Anakim of TAHI sometimes wore a crest of one or two eagles' feathers on the crown of their head-piece, but there is not an instance of the RBO wearing any such ornament: on the other hand, the RBO never appear without the side lock, but the TAHI did not always wear it.

The chief of MASHUASH wears his lock behind the ear; moreover his round skull-cap and circlet, totally different from the genuine and invariable Anakim helmet and strap, but strikingly resembling those of his fellow captive of AMĂR (Ros. pl. 143), indicate that he was the local ruler of an Amorite dependant district, though a son of Anak by race. Other instances of blendings of costume will be found to occur in regions by a mixed population.

The sculptured representations of the Anakim plete in illustrating their armour. In the great Rameses III. they are entirely unarmed; in that nephtah and the TAHI, their only weapons are bows

The form of their shields, if they ever used any, is unknown. In the scene last referred to it appears that in pitched battles they removed their mantle in order to fight more freely.

In their personal appearance the children of Anak of the monuments fully realise the description of the Hebrew spies, that they were ' men of great stature.' They are generally delineated as tall, spare, and long-limbed, to a degree often bordering on caricature.

§ B. The Emim.

The geographical range over which the rule of the Emim extended was so wide, and the mixture of races they counted as their vassals so various in origin, that we must expect to find a considerable difference of costume prevailing in the different regions of their domains. Yet even these variations are systematic and consistent. The attire of the people of the primary and metropolitan district—the plains of Shittim northward of the Arnon —is only a partial modification of that worn by the Anakim; both are obviously derived from one common primitive type. The southern section of the nation—those at least who garrisoned and ruled the Horite dependencies—appear in garments of a Horite fashion; nevertheless, the Shethite rulers are clearly distinguishable from their Horite subjects and their allies of Edom, by the broad line of national demarcation, the custom of *destroying the sides of the beard.* Indeed, they more frequently shaved it entirely away.

The monumental illustrations relating to the Emim will be found in the following series of plates in Rosellini's work, from which the leading forms of costume are given in our plate IV., upper line of figures.

Ros. Mon. St.

1. Symbolical group: Seti-Menephtah devoting the enemies of Egypt to destruction (*from Karnak*) . Pl. 60
    The kneeling figure in front of this group represents the Emim nation.
2. Seti-Menephtah engaging with the SHET'TA and the AMĂR before ATESH (*from the same*) . . . Pl. 53
3. The same king defeating the SHET'TA and killing their chief (*from the same*) . . . . . . Pl. 57
4. SHET'TA captive chiefs of various tribes presented by Seti-Menephtah to the Theban Gods (*from the same*) . . . . Pl. 59
5. Rameses II. devoting the enemies of Egypt to destruction (*from Abou-Simbel*) . . . . . Pl. 79
6. Great expedition of Rameses II. against the SHET'TA (*from the same*) . . . . . . Pl. 87–103
7. The surrender of ATESH (*from Luxor*) . . . Pl. 104–107

The Emim differed from the other Rapha nations in that they allowed their hair to grow long. Those of the metropolitan district wore it parted into three locks, one hanging on each side, and one down the back. This is the style of the tribe engaged with Seti-Menephtah, in the battle-scene, Ros. pl. 57, and of the chief embodying the nation in the symbolical groups, pl. 60 and 79. The head in our Pl. IV. fig. 26, is copied from the former; it exhibits to great advantage the physical characteristics of this tribe, without the repulsive individual traits of the Medinet Abou captive, whose costume shows that he belongs to the southern or Kenite region. These wore their hair in a single long lock or *queue*, hanging down behind; see our Pl. IV. fig. 20, which is that of a warrior slain at the siege of POUN or Punon. Sometimes the hair was simply combed back from the forehead and confined by a fillet or circlet either of gold or scarlet; sometimes the whole anterior half of the head was shaved, the long back hair only remaining.

The Emim hardly ever are represented with beards; those who did not shave the face entirely never exceeded the limits of a very small tip and moustache.

In the right-hand division of the vast Abou-Simbel subject (Ros. pl. 103), where we see the chiefs hastening from the south to the assistance of their brethren of ATESH, we recognise some of the long-haired tribes, as well as some with shaved foreheads. Among them also are those who 'cut away their hair all round and shave it off the temples,' in imitation of the god Orotal (see our Pl. IV. fig. 16). Their tufted crests so curiously resemble the tufts on the skull-caps of the Shethites of ATESH, both in the siege of the city by Seti-Menephtah (Ros. pl. 53 and 57), and by Rameses II. (Ros. pl. 91), that we are perhaps not very rash in conjecturing that this peculiar cap, worn only in battle, was quite as much a religious signal as the two-horned Ashtaroth helmets of the Rephaim of Bashan, or the Onka-crested ones of the Philistines.

In the part of the picture above referred to (pl. 103) the colours are still in good preservation. We thereby recover many valuable details, which convey a rather striking idea of this people's luxury and splendour. As they are only marching to the battle, we have the advantage of seeing them in full costume, with their mantles on, which we see, by Ros. pl. 57, they sometimes took off for the fight. This mantle, in form, does not materially differ from that of the Anakim (see our pl. IV., fig. 16, 17, 19). It is cut a little shorter, richly bordered, and striped in various splendid colours. This is the attire of most of the chiefs slain before ATESH. The fig. 19 in our pl. IV. represents one of these, a chief named TAATUR; fig. 17 is one of the two Shethite ambassadors brought before Rameses II., who were beaten as spies: fig. 18 is a somewhat different form of costume; it is that of the tribe contending with Seti-Menephtah (Ros. pl. 57), and is taken (with the exception of the head attire) from the chief TAR·KANUNASA, killed before ATESH. The upper part of the figure is covered by a close corselet with short sleeves; the charioteers in fig. 16 have one of a similar make under their mantles, but apparently folded or quilted: their under tunic is exactly like that of the kneeling ambassador behind them. The robe of the chief in fig. 18 is a substitute for this tunic, worn only by persons of great distinction; it is somewhat longer, and richly bordered. The Assyrian sculptures display kings and gods clothed in a similar garment, fringed and bordered: it is in all probability the אַדֶּרֶת שִׁנְעָר, 'Babylonian garment,' referred to in Josh. vii. 21. It appears that the corselet was worn only in battle, when the upper mantle was discarded. The wearing of an under tunic with the mantle was quite optional, for the Shethite Rephaim are as often delineated without one—like the TAH·N·NU—as with one —like the RBO. The material of this under tunic, as well as its length and the richness of its adornments, were evidently regulated by no custom but the convenience, taste, and rank of the wearer.

The arms of the Emim were bows and arrows, and long spears. They carried shields of various forms, which, from their markings in the pictures, appear to have been made of wicker. They never appear in helmets, save the close skull-caps above referred to, worn only in battle, which were either quite plain, or were finished at the top with a short tail or tuft.

The various battle-scenes in which they appear, represent them as fighting on horseback as well as on foot. The chiefs used war-chariots drawn by a pair of horses. These were not very unlike the Egyptian chariot in make. The horses were magnificently caparisoned, with embroidered cloths and ornaments of gold, blue and scarlet. It is difficult to understand how a people presenting so elaborately luxurious an array could ever have been referred, on the strength of a half-resemblance of name, to the rude nomadic troops of barbarians described under the name of *Scythians* by Herodotus.

§ c. The Rephaim (*of Bashan*) and Philistines.

The costume of the Zuzim is so exactly the same as that of the Philistines, that one description will suffice for both. They are depicted in the following subjects :—

Ros. Mon. St.

1. Seti-Menephtah routing the SHAS·U before PAIROU (*from Karnak*) . . . . Pl. 48
2. The same attacking the SHAS·U before a fortress on a hill (*ibid.*) . . . . Pl. 49
3. Presentation of the captives and spoils (*ibid.*) . . Pl. 50, 52
4. The SHAS·U surrendering to Rameses II. (*from Abou-Simbel*) . . . . Pl. 101
5. Philistines and Amorites, in a boat, coming to aid the Shethites of ATESH against Rameses II. (*from Luxor*) . . . . Pl. 104
6. The PULSA·TA aiding Rameses III. against the RBO (*from Medinet-Abou*) . . . . . . Pl. 136
7. The Rephaim (SHAS·U) aiding Rameses III. against the T·AKKR·U (*ibid.*) . . . . . Pl. 127-8
8. The same fighting in the ships of the PULSA·TA against Egypt (*ibid.*) . . . . Pl. 131
9. T·AKKR·U and RBO prisoners (*ibid.*) . . . . Pl. 134
10. PULSA·TA and TUINU·NA prisoners (*ibid.*) . . Pl. 144
11. Portraits of the captives of Rameses III. :—the chief of T·AKUR·I,— of SHAIRTA·NA,— of SHA·· (partly effaced, SHAS·U or SHALĂMU?) . . . Pl. 143

Figs. 1, 2, and 3, in our Pl. III. are, respectively, the Rephaim of the central Judea region, of PAIROU or Pelusium, and of Bashan, from Ros., pl. 50, 52, and 127. Figs. 10 and 11 are an Amorite and a Philistine, from pl. 102. Fig. 12 is a Philistine, from a painted vase in the tomb of Rameses III.

The Zuzim and Philistine costume consisted of a short kilt like that of the RBO Anakim. It opened in front; the hem, which often had a double border, was sometimes straight, but often cut so as to make the skirt dip in front into a point. Their bodies were protected by a low corselet, quilted, or made of bands or plates, and reaching no higher than the arm-pits. Sometimes two broad straps of the same material or pattern went over the shoulders to keep it on. This corselet was an Egyptian fashion.

Neither the Zuzim nor the Philistines ever appear on the monumental sculptures in their upper robe. Yet we have extraneous evidence that this garment was also part of the full costume of both these nations. In a vase delineated in the tomb of Rameses III., supported by two Philistines, the figures are attired in a mantle with a deep fringed border, which is worn in the fashion characteristic of the Rephaim, passing under one arm and fastening over the other shoulder. As it is made a little more ample than the corresponding garment as worn by the Anakim, it does not appear open at the side, but the upper edge laps over the under edge of the opening in a very graceful manner. A Philistine chief in this elegant costume, with his tall feathered coronet, must have presented an appearance equally gorgeous and imposing.

The SHAS·U who surrendered to Rameses II., in the war with the SHET·TA, present a strange exception to the rest, in being dressed exactly like the Egyptian soldiers coming to their rencontre, —in all but their Ashtaroth-crested helmets. Whether on this occasion they really donned the Egyptian uniform,—or whether it was gratuitously bestowed upon them in the painted relievo, as a compliment, to indicate their assimilation with ' the pure race ' of Egypt, we cannot decide. It is quite a solitary instance. This incident is repeated in the Luxor version of the memorial, Ros. pl. 106, lower line of figures.

The Zuzim and the Philistines used the same arms, offensive and defensive. The foot-soldiers had either straight double-edged swords, shaped like wedges, or smaller curved ones, single-edged ; they also used battle-axes of an Egyptian pattern. Those who rode in chariots used spears, javelins, and bows and arrows ; they carried large round shields. There is no representation of the SHAS·U in chariots ; those of the Philistines were exactly like those of the Emim ; but the quiver was attached to its side, after the Egyptian fashion.

We observe the same variations in the shaving of the beard among the Zuzim and Philistines, as among the other tribes of Rephaim. Sometimes they wear it pointed, without a moustache, like the chief of SHAIRTA·NA or Zarthan in our plate 3, fig. 13 ; sometimes they wear a moustache and no beard, like the SHAS·U who surrender to Rameses II. (plate 101) ; sometimes they are quite shaved, as the warriors in the Medinet-Abou battle-pieces. The Ekronite chief of the Medinet-Abou portraits has a pointed beard, yet the warriors in the battle-scene have none. But these people never wear a full beard, nor show any hair. The shape of the Ashtaroth-crested head-pieces worn by the Rephaim of Bashan necessarily exhibits the back of the head ; and it is there-fore evident, from all the representations of them, that the hair was shaved off or clipped away quite close.

The only difference in the costumes of the Rephaim of Bashan and the Philistines is in the form and symbol of their helmets ; yet there is an agreement even in this difference, since both wore the badge of their respective tutelar goddesses.

There is a part of the SHAS·U nation who did not wear the token of Ashtaroth; those against whom Seti-Menephtah made war in their own land (Ros. pl. 49), after expelling their forces from PAIROU (Pelusium). Their city was near a high hill—but its name is lost. The costume of this tribe is given in our pl. 3, fig. 1; but the shapes of their helmets vary considerably: some project behind in a form strongly resembling the head-gear of a captive of Rameses III. at Medinet-Abou, whose name, SHA-.., is partly erased. His likeness to the chief of SHAIRTA·NA is so strong, that he must have been of the same nation; but it must remain doubtful whether SHASU, or SHALAMU be the restoration of the name on his legend. It is more likely to be the latter, because SHALAMU is registered by name among the conquests of Rameses III.; whereas the SHAS·U are not mentioned by that name in his inscriptions, being comprehended under the general designation of TEMAH·U.

The similarity of costume between the Philistines of the later monumental period, and the elder branch of the Rephaim nation, is quite consistent with the Scriptural intimation that those Philistines were a people who had become closely identified with the remnant of Caphtor or Lower Egypt. The dissimilarity in costume between the Zuzim and the two other Rapha tribes, and its approximation in all such points of dissimilarity to that of the Delta, is also fully explained. For more than five centuries they ruled in Memphis; for three out of the five they held all Upper Egypt under tribute. It is perfectly natural to suppose that during such a long lapse of time they took up many Egyptian observances of costume more adapted to the climate of the country, and which they did not afterwards wholly cast off. And when the kindred race of Caphtor, who shared their exile, joined the small Philistine tribe, we can easily perceive how, although the ancient name of the tribe continued, its national characteristics and predilections became modified by the connection of the new-comers with the Rephaim of Jerusalem; assimilating rather with these, than with the Rephaim of Anak or of Shittim, whenever, in their subsequent relations with Egypt, their political interests happened to clash.

But although in the last phase of their national existence, certain outward tokens of nationality were thus sunk, in the elder family of the Rephaim, there is reason to believe that a most valuable record of their primitive type still exists in the well-known subject from the grottoes of Beni-Hassan, which represents an embassy of unknown foreigners, headed by their HK, named ABSHA, and accompanied by their wives and children, bringing gifts to an officer who lived in the reign of Sesertasen II., one of the earlier kings of the XIIth dynasty (Vide Ros. pl. 26 to 28).

This monument accordingly belongs to a period a little preceding the Hyksos invasion, since the 'six foreign Phœnician kings who took Memphis' are now found to have been contemporaneous with the latter part of the XIIth. Manetho limits the rule of the Hyksos in Egypt to 511 years. This interval is quite sufficient, though not too long, for the XVth Phœnician dynasty, the XVIIth of 'other Shepherd-kings,' who laid Thebes under tribute, and their contemporaries, the tributary XIIIth of Thebans, and VIIIth Memphites. By placing the Exodus at the close of the XIXth dynasty, the expulsion of the Shepherds by Amosis or Aâhmes, leader of the XVIIIth, falls at about the time of Abraham's death. Thus we are not exaggerating the antiquity of this curious old Egyptian picture, when we say that it was painted nearly four hundred years before Abraham was born!

A reference to the figures themselves will, I believe, satisfy the inquirer that in all elementary and characteristic forms of their costume, these foreigners strikingly resemble the Shethite and Anakite Rephaim. Figs. 4, 5, 6, in our Pl. III., represent the three principal persons in the procession. They wear the peculiar mantle, striped with rich variegated patterns and colours, and passing under one arm and fastened over the other shoulder, just like the Anakim of RBO and TAHI, and the SHETTA, but a little shorter than the former. Instead of the loose tunic of the SHETTA, our unknown people wear the short close-fitting kilt of the RBO. The only figures showing this part of the costume are the attendants behind ABSHA, who do not wear the mantle of distinction. They are all in their civilian costume, and wear no helmets; but the form into which their hair or wig is trained reminds one strongly of the caps of some among the SHASU of Pelusium and of the upper SHASU country (compare pl. 49, 50). Their beards are very curiously cut and trimmed to a point; the side of it, according to the invariable custom of the Rephaim, is partly shaved away.

Again, the remarkable outline of their profiles is worthy of attention, viz. the *retiring forehead and chin* peculiar to that nation. The latter feature is particularly well displayed in the female faces. Compare the head of the chief woman with that of a RBO captive of Rameses III. next to it, in our pl. III., figs. 4, 5. By the likeness of their features, she might be taken for his daughter, yet an interval of eight hundred years separates these two individuals.

The costume of the women was very like that of the men; but as all the figures are turned sideways, we cannot see whether their tunics or mantles are open at the side. The fringe down the opening of the HK ABSHA's mantle shows that the men wore this garment open. The hair of the women is dressed in the most archaic Egyptian fashion. See the head of Neith in our pl. II., fig. 10. The men wear sandals, the women boots. The chief, ABSHA, carries the hook-shaped sceptre, which by the way is the initial letter in his title HK, a ruler, equivalent to the Hebraized title עוֹג (Og). The other men carry bows, spears, and a club of a very remarkable shape.

This resemblance in their general characters of person and costume seems to justify our believing that, in the hitherto unknown Beni-Hassan foreigners, whose identity has given rise to so much speculation,[f] we behold an authentic contemporaneous representation of the primitive type of that ancient people, the REPHAIM of the Bible, in its very earliest stage of nationalization, prior to its conquest of Egypt, perhaps even prior to its subdivision into the branch nations known in Bible-history as the Emim and Anakim, since each of these tribes appears to have adopted to itself certain special modifications of the original national costume, sufficiently marked to distinguish one family or tribe from another, yet not sufficiently different from the primary type to obliterate its essentially characteristic points.

§ D. THE ARAMITES.

The last group to be described presents characters of feature and costume so different from those of the Rephaim, that we must have recognised in them another nation of another race, even if their lands had remained unidentified, and their origin unascertained.

The series of subjects in which this race appear, and from which the figures 21 to 25 of our plate IV. are selected, are as follows:—

		Ros. Mon. St.
1.	SHEM·U group; tomb of Seti-Menephtah (*Biban-el-Moluk*)	Pl. 155
2.	Same, in full dress; tomb of Menephtah (*from the same*). See our fig. 21	Pl. 157
3.	Same; tomb of Rameses III. (*from the same*)	Pl. 158
4.	The lower LT·N·NU and RMN·N submitting to Seti-Menephtah, and cutting down trees (*from Karnak*). See fig. 22	Pl. 46
5.	Attack of a city, name partly lost	Pl. 46
6.	Defeat of the upper LT·N·NU by Seti-Menephtah	Pl. 47
7.	Captives and spoils of the upper LT·N·NU	Pl. 48

---

[f] The favourite hypothesis that the picture represented the arrival of the Hebrews in Egypt is of course demolished by recent chronological research. An interval of seven centuries elapsed between the reign of Sesertasen II. and that event. If the Exodus happened at the end of the nineteenth dynasty, the elevation of Joseph must have taken place under one of the early reigns of the eighteenth; most probably under the regency preceding the reign of Thothmes III., or during his minority.

The epithet SHEM·U, which describes the tomb-figures of the three first subjects referred to, is evidently the primary designation of the Aramite race, 'the Shemites.' In those early ages, when the great Asiatic migration from the region of the upper Euphrates was only beginning to direct itself southward, the Shemites of the eastern line of population were the only tribes touching upon the Hamites of the western line, who were not of the same paternal stock. Thus their early patronymic, 'SHEM·U,' seems, by an easy transition of ideas, to have passed into the language of the Mizraim as a common appellative for *strangers*—those of a different race. By the Canaanites of the West, they were geographically designated 'the children of the East.'

The fundamental points of resemblance between these SHEM people of the tombs and the monumental groups of the succeeding subjects, clearly show that they are of the same stock—that the SHEM·U are the typical figure of which the monumental nations are as many local and unessential variations. The SHEM·U may be the metropolitan tribe, for Damascus and Shem were both names of the same city; and therefore the people bearing that name would be pictorial representatives of the monumental NAHARI·NA (River-land, Aram Naharaim); while those figured in the historical illustrations appear, by the names of their localities, to belong to the southern region of this ancient establishment, and to represent its provincial members, though at a period when its power had been superseded by the Shethite Rephaim, and its population had given way to the Edomites.

The figure in the tomb of Seti-Menephtah does not give the full costume—it only wears the short under garment of inferior people, like the attendants of Absha in the old Beni-Hassan subject; but in the tomb of Menephtah, son of the great Rameses, and contemporary of Moses, we find a repetition of the figure in full attire, with the same name, countenance, and head-dress as the others (see fig. 21 of our pl. IV.). We are thereby enabled to connect this typical figure with the monumental group to which it belongs.

The people comprised within this group all affect the following peculiarities :—

They do not clip or shave any part of the beard, like the Rephaim ; but wear it full and round.

They do not go with their limbs bare, like the Rephaim ; but wear a long robe, which either folds over the person in front, or is twined spirally round the figure, fastening at the waist with a short girdle.

They do not wear a mantle, like the Rephaim ; but the upper part of the body is covered by a short cape, rounded and open in front, which never reaches lower than the waist. The aperture for the throat is sometimes cut and bordered in a peculiar form which gives it the appearance, in the sculptures, of a cross hanging from the neck. In the SHEM·U of the two first tomb-subjects, the hair seems to have been powdered, or enclosed in a white bag or net spotted over with blue. A fillet with a bow behind encircles the head.

The faces of all the people wearing this costume present as great a contrast to those of the Rephaim as their attire. Their profile exhibits a much more upright outline, with a genuine aquiline cast approximating to the Hebrew countenance. See our fig. 27.

Four Biblical names are found in one region, corresponding to the four names of the people whose costume answers to the above description, viz. SHAR, Seir ; LET, Elath ; RMN, Rimmon-Parez ; and POUN, Punon. This fourfold correspondence of name and costume is a coincidence of great value as a test of the people's identity ; while, on the other hand, the general resemblance they all bear to the SHEM of the tombs is a striking confirmation of the conclusion founded on a great number of Scriptural references already quoted—that the original settlers in the Horite valley were an Aramite race.

The individual variations of costume between the people bearing these names are very unimportant, and chiefly consist of a slight difference in the head attire. Some wear the back hair full and round, with the fillet and tie behind : the LET, Elath (Ros. pl. 46, 47, 48), SHAR, Seir (pl. 49), and the Luxor captive chieftain (pl. 141), are so represented. The REMEN, and some of the SHAR, have a close round skull-cap with a flap over the back of the neck, and they seem to have cut off their back hair. The garrison of the nameless fortress in the Beit-el-Wally subject (fig. 24) shave their heads, though their chief wears the SHEM·U coiffure. Some wore the back hair full, but shaved the crown of the head, and cover it with a cap. But amidst all these variations of individual fancy, the great line of demarcation between the Shemite and the Rapha

races remains inviolate. None of these people *shave their beards*.
The Scripture history constrains us to recognise the Edomite rulers
and successors of the Horites in the chiefs of the people whose
costume we have described; and it appears established, from the
evidence of these interesting representations, that the children of
Esau, although in all their political relations they proved themselves true friends and faithful allies of the Shethite people, among
whom their first establishment was formed, had not assimilated
themselves with that idolatrous race so far as to adopt their external badge of nationality by shaving their beards.

The only exception to this rule would seem to be the shaved
garrison of POUN, or Punon, who wear the genuine Horite robe
and cape (see our fig. 26); but the monumental picture which records the event, also records the fact that the masters of Punon
were of the SHET'TA people, and thus proves the rule to be without
exception.

The fortress in the subject (pl. 68) exhibits the female costume
of the country, in three women on the battlements: one is beating
her head in despair, another offering her child to the victors, or
throwing it over the walls. Two of them wear capes like the men;
the third, apparently a young maiden, has her neck and shoulders
unclothed. Their hair is long, hanging down, and from the
shoulders the ends are braided into three tails. See fig. 25.

In these battle-pieces, most of the enemy are represented without weapons. This ingenious Egyptian expedient to suggest their
absolute helplessness, unfortunately deprives us of the means of
knowing how they really did defend themselves. Here and there
we see a figure with a broken bow; and in one of the battles of
Seti-Menephtah (pl. 46), a chief is looking out of a circular
window or loophole, with one hand on his head, and his sword
pointing downwards in the other, as a token of submission. This
sword is the same double-edged and wedge-shaped weapon as that
borne by the Philistines, and the Zuzim surrendering to Rameses
II. in the great picture of Abou-Simbel.

The costume of the Amorites may be gathered from the only
three subjects in which they appear by name. In the attack on
ATESH by Seti-Menephtah, the city is evidently defended by an
Amorite garrison; for although their costume resembles that of
the Shethites as to the military uniform—the corselet, and a skull-
cap crested with a tail—they have full beards, and moreover are
commanded by a bearded chief who wears the same head-attire
as the chief of AMAR, captive of Rameses III., in the harem at
Medinet Abou (Ros. pl. 143). The same *bearded* people, in plain
long robes, accompany the Philistines coming to aid the Shethite
garrison of ATESH against Rameses II., in the Luxor subject, from

which the figure 10 in our plate III. is taken; and we know from Scripture, on the one hand, that the Philistines ruled over an extensive Amorite district, and could therefore command the services of its population in case of war: on the other hand, the AMARU are mentioned by name with the people of CHERBU (Hebron), in the Egyptian inscriptions of these subjects, as allies of the SHET'TA in the war. Finally, in the captive chief of Rameses III., a distinct idea of the physique of this race is handed down to us. This chief has a longer face than the Rephaim, and a much straighter line of profile. The Ekronite chief is not unlike him. The Amorite has a fine long full beard, and the sides of his face are not shaved. His hair is arranged precisely like that of the SHEM'U and LET people, and bound by a similar fillet and tie. As the Edomites themselves were half-breed Canaanites, descendants of Seir the Hivite, co-settler with Esau, it is interesting to find the similarity of their respective fashions thus in harmony with their origin.

F. C.

MOSES STUART.

THE memory of a man who has exerted so prominent an influence as Professor Stuart upon the study of Biblical Literature in the great American Republic, is entitled to some record in a Journal which claims the function of registering its history and condition. The simple fact, that the studies connected with this literature may be considered to owe their origin in that country to his exertions, and that its progress there has been throughout illustrated by his labours, so connects his name with its national history, that it would even on those grounds alone be unpardonable to neglect the opportunity of producing what we have been able to learn of a man so remarkable for his influence and character, and so eminent for his talents and his labours.

Sufficient materials for such a record as we desire to furnish lie before us in two exceedingly able funeral discourses, one by Professor E. A. Park, of Andover, and the other by Dr. William Adams, of New York.[a] The discourse of Professor Park was preached at the funeral of Moses Stuart; and that of Dr. Adams at the request of an association composed of upwards of thirty clergymen of New York. From these sources we shall take the facts which bear directly upon the career of the departed, using Professor Park's discourse for the basis, but resorting to the other for additional particulars, and preferring it where, from greater fulness or from more conciseness, its statements of particulars common to both may seem preferable. The opinions as well as the facts are those of the authors.

It is, therefore, to be understood that the following statement is given in the very words of these two authorities, except where some of the details, less important than others from our point of view, are exhibited in a condensed form.

Moses Stuart was born of honest but humble parentage, in Wilton, Conn., 26th March, 1780. At sixteen years of age he entered Yale College, in the second year of the presidency of Dr. Dwight, where he sustained the character of a diligent student and excellent scholar. Graduating in 1799 with the highest honours of his class, he taught an academy in Fairfield, bestowing some attention at the same time on the study of the law. In

---

[a] *A Discourse delivered at the Funeral of Professor Moses Stuart.* By Edwards A. Park. Boston, 1852.

A Discourse on the Life and Services of Professor Moses Stuart. Delivered in the City of New York, Sabbath Evening, January 28, 1852. By William Adams, Pastor of the Central Presbyterian Church. New York, 1852.

1802, three years after his graduation, he was chosen tutor in Yale College, in which capacity he served for two years. While a tutor he entered himself as a student of law, and prosecuted with diligence and success the studies connected with that profession. He, however, never opened an office for the prosecution of his legal profession; but in subsequent life he was always ready to testify to the great advantages he had received from legal study as a very important part of his intellectual discipline. Seriously impressed, under the preaching of Dr. Dwight, with the importance of personal religion, and experiencing a decided change in his religious sentiments, his preference was given to the sacred profession, and after a comparatively brief season of preparation, on the 5th of March, 1806, two years after resigning his office as tutor, he was ordained pastor of the Centre Church, in the city of New Haven. The fervour, fidelity, and success of his career as a pastor are still matters of grateful remembrance and distinct tradition. Distinguished as is the reputation which he subsequently acquired as a scholar, there are many who think that his best efforts were in the pulpit. The congregation over which he was ordained, accustomed for a third of a century to a style of discourse, clear, cold, and philosophic, which deserves to be designated as 'diplomatic vagueness,' were startled from indifference by the short, simple, perspicuous sentences of their new pastor, and more than all by the unaffected earnestness and sincerity with which they were delivered; as the result of which, by the blessing of God upon his labours, some two hundred individuals were added to the Church under his brief ministry of four years; among whom was the celebrated Noah Webster, then in his fiftieth year, who, thirty-five years after, on his death-bed (Mr. Stuart being at the time on a visit to New Haven), expressed to his former pastor the liveliest gratitude for the fidelity of his early ministrations. At the end of this time—in 1810—Mr. Stuart, then thirty years of age, was appointed to the professorship of Sacred Literature in the newly organized Theological Seminary, at Andover, Massachusetts.[b]

This institution had been organized on its existing basis as a College for *exclusively* theological education in 1808, and the Rev. Eliphalet Pearson, LL.D., became its first professor of Sacred Literature. He continued in this office but a single year, when Mr. Stuart was elected as his successor. Though not one of its original founders, Professor Stuart may be said to have been associated with Andover Seminary from its organization. It was not because of extraordinary proficiency in Oriental languages

[b] Adams, pp. 14-17.

that he was chosen to this office, for his knowledge of Hebrew was at this time very limited. Two years preparation for the ministry, and five years in the diligent prosecution of his profession, had not furnished large opportunities for exact and extensive study. Choice was fixed upon him, because of the general qualities which designated him as one able and willing to furnish himself for any station; and upon that thorough qualification he entered, with characteristic enthusiasm, immediately upon his transfer to this new office.

Rightly to estimate the nature and extent of those services which he subsequently rendered to the world, Dr. Adams deems it necessary to take a survey of the state of Biblical learning in America prior to the time when his labours were commenced.

Many of the earliest ministers of the New England colonies were men of extraordinary scholarship. They had been trained at the English universities, and that at the golden age of Biblical learning. It would be difficult to designate in English history any other time when such constellations of talent were shining upon the earth. Whatever was his opinion of poetry and lighter literature, Cromwell, it must be admitted, was a warm admirer and patron of solid learning. Not to mention the many names which are eminent in general literature and science, the period of the Commonwealth is distinguished by the honoured names of Selden, Usher, Chillingworth, Taylor, Pococke, Cudworth, Leighton, Baxter, Castell, Lightfoot, Brian Walton, Prynne, Owen,—and others of scarcely inferior renown. The catalogue of evil spirits in the first book of Paradise Lost evinces what acquisitions Milton had made in Rabbinic literature. The 'Syntagmata de Diis Syris,' by his friend Selden, demonstrates that Oriental studies were not superficial. It was then that Walton compiled his Polyglot, Cromwell permitting the paper to be imported free; that Castell published that Herculean work the 'Lexicon Heptaglotton;' that Lightfoot in his retired parsonage, and Pococke in Oxford, were prosecuting their thorough researches in all the Oriental tongues. With these men the first clergymen of New England were contemporary. They had been associated together in schools, in parishes, and colleges. They shared the enthusiasm of their studies. The sympathy of scholars was not sundered by exile. Harvard College, at its very origin, included in its course of studies Hebrew, Chaldee, and Syriac. Dr. Lightfoot bequeathed his invaluable library of Oriental books to that College, which unfortunately were consumed by fire about a century ago. Mr. Chauncy, the second President of Harvard College, was the intimate friend of Archbishop Usher, and had served as Professor of

Hebrew and Greek in the English University at Cambridge. Cotton, the first minister of Boston, was able to converse in Hebrew. The thesis of Cotton Mather, when taking his second degree, was the 'Divine origin of the Hebrew points.' There was an intimate connection kept up for many years between the heads of Magdalen, Trinity, and Emmanuel Colleges, and the humble pastors of the small villages around Massachusetts Bay; and at no time in our history has a greater attention been given to the study of Biblical languages than in the first fifty years after the settlement of the colony. The clergy were accustomed to read the Hebrew and Greek Scriptures to their families at morning and evening worship.

It would be idle to speculate as to the causes which led to a rapid and general decline in this department of study. The habits of the colonists were necessarily to a great degree provincial. The attention of the learned in the Old World had assumed a new direction. Cudworth and Locke, Samuel Clarke, Shaftesbury, Hobbes, Leibnitz, and Butler had eagerly entered upon the analysis of mental laws and moral actions; and the great questions of ethical philosophy were fairly before the world. Butler's Analogy was presented to his royal mistress, Queen Caroline, in 1736. The treatises of Jonathan Edwards on the Freedom of the Will, and Original Sin, were written between the years 1751 and 1757. Never was there a body of men who, by nature, constitution, and external circumstances, were more disposed to follow the lead of their distinguished countrymen than the clergy of New England. Their habits inclined them to great independence of thought. They had little reverence for antiquated authority. They would have reasons for their faith. We have no occasion to be ashamed of them. It would be difficult to find men superior to many of the rural ministers of those days in metaphysical acumen. Whatever may be thought of their particular dogmas, no American can fail to honour Edwards, Hopkins, Bellamy, and Emmons. But the fact to be observed is, that for two-thirds of a century metaphysical theology had gained the entire ascendancy. The study of the original Scriptures had passed into a very general desuetude. Professor Sewall, at Harvard, President Stiles, of Yale College, and Professor Smith, of Dartmouth, were rare exceptions to the common condition. The effects of this state of things are apparent in the writings of the most distinguished men of that period. Not only are there few references to the original languages of the Scriptures, but fanciful modes of quoting and applying the common version are not infrequent. With the exception of occasional references to Pool's Synopsis and Buxtorf on the etymology of particular words, no instance is remembered of what may be called Biblical criticism in the writings of Edwards. In his celebrated letter to the Trustees of Princeton College, on occasion of being elected President of that Institution, he mentions, as a reason why he should decline the appointment, his ignorance of the Greek classics. So uniformly severe were the studies of this illustrious man, that it is doubtful whether his voluminous writings contain many quotations from Milton, or the whole range of classical literature. It is even said of Chauncy, his contemporary and acute opponent, that he was accustomed to wish that Paradise Lost was *translated*. This exclusive attention to one study was preparing the way for serious mischief.

Such was the state of things when Professor Stuart entered upon the Professorship of Sacred Literature at Andover.[c]

Thus far we have mainly followed Dr. Adams, but we now turn to Professor Park, who cites Stuart's own statement of his biblical standing at the time he took this charge upon him :—

'I came here,' he says, 'with little more than a knowledge of the Hebrew alphabet, and the power of making out, after a poor fashion too, the bare translation of some [five or six] chapters in Genesis and a few Psalms, by aid of Parkhurst's Hebrew Lexicon, and without the vowel-points. I had not, and never have had, the aid of any teacher in my biblical studies. Alas! for our country at that time (A. D. 1810); there was scarcely a man in it, unless by accident some one who had been educated abroad, that had such a knowledge of Hebrew as was requisite in order to be an instructor.'[d] The youthful professor's acquaintance with the Greek language was far inferior to that now obtained in American colleges. He was to be a self-made man. In about two years, amid all the heterogeneous cares of a new office and a new seminary, he prepared a Hebrew grammar, without the points, for the immediate use of his pupils. They were obliged to copy it, day by day, from his written sheets. In the third year, he published it at his own expense. To print a Hebrew grammar was then a strange work. He was compelled to set up the types for about half the paradigms of verbs with his own hand. He taught the printers their art. Is he not fitly termed the father of biblical philology in our land? Eight years afterwards he printed his larger Hebrew grammar. This he soon remodelled with great painstaking, and published it in a second edition, two years after the first. Not satisfied with it, he reëxamined all its principles anew, wrote 'some of it three, four, and a small part even seven or eight times over,'[e] and published the third edition five years after the second. Professor Lee,

---

[c] Adams, pp. 19-24.   [d] Christian Review, vol. vi. p. 448.
[e] See Preface to Hebrew Grammar, 1828.

of the University of Cambridge, England, while speaking of this edition, says, ' the industry of its author is new matter for my admiration of him.'[f] When called to prepare a seventh edition of this work, on which he had already expended labour enough to fill up half the life of an ordinary man, he preferred to introduce the amended system of younger grammarians; and therefore, in his sixty-seventh year, he translated the grammar of Gesenius as improved by Roediger. As early as 1821 his enterprise had procured[g] for the seminary a Hebrew press, then unrivalled in this land; and as early as 1829 he had at his command fonts of type for eleven oriental languages and dialects. The works which he sent forth from this press gained the notice of scholars who had previously looked upon American literature with indifference, if not with disdain. He awakened a scientific interest in biblical theology.

When he began his course in the seminary, he often consulted Schleusner's Lexicon, and was troubled by the German terms occasionally introduced into that work. No one could explain their meaning to him. His curiosity was thoroughly roused. At an exorbitant price he obtained the apparatus for German study, and in a single fortnight had read the entire Gospel of John in that language. A friend presented him with Seiler's Biblische Hermeneutik, and this work introduced him to the wide range of German literature.[h] He felt himself to be in a new world. It was the suggestions and references of that one volume which enabled him, through the liberal aid of the trustees of the institution, to fill our library with the richest German treatises then in the land. ' Before I obtained Seiler,' he writes, ' I did not know enough to believe that I yet knew nothing in sacred criticism.'[i] For ten years he performed the rugged work of a pioneer; and in his maturer life he often said that he did not know how to begin the study of the Bible until he was forty years old. For forty years he had been in the wilderness. He entered late in life upon the promised possession.

Nor was he merely alone in the efforts of the first ten years of his professorship. To have been simply friendless would have been to him a relief. But the anxieties of good men were awakened with regard to the results of his German study. He endured the whisperings of his brethren. Many of them met him with an averted face. ' Solitary,' he says of himself, ' unsupported, with-

---

[f] See North American Review, vol. xxxvii. p. 295, and American Biblical Repository, vol. i. pp. 776-786.

[g] Through the generosity of Rev. John Codman, D.D., of Dorchester, Ms., donor of the Codman press.

[h] Of this work a translation by the Rev. W. Wright, LL.D., was published in London in 1835, under the title ' Biblical Hermeneutics, or the Art of Scripture Interpretation.' From the German of George Frederic Seiler, D.D.—Ed. J. S. L.

[i] Christian Review, vol. vi. p. 449.

out sympathy, suspected, the whole country either inclined to take part against me, or else to look with pity on the supposed ill-judged direction of my studies,'—'admonished by my bosom friends,'— 'warned of my approaching ruin,'—'very sensitive on the point of character,'—'many a sleepless night have I passed, and many a dark and distressing day, when some new effusion of suspicion or reproof had been poured upon me.'[k]   Morning after morning he sallied forth from his house at five o'clock, through rain, hail, snow, storm, and, as his attenuated figure breasted the winds of our cold winters, it seemed a type of his spirit, encountering manfully the opposition not of foes only,—this were easily borne,—but of friends. Night after night he repeated the sentiment which at the age of threescore years he expressed in a public prayer, and which many an ingenuous youth will hereafter read with a tearful eye: 'God in mercy keep me, by thy Spirit, from falling,—from denying the Lord that bought me, and from refusing to glory in the cross of Christ!   A poor, dying sinner has no other hope or refuge but this; and to forsake his last and only hope, when he is approaching the verge of eternity, would be dreadful indeed!'[m] [n]

It was not, however, to be always thus.   The part he took in the Unitarian controversy, in his celebrated Letters to Dr. Channing, not only evinced the soundness of his orthodoxy, but made manifest the advantages he had derived from 'his communion with the Teutonic mind.'   The result, in removing the suspicions which had previously attached to the cultivation of German literature, is, as recorded in the Discourses before us, very remarkable.

Stuart's opponents acknowledged and admired his learning. His friends confessed their error in resisting his German progress. They felt the importance of it for the church.   'No,' said the venerated Porter to him, 'you could not' have written that volume without your German aid.   'You are in the right in this matter, and your friends are in the wrong; take your own way for the future.'[o]   Before this contest of the intrepid student, scarcely one of our divines was acquainted with German literature.   He has made it common.   With a great sum he obtained for us this freedom.   For it he endured a great fight of afflictions.   But he fought a *good* fight.   He kept the faith.   He came off a conqueror, and more than a conqueror, through Him that loved him.   Thousands of trembling Christians now triumphed in their strong deliverance. They honoured him who had honoured Christ.   'At this time,' says Mr. Park, 'he entered upon a career of popularity as a scholar, which was perhaps unexampled in our religious annals.   He disap-

---

[k] Christian Review, vol. vi. pp. 455, 456.   [m] Ib. p. 460.   [n] Park, 25-29.
[o] Christian Review, vol. vi. p. 458.

proved of the adulation that was offered him. Such encomiums ought not to be pronounced upon a mortal.'

Flatteries, however, more than frowns, did not deter him from his studies. In a few years he published his Commentary on the Epistle to the Hebrews. At once this work was honoured in the high places of letters, where so few of our theological treatises had been previously noticed. The most eminent scholars of Great Britain have confessed their obligations to it. The North American Review predicted that it would be translated into the German language.[p] It was lauded as an American treatise had seldom been in the German periodicals.[q] Within five years the Commentary on the Epistle to the Romans followed that on the Hebrews, and awakened a still deeper interest, not only among critics, but also among metaphysicians. It is unwonted for a treatise to touch so many salient points in the creeds, and to stir up so many classes of men. It reached the hidden springs of intellectual and of moral life. If some Expositions of this Epistle be more accurate than his, are many of them more learned? If some be more learned than his, are many of them more accurate? In originality of thought and feeling, it excels those by which it is surpassed in logical order and chaste style. It exhibits no more of piquant idiom, nor of good sense, nor of pious feeling than are to be found in some other Commentaries, but it exhibits an unusual combination of these excellences; of thoughts which are to be remembered, with phrases which are to be quoted. The erudite and pious Tholuck commended it to the 'learned Germans,' and said, 'In preparing this work its author was able to avail himself of a rich exegetical literature; he himself examined every point independently and carefully; his remarks bear testimony to a keen and practised judgment; he is particularly careful in deciding the most important doctrinal points of the Epistle; and what is in the highest degree attractive, is the Christian mildness and moderation which he everywhere manifests; as also the expression of his warm Christian feeling which here and there breaks through.'[r]

No sooner had Professor Stuart completed his Exposition of the Romans, than he began his Exposition of the Apocalypse. With what enthusiasm he searched into the dark sayings uttered on Patmos, his exhilarated pupils know right well. Professor Park declares that he shall never forget the tones almost of inspiration with which he exclaimed, 'Oh that I might have seen Michael An-

---

[p] North American Review, vol. xxviii. p. 150.

[q] Although the preparation of this Commentary cost its author years of toil, yet he formed the plan of it in fifteen minutes, and wrote the entire first volume with a single quill.

[r] Literarischer Anzeiger, 1834, No. 22, S. 170.

gelo or Guido, and besought them to transfer to the canvas three or four scenes which John has suggested to my mind. I am on the point of writing to Washingston Allston and proposing to him these subjects for his pencil.' 'So large,' adds the preacher, 'were the conceptions, so vast the plans, of our many-sided critic ! Whether the details of this, which he regarded as his most elaborate Commentary, be true or false, it will effect a revolution in our mode of interpreting the prophetical style. Many will resort to it for information, if they will not admit it as an authority. Many a finished treatise will be cut out from it, as a statue from a marble block. It is a pyramid of labour. One of its most eminent opposers has said that, "if it were compressed into two-thirds its present bulk, it alone would bear the name of its author to a distant age."' In rapid succession followed this veteran's Commentaries on Daniel and Ecclesiastes ; both of them abounding with hints and references of rare worth. On his seventy-second birthday he began his Exposition of the Proverbs. In four months it was prepared for the press. Five weeks before his death he fractured his arm by a fall upon the snow, but he persevered a full month in correcting, with his lame hand, the proof-sheets of this his final work, and sent the last pages of it to the press two days before he died. During his life he printed more than twenty volumes, and carried several of them through the second and third editions ; and whenever he republished any one of his writings, he verified anew its accumulated references to other works. His pamphlets and periodical essays occupy more than two thousand octavo pages. All the labour immediately connected with these voluminous publications has been performed, amid physical pain, during three, or at most three and a half, hours of each day. He has never allowed himself to engage in what he called study for a longer portion of the twenty-four hours. These were his golden hours. No mortal man was allowed to interrupt them. They were his sacred hours. He was wont to commence them with secret, but sometimes audible, prayer, and occasionally with chanting a Psalm of David in the original Hebrew. While in his study, his mind moved like a swift ship. He bounded over the waves. It required a long time each day to repair his dismantled frame, his exhausted energies. He made all his pecuniary interests, all his plans for personal comfort, all his social enjoyments, tributary to his main business, that of investigating the divine word.[*]

---

[*] During a large part of his professional life at Andover he would not allow himself to sit in his study-chamber after eleven and a half o'clock in the morning. At the stated minute, even if he were at the height of his interest in a theme, he would leave a sentence unfinished, drop his book or manuscript, and go to his physical exercise. He was once invited to perform the marriage ceremony for two friends, who had long enjoyed his esteem. He desired to gratify them, and consented to do so, on condition of their having the ceremony *after* half-past

But although his writings have been read on the banks of the Mississippi and of the Danube, it is not by them that he has achieved his greatest triumphs. He lives in the souls of his pupils. He has stamped an image upon them. He has engraved deep lines on the character of the churches through them. Many a professor in our colleges has reiterated the saying, ' I first learned to think under the inspiration of Mr. Stuart. He first taught me how to use my mind.' The excellence of a teacher does not consist in his lodging his own ideas safely in the remembrance of his pupils, but in arousing their individual powers to independent action, in giving them vitality, hope, fervour, courage ; in dispelling their drowsiness, and spurring them onward to self-improvement. The vivacity of Mr. Stuart when he met his pupils, his exuberance of anecdote, his quick-thronging illustrations, his affluent, racy diction, his vivid portraiture of the prominent features of a theme, astonished his class, and animated their literary zeal. If all his writings had been burned in manuscript, the preparation of them in his own mind would have been a sufficient publication of them through the minds of his scholars. By his enthusiasm in elaborating them, he disciplined himself for his oral instruction. Daily he went from the scene of their influence to his class-room. His words in the afternoon betokened his morning struggles, and quick was the sympathy which they awakened. He verified the adage, that instructors must be learners, and they cease to impart when they cease to acquire. The fresh, versatile, easy, open-hearted way in which he discoursed before his scholars on every science and every art, raised their admiration of him often to an excess. Some of them almost looked upon him as a being from a higher world. The hour when they first saw him was a kind of epoch in their history. ' Never shall I forget my first interview with him,' has been said by hundreds of young men. No teacher in the land ever attracted to himself so many theological pupils. The number of our Alumni is eleven hundred and eleven. But the number of his scholars has been more than fifteen hundred. Men came to him

eleven of the forenoon. They urged him to perform it at ten. 'But that is in my study-hours!' was his reply, and, of course, another clergyman was called to the service. It will not be surmised that Mr. Stuart was divorced from books during the afternoon and evening of each day. His pupils were early familiarized to his distinction between 'reading' and 'studying.' For his mental relaxation he was daily perusing books of geography, history, biography, literary criticism, etc. Among the works which he 'read' in his parlour were such as Brown's Philosophy of the Mind, Brown on Cause and Effect, Bishop Butler's Sermons. He interdicted all 'study' during his seminary vacations, but in the five weeks' recess of 1841 he read thirty volumes through. He exemplified the law, that change of mental action is mental rest. The irrepressible instincts of his mind for progress in knowledge illustrated the reasoning of the old philosophers for the immortality of the soul.

from the Canadas, from Georgia, and the farthest West. Members of eight differing sects congregated around him, and did one ever suspect him of a proselyting spirit? They loved his freedom in dissenting from their views, but perhaps no man who knew him ever stigmatized him as a sectarian. More than seventy of his pupils have been the presidents or professors of our highest literary institutions; and in their persons he has given an impulse to classical study among the colleges of our land. Nowhere is he more gratefully remembered than in our halls of science. More than a hundred of his disciples have been missionaries to the heathen; about thirty of them have been engaged in translating the Bible into foreign languages, and have borne the results of his grammatical study to men who are to be civilized by means of it. It cheered his declining years to reflect that he had been preaching the gospel, through his missionary pupils, in ancient Nineveh and under the shadow of Ararat, as well as amid the wilds of Oregon, and on the islands of the sea.

The great work of Mr. Stuart may be summed up in a few words. He found theology under the dominion of an iron-handed metaphysics. For ages had the old scholastic philosophy pressed down the free meaning of inspiration. His first and last aim was, to disenthrall the Word of life from its slavery to an artificial logic. He made no words more familiar to his pupils than 'The Bible is the only true and sufficient rule of faith and practice.' In his creed the Bible was first, midst, last, highest, deepest, broadest. He spoke sometimes in terms too disparaging of theological systems. But it was for the sake of exalting above them the doctrines of John and Paul. He *read* the scholastic divines, but he *studied* the prophets and apostles. He introduced among us a new era of biblical interpretation. The Puritan fathers of New England were familiar with the Greek and Hebrew tongues. But they never devoted themselves to the original Scriptures with that freshness of interest which he exhibited, that vividness of biographical and geographical detail, that sympathy with the personal and domestic life of inspired men, that ideal presence of the scenes once honoured by our Redeemer, that freedom from the trammels of a prescriptive philosophy or immemorial custom. Because he has done so much and suffered so much, in persuading men to interpret the Bible, not according to the letter, but the spirit, not in subjection to human standards, but in compliance with its own analogies, not by conjectures of what it ought to mean, but by grammatical and historical proofs of what it does mean, he has received and deserved the name of our patriarch in sacred philology. Several weeks before he was publicly named for the professorship which he afterwards adorned, a sagacious observer remarked to him incidentally, 'You, of all men whom I know, are just the man for that professorship. Biblical literature is now at a low ebb throughout the country, but if you were to teach it at Andover you would make the students there believe, in three months, that sacred criticism is as necessary to the successful progress of a theologian as air is to the support of animal life.' For more than forty years the man who uttered this prophecy has been an instructor in one of our most enterprising colleges, and he is, perhaps, more familiar than any living man with the history of our philological literature, and he now writes, 'No one has rejoiced more heartily than myself at the success which has attended Mr. Stuart in his office at Andover. He has done a work there, and in the whole of our country, which no other man, as I believe, could have accomplished. Those who have come forward as theological students within the last thirty-five or forty years can form but a very imperfect idea of the difficulties which he had to encounter at first. But he seemed not to regard them, and they disappeared.'

As it was the aim of Mr. Stuart to present theology in a Biblical form, so it was one of his chief aims to exalt the doctrine of a Saviour's atoning death. One of his reviewers, the devout and quick-sighted Tholuck, has said of him, 'In respect of his theological views, he believes in all the fundamental doctrines of the Christian Church of the Reformed [Calvinistic] confession. In these his extensive study of German literature has in no degree shaken his faith; though it should seem to have exercised an influence upon his method of establishing them. He forsakes the ways prescribed by those of the same faith, and the dogmatic interpreters of his own Church, and seeks new paths; being led to this sometimes because scruples have occurred to him, which were unknown to them.'[t] In a new path, however, or in a beaten one, he never went away from the scene where his Lord was crucified. Lutheran or Reformed, either, or both, or neither, he was determined to know nothing among men, save Jesus Christ and him crucified. Firm, indeed, was his faith in the sovereignty, the decrees, the universal providence of Jehovah. But these were not the heart of his theology. In his view, all other truths clustered around the doctrine of Redemption. To make this doctrine prominent, he would depress any formula invented by man. Around the cross he gathered all his learning. At the foot of the cross he strewed his many honours. Here his quick-moving, his indomitable spirit lingered in a childlike peace. If men trusted in the Redeemer, they were welcomed to his sympathy, let them err as they might on the metaphysical theories of religion. And

---

[t] Literarischer Anzeiger, 1834, No. 22, S. 169.

when he uttered censures, too severe perhaps, upon the abstractions of our divines, it seemed to be not that he loved philosophy less, for he aspired after a true philosophy, but that he loved Jesus more.

Mr. Park states that several years ago he heard him say incidentally, ' No greater injury can be done to me than to hold me up as faultless in my mode of thinking and living.' — ' The thought,' says the preacher, ' never occurred to my own mind, until three days ago, that I should be called to heed this admonition while standing over his bier. He was not faultless. The sun never shone on all parts of the same body at one and the same time. If it illumine one side, it must leave the other shaded. But the frailties of our revered friend were intimately combined with his excellences. The former suggest the latter. If he made minor mistakes, it was because he gazed too steadfastly at the great principles of things. In the celerity of his thought, he was sometimes led to overlook important incidents. Did he commit errors which he had the power to avoid? It was because he seized upon pressing exigencies, and hurried forward to meet the demands of the people. He launched his vessel when the tide was up. It is one characteristic of true genius to find out and then to meet the crisis; to put forth the influence which is demanded, and *when* it is demanded by the occasion. Mr. Stuart was always at the post of danger. When the Education Society was attacked, he was at once upon the ground. When the cause of Temperance was assailed, he was speedily in the field. When the laws of hygiene were discussed, his essays were in the newspapers forthwith. — Did he make more inaccurate statements than some other men? And did he not utter many more truths than most other men? The most luxuriant tree needs most to be pruned. Habitually was his mind on useful themes. Sometimes this, sometimes that, but always one important idea was revolving before him. When the missionary Judson, on his recent visit to this place, came out from the chamber of our departed friend, he said, with a full emphasis what has been repeated by many a pilgrim on the threshold of that same chamber — ' I feel that I have been conversing with a great man.' In Mr. Stuart's conversation with a farmer, he imparted new ideas on the implements of husbandry. To the mechanic, he often seemed to have learned the trades. To the merchant, he gave instruction on political economy. To the philanthropist, he proposed new schemes of beneficence. Medical men were often surprised at the extent of his reading in their own department. If there were better metaphysicians than he, more accurate classical scholars, more correct historians, more profound statesmen, — as there doubtless were,—still, where is the man who knew so much of philology *and* philosophy *and* history *and* practical life, all combined,—who had so many knowledges of such multifarious things, and applied them all to a better purpose? If there be such a man (and there *may* be such), I am too ignorant to have learned his name.[u]

As to the personal character of Professor Stuart, it was read and known of all men. Whatever faults he had, never did he subject one to the necessity of ferreting them out. Frank, confiding, and impulsive, he abhorred dissimulation. Never could he afford the time, nor subject himself to the trouble, of accomplishing an end by circumvention, so long as he believed that a straight line—that beautiful symbol of righteousness—was in morals, as in mathematics, the shortest between the two points. He would rather have been accused of imprudence than suspected of trickery. Familiar with his person and domestic habits from my infancy, says Mr. Park, it is something for me to say that he was always the favourite of the young. Ardent in temperament, transparent in character, simple in manners, there were a thousand points where his manly sympathies touched the affinities of boyhood. The necessities of a nervous temperament obliging him to be methodical in physical exercise, his ardour in working his garden, plying an axe and saw, or accomplishing his daily walk, had a charm for the people of simple habits among whom he lived; revealing to them that he was ambitious of nothing beyond sound health of body and mind, for the better prosecution of his professional pursuits. Never overstepping the proprieties of his profession, he was not suspected of anything bordering on the artificial and sanctimonious. Leaning over a fence, when taking his accustomed walk, he had something to say to a labourer which would make him his admiring friend for life. The correspondent and friend of distinguished men across the sea, who will hear of his decease with great grief, no mourners at his funeral were more deeply moved than the farmers and mechanics whom he had accosted with kind greetings every day for forty years. Addicted to the life of a student, study was his delight. Adopting a few hours for severe and uninterrupted study, rarely exceeding three and a half—and these in the early part of the day—(his varied and immense reading in other hours would have been called study by others)—he never worked with a jaded, strained, and wearied mind; consequently, hardship was never associated with his pursuits, but delight always.[x]

We look for no perfect one on earth, adds the preacher; and

---

[u] Park, 29-43.   [x] Park, 48, 49.

had the master who is taken from our head to-day been more punctiliously accurate, he would have been less impulsive ; and had he been less impulsive, he would not have stirred up the mind of the clergy ; and had he not aroused men to biblical studies, he would not have fulfilled his mission ; for his mission was to be a pioneer, to break up a hard soil, to do a rough work, to introduce other labourers into the vineyard which he had made ready. If, then, he lapsed here and there in sacred literature, who are the men among us that correct him ? Chiefly, the men who are in some way indebted to him for the power to make the correction. Chiefly, the men who have received from him the impulses by which they have learned to criticise him. Chiefly, the men who would have remained on the dead level of an empirical philology, had they not been quickened to an upward progress by his early enthusiasm. If the eagle in his flight toward the sun be wounded by the archer, the arrow that is aimed at him is guided by a feather from the eagle's own broad wing.

He who now lies before us had faults of character. But he might have concealed them, if he had possessed more cunning and less frankness. He was ready to acknowledge his errors. Had he been adroit in hiding them, he would not have been a man of progress, nor that transparent, open-hearted man who won to himself the general love. Spreading himself out over various departments, he was free in his speech upon them all. Had he not been thus adventurous, he would not have roused so many classes of minds to such diversified activity. He wore a glass before his heart. He spoke what he felt. We know, and the world know, the worst of him ! and this is his highest praise. He had no hidden mine of iniquity. His foibles do not lie buried beneath our soundings. But it is no common virtue which is honoured in every farmer's cottage of the town where he has lived for two-and-forty years, and which is venerated by missionaries of the cross on Lebanon and at Damascus. I have heard him praised by Tholuck, and Neander, and Henderson, and Chalmers, and by an Irish labourer, and a servant-boy, and by the families before whose windows he has taken his daily walks for almost half a century. His influence as a divine is to be widened and prolonged by the fact, that on the hills and in the valleys around his dwelling there is neither man, nor woman, nor child, who has known him, and does not feel that an honest Christian rests from his labours, —an Israelite indeed, in whom was no guile.

The old age of Mr. Stuart honoured God in illustrating the wealth of the inspired word. In his sixty-seventh year he read all the tragedies of Æschylus, for the sake of detecting idioms and allusions explanatory of the Bible. There were three hours in every day when he forgot all the pains of advancing years, and all the turmoils of the world. More than once, with his wonted vivacity, has he repeated the sentiment of Heinsius: 'I no sooner come into my library than I bolt the door after me, excluding ambition, avarice, and all such vices, and in the very lap of eternity, amidst so many diivine souls, I take my seat with so lofty a spirit and such sweet content, that I pity all the great and rich who know not this happiness.' A few years ago, when he made a certain discovery with regard to the book of Job, he could not sleep for more than thirty-six hours. They were hours of a grateful interest in the wonders of the Bible. At his death he had formed the plan for several commentaries which would have engrossed three years of his time.[y] His solace was in the book of books: it never tired him. Not seldom was it his meditation all the night. It presented to him exhaustless stores. Near the end of his life he expressed a religious gratitude that the Hebrew language had become to him like his mother tongue, and that the simple reading of the Hebrew text opened the sense of passages which had before been closed against him. When asked whether he retained his confidence in the great system of truths which he had defended, he answered with a strong emphasis, 'Yes.' Have you any doubts with regard to your former principles? was the question; and the energetic answer was given at once, 'No.' As he approached the grave, he became more and more hopeful that these principles would soon triumph over all opposition.—'I have long since learned,' he said, 'that feelings in religious experience are deceptive. I look mainly to my life for my evidence. I think that my first aim in life has been to glorify God, and that I have been ready to labour and suffer for him.' When afflicted with severe pains he loved to repeat the words, 'Wearisome days and nights hast *Thou* appointed unto me.' He had thought of death long and carefully. He was familiar with it. He was ready for it. It was less to him than a Sabbath day's journey. 'This is the beginning of the end,' was his placid remark with regard to his broken arm, and, after alluding to the pains which it caused him, he added, 'Such troubles make the peaceful asylum of the narrow house look very inviting.' When he heard the hope expressed that his last sickness would be unto life and not unto death, he replied, 'Unto the glory of God, but unto *death*'—'I am prepared to die.—O God! my spirit is in thy hand! Have mercy, but thy will be done.' On the first

---

[y] He intended to write soon a second Exposition of the book of Proverbs. It was to be popular in its character. Its plan was admirable. He recently collected the materials for an Exposition of the book of Jonah, and also for the book of Job. He left written notes on the Epistles to the Corinthians.

Sabbath of the new year, when the storm was howling around his dwelling, he fell asleep. Peaceful, as to a night's repose, he entered on his long rest.[z]

Having latterly followed chiefly Professor Park's account of his distinguished master, we have not interrupted it by referring to a matter which he omits to notice, but to which Dr. Adams very properly calls attention,—a matter no less painfully suggestive in this country than in the United States :—

The Commentaries of Professor Stuart not being adapted for popular use, but designed for professional students, their sale was never very lucrative to him. In their disposition, the noble enthusiasm of the scholar was always uppermost, often, as he has been told by others, to his pecuniary loss. With a morbid sensibility did he shun, as a thing to be loathed, the imputation of making a book for the sake of money. If the choice had been for him to make between a scholarly book, which would do honour to his profession and his country, with no gain but even a loss of money to him, and a commonplace volume, designed for popularity, with immense

---

[z] Park, 43-48. 'Although he had reached the limit of threescore years and ten, many circumstances combined to create the hope that Prof. Stuart would prosecute his studies for several years to come. A slight accident, as we say, decided the case otherwise. Taking his daily walk, the sled of a boy occasioned him a fall in the street, by which the bone of the wrist was fractured. The pain and confinement which followed rendered him unable to withstand a severe cold by which he was subsequently seized, and which, passing into a typhoid fever of several days, terminated his earthly life. At times during his illness his mind displayed its usual vigour, and he conversed on subjects of public interest with that vivacity which was common to him. No apprehensions of immediate danger were felt by his family until the day on which he died.'—*Adams*, pp. 56, 57.

Professor Stuart died at ten minutes before twelve o'clock on Sabbath night, January 4, 1852, aged seventy-one years, nine months, and nine days. He had been a preacher of the gospel forty-seven years, a teacher of youth forty-one years, a Professor in the Theological Seminary thirty-eight years. His death was so sudden and tranquil, that but few of his family were apprised of it before the morning. The tolling of the chapel, and of the village bells on Monday, announced the sad event to his townsmen, many of whom did not know that he had been dangerously sick. His disease was the influenza, accompanied with a typhoid fever. His funeral was attended on Thursday afternoon, January 8, 1852, by a large concourse of clergymen, pupils, and friends. Rev. Prof. Stowe, of Bowdoin College, introduced the exercises with an invocation and the reading of select passages from the Bible. Rev. Prof. Emerson, of Andover, offered the funeral prayer. The choir then sung the four hundred and fifty-fourth Hymn of the Church Psalmody—

'Thine earthly Sabbaths, Lord, we love.'

This was a favourite hymn with the deceased, and one which he had sung on every Sabbath of the past two years. After the sermon the choir sung the last three stanzas of the seventeenth Psalm, Long Metre, Third Part, in the Church Psalmody—

'This life's a dream, an empty show.'

These were also favourite stanzas with Mr. Stuart. On the Sabbath after his interment many clergymen of various sects, and in distant parts of New England, noticed his death in their pulpits.—*Park*, p. 56.

sales and immense profits, he could not have hesitated for a moment. A love for his profession, and a religious ambition to elevate and honour it, compelled him to turn from proposals, frequently addressed to him, to prepare a series of more popular publications, and the high-toned purpose which forbade his concession to a more lucrative employment was not without some fears, shadows, and anxieties as to future support, which only rendered his persistance the more manly and heroic.[a]

These anxieties, creating more or less of despondency, were never known beyond the confidence of private friendship. The public never suspected that his latest labours were projected and prosecuted with a secret hurt in his heart. Less we cannot utter than this decided testimony, that it would have been more for the honour of our Alma Mater to have retained this distinguished Professor in the full emoluments of that office upon which his name had shed such renown, to the very end of his days, rather than, by accepting the resignation which his own nice and delicate sense of honour had volunteered, in view of declining health, to have entailed the possibility of wounding, in the evening of his life, the man to whom so much of her fame was owing.[b]

But here is a disparity—the inadequate rewards of literary talent and attainment—which, for its explanation, demands all our philosophy and all our religion. A man with no thirst for knowledge, and no taste for letters, rises to affluence, though unable to read

---

[a] ' That I speak not unadvisedly on this subject will appear from the following extract of a letter addressed to Prof. Stuart by one of the largest publishing houses in the country. It has reference to negotiations for the publication of his work on Proverbs.

' We had supposed that the work referred to was a *popular* commentary. With a work of this kind, from your pen, and on such a subject, we could "take the country." But, creditable to us as it certainly would be, we are really afraid to commit ourselves for the publication of the more learned and critical work now proposed.'—*Adams*.

[b] ' The writer is aware of the explanation given of this measure—that the endowments of the Seminary yielded but a certain amount of income, and that this amount was necessary to remunerate the actual services of instructors, with no surplus for the support of others, beyond the meagre sum which was allowed the two oldest Professors on their retirement, after having been connected with the Institution for nearly half a century. The General Assembly of the Presbyterian Church generously insisted that Dr. Miller, on resigning his connection with Princeton Theological Seminary, should continue to receive the full amount of his former salary for life. And we cannot but think, had the fact been known to the churches of Massachusetts that Prof. Stuart, when a year's illness, by which he had been deprived of the power to study and instruct, led him to tender the resignation of his office, was at once reduced from the ordinary stipend which habits had made essential to his comfort to a small fraction of the amount, they would have spontaneously furnished the Seminary with the means of a more just, not to say liberal procedure, and so have saved one of the most distinguished scholars of our land from a state of mental depression which, for two years, was as the valley of the shadow of death.'—*Adams*.

the inscription emblazoned on the panels of his equipage; while another, devoting a whole life to studies which advance learning and religion, and reflect honour on the land of his nativity, poorly compensated at the best, must bear up, at last, with the despondent fear that an unrequited toil may terminate in an old age of dependence. The essay of Epictetus explains the mystery in part: all these things are commodities in the market of life, and it is by exchanges and barter that one is procured at the loss of another; and the attainments and rewards of Christian scholarship are cheaply bought at any price, even if the Word of God did not decide the balance by the promise of future reversals and promotion. ' *Their works do follow them.*'c

It is regretted by Professor Park that a complete list of Mr. Stuart's published works cannot be made out at present; but he offers the following as an imperfect catalogue of them:—

Two Sermons, preached at New Haven, one immediately before, another soon after, his resignation of his pastoral office. 1810.
Grammar of the Hebrew Language, without points. 1813.
Sermon before the Salem Female Charitable Society. 1815.
Sermon at the Ordination of the Missionaries Fiske, Spaulding, Winslow, and Woodward. 1819.
Letters to Dr. Channing on the Divinity of Christ. 1819. Fourth American edition in 1846.
Sermon at the completion of Bartlet Hall, Andover. 1821.
Grammar of the Hebrew Language, with points. 1821. Sixth edition in 1838.
Letters to Dr. Miller on the Eternal Generation of the Son of God. 1822.
Two Discourses on the Atonement. 1824. Four editions.
Winer's Greek Grammar of the New Testament. Translated by Professors Stuart and Robinson. 1825.
Christianity a Distinct Religion. 1826. A Sermon. Two editions.
Elementary Principles of Interpretation. From the Latin of Ernesti. Fourth edition in 1842.
Election Sermon. 1827.
Commentary on the Epistle to the Hebrews. 2 vols. 1827-8. Second edition in one volume, 1823.
Hebrew Chrestomathy. 1829. Second edition, 1832.
Practical Rules for Greek Accents. 1829.
Sermon at the Funeral of Mrs. Adams. 1829.
Course of Hebrew Study. 1830.
Letters to Dr. Channing on the subject of Religious Liberty. 1830. Second edition with Notes. 1846.
Prize Essay respecting the Use of Spirituous Liquors. 1830.
The Conversion of the Jews: A Sermon at the Ordination of Rev. Wm. G. Schauffler. 1831. Two editions.
Commentary on the Epistle to the Romans. 2 vols. 1832. Second edition, in one volume, 1835.
Grammar of the New Testament Dialect. Second edition improved, 1834.
Notes to Hug's Introduction to the New Testament. 1836.
Cicero on the Immortality of the Soul. 1833.
Hints on the Prophecies. Second edition, 1842.
Commentary on the Apocalypse. 1845. 2 vols.; pages 1008. This, and five of his other most important works, have been reprinted in Europe.

---

c Adams, pp. 51-55.

Critical History and Defence of the Old Testament Canon. 1845.
Sermon on the Lamb of God. 1846.
Translation of Roediger's Gesenius. 1846.
Sermon at the Funeral of Mrs. Woods. 1846.
Scriptural View of the Wine Question. 1848.
Commentary on Daniel. 1850.
Conscience and the Constitution. 1850.
Commentary on Ecclesiastes. 1851.
Commentary on Proverbs. 1852.

Several of the preceding works were republished in a volume of Miscellanies in 1846. Among the anonymous Essays written by Mr. Stuart are twenty or twenty-five in the Panoplist, the Christian Spectator, and the Spirit of the Pilgrims. Among his articles for the American Quarterly Register are one on the Study of the Hebrew, and one on the Study of the Classics, in 1828; one on Sacred and Classical Studies, in 1831, and an Examination of Strictures upon the American Education Society, and a Postcript to the Examination, in 1829. Among his articles for the North American Review are a Review of Roy's Hebrew Lexicon, in 1838; of Robinson's Greek Lexicon, in 1851; of Gilfillan's Bards of the Bible, in 1851. In 1851 he also published two Essays in the Quarterly Review of the Methodist Episcopal Church, South, on the Traits of History and Doctrine peculiar to Christianity. The larger part of his Essays for Periodicals, however, he published in the Biblical Repository and the Bibliotheca Sacra. The following is an incomplete list of them. His anonymous and his briefer articles are omitted.

Biblical Repository.

1831. Interpretation of Psalm xvi.; pages 59.—Remarks on Hahn's Definition of Interpretation, and some topics connected with it; pages 49.—Creed of Arminius, with a Sketch of his Life and Times; pages 83.—Interpretation of Romans viii. 18-25; pages 44.—Meaning of ΚΥΡΙΟΣ in the New Testament, particularly as employed by Paul; pages 43.—Remarks on Internal Evidence respecting the various Readings in 1 Tim. iii. 16; pages 23.

1832. Are the same Principles of Interpretation to be applied to the Bible as to other books? pages 14.—Notice of Rosenmuelleri Scholia in V. T., in Compendium redacta; pages 5.—On the alleged Obscurity of Prophecy; pages 29.—Hints on the Study of the Greek Language; pages 20.—Samaritan Pentateuch and Literature; pages 43.

1833. Hints respecting Commentaries upon the Scriptures; pages 50.—Is the Manner of Christian Baptism prescribed in the New Testament? pages 103.

1834. Hints and Cautions respecting the Greek Article; pages 51.

1835. On the Discrepancy between the Sabellian and Athanasian Method of representing the Doctrine of the Trinity: Translated from Schleiermacher, with Notes and Illustrations; pages 88.—Second Article on the same; pages 116. [Both of these articles were afterwards republished in a distinct volume.]—How are Designations of Time in the Apocalypse to be understood? pages 50.—On the use of the Particle ἵνα in the New Testament: translated from the Latin of Professor Tittmann of Leipsic, with Notes; pages 28.

1836. What has Paul taught respecting the obedience of Christ? Translated from the Latin of Tittmann, with Notes and Remarks; pages 88.—On the meaning of the word πλήρωμα in the New Testament; and particularly on the meaning of the passage in which it occurs in Col. ii. 9; pages 56.—Hebrew Lexicography; pages 46.

1837. Critical Examination of some Passages in Genesis i.; with Remarks on Difficulties that attend some of the present Modes of Geological Reasoning; pages 60.—Have the Sacred Writers anywhere asserted that the Sin or Righteousness of one is imputed to another; pages 89.

1838. The Hebrew Tenses: Translation from Ewald, with Remarks; pages 43.—Review of Prof. Norton's Evidences of the Genuineness of the Gospels; pages 78.—Inquiry respecting the Original Language of Matthew's Gospel, and the Genuineness of the first two chapters of the same; with particular reference to

Prof. Norton's 'Genuineness,' etc.; pages 44.—Second Article on the same; pages 41.

1839. Genuineness of several texts in the Gospels; pages 26.—What is Sin? pages 34.—Second Article on the same; pages 45.

1840. Christology of the Book of Enoch; pages 52.—Future Punishment as exhibited in the Book of Enoch; pages 34.

1841. Correspondence with Dr. Nordheimer on the Hebrew Article; pages 8.

1842. Examination of Rev. A. Barnes's Remarks on Hebrews ix. 16-18; pages 26.

Bibliotheca Sacra.

1843. Sketches of Angelology in the Old and New Testament; pages 66.—On the Manuscripts and Editions of the Greek New Testament; pages 28.—The number of the Beast in the Apocalypse; pages 28.—The White Stone of the Apocalypse: Exegesis of Rev. ii. 17; pages 16.—The Lord's Supper in the Corinthian Church: Remarks on 1 Cor. xi. 17-34; pages 32.

1844. Patristical and Exegetical Investigation of the Question respecting the real Bodily Presence of Christ in the Elements of the Lord's Supper; pages 42.—A Second Article on the same theme; pages 55.

1848. De Wette's Commentary on Rom. v. 12-19; pages 20.

1850. Exegetical and Theological Examination of John i. 1-18; pages 41.—A Second Article on the same theme; pages 47.—Doctrine respecting the Person of Christ: translated from the German of Dr. and Prof. J. A. Dorner, with remarks; pages 37.

1852. Observations on Matthew xxiv. 29-31, and the Parallel Passages in Mark and Luke, with Remarks on the Double Sense; Review of Mornings among the Jesuits at Rome. (Now in press.)

Z.

EWALD ON THE PROPHETS:

BEING A TRANSLATION OF THE FIRST TWO SECTIONS OF THE GENERAL INTRO-
DUCTION TO PROFESSOR HEINRICH VON EWALD'S WORK, ' DIE PROPHETEN
DES ALTEN BUNDES ERKLÄRT.'

[The first numbers of this Journal contained translations from Ewald's
Dissertation of Hebrew Poetry prefixed to his Work on the Poetical
Books of the Old Testament. The following pages are a translation
of the first two sections of the Dissertation which, in like manner,
precedes his Version of the Prophetical Books. We believe that, when
our readers have acquainted themselves with what we thus put before
them, they will find our sufficient justification in the Dissertation
itself, however much they may object to particular statements in it;
but, as it has been referred to by very eminent evangelical commentators, German as well as English, in terms which seem to class it
with the works commonly called rationalist, it is due to them, as well
as to our readers and ourselves, to say a word on the subject beforehand.

These learned and Christian writers are—as the Church has need
they should be—mainly controversialists, in as far as they come into
contact with Dr. Ewald's views of prophecy. He accepts, as critically
proved, those conclusions as to the genuineness of various portions of
Isaiah and other prophets, which we quite agree with Hengstenberg
and Alexander, and other commentators, in considering as no less
opposed to the method of scientific criticism than they are to our
old feelings of reverence for the Word of God: and therefore
these commentators class his views of prophecy with those of such
writers as Rosenmüller, Gesenius, De Wette, Winer, or Strauss. But
though this may be just for certain critical and controversial purposes,
we think nothing is clearer than that in other respects the difference
between him and them is not less marked, than between them and the
evangelical commentators. The whole temper and spirit of the man is
different. The writings of those rationalists are characterized by the
absence of properly religious interest in the Bible. They have devoted their lives to the study of it, but they study it more as a dead
subject for intellectual anatomists, whose main design is the exercise
of their anatomical skill, and who show little or nothing of that lively
sympathy which even the records of Greece or Rome awaken in a
Niebuhr or a Grote. Dr. Ewald, on the contrary, while he has all that
lively personal sympathy in the Hebrew literature which the last-
mentioned authors have in the classical, constantly asserts that the
main interest of the Bible—and that which it is the aim of all his
learned labours to promote—is the practical one; that it is the book of
eternal life for his countrymen and the world; that in the midst of the
worldliness and scepticism which he sees around him, he discerns signs
also that the Lord of grace and of light is employing this Bible to make
His will known; and that as long as it remains open to us, and its clear
voice is heard by individuals as well as through churches and kingdoms,
we may confidently declare that the Prophets will never prophesy in
vain, but that their Lord will appear to us also in His glory: and if

we are unable to approve the unlimited liberty he claims, any more than the particular conclusions he may arrive at, in his investigations of Scripture, we must not overlook that he maintains that neither in this, nor in anything else, is there any true liberty except what a man can have as the servant of God and of true religion—which latter he farther explains to relate not to some one department of knowledge or of morals, but to the seeking and finding, in all and everywhere, that salvation and life whence itself proceeds. While he complains that he has been condemned no less by his evangelical than by his sceptical countrymen, he declares that his sympathies are with the former, as well as his aims and purposes, and that his conscience tells him that they will one day see that he is no sceptic, nor doing the work of sceptics, but only what they will rejoice in, and no longer mistakingly grieve over, when the Lord whom they honour, though not in this matter with full knowledge, shall open their eyes to see the case as it actually is. And, in the preface to his Translation of the Gospels (dated May, 1850) he states that he has hastily published this, without waiting to finish the 'History of Israel' (on which he had been long engaged), in order that he may, if possible, add something to his countrymen's means of studying and understanding these records of the Christian faith; because their fathers', and still more their own, sins have brought Germany to that condition in which nothing can save it from utterly perishing—though, possibly, by a slow, Byzantine-like decay—except the power of Christianity, spreading itself through all forms of life, personal and social, and becoming the actuating spirit alike of the prince, the statesman, the judge, the lawgiver, and of the people: 'and this blessing,' he goes on to say, 'we may attain to, if Christ himself shall come again in His own light from out of the darkness into which the evil times, and the various forms of human self-seeking, have driven Him, and shall appear among us as though risen a second time from the dead:'—' In religion, in philosophy, in the state, and in our homes, there is some one thing worthy of our devoting to it all our wisdom and strength, and giving ourselves to it with ever more direct, and, if possible, more earnest desire and joy, throughout our whole life: to help forward such a zeal for the knowledge and practice of Christianity among us is the object of my publishing this little book: Christ will come again among us with greater might; O bow yourselves before Him alone, and hear his words of love as well as of judgment!'

Dr. Ewald has given us a translation of the Prophetical Books which is said to be worthy of his pre-eminent Hebrew scholarship; and, if he had done *only* this, we should not have failed to see how important this earnest, religious frame of mind must have been to the effectual accomplishment of his task, and how much more he must have been able to apprehend of the meaning of his text, because he entered so deeply into, and must have therefore been guided by, the Spirit which directed the original writers: and if so, may we not—nay, must we not—apply the same rule in our consideration of what he has done in a province beyond that of translation? This province is not primarily that of the divine or theologian, much less of the minister of the gospel: it belongs, just as the critical investigation and translation of the original text do, to the *human* side of the Bible. 'God spake by the mouth of His holy prophets;' and it is what GOD spake that the divine and the minister have primarily to do with: yet, since the prophets were men, and God did employ them as human, and not as mere mechanical, means of uttering His word, there must surely be a right (as well as a wrong) way of investigating the human character of the prophets, and the human element of prophecy, and one which, if we could properly avail ourselves of it, must be full of instruction—so that the minister who is furnished with this will be as much aided in his own work as he admits himself to be by the translations of scholars whose knowledge of languages and grammar he does not possess. And such help, we are bold to say, will be found in this dissertation on prophecy. In its main views—not, we repeat, in all its details—it stands not in rationalist and sceptical contradiction to the Christian view of prophecy, but in real harmony with it, and could plainly only have been written by one who entered into the spirit in which prophecy is viewed by our Lord and his Apostles in the Gospels and in the Epistles.

If we turn to the biblical commentaries of Luther or Calvin, we find them always presenting the human as well as the divine side of the Bible, with a life and sympathy which show how important they felt the former to be, for the sake of the latter: and the absence of this element in so many of the modern evangelical commentators is notoriously one of the things which drives men to the neologists, in the hope of finding something which will be less drily doctrinal, and more real—though, in fact, what they find there is for the most part less real and living, even on its human side, than what they have left. And though we must class Dr. Ewald's dismemberments and reconstructions, and consequent substitutions of a mechanical and fictitious for an organic and living unity, of the Psalms and Prophets, among the criticisms which are as little human as divine, the contrary must be asserted of his general dissertations, and especially of that now before us. It is full of true life and unity, and, though open to objection as to details, will, we are persuaded, help every one who studies—not takes for granted—its statements, to a clearer understanding of what manner of men the Hebrew Prophets actually were, than he had before. The whole turn of thought is no doubt different from what we are accustomed to in the English way of looking at such subjects: but we must remember that it is the appointment of Him who divides and apportions faculties to nations and churches, no less than to individuals, 'severally as He will,' that, if we are really to understand such subjects as that now under consideration, we must learn from the Germans, and therefore be content with their way of looking at them, at least until we are able to reproduce them in our own. The Germans have received the gift of imagining and bodying forth the forgotten past in a manner we are of ourselves not capable of: though to us, on the other hand, has been intrusted—and we must use for them as well as for ourselves—the common-sense faculty of distinguishing those images which really restore the past, and those which are mere figments of the fancy.

The third and last section of the dissertation (on the Canon of the Prophetical Scriptures) would require so much criticism, in order to dissever what is positive from what is merely hypothetical in it, that we abstain from translating it. But if, here especially, we cannot accept certain of Dr. Ewald's critical *results*, we may heartily accept that which is the essential characteristic of his *method ;* and which he sets forth, when he insists on the importance of a thoroughly accurate and complete investigation of the several books of the prophets, of each in all its details, and of each as a whole, and in its relation with the rest,—and then concludes by saying, 'He only who has in himself no apprehension of the reality, the nature, and the majesty of true prophecy, and who has acquired none from the prophetical writings; he who will learn nothing from the Spirit of God, and who never has experienced, even remotely, what it is to feel that impulse and hear that voice within him ;—he will always remain no less unsuccessful than unworthy, whether as reader, as enquirer, or as expositor, on this subject.'—Tr.]

I. THE PROPHETS IN THEIR LIFE AND ACTS.

IT is not proposed to give such a complete description of what prophets were in their life and acts as would involve an investigation of all the religions of antiquity, in all of which the ministry of prophets is an essential feature : nay, many demonstrable truths concerning the nature, history, and end of the religion and the polity of the ancient nation of Israel itself, must here be taken for granted without entering into full details.

Nor do the limits of this work permit us to elucidate all the notices of the prophets scattered through the Old Testament, and especially in the historical books. It is, indeed, incontestable, that every such notice, though derived from tradition never so remote, contributes to the right understanding of the whole character of the ancient prophets, as soon as we can ascertain its original purport ; and to this extent the non-contemporary narratives relating to prophets have not been overlooked. But the object of this work is to elucidate, not the historical, but the properly prophetical, literature of the Hebrews, while a complete explanation of those narratives, pointing out the amount of proper historical matter contained in them, belongs in part to an exposition of the historical books of the Old Testament, and in part to a general history of this ancient people.

But in truth it is better for us to begin our study of the prophets in what they have themselves written, and where we may see their spirit expressed with most clearness and certainty, rather than in the scattered, and frequently very scanty narratives of others, about them and their deeds and words. Let him who desires a really intimate acquaintance with these heroes of the truth of God, first learn to understand their words and deeds as they themselves have recorded them ; for here they approach us most closely and confidentially, and irresistibly invite us to know them. Those accounts of the older prophets, and their striking or important sayings and acts, which have been preserved by other and often long subsequent writers, will be more certainly intelligible to us, if we have first learnt to comprehend rightly and thoroughly those which the later prophets have themselves delivered to us.

We therefore give here a few general propositions, which will be completely established in the subsequent detailed commentary on the writings of the several prophets, while they serve to make many particular points more intelligible at once.

1. *Of the Prophets in general.*

1. The universal truths which govern the world, or (to say the same thing in other words) the thoughts of God, lie ever beyond the reach of change or interference, wholly independent of the vicissitudes of things below, or of the will and act of man. Yet man was not originally created nor intended to remain a stranger to them ; but, on the contrary, he has an innate capacity and ability—though never so small, or in many individuals never so weakened—to lay hold of these same truths, and to receive them through his thoughts into his will, and so into his acts ; and thus, by a voluntary participation in them, to think, to resolve, and to act with God, and thus attain to his true end. The spirit (that is, the purely divine life) which is originally in God alone, has, through the creation, been implanted in man as a germ—a germ which by itself remains unquickened, like the germ of a plant without its earth. And in accordance with this twofold truth is it declared that God is ever calling and inviting men, stirring and moving them to take part in His own life, will, and deed, to know Him, and to follow Him : and while this call goes forth without restriction and continually to all men, it precedes, for it first makes possible, and supplies the primary condition of, all prophetic action (Isa. vi. ; Jer. i. ; Ezek. i., ii., iii.).

Now this call, which goes forth to all men, in accordance with their original constitution, cannot always remain without a corresponding answer on the part of man, nor this innate capacity without its fulfilment : it were no original, no divine capacity if it did always so remain without reaching its goal—nay, without a beginning or an endeavour in that direction. On the contrary, that spiritual germ is incessantly stimulated by the whole course of the world, and by the divine energy hidden therein, not to continue wholly dead and inert ; and it could only then remain unfruitful if the divine energy were itself to cease. Each of the violent concussions and commotions of the world (as we actually see) necessarily communicates itself to this germ, and tends to draw it out of the dull earth towards the light : for every concussion of the world awakens at the same time the impulse to ascertain its cause ; and no sooner is the impulse to inquire, to observe, and to draw conclusions, awakened in this germ of man's spiritual life, than it begins to grow up more and more vigorously, and to put forth its proper blossoms and fruit; and so, as history unfolds itself, that innate capacity is unceasingly stirred to ever stronger and deeper movement, and that divine call ever more irresistibly uttered, till at last—far as our own age is yet distant from it—mankind will have reached its goal, and the appointed measure of the capacity of human will and deed be full.

If, now, any man consents to the purpose of God, who is ever calling on him personally, and always ready to draw his mind from its natural dulness and apathy into intercourse with His own, and thus to lead him on to will and to do accordingly, there is then built up in him a new life in which he finds that he is no longer alone and forsaken, but in fellowship with God, and with all truth, and ready to proceed from one truth to another without end. This is essentially another life, a second and higher life in the same man, when his individual will finds itself directed and led by a higher universal will, and his acts are no longer worthless or isolated, but grafted into the divine activity itself, and so made to bear the good fruit of an eternal result and reward. Thus does the Spirit, the true and divine life, first manifest itself in action ; at least, thus first, in the course of our earthly existence, the work of the Spirit begins in man, and is able to proceed on firm ground. And this is no strange and forced life, but only the fulfilling of that originally appointed for man's free and holy enjoyment, only the perfection of life as it should be.

But the sign and the proof that such a fellowship with the pure Source of all energy has been really formed in a man, are not found in the mere growth and life of certain definite truths in him, but chiefly in a clear and distinct view of the whole time and state of things ; in wisdom and readiness to oppose the darkness and complications of circumstances ; in a firm and vigorous activity in overcoming the hindrances of what is good ; and in the final and certain victory in which the good things of God are won. He who finds in himself a light with which he triumphantly disperses the darknesses of the present time, will not deceive himself as to the life of that fellowship within him ; and he who approves himself by this test will, sooner or later, be recognised by others also as a sharer in this fellowship.

But we have in this place less to do with this universal truth of the relation of the human and divine spirit, than with the great diversities which are possible therein on the side of man. Not only are there differences in the duration of this fellowship, inas-

much as many are faintly roused for a moment by the light of this
fire of a higher life, and few permanently illuminated by its beams;
not only in its inward energy, which in so many accomplishes but
half its work, and in few attains a might which overcomes everything; not only in the activity with which he in whom this fellowship is already established endeavours to direct and to draw
others into the like fellowship, since this power is not given to
all men: but this fellowship between God and man also manifests itself as different in kind, in accordance with the great differences of historical periods, and this is precisely what we have
here to investigate further.

If, as has been said, it is generally possible for the human to
sink itself in the divine spirit, and to apprehend the divine will, it
must also be possible, at one stage of this higher life and more
inward energy, for a conception originating in the mind of God
to possess the mind of a man so wholly that he feels it to be not
at all his own, but only that of his God. This is not merely possible, but to be desired, since the divine thoughts and conceptions
are indeed mighty enough to fill the soul; and truly, when they
do alone and entirely guide it, they guide it even to salvation.
And thus shall the man sacrifice his own thoughts to the thoughts
of God—blessed in that he receives the higher in exchange for
the lower, and can continually think and find himself again in
God; and that God is so present with him that he hears the voice
of His word, converses with Him as with the most intimate friend,
and finds that He reveals His mind to him more and more
clearly. As he who has accustomed himself to evil thoughts finds
an oracle in himself which ever crowds new conceptions and reso-
lutions of wickedness upon him, and seduces him to wicked deeds
(Ps. xxxvi. 1), so in the inner being of the good man the properly divine oracle establishes itself, loudly proclaiming to him all
pure truths, setting their corresponding conceptions and resolu-
tions clearly before the eyes of his spirit, and impelling him with
almighty power to all good works—of which Ps. xci. gives a sublime example.

But it is not always with his own concerns that a man is interested and occupied, whether in public or in private. He may
also be stirred up, interested, and moved by what he sees of the
concerns of others, since all are at bottom of the same kind, and
there is after all something common in origin, operation, and
consequence in all human interests. And if an event which relates in the same or a greater degree to others, kindles in a man
an idea so full of divine life that he feels it to be not his own, but
that of his God alone, its irresistible inward power will impel him
to utter it as such, and to impart it to those who gave occasion
for it, and for whose good it seems needed, with all the imme-

diateness and strength with which it lives in himself. A man
cannot relieve himself from the throng of ordinary ideas when
they crowd into his mind, except by transferring (or endeavouring to transfer) them into will and action : and how much more
is it impossible that such a divine idea as we speak of should,
when it has once taken possession of a man, suffer him to rest or
pause, till he has put it forth where its truth and its might can
work, and ought to work, most effectually?

And thus it is that we arrive at what we call *Prophecy*. A
prophet, according to its original idea, is a prophet not for himself but for other men; he has seen or heard something which
concerns not him, or not him alone, and which will not let him
rest till he gives it effect by uttering it in words. He is completely overpowered by a certain divine truth and idea which he
sees as a distinct form, as a vision floating before his spirit : it
possesses him wholly, so that as man he disappears before it, and
believes that he hears the divine voice alone, neither hearing nor
feeling himself any more, but only the loud and distinct voice of
another who stands higher than he. And thus, when, concerning
some event important for the world, he hears the mighty voice of
this Higher One, so exclusive of the world that he can no longer
escape from it, nor resist its call—then he must utter at the right
place what is irresistibly pressing him within, and he finds no rest till
he has discharged the obligation. He has a true sense of having
a special charge, mission, and errand from his God straightway
to proclaim, in spite of all hindrances, and at the right place, the
words of that higher voice which he can no longer hide and repress within himself; he acts and speaks not for himself; a
Higher moves him, whom it is sin to strive against—his God,
who is also the God of those to whom he has to speak : and
they in their turn readily feel, at his words, that *their* God is
living in them ; they hear what they sought and did not find, and
in him who thus makes clear to them what they had so long
sought, they recognise, as by a secret instinct, the proclaimer and
interpreter of his and their God, the mediator between them and
God. In this irresistible something which moves the prophet as
well as his hearers—in the extreme power with which the divine
truth and idea break forth from the one as from their active
organ, and operate on the others as on their passive recipients—
in this consists genuine Prophecy.

This view of the ancient world as to the nature of prophecy is
also expressed in the names by which its language designates the
prophet. Keeping here to the Hebrew only, we may observe
that the word נָבִיא which runs through all the Semitic languages
as the oldest and most frequent name for a prophet, and which
even already in the Hebrew appears without a root and as itself

the root of derivatives, originally signifies a *Speaker*,[a] and a speaker who declares the mind and the words of another who does not speak. As the dumb or the recluse must have a speaker who speaks for him and explains his meaning, so must the God who to the multitude is dumb have his messenger or speaker; and thus the word, in its religious sense, signifies him who speaks not for himself, but as he is commissioned by his God: in one place, indeed, it signifies, in a somewhat lower sense, one who acts as the speaker of a holy man who is his superior, and whose mind he explains to the multitude (Exod. vii. 1; compare iv. 10-17). Later writers explain this original word by the more obvious expressions מֵלִיץ *Interpreter* (Isa. xliii. 27), and מַלְאַךְ יְהוָה *Messenger of Jehovah* (Hag. i. 13; compare Judg. ii. 1-5, with vi. 8-10). It is also exchanged for the name *Man of the spirit* (Hos. ix. 7; compare Ezek. ii. 2, ff.): the name *Man of God*, which is especially given by the historical writers to the great prophets of the earlier times (1 Sam. ii. 27; ix. 6, ff.; 1 Kings xiii.), is more distinguishing, yet less definite. And what the prophet utters is called דְּבַר יְהוָה the *Word of Jehovah;* a lesser oracle bears merely the name מַשָּׂא, properly a lifting up of the voice, an *Utterance*, or rather, since the word only occurs in the prophetical sense, a *Lofty Utterance* (compare 2 Kings ix. 25), a name which Jeremiah (xxiii. 30-40, compare Lament. ii. 14), on account of its serious misuse by the bad prophets of his time, wished to be everywhere replaced by that plainer name the *Word of Jehovah:* and in fact he never uses it, and in this he is followed by Ezekiel. And from the very old times is derived the word

נְאֻם, properly *Sound, Utterance, Word* (compare the Arabic نام *nam* and نَحَم *naham*), which even the earliest prophets of whom we have any written remains employ only in strict conjunction with יְהוָה, and only then at the end of a passage where there is more or less pause; and especially at the end of a complete period, in order once more to declare expressly that what they have now spoken is to its conclusion the word of Jehovah. Some of the poets begin to use the word again somewhat more freely in the sense of *Oracle* (2 Sam. xxiii. 1; Numb. xxiv. 3 ff; Prov. xxx. 1; Ps. xxxvi. 1); and Jeremiah (xxix. 31) on one occasion even ventures, for particular reasons, to make a new verb from it.

---

[a] The Author quotes in evidence the ordinary use of the word نَبَأ *naba'* in Arabic, for a *message*, or *information;* and adds that προφήτης, *vates*, and the Sanskrit वादि *vádi*, or वादिक *vádica* (Latin and Sanskrit being derived from वद् *speak*), all perfectly correspond with the Semitic terms in meaning.

Now it is quite impossible to doubt that the mind of God could draw nearer to man, and actually did so, by this method of prophecy. For he who has ever thought carefully upon the way in which it is possible to make a living application of divine truths to human confusions, will perceive that this way leads across the boundary at which the human and the divine spirit meet, and, by their meeting and mutual sympathy, kindle the spark of right thought and fitting conception as to those questions of the life of man which are under consideration : every one even in the present day whose object is to attain to an assured and personal certainty in this matter, and to strengthen himself in an immoveable position against the world and its confusions, must still strive to attain it by this same way ; and whatever may be yet in store for us from the like truths (and the application of truths once given is easier than their first discovery) will come from this same source which we have here first learnt to recognize as the source of prophecy.

The only distinctive peculiarity of this way of prophecy is the vehemence and immediateness of the whole prophetic activity, the irresistible impulse from God himself, the manner in which the inner and the outer man alike are constrained and carried away. The prophet must speak what his God wills, and as He wills ; he must speak as he is required, without respect of any man ; he disappears in the presence of his God, hardly knowing or feeling his own existence any more. Now we readily grant that this vehemence and immediateness, if one looks only to the inmost truth of things, is merely phenomenal or formal ; for though the first test of the truth and suitableness of what a man brings forward with such urgency, as coming from God himself, must be its manner of operation, yet the dress and the fashion are not the idea itself. But still this phenomenon is essential to all prophecy : prophecy, in its greatest and eternally fruitful works, is not possible without this form ; and, historically, this form must have flowed from an unavoidable necessity.

Thus, then, we come to the fundamental principle, that prophecy is the first form in which it is possible for the higher order of divine truths and ideas to find a living expression, and that it therefore properly belongs to the earlier times of antiquity, and of the youth of the whole human race. In the early times prophecy must needs come, and precisely in this way ; for we have to realise to ourselves a time when the higher truths had not yet begun to live among men, at least with any adequate consistency and clearness, and when their application to the confusions of human existence was still less familiar. And this will also have been a time when these truths, and their applications to practical

life, had to open themselves a first path, and to establish for
themselves an existence and a value among men. And where
any such truth breaks forth, and makes itself a path, for the first
time, it lays hold of the individual through whose spirit it is forcing
its way with a strength and vehemence in proportion to its original, fresh, and as yet wholly undivided power. It comes to the
man with no derived, weakened, half force; but when it really
comes for the first time, it comes with a force altogether immediate and overpowering: and when it comes thus, then there
comes with and in it God himself; for to separate God from the
truth is impossible. Thus is explained the inward impulse of the
prophet, his certainty of the immediate presence of God himself,
his being filled and possessed by one higher than himself, whom he
cannot resist. And meanwhile, in the rest, in the mass of men,
the exactly opposite condition prevailed from that of him in whom
these truths were kindled with such entirely new and wonderful
power; and the greater and more marked the opposition between
the one man and the many, the more forcibly and vehemently
was the former obliged to work the new idea into utterance, and
to urge upon others to receive it with the same sense of its having
come immediately from God himself, as was already awakened in
the prophet. Where the internal pressure and movement of an
idea is thus irresistible, its efforts at expression will be vehement
in proportion; and thus two causes combined to make the utterance of the prophet as extraordinary and as wonderful as the
work within him.

Thus the phenomena of prophecy were (if we look at the whole
course of them) the first mighty strokes and wonderful movements
of the higher ideas themselves, in their application to human
problems and perplexities—the first sparks which fell, like sudden
flashes, into the darkness of human endeavours; the movements
could not be more gentle nor the flashes slower than they were;
the extraordinary and the wonderful lie in the thing itself, and
without going forth in this manner no truths could be awakened
among men. Moreover the beams of light which broke forth
here and there were very scattered; there appeared but few original and real prophets, and these few stood all alone in contradistinction from the mass of men. Yet the mass saw the beams,
and could not for ever fail of understanding that such a light
was pleasing to their God, and a means of illuminating and com-
forting themselves: a wider or narrower circle would be certain,
sooner or later, to form itself about a real prophet, whom they
would gladly hear as a speaker and interpreter; and thus would
be knit up the manifold threads of prophetic action. Consequently, since the example of the rightly human and divine life

was first exhibited by the few who were prophets, their office and manner of filling it were of the greatest importance for whole races and nations; and while a true prophet became the salvation and blessing of a wide circle, a corrupt one contributed mightily to the general depravity and ruin of the land (Jer. xxiii. 9-14). And it was always held a happy thing if the Oracle did not cease, but continued with living activity (Prov. xxix. 18; Ps. lxxiv. 9); and in the earlier times of antiquity it was readily expected that he who was bound by position and office to aim at a nobler character, would become, as it were, a prophet,—as is shown by the beautiful story of Saul among the prophets. A kind of intermediate place between the prophets and the people was held by the Nazarites (devotees), who, without being speakers, yet engaged themselves to lead a holy life (Amos ii. 11, f.; Num. vi.).

In our time everything is altogether different. The truths which come from God (that is, the religious and moral ones, for we are not speaking here of historical and natural truths) have now, thanks to the prophets, become universally known and familiar, and we have to occupy ourselves with little more than their due development and endless applications. Established by tradition and by written records, recognised by schools and the laws of nations, honoured by thousands, these truths now come forth and meet men as an external power; and that which at first glowed only in the inmost soul of holy men as a fire still hidden, though struggling mightily to break forth, is now become a visible light set up in the world. In these wholly changed circumstances we are, it must be admitted, liable to a danger altogether peculiar to them, and which in modern times has been developed to the utmost;—namely, that a strong external position between God and man having been established for these truths, and not only for these (which are few, simple, and universal), but also for a mass of mere derivative, temporary conceptions and customs which have acquired sacredness and the force of law, it has now again become hard to raise ourselves to the living fountain of pure truth, to God himself, and to find our way along to its right ending, through the great confused mass of the produce of men's minds which lies before us. But, turning from the disadvantages which so easily arise from this cause, we find the advantages much greater and more permanent. The established results of the work of prophecy, the truths which have been proclaimed to the world, are now known and possessed—with more or less clearness of comprehension—through a wider circle, and are spreading, and will spread, themselves more and more widely for ever: each individual, even in the mass of mankind, may know and apply them without the creative effort originally required, and may distinguish

the primary and essential grounds of things ; and thus from prophecy is evolved doctrine properly so called, which tranquilly
deals with fundamental truths as already settled, compares them
with each other, estimates and arranges them, and makes the
longest established truths as clear and as certain to the hearer
and scholar as it is possible to desire. The vehement and the
immediate cease because they have attained their end, and their
time is over ; but for the truth itself, and its necessity for men,
this makes no real difference : we must behold the truth in God
just as clearly and immediately, and maintain its application to
the whole world just as firmly, as ever ; but we must not expect
it to be revealed either to us or to others with the old immediate
vehemence, which in its outward form already exists for us.

2. Thus then there was a proper time and season for the existence of prophecy : we may say generally, that it was a phenomenon only necessary and suitable to the earlier ages of antiquity.
It would therefore have originally prevailed among all nations ;
and we are sufficiently aware how the oldest records and legends
of all ancients nations tell of such speakers and messengers of
their gods, and with what wonderful eagerness great tribes and
nations many times hung upon the inspired and trusted lips of a
prophet. The Bible everywhere expressly allows that the gods
of the heathens also might have their prophets.

But it is not the less certain that prophecy might easily dege-
nerate, and err from its proper end. History shows how early
and how universally this happened among the nations of antiquity,
and a closer investigation into the nature of prophecy explains
how this was possible. If indeed the outward signs of prophecy,
its impulse and passion, its vehemence, and its constant appeal to
an immediate, divine certainty, were truth, or religion, itself, we
should be unable to conceive the possibility of its degeneracy ; but
since we have seen how all these, though good and necessary for
their purpose, belong only to the temporary phenomena of prophecy, we even expect its occurrence ; for we know that even religion and justice, Church and State, when embodied and established in the various forms of existence in time and place, are
liable to great degeneracy, without this being a reason why we
should reject or despise the inward life and object of these chief
human blessings.

There are several kinds and occasions of this degeneracy
possible.

a. A very peculiar, and at first hardly perceptible occasion of
such degeneracy, lies in the stormy excitement which characterizes this phenomenon of prophecy. It is a characteristic of
the prophet that he is overpowered by the divine truth and idea

which have taken possession of him—overpowered from the first moment in which they seize and agitate him, fill and constrain him—and still overpowered when he proceeds to carry them into act, when the mind and the word of his God force themselves through him into the world : the state of inspiration is one which expands and stimulates his whole being in an extraordinary manner, and in which he can and must say and accomplish the most wonderful things. But this state of most extreme expansion and elevation, in which, in very deed, the deepest powers of man may be drawn from their last recesses, and the most unexpected sparks of the Spirit flash forth, is yet a state of great peril, inasmuch as the power of clear, lucid expression does not always answer to the vehemence of the impulse ; and if in these incongruous circumstances the prophet is unable to control himself, his mind is liable to over-tension, and judgment and complete self-consciousness give way together before the vehement commotion within, so that the inspired person, misled for the moment by confused, though overpowering ideas, says and does what he would not have done if he had retained his full consciousness. And no sooner is the slender boundary thus overleaped, than *madness* or frenzy proves to be the dark, gloomy, side of prophecy,—whether it be the case of a true prophet, who can ordinarily govern himself rightly, as well as highly value a sound judgment, though he may on some one occasion sink under too great an excitement and disgust with the obstinate resistance of the world (Hosea ix. 8) ; or of one who is really too weak to maintain his full self-possession in the awful moment. There are indications that even the more able prophets often fell into violent convulsions at the moment of being surprised by some new idea (1 Sam. xix. 24 ; Numb. xxiv. 4, 10), and the strange signs of elevation and ecstasy easily made the most impression on the hearers, so that they were unable to think of a prophet except as half insane. Hence arises the usage of words which mixes the notions of insanity and fanaticism with the conception of a prophet : מְשֻׁגָּע a *madman*, is a prophet who can find no rest (2 Kings ix. 11 ; Jer. xxix. 26 ; compare the right interpretation of Deut. xxviii. 34) ; and thus also from the ordinary name נביא—the original meaning of which, as was shown above, has no such connection—are derived the reflective verbs נִבָּא and הִתְנַבֵּא ' to show oneself like a prophet,' which occasionally take the bad secondary sense of madness and frenzy (1 Sam. xviii. 10 ; Jer. xxix. 26).[b] It is also easy

---

[b] It is somewhat different when the word, like our (the German) ' Phantasiren,' is used of great musicians, who first conceive the tunes themselves in a kind of inspiration, and then give them forth again by an inspired performance on an instrument. 2 Chron. xxv. 2 f.

to understand how powerfully such a vehement inspiration, whether pure or impure, would work on the spectators, and excite them to like convulsions, especially if the phemonenon were still new and unusual (1 Samuel x. 4, ff. ; xix. 20-26).

Now, through these easy and obvious aberrations, prophecy, in many of the nations of antiquity, fell away from its true object at a very early period, and sank very low in the opinion of men. But no one can maintain, or prove, that this was in every case inevitable : the prophet could keep within those bounds, slight as they were ; the demand for moderation and discretion, which is always made upon all men, was made upon him also, only with a clearer necessity for him than for others. And prophecy then first attains to perfection, and reaches its true goal, when the prophet loses not his self-consciousness, even in the midst of the utmost ecstasy and inspiration. Then the previous ecstasy and inspiration are only the holy but hidden fire which—spontaneously and suddenly kindled—imparts light and warmth till its purpose is accomplished : the corresponding utterances in word and act are wholly illuminated and warmed by that inner fire, and suffer themselves not to be weakened or troubled by hostile influences from without ; but the prophet knows and respects above all the divine rule which in no conceivable circumstances allows man to sacrifice his self-consciousness, and with it the possibility of being a rational and true fellow-worker with God.

b. The prophet appeals to his God as having moved and compelled him to speak : and though evidence in his behalf may be subsequently derived from the result of his words (not to mention the assent with which his hearers may possibly meet him at once), still he must, in the first instance, be himself his only witness, and must feel and know in his own soul whether his God does actually and irresistibly move him or no. Here he is in great danger of *self-delusion :* and many a man might give himself out for a prophet, and adopt the prophetic deportment and occupation, who heard the divine voice very confusedly and doubtfully, or not at all. The oldest prophets, indeed, who now lie beyond the reach of all our histories, cannot have deceived themselves : their conviction must have been a true one, and the impulse really irresistible, else the office and act of prophecy had never originated ; but when the example was once given, it might find a multitude of unfit imitators ; and thus in this quarter too, what was at first a pure fresh power, would gradually sink into a more and more spiritless form.

Even over the first movements of inspiration self-deception might hover : for a man might often rightly believe that he perceived something to have come from his God, and yet perhaps perceive

it in a half and confused manner; and he would himself discern
that he must not take this for the true voice of God, if he first
quietly considered, and followed it out with himself, and did not
hastily allow himself to be carried away with excitement. Thus,
in ancient times, dreams were valued as a means by which the
more purely spiritual influences found their way to man; and it
cannot well be denied that it was possible for ideas of a high and
very spiritual order to be brought together in the tranquillity of
a dream, and there be formed into poetical conceptions. But
wherever in the Old Testament this kind of revelation is recognized as of God, it is at the same time looked on as belonging to
an inferior grade:—as, for instance, as proper to the remote
patriarchs, or to old men whose spiritual powers have lost their
vigour (Gen. xv. xxviii. 12, ff.; xxxi. 24, 29; xlvi. 2; Job iv. 12;
Joel iii. 1); and it is expressly maintained (Jer. xxiii. 25-29)
that mere feeble dreams and fantasies not only are of no worth
in the estimation of the true prophet, but may contain mischievous
delusion in them.

Moreover, it is true of prophecy, if of any operation of the
human mind, that it wholly depends on an original spiritual
power, a special experience and conviction, a direct capacity;
and that in itself it is less than anything else to be learned,
or handed down by tradition. Yet in this, as in every other
human thing, tradition and succession have from very early times
connected themselves with original ability: it often happened,
whether right or wrong, that the prophetic office was subjected to
the conditions of inheritance, and many nations recognized hereditary families of priests and soothsayers; and oftentimes a more
or less competent disciple was put in the place of an older prophet; and schools of the prophets were formed more or less extensively. With this is often connected the limitation of the exercise
of the prophet's powers to a holy place, and the belief in some
spot set apart for an oracle,—as though the place itself bore some
share in his solemn state of mind, and thus charmed forth truth
for the prophet. But in this way the free and pure movements of
the spirit of God were more and more lost, and the prophet who,
without any real gift of prophecy, represented himself as having
received free and immediate communications from God, led himself into stronger or weaker self-delusion.

A farther occasion for the degeneracy of prophecy lay in overstepping its true object. For it is clear from what has been
said, that what the prophet is fully justified in publishing as
the word of his God, is in itself an application of some universal and divine truth to a given set of moral circumstances,—a
distinct intuition going forth from the clear light of the Spirit

upon the surrounding confusions and irregularities of the moral life : all that belongs to these falls into the province of the operation of the pure, that is the divine, Spirit ; and if a prophet can in addition understand and decide other questions, this is an accident : at least, it will be shown hereafter that the great prophets who exhibited the prophetic character and office in their most perfect form, limited themselves in this respect. But when once the prophetic power has come into activity and estimation, curiosity soon leaps these bounds. The people, in their indolent desire to get an easy means of information about the things of common earthly life, and of obtaining outward decisions and directions about everything possible, and also in their imperfect conception of the true nature of prophecy, are ready to inquire every sort of thing of a prophet in whom they have once put their trust,—demanding, for instance, to what place a colony should be sent out, and whether the expedition would be prosperous (Judg. xviii. 5 ff), and where and how lost things were to be found again (1 Sam. ix. 6). And in earlier times, and as long as no gross abuses had arisen in consequence, even the superior order of prophets seem to have often entered into these worldly questions, in order to connect higher thoughts and consolations with them ; but still, where this transgression of the proper bounds of prophecy was the rule, as it was among many ancient nations, the whole prophetic character and function of necessity sank deeper and deeper from its original height.

When, at length, both the speakers have sunk to this stage, and the questioners are so easy to satisfy, though so eager to have answers on all possible subjects, it is then no longer remarkable if the prophet's power of vision fell more and more from its spiritual acuteness and vitality into the use of charms and other external aids, on the employment of which he then became dependent for acquiring any tolerable appearance of having been put into the prophetic state of mind. He avails himself of the help of idols (Judg. xvii.), or merely of a sacred ornament to which he directs his eyes at certain solemn times (the *Urim*) ; he employs the lot in its various forms, or even a consecrated drinking cup (Gen. xliv. 2 ff.) ; he waits for omens or auguries (Numb. xxiv. 1) ; and, lastly, he has recourse to the jugglings of necromancy and the like magical arts, and finds weak and timid believers, nay himself weakly believes in the effectiveness of his means.

Thus arise countless deviations from the better kind of prophecy, which this is not the place to attempt to reckon up.

c. At last, even deliberate fraud is introduced into the prophetic function : that which should have served the truth alone against every man, becomes changed into its exact contrary, and made the instrument of flattery and untruth, and thus even of fraud. This extremest degeneracy is only explicable by the universally high consideration which the prophetic function had already obtained in many places: in the view of the ancient world the prophet was recognized as being also *a Giver of decisions,* and—in conjunction with the priest and the sacrifice—as the worthy *Beginner* of any difficult undertaking; in the weightiest affairs of the government and of public life, no one would willingly hazard the acting on a resolution without him; but when he and the priest (Isa. xxviii. 7, ff.) had approved it, its commencement was held to be fortunate, and pleasing to the gods.[c] According to this general view, the prophet is also called קֹסֵם *Decider,* above whom there sits no higher judge; his decision is a קֶסֶם a word which is used in Prov. xvi. 10, for an oracle, in a good sense, although—as an Aramaic word derived from heathen Syria—it usually signifies soothsaying, in a certain bad sense (Numb. xxii. 7; Josh. xiii. 22; Isa. iii. 2; xliv. 25, &c.). We see also, from the interchange of the word *vision* or *prophecy* with the word *covenant* in Isa. xxviii. 15, 18, how deep the ancient belief was, that every more weighty design—as, for instance, the conclusion of every treaty—required the decision and sanction of a seer. If then such great power was given into the hands of the prophet even in the greater and more civilized states, it is easy to understand to what a perilous temptation he would be exposed, and how easily he might, from servility and desire of gain, say what would please the great and powerful, who needed him for their plans regarding the people: see especially Isa. xxviii. ff., and many passages in Jeremiah. But this is the complete reversal, the criminal destruction, of the very nature of prophecy; and nothing worse can be said of a prophet than that he speaks *out of his own heart and mind,* while God is purposely holding him back, and imposing silence on him within (Jer. xiv. 14; xxiii. 16; Ezek. xiii. 2, ff.); or that his God has not commissioned nor sent him, and yet he speaks and deals as though he held a commission and message from Him (Jer. xiv. 14, ff.; xxiii. 21, ff.; xxvii. 15; xxviii. 15; xxix. 31; Ezek. xiii. 6.). And we know well enough in how many ancient peoples prophecy did sink down to this lowest stage without any vigorous and public remonstrance, and so perished in its own ruins.

3. But it cannot be maintained that prophecy must have thus perished, in every people, through its own aberrations: on the

---

[c] [Though the priests and prophets here denounced by Isaiah had turned to the worship of false gods, they would probably retain the old national customs and rites.—T.]

contrary, it was quite possible for all such defects and perversions, when they occurred, to serve the purpose of pointing out with more clearness the dangers to which true prophecy was exposed, and of freeing it more completely from all that contradicted it; and somewhere on the earth it was certain to attain to this its perfect end, since it is inconceivable that the efforts of a power, in itself good and necessary, should in every case be directed towards its object, only to fail of reaching it. And though it is admitted that prophecy is only one special, though very important phenomenon in the wide sphere of religion, it is easy to understand that it could only raise itself out of its shackles and errors to true freedom, power, and majesty, where the whole religion of a people was engaged in elevating itself to complete spiritual life, and had already triumphantly passed the lower stages of its existence.

Here history comes in to show that prophecy, at least in *one* ancient people, did not fail of its end, but unfolded itself in ever-increasing purity and excellence, through an ascent from the lowest to the highest stage. The Hebrews are this one people of antiquity: and to them alone were all the requisite conditions of prophecy available, as we must here point out very briefly. The covenant with Jehovah (the public, recognized religion), which we now call the Old Covenant, was, even at the time when it originated, a form and institution of religion which left still older and simpler forms far behind it, and surpassed all other ancient religions in excellence. It was indeed a raising of men up to purely spiritual religion, an elevation of the spirit of the nation to the most purely divine thoughts and endeavours, a continual and persevering call and incitement to a life of true insight, power, and freedom, and to the mastery and triumph of this life over all opposing darknesses and hindrances; and accordingly it was from the first an essential law of the community, that the free course of the spirit was not to be restrained, when and howsoever it was directed: nay, the community was to be at bottom nothing else but the constant and living fellowship of the people and Jehovah in the bond of one spirit (Exod. xix. 5, ff.; Numb. xi. 29; Isa. lix. 21; lxiii. 11); how much more ought this fellowship to live in the individual man! And yet this institution, with this immoveable foundation, for every sort of good progress, arose in the earliest and most childlike times of antiquity, and so in a period in which comparatively very few fundamental truths could have been fully established, when a multitude of new truths had yet to be educed in their application to the errors of practical life, and the office of the prophet was still absolutely indispensable. The prophets, then, who were raised up in this state of things, and in this community, and who did not come short of the high standard already established there by law and custom, but who answered its requirements, and suffered themselves to be influenced by its purer spirit, were necessarily altogether different from the prophets who appeared in the rest of the nations. They advanced from truth to truth, and from one divine intuition and certainty to another, and were able—so that they only remained tolerably faithful to the old and main truths already given them—to realize a continual inward strength and confidence; and could not utterly sink back again, unless they renounced themselves and their whole consciousness, and every historical tradition. A never-failing charm lay for them in the name of Jehovah, and in the thoughts and traditions interwoven therewith: they felt that to lose themselves in Jehovah, to discover and hold fast to His designs, to utter His clear word when it came to them, was an irresistible attraction, calling, and task to them, and that they must offer up in sacrifice all their earthly and merely human conceptions, in order to perceive, to make their own, and where necessary to make clear to others, the pure mind and will of God: they felt that the power which moved and agitated them as prophets was in very truth the power of the Spirit which it was sin to resist. In this nation, and under the guidance of this faith, the prophetic order attained more and more its true destination, and fulfilled its calling to become the living centre and the ever active consciousness of the pure and spiritual religion which was being developed: whoever proved himself to be a real prophet had a right to be heard (Deut. xviii. 15, ff.). In this nation, it achieved freedom, and influence over men's hearts from a purely internal source;—for although many prophets' schools existed, it was nevertheless lawful for every individual of the nation, without distinction of rank, age, or sex, on proof of possessing the qualification, to act as a prophet,—whether a herdsman taken from the field (Amos vii. 14, ff.), or a woman,—though the instances of women are not very numerous (Judg. iv. 4, ff.; 2 Kings xxii. 14; Nehem. vi. 14; Ezek. xiii. 17-23): and although Jerusalem was, from the circumstances of the case, the seat of the greatest number and the most eminent of the prophets, and the place where the sublimest of their orations were first heard, so that the lower city is called, as of course, the *valley of prophecy,* in Isaiah xxii. 5, yet prophecy was never restricted to a holy place; and it freed itself more and more from all external aids and supports. In this nation, from an early period, the prophets rightly comprehended the final aim and object of their office, which were nothing else than the arrival of all the members of the community at the prophet's state of personal faith and holiness in

Jehovah, when the special form of prophecy would cease of itself, because its work was done (Numb. xi. 29; Joel iii. 1, ff.): and that it did attain to this knowledge of its own end, is shown most manifestly in its lofty freedom and perfection. In this nation, lastly, did the prophetic institution refine itself to the purest form and condition; mount to the highest step which its aim proposed to it; and prove to be of the greatest importance—of eternal value— in its consequences and results. All prophecy in the ancient world was glorified and fulfilled in it as in its noblest pattern, and its full-blown flower; and while prophecy ceased in the other nations because it had become by degrees utterly corrupt, in this nation the time of its outward cessation was only that of its inward perfection and accomplishment of its purpose: while we possess only a few very scattered traces and evidences of the prophecies of the heathens,[d] those of the Old Testament continue ever to live, complete and indestructible, and can never be known and valued enough by later ages.

2. *Of the Prophet of the Old Testament.*

Confining our attention to the prophet of the Old Testament, we now proceed to consider firstly his essential characteristics.

1. *How* the Spirit breathed upon the true prophet, and enabled the eye of his spirit to see amid the darkness of human things, is, in any particular instance, a mystery of the inner life, which is as little within the reach of description as the state itself was within the power and control of the prophet's own will: for the Spirit of God, who is higher and mightier than man while dwelling in him, does indeed establish in that soul in which He has actually made himself a place, a power reaching into the infinite, and able to penetrate through all the darkness which human weakness and confusion have created; but He comes neither invoked by name, nor haled hither by force, but spontaneously and unnoticed, breathing in a moment, like a favourable wind, upon the spot which He finds prepared for him, as a field ready for its seed. If even now, when, through the course of all the previous ages, so many ideas have been brought into operation, it still remains impossible to call up at our own will any thoughts but those which are traditional and derived from others, how much less was it possible for a true prophet to summon and control the Spirit as his servant! But nevertheless we may be allowed to follow out more closely what must have taken place in him

---

[d] It were well worth the labour to collect all that relates to the prophetic institution in the different heathen nations. Eichorn has collected much as to the Greeks in the preface to the last edition of his *Introduction*, vol. iv. We might now make use of the Indian and old Egyptian sources.

before the favourable moment in which the light of the Spirit could effectually possess him.

And here we must before all give prominence to the fact, that there is no instance of a true prophet of Jehovah who did not from the first direct his eyes to the full majesty and holiness of Jehovah Himself, and thus so inwardly realize the true and eternal life that it was thenceforth established and manifested in him as his new life. Once must he, who was to be a prophet, have become absolutely certain of the true relation of the world and Jehovah,—must have beheld, as in a distinct form, the sublime and holy character of Jehovah,—and felt that he was directed by Him alone : once must he have recognized the divine power of truth against the whole world, and himself as living and moving in it alone : once must he have entered, with the effectual operation and act of his whole inner being, into the counsels of God, and found himself for ever bound by them and endowed by these bonds with true power and freedom :—this was the first condition, and the true beginning of all the work of the prophet, the holy consecration and the inner call without which none became a true prophet ; and only he who has thus first turned his eyes within, and there found clearness and strength of sight, can afterwards look clearly and firmly into the world without, and there do his work as a prophet. Therefore on the nature and strength of this beginning depended the whole subsequent life and work of a prophet : for though it is true that there would afterwards be moments in which the look would again be turned inwards, again to seek and find Jehovah (compare Amos ix. 1, with vii. 1 ; Ezek. x. with i.) ; yet, where the true and vigorous beginning of the work was wanting, all subsequent endeavours were weak and defective, empty and unfruitful, while in the true prophets that beginning never ceased to be operative, and the recollection of it bloomed without fading in later years. If such a prophet undertook to record his more important prophecies in writing, he put at the head of them, and with a just consciousness of its significance, a description of that holy moment—often of a time long gone by— when he had first known Jehovah in His true majesty, and felt that he was called, sanctified, and endowed with strength by Him. (Isa. vi. ; Jer. i. ; Ezek. i., ii., iii.)

It scarcely belongs to the present occasion to follow out the truth that this beginning of the prophetic office could not have been wholly arbitrary and abrupt in the case of the individual who became a prophet ; and that there must have been threads of connection, however unknown to him and difficult to trace, which reached far back, beyond that beginning of office to the limits of the consciousness, and from thence to the commencement of his life and his divine destination :—for he who, on becoming a prophet, reflected on the original course and circumstances of his whole moral and mental existence, would find that there never was a period of his previous internal history which did not include the possibility of his subsequent special call: whence it is said (Jer. i. 5) of a true prophet, that he was marked out by the eye of Jehovah for the prophetic office from his birth.

But what is much more essential to be considered here is, that while that special beginning of the true prophet's office was no reason for his breaking off the main threads which connected him with his previous life, he was not now become able to employ at pleasure a spiritual power formerly unpossessed by him, and with no necessity for turning his eyes back to the original sources of his light, unless he happened to feel the external pressure of some new and doubtful event. On the contrary, he was required to make that beginning the standard and the motive for testing his new and higher life, whether it always continued to be as pure and vigorous as he had once beheld it with the eye of his spirit, and had received it into his will and act. As he had once turned, with purely inward glance, from Jehovah to the world, and from the world to Jehovah again, so was he thenceforth constantly to look on both, with an eye alike clear and watchful. He must indeed look on the world, and take an oversight from his lofty position of all human things, so as to understand the old and new destinies of nations and rulers, at every stage, and according to the order which the Spirit of God has appointed, and is continually appointing, for them: but woe to him if he ever allows his sight to lose itself in the tumult of the world, and with over haste or else perverseness takes up some view or idea of his own; if he does not, on the contrary, revert again and again continually to Jehovah alone, and, like one set on a high watch-tower (Hab. ii. 1; Isa. xxi. 6-8), ever look untiringly to Heaven, watch anxiously for every gentle movement of the divine will, as for a sign to direct him, and give himself up at every movement to be warmed and led by the pure spirit of God. Down there below, all things are in perpetual change; but he must be ever on the watch for what the eternally unchanging voice of God will say in each change and each relation of human affairs,—and never can he think that he has seen and heard enough; his eye must be always clear, his ear always open, as is beautifully said in Isa. l. 4 ff.; and if he thus explores continually the mind of Jehovah, he is then perhaps also able to descry even the coming destinies of nations, and to look far into the future. For this reason are the names צֹפֶה *Spy*, or *Observer*, and שֹׁמֵר *Watchman*, so forcible, though they do not occur in common discourse, because they express rather the prophet's own feeling of the nature and direction of the prophetical spirit. (Isa. xxi. 11 ff; lii. 8, compare lvi. 10; Micah vii. 4, compare verse 7; Jer. vi. 17; Ezek. iii. 17, compare the further explanation in chap. xxxiii. 2-7.)   Or, as the shepherd watches anxiously and untiringly over his whole flock, so must the prophet also embrace with his watchful love the community to the care of which he has directed the eye of his spirit, yet so that he looks continually to the true and only Shepherd, and from him obtains, as it were, his charge and authority anew every moment. (Zech. xi. 5 ff.)

But this steadfast direction of the soul upon Jehovah alone, can be fully established only in him who brings into captivity all that opposes it with hostile intent within, and who allows himself not to be frightened and restrained by anything external, but maintains a divine confidence and strength in the conflict, though it be with the whole world if necessary.   This is expressed exactly in the noble picture Isa. l. 4 ff., and especially verses 6-9; and in fact, according to the older descriptions of the original commencement of the prophetic office, the divine consecration of the prophet is followed immediately by a new and wonderful energy, setting itself strongly and courageously against the whole world, and annihilating every human weakness and fear (Isa. vi. 5-8, Jer. i. 6-8, 17-19).

Thus the previous conditions required for all prophetical functions are of that kind, that they might be laid down—in their essential characteristics, if not in their fullest development—for all men, as the law for the commencement of all higher action; just as, in fact, the beautiful description in Isa. l. 4-9, although borrowed from the picture of an actual prophet, is yet exhibited in that passage as an universal type and distinct example of every man in whom the divine and human life are united; and just as it is surely declared that at last all men shall become as prophets,—that is to say, not only as to the external and temporary forms, the speech and the demeanour, of the prophetic office, but as to the true inward life which depends on those previous conditions.   Only the principles and motives of the higher life, in all its forms, necessarily manifested themselves with greater originality and purer vigour in the prophets than in other men; yet they were the indispensable receptacles which the divine Spirit must first find, to put the seed of prophecy therein; and if they could not possibly be dispensed with, even in the case of a prophet, who, like Amos, was only once in his life stirred by the power of prophecy, and whose ministry lasted but a short time, much more was it necessary that they should become the perpetually fresh and ever living sources of all the very various functions of those who, like Isaiah, Jeremiah, and others, devoted their whole lives to the prophetic calling.   And it is here of great importance that we are often able to make out from particular historical traces, how these prophets, even when they had exercised their office longest, used continually to yield themselves anew to the warnings and instructions of the divine Spirit, and by this means advance from one step of prophetical certainty and power to another.   Thus Isaiah had long been a prophet when, in a new and perilous obscurity of his times, he was conscious of a new hint of warning from Jehovah, and professes his readiness to follow it without reserve (chap. viii. 11); and Jeremiah's whole life as a prophet—as he himself describes it—was properly an unceasing intercourse with Jehovah as with his Friend and Lord, only interrupted when he was required to carry into action in the world those truths of which the certainty was perpetually renewed to him within.   This intercourse is often penetrated with the prophet's grave human doubts, and threatens to sink into lamentations and complaints against Jehovah, but he always at last draws comfort and strength again from the divine voice, which loudly speaks to him from on high; and the true prophet's character grows in him, through all the extremest dangers, from stage to stage, till he shines as the last great prophet of the Old Testament recognised and honoured in history.

2. Thus was opened the way by which it was possible for him who became a prophet to be possessed by the mind of God, or, in other words, to have a part in the secret councils of Jehovah, and to know His voice and His resolves, like a trusted friend. (Jer. xxiii. 18, 22; compare Amos iii. 7, iv. 13.)   For the region of pure, that is, divine, ideas, which stands above all times and all human things, lies indeed ever near to man, but floats above him like a treasure which he cannot reach nor appropriate, unless a bridge is set up from it to the vicissitudes and darknesses of the actual life:—like a piece of touchwood, which will kindle in a moment if the appropriate matter comes near it, but which otherwise remains for ever without fire and action.   But if the human spirit, prepared in the way described above, turns, full of zeal and fire, from the contemplation of the confusions of the world to that region above, there opens before it—at the contact of the inflammable matter—on both sides, with the suddenness of a flash of lightning, a picture, a view, and a distinct image, which it had not previously: instead of the confused images which present themselves to the eye of sense in the actual world, there appears before the spiritual eye a clear image of that which is essential and real before God; and the realities of the spiritual world throng in distinct shapes and forms before his soul.   The true character of the Past

appears to him as in a single and distinct image, the Present is
seen with no delusions, and that which is to come in the Future
presents itself before his spirit as with palpable form and features :
what Jehovah wills and prepares, the prophet beholds as with the
clearest eye, while the world about him sees nothing of this wondrous light.   This is the atmosphere in which the prophet feels, as
it were beforehand, sooner and more acutely sensible than all other
men, the approaching Future, and is able with delicate perception
to anticipate that which others arrive at later and more roughly
by experience:—in which he discerns the inevitable calamity
which comes from God, while none else has yet marked anything
of it, and is conscious of the divine wrath beforehand, from the
fire which glows within his own soul (Amos iii. 7 ; Jer. vi. 11) ;
but also rejoices and shouts with a divine joy, though lamentation
and despair reign round him (Isa. xxi. 10 ; xl. 1 ff.)   There first
appears to him a single compact image ; but this, when followed
out further into its practical applications, soon breaks up into a
multitude of distinct images.

At this stage of intuition the prophet of the Old Testament
takes his stand ; he knows of a certainty that this is his proper
sphere and region, and that his highest object is just this,—to obtain the purest and clearest intuitions of Jehovah, without employing external helps, and still less frauds, for the purpose.   The name
חֹזֶה of *Seer* in this way becomes one of the most exactly suitable
for these prophets (Amos vii. 12 ; 1 Chron. xxi. 9 ff.), and what he
utters is usually called חָזוּת *Sight*, or *Vision* (Isa. xxix. 11 ; xxi.
2) ; nay, so very suitable did these expressions seem, that any
prophetical discourse is called *a Vision* (חִזָּיוֹן 2 Sam. vii. 17 ; Isa.
xx. 5 ; חָזוֹן Isa. i. 1 ; Prov. xxix. 18), even though the reference
is rather to what is spoken and written ; and the verb חָזָה, *to see*,
(oracle,) is used by itself for prophecy, or the utterance of a prophetic discourse (Isa. ii. 1 ; xiii. 1 ; Hab. i. 1, &c.).

Now, together with such vision, comes also an intellectual
idea ; since that which is seen in Jehovah as necessarily existing,
or coming into existence, must have a divine ground, that is, a
corresponding truth : the prophet does not merely see what Jehovah shows him, but also hears His clear word sounding loudly in
his ears, and what he thus hears from God must stand even
nearer to the utterance of pure truth (Isa. v. 9 ; xxii. 14, &c.).
Only the prophet, properly so called, never contemplates the idea
as superior to the image, or as pushing itself into its place ; the
idea remains rather as the mere ground-work, and only here and
there comes forward more and singly : (as in Isa. i. 16 ff.), in the
same way as the poet's office is to picture images and not abstract
thoughts.   If this order were reversed by the predominance of

such abstract thought, the prophet would become a mere teacher, and thereupon enter into a wholly different sphere. That purely intellectual thought was brought down, established, and spread among men, is a consequence of the prophecy of the Old Testament.[e]

But the great advantage of a vision over a purely doctrinal proposition lies in this, that the former springs directly out of the living facts around it, and as directly realizes and embodies them. The intellect inquires into definite relations of human life, and gives specific conceptions and representations of these, and labours in this way to establish its truths practically in the actual world. In the vision which the genuine prophet declares, there is already a clear view beforehand of the manner in which some confused and oppressive condition of men is to be resolved; and if it is to be resolved, according to God's design, thus and not otherwise, then there is no less in it the powerful motive to corresponding activity, and to the reception of the intuition into the will and deed. The true intuition bears within itself the germ of an active apprehension of the needs of the present time, both for the prophets in whose spirit it is kindled, and also for the hearers who receive it; in this respect it stands infinitely higher than mere doctrine.

The prophet's vision also stretches back into the Past, since much which has been told from ancient times appears to him in a wholly new light, as in Amos v. 25 f.; Jer. vii. 22 f. But the region of antiquity was not so wide nor so hard to understand in those times; and the prophet is more oppressed by the darknesses of the present and the future :—the future especially must be embraced by his view, and he can deliver no discourse in which he does not exhibit the picture of its deliverance which floats before his eyes. But what the prophet beholds of the future is, as to its substance, of a twofold character. The prophets of whom we here speak—namely, those subsequent to Moses—had already received the ground-work of eternal hopes and firm confidence as to the end of all things, through the Church in which they laboured, and the holy truths of which had met them on their entrance into it; for where the eternal truths are once known as clearly and certainly as they were in the ancient Church of Israel, and are recognised as the foundation of man's whole life, the strong consciousness will prevail that they can never again be wholly lost, but will, on the contrary, continually become more effective towards a greater salvation, and that the Church which possesses them does

---

[e] Thus, we may easily deduce an intellectual idea from Isaiah's words (xxii. 14), 'This mortal sin shall never be forgiven you, saith Jehovah:' yet, in as far as the words made an immediate impression on the original hearers, they did so in their character of vision, or prophecy, and not as simple doctrine.

2 A 2

therein possess the germ of a life ever new and capable of endless developments, nay, gives a pledge of the eventual fulfilment of the whole struggle of humanity. The force of an imagination full of earnest desire might follow out at large the expectations thus presented, and embody them in forms no less living than true,— as in fact the whole multitude of the so-called Messianic expectations, with all their sublimity and truth, were gradually developed from this source by the glowing and varied longings of the imaginations of these prophets; but the original ground of all these expectations belongs not to them, but is, as it were, an old and indisputable inheritance of good, in which the anxious and longing soul can freely expatiate on all sides. And this is certainly a main advantage of these prophets, that they all enter from the first into a circle which begins with the sublime history of the establishment and maintenance of the true Church, and concludes with the certain prospect of its eternal duration, and of the fulfilment of all good as the necessary result from that beginning. Yet the present time is often very far from the goal of this fulfilment, nay, the road to it seems quite darkened or else cut off: here comes in the proper work of the prophet; and according as a prophet shows God's way out of the obscurity which surrounds the present and the immediate future, and to the fulfilment of those eternal hopes, so is his greatness and truth to be estimated. For it is essential that his mind should form an image, a distinct conception of this immediate future, though a conception extending itself into the unchangeable ideas and expectations of the distant future. And this conception of the nearer future is evidently for the moment much more distinct and important than that of the more distant, since it includes a definite view and summons as to what is to be done, or left, at the present time, and thus exercises an immediate influence on the determinations of the will and the line of conduct. This is the first test of the genuine prophet.

But every conception of the future is essentially a foreboding,— that is, an attempt and effort of the spiritual eye to employ some ascertained truth as the means of bringing before itself the distinct form of the future, and thus break through the veil of the unseen: it is no description of the future, with the strongly marked historical features which will afterwards begin to unfold themselves in actual fact. The foreboding takes the direction of the whole, the large, and the final: the prophet who rightly forebodes calamity, sees floating before his imagination the ruin as a final punishment; and though this does not come so immediately or so completely as he seems to expect, yet the essential truth of the threatening remains, so long as the rebellion which called it forth continues to work, be it accomplished somewhat earlier or later. Or, if the glance of the prophet, expanded with joyful hope or holy desire, dwells on the contemplation of the so-called times of the Messiah, these float before him as though they were coming soon and with haste, and there seems to be no longer any great distance between him and what he sees so distinctly and certainly; but then, the course of things, as it unfolds itself, shows how many obstacles heap themselves up in the way of the fulfilment of his eager anticipation, which dwindle further and further continually before the face of present circumstances: and yet the absolute truth, that its fulfilment will come, and must come under precisely those conditions which the prophet specifies, remains unchangeably the same, and reasserts its worth in each successive period; while something of the great expectation is insensibly fulfilled in each. The prophet moreover endeavours to give as much clearness and definiteness as possible to the substance of his anticipations, and avails himself of the images and comparisons which past events and popular notions suggest to him, in order to picture that which is itself invisible; his anticipation of calamity suggests the thought of Sodom and of all the convulsions of nature,—his bright hopes and longings, that of the times of Moses and of David; yet he does not—if we look into the matter—say that there is to be nothing more than a return of the former things of Sodom, or of Moses and David, or than earthquakes and thunderstorms, but, while employing these similes in his discourse, he still means something higher. In certain pressing circumstances, indeed, he endeavours to penetrate more completely into the future, and ventures even to fix times and seasons in the evolution of those future events, which are foreseen with certainty; but all such minuter calculations and determinations are only essays of the same faculty of anticipation, and must be understood and judged of within their own sphere, and in accordance with their own nature and intention. Not to mention that all that the prophet threatens or promises is limited to the successful results of his counsels and his exhortations, nay, of his silent, though necessary, and in themselves intelligible, assumptions. Wherefore the ultimate force of the prophetic imagery depends not on its drapery, but on the meaning of the thoughts and exhortations which are hidden in it; and we should err continually if we were not to understand and to judge of such forms of expression and of anticipation according to their own nature. Jerusalem was not destroyed so soon as Micah (i.-iii.) anticipated; but yet, since the causes which occasioned that anticipation were not radically removed, the destruction did not fail to come at last: the Jerusalem of Isaiah's day was neither besieged nor delivered literally in the way he anticipated in chap. xxix. 1; but yet, even in his lifetime, an imminent danger, followed by a wonderful deliverance, did occur to fulfil that anticipation. If we compare Isa. xxxii. 14 ff., with verse 10, and with xxix. verse 1, and still more verse 17, we perceive a minute contradiction, if we take the words slavishly; but this easily and at once disappears before a living union of all the images, such as that in which they would have presented themselves to the prophet's spirit: in Hosea, chap. ii., the punishment of Israel consists in expulsion into the wilderness, but in chap. iii. in other things, such as subjection to Assyria and Egypt; yet all these anticipations were alike possible, and are only really contradictory when they are confounded with historical declarations, or external directions. We see from Jer. xxvi. 1-19, that in the middle period of the Hebrew nation there was still, in this respect, a just appreciation of the true meaning of prophetical declarations, and that they were not then so misunderstood as was the case in the middle ages, and is still the case in many places.

3. If now such higher thoughts take the true prophet by surprise, it is as if he were forcibly seized from above, and held fast by a mighty hand, the mastery of which he cannot resist: it is a holy moment, in which a new and clear truth presses into his soul, and so fills him that by it he becomes another man, and would rather lose his life than it:—'*the Hand is mighty upon him*,' has become the standing phrase to indicate the ecstacy of this moment. (Isa. viii. 11; Ezek. iii. 14; compare 2 Kings iii. 15.) It is possible that he has been asked for advice; and then his words are only in answer to the previous questions,—supposing he then actually finds the answer in the mind of God (compare Isa. xxx. 1 ff.; xxxvii. 1-7; Jer. xxxvii. 3, 17; Ezek. xx. 1 ff.; Zech. vii. 2; and the narratives in the Historical Books): but the mighty Hand may also lay hold of him without any such outward occasion, nay, the inspiration is then strongest and freshest from its source; nor indeed could questions be directed to a prophet, unless his own inward impulse had first proved him to be a real prophet. Nor does the true prophet remain at some place of an oracle, and haughtily wait for men to seek him out: on the contrary, since he cares for all, and bears at his heart the destinies of his people and of all mankind, he is—when he actually sees and hears what Jehovah is irresistibly bringing before his eyes and ears with respect to some problem of the time—as one *sent* by Jehovah, his Lord, into the world, there to speak and to act according to the truth which alone lives in him. This is of the greatest significance, that the divine office of the true prophet is counted as a mission into the midst of the storms and floods of the world, so that the truth, and the prophet as its instrument, prove themselves and their practical worth, through conflicts, sufferings, and triumphs, and

the prophet exercises his function not for himself, but solely for the kingdom of God, and its advancement (Isa. vi. 8). Therefore the prophet comes forward in public on all occasions, in the place in which he may hope to be able to declare most effectively that which he has to declare,—chiefly in the temple, where the priests and a great part of the people were accustomed to assemble (Joel i. 2 ff.; Amos vii.-ix.; Hos. ix. 8; Jer. vii. 1 ff.; xix. 14; xxvi. 1 ff.; Zech. vii. 2), or in the market-place, near the court of justice (Amos v. 10; Isa. xxix. 21); but he also appears where he is least expected, and allows nothing to repulse him (Isa. vii. 1 ff.; xxii. 15 ff.; xxviii. 7 ff.). No incident in the moral and political life of his countrymen can be too remote or too unpleasant, no person too high or too powerful for him: priests, nobles, and kings must alike hear his voice, for he is moved to speak by Jehovah himself, and where the greatest danger prevails, there is he most certain to be found in the breach (Ezek. xiii. 5): and, lastly, he exercises his office not only for his own people, but, since all peoples are alike before Jehovah and His Spirit, the prophet too looks from his elevated station over the destinies of all the nations round the true Church of that time, and speaks concerning them those things which, whether threatening or joyful, are presented unavoidably to his spirit in the moment of the vision (compare 1 Kings xix. 15 ff.; Jer. xxviii. 8).

As the true prophet will not utter the word of Jehovah which has come to him until it has become quite clear and certain in him, and, as it were, a part of his inmost life and thought, so on the other hand would he utterly fail of his duty, if he were to repress the divine voice which is actually moving him, through mere human fear and other base considerations: this were on his side the sin against the Holy Ghost, and in the old Church there prevailed the liveliest feeling that for no price dare the prophet venture to do other than discharge his divine commission without hesitation or abatement, and exactly as it had been intrusted to him in the holy moment of inspiration (Amos iii. 8; 1 Kings xiii., especially verses 21 and 26; and the Book of Jonah). And as he neither may nor can resist the spiritual impulse, so must every member of the Church give him opportunity for the exercise of his office, whether he announce what is pleasing or unpleasing: he is recognised even by the external law as the inviolable ambassador of One on high (Deut. xviii. 15 ff.; Jer. xxvi. 1-19). His responsibility indeed, is, in consequence, greater than that of other men; the result alone can fully justify him (Jer. xxviii. 8 f.), and the law rightly holds him guilty of the greatest crime who has proclaimed what is directly false and ungodly, and thus misled the people (Deut. xviii. 20-22): but the true prophet, who wholly breathes, speaks, and acts in the mind of Jehovah, can in truth bring forth nothing but what—because it has been purposed by Jehovah, and in Him is sure—will in the main be confirmed by the result. The word of Jehovah stands for him in the stead of all other orders; he has no other weapon either for attack or defence, and when he has done that, which not to do were sin in him, he must quietly retire and wait the result,—of which dignified composure and waiting in its sublimest form, we have an example in Isaiah (chap. viii. 16 ff.; xxx. 8 ff.). And this word penetrates like fire, and breaks in pieces like a rock, and the prophet feels in himself that the Spirit of God rules all things in the world with irresistible power, raising up and destroying kingdoms, and punishing or delivering nations (Jer. i. 10; xxiii. 29; Hos. vi. 5; Isa. xxxi. 2).

And therefore also is it, that this word of Jehovah is so often uttered with an immediate 'I' in the discourses of the prophets, who lose all sight of themselves in the presence of Him whose mind is so living within them. The pure Spirit of God begets in them its own clearness, its own infallible and fruitful mind: in the hour of action this mind of God's Spirit comes forth, and reveals itself to the world through its organ, the prophet, with the same immediateness, power, and disregard of obstacles, as in the first instance to the prophet himself: and those are the highest places, the tops and summits of a prophet's discourse, where his own personality vanishes before the 'I' of One higher than himself, and the whole truth and power of the eternal Spirit himself speaks through his passive mouth. Yet the true prophet does not at such times by any means so forget himself as to begin his discourse without self-consciousness, or end it in frenzy and the loss of such consciousness: he has in truth, from the first, a real—though not the common, worldly, God-lacking—consciousness, which recognises alike the divine subject-matter and the divine power of his discourse: nor does his utterance of the words of God in the first person become a mere pedantic, and therefore empty habit, like that of Mahomet, who in his later *Surats* can never leave off his pedantic and conceited use of this form. The prophet sets out from himself in proclaiming that which he has already seen in the Spirit, and ends again with himself; nor, in the course of his utterance, does he ever lose his consciousness of the delicate boundary between the divine and the human—he changes the language where it seems necessary, and intermingles new arguments, images, and reflections of a purely human kind, and is not ashamed to show his human feeling in the proper place. But when the most inward and spiritual thoughts have reached their height, and the divine power allows no further restraint on itself, or when the prophet is wholly immersed in the holy vision of everlasting hopes, then the eternal ' I,' whether speaking to the surrounding hearers, or in dialogue within the prophet himself, utters itself spontaneously from his breast, asserts its unchangeable truth and its irresistible energy, and proclaims thoughts before which no one feels more godly and religious fear than the prophet himself. Thus there is in the prophetic discourse a continual undulation between high and low,—vehement excitement and elevation alternating with composure and calm; and it is only on the heights and summits of the wave that God shows himself openly, and in all his might.

In other respects, however, and apart from this internal necessity for such a mode of utterance, it is the characteristic of prophetical discourse to have no one definite manner, but, inasmuch as it has reference to all kinds of human interests, to use all manners, as they may best answer to these. The poet has his own definite manner, and cannot suddenly vary it; for his immediate object is not to work upon others, but to satisfy himself and the demands of his art. The prophet has to work upon others, and that in the most direct and peremptory manner; and therefore every means, and every mode of expression which goes straight to this object, is right for him.

a. The chief of these means is always discourse, and, especially, copious, exhaustive discourse, which does not at first seem to recognise the need of proving its assertions, though in reality it never deals in mere commands and directions, but, in accordance with a law, applicable alike to its human and divine character, does explain and justify itself to its hearers, labouring to support and establish itself in the most various ways, and never being weary of condescending from its own lofty position in order to make itself thoroughly intelligible to them. This discourse is the most comprehensive and most powerful of the prophet's instruments, which he has again and again continually to return to in the last resort, since it is by this that he can most completely interpret the inward meaning of his soul. Hence the art of discourse was certainly cultivated to the utmost by the prophets, as we are still able to conclude from their written pieces. The prophet was the true and trained popular orator, and all the public eloquence of this ancient nation was united in him. And this discourse is capable of rapid transitions to express every sentiment and every requirement;— lamenting or rejoicing, threatening or exhorting, raising itself more or less completely to the height and repose of pure poetry, and even at times passing into actual song. (Amos v. 2; Isa. i. 21; v. 1.)

b. Such full and detailed discourse, however, does not always find its proper time and place on the side either of the prophet or of his hearers. A truth comes home to the prophet (as was shown

above), not in the way of mere words or discourse, but in
the poetical and lively form of intuitions and images which
hover like living beings before his spirit; and since his mind, as
has been said, continually abides, desires, meditates, and endeavours, in Jehovah, it is not possible but that Jehovah himself
should constantly enter into these *Visions* of the imagination, as
the predominating and all-moving person in them.   Does he, for
instance, forebode calamity?—he sees in spirit Jehovah causing and
bringing this or that kind of judgment: in the beginning, when
the image first forces itself upon him, he is perhaps terrified at the
greatness of this judgment which is to come, and ventures to bring
forward another image, another possibility as it were, in dialogue
with his Lord and Friend, but in the end he comes back again to
the higher and divine necessity of the case, till its certainty stands
clear before him, and he must declare it aloud.   Now the prophet
begins his public utterance with the description of that which had
first so stirred him to animated though secret dialogue with Jehovah, and had so shaped itself before his spirit; and his hearers, on
their part, are very often more easily laid hold of, and their hearts
moved, by means of such sensuous representations of short,
striking images, and by the simple tone of the whole.   And as
the prophet's internal activity begins with images, so, on the other
hand, do the most distant and least easily intelligible of the
things which his exploring mind lays hold of, readily shape themselves into images, like far-off clouds in its heaven; so that one
might well say that the prophet begins and ends with visions.
Such visions indeed were often depicted by the prophet, just
as they floated before his mind (as Amos vii., ix. 6; Jer. xxiv.;
1 Kings xxii. 19-23): yet they were hardly sufficient without
further elucidation and application in discourse properly so called,
and were rather preliminaries or essays which must have a place
in the prophet's own mind, but were not necessary to be uttered
to others, and which were so uttered the less frequently as the
prophet was the greater:—as is clearly shown in the instance of
Isaiah, who, when he appears in public, almost invariably works
up his inward intuitions into a clear stream of pure discourse, and
thus in truth is more powerful as well as more clear; for the
image required a further explanation, and was not very different
from the riddle.   (Compare Numb. xii. 6-8.)

At the same time, cases might occur in which the prophet had
a special cause for first exhibiting such an image by itself.   For
the open declaration of the very things themselves might perhaps,
for the time, if the hearers were incapable of understanding them,
frustrate the object in view: the prophet, for instance, might prefer
first to arrest his hearers by some simple but attractive image,

and then suddenly surprise them with the application drawn therefrom.   Thus Michaiah (1 Kings xxii. 19-22) first presents a vision
of heavenly appearances, in order immediately to draw a dangerous
application from it : if, on the contrary, the image is still more
simple, clothed in shapes from the earth below, and all in accordance with the sphere of the hearers to whom it is presented, it is
then to be considered as a similitude or parable—a mode of representation in which the prophets show high and successful art.
(2 Sam. xii. 1-9; Isa. v. 1-7; Hos. xii. 11.)   Or, at other times,
the prophet may, designedly, and with propriety, when addressing
wicked and scornful hearers, give his vision wholly in its original
close and enigmatical form, in order to confront their hostile attitude, by proposing to them a riddle, of the solution of which they
will despair,—of which we have a noticeable example in Isa. xxix.
1-9 ; compare verse 11.

    c. Moreover, the true prophet's mode of setting forth the truth
shows clearly how thoroughly he is a man of action and practical
energy—one who will indeed declare nothing but the word of
Jehovah, but who does not merely declare this with his lips, but
shows it forth by his whole life and conduct.   The true prophet
knows his proper limits ; but within these, life and speech, word
and action, are all alike to him, and each inseparable from the
others : he must immediately act in a manner answerable to the
inward movement of his soul, and, above all, verify that movement
by action ; nay, action first connects his words indissolubly with his
life.   This is shown in the most various ways.   There is often an
unavoidable necessity laid on the prophet to exhibit, in his own
person and acts, an external type and sign of the thought which
he desires to declare : his too full mind flows over into some visible
sign which all can understand, which comes direct from an inward
impulse unmixed with any inferior motive, and is less a mere type
than the actual commencement of the future.   Is his prophetic
soul overflowing with the foreboding sense that calamity and captivity must follow? he puts a yoke on his neck, or goes barefoot
like a prisoner ; or is his mind too full of the expectation of success
and victory? he wears horns like an all-crushing conqueror ;—as
though he himself were experiencing the state of things, of which
he feels, as no other does, the God-appointed certainty.   This may
be an impulse of the prophet, occurring suddenly, and quickly
reaching its object ; but he often remains for a long while in this
unusual appearance, until his anticipation and foreboding are fulfilled in the world.   (1 Kings xi. 30 f.; xxii. 11 ; Isa. xx. ; Jer.
xix. 1 ff.; xxvii. 2 ; xxviii. 10-12 : compare the way in which a
prophet exhibits a hazardous parable in his own person, 1 Kings
xx. 35-43.)   He also turns to his use natural occurrences and

indications, for his soul is so thoroughly possessed by mighty thoughts, full of life and meaning, that he feels those to be the signs and proofs of these spiritual truths; and along with him, a wide circle of hearers are often full of the same sentiments: only a slight resemblance and association of thoughts are requisite, and the external occurrence has at once an existence for him which is neither dead nor isolated, though on such occasions the danger of delusion is very near at hand. (1 Sam. xii. 16-19; 1 Kings xiii. 3; 2 Kings xiii. 15-19.) But in this respect, the most important matter of all is, that to a prophet, who consecrates a long life to his spiritual calling, his whole house, his wife, and his child, and all the like things of private life, become holy and full of bright light, through his various experiences in the light of spiritual truth; and the longer he lives, the more of these external witnesses, tokens, and memorials of that truth which proceeds from his spirit, and into his spirit from Jehovah, does he surround himself with, as will be hereafter illustrated at greater length, in the instance of Isaiah. (Compare Hos. i. 3; Jer. xiii. 16; xviii. 32.) Is there, for instance, some truth revealed, higher than that the people can at once apprehend it?—he makes himself, or one of his children, the sign and pledge thereof, summing it up in some one short and intelligible name, by which he calls either himself or the child; and then, as certainly as he himself, or his child, lives and breathes, does the idea which is indissolubly joined with the significant name, life, and existence of a person, maintain its own existence, and all the members of the prophet's family become as living signs and pledges of the truths connected with their existence.

It is this anxious effort to connect and confine prophecy as closely as possible with and to living proofs, and so with the life itself, that so frequently impels the great prophets to confirm with a sign—a kind of prognostication and beginning of the thing itself—that which, in the sight of Jehovah, is already true and valid in and for itself. The prophets give, and the hearers desire and receive, it, in a simple sense; and so long as the truths themselves have but little place and firmness, such a help is good and innocent on both sides. But it never appears as the main point with any true prophet of the Old Testament; it is always an accessory, a help, only; never the thing—that is the truth—itself: and as soon as this becomes strong enough, the other is certain to fall off of its own accord. Compare what is said further on this subject hereafter. But completely to understand *how* the prophet gave such signs, would in many cases require an observation of the signs themselves which is now impossible for us; but certainly no sign ever played more than a subordinate part in the life and acts of the prophets.

Since, then, the true prophet showed himself not merely in words, but still more in his whole life, actions, and practice as the messenger of Jehovah, the world rightly expected from him not mere advice, but also more important help in the troubles of life: and in a time when other means were too weak to afford health and the like important aids, these would be eagerly sought, in each vital form, from him. And without dispute, the great prophets were in this way real instruments of restoring health, and gave proof how much of the knowledge and the alleviation of human suffering, even in its earthly forms, proceeds from the living action of the spirit of Jehovah: only the ancient narrative in 2 Kings v. 11, shows us how easily all kinds of wrong understanding and false desires might prevail on such occasions, especially on the part of the receiver of the benefit. But this is not the place to follow out this point any further.

3. *Of the Old Testament Prophet considered historically.*

It is easy to understand that these universal characteristics of a true Old Testament prophet took very different forms in different individuals, as regarded their merely human and poetical side: but they also partook of all the important changes in the course of the general historical development of the nation; and it was only by degrees that this wonderful phenomenon of Prophecy elevated itself to its highest and purest form.

1. The many centuries between Moses and Amos may be designated as the first period of the Old Testament prophets. Of this period we have indeed no writing from a prophet's own hand except the small book of Joel; but from this, and from the scattered historical notices of other prophets, we may nevertheless form a tolerable conception of the character of this earliest period. We see there the natural state, as it were, of Hebrew prophecy, of which the wonderful, but wild and almost unapproachable greatness of Elijah is a valuable example. The sublime truths of the true religion and church move the prophets of this earliest time in the mightiest manner; and the most ancient of these, who acted wholly by their own innate energy, developed the most enormous power, and an activity most rich in its results: it is only one of the consequences of their great efficiency that first under Samuel, and then especially in the northern kingdom under Elijah, there grew up a constantly increasing multitude of schools, by means of which the prophetic office lost indeed much as to inward energy—as even Elisha stands far below Elijah—but gained the more in a wider and more rapid diffusion of its truths (1 Sam. x. 5, ff.; xix. 21, ff.; 1 Kings xviii. 4, 13, 19, ff.; xxii.

6 ; 2 Kings ii. 7, 16, ff. compared with 1 Sam. iii. 1). But even yet the prophet remains standing wholly in his original, unshared, and unbending might : if he speaks and directs, the whole people submit at once without contradiction or hesitation, or, if they do resist, he terrifies them with strange portents; his word is almost entirely as a command—in the state as the word of a lawgiver, in war as that of a general; and Joel still exhibits in his language and its successful results this stern greatness of an ancient prophet. Prophecy is indeed as yet wanting in the gentler forms of sensibility and sympathy ; it still stands rather as a strange, unbending power, as an external force over against the nation, and as yet enters too little into its inward spiritual life. It fights indeed with most enormous and triumphant energy against heathenism in all its forms, against the kings, and against the whole people. Elijah is the giant of prophecy, who wars with heaven and earth, and, after the most wonderful battles and labours, triumphs over all, and enters into his glory : but still prophecy is as yet little aware of its own secret defects and dangers, and thus it still stands in many respects under the hard law of mere nature, and is not yet made wholly conscious of its full and purely spiritual greatness and power. Sudden and enigmatical impulses still play an important part in the prophecy of this period. Thus Samuel elects Saul ; a prophet, apparently well aware of the danger of what he undertakes, hastens out of Judah in order to proclaim words of threatening with all speed in the northern kingdom, and then instantly returns homewards without stopping (1 Kings xiii.) : a disciple of Elisha's anoints Jehu king with the haste of flight, and as though he were treading on burning ground (2 Kings ix. 1-11). But the prophetic frame of mind is often obtained with difficulty, and then prophets who do not altogether belong to the highest order employ charms, (such as music)—especially since the prophet still, according to the ancient custom, sought an answer to every possible question (1 Kings xxii. 14 ; 2 Kings iii. 15) ; and when the prophetic frame is thus obtained at last, it easily passes in such recipients into some vehement mental excitement which they cannot control (1 Sam. xix. 24 ; Num. xxiv. 4-16). Before the universal power thus exercised by the prophets all other powers at once give way : only a truly royal spirit such as David's might maintain itself in their presence without being suppressed or annihilated, and thus was given to the world the first great instance of that most happy co-operation of the kingly and the prophetical powers ; but their words alone were enough to make all the might of the weaker kings, Saul, Rehoboam, Jeroboam, and the house of Ahab, give way :—nay even a David was not always above the reach of their indignation, the house

of Jeroboam fared no better than that of Rehoboam, nor was the
house of Jehu long respected more than that of Ahab. Therefore, notwithstanding all the great excellences which prophecy,
impelled by the sound moral spirit of true religion, already reveals,
we cannot see it fully developed in all this long period : but the
defects which still adhere to it spring necessarily from the
heathenish times anterior to Moses, and were only not yet completely overcome.

2. Another form of prophecy shows itself in the century from
Amos and Hosea to the times of king Manasseh. The simple
and awful reverence of the people for a prophet is now broken
down : thus, for instance, in Israel, the nation of prophecy, there
were many who ventured to mock at the non-fulfilment of the
prophetic threatenings, because the *Day of Jehovah*, that is, the
great Day of Judgment and punishment, the approach of which
the prophets had so often foretold, seemed—especially before the
destruction of Samaria—as if it would never come—(Amos vi.
3 ; ix. 10, compare v. 18 ; Isa. v. 19 ; xxviii. 9, ff. 22) : nay,
many did not blush even to treat as mere abuse the truest words
of a prophet, because they were inconvenient to them, and to
bring accusations on this account against the best prophet and
the most conscientious in discharge of his duty (Micah ii.
6, ff.) ; or else they would under some pretext withdraw themselves out of reach of his words (Isa. vii. 12). And whilst the
people now begin thus strongly to assert their independence, a
dangerous schism breaks out among the prophets themselves,
very many of whom—though still professing to serve not
heathen gods but Jehovah himself—forget the true prophetical
severity and virtue, take to flatter the passions and disorders
of the great, to set themselves in opposition to the better
prophets, and to think that in this they are doing what is most
suitable to the times (Isa. xxviii. f. ; Micah ii. f.). The position of the true prophet of Jehovah consequently now becomes
very different : if true prophecy, of which the very existence is
thus violently attacked both within and without, is not to give
way and perish, it must draw forth all its most hidden powers and
capabilities, and strain them to the utmost in fighting for the
good cause against all enemies, whether they are scoffers without,
or its own false professors within. And, in fact, it does at this
period succeed in this task ; it raises itself to meet its peculiar
dangers as though it were born again, and its youth renewed with
the most wondrous power ; it gains extraordinarily in self-denial,
freedom, and sensibility, and arrives at that stage at which its
activity is most spiritual and most rich in blessings for its own
age, and most imperishable and most sure to be had in remem-

brance for all ages. This century is the golden age of Old
Testament prophecy, and we see the most perfect expression of
the height it has attained, in Isaiah, the greatest among a multitude of prophets great in a like kind. Now, first, is it possible
for us to discern how deep and strong must have been the original
roots of this prophecy, to have made it possible for it to attain such
a height. At the same time we still find even in Isaiah, the type
and representative of this age, that favourite offering and giving of
signs, as well as other remains of the impulsiveness and unperfected
action of the earlier centuries; and have thus a proof that the
highest conceivable stage of prophecy was not yet quite reached.

3. Immediately after this fairest period of ancient prophecy, we
notice a singular pause in its progress, apparently owing to the
severe persecution of the prophets of Jehovah which king Manasseh took delight in (2 Kings xxi. 16). But yet no real pause
was possible, in a period in which the noblest energies of prophecy were opening out in their utmost power. From this
time to the end of the then kingdom of Jerusalem, under king
Josiah and his successors, prophecy raises itself with new resolution,
and maintains itself thenceforward to the Exile with indestructible energy: and it does actually in this its third period establish
itself in full vigour in that purified and perfected form after which
it strove so mightily in the second period. Those few remains of
the violence and imperfection of its youth, which are still visible
in Isaiah, it now lays aside, and confines itself in entire purity to
its true and inviolable sanctuary, to the clear and pure Word of
God, which, on the one hand, thoroughly asserts its distinctness
from the imperfect kinds of revelation, (such as dreams,) and thus
establishes a lively sense of its own absoluteness, and on the other
hand is content with itself, will urge itself on no one by force
(Jer. xxiii. 28, f.; Ezek. iii. 17-21; xxxiii. 2, ff.). It is wonderful to see how Jeremiah, the representative of this last form of
prophecy, and his disciple Ezekiel, even in the midst of the commencing decline of the prophetic office and order, are the first to
declare the true view of its character, and to establish it by the
example of their whole life. In like manner, too, has true prophecy now gained the victory over all corruptions and all half-
knowledge in the belief of the people. In the first period the
priesthood is still greatly mixed up with the prophetical order,
since the oracle (the Urim) belonged by law to the high priest,
and every other priest was readily supposed to share his compe-
tence in this respect (Judg. xvii. f.); and since so many other
heathenish kinds of oracles maintained themselves, though contrary to the law, alongside of the prophetical institution of Jehovah. In the second period, that of the great prophets, the

prophetical was so distinctly separated from the priestly office, that the division was never again to be filled up, while the heathenish oracles sank so utterly below the dignity of true prophecy as to be considered hardly worth its further notice (Isa. viii. 19, f.) : scarcely anything is now known of the Urim in the popular creed, and after Manasseh no one any longer applies to necromancers or other heathen soothsayers. In the first period prophecy still enters into unimportant and rather accidental questions; in the second it still utters direct threats against men in high positions (Isa. xxii. 15), but shows a visible tendency to devote itself more and more decidedly and entirely to the questions of high and universal interest for the whole age; in the third it is content to develop its universal intuitions in a tranquil and purely spiritual manner.

Yet the visible and inevitable decline of ancient prophecy stands close by this its rise to its highest perfection; and already in Jeremiah and Ezekiel we have the most evident traces of it. For the whole spirit of the ancient people now began to show signs of a certain relaxation and languor, as though it had overstrained its powers in the great battles of former times; and indeed the entire dissolution of the external kingdom was unavoidable: this universal languor was felt also by the prophetical spirit of the nation in the midst of its highest elevation; and since the whole institution of prophecy had hitherto been connected most intimately with the existing kingdom and with the whole life of the nation, and had unfolded its noblest powers in public speaking and action, it could not fail to be crippled by the decline and dissolution of the state, which reduced the prophet from a public speaker to a mere author, as we see clearly, if but partially, in Ezekiel. For though it is certainly true that the greater number of prophets in the previous century were writers as well as speakers, yet their writings, as will hereafter be further explained, were only the consequence and fruit of their previous public speaking and acts: but now there remained only one of these two occupations, namely, the secondary, and that less full of original power. And consequently a gradual change in the character of the writings themselves became inevitable: what the author wrote was now no longer the real counterpart of a powerful, and directly effective, public discourse; and he was therefore the more ready to throw out the thoughts and images proper to a spirit musing in solitude, while he found it expedient to help the effect of these by the aid of external art: and thus at last return the visions which the great prophets confined within such very strict limits, only now more artificial and prominent than ever. And then, since the highest art of authorship could never com-

pensate for the want of that living breath with which the old prophecies were uttered, it was inevitable that this mere written
composition should decline more and more continually from the
living characteristics of prophecy.

It is true that prophecy—fashioned through long centuries
to ever purer and more vigorous perfection—was too mighty now
to perish on a sudden. At the time of the liberation of the
nation from the Exile, and of the founding of the new Jerusalem,
it suddenly blossomed once more, and bore many fruits worthy of
the great times of old : that it produced a multitude of very
active prophets at that period, we may see, among other indications, from Zech. vii. 3 ; viii. 9 ; Neh. vi. 7-14. But the germ
of death was too surely within, and this after-blossom was
without abiding fruit. Even when all public ministry of prophets had wholly disappeared from the nation in the fifth and
fourth centuries before Christ, there were still many germs and
shoots of the old prophecy which came forth in a written form ;
but from this cause arose a literature of so very different a kind
that it will be necessary to speak of it hereafter in an appendix
to this work.

But besides these external difficulties, there existed, from the
beginning of this third period, in prophecy itself, a perhaps still
more powerful cause of its gradual decline and ultimate destruction. This is a cause which at first seems cheerless, but is in
truth most cheering. For it was necessary that the whole institution and work of prophecy should at last reach its object and issue :
prophecy was, as has been shown above, only one of the many
possible forms in which the Spirit of God reveals Himself to men :
the form was essential, until the object which could only be reached
through it was reached ; but when that object, the nature of which
has been explained above, was reached—when it had fully established, in actual and eternal operation, those truths which through
it alone could be established among men—then it fell into dissolution of itself, and disappeared, leaving only its imperishable
creations behind it. It had already, by this time, brought to light
the greatest treasures ; its very riches were in the way of its further operations, and many old oracles were reproduced with more
or less of change by the later prophets, as though from a real
feeling of the impossibility of giving anything better :—reproduc-
tions of a wholly different character from those of the great prophets of the middle period, who deliberately and without concealment repeat the exact words of some old prophecy, simply in
order to connect their own views with it (Amos i. 2 ; Isa. ii. 2-4 ;
xv., xvi. ; Micah iv. 1-4), and in no degree in consequence of
an innate poverty which contented itself with the wealth of its

predecessors. And the whole path of prophecy, which it evidently cost the old prophets such extraordinary conflicts to open successfully by, and for, those great truths they taught, was now made so level and easy, that on the one hand the hearers are become proficient, and prophetical discourse has laid aside its vehemence and gradually passed into doctrinal statement, while on the other hand a host of incapable imitators arise, such as would gradually corrupt the most beautiful form. The prophets kept free from external peculiarities in a way deserving of admiration under the circumstances: from the time of Elijah they were barely distinguished by a kind of rough clothing consisting of a mantle and girdle (Zech. xiii. 4; 1 Kings xix. 13, 19; 2 Kings i. 8; ii. 8; Isa. xx. 2, compare Matt. iii. 4), and the prophet who was unable to live by his own means received at most free-will gifts of no importance (1 Kings xiv. 3; 2 Kings iv. 42; v. 5; viii. 8, f. compare Numb. xxii. 7). But the peculiar phrases—such as the weighty expression נְאֻם יַהְוֶה and the like—which had grown into use in the discourses and writings of the prophets, obtained by degrees so wide a circulation, and consequently so high a value, that very many ambitious persons were induced, notwithstanding their incompetence, or even their evil purposes (such as the flattery of the great men), to imitate these externals of the old and honoured prophets. Isaiah and Micah had already begun to contend with the false prophets of Jehovah; and, in a way entirely different still, Jeremiah (in many places, and especially xxiii. 9-40) and Ezekiel (xiii., compare Neh. vi. 7-14) speak against the great multitude and the complete degeneracy of prophets and prophetesses; and one prophet expressly wishes that in future no one else might arise as a prophet (Zech. xiii. 3-6): whilst the people, on their part, became more and more suspicious of prophecy, and no longer received it with anything of the ancient childlike trust (Ezek. xii. 22-28). Thus prophecy was, at this period, in its decline, as the true and great prophets themselves perceive; its creative power was checked, and its forms, through excessive use, were now abused; its final purpose was attained, and its gradual and complete exhaustion no longer a misfortune. It was necessary that a wholly different time should come, in which the multitude of truths which prophecy had brought into the light of day, were first properly considered and applied; a time not of origination, but of elucidation and application; a time during which, after all living prophecy had long disappeared, excessive drought and unfruitfulness followed that abundance, till in the end came that greatest and eternal Prophet to fulfil the whole Old Testament,—of whom, however, does not belong to this work to speak.

II. The Prophets in their Writings.

I. It follows, from what has already been considered, that writing was no original or essential part of the prophet's office. At the same time certain causes might, at a very early period, lead a prophet to the resolution of binding the fugitive thoughts of his discourse by means of writing. In this respect nothing is more instructive than the instances actually recorded of Isaiah. When his contemporaries would not accept and believe some great truth which he had repeatedly declared in public, the same prophetical spirit which had moved him to speak, then led him by its mighty impulse to write, in order that he might thus both serve his own age, and also leave as an eternal testimony for all ages that which he felt to be as true as his own life (viii. 1, 16; xxx. 8). Or when a prophet had now long exercised his office, and acquired much experience, he might well hold it worth while, on looking back on his whole prophetic ministry, to perpetuate by writing the weightiest of his discourses and acts, and so to leave behind an enduring memorial for the instruction of the near and the far off, the present and the future; and in order to see the importance of a well-chosen collection of such pregnant passages, and other fruits of a long prophetical life, we have only to remember the note-worthy account in Jerem. xxxvi. Thus all prophetical writing (or dictation) sprang originally from the innate vigour of the prophet's life, and was the fruit and consequence of his practical work in general: it was a beautiful continuation and completion of the true prophetical activity, and only by degrees, and not entirely until the latest period, could it have passed into a mere authorship unpreceded by any public speech and action.

There were two modes of recording prophecies; either short heads and striking words of a discourse which the prophet wrote for the people, in large letters and on a tablet put up in public, to be like inscriptions and notices for every one, such as are mentioned in Isa. viii. 1; xxx. 8; or else detailed statements in books properly so called, which latter alone have preserved their existence, and have here to be further spoken of. That such proper prophetical books were not seldom composed, even in the earliest period, may be inferred from many grounds: for shortness we here confine ourselves to the following. In the Book of Joel, which itself belongs to that period, not only are the most peculiar ideas and phrases of prophecy (such as the weighty conception of the Day of Jehovah) already employed, so that one may see that Joel only continues a chain of thoughts which had been woven long before by other prophets, but there is manifest refer-ence to earlier oracles, partly in express words (*as Jehovah has said*, ii. 32, compare Hos. vii. 12), and partly in the general colouring of the language (iii. 1, where the idea of redemption is set forth); but a prophet is not accustomed to quote his own earlier oracles, and the words must therefore refer to known de-clarations of prophets still earlier than Joel, which we may very easily suppose to have been written, since Amos refers to the written oracles of Joel, and since we have no reason for supposing that the little Book of Joel, which now alone survives, was the only book which had been written at that early period : moreover Isa. ii. 2-4 ; xv., xvi., and Micah iv. 1-4 (to confine ourselves to the prophetical books), are fragments just saved out of this earliest period.   But certainly it was in the middle period, in which the greatest prophets lived, that this prophetic literature flourished in its chief beauty, whilst in the latest times it plainly spread itself too luxuriantly, and this became the more frequent the more the true prophetical character declined.

ii. If now we consider the prophet when he passes from dis-course to writing, we naturally expect that the same general features will be found in his written as in his oral discourse. And this proves, on inspection, to be actually the case.   The written discourse has all the life and spirit,—striking in a moment, di-gressing and returning, surprising and startling—of the oral discourse.   And as the prophets, in their public ministry, spoke in the first place only to the men assembled round them, but yet might in some pause, or at the conclusion of their discourse, direct a word to the distant women, so in their writings also there occur the like short addresses to the women, at the end of some of their longer speeches (Amos iv. 1-3 ; Isa. iii. 16—iv. 1 ; xxxii. 9-13 ; Ezek. xiii. 17-23).

At the same time there can be no mistake as to their writings taking a form which in many respects varied considerably from that of their oral discourse.   The oral delivery, though necessa-rily elevated above ordinary discourse by the inspired tone and sublimity of the prophetical ideas, must have been less regular and rounded, and must moreover have been often interrupted by the objections of the hearers (compare Isa. vii. ; Jer. xiii. 12, f.) : the written statement would not be tied down to a slavish repro-duction of the very words that had been spoken, but would give their sense with more regularity and method, and in many places with considerable enlargement as well as greater preci-sion.   And since the writing down such long, copious, and well-arranged discourses as (for instance) the Book of Amos, Isa. xxviii.-xxxii., and the Book of Micah, manifestly requires much

reflection and skill, we must suppose a period of greater leisure after that in which the prophet had been induced by great
events to exercise his public ministry; and thus the experiences
which he had made during that public ministry often influenced
the prophet while writing, and imperceptibly passed into, and
affected, the colours and keeping of what he wrote. Of this there
is a distinct instance in that passage of Isa. xxviii. 1, ff.—in
which all the past experiences of the prophet are reproduced in
the liveliest manner, as if he were surprising a luxurious banquet
of powerful mockers with his threatening word. But the object
of the written record was often that of collecting the thoughts of
several discourses delivered at different times, or even the results
of a long prophetical ministry; and then there was need of still
more latitude in the mode of employing it. In this case certain
historical notices were introduced, either in order to distinguish
more clearly the several records of the discourses delivered at
different times, or else to make the discourses themselves more
completely intelligible; we see the faint beginnings of this method
in the Books of Joel, Hosea, and Amos, and its more extended
use in the larger Books of Isaiah and Jeremiah:—if the prophet
would record in writing the acts and other matters which had
resulted from his prophetical inspiration, he could not but avail
himself of an historical clothing for them. Moreover, if, at the
moment of writing, the events were already long past, and a large
circle of prophetical words, acts, and experiences were crowding
together before the author's eyes, a verbal report was no longer
possible, it was necessary to select the weightiest points with more
precision from the mass, and the knowledge derived from later
observations and experience would easily be mixed up with these:
the Books of Jeremiah and Ezekiel show very clearly that the
written works aimed at general historical points of view and a
kind of arrangement according to subjects, rather than at a strict
chronological sequence. Lastly, ideas and statements which had
never been touched on in oral discourse might easily occur in
such written works: for the true prophet, who had long exercised
his ministry, would certainly have many more thoughts and experiences in the sanctuary of his own heart, than he had ever
spoken, or could speak, in public; and when the time for a full
utterance of these did arrive, his heart would be opened the more
freely, and its deeper secrets drawn forth. Thus, while the prophet looks back on his past experience, a new and striking picture
forms itself before his spirit, as though his own earlier life in the
world and in Jehovah had come to meet him in the new and
clearer light of a spiritual and divine history: and thus arise glorious narrations of the more spiritual kind, in which earthly expe-

riences and recollections are wonderfully united and reconciled
with divine truths and views :—histories not regarding things as
they occurred to the senses, but as they lay clearly revealed to the
divine mind in their inmost essence (Hos. i. 2-11 ; iii. 3 ; Zech.
xi., xiii. 7-9 ; 1 Kings xix. 9, ff.) ;—histories which would have
been the material for divine dramas, if they had been taken and
worked up for that purpose by art. And still more would the
prophet thus look back on the holy moment of his first calling
and consecration, and prefix to his greater writings a description
of the feelings which thenceforward sustained and directed his
whole prophetical life (Isa. vi. ; Jer. i. ; Ezek. i.-iii.). On the
other hand, a prophet might, in the composition of a long written
work, look more widely into the world about him, and (for instance) admit into the frame of his main divine view and description of things, much relating to the condition of foreign nations
which he would scarcely have thus treated orally.

Thus the written book was an intellectual revival and new
creation of the spoken discourse,—a creation which indeed would
not have been possible unless the discourse, with its life and its
results, had gone before ; but which yet went beyond it in many
respects, and had not only advantages, but also an object, of its
own : whence it is easily understood that some prophets (for instance Amos in particular) kept themselves more closely to the
form of their oral discourse than others,—such as Hosea especially.
Each prophecy is a work of itself, with its own plan and arrangement : each, the least no less than the greatest, must, for instance,
refer to the Future, or rather—to speak more exactly in the sense
of the prophets—to the great decisive Day of Jehovah, whether
this reference be precisely declared, or only indicated ; but at
what place of the whole this summit of the discourse can be most
advantageously made prominent, that depends only on the well
considered plan and structure of the whole. In like manner, every
greater book is arranged on a well-considered view of the whole,
never quite neglects, if it never rigidly adheres to, the limits it
has laid down :—as, for instance, by opening the whole with the
prophet's consecration as the most suitable introduction ; crowding
together towards the end grand sketches in which the predictions
of the Messiah are set forth ; collecting in another appropriate
place all the oracles concerning the foreign nations ; and so on.

III. How great, then, the distinctive peculiarities of the prophetical literature were becomes most evident when we investigate more closely its nature and colouring, its origin, and
its constituent parts. The prophet, indeed, is by no means tied
down to one kind of style in his writings : he employs the ordinary style, as has been observed above, for historical narration,

while in certain places his discourse rises into song with distinct verses and purely poetical language (see page 361); and the later authors, whose writing was less after the life, introduced even long hymns (Hab. iii. 3–15). But both the one and the other of these are exceptions; and the peculiar discourse which, as the copy of the solemn oral discourse, formed the broad ground of a prophetical literature, has a form and a mode of expression wholly peculiar to itself. It is, namely, on the one hand, too elevated in its subject and its range to sink down into common prose; but, on the other hand, again, its object is too directly and completely that of practical life, for it to retire into anything so wholly remote as the strictly poetical form. Consequently it fluctuates between the two in such a way, that as to its inclination and endeavour it everywhere struggles upwards to the heights of poetry, while for its outward expression it makes use of freer and more usual means, both that it may be more directly practical, and also not to lose the proper fulness and flexibility of oratory. From the fusion of these two elements is produced that peculiar form which prophecy has appropriated to itself, the difference of which from that of strict poetry may be felt most strongly where the two come into immediate contact, as in Hab. iii. This form is in the main invariable, and rigidly carried through all details of phrase, proposition, and evolution of the whole through its parts; at the same time it is in the very nature of such a composite style that it should rise more with one prophet, and less with another, to the elevation of pure poetry. It was certainly essentially the same in the oral discourse as we now find it in the written, especially as to the form of phrases and propositions, only that in writing everything was made more finished and regular.[f] Nay, so constantly was this the case, that even what was perhaps a written composition from the first, still followed the same pattern; until at last, under the hand of authors who seldom or never continued the practice of public speaking, it lost its fresh colour and true life, and—partly, too, from the intractableness of the materials—degenerated more and more into prose, as in the long visions of Ezekiel, chapters xl. ff.

1. As regards *Language*, the prophetical style is less fond of those unusual forms by which the language of poetry is distinguished from that of prose. (*Hebrew Poetry*, in *Journal of S. L.*, 1st Series, i. 295). Still it follows in the main the history and the changes of the poetical phraseology: so that from the seventh century it shows the same inclination for a short elegant manner, as for

---

[f] Very similar is the more elevated prose of the Arabs, which also appears in their solemn oral discourses—in the pulpit for instance; the most beautiful specimens are in the older *Surats* of the Koran. Comp. 'Arabic Grammar,' § 777.

instance in Jeremiah (*Hebrew Poetry*, in *J. S. L.*, i. 88), only that
a multitude of words and forms in which the language of poetry is
most remote from that of prose (such as the *î* of the *stat. c.*, and
such expressions as אֱלוֹהַּ for אֵל, or the word יָהּ, or שַׁדַּי, for
God), either do not occur in the prophets, or only rarely and for
some special reason (as, for instance, the *î* of the *st. c.* in
Isa. i. 21, because a kind of song is begun there, or שֵׁדִי in
Joel i. 15, for the sake of a play on the word); whilst, indeed,
oracles which are purely literary compositions in their form, very
soon overstep these limits (Numb. xxiii. f.).

But apart from this greater amount of external ornament, the
prophetical language has all the fulness and sublimity of the
poetical: it begins, indeed, prosaically in its announcements, such
as *Thus speaks Jehovah*—which expression is very rarely found in
immediate combination either with the poetico-oratorical openings
(Zech. ix. 1; Isa. ix. 8 f.), or the prophecies which are more
purely poetical in form (2 Sam. xxiii. 1 f.; Numb. xxiv. 3 ff.);
and it often sinks back into the same tone, with such remarks
as *saith Jehovah*, in the course or at the conclusion of the whole
piece; but when it rises freely it at once reaches the fulness and
power of the properly poetical language.   At the same time, however, it is not false to its character as oratory, one proof of which
we may observe in the frequent play on words and thoughts, which
is never so much in place as in that lively discourse of which the
object is to strike and to convince in a moment—be the play that
which is produced merely by the antithesis of opposite meanings,
or that which turns at the same time on the sound.[g]   In proper
lyrical poetry such usages would be greatly amiss; for the poet
does not aim at striking others by surprise, but lives and moves
entirely in his own sad or joyful feelings: when, however, poetry
proper is mixed with oratorical discourse, as in the drama, such
plays on words are employed with much suitableness—as is shown
in the Canticles and Book of Job; and they have often a fine
effect in giving point to proverbial maxims.   And they find their
place in the writings of the prophets chiefly because these are the
counterpart of their public speaking; and there would be no considerable discourse into which they did not enter with their quick
and effective point, in order to surprise and to fix the hearers:
it even occurs in those discourses which fall more into the tone of
lamentations (Joel i. 15; Isa. xv., xvi.).   Moreover the greatest
prophets always employ them in the right place only, when the
thought leads irresistibly to it, and when they will complete some
whole and elaborate passage by a single stroke: of this Isaiah

[g] Isaiah x. 30 affords an instance of the former; xxx. 7 of the latter.

may serve as the example; while that certainly very old prophet to whom the 15th and 16th chapters of Isaiah are to be ascribed, and still more Micah and many later authors, have no such regard to rule and purpose, but employ them in a long series without interruption, and thus really weaken the effect: long strings of such allusions, to names of places especially, occur in Isa. xv., xvi., x. 29-31; Micah i.; Zeph. ii. 4-6. And since this is everywhere a characteristic mark of the proper tone and colouring of prophetical discourse, it is obvious that in translation it should be expressed as easily and imperceptibly as possible.[h]

2. The prophetical discourse has the same *rhythmical structure* as poetry proper, so that we might here repeat almost everything that was formerly said at length on the poetical Rhythmus, (*Hebrew Poetry*, in *Journal of Sacred Literature*, i. 298-321): nay, since there is less external ornament in the greatest prophets than in the poets, the prophetical discourse shows the movement of the rhythm the more clearly of the two. Thus a thought is very often so divided between the two members of a verse that the one would not give a perfectly complete sense without the other, as is most noticeable in certain places (Isa. iii. 12; v. 17; xi. 7, 14; xvi. 5; xxi. 14; Jer. iv. 15; Ezek. vii. 26), while the consideration of it is often most important for their correct explanation. And when a similar, or even the same word is repeated in the second member, there is still usually a small change of expression, were it only in the sound, or in the change of the person and the suffix, when the sense will bear different forms and personifications (Amos v. 16; Jer. vi. 23; ix. 16; Isa. xv. 3, 7; xvi. 3; xxi. 11; xxiii. 13),—in which last the suffix is changed three times, since the sense actually bears three variations, though all in the end referring to the same: but a great prophet like Isaiah does not everywhere use to care anxiously about these lesser embellishments of the rhythm of the parts, which is already distinct enough.

Nor is it less plainly to be observed, that the rhythm changes decidedly and beautifully with the subject and tone of the discourse. Thus, an uneven triple rhythm is introduced with great effect when the discourse sets itself on a certain proud height, as if to subdue the excited glow of the imagination (Isa. iv. 2-5; ix. 5 f; xxx. 25 f; xix. 18; Micah iv. 7-9; v. 4-7), while a very short and compressed verse, after a loftily-moving passage of the discourse, beautifully prepares the way for its rapid conclusion (Micah v. 8). All the various kinds of rhythm, too, are changed

---

[h] Modern readers, however, have often mistaken merely accidental coincidences of sound for intentional plays on words, not considering that a real play of words must at the same time be a play of thoughts.

with each verse, according to the disposition of the moment, and one rule is never constantly followed.

But that in which the prophetical differs especially from the properly poetical rhythm, and takes in some degree a form of its own, is the length and extension it is capable of. It cannot forget the oratorical sentiment and feeling in which it has originated: the free discourse which aims at producing an effect on others, longs for greater fulness and breadth, stronger emphasis, and readier repetitions of its thoughts and words, than the language of pure poetry: and thus that kind of verse-rhythm was appropriated to prophecy, the general laws of which permitted the widest extension and the most various modes of handling. Verses with two or three short members occur but seldom: the most usual construction is that of verses with members extended to great length, of which the origin is described in *Hebrew Poetry*, in *J. S. L.*, i. 314, 318; and also that of verses with three such long members, each of which is equal to two or three short ones, as Isa. xxxiii. 15, *A B C = ab, cd, ef*, verse 20, *a B C*. But here, too, is its limit; the prophetical verse may no more extend itself indefinitely than the poetical. Verses with only one member, or so short as to seem such, are only found in the older and intermediate prophets, at the beginning, at the conclusion, or at a pause (*Hebrew Poetry*, in *J. S. L.*, i. 210)—a rule which even the later writers pretty strictly adhered to (Jer. v. 30; vi. 2): verses hardly divided into members, and gradually sinking into prose, were just beginning in Jeremiah's time (Jer. vii. 33; Zech. xii. 11).

While we are able to point to indications that the purely poetical books of the Old Testament were originally written versewise (*Poet. Bücher*, i. p. 91), there is no trace of such a mode of writing in the prophetical books, so that we must conclude that the ancients made a fixed distinction in this respect between the prophetical literature and poetry proper.[i] Modern German translators have, it is true, written the prophetical verse in regularly divided members, just like the poetical: but this introduces an innovation which takes away a valuable and essential distinction of the ancients, and imports something foreign into the words of the prophets. I have therefore preferred a more simple indication of the rhythmical members of the verse, by strokes and the usual points, which at the same time saves much room in printing.

3. Lastly, a kind of *Strophe* is very prevalent, just as the strophe-structure runs through the whole of the poetry (*Poet.*

---

[i] Exactly as the half-poetical language of the Arabs is never written in lines like a poem.

Bücher, i. pp. 92-119). An accurate investigation and acquaintance with all the prophetical works before us, shows this to be a
truth of the utmost importance for a right view of the whole, as
well as for the elucidation of details : and at the same time there
is no inherent difficulty in supposing the use of such strophes in
the prophetical style of composition. For as the prophetical discourse endeavoured to raise itself to the poetical, and to become
a free copy of it in language and in rhythmical form, it might
certainly seek to resemble it also in this last characteristic,
especially as every great prophet was also a poet, and understood
music. We may also suppose that in the earlier times, during
the public delivery, an appropriate musical performance was
introduced at each pause, and after every strophe, either by the
prophet himself or by his attendant, as is still done by the public
story-tellers in those countries :[k] that music played an important
part in the earliest ages in exciting and accompanying the prophets is manifest (1 Sam. x. 5 ; 2 Kings iii. 15), and at times the
prophetical discourse itself passes completely into song, and then
frees itself therefrom again (Isa. v. 1-3). And if the possibility
of the use of the strophe in the oral discourse of the prophets be
admitted, we cannot wonder at its employment and complete
development in the corresponding literature. It does, however, in
the prophetical books actually take a somewhat different form
from that of the poetical : it is not so fresh and lively, so varied
and so ever new, as in the latter, but much more uniform and
inflexible.

The *non-symmetrical* strophe-structure is rare, and is found only
in the higher *ascending* form (*Poet. Bücher,* i. p. 104 ff.), and in
the longer pieces, such as that very ancient one of Joel i. f., and
also Micah i.-iii., and Zeph. i. In these a most impassioned eloquence expands itself with vehemence into ever-widening circles,
till it is spent in the last and widest.

In the *symmetrical* strophe-structure we find (1) two and two,
or at most three, verses in quite short utterances of two strophes,
as Isa. xiv. 29-32 ; xxi. 13-17 ; or in one strophe, as Isa. xxi. 11 f. ;
or, somewhat more strongly marked, three and three verses in four
strophes, of which one has only two verses (Isa. xvii. 1-11) ; or
else in seven strophes, of which only a few have two verses (Amos
i. 3—ii. 5) ; in five strophes very commonly (Hab. ii. 6, *B*—20) ;
in four strophes, of which one has four verses (Zeph. iii. 8-20).
These forms we may call the small strophes. (2.) Four and four,
or at most five, Masoretic verses, in three strophes (Zeph. ii.
4-15) ; in four strophes (Isa. ix. 7—x. 4) ; in five strophes
(Micah ii. f. ; Mal. i. 2—ii. 9) ; more strongly, five and five

---

[k] Lane's ' Modern Egyptians,' vol. ii. p. 116.

verses in three strophes, of which only one has four verses (Isa. xxiii. 1-14) ; or fluctuating between four and five, in four strophes (Hos. iv.) ; in five (Hos. v. 1—vi. 11) ; and between four and six, in four strophes (Zech. xii. 1—xiii. 6 ; and also xiv.). These forms we may call the middle strophes. (3.) The great or long strophe originates in the combination of either three small, or two middle strophes, producing a whole which usually contains seven or eight verses, but is at times somewhat stronger, though seldom contracted to six verses. This use of the strophe-structure occurs without end : nay, we must say that it is the peculiarly prophetical form, within which important circle the weighty ideas of prophecy are poured forth most delightfully. It exhibits a somewhat rough shape with Amos, but attains a great degree of cultivation and firmness with Hosea (vii.—xiv.), prevails decidedly with Isaiah, and almost all others, and still shows itself with Jeremiah and Malachi. It allows every number of strophes, and it is content to find itself alone with one (Isa. vii. 18-25). We may see most plainly how it first originated in the consolidation of two or three smaller strophes, in such old pieces as Isa. xv., xvi. 7-12, and in much of Hosea, vii.—xiv. The last strophe of each kind is often compressed, as though shortened from the weariness of speaking ; the first is very seldom only a half (Isa. v. 8-10).

The construction of strophes with a *refrain*, or repetition of the same beginning or ending, is more frequent and characteristic with the prophets than with the poets, since it is more properly the task of the former to follow out the several sides of a truth, and to exhibit the homogeneous and the permanent in the manifold. This repetition is often distinctly marked through whole periods (Amos i. 3 ff. ; Isa. ix. 8 ff.), while at other times it is not so strongly expressed in form, but still is manifestly involved in the sense of the whole passage. (Isa. v. 8-24 ; Hab. ii. 6 *B*—20.)

All this may be further multiplied ; so that (for instance) the last strophe of an *ascending* series, when it becomes too extended, is resolved into smaller symmetrical forms (Micah ii. f.) ; or else — and this is especially important—a succession of symmetrical strophes which constitute the substance of a particular prophecy may have a special introduction or conclusion, and thus form a peculiar whole (Hab. ii. ; Amos i. ii. ; v. vi. ; Isa. v. 25 ; ix. 8— x. 4 ; v. 26-30 ; Zeph. ii. 1—iii. 7. Comp. *Poet. Bücher*, vol. i. p. 123 ff.)

Lastly, it is by no means asserted in all this, that every single prophecy must necessarily exhibit the strophe-construction : a close investigation proves that it is sometimes wholly wanting. In the prophet who belongs to the earliest times—namely Joel—we find, indeed, in the first and lyrical portion of his writings the simpler ascending form of strophe-structure; but in the second, and more purely prophetical, portion no such construction is discoverable with any certainty.[m] On the other hand, it gradually ceases as the later literature declines more and more; it is still found in Jeremiah and even Malachi, but is almost wholly lost by Ezekiel, and quite so by Haggai and Zechariah, whilst these latter throw out their thoughts more freely and in mass, writing now in longer, now in shorter, sections, and introducing into every section, even the shortest, the remark, '*and Jehovah said*'—a remark which was very seldom introduced by the prophets who wrote in strophes (Isa. iii. 16), because the whole discourse manifestly turned in another direction with the new strophe. When a prophet is merely narrating, or explaining what has been narrated, the strophe-construction is either unsuitable or unnecessary (Hos. i.-iii.; Zech. xi.); it may also be absent if a marked interchange of different sentiments is expressed (Hab. i.). On the other hand, the readiness with which the strophe-form imparts a beautiful regularity like its own to the expression of the prophet's thoughts, is plainly seen in the manner in which a series of visions, following each other, adapt themselves to it (Amos vii. 1-9). And nothing proves the reality of the strophe-construction more than the fact, that the thoughts often perceptibly crowd together, and hurry to a close, towards the end of a strophe already becoming too full and too extended (Isa. x. 5-15); while, on the contrary, on one occasion, they expand themselves in a striking manner, in order to fill the proper measure (Isa. xxxii. 1-8)."

E. S.

---

[m] It would indeed be possible to divide the second portion of Joel into three great strophes of the somewhat crude form which we find in Amos:—namely ii. 19-27; ii. 28—iii. 8 (where there is certainly a strong pause, marked by the words, *the Lord hath spoken*): and iii. 9-21. But this division, being strongly opposed by the sense, is not probable.

[n] In the latter pages of this article there are many references to Dr. von Ewald's work on the Poetical Books of the Old Testament. A translation of a portion of the Introductory Dissertation prefixed to this work is given in the first volume of this Journal (first series), published 1848. The references in the present article are to *this* translation so far as it extends, and to the original (*Die poetischen Bücher des Alten Bundes*) of those portions which that translation does not reach. —Ed. *J. S. L.*

THE RESURRECTION OF THE BODY.

Commentarius perpetuus in prioris Pauli ad Corinthios epistolæ caput quintum decimum, cum Epist. ad Winerum Theol. Lips. auctore W. A. van Hengel. Sylvæ Ducis (*Bois le Duc*), apud Fratres Muller. 1851.

THERE are two important considerations,—important in the investigation of every subject of which we are either in doubt or ignorance—to which we feel constrained to attend at the very outset of our inquiry.

First. It is no argument against the existence of a doctrine in Holy Scripture to prove that it is not laid down formally, and in the precise terms in which we have chosen to express it. It is ours to collect, compare, arrange, and classify the words of Scripture, and then to describe in our own language the result, or the truth thus discovered. Occasionally, indeed, a doctrine is formally propounded in the Bible, but in how large a majority of cases have we to gather the mind of the Spirit by laborious research and careful induction! Doubtless this is well and wisely ordered:—mind, like the sea, would stagnate but for the constant activity and motion which are prescribed to it: the bee must gather its honey from a thousand flowers scattered over the plain: the silver is hidden and the gold is buried, and the secret treasures so necessary for man are laid down deep beneath the surface of the earth: every provision of nature requires labour to adapt it to our use, and it is as really necessary in order to the discovery of truth, and its adaptation to practical uses. We even find that truths of universal interest and of an eminently practical tendency, such as we might expect to have placed immediately before us and prepared for application to the purposes of life, are only to be acquired by a process like this. It would therefore be no disproof of the resurrection of the body, nor any disparagement of its importance, to show that we have no formal enunciation of the doctrine, or to admit that research is necessary to bring it into clear light, and exhibit its practical tendency.

While however we thus speak, we by no means think it a doctrine which requires the same amount of investigation as some others; it will *bear it*, and the more thorough the investigation is, the less of obscurity and uncertainty will remain; but an article which has been so uninterruptedly held from the first promulgation of the gospel, with so little variety of detail in its explanation, can scarcely be denominated obscure or doubtful.

Neither, *secondly*, is the truth of a doctrine determined by the ability of its advocates. Many a bad cause has been gained by the talent of its promoters; many a good cause has been lost through the inefficiency of those who undertook its defence: and this will apply to Scripture as well as other things. Richard Baxter puts this very well when describing those 'who turn to errors and heresies. They took up the truth in the beginning upon either false or doubtful grounds, and, when their grounds are overthrown or shaken, they think the doctrine is also overthrown, and so they let go both together; as if none had solid arguments because they had not, or none could manage them better than they.'[a] It is very probable that such has been the case with some who have denied the resurrection of the body. They could not find it formally propounded in Scripture, and, going with all their physical and metaphysical difficulties, and with their philosophical objections, to its defenders, they have met with what has repelled and shocked them. They have been less arrested by the proofs than by the fable of the phœnix, the minute and rigid particularity of Jerome, the untrue statements made, the unphilosophical arguments employed, the unsound exegesis adopted, the absurd views put forth, and the host of other objectionable circumstances which are encountered—from Clement of Rome to Dr. Edward Young—in poets, philosophers, and divines.

All this we lament, but do not wonder at. Still, we no more justify the conclusion which has too frequently been arrived at in such cases, than we do in those where feeble advocates of a good cause have estimated that cause by the standard of their own powers, and in consequence have abandoned it. And we complain that in the majority of instances in which the resurrection of the body has been denied, it is owing to inattention to one or both of the important considerations which have been set forth.

Be this as it may, the doctrine in question is repudiated in the book placed at the head of this article, upon which, before proceeding, we will bestow a few remarks. It is dedicated to Professor Winer, for whom the author entertains profound respect. It is written in Latin, for which (to us) a singular reason is assigned—the small extent to which the writer's vernacular (the Dutch) is now cultivated among the learned. This circumstance we regret on several accounts, especially because there are theological treatises of sterling value in that language, and because

---

[a] Saint's Rest, pt. 3, ch. viii. § 6, p. 163, 3rd edit. 1652.

its affinity to our own renders it an interesting study for philological purposes, while it is by no means of difficult acquisition. To return: the work under notice is a connected commentary upon the consecutive verses of 1 Cor. xv., and is quite a repository of ancient and modern opinions upon the chapter. The style is simple, clear, calm, and dispassionate, but the views advocated are such as we can by no means always receive. As is too frequently the case, there is a liberty taken with the word of God to which we are not yet reconciled. There is too much measuring of the divine by the human with writers of this class, and, with an appearance of the utmost candour and honesty, we fear there is a 'handling of the word of God deceitfully,' of which they are themselves unconscious. Yet we commend this book to the serious attention of our readers, and express a high opinion of the author's industry and ability, which, while they may render some of his errors plausible, bring into clearer light the interesting views of truth which are frequently presented to our notice in his pages.

In the Introduction (pp. 1-12) three questions in particular are treated.

1. Whom had the apostle in view when he wrote this chapter? To this no definite answer is returned.

2. What is the scope of the apostle's reasoning?

To this he thus in effect replies:—Paul did not intend either to prove the immortality of the soul, or *the resurrection of the body*, as Tertullian thought[b] with many since. Still less is *the resurrection of the flesh* attempted to be proved, though many moderns thus explain the formula ἀνάστασις νεκρῶν (*resurrectio mortuum*), treading in the steps of the ancients, who by common mistake placed the *resurrection of the* FLESH among the cardinal doctrines in the (so called) apostle's creed.[c] This view, he says, was the more readily received, inasmuch as σάρξ and σῶμα (*flesh* and *body*) were generally recognised as synonymous in many places of the New Testament. Griethuysen did much toward removing this error, but his success was only partial. Understood or not, it has been more than sufficiently proved that the resurrection of *the flesh* is not taught here or elsewhere in the New Testament. Even those who understand the chapter as teaching the return of the body to life, often abandon the correct interpretation. It remains therefore only for us to believe that the apostle wrote to prove that man is destined to immortality.

---

[b] For his view of the intention and scope of this chapter see *de Res. Carnis*, 42, 48, *seq.*, and *Adv. Marcion*, lib. v. 9, 10, 15.

[c] In the English Book of Common Prayer the version of this creed reads 'resurrection of the body;' the Latin is ' *carnis resurrectionem.*' Why *carnis* was rendered 'of the body' we cannot decide; the difference, however, is observable.

3. When did Paul believe that the return of Christ's followers to life would take place? Our author answers, that at first sight we shall understand the apostle to say 'immediately after death;' but if it be so, we must assume what is contrary to ver. 51, 52, where he plainly teaches that all the followers of Christ will together be recalled to life. 'Therefore I doubt not that in the whole of this chapter Paul holds out to the followers of Christ the hope of future blessedness which awaits them all at one and the same time.' 'Not seldom Jesus and his followers spoke as if they believed each person's return to life must be immediately consequent upon death' (Luke xxiii. 43; Acts vii. 59; 2 Cor. v. 1, seq.; Ph. i. 23; Heb. xii. 23; Rev. iv. 10; vii. 14, &c.). And hence he infers, 1, that it is no wonder some have thought that at death we are made partakers of another life whose beginning is called the ἀνάστασις: and 2, that the opinion that souls remain in heaven till some future day of reunion with the body is wrong. No separation of soul and body in death is taught in the New Testament. And again, each Scripture writer propounded those views which were most agreeable to himself (*quæ sibi maxime arridebant!* p. 11), but still they were so directed as to raise in their followers the certain hope and expectation of future bliss.

To refute all the errors of the previous summary is beside our present purpose, and would require more time and space than we can now command, not that it would really take up very much of either. Our readers will remember the shield in Martin Scriblerus; the 'precious ærugo,' 'the beautiful varnish of time,' the 'venerable verdure of so many ages,' was all removed in a few minutes by the scrubbing of the servant-maid. But we will make no comparisons; our business is of a more serious character, and it is to show what kind of reasons may be given for believing in the resurrection of the body, and of the same body to all intents and purposes. This we consider to be safe and Scriptural ground, and we are not sufficiently punctilious to maintain the phrase '*resurrection of the flesh,*' because we consider it a question with which we can have very little to do—'with *what sort* of (ποίῳ) body do they come?'

The *first* position we assume, and which will scarcely be disputed, is that the Scripture teaches a resurrection of the dead (τῶν νεκρῶν and ἐκ τῶν νεκρῶν), both of the righteous and of the wicked. The words most commonly employed to describe this doctrine in the New Testament are ἀνάστασις and ἀνίστημι (*resurrectio* and *resurgo*). The verbs ζωοποιέω (*vivifico*) and ἀναβιόω (*revivo*) have also been used to convey the same idea, but the latter not in the New Testament. The terms employed in the

Hebrew, Chaldee, Syriac,[d] and other Oriental languages, simply denote to arise or quicken (like our author's Dutch, *opstaan, opstanding* = Germ. *auferstehen, Auferstehung*). Nor let it be thought that the meaning of the words employed in this case is of small importance; they convey an idea, and, as has frequently been noticed, make an instructive suggestion respecting the character of that future fact which we call the resurrection of the dead. 'When I hear,' says Tertullian, 'that a resurrection awaits man, I must ask, of what part of him it is the lot to fall (*cadere*), for he will expect nothing to rise again (*resurgere*) which has not previously fallen. He who knows not that the flesh falls by death, cannot know that it stands by life,' &c.[e] 'The body alone is called πτῶμα (a thing fallen, a corpse), because it alone πίπτει (falls). And it would be so far from possible to say we rise again, that we should rather be said to descend, and fall from heaven at the resurrection, if those celestial bodies which some have appointed for us there have never fallen by death,' &c.[f] 'Resurrectio est ejus quod cecidit,' said Ames,[g] and the old divines almost universally repeat the sentiment.

If we said the resurrection of the soul is an impossibility, we might be regarded as making a superfluous assertion, because, unless (in opposition to Eccles. iii. 21, and xii. 7) the soul goes downward into the earth (as the New Zealanders suppose) 'to sleep, perchance to dream,' to speak of its rising again would involve a contradiction. It would be as absurd to affirm that the phrase 'resurrection of the body' is an impropriety of language, as to say that we can properly speak of the resurrection of the soul. The soul does not die, nothing of man dies but the body; nothing else therefore can be said at the resurrection to be made alive, or to live again: we do not now refer to the *first* resurrection (Ephes. ii. 5, &c.).

In referring to passages of Scripture which teach a resurrection we shall limit ourselves to but few. Passing over Job xiv. 15, and xix. 25, &c., we refer to Dan. xii. 2, which says, 'many of them that sleep in the dust of the earth shall awake, some to everlasting life, and some to shame and everlasting contempt.' A resurrection is frequently and distinctly alluded to in the Gospels, *e. g.* Luke xiv. 14; xx. 27, *et seqq.*; John v. 21-29; xi. 23, &c. In the Acts of the Apostles, when the doctrine had become

---

[d] The Syriac also uses the word ܢܘܚܡܐ *consolation*, the reason for which is thus given: '*Quia perfectam consolationem et gaudium afferet piis.*' See Schaaf's Lex. and the Notes of Tremellius, Piscator, &c., on John xi. 24, 25.

[e] Tert. de Res. Carnis, sec. 18, vol. iv. edit. 1841.

[f] De Resurrectione, in Thes. Salmur., pt. 3; Thes. 64, p. 894, edit. 1651.

[g] Medulla Theol., p. 190, edit. 1648.

2 c 2

a fact, and had assumed a tangibility from the resurrection of Jesus, previously unknown, it is still more strikingly exhibited; *e. g.* chap. ii. 31; iv. 2; x. 41; xiii. 33, 34; xvii. 18-32; xxiii. 6; xxiv. 15; xxv. 19; xxvi. 23. The prominence given to the subject, and the weight attached to it by the apostles in their teachings, sufficiently prove the importance of the doctrine, and of correct views of it. Peter preached it on the day of Pentecost; the apostles generally taught it to the people: Paul proclaimed it as a new doctrine on Mars' Hill among Athenian philosophers; he used it as a plea for justice to himself at Jerusalem; he confessed it before Felix at Cæsarea, and referred to it in his noble apology to Agrippa. The apostolical epistles similarly bear witness to this great principle. To the Romans (viii. 11) Paul said, 'He that raised up Christ from the dead shall also quicken your mortal bodies.' To the Corinthians he addressed the fine chapter, the 15th, the resurrection chapter *par excellence.* In chaps. iv. and v. of the 2nd Epistle to the Corinthians very direct reference is made to it. To the Philippians, in expressing his own hope (iii. 20, 21), he set forth theirs. To the Thessalonians he exhibited it as the common expectation. Elsewhere in the epistles it is often referred to, while John finely brings up the rear in the closing chapters of the Apocalypse. Thus the idea of a resurrection runs through the whole of the New Testament; it pervades the entire texture of the book, and is so interwoven with its teachings and facts, that if all reference to it were removed, many a dreary blank would appear on the pages of the Scriptures of truth which are now studded with gems of doctrine on which the Christian's eye rests with delight.

After what has already been said of the intention of this article, we need not dwell on our *second* point—that the resurrection of the body is *a possibility.* Yet various arguments have been advanced to show what (for want of a better word) we must call the *comparative* impossibility of such an event. Perhaps the indiscreet zeal of some supporters of this doctrine, who maintain that the same body of flesh, identical in every point—the very hair, teeth, and nails remaining unchanged—has made the general doctrine more difficult of reception. Hence some, like Locke,[h] believe the identity of the body next to impossible. Others, going further, have thought it will be simply enough to clothe the soul with a body, the same as that of Christ, in age and appearance; but this, which places the whole of personal identity in the soul, is little better than the metempsychosis, for it denies the resurrection of the *same* body. In whatever identity, as regards

[h] On the Understanding, bk. 2, ch. xxvii.

the body, consists, we doubt not it will remain and reappear on that day: and when unbelief presents all the difficulties of the case, and asks, 'Against so many enemies, what remains to you?' we may safely answer in the words of the same writer (Corneille), '*moi; moi, dis-je, et c'est assez*'[i]—'myself; myself, I say, and that is *enough*.' But the possibility of the resurrection of the same body can always be safely intrusted to infinite wisdom and boundless power: 'all things are possible with God.' Therefore He can watch over, collect, restore and reanimate the scattered dust of man. If we are asked *how* this can be, we are not careful to look for a reply; our chief concern is to establish a *fact*, and we have nothing to do with the *means by* or the *mode in* which it is to be brought about. Of such as doubt the absolute possibility of a resurrection of the same body, we would inquire whether they believe this to be more than the creation of a universe? The one is the restoration of existing matter to a form it previously possessed;[k] the other is the calling into existence of what before had no being. The example of even Seneca ought to teach such to pause. Speaking of the future destruction of the world either by fire or water, he says, 'Nothing is difficult to Nature when she hastens towards her end:'[m] and again, 'All things are, as I said, easy to Nature, certainly what from the beginning she determined to do, which she comes to not suddenly but by previous announcement.' To all and sundry who with a doubting or an unbelieving heart look upon the tomb as closed for ever, and despairingly ask over again the question, 'Who shall roll us away the stone from the sepulchre?' we say, 'Why should it be thought a thing incredible with you that God should raise the dead?'

We now arrive at the *third* and main point, which is to show that *the Scripture teaches the resurrection of the body.*

The Bible testimony on this head may be thus exhibited :—

I. *Direct*, which includes general declarations; particular references to the righteous; and comparisons of the resurrection of man with that of Christ.

II. *Indirect*, which includes those passages in which the resurrection of the saints is connected with that of Christ; then those from which the resurrection of the body is a necessary inference; and, lastly, those from which it may be probably inferred.

Perhaps a better arrangement might be made; but this will answer our purpose and enable us to assign separate passages to the positions which we regard them as occupying. But we shall invert the order of this plan, and invite attention—

I.—To indirect Scripture evidence, and those passages from

---

[i] Médée, act. 1, sc. 4.   [k] Comp. Tert. de Res. Carnis, sec. 11, p. 104.
[m] Nat. Quæst., lib. iii. 27, 30. Comp. M. Felix, Octavius, sec. 34.

which we infer *the probable resurrection of the body.* We are led to believe that the soul of man shall exist hereafter in bliss or woe according to its merits while in the body. But this future state seems but the continuance, development, complement, or necessary end of this present, which is as really a state of rewards and punishments to a certain degree.[n] Now the soul here acts in and by a body which attends all its movements and follows all its fortunes: it is affected with honour and dishonour, rejoices in safety, trembles in peril, is gladdened by health, grieved by sickness, and dissolved in death. Gen. iii. 19, clearly teaches us that soul and body have like experience here, and why should not the principle be carried out hereafter by the resurrection of the body to share the same fortunes in eternity? Further,

The original curse or sentence pronounced against sin had respect to the body equally with the soul; why should it be temporal in one case and eternal in the other? The condemnation in this life certainly affects the whole man as consisting of body and soul, and we have no reason to believe that in the next state of being it will be limited to the soul.

Again, Christ is called 'the Saviour of the body;'[o] but how can he be this, if it rise not from the dead? The members are of the same nature as the head, and we know that Christ our Head has a body equally with a soul. A comparison of the words last cited with 1 Cor. vi. 13, &c., seem to render the conclusion inevitable that the body equally with the soul will for ever reap the blessed fruits of the Saviour's incarnation, death, and resurrection.[p]

In many passages the body is spoken of as capable of undergoing a remarkable change, so as to become holy and a temple of the Holy Ghost in this life, and fitted for the heavenly state.[q] As illustrative of this idea we refer to Enoch and Elijah as now actually existing in the body somewhere; the narratives of the temporary resurrections effected by prophets, apostles, and Christ; and the resurrection of the Lord himself. By all such passages and facts, the idea of the resurrection of the body is rendered prominent, and its expectation probable.

Another class of passages is those from which the resurrection of the body is *a necessary inference.* They are not rare, but they turn upon the form of expression, or upon a single word, or upon a comparison with other scriptures.[r] Those which follow are selected rather as specimens, than presented as a complete collection of the various forms in which this doctrine meets us.

---

[n] *Vide* Butler's Analogy, pt. 1, chap. ii., &c.
[o] Eph. v. 23.   [p] We shall return to this passage in the sequel.
[q] 1 Cor. vi. 13, &c.; Rom. viii. 10, 11; Ph. iii. 20, 21. *Vide* Tert. de R. C., 15.
[r] Like Paley's 'undesigned coincidences' in the *Horæ Paulinæ.*

Dan. xii. 2. 'Many of them that sleep,' &c.   Is it the *soul* or
the body which sleeps? Certainly not the soul. If, however, the
soul slept, would it be in 'the dust of the earth'? Certainly no
fair exegesis can apply these words to the soul as distinct from the
body. Those 'which sleep in the dust of the earth' (אַדְמַת־עָפָר
earth of dust) shall awake. We ask again, what *can* be referred
to if the body that died is not? Not the soul therefore, but the
body is chiefly in view, which accords with Eccl. xii. 7, a passage
which shows that at the resurrection, the soul, in order to reunion
with the body, must be recalled to this world, where it does not
remain after death.

Matt. v. 29, 30, is an instructive incidental proof. How can
the *body* be cast into *hell*, unless it be first raised from the dead?

Matt. x. 28. 'Fear not them,' &c.   Here we are taught that
there is one who can destroy both *soul and body in hell*. If the
body of the sinner can be destroyed in hell, we must infer a
previous resurrection of the body. To say that Gehenna here
denotes, according to Jewish notions, some underground habitation, but not the place of future torment, does not remove, but
rather increases, the difficulty. The terms require us to regard
soul and body as liable to destruction in one place at one time;
and how can this be but by the resurrection of the body in order
to its reunion with the soul? Tertullian felt the force of this,
and therefore he observes, that ' there is a resurrection *of the flesh*
of the dead, which cannot be destroyed in Gehenna if it be not
resuscitated' (*de R. C.* 35).

Acts ii. 31, represents the resurrection of Christ as involving
two distinct points—his soul was not left in hell ($\varepsilon i \varsigma \, \ddot{q} \delta o \upsilon$); and
his body did not remain under corruption. His human soul re-
animated his body after he had expired[a] upon the cross, and that
body became again the *ministra et famula animæ*. Why should
not the resurrection of man be similar to this?

Rom. viii. 23 is still more to our purpose. What is the 'adoption, the redemption of the body'? The entire context forbids our
referring it to anything in this life. Neither can we apply it to
deliverance *from* the body. The *adoption* is the resurrection and
its consequents, just as the resurrection of our Lord, in Acts xiii.
33, &c., is explained to be the fulfilment of Ps. ii. 7. The deliverance *of* the body from the power of death is meant therefore,
and the use of the word 'redemption' in Ps. xlix. 7, and Hos.
xiii. 4, favours this view. Now, just as our Lord received the
adoption and was *delivered* from the bands of death (Acts ii.
24), and freed from its captivity (Eph. iv. 8), so Christians shall

---

[a] This word ἐξέπνευσεν should have prevented van Hengel from denying that the
New Testament teaches the separation of the soul and body, pp. 10, 11.

reach the summit of human perfection when soul and body are glorified together at the resurrection.[t]

Heb. xi. 35. ' Women received,' &c. Was not this a resurrection of the body? and is not the ' better resurrection' similar in character, but followed by more glorious results? We must infer a resurrection of the body, and its constitution, as the eternal *consors et cohæres* of the soul.[u]

1 Thess. v. 23, is another of those incidental expressions which come with all the force of demonstration. It will be sufficient to repeat it,—' Your whole spirit and soul and *body* be preserved blameless unto the *coming of our Lord Jesus Christ!*'

Rev. xx. 13. ' The *sea* gave up the dead which were in it.' And what dead are there, if not the bodily remains of those who have found in it a grave? The immediate mention of death and Hades rather confirms than weakens our inference: the dead bodies of men from earth and sea are to rise again, and the power of Death abolished, all his captives delivered (1 Cor. xv. 26), and the souls in the separate state now united again to their bodies,— see and compare Isa. xxvi. 19.

Those passages which *connect the resurrection of believers with that of our Lord* are next to be noticed, and certainly the impression they produce is, that in all essential particulars there will be a resemblance. We have already seen wherein the resurrection of Christ consisted.[x] When therefore our resurrection is inferred from his, and proved by it, we necessarily compare them. It would perhaps be difficult to prove that the resurrection of *the body* of Jesus formed no essential part of His resurrection, and still more hard to show that it is not often and chiefly alluded to by the apostles when they speak on the subject.

When we are told of His resurrection from the dead, we naturally conclude that, as man, He had been one of them (the dead) and like to them. The dead still remained, but he arose and gave the world an example, a pledge, and a hope of the resurrection of the body at the last day. See Acts iv. 2; xvii. 18, 31, 32; xxvi. 23;—1 Cor. vi. 14; xv. *passim.*—2 Cor. iv. 14; Col. iii. 3-5; 1 Thess. iv. 14.

In Rev. i. 5, Christ is the ' First-begotten from (ἐκ) the dead,' and in Col. i. 18, he is the ' Beginning' or first fruits, as well as the 'first-born from the dead,' with which other passages admit of close comparison.

II. But we have Scripture testimony of a more *direct* character, the first portion of which consists of passages which *compare* the

[t] Comp. 2 Cor. v. 2. See also Luke xxi. 28; Eph. i. 14, iv. 30; Heb. xi. 35; and Rom. viii. 2, 21.
[u] See the Greek of this passage.　　　[x] On Acts ii. 31.

resurrection of our Lord with that which awaits believers. Waiving the question of their primary application, do not the *terms* of Rom. vi. 5; viii. 11; 1 Cor. xv. 20, 23, 48; Phil. iii. 10, 11; 1 Th. iv. 14, &c., all go to confirm the views we have taken? It is trite to say we cannot compare things which differ,[y] and therefore that there can be no essential difference in the present instance. The drift of these texts is, that Jesus arose, and that therefore we may expect to rise, and that his resurrection was a pledge, earnest, and *pattern* of ours.

The next class of passages relate to the resurrection of the righteous. As specimens take first 1 Cor. xv., where we have a series of arguments, intended, says Van Hengel, not to prove the resurrection of the body, but man's destiny to the possession of a happy immortality. Our limits will not permit a particular investigation (which, however, we should not fear), but we appeal to the impression which its perusal must have on those not previously biassed by doctrinal prejudices. If it were read aloud deliberately in an assembly ignorant of the controversy, we could venture to abide by their verdict. To reach the truth in a connected and intricate argument, it is not needful always to dissect and analyse, refine and sublimate each particular phrase and word. Apply the principle:—is the *whole* chapter declaratory of the resurrection of the body? We think so. But neglect the principle, and, as a man might prove an oak-tree not a tree, by proving that neither the root, trunk, bark, branches, nor leaves could be a tree; so might we show perhaps that no verse, phrase, or word in this chapter, separately proved the resurrection of the body. However, as the tree would remain in the one case, so would the doctrine in the other, in spite of sophistry and false logic.

Writers of the school of our learned author have an easy method of escaping from their difficulties: a quotation from the Old Testament is 'an accommodation' (see pp. 112, 113, 115, 231, 234, &c.); in other cases the apostle had 'not given up his erroneous expectation of what is called the resurrection, during his lifetime' (see pp. 104, 106, 218, 224); sometimes the inspired penmen are 'mistaken,' and at others 'inconsistent' with themselves or one another. Perhaps they have as easy an escape from the difficulty *we* feel in harmonising the view of the resurrection

---

[y] Barnes has a judicious note on Isa. xxvi. 19-21, which is opportune: 'Though, therefore, this does not refer primarily to the resurrection of the dead, yet the illustration is drawn from that doctrine, and implies that that doctrine was one with which they were familiar. An image which is employed for the sake of illustration must be one that is familiar to the mind, and the reference here to that doctrine as an illustration is a demonstration that the doctrine of the resurrection was well known.' *Vide* also Tert. de R. C., 29.

(for instance) maintained in this book, and of the supposed expectation of the apostle, with such passages as these :—' When the sound of the last trumpet is heard, as the followers of Christ who are already dead shall be raised from death without corruption, so we also, who now live, shall be changed, *whether* we previously depart out of this life, *or* remain in this life until then' (on verse 52, p. 225). Again (p. 226), ' For since in each member [of the verse] the apostle directs his reader's attention *to his own body*, the thing speaks for itself, that in the former equally with the latter he refers to the change destined to pass upon himself and his coevals. This most interpreters have supposed after Œcumenius . . . . CORRECTLY also with Chrysostom, not a few have hence inferred, that *the same bodies which we have in this world will return to life.*' Still again (on ver. 54, p. 227), ' Now, when *this* body, which is liable to corruption and mortal, shall be changed so that it will become incorruptible and immortal.' These expressions are amply sufficient to show, not that ' *bonus dormitat Homerus,*' but that as he advances he wavers under the accumulated weight of evidence, and, though he does not (like one well-known name) become a convert to that doctrine which he undertook to refute, he in effect says, ' " Almost persuadest thou me" to believe the resurrection.' We regard the two last quotations as a virtual abandonment of the position taken up. If the same bodies as we have in this life are to return to life, it is unmeaning and useless to deny the resurrection of the same body. By our author's own admission, then, 1 Cor. xv. does teach our doctrine.

Phil. iii. 20, 21, is a passage (not cited nor referred to, so far as we can observe, in Van Hengel's work) to which we attach much importance. ' What is more evident than that the words signify that these bodies of ours, which we carry about with us in this life, pursue by holiness the way to heaven, and so render themselves qualified for the citizenship which is in heaven? (ἄξια τοῦ πολιτεύματος ὃ ἐν οὐρανοῖς ὑπάρχει.) For there is great force in the words ἐξ οὗ καὶ—' *whence also* we look for the Saviour,' where mention of the heavenly citizenship and of a life worthy of it is connected with the hope of the coming of Christ, who shall change our vile bodies. This connection amounts to absolutely nothing, if the heretics against whom we contend speak truly. For these bodies of ours which strive to qualify themselves for heaven, will never possess heaven, and those bodies which they say shall be ours, and shall inherit heaven, have not striven for that citizenship by sanctity of life. Again, what is ' the body of our humiliation' but this humble and base body, endued and attended by so many infirmities and earthly qualities, and derived from Adam ?

Now, how will that body of ours be transformed so as to become like the glorious body of Christ, if it perishes for ever? But of those bodies which await us in the opinion of these persons, how can we say they shall be transformed, when they have not previously existed, &c.?'[z]

Rom. viii. 11, also remains unnoticed. We are quite aware how often this verse has been applied to a moral and spiritual resurrection, both by older and more recent commentators. This view cannot be more clearly expressed than it is by Piscator, 'God raised up Christ from the dead by his Spirit: therefore by the same spirit he will also raise up you (*i. e.* members of Christ) from the dead: that is, he shall quicken your bodies to sanctity of life.' Again, 'It is certain the apostle here does not speak of the resurrection of bodies, but of souls.'[a] Stuart[b] takes the same view, because a statement or promise of the resurrection, here made to believers, would leave us to infer that unbelievers will not be raised; a reason which it will be needless to refute; as also that the application of the passage in this way reduces it to comparative insignificance. What! is God's declaration that he will raise up the mortal ($\vartheta\nu\eta\tau\acute{\alpha}$) bodies of believers, *because*[c] his spirit dwells in them, an insignificant thing? To take the words in any other sense involves a serious difficulty,—that God will quicken those whom he has quickened. Dr. Doddridge saw and felt this,[d] and maintained the view we take, as did Dr. Hammond, &c. The translators of the old Dutch version (or rather its annotators, from whom Van Hengel seems often to have borrowed, even without being aware of the fact) appear to unite both views as others have done :— 'Weder opwekken tot een eeuwig leven, daar geen sonde noch dood meer plaatse en sal hebben ;'—'To raise again to an eternal life where no sin nor death shall any more have place.' The Theses Salmurienses, already quoted, uphold our view, and Fritzsche[e] presents us with a learned and elaborate defence of the same, to which we refer our readers. On carefully weighing the evidence on both sides, we are persuaded that the plain and natural sense of the verse is, that the body of the believer shall be raised from the dead, because that body has been honoured as the temple of the Holy Spirit. Tertullian[f] argues, from the honour put upon the mortal body of the Christian here, that there will be a resurrection of the same hereafter.

A few words must suffice upon the passages which remain. On 1 Thess. iv. 13, &c., Tertullian says, 'What archangel's voice, or

---

[z] Theses Salmur. de Res., xx. p. 898. [a] Piscator in loc., p. 904, edit. 1613.
[b] Comm. in loc. [c] We are compelled to adopt this reading.
[d] Comm. in loc., and note *b* on v. 10. [e] Comm. in loc., tom. ii. pp. 117–131.
[f] Tert. de R. C., 10.

trump of God, is heard now, except perhaps in heretics' dreams? For though the preaching of the gospel can be called the trumpet of God, &c.'[g]

As Rom. viii. 11, is applied by some to a spiritual resurrection, so Ezek. xxxvii. 1-14, is generally referred to a political one. But even if it were true in both cases, and it may be in the latter, we should still infer from them the resurrection of the body, on the principle which seems to have influenced Calvin on Rom. viii. 11, and which has been already laid down in the quotation from Albert Barnes. (See note [y].)

2 Cor. iv. 13, to v. 10. The whole texture of this passage, as well as several separate phrases in it, require us to apply it to our doctrine of the resurrection. We particularly call attention to ver. 10, ch. v., which in the English version reads, 'That every one may receive the things done in his body, &c.,' but the sense conveyed by the Syriac Peshito, 'For all of us must stand before the tribunal of Christ, that every man may *in his own body* receive the reward of what has been done by him, whether good or bad,' deserves especial attention. Tert. de Res. Car. 43, gives this passage, *per corpus*, observing that the passage may be read both ways, preferring this, but inferring the resurrection of the body even from the other. Even if the English version be correct, we learn from the other the views of the translators of the venerable Peshito. In any case, since the body comes into account, and the things done by the body (τὰ διὰ τοῦ σώμ) are set forth, certainly it suggests the highest probability of its resurrection from the dead.

Rom. iv. 17. God is he that quickens the dead, because he shall hereafter do so, just as Christ is judge of living and dead, because he shall hereafter judge them.

John v. 21 seqq.; viii. 51 seqq.; and xi. 21 seqq. The many striking expressions found in these passages deserve most careful attention, which will be abundantly rewarded. And even if it should be concluded that a spiritual resurrection is chiefly taught, we may still apply the principle already referred to in note [y]. On John v. 28, 29, Van Hengel (p. 64) says, 'Those who shall go forth are *men*, not bodies or souls, even if that be true which is commonly assumed, that there is set forth here the common egress of the dead from their sepulchres.' Again, p. 92, 'For even if I concede that the dead shall return to life, from John v. 28, 29; and Acts xxiv. 15 (where νεκρῶν is to be expunged), yet they cannot relate to the whole human race (as to infants and children)—on moral grounds.' While our author sturdily denies the resurrection

---

[g] De R. C., 24.

of the *body* and of the *flesh* as something incredible, he clearly
admits that the dead who return to life will have a body of some
sort, for, says he, 'The apostle returns to his disputation concerning the body destined to followers of Christ, by denying that
it can be of flesh and blood;'[h] in which he scarcely differs from
ourselves and the orthodox generally, as represented by the Dutch
vernacular already cited, which here remarks, 'Flesh and blood,
i. e. such bodies as are corruptible, as flesh and blood are in this
life, and in respect to their being such, as is explained in the verses
following (see Gal. i. 12 ; Heb. ii. 14).' And again, 'The apostle
speaks only of *qualities*, to show that it is of *qualities* he speaks,
and not of the *form* of bodies.'

The remaining class of texts is of a more general character.
Various parables, representations of the future judgment, and
other scriptures, render it highly probable that both wicked and
righteous will possess a body through eternity ; see, for instance,
Luke xvi. 23, 24. But passing by these, we observe that, while
over every man '*mors quasi saxum Tantalo impendit*,'[i] something
still more terrible awaits the wicked, even the resurrection of the body
in which he sinned, to be his partner in eternal shame and suffering,
as in earthly guilt. From Dan. xii. 2, before quoted, we learn
that some will awake 'to everlasting life, and some to shame and
everlasting contempt.' In Acts xvii. 32, we see, not merely how
the Athenians ridiculed the idea of a resurrection, but are taught
to infer that they certainly understood it of the body, a doctrine
which they as certainly did not generally believe ; for although
the idea was not new to them, they had been wont to allude to it
as an impossibility, or an insurmountable difficulty. That the
ἀνάστασις was by them understood in the comprehensive sense in
which we have used the word, we have conclusive evidence in the
Eumenides of Æschylus, 647, 648, where Apollo is made to say—

ἀνδρὸς δ' ἐπειδὰν αἷμ' ἀνασπάσῃ κόνις
ἅπαξ θανόντος, οὔτις ἐστ' ἀνάστασις.

This quotation sets at rest the question as to what idea is to be
attached to the word ἀνάστασις when applied to that future event
which we call the resurrection.

Acts xxiv. 15. Here the Apostle Paul declares his hope of
a 'resurrection of the dead,[k] both of the just and the unjust.'
There ought to be but one opinion upon this passage, and we are
surprised that so many have interpreted John v. 28, 29, otherwise

---

[h] On ver. 50, p. 207; and Dutch Annotators on 1 Cor. xv. 50.

[i] Cicero de Finibus, i. 18.

[k] We do not feel justified in departing from the received text here; the
authority is too strong in its favour.

than literally. Van Hengel has a note on this text,[m] in which he tells us that 'Tittmann admits that the *usus loquendi* allows us to explain τοὺς ἐν μν. of the impious, some of whom should receive the doctrine of salvation with a ready mind and be saved, but that others should reject it and miserably perish. Very recently Jentink has attempted to refute the common notion. Of his essay our author partly approves and glances at the arguments which seem to himself to require a figurative interpretation :—

1. The intention of the whole line of argument.

2. The argument has respect to this life, ver. 17 seq., 30 seq.

3. The antithesis between ' resurrection of life,' and ' resurrection of judgment,' which cannot agree with the opinion that all men shall come to judgment.

4. The use of the aorists ποιήσαντες and πράξαντες, and not of the perf.: see Acts xxv. 11, 25.

5. The sense of the words, ' shall hear his voice,' which ver. 25, &c., require us to explain of their hearing him divinely proclaiming to them the way of salvation.

6. The οἱ ἐν τ. μν., which does not mean those *who shall be* but *who are now* in their graves.

7. The word ἐκπορεύσονται, by which, since men are denoted who are already recalled to life and so prepared to go forth, it cannot follow that ' the resurrection of life ' respects persons who are to return to life to become partakers of blessedness.

We shall bestow a word on each of these arguments, which the writer promises hereafter to develop and maintain. In our opinion he must rely rather on their number than their weight.

1. Jesus had restored a *sick man* to *health*, which offended the Jews, who thereupon sought to *kill* him. So the Lord said, in effect, ' You wonder to see me raise a *sick* man to *health*, you shall see more than this (ver. 20), you shall see the Son of Man raise the *dead* to *life*, for I am constituted Judge (ver. 22), and will raise the dead in order to execute my high commission ' (ver. 27-30).

2. The remark last made is sufficient to show the transition of the argument to a future life, and its connection with both the present world and that which is to come.

3. The antithesis in ver. 29 certainly does *not* contradict the opinion that all men shall come to judgment. There will be and are but two classes of men, and there are but two destinies. Every man will rise either to the resurrection of life, or to that of condemnation.

4. This objection is wholly without force. The aor. is used in numerous instances, where we should perhaps expect the perf.

---

[m] Pp. 8, 9.

Thus, in 2 Cor. v. 10, we have the aor. in precisely the same sense and similar connection. Moreover, there is a propriety in the use of these forms, in their *indefinite reference to past time.* The perf. properly brings up the idea to, and connects it with, the present in the speaker's mind; the aorist refers to some period antecedent: which is the more appropriate here, it is superfluous to say. If our Lord spoke in the Syriac, he used the pret., which the Latin expresses more accurately than our English,—'qui fecerunt bona, in resurrectionem vitæ, et qui fecerunt mala, in resurrectionem judicii.' But the application of Van Hengel's own remarks on 1 Cor. xv. 49, would alone suffice to remove his objection to the aorist. 'Now the common opinion is, that the apostle wrote ἐφορέσαμεν in the aor. because he had present to his eyes the time in which this terrestrial life should end: this opinion is also approved by our translator, who rendered the word 'gedragen hebben' ("have borne," as English version). However, as I greatly doubt whether, *per loquendi usum*, it be right to assign to the aor. the power of the perf., so I know not whether the whole of this earthly life, as well present and future as past, be comprehended by it. If I mistake not, the aorist is similarly used, Matt. iii. 17; xxiii. 2; Luke i. 47; Rom. viii. 29, 30; James i. 11.'[n] This is not quoted because we prefer it as an explanation, but to show that in other cases the author can find one which satisfies himself, partly, at least.

5. Why limit these words to Christ's preaching to the living? The dead did hear his voice (as proved by Matt. ix. 25; xi. 5; John xi. 43, 44, &c.). And if then, why not now, or hereafter? Even if they had not heard it, he from that time had the power and authority requisite. Our Lord sometimes used the word *now*, or its equivalents, in a peculiar manner—including the entire dispensation of the gospel.[o] If we are to limit the words to Christ's personal preaching, what becomes of *the dead* now? whose voice do they hear when they are called upon? not the voice of Christ, if we *must* be literal.

6. This objection is trifling. Every one knows that the tenses of the substantive verb are to be supplied according to circumstances. This quibble would exclude all reference to those that went before and to those that came after, alike. The plain meaning is, that those who *are* in the graves *when the voice is uttered* shall hear it, &c.

7. This objection, if it means anything, means that the dead who shall hear the voice of the Son of Man, are not dead but alive!

[n] P. 204.
[o] A reason for this may be found in 2 Pet. iii. 8.

and this is to avail ourselves of the imperfections of language, in order to show that we are wiser than the word of God.

Matt. xxii. 23, &c., presents an interesting circumstance which gave occasion to our Lord to state, in plain and significant language, the doctrine of the resurrection. Tertullian's satirical remark upon this text shall close what we have to adduce upon scripture evidence for the resurrection of the body. 'You have here the Lord, confirming, against the *heretics* of the Jews, what is now also denied among the *Sadducees* of the Christians—a real and veritable resurrection.'[p]

These testimonies, when carefully weighed, appear to us so clear, conclusive, and satisfactory, that we feel there is no need for philosophical subtleties and metaphysical abstractions; they form a true sorites, which rapidly accumulates as we proceed, until we are constrained to submit that no physical difficulties or antecedent objections ought to influence us, so as for a moment to prevent our receiving a doctrine for which so much is said, and in support of which so much concurrent and collateral evidence can be adduced from analogy and history alike. Verily, if in this matter we 'hear not Moses and the prophets,' Christ and his apostles, 'neither shall we be persuaded though one rose from the dead.'

We shall conclude this already protracted article, by giving a brief sketch of the opinions of the ancients,—heathens, Jews, and Christians, upon the doctrine of the resurrection.

1. The ancient heathen seem to have perceived some shadow of this doctrine, those of them, at least, who believed that the world would hereafter be purified by fire, and so renewed that every man would live again. This opinion, which most prevailed among the Stoics, was clearly borrowed by them from other, and most likely eastern sources. We learn from Clement of Alexandria[q] that Zoroaster received it, and Diogenes Laertius informs us that Theopompus, a Peripatetic philosopher, derived the same opinion from the system of the Magi. Clem. Alex. also ascribes the same sentiment to Heraclitus, who received it from the barbaric (*i. e.* foreign, *not* Greek) philosophy, and it is ascribed to the idea which God had given his Church of the future destruction and restoration of the world.[r]

In the writings of Seneca we meet with some remarkable expressions, as also in other Latin and Greek writers. Thus, *Sen. Ep.* 36, 'The death which we fear and avoid only intermits life, and does not take it away.'[s] Again, *Nat. Quæst.* 3, 30,

---

p De Res. Car., 36.   q Strom., lib. v.
r See Thes. Salm. ut supra, pp. 890, 891.
s See Lipsius's note on this passage, pp. 448, 449, edit. 1615.

'Omne ex integro animal generabitur, dabiturque terris homo inscius scelerum'—'Every animal shall be born again, and man shall be restored to earth ignorant of crime.'[t]   The doctrine thus broached involved the idea that in the natural order of things, by the revolution of some cycle (see *Sen. N. Q.*, 3, 27-30), this return would occur, and as naturally be followed by sin.   It was inferred from the constant revolutions of nature : all things seem to move in circles; alternate production, progress, and decay, and the constant interchange of death and life, as we all observe.   The fathers used the same argument for the resurrection, *e. g.* Clemens Romanus, Tertullian, and Minucius Felix.

But of the Scriptural resurrection they seem to have had no expectation.   The passage already quoted from Æschyl. Eumen. well illustrates this remark, and in the Antigone of Sophocles a similar sentiment is expressed.[u]   Lucretius (*de Nat. Rerum*, 3, 859-862) thus shows his incredulity :—

> Nec si materiam nostram collegerit ætas
> Post obitum, rursumque redegerit ut sita nunc est
> Atque iterum nobis fuerint data lumina vitæ,
> Pertineat, &c.

Cicero, in his *Consolation*, is similarly confident on the side of scepticism, or rather disbelief: 'No one can wisely believe that their bodies have been taken to heaven; a thing which, because nature does not suffer that which is of the earth to remain elsewhere than in the earth, necessarily ought not to be credited; but that their souls . . . are carried away to heaven.'   'The body, naturally mortal, remains in the earth, and what is earthly can on no account put off its own nature and put on another.'   Similar sentiments are elsewhere expressed in the same book, and also in the *de Natura Deorum*, 3, 12-14.   No doubt the classical reader will be able to add many other passages, but we can only quote one, which may be found in Grotius *de Veritate*[v] and Dr. S. Clarke's *Evidences of Religion*.[x]   Lactantius originally cites it from Chrysippus, who flourished above 200 years B.C.   'It is evidently not impossible that we also, after death, when certain periods of time have revolved, should be restored to that form ($\sigma\chi\tilde{\eta}\mu\alpha$) in which we now are.'

As we said, the oriental nations seem to have earliest held opinions related to the doctrine of a resurrection; the doctrine

---

[t] See also Sen. Consol. ad Marc., 19; Lipsius, note 269, on the place.

[u] See Antig., 1337, 1338.   Such expressions make Acts xvii. 32, very significant.

[v] See Grot. de Ver. 2, 7, 11, pp. 107, 118, Oxon. 1827, for further references.

[x] Edit. 1724, pt. 2, p. 204.

has also been most clearly broached by them. The following quotation from a recent work will amuse :—

' The resurrection is the triumph of Ormuzd and his worshippers, and an essential article of their belief. The judgment of men is to occupy a space of 57 years. Then will the genii of the elements render up their trust, the soul re-enter its former earthly dwelling-place, and the juice of the herb hom and the milk of the bull (!), Heziosk, restore life to man, and render him immortal.' [y]

2. We now turn to *the Jews*, whose doctrine may be partly learned from the New Testament, Matt. xxii. 23, &c,; Acts xxiii. 6-9 ; and xxiv. 15. The notes of Grotius on Matt. v. 20, and xxii. 32, will illustrate both this and the previous particular. The statements of Josephus,[z] and the Jewish writers generally, accord with those of the New Testament. The Jews have now for a long period only admitted that there will be a resurrection of the just, resting their faith on Ps. i. 5. In the Apocryphal books there are several references to the doctrine, *e. g.* 2 Esd. ii. 16, 23 ; vii. 31, 32, 39, 43 ; 2 Macc. vii. 14 ; xii. 43, 44. In the Septuagint a curious addition has been made to the book of Job at the end, ' And it is written, that he will rise again with those whom the Lord raiseth up,' &c. We may also refer to the Targums, *e. g.* on Jer. xxxviii. 16 ; Hos. vi. 2 ; and Zech. iii. 7 ; but it will not be requisite to dwell upon the evidence which in this case is so free from doubt or partiality.

3. Therefore we proceed in the last place to the *Christians ;* the Scripture evidence need not be repeated. Now, as it is most evident in what light the resurrection has been understood both by Jews and heathens, so it will soon appear that from the earliest period of Christian history the followers of Jesus regarded the resurrection of the body as an article of faith.

Barnabas[a] says, ' Now, since it became Him to appear in the flesh, that he might abolish death and show forth the resurrection of the dead, He suffered in order to fulfil the promise to the fathers,' &c. Clemens Romanus,[b] ' Let us consider, beloved, how the Lord shows to us perpetually that there shall be a resurrection, whereof he made the Lord Jesus Christ the first-fruits, having raised him from the dead. Let us contemplate, beloved, the resurrection which takes place at every season. Day and night exhibit to us the resurrection,' &c. The arguments previously referred to as used by Seneca, Tertullian, &c., are then given, and these are followed by the story of the Phœnix, which

---

[y] Nineveh and Persepolis, W. S. W. Vaux, M.A., 1850, p. 101.
[z] *e. g.* Antiqq., xviii. 1, 3-5.
[a] Ep., sec. 5.   [b] 1 ad Cor., 24-27.

is also repeated by Tertullian, but of which too much has been made. Their knowledge of natural history was limited, and they sometimes accepted as true what we regard as fable.[c]

Again (sec. 50), Clement says, 'They who by the grace of God are made perfect in love shall possess the place of the holy. They shall be manifested in the visitation of the kingdom of Christ. For it is written, "Enter into thy chamber a very little time until my anger and wrath pass away, and I will remember the good day, and will raise you from your graves."'

Again, in 2 Clem. *ad Cor.* sec. 8, 9, Christians are exhorted to preserve the purity of the flesh, and admonished not to 'say that this flesh shall not be judged.' The writer proceeds to argue from our salvation while in the flesh, and from the fact of its sanctification, 'for as ye are called in the flesh, ye shall also come in the flesh, even as Christ the Lord who saved us, though he was spirit before he became flesh, and so called us; so also we shall in this flesh receive the reward.'

Polycarp (*ad Phil.* 2.) thus expresses himself: 'Now he who raised Him from the dead shall also raise us, if,' &c.; and further (sec. 7): 'He who perverts the words of the Lord to his inclination, and saith that there is neither resurrection nor judgment, is the first-born of Satan.' In the *Martyrium Polycarp.*, sec. 14, the martyr, in the touching prayer there recorded, and which he offered at the funeral pile, is represented as saying, 'I bless Thee that on this day, and at this hour, Thou hast counted me worthy of a portion in the number of thy martyrs, in the cup of thy Christ, for the resurrection of eternal life, both of soul and body, in the incorruptibility of the Holy Spirit!"

Hagenbach[d] states, that the Apologetic Fathers keep the resurrection of Christ in the background, in contradistinction from Paul, referring especially to Athenagoras and Min. Felix. This opinion we believe to be too indiscriminately applied. The references already given show that it was not so with the *Apostolical* fathers, while in the cases of Athenagoras and M. Felix it can readily be accounted for.

The phrase 'resurrection of *the flesh*,' as more definite and precise than that of '*the body*,' was soon generally adopted, and appears, as already seen, in the so-called Apostles' Creed.

Justin Martyr maintained similar views to Clem. Rom. Athenagoras believed in the resurrection of the same body, and in a similar state. Theophylact (*ad Autol.* i. 8) uses similar language;

---

[c] Witchcraft and apparitions were believed by Baxter, but who would thence infer the worthlessness of the Saints' Rest? See the Rest, pt. 2, ch. vii. 2–4, and pt. 3, ch. vi. 24; also Tert. de Anima, 51.

[d] Hist. Doct., vol. i. p. 212, Clarke's edit.

and Irenæus (*adv. Hær.* v. 12, 13) asserts that it will be a *revivification*, and not a new creation. The views of Tertullian, whom we have already so frequently cited, resembled these, though he asserted the materiality of the soul. Cyprian agrees with Tertullian, and Min. Felix also taught the resurrection of the same body.[e]

The Alexandrine school, says Hagenbach (*loc. cit.*), endeavoured to clear the doctrine of additions, and to refine and spiritualise it. It is true there is no definite expression of opinion in Clem. Alex. on this subject, but from various expressions in the 5th book of the *Stromata*—as when he sets forth the opinions of the Stoics and of Zoroaster, and quotes from the 10th book of Plato's *Republic* the story of the dead man restored to life—it is clear that he received the doctrine mainly according to the general understanding of it.

Origen, while admitting it to be not an essential article of faith, defends it against Celsus.[f] His idea of the resemblance between the buried body and a seed planted in the earth, and between the resurrection body and the plant produced from the seed, has found adherents even in modern times.[g]

The Gnostics, while they admitted the soul's immortality, denied the body's resurrection. Some in Arabia held that soul and body sleep till the resurrection; these were opposed by Origen, and are called *Thnetopsychites* by John of Damascus. Eusebius (*Hist. Eccl.* vi. 37) describes the opinions of this sect, who, be it observed, believed in the resurrection of the same body. Lactantius[h] and others believed in a two-fold resurrection (see Rev. xx.), but Augustine[i] speaks of this view slightingly. The views of Origen were afterwards adopted by Basil the Great, as well as by the Gregories of Nazianzum and Nyssa, though opposed by Methodius. Chrysostom, who asserts the identity of the resurrection body, also maintains its superiority, *e. g.* in *Hom.* x. on 2 Cor.

Jerome, with his wonted rigidity, maintained the doctrine of the orthodox with minute precision and severity against (among others) Rufinus, who yet received the *resurrectio hujus carnis*, and still more against John of Jerusalem, who distinguished between *flesh* and *body*; in this he would now find many followers.

Augustine,[k] who at an earlier period held the doctrine with some deviations from the orthodox, gradually settled down in the

---

[e] Octavius, sec. 11, 34. [f] Contra Cels., 4, 57; 5, 18, 23, &c.

[g] It seems a result of this opinion that Van Hengel takes the word σπείρεται in the sense *procreare*, p. 182, &c.

[h] Lact. Instit., lib. vii. 20. [i] De Civ. Dei, lib. xx. 7.

[k] De Fid. et Symbol, c. 10; Retract.; Enchirid. ad Laur.; and C. D., xxii. 11.

more common views. These views, being confirmed by Synods and adopted into Creeds and Confessions, in a short time prevailed, and no room was left for discussion except in regard to some of the circumstantials. From the period of Jerome and Augustine, therefore, we may say that the resurrection of the same body was universally owned by the Church.

The Reformers, while they rejected so much that had been so long implicitly received, did not touch this article of the faith. Amid the sifting of the Church then, it was recognised by them : ' I cannot,' said Calvin, on 1 Cor. xv. 1, ' be induced to apply the language of Paul otherwise than to the resurrection of the flesh.' He believed that, ' if their faith in the resurrection be not well-founded, Christians are of all men most miserable' (on 1 Pet. iv. 17) ; that, in fact, the ' very foundation of religion is undermined' (on 2 Pet. iii. 4) ; and that ' those who instil doubts into men's minds on this matter are deceivers.' [m]

The history of the Protestant doctrine is the echo of Calvin's words, and with marvellous unanimity have the Reformed Churches subscribed to his sentiments in this particular. 'Shall these dry bones live ?' is a question to which Jew and Christian alike give in reply an emphatic affirmative. Surely the voice of Scripture can be no uncertain sound here where those who differ from each other so much are at one! 'How can these things be ?' is a question which a Christian should never put when he has the promise of God. Sarah laughed in her incredulity, but the power of Him that promised checked her doubting smiles. Martha was dubious of her brother's speedy return to life, but the summons, ' Lazarus, come forth!' soon dispelled her fears. The Apostles trusted that it should have been He, but He had been crucified—how their faith rallied when he manifested himself to them ! Thomas refused credence till he had tangible proof; but the Lord blesses those who believe and have not seen.

The practical tendency of this doctrine cannot be otherwise than salutary—to the Christian and to the man of the world alike. It speaks to the believer patience and hope. He can bear quietly all the rebuffs of an unsympathizing world, and all the burdens of this transitory scene, because he knows that he shall at length appear in the likeness of the Redeemer. He feels more strongly induced to adorn his body—the living temple—because he knows that though destroyed by death it shall be built again. He looks forward to this restoration of the tabernacle wherein he has worshipped in this wilderness, but its restoration in a more glorious form on the other side of the dark valley.

---

[m] Besides many others see Calvin's note on Matt. xxii. 23, which is very emphatic.

The application of this doctrine to bad men is equally apparent. How it magnifies the importance of sin in the members! How it augments the terror of the future prospects of the wicked! 'Who shall deliver me from the body of this death?' will be the everlasting and never answered question of despair.

But in another aspect such a doctrine is wonderfully consonant to our circumstances, but in direct contrariety to the opinions of those who 'sorrow without hope' for their departed friends. It gives a sacredness to the sleeping dust, and adds a solemn charm to the sepulchre which we cannot but feel.

'Therefore,' says the darkness of nature, as it closes the tomb above its buried friend, 'does sleep perpetual rest upon Quinctilius?' [n]   O! that *iron sleep*, that *brazen sleep!* [o]   Christianity alone can answer the question by Him who 'brought life and immortality to light.' He who gives this sleep shall also remove it: 'Our friend Lazarus may sleep, but he will come and wake him from his sleep.' *Reposita est hæc spes nostra in sinu nostro!* [p]

C. H. B.

---

[n] See Hor. Od., i. 24, 25.   [o] Virg. Æneid, iv. 244; x. 745.
[p] See the Vulgate of Job xix. 27.

AURICULAR CONFESSION.

THE practice of Auricular Confession, now universal in the Church of Rome, had no existence till several centuries after the establishment of Christianity. We find no trace of it either in the writings of the New Testament, or in the works of the early Fathers of the Church. Its origin must be assigned to the ninth century. It did not become obligatory until the commencement of the thirteenth.

The only acknowledgment of sin which the Scriptures recognise, besides confession to God, is that of Christians mutually acknowledging to each other in private their failings and sins. 'Confess your faults one to another' (James v. 16). In very early times, however, the practice of public confession arose in the Church. Those who subjected themselves to penance were accustomed to confess their sins in the presence of the faithful. They stood in the entrance of the church, in the posture of suppliants, covered with sackcloth and ashes. They groaned aloud, imploring forgiveness of their sins, and the favour and prayers of all present. They fell prostrate on the ground, beat their breasts, and kissed the very feet of their pastors. When the period of penitence was ended, they were introduced into the church by one of the presbyters, where, in the presence of the assembly, they again expressed their penitence, and again recommended themselves to the prayers of the faithful.

Public confession was continued for some time in the Christian Church, from the belief of its salutary effects. 'There is nothing so likely to prevent sin,' says Chrysostom, 'as the obligation to confess it.' It gradually came, however, to be regarded as of little use in deterring from crime, and the scandal which followed the confession of certain sins at length led to its abolition. Nestorius, a deacon of the Church, having publicly confessed his connection with a Roman lady, brought so much discredit upon the order of the clergy that the practice was prohibited by the bishop. The fear of frightening away those converts who trembled at the idea of a public acknowledgment of guilt had some influence too in producing this result. 'The sins of those who come forward for penance are not always of a nature not to dread publicity. We must therefore lay aside this custom, which for this reason cannot be approved, lest we should drive away many persons who blush to avow their sins, or fear to expose them to their enemies, and thus incur the punishment of the laws.' [a]

---

[a] St. Leon, Epist. 80, ad Episc. Camp.

The practice of auricular confession to priests began to be introduced in the ninth century; it was, however, far from general for some ages. The state of opinion when the Council of Châlons was held, in the year 813, may be gathered from the following canon:—'Some say that they ought to confess their sins to God alone; others think they must confess them to the priest. Either may be done to the great advantage of the holy Church; but only in case we confess our sins to God, who remits sins, and say with David, "I have acquainted you with my sin, and I have not hid my unrighteousness," &c.; and according to the instruction of the Apostle: "Let us confess our sins to one another, and let us pray with one another that we may be saved."' [b]

It was not till the thirteenth century that this practice was formally and authoritatively established by the Roman Church. Indeed this could not happen until the doctrine of priestly absolution assumed the monstrous form which it now exhibits in that corrupt community. For many centuries no one pretended to ascribe to priests the power of forgiving sin. All the ancient forms of absolution previous to the thirteenth century are *deprecatory*, not *judiciary*: in other words, they implore forgiveness from God, instead of declaring it to be already granted. 'Until the twelfth century,' says Gieseler, 'the confession of private sins had not been considered *an indispensable condition of forgiveness*, but only a means of amendment; and no peculiar power of absolution being attributed to priests, it was allowable also to confess to laymen. But after confession had been included among the sacraments, the opposite views began to prevail, at first only in opinion, but afterwards sanctioned by the ordinance of Innocent III., that every one should confess to a priest at least once in every year. From this time the notion grew up that confession was the only means of obtaining the forgiveness of deadly sins, and that *the priest, as God's representative, could bestow such forgiveness, and the priest only.*' [c] Up to this time the *form* of absolution was, ' THE LORD GRANT THEE absolution and remission' ('Absolutionem et remissionem tribuat tibi Deus'). In the thirteenth century, however, the priest in the most open manner usurped the place of God, and instead of *imploring* forgiveness, *bestowed* it, by the power of the keys. The form henceforth in use was, ' I ABSOLVE THEE from thy sins, in the name of the Father, and of the Son, and of the Holy Ghost' ('Ego te absolvo a peccatis tuis, in nomine Patris,' etc.).

The practice of auricular confession is one of considerable advantage to the Church of Rome, in magnifying the priestly

---

[b] Synodus Cabilionensis ii. an. 813.   [c] Text-book of Eccles. Hist. ii. p. 353.

office. The head must bow and the knee bend before him who has the power of consigning you to an abode of eternal torture, or of opening for you the gates of the kingdom of Heaven. Those who believe such opinions must necessarily regard priests as above all other human beings, and feel compelled to submit to the laws of the Church as authoritative and divine. But in addition to the increase of power and dignity which this institution produced, it constituted a great source of wealth. The writings of Gratian (A.D. 1154) may be referred to. After asking whether any one can satisfy God in secret by the confession of the heart alone without the confession of the mouth, he replies, ' there are persons who hold that all may deserve pardon for their sins without church confession and the judgment of the priest.' Having produced the different opinions upon the subject, he adds, ' But which must we rather embrace? This we must leave to the choice and judgment of the reader, because both opinions have found defenders among wise religious men.' [d] It appears to have been the practice in the middle ages to pay for the sacrament. There is a charter of the city of Paris still extant, dated A.D. 1224, in which mention is made of *denarii qui dantur in confessionibus.*[e] A passage quoted by Carpentier refers to the same practice as existing in the year 1476. ' The same Havart demanded of this same Thomasin to lend him five sous and a half, ' pour soy confesser et ordonner a Pasques.' [f] What is worse, as showing the fearful ignorance and gross superstition of those times, it appears from the following extract out of an old chronicle, that *girls prostituted themselves in order to obtain money to get the remission of their sins.* ' The supplicant having met a young girl of fifteen or sixteen years of age, lui requist qu'elle voulust qu'il eust sa compagnie charnelle: to which she consented: among other things he had promised to give her a robe and chaperon, and money to buy shoes for her to go to confess at Easter.' [g]

The custom of paying for confessions is still practised in Ireland, and is the source of vast gain to the priesthood. When the priest attends on the sick and dying on the continent, and pronounces the final absolution, a charge is made, though not, we believe, for ordinary confessions.

The considerations just adduced naturally led the Roman hierarchy earnestly to recommend the frequent use of confession to a priest-ridden and superstitious people. They found that the confessional was a place where they could dictate from time to time those opinions and commands to which they wished the

---

[d] De Pœnit. c. 89.   [e] Hist. of Auric. Conf. i. 169.
[f] Glossar. Nov. sub voc. Confessio, No. 4.
[g] Carpentier, Supplém. à Ducange, in voc. Confessio.

people to submit: and they also found it a source of pecuniary profit by no means to be despised. Various treatises were written on confession and penance, in which the most cogent arguments were brought forward in support of this mischievous practice. ' Every time you confess,' says a distinguished theologian, ' when you have sinned, you obtain grace and the remission of your sins. If you confess four times a year, grace is increased four times, and if you confess more frequently, grace is increased in proportion. It is difficult to know of what value grace is. But it cannot be denied that the least particle of grace is more desirable than the possession of the whole world.' The Council of the Lateran[h] only insisted on an *annual* confession as indispensable, but weekly attendance on this sacrament was enjoined on all the faithful in the sermons and devotional books of the day. ' Shryve you ever weke to your curate,' says the Prymer, ' except ye have grete lette ; and beware ye passe a fourtnyght except veray grete lette.'[i] Dens also, in his Text-book of Theology, recommends weekly confessions of sins, and pronounces it impossible to live a devout life without confessing every month.[k]

We must not forget to notice the numerous miracles which were constantly related in the pulpits, in order to prove, that confession was a necessary condition to salvation. Bede informs us, that a soldier, after having led a very abandoned life, fell sick. The king, says Bede, had exhorted him often to confess his sins, in the manner customary among Christians, before he departed from this world ; but all to no purpose : he had, however, before his death, a vision which warned him that he was justly condemned to eternal torments, as the consequence of having neglected and deferred the confession of his sins.[l] Bellarmine refers to this miracle, in proof of the obligation of the sacrament.

The writers of the Life of St. Bernard inform us that this saint performed a miracle to prove the same. A nobleman fell dangerously ill, lost his senses and the use of his speech ; then his children and friends sent for St. Bernard, who finding him in this state, addressed the bystanders as follows :—' You are not ignorant that this man, by vexing the church and oppressing the poor, has grievously offended God ; if you will believe me, and do what I tell you, restore to the church whatever has been taken from them, the patient will recover his speech, make a confession of his sins, and receive devoutly the divine sacrament.' They followed the advice of the saint, who began immediately to pray : he performed mass ; but scarcely had he finished, when they came to tell him

---

h Held A.D. 1215.   i Prym. pref. Rouen, 1556.   k Tom. vi. p. 91, Dublin, 1832.
l Neglectæ dilatæque confessionis pœnas pestissimas dedisse, Hist. Britan. cap. 14.

that Jubert—this was the name of the patient—was speaking, asking to confess his sins, which he accordingly did.[m]

Innumerable other miraculous stories are found in the legendary books of Rome; we shall only give the following :—A brigand having been beheaded by his enemies on the top of a hill, his head rolled down to a village situated at the foot, and began to cry 'Holy Virgin Mary, give me a true confession ;' some persons hearing this exclamation, went to fetch a priest, who on his arrival sat down and received the confession made by the head; at which astonished, he immediately granted absolution.[n]

Such is a sample of the lying wonders invented by those interested in the practice—for the purpose of rendering confession to the priest general throughout Christendom. The efforts of the Hierarchy were successful, and it is now our painful task to point out the pernicious effects of that Antichristian practice upon both the priesthood and the people. Let us consider,—

1. *The influence of Auricular Confession upon the Priesthood.*

There can be no question as to the fearful influence of this practice in depraving the monks and secular clergy of Rome, and thus spreading on all sides a shameless and boundless licentiousness. As practised at its first introduction, auricular confession to the priest was comparatively harmless. When it became universal—about the twelfth century—it also underwent some change in the mode of its performance—sins being confessed with all the circumstances which attended them; and to this we must ascribe the subsequent horrible results of the Romish confessional. Up to the twelfth century, it was chiefly individuals possessing some regard for morality that frequented the tribunal of penance. There being no external obligation to compel the practice, the profligate and licentious naturally avoided the avowal of their guilt. But after the decree of the Council of the Lateran had been issued, and the rites of the Church, and even Christian burial denied to all who neglected this sacrament, the most abandoned persons were driven to the confessor's chair; and the results of the circumstantial disclosure of their sins upon the priest may be easily imagined. It should be remembered, too, that the men into whose ears the abominations of every parish in Christendom were poured, lived under the irritation of forced celibacy. In direct variance with—not the permission—but the recommendation that the minister of Christ should be ' the husband of one wife '— the Church of Rome consigns to perpetual celibacy a body of men taken indiscriminately from the mass, at an age when it is impossible to ascertain their fitness or unfitness for that state. The.

---

[m] Hist. Auric. Confes., i. p. 166.   [n] Ibid.

frightful consequences of confession upon the clergy are thus multiplied tenfold.   In the graphic language of a philosophic writer, 'the wretched being within whose bosom distorted passions are rankling, is called daily to listen to tales of licentiousness from his own sex, and infinitely worse to the reluctant or shameless disclosures of the other! . . . . Each sinner makes but one confession in a given time, but each priest in the same space listens to a hundred! What then after a while must that receptacle have become, into which the continual droppings of all the debauchery of a parish are falling, and through which the copious abomination filters! It is hard not to suppose that the Roman Church, in constituting her Hierarchy, had wittingly kept in view the purpose of rendering her clergy the fit instruments of whatever atrocity her occasions might demand them to perpetrate; and so had brought to bear upon their hearts every possible power of corruption.   Not content with cashiering them of sanatory domestic influences, she has by the practice of confession made the full stream of human crime to pass, foul and infectious, through their bosoms. Having to construct at discretion the polity of the nations, the Roman architects have so planned it, that the sacerdotal order shall constitute the *cloacæ* of the social edifice; and thus they have secured for Rome the honour of being, through these channels, the great stercorary of the world.'[o]

It is then, we think, difficult to overrate the guilt chargeable upon the Romish Church during those centuries in which auricular confession was of universal obligation.   The awful depravity of the priesthood thus engendered in the confessional is attested even by members of the Romish communion.   'Confession,' says Erasmus, 'tends to deprave the morals of young priests, by the detailed accounts of the obscenities which excite their curiosity and inflame their passions.   They converse of these things with their penitents, or with their fellow ecclesiastics, which talk necessarily leads to evil.   The knowledge of the general corruption tends to corrupt them; these shameless practices being every day presented to their mind.   The irregularities of the priests, which the clergy, and even governments carefully conceal, transpire nevertheless; and these examples deprave the laity.'[p]

We now proceed to consider

2. *Its influence upon the People.*

The pernicious results of auricular confession upon the members of the Romish Church arise from divers causes, foremost

[o] Fanaticism, pp. 164–5.
[p] Erasmi Exomologia, quoted in Hist. of Auric. Conf. ii. p. 255.   Cod. MS. Penitentiale, apud J. Morinum, Com. Pœnit., p. 23.

among which must be ranked the plan, universally adopted by the clergy, of addressing questions of the most disgusting nature to their penitents at confession. We have already seen that the Church required a ' minute and circumstantial disclosure of all the circumstances of sin, without which,' says the council, ' the sacred physician cannot be qualified to apply the remedy.' But in how many cases might ignorance, negligence, or shame, lead the penitent to omit this condition? The Church, therefore, undertook to provide the remedy. Formulæ of interrogation were drawn up for the use of confessors, in which might be found all imaginable forms of human depravity; and these were addressed to the individuals who came for confession, in order that sins might be confessed with all the circumstances attending them. The frightful result of such a procedure may be more easily imagined than described. The knowledge of sin in its vilest and most loathful forms was communicated to individuals who were previously uninformed on such topics—and all but the vile and the debauched left the confessional with ideas of wickedness to which they were altogether strangers.

It appears that certain *formulæ* of interrogation intended for the use of priests were in existence long before the Council of the Lateran. The *Penitentiary* of Egbert, archbishop of York, in the 8th century, given in *Wilkins' Concilia*, may be mentioned as the earliest known. Another, belonging to the ninth age, may be seen in Morinus' well known work on this subject. It was not, however, till the 13th century that these works reached the climax of monstrous iniquity which they have since exhibited. That composed by Albert of Ratisbon stands foremost amongst these abominable productions. In his work, entitled a ' Commentary on the Fourth Book of Sentences,' he enters into the most gross and licentious details of the crimes against the seventh commandment; pleading as his excuse ' *the monstrous acknowledgments which must necessarily be heard in confession.*' Jean Benedicti, a Franciscan friar, published a book at Lyons in 1584, under the title of *La somme des Pechés, et la Remise d'iceaux; dediée à la Saint Vierge ;*—' a dedication,' says Count Lasteyrie, ' which would not be accepted in these days by a harlot of Paris or London.' He adds, ' the licentious manœuvres described by this monk and the picture he gives of them are of such lubricity, that it is impossible for us to give them in spite of our wish that the reader should be made acquainted with their excessive baseness.'[q] The celebrated work of Sanchez, *De Matrimonio*, appeared soon afterwards, in 1592. This is said to be the great storehouse

---

[q] History of Auricular Confession, by Count Lasteyrie. Translated from the French. 2 vols. 8vo. Lond. vol. i. p. 214.

from which subsequent casuists have drawn the details with which
their works are polluted. Those who have read it appear quite
at a loss for terms to express the exceeding turpitude of its pages;
yet this infamous book was dedicated to the Archbishop of Grenada, and approved of by ecclesiastical censorship even with extreme delight. ' *Legi, perlegi maxima cum voluptate,*' are the
words in which the licence is expressed. The author already
quoted mentions also another work of a very similar nature, published by a priest named Sœttler, and reprinted in 1840, in the
Seminary of Grenoble, by a professor of theology. It bears the
following title:—*Joannis Gaspari Sœttler in Sextum Decalogi
præceptum, &c.* 'We find,' he adds, 'on pages 17, 23, 28, and
37, cases of conscience so very disgusting upon such unheard-of
crimes, that we should not dare to mention them in any language.'[r] We will only further specify the theological treatise
of Peter Dens—the text book, as is said, in the Roman Catholic
colleges of Ireland. A large portion of the sixth and seventh volumes of this work is devoted to the subject of confession; and
the instructions given for the examination of the penitents, male
and female, are so disgusting that no profligate would venture to
translate even a fractional part of these pages before any decent
assembly. Were not the book in Latin, it would be in danger of
being seized by the police, as an immoral and indecent publication. It would be difficult to overrate the pernicious results
arising from this custom in the present day. In the words of a
recent French writer, ' priests, monks, and even bishops, have exposed, in works of morality and theology, designed for the instruction of seminarists, all the lewdness that the most licentious and
audacious casuists have imagined to guide young seminarists in
the practice of confession. It is impossible to feel too indignant
when we see these works are intended for the instruction of some
50,000 priests or monks, who may daily propagate in every part
of France ideas and practices of unparalleled depravity.'[s]

It must be admitted, then, that auricular confession as practised since the 13th century all over Papal Europe, is most demoralizing to society. By putting interrogations to the penitent,
the priest must necessarily communicate ideas of sin to which they
were altogether strangers.[t] Those who know best the corrupt
state of the heart, and have the deepest practical acquaintance
with human nature, will be best qualified to estimate the fearful
consequences of such a plan of procedure. One cannot but shudder
at the thought of modest and virtuous females having such ques-

---

[r] Hist. Auric. Conf. vol. i. p. 215.   [s] Ibid. vol. i. pref. p. xvii.
    [t] See the forms of confession in use in the middle ages in ' Popery, its Character
and its Crimes,' part i. chap. i. Second Edition. Partridge and Co., London, 1850.

tions addressed to them in confession as those contained in the volumes of Dens.

It is not merely the *knowledge* of vice in its most loathsome form which is thus communicated; but the *familiarity* with guilt, the destruction of all virgin purity which are the necessary results of confession. It is, indeed, marvellous to think how decent females can converse with persons of the opposite sex on such topics. But it will be admitted that the unavoidable result of such habits must be insensibly to destroy that modesty which is one of the safest preservatives of female virtue. 'Confession,' says the Catechism of the Council of Trent, ' contributes powerfully to the preservation of social order. Abolish sacramental confession, and that moment you deluge society with all sorts of secret crimes.' So far from this, the confessional is unquestionably a school of licentiousness, and proves the means of propagating amongst mankind ideas and practices of unheard of wickedness.

It should be remembered, too, that books—*devotional* books—for the use of the people contain, under the head of 'Questions on the Decalogue,' a perfect encyclopædia of lusts. In the London ' Times ' of November 26, 1850, we read a long extract of this kind from a book borrowed from a young lady, entitled ' The Catholic's Daily Companion,' published by R. Rockliff, Liverpool, 1845 ; but we cannot defile the pages of this Journal by transcribing it. Some editions of ' The Garden of the Soul,' a popular English book of devotion, contain the same. In other editions we have found it wanting.

Lastly, the sacrament of confession depraves society by holding out the strongest temptations to sin. It would hardly be believed by persons ignorant of the fact, that a priest, in the performance of a sacrament in which ' he represents the character and discharges the functions of Christ,'—should entice his female penitents to the commission of sin. But there are too evident proofs of the constant occurrence of the crime to allow it to be a matter of doubt. The marvellous combination of circumstances in which the clergy are placed amply account for the fearful fact. The unnatural and constrained celibacy in which the priests live—the open and intimate disclosures of the female penitent—the secret retirement of the confessional—and the superstitious reverence in which the clergy are held—all conspire to render this crime a not infrequent result of this *holy* sacrament. We must cease, therefore, to wonder at what otherwise would be incredible ; and regard the seduction of females, in Romish countries, as an almost inevitable consequence of that monstrous perversion of Christianity termed the ' Catholic Faith.'

Abundant evidence, and that of the most unexceptionable kind, may be adduced to prove this assertion. The celebrated Erasmus says, 'Penitents often fall into the hands of priests who under the pretence of confession commit acts which are not fit to be mentioned; they who ought to correct morals become the accomplices, the teachers, and disciples of debauchery. Would to God that my warnings were unfounded; and that there did not exist so many examples of these irregularities everywhere, of which I speak only in sorrow, and cannot mention without blushing.'[u] The famous casuist, Escobar, says, 'In these calamitous times we have frequently seen the sacred sanctuary, where the remission of sins is given, defiled, which ought to make us fear a signal vengeance of the Lord upon his ministers;' and, again, 'This enormous crime has spread to such an extent in these days, that every one ought to oppose it with all his might, and apply a fit remedy.'[v]

In the year 1556 Pope Paul IV. addressed a bull to the Inquisitors of Grenada, in Spain, in which he stated that he had heard that several priests had been guilty of the crime of seducing their female penitents, and called upon them to prosecute all those confessors whom the public voice accused of this detestable offence.

This bull of the Pope, from prudential motives, was never published. Its contents, however, were communicated privately to those engaged in receiving confessions; and they were enjoined to conduct themselves with greater propriety for the future. An inquiry was also instituted against those priests and monks who had incurred suspicion, and several notorious offenders were punished privately, for fear of occasioning scandal. 'The discoveries that were made,' says Llorente, 'proved to the Pope that the abuse in question was not confined to the kingdom of Grenada, and that there was an urgent necessity of subjecting all the other provinces of the kingdom to the same law. Accordingly, on the 16th of April, 1561, he addressed a bull to the grand Inquisitor Valdez, by which he authorized him to take proceedings against all the confessors in the kingdom and domains of Philip II. who had committed the crime of seduction, as if they had been guilty of heresy.' The measures taken on this occasion not appearing, it is supposed, sufficient to remedy the evil, Pius IV. sent a new bull in 1564, which was successively followed by several others, in order to extirpate an evil which had taken deep root, not only in Spain, but also throughout Christendom; since in one of these bulls we find the words: '*in illis Hispaniorum remotis, et a quibusvis Christiani orbis partibus.*'[x]

'An edict, published at Seville in 1563, gave rise to such a number of denunciations, that the recorders of the Holy Office were

---

[u] Erasmi Exomologia, p. 129, apud Lasteyrie.

[v] Escobar, Tract. de Confes. Solic. p. 1, col. 1.

[x] Llorente, Hist. Critic. de l'Inquisit. d'Esp. (Paris, 1818), quoted in 'Popery, its Character and its Crimes,' by W. Elfe Tayler, second edition, part i. chap. i.

no longer able to receive them, which obliged them to assign a term of thirty days to every female accuser to come forward a second time. As this postponement was followed by several others, it took no less than 120 days to register all the denunciations. But the Inquisitors, alarmed at the prodigious number of guilty persons, and the scandal which was occasioned, resolved to abandon that undertaking, and renounced the prosecutions of the delinquents. Indeed, there were in this vast crowd of females some very respectable persons, nay some of illustrious birth. Ashamed of all that had taken place, they used to disguise themselves and muffle up their heads, in order to repair to the Inquisitors, who occupied the castle of Triana, for fear of being met and recognized by their husbands. In spite of these precautions several were informed of what was going on; and this affair was near occasioning a great disturbance.'[y]

Several other bulls of the same nature were issued by subsequent Popes, with as little success. Gregory XVI. published one under the title ' *Universi Domini,*' in 1622.[z] Benedict XIV. confirmed the bull of Gregory, by issuing another in 1741. Another mandate was published in 1745 by the same Pontiff, repeating and confirming former enactments against this crime.[a]

The evil results of auricular confession, in leading to the seduction of females, have more extensively prevailed in convents, the privacy of which renders the crime of more easy commission and of more difficult detection. Clemangis, Doctor of Theology in Paris, in the fifteenth century, describes the nunneries of his time as ' execrable brothels of Venus, rather than sanctuaries of God; and houses of resort for filthy and lascivious gallants to satiate their lusts,' adding, ' so that now for a nun to take the veil is nothing less than to become a public prostitute.'[b] Erasmus says, that a Doctor of Theology had related to him, that he had heard a priest, a director of a convent of nuns, boasting that he had seduced two hundred virgins, and that this Doctor justified his own bad conduct by his example.[c]

To come down to later times, the horrible licentiousness which prevailed in the convent of St. Elizabeth de Louvieres, in France, in the seventeenth century, affords the most convincing evidence on this subject. The valuable work on auricular confession, which has been already quoted, contains the following extract from the confession of Elizabeth Bavant, one of the nuns of the convent :— ' I found,' says she, ' debauchery established in the convent. David, our confessor, was a horrible priest, and quite unworthy of

---

[y] Hist. of Auric. Conf. i. p. 237.   [z] Dens, tom. vi. De Cas. Res. No. 216.
[a] See Bullarium Bened. XIV., tom. i. p. 100, and tom. iii. p. 416.
[b] Apud Wolfium, Lect. Mem. i. p. 775.   [c] Erasmi Exomolog. p. 154.

so divine and holy a profession. He used to read to us "The Book of the Will of God," composed by a Capuchin friar, which then served for our particular and only rule in the establishment; but he explained it in a strange manner, which was nevertheless approved of and followed by the matrons who governed us. This bad man and dangerous priest, under pretence of introducing perfect obedience, which ought to extend even to what is most repugnant to nature, introduced abominable practices, by which God has been dishonoured and insulted in an extraordinary manner. Can I dare even to name them? He used to say that we ought to exterminate sin by sin—to return to innocency, and resemble our first parents, who were not ashamed of their nudity. Under this language what impurities and disgusting actions did they not cause to be committed? Those nuns were considered the most holy, perfect, and virtuous, who stripped, and danced, or appeared in the choir and went to the garden in that state. This is not all—they accustomed us to do what I dare not relate; to commit the most horrible and infamous sins, which my confessor told me were spoken of by St. Paul, in his Epistle to the Romans, as instances of the most excessive immorality. I have seen them profaning the most holy sacrament of the altar, which was at the disposal of the nuns. What penance must they have recourse to in order to obtain pardon for so many and so horrible crimes!'

A great deal more to the same purport, together with the particulars of the trial of Elizabeth Bavant, for whose destruction the nuns and confessors leagued together, may be seen in the work of Count Lasteyrie. 'Never,' says the author, 'did a prosecution present scenes in which ignorance, superstition, and immorality were more grossly conspicuous than that brought against the convent of St. Elizabeth de Louvieres, but principally against Elizabeth Bavant, a victim alike of the directors who had been inflicted on her, and of the unchaste nuns of that convent. We find in this trial a series of facts, denunciations, and testimony, in which abominable priests are the chief performers, and a young pious, virtuous maiden is corrupted and becomes the victim of guilt. Corruption of the confessors; credulous bigotry on the part of the accused; barbarous prejudices of the judges, and of the civil and religious authorities; such were the component parts of this affair. All these iniquities were, as we shall see, the result of sacerdotal confession in a house where fifty nuns were secluded.'[d]

The excessive depravity which long prevailed in the convents of Tuscany, and which was the subject of official investigation in the eighteenth century, is too important to be passed by. It appears that for more than a century and a half previous to the French

---

[d] Hist. of Auric. Conf., vol. ii. p. 54.

Revolution, the vicious conduct of the nuns had been the cause of much scandal. In the year 1642 a petition was addressed to the Grand Duke of Tuscany, signed by one hundred and ninety-four individuals in Pistoia, entreating that a remedy might speedily be applied to the gross indecencies of which the monks were guilty in two of the convents of that place. But towards the close of the eighteenth century the frightful depravity committed in those nunneries became the subject of official investigation. Two of the nuns of the convent of St. Catharine of Pistoia denounced the authors of these iniquities, and entreated him to save them from the execrable principles professed by the Dominican monks, their directors. The Grand Duke immediately instituted an inquiry into the matter. He caused all the nuns to be interrogated by the prefect of the police, and forbade the monks, on pain of imprisonment, to approach the convents.

In the petition addressed to Leopold by the nuns we find the following statements :—'The monks often come to meet us at the side of the sacristy, of which almost all have the keys ; and there is an iron grating sufficiently large, where they conduct themselves in the most shameless manner. If, besides, they find an opportunity of entering the convent under any pretence, they come and remain alone in the chambers of such as are devoted to them. All of them, even the provincials, are of the same stamp. They give utterance to brutal maxims which imply the utter absence of all moral feeling. They are incessantly repeating that we are too happy in being able to satisfy all our inclinations. They say that after we have left the world everything is ended with us ; and that even the writings of St. Paul ought to serve to enlighten us. All sorts of indecencies are committed in the parlour.'

The horrid licentiousness prevailing in this convent is further established by the letters which the Prioress, named Peroccini, wrote to the Rector of the Episcopal Academy in Pistoia. 'To answer the questions,' says she, 'which you ask me, I should require much time and an excellent memory to remember the many things which have happened during the five and twenty years that I have spent among monks, and all those things also which I have heard related about them. I shall not speak of friars who are no more. As to the rest, whose conduct is blameable, there are more than you imagine ; among others (here nine are named.) But why enumerate any more? Excepting three or four friars among so many monks, whether living or dead, whom I have known, there is not one who is not of the same stamp. They all profess the same maxims, and their conduct is the same ; their intercourse with the nuns of the utmost familiarity.[e] When

---

[e] Si tratta con le monache con piu confidenza che se fossere amogliati.

the monks come to visit a sick person, it is the custom to sup with the nuns, to sing, dance, and play with them, and they sleep in the convent. Their maxim is that God has forbidden hatred, but not love. I affirm that they have the art of corrupting not only the young and innocent, but even the most circumspect and knowing; and without a miracle no one can frequent their company without at length yielding to this species of diabolical temptation.'

From a letter published in Leopold's correspondence, it appears that the Dominican friars were not the only corrupters of nuns. A nun of Castiglione Fiorentino thus addressed the Grand Duke :— 'Our convent is under the direction of the Franciscan friars, or Minor Observatines, and consequently in the greatest laxity, and in extreme immorality. . . . . The nuns are obliged to allow such enormous sins to be committed if they do not wish to be shut up for life under any pretence. The Commissioner is invited to the convent and goes with the young nuns into their chamber, with one of them at a time, or with two at most, if they are such as may be trusted, and then he locks himself in. . . . . The monks who are intimate with the nuns make them bolder than lackeys.'

The above details are all taken from the well-known work of M. de Potter, entitled 'Vie de Scipion de Ricci, Evêque de Pistoie et Prato' (Bruxelles, 1825). It should be added that the iniquities here exposed prevailed not only in the convents of Pistoia and Prato, but also in those of Florence, Pisa, Sienna, Perugia, Faenza, and others.

A vast number of other instances of the seduction of females in confession, some of the most horrible kind, may be found in a work already often quoted.[f] With reference to the present time, this author makes the following observations :—'This species of wickedness, as I have had opportunity of convincing myself, from information derived from different journeys in Italy and Spain, is less uncommon than is supposed, especially in countries where the priests, and principally the monks, have much influence and enjoy the consideration of the people. Most of the seductions that take place in what is called the tribunal of penitence remain unknown to the public, even when denunciations, avowals, or still more positive results, exhibit proofs either to families or to the superior ecclesiastics, whether regular or secular. For, on the one hand, the honour of the persons compromised, and that of their parents, and on the other the interests of the Church, and even an ill-understood reserve, which civil authority thinks proper to use on these occasions, as well as the impunity usually attached to so great a crime, are so many causes that prevent it from coming to the knowledge of the public.'

---

[f] Hist. Auric. Conf., vol. ii. pp. 1–106.

The crime *solicitatio mulieris* is said to be not of rare occurrence in Ireland in the present day, and would be very common but for the dread of detection.[g] It has been found necessary to publish the most stringent laws in that country for its prevention. The following extract we have taken from the *Diocesan Laws*, &c., reprinted a few years ago by the Rev. Mr. M'Ghee :—'It must be confessed how great is the burden and danger of those who undertake so formidable an office, since experience proves that this remedy, so salutary to the fallen, is sometimes so perverted by the ignorance and negligence of confessors, that this fountain of grace is turned into an occasion of perdition. We fear that there is no time in which the melancholy saying of St. Thomas of Villanova is not fulfilled in some confessors, that they send themselves and sinners down to hell.' In the list of reserved cases we have the following :—

'The priest who shall attempt to absolve his accomplice in the foul sin against the sixth commandment incurs, ipso facto, the greater excommunication reserved to the Pope, and such absolution is altogether null and void, except in the article of death, and even then unless no other confessor can be had.

'The priest who shall attempt to solicit or entice to the commission of dishonourable and base sins, either by words, or signs, or nods, or touch, or by writing, then or afterwards to be read by any penitent, whatsoever person she be, either in the act of sacramental confession, or before or immediately after confession, or by the occasion or pretext of confession, or even without the occasion of confession, in the confessional or in any other place destined or chosen to hear confessions, with the pretence of hearing confessions there, or who shall have held with presumptuous audacity any unlawful or dishonourable conversation or intercourse with them, is ordered in the bull of Benedict XIV., entitled *Sacramentum penitentiæ*, to be suspended for ever, and the same Benedict XIV. decrees that the priest so soliciting shall be for ever incapable of celebrating mass.'[h]

We have thus considered the fearful effects of the practice of confession in corrupting the morals of the people, and occasioning in very many instances the most flagitious and horrible crimes. It now remains to bring before the reader the demoralizing influence of the ABSOLUTION from sin, which is granted to penitents at the close of their confession by the power of the keys.

Christianity reveals to sinful man the great doctrine of forgiveness of sin—a full, free, and perfect absolution from all sin, through the blood of the Lamb. It is, however, universally connected

[g] O'Croly's Inquiry, p. 153.
[h] Quoted in 'Popery, its Character and its Crimes,' part i. chap. i.

with a change of heart, a reformation of life. Popery on the contrary teaches the doctrine of absolution from sin by the priest, but requires no change of heart or life ; and hence, whilst the one pardon—that which God gives—sanctifies and saves, the pardon which man professes to bestow corrupts and curses the soul.

Ever since the twelfth century, as we have already seen, auricular confession has been compulsory upon all persons, without exception. The great majority of individuals who attend at the confessional must, of course, in the present state of the world, uniformly consist of unconverted persons, 'afar off from God by wicked works.' The unavoidable result of giving to such persons what they believe to be the absolute remission of all their sins, it is easy to see, will be to encourage them to continue in sin under the full belief of again obtaining similar forgiveness.

It is granted that if true contrition of heart were required, and absolution were never pronounced where any doubt existed as to the possession of this grace, such consequences would not follow. But it is notorious that the Church of Rome does not require this godly sorrow for sin from her penitents. Indeed her doctrines on this subject are so monstrous that the Council of Trent declares that no hatred of sin, no love to God, is necessary. *Attrition*, proceeding either from consideration of the turpitude of sin, or *from the fear of hell*, if it excludes the present will of sinning, and be accompanied with the hope of pardon, is sufficient with the sacrament of penance. Before the Council of Trent, the attrition necessary to obtain the grace of God in the sacrament of penance was commonly described by divines as not altogether separated from at least some slender feeble initial love of God. The Dominicans, Vittoria and Soto, first taught that *servile attrition*, that which arises *solely from the fear of hell*, provided the penitent believes it to be contrition, is sufficient. This opinion was followed by Melchior Canus, who extended it even to servile attrition, when known by the party to be such ; that is, to be not true contrition. And Melchior Canus's judgment was no sooner made public than it spread through all the public schools, and was eagerly adopted by a great majority of divines, and those of the highest reputation ; some of the wiser and more learned among them subscribed to this opinion at first with great caution ; but their successors, confident in the numbers of those who maintain it, have not only affirmed it without any doubt or limitation, but have not scrupled to brand the contrary opinion *with a formal censure as* '*utterly improbable, dangerous, and implicitly and virtually proscribed by the Council of Trent.*'[i]

In addition to the above testimony, a decree of Alexander

---

[i] Benedict XIV., quoted by Delahogue, Pœn., p. 101.

VII., dated 5th May, 1667, declares ' that the more common opinion is, that which denies the necessity of any love of God in attrition to obtain the grace of God in the sacrament of penance,' and forbids any one to speak in contemptuous or offensive terms respecting it. In the celebrated bull ' Unigenitus,' the Pope condemned sixteen propositions, which were in favour of, or affirmed the necessity of the love of God. Still more recently, a Synod, held in the early part of the present century at Dublin, describes the qualifications for absolution in such terms as totally excluded the necessity of our love to God. Lastly, during the examination of Romish bishops and clergy, which took place in the House of Commons, on the occasion of the passing of the Catholic Emancipation Bill, in 1829, Mr. Phelan referred to *attrition* as a substitute for contrition, and described attrition as ' a sorrow for sin, arising merely out of a consideration of the punishment which may be annexed to it; and this feeling,' says he, ' is at present admitted by the highest authority in the Church of Rome as ENTITLING TO ABSOLUTION.'[k]

The obvious result of absolution then upon a superstitious people is to remove that dread of future punishment which constitutes the sole preventive or check to wickedness in the case of ungodly men, and thus encourage the continuance in sin.

It is absurdly pretended by Romish theologians, that the penances imposed upon sinners by the confessors ' tend powerfully to preserve and restrain penitents from sin, and render them more cautious and watchful in future.'[m] None, however, who have any knowledge of what these boasted penances consist in, will be disposed to give any credit to such a statement. If the ancient system of canonical penance which prevailed in the Church during the fifth and some subsequent centuries were still in use, such an assertion would carry with it some appearance of truth; but as Jeremy Taylor quaintly observes, ' the penances are reduced from the ancient canonical penances to private and arbitrary, from years to hours, from great severity to gentleness and flattery, from fasting and public shame to the saying over their beads, from cordial to ritual, from smart to money, from heartiness and earnestness to pageantry and theatrical images of penance; and if some confessors happen to be severe there are ways enough to be eased.'[n]   K. L.

---

[k] Commons, p. 491.   [m] Catechism. Conc. Trid.
[n] ' Dissuasive from Popery,' quoted in ' Popery, its Character and its Crimes.' Second edition. Partridge & Co., London, 1850.

HEBREW LITERATURE.

THE victories of Jena and Auerstädt, on the 14th of October, 1806, were succeeded on the 17th by the capture of Halle. The suspension of its University and the dispersion of its students almost immediately followed. Amongst the terrified fugitives, whose flight was hastened by the burning of Nordhausen and other towns by the enemy, were two penniless youths, who had but recently joined the University. Dejected and on foot they sought for safety in the direction of Gottingen, and hurried on, impelled by their fears, until one of them sunk down from utter exhaustion, and could proceed no farther. In this destitute condition they were fortunate enough to excite the sympathies and receive the aid of a youthful stranger, who was himself returning from his native town, then in flames, to his duties in the University of Gottingen. That stranger was Gesenius—the youths Neander and Neumann.[a]

How strangely at times does the calm determination of the student contrast with the excitement and turmoil of the world around! The pulpits of London were resounding with the 'crowning mercy' of Worcester while Walton was projecting his Polyglot. Amid the din and bloodshed of the seven-years' war, the modern German school of philology struggled into existence. So, while Napoleon was scattering dismay and ruin around him, and destroying the Prussian power, Gesenius was addressing himself to his self-imposed and life-long task of elevating the study of Hebrew from the disrepute and neglect into which it had been suffered to fall. Who would have thought, at that time of all-absorbing terror, that a great and vastly important movement was lying, in recently-formed design, in that youthful Professor's breast?—Yet so it was.

Gesenius, but twenty years of age, had just become *Magister legens* and *Repetent* in the University of Gottingen. Hebrew learning was then at a very low ebb in Germany. Michaelis, who had been Oriental Professor in the University of Gottingen from 1745 to 1791, had disgusted very many by his low wit and tedious discussions;[b] while Vater, who at the time was Professor at Halle (1800-1809), was lecturing on Genesis to a class of but seven. Dissatisfied with the little interest taken in his favourite

---

[a] Chamisso's Leben, i. ap.—Bibliotheca Sacra (American) for May, 1847.

[b] See Biographical sketch appended to Heeren's Historical Researches, vol. i. p. xi.

study, and with the manner in which Hebrew grammar[c] and lexi-cography were then treated, Gesenius formed the determination of giving an impulse and direction to the pursuit of Hebrew lite-rature, and of trying to bring those principles of philology to bear upon it which Heyne, Wolf, Buttmann, and Hermann had so successfully introduced into classical studies.

After a residence of three years at Gottingen, Gesenius was transferred to the Gymnasium of Heiligenstadt, and in the fol-lowing year to the University of Halle, of which he continued until his death the brightest ornament.

No sooner had he settled at Halle than he commenced putting into execution the design he had formed, by publishing the re-sults of his studies. His labours there, during a period of thirty-two years, are themselves, in some degree, the history of that extraordinary impulse which he communicated to the study of Hebrew, and must be known, in order to ascertain how well he redeemed the pledge of earlier years, and how nobly the students of Germany responded to his call, and caught his enthusiasm. We think it desirable, in order that this important movement may be better understood amongst us, to give a list of his Hebrew publications, with their dates. This list will speak for itself:—

1810. Hebräisch-deutsches Handwörterbuch des Alten Testaments. Vol. 1. Published the first year of the author's residence at Halle, at the age of 24.

1812. ——————— Vol. 2. The whole work was translated by Leo and published at Cambridge in 2 vols. 4to., 1825.

1813. Hebräische Grammatik. First edition.

1814. ——————— Second Edition.

„ Hebräisches Lesebuch. First Edition.

1815. Neues Hebräisch-deutsches Handwörterbuch, einer für Schulen umgearbeiteter Auszug. An edition of 3000. This work was translated by T. W. Gibbs, and published at Andover, United States, afterwards republished in this country by Duncan, Paternoster Row.

„ Geschichte der Hebräischen Sprache und Schrift.

1816. Hebräische Grammatik. Third Edition.

1817. Lehrgebäude der Hebräischen Sprache. A vast repository of the phenomena of the language which did not, however, satisfy its author in after years.

„ Hebräisches Lesebuch. Second Edition.

1818. Hebräische Grammatik. Fourth Edition.

1820. Der Prophet Jesaia; übersetzt und mit einem Commentar beg-leitet. The first part appeared in 1820; the others in 1821.

„ Hebräische Grammatik. Fifth Edition.

---

[c] The Grammars of Dauz and Vater were in most repute at the time. Of these authors the former treated the subject very arbitrarily, while the latter followed no definite plan, and was often led astray by false views.

1821. Hebräisches Lesebuch. Third Edition.
1822. Hebräische Grammatik. Sixth Edition.
1823. Hebräisches und Chaldäisches Handwörterbuch über das A. T. An edition of 3000. With this improved edition of his Manual appeared Gesenius's Essay on the Sources of Hebrew Philology and Lexicography. It was translated for the American Biblical Repository, iii. 1-44.
1824. Hebräische Grammatik. Seventh Edition.
  ,, Hebräisches Lesebuch. Fourth Edition.
1825. Gesenii (G.) et Hoffmanni Rudimenta Orientalia. Part I. Dialectus Aramaos cum Hebræa complectens.
1826. Hebräische Grammatik. Eighth Edition.
1828. Hebräisches und Chald. Handwörterbuch über das A. T. An edition of 3000.
  ,, Hebräisches Lesebuch. Fifth Edition.
  ,, Hebräische Grammatik. Ninth Edition.
  ,, Genesis, Hebraicè ad opt. exemp. accuratiss. expressus.
1829. Thesaurus Philologicus, &c. First Fasciculus. On this work, which is a storehouse of Hebrew archæology and geography, as well as of philology, Gesenius wished to rest his claims as a Hebrew scholar.
  ,, Jesaia der Prophet. The translation of Isaiah taken from his great work on that prophet, published 1820-21.
  ,, Job, Hebraice ad opt. exemp. accurat. expressus.
1831. Hebräische Grammatik. Tenth Edition. The delay between the publication of the ninth and tenth editions was caused by the influence of Ewald's grammar. The improvements in the tenth edition are more valuable and much greater than those made in any previous edition.
1833. Lexicon Manuale Hebraicum et Chald. in Vet. Test. libros. This was compiled by Gesenius from his third German edition with many improvements and additions. Translated by Dr. Robinson and published in Boston, 1836.
1834. Hebräische Grammatik. Eleventh edition. The first edition translated into English by Dr. Conant, 1839, reprinted in London, 1840.
  ,, Hebräisches und Chald. Handwörterbuch über das A. T. An edition of 3000.
  ,, Hebräisches Lesebuch. Sixth edition.
1835. Thesaurus Philologicus, &c. Second fasciculus.
1839. Hebräische Grammatik. Twelfth edition. The long interval between this publication and the last is accounted for by the appearance of the author's inestimable work, 'Scripturæ Linguæque Phœniciæ Monumenta quotquot supersunt,' 2 vols. 4to. 1837.
  ,, Thesaurus Philologicus, &c. Third fasc.
1840. ——————————— Fourth fasc.
1842. ——————————— Fifth fasc.
  ,, Hebräische Grammatik. Thirteenth edition.

This extraordinary call for grammars and lexicons by thousands, after an almost utter neglect of Hebrew study, sufficiently proves that Gesenius had anticipated one of the demands of the age, and had admirably met it.

While thus indefatigably engaged in the publication of Hebrew works, Gesenius was not unmindful of the claims of cognate tongues. His treatise on the Maltese dialect, his first production, was published in 1810. In 1815 appeared his 'De Pentateuchi Samaritani Origine, Indole, et Auctoritate.' This was followed, seven years after, by the treatise 'De Samaritanorum Theologia ex fontibus ineditis;' and two years after that by the 'Carmina Samaritana, &c.' In 1834 he printed his work on Bar Ali and Bar Bahlul. But of all his labours in this direction, those connected with the Punic language presented to him the greatest attraction. In 1825 and 1835 he published works on this dialect, which were however superseded by his noble and elaborate production, 'Scripturæ Linguæque Phœniciæ Monumenta quotquot supersunt,' which was given to the world in 1837. In addition to these labours, Gesenius was a frequent contributor to the 'Literatur-Zeitung'[d] and other periodicals; and wrote many of the most admirable articles in Ersch and Gruber's Encyclopædia.[e]

Nor was this indefatigable scholar content with facilitating, by his publications, the acquisition of Hebrew, he was, by his daily lectures and classes, inspiring thousands of eager and admiring students with his own enthusiasm. His lecture-room was thronged. Five hundred students at a time listened, with almost breathless attention, to the lucid and animated statements of their favourite lecturer, and to that fluency of utterance by which he gave to a dead language the instinct of a living, spoken tongue. Every important remark and felicitous explanation was treasured up by them in their note-books—those indispensable companions of German students—as of great and permanent value, while the necessity for thorough research and impartial investigation was daily urged upon them, no less by the example than the words of the celebrated Hebraist. Students from all parts of the Continent, and even from America, attracted by his fame, sat at his feet; and Halle became the acknowledged seat of Hebrew learning.

While he lived, Gesenius continued to be the most popular lecturer in Germany, and the honoured instructor of thousands. When he died, his country mourned, and wondered where a fit

---

[d] See his excellent critical examination of the Liber Adami of the Zabians, in the Literatur-Zeitung for 1817, Nos. 48-51.

[e] For instance, the articles, 'Arabische Sprache,' 'Amharische Sprache,' 'Ethiopische Sprache und Literatur.'

successor could be found. Would that we could speak as favourably respecting the religious views of this learned man, and the influence which he, as a theological professor, exerted on the minds of those who were preparing for the solemn duties of the Christian ministry. Alas! in this respect the pure gold becomes dim indeed.

In surveying the whole course of Gesenius, comparing his various works, and estimating the influence he exerted on the study of Hebrew, a few thoughts suggest themselves. He has himself informed us that two things are required of those who attempt to exhibit the grammar of an ancient language. First, a correct observation and systematic arrangement of all the phenomena of the language; secondly, the explanation of these phenomena, partly by comparing them with one another, and with analogous appearances in the cognate tongues, partly from the general analogy and philosophy of language. The first is the *historic*, the second the *philosophical* element in grammar. Now it is evident that the former is, in order of time and succession, prior to the latter. The *facts* of a language must be sufficiently known, and its study be made sufficiently attractive, before the materials for comparison and general analogy are at hand. For the discharge of this duty, Gesenius was pre-eminently qualified. The bent of his mind was towards the historical in language. His favourite pursuits were palæography and lexicography. His great excellence lay in his unwearied collection of facts, the admirable method by which they were arranged, and the clearness with which they were stated. This was his high vocation, one especially needed at the restoration of Hebrew learning, and nobly did he discharge his self-imposed duties. He was the man for the thing at the time.

Yet these qualifications, admirable as they were, would not alone have enabled Gesenius to maintain the ascendancy he had gained, or to direct the progress he had originated. So rapid was the advance of the study during his residence at Halle, that he would have been left far behind the movement he had commenced had he not been able, by comprehensiveness of mind, untiring efforts, and impartial examination, to maintain his position. 'Unwearied personal investigation,' said he, 'and impartial examination of the researches of others; the grateful admission and adoption of every real advance and illustration of science; but also a manly foresight and caution, which does not with eager levity adopt every novelty thrown out in haste and from love of innovation: all these must go hand in hand wherever scientific truth is to be successfully promoted.' Well did he prove that this language was sincere. He never refused to acknowledge the labours of others, however much and bitterly they opposed him. A comparison of his latest works with his first publications will go far to prove that, however valuable the suggestions he derived from others, the improvements he himself made on his earlier works were still more so. Indeed, the rapid progress of Hebrew study may be best learned from his own publications,[f] and from the well-known dissatisfaction with which he regarded his first efforts. He was the first, with any success, to point out the lexical connection between the Sanscrit and the Hebrew, and to lead the way to a more thorough investigation of Hebrew roots. His Grammar, revised by his pupil Roëdiger, still continues to be the favourite school Grammar in Germany; and his Lexicons, while they maintain their popularity, have, by their careful research and logical treatment, been the models by which Passow and Freund have illustrated the languages of Greece and Rome.

While Gesenius was thus giving importance to Hebrew literature, and facilitating its acquisition, the study of the Indo-European languages had been making rapid advances. Buttmann, Matthiæ, Thiersch, Zumpt, Bopp, Humboldt, Rosen, Schlegel, and Grimm, had been striving for higher aims and more sound results. Grammar was no longer a mere collection of phenomena, but a science demanding and deserving philosophical investigation and analysis. The advancement in classical philology necessarily brought with it a desire that Oriental literature might share in the benefits thus largely enjoyed and highly prized. This wish, as far as Hebrew was concerned, was strengthened by the improvements introduced into the study of Arabic by Rosen, Kosegarten, and especially De Sacy; and into that of Ethiopic by Hupfeld. The honour of having, to any considerable extent, satisfied these new demands, belongs undoubtedly to Ewald.

This distinguished scholar was, at the time when he published his 'Kritische Grammatik der Hebräischen Sprache ausführlich bearbeitet,' Professor in the University of Gottingen—the same University in which Gesenius had commenced his learned labours. Thirteen years after the latter scholar had published the first edition of his Grammar, Ewald's work was printed, 'from the appearance of which,' says Nordheimer, 'dates the commencement of a new and important era in Shemitish philology.' Such was the space of time, and no more, between the first and second epochs of Hebrew study. This great work of Ewald's was followed, in 1828, by his 'Gram. der Heb. Sprache in vollst. Kürze;' and in 1835 by the 'Gram. der Heb. Spr. des A. T.;' and in 1844 by the 'Ausführliches Lehrbuch der Hebräischen Sprache.' His

---

[f] How great is the difference, for instance, between the first fasciculus of his 'Thesaurus' and the last! What an advance *he* had made within thirteen years!

smaller work, ' Hebräische Sprachlehre für Anfänger,' appeared in 1842. In all these Grammars the historico-genetic method of Grimm and Bopp has been followed with brilliant success. Basing his investigations on the philosophical views of language in general, he has elucidated some of the deepest obscurities of Hebrew grammar, and raised the study to an equality with that of the Indo-European tongues. ' I myself,' he says, ' may only have the merit of the first impulse to improvement, if even that may be called a merit, since the idea of an improvement in this science is less owing to me than to the claims of our time ; and this idea has perhaps only been awakened somewhat sooner and more vividly in me.'

Applying the doctrine of sounds to the language, Ewald has eminently succeeded in giving a life-like character to this ancient tongue. In treating on the accents, his bold and keen spirit of research has led to most valuable results, and enabled him to show the ' beautiful harmony between the accentuation and the syntax.' His sections on ' nominal stems ' and ' verbal flexion ' are invaluable, while his treatment of the syntax is such as scarcely to leave a difficulty untouched. ' The masterly syntax of Ewald,' writes Prof. Stuart in his last work,[g] ' in regard to the most obscure and difficult points of the Hebrew language, affords peculiar and, in general, adequate aid—aid which can scarcely be found to such an extent in any other work of this nature. I acknowledge myself indebted to him for illustrations of some points elsewhere either overlooked or imperfectly exhibited. There is scarcely an anomaly in the Hebrew Scriptures on which he has not touched, and not only so, but adduced illustration and confirmation of his method of solving it.'

Ewald's elucidation of the language is not, however, confined to his grammatical works. The researches necessarily required for his ' Geschichte des Volkes Israel ' have enabled him to supply much interesting information respecting the history of the language, and the preparation of his Commentary, ' Die poetischen Bücher des alten Bundes,' has led him to consider at length the nature of Hebrew poetry.

The influence which this eminent scholar has exerted has been very great, and this influence is on the increase. Scarcely any German commentaries on the books of the Old Testament are published which have not numerous references to his various works. Indeed, in some of the most recent, Ewald's last grammar is almost exclusively cited, and this is the case not only in the Commentaries of his pupil and admirer Hitzig, it is also

---

[g] Commentary on the Book of Proverbs, p. 4.

characteristic of the latest works of Heiligstedt, Keil, Thenius, and others. The views of Ewald on the Hebrew tenses have become very generally received. Roëdiger has adopted them in his editions of Gesenius' Hebrew Grammar, so has Professor Stuart.[h]

Yet, although esteeming Ewald's efforts so highly, his insatiable thirst after novelty, his determination to ignore the opinions of previous grammarians, and his obscure and involved style, so obscure that Delitzsch says respecting it, 'you must toil as though you were reading the Parmenides of Plato,'[i] render his grammars essentially unfit for elementary purposes. They are books for the student and the scholar, not for the beginner. The facts of the language should be learned from Gesenius, the philosophy from Ewald.

While Ewald, the uncompromising and sometimes bitter opponent of Gesenius, was thus prosecuting his researches and publishing his works, Hupfeld, a pupil, and, subsequently, the successor of the great Halle Hebraist, was preparing a new Hebrew Grammar, 'which,' says Tholuck, 'must surpass that of Ewald in the fundamental character of its researches.' As early as 1825, the year after the seventh edition of the Grammar of Gesenius appeared, and three years before Ewald's first Grammar was published, Hupfeld printed his first work, 'Exercitationes Æthiopicæ,' in which he presented to the world his researches into the doctrine of sounds, and well illustrated the quadriliteral and quinquiliteral forms in Hebrew from Ethiopic sources. His investigations on sounds were afterwards more thoroughly carried out, and his views more fully unfolded in his admirable essay, 'Von der Natur und den Arten der Sprachlaute,'[k] to which both Gesenius and Ewald have honourably expressed their great indebtedness. Hupfeld's treatise, 'System der semitischen Demonstrativbildung und der damit zusammenhängenden Pronominal- und Partikelnbildung,'[m] has thrown much light on the older formation of the language. Indeed all the writings of this eminent scholar are of the greatest value to the student of Hebrew.

---

[h] On the Hebrew tenses many excellent articles have recently appeared on the Continent. Krook has written one, 'De formis Futuri linguarum Hebraeae et Arabicae. Lund. 1841.' The best is perhaps by Dietrich, in his 'Abhandlungen zur hebräischen Grammatik. 1846.' It is styled, 'Ueber den Character des hebräischen Futurum,' pp. 93-192, and will well repay perusal.

[i] 'Ewaldus tantopere philosophatur, ut, cum grammaticam ejus criticam legis, saepe quasi per daedaleos labyrinthos corde trepidans rapiare; stylus ejus multi sudoris est, majoris etiam ejus inquisitio. Sudandum est tibi, ac si Parmenidem Platonis legas.' Jesurun, p. 31.

[k] Published in Jahn's Jahrbuch der Phil. und Päd., 1829. Translated for the American Bib. Sac., 1851.

[m] In Zeitschrift für die Kunde des Morgenlandes, bd. ii. 124, 427.

Would that they were not in a measure lost to us in the periodical
literature of Germany! Distinguished as they are for profound
erudition, they are not less marked by a careful avoidance of
extreme views, and by an elaborateness of scholarlike finish. We
cannot forbear referring to some of these articles not already
mentioned above—to his admirable paper in the 'Stud. und Kritiken' for 1830, his valuable critique on Ewald's Grammar in the
Hermes, xxx. 1, s. 11, 12, and his essay, 'Uber die hebr. Laut-
system,' in the Hermes, xxxi. 1, s. 10-12, 15, 16. His treatise,
'De emendanda ratione Lexicographiæ Semiticæ,' published 1827,
is worthy of more than a passing reference. In this work Hupfeld rejected the doctrine of primitive triliteral roots, and maintained that they originally consisted of fewer elements increased
by prosthesis, epenthesis, and paragoge. The last work issued by
Hupfeld is a fragmentary one on the language, entitled 'Aus-
führliche Hebräische Grammatik,' 1841, containing eighty pages
printed many years ago, and forty-eight additional pages. The
first part is taken up with the history and literature of the language, the second contains the unfinished researches of the author
on the accent system. Alas! that the ill health and fastidious-
ness of this learned man do not permit us to hope that his task
will ever be completed. He contemplates, he tells us in a letter
written to a friend, 1847, continuing his larger Grammar, but as
he is now preparing a smaller Grammar, and thinks of collecting
his detached pieces, those who know him will almost cease to
cherish hope.

Shortly after the publication of Ewald's Critical Grammar, the
increasing attention paid to philology led to so successful a comparison and classification of languages as to call for the formation
of a new science—that of Comparative Philology. Bopp, Pott,
and W. de Humboldt were the great leaders of this movement.
The connection between the so-called Semitish tongues had been,
at least to some extent, long known, and valuable aid in the
study of Hebrew had been afforded by means of the cognate
dialects. The union between the Indo-Germanic languages was
a discovery of later years. It could not but be that the impulse
given to the study of these two families of languages should lead
to the desire to inquire into their relationship. The result was
that the Semitish family was no longer found to occupy an isolated
position, but was connected with the other great families of
tongues, and with them forms the great object of comparative philology. It was beginning to be felt 'that,' to use the language
of W. de Humboldt, 'the true solution of the contrast of stability
and fluctuation, which is found in language, lies in the unity of
human nature.' The question, however, still remained and it is

not answered yet—what is the connection between the Semitish and Indo-Germanic families?

Gesenius, who in his Latin Manual, 1833, was the first to deduce lexical analogies from the Indo-Germanic tongues, asserted at the same time that the connection between the languages was but remote. Roëdiger, the pupil of Gesenius and the editor of his Grammar, is still more decided. He says, that though a remote relationship exists between these families, which renders comparison valuable for lexicography, they 'do not stand in a sisterly or any close relationship to each other.'

Other scholars have been induced to think differently. In 1834 Lepsius[n] traced some striking resemblances between the Hebrew and the Sanscrit, and the year after, in letters to Chev. Bunsen, proved the remarkable agreement between the numerals in Coptic, Semitic, and Indo-Germanic, and announced that his discovery of the meaning of the ancient numeral roots had placed the whole cycle of Semitic and Indo-Germanic languages 'in a very remarkable harmony with one another.' Three years later Nordheimer, in the preface to his excellent Hebrew Grammar, affirmed it to be one of the objects he had in view in treating of the Hebrew language 'to point out its surprisingly intimate connection, both lexicographical and grammatical, not only with the other Shemitish languages, but also with those of the Japhetish or Indo-European stock.' This object was still more steadily pursued by Fürst, who may be said to have founded the third school of Hebrew study. He, Delitzsch, Caspari, and others, while they style the school of Gesenius the *empiric,* and that of Ewald the *rational,* term their own the *historico-analytic,* making, as they do, equal use of the writings of the Rabbins, the philosophy of speech, and the comparison of languages. Cultivating with the utmost assiduity and success Talmudic learning, they at the same time boldly, and sometimes rashly as it appears to us, make the greatest use of the Sanscrit, claiming for it a close and sisterly relation to the Hebrew. Dr. Julius Fürst, the great leader of this movement, published his views as early as 1835, in his valuable work, 'Systema Linguæ Chaldaicæ,' defended them against the attacks of Ewald in the 'Charuze Peninim,' 1836, more fully unfolded them in his profoundly learned Hebrew Concordance, 1841, and is now perfecting them in his 'Hebräisches und Chaldäisches Handwörterbuch,' of which beautifully printed and learned work the second part is just issued from the press of Tauchnitz. Fürst boldly asserts that of the list of 375 Sanscrit roots given by Pott in the 'Etymologische Forschungen,' whose

---

[n] Paläographie als Mittel für die Sprachforschung, zunächst am Sanskrit nachgewiesen.' Berlin, 1834.

meaning is established beyond a doubt, there is not one which is
not also Shemitic. In defence of the same views, Delitzsch wrote
his 'Jesurun—Isagoge in Grammaticam et Lexicographiam Linguæ Hebraicæ contra S. Gesenium et H. Ewaldum,' 1838, in
which, after dwelling upon the history of Hebrew literature and
the use of tradition in philology, he, in the third book, treats of
the affinity between the two languages at considerable length,
tracing it not only in the roots of the respective tongues,[o] but also
in their grammatical flexion and nominal endings.

It was reserved, however, for Meier to theorize most daringly
in this direction. In his large work 'Hebräisches Wurzelwörter-
buch, 1845,' after finding fault with all preceding attempts at
comparison and derivation between the two classes of languages,
he propounds at length his own views. He asserts that the
simplest form of the verb in Hebrew in the perfect, has been
formed from monosyllabic roots by the *reduplication of the radical
syllable*, just as in Sanscrit, Gothic, Greek, and Latin. While
presenting this theory, which he evidently regards with the
greatest complacency, as about to change the whole aspect of
Shemitic philology ('Die ganze Art der semitischen Sprachver-
gleichung wird künftig eine wesentlich andere werden.' Pref. xx.),
he takes care to say that this augmentation of the simple root
takes place in the Shemitic languages, in a manner peculiar to
itself. He tells us that while it exhibits a *pre-reduplication*, like
the Indo-Germanic, it also very frequently displays a *post-redupli-
cation*, and that in order to avoid the repetition of the same letter,
both in the beginning and end of a word, it changes the redupli-
cated letter for one nearly allied to it. All this, Meier affirms,
gives rise to great variety in the development of stems, and in the
secondary signification of the verbal idea, since the same end is
thus accomplished which the Indo-Germanic languages attain by
prefixed prepositions. Thus, while he asserts that the final letter
of the monosyllabic root gives the primary signification to the
word, those ending with a *dental or lingual* giving the idea of
separating, splitting; those with a *labial*, that of drawing together,
fitting, joining; and those with a *guttural*, that of being dense
or firm—the secondary idea is conveyed by the re-duplicated letter.
For instance, while בטח‎, בטל‎, and בטן‎ have the same fundamental
idea suggested by בט‎, their secondary meanings differ. The conclusion to which Meier comes, is that in general the fundamental
roots in the Shemitic, together with their simple, primary signifi-

---

[o] Boetticher (P.) has also thrown some light on the connection between the two
families in his works:—'Rudimenta Mythologiæ Semiticæ Supp., &c.' 1848, and
'Wurzelforschungen,' Halle, 1852, containing a comparison between the Coptic,
Semitic, and Sanscrit.

cation, occur also in the Indo-Germanic. He therefore regards the languages as nearly related, or twin-sisters.

Since the publication of this work, which has been fiercely attacked by the rival schools of Germany, the same author has defended his views against Ewald, and has endeavoured to trace the close affinity between the Indo-Germanic and Shemitic families, in the form and signification of their plurals.[p] Much learning distinguishes all the writings of this scholar,[q] but surely it is going too far in the direction of mere theory to affirm as he does that the number of primary roots in Hebrew is reducible to twenty-four![r] All that it seems at present safe to attest is, that there is a more intimate connection between the two families than has been supposed, and that the connection is especially to be sought in the comparison of monosyllabic roots.[s] Doubtless rich discoveries await us in this interesting field of research, but profound learning and a more earnest desire for truth than novelty must lead.

It is worthy of remark that while an almost exclusive reference to tradition distinguished the first students of Hebrew, and a peculiar fondness for the use of the cognate dialects marked the scholars of the Reformation and the Dutch philologians, all the sources of information are now open, and are alike and in union brought to bear upon the study in question. Thus while Ewald and his followers are with the greatest success pursuing the philosophical study of Hebrew, and while Winer, Hupfeld, Bernstein,[t] and Roediger are displaying the riches of the cognate dialects,

---

[p] 'Die Bildung und Bedeutung des Plural in den semitischen und indogermanischen Sprachen.' 1846.

[q] Meier has published several Commentaries, viz.: 'Kommentar zum Propheten Joel,' 1841; 'Schrift (die heil.) des A. T. übersetzt und erläutert,' parts 1 and 2; 'Der Prophet Jesaia erklärt, Erste Halfte,' 1852.

[r] Meier gives these roots in tabular form, pp. 747, 748. They are thus classified :—

I. *Roots with final guttural and palatal.*

תק   רק   לק   נק   פק

II. *Roots with a final dental and lingual.*

קט   רת   לת   נת   פת

III. *Roots with a final labial.*

קם   תם   רם   לם   נם

IV. *Roots with a final liquid.*

קר   קל   קן   תר   תל   חן   פר   פל   פן

[s] The deciphered cuneiform inscriptions of Behistun prove that the Babylonian roots are chiefly biliteral and allied to the Shemitic :— *Sib*, to dwell, יָשַׁב ; *rad*, to descend, יָרַד ; *duk*, to smite, דָּקַק ; *ten*, to give, נָתַן.

[t] We are glad to find that Bernstein, the most eminent Syrian scholar alive, is about to publish his long-expected Syriac Lexicon. Until that appears, 'Syriac lexicography is still,' to cite Bernstein's own words, as used in the Journal of the German Oriental Society for 1849, 'in its infancy.'

Zunz, Sachs, Lebrecht, Kämpf, Forkel, and Luzzatto[u] are placing their researches in ancient Hebrew literature within the reach of students, and Fürst, Delitzsch, and Lassen are throwing light upon the ancient Scriptures from the sacred tongue of the Hindoos. Especially active at present are the Hebrew scholars in Germany, in the direction of comparative philology and the early literature of the language. In proof of this assertion, we need but refer to Dietrich's 'Abhandlungen für Semitische Wortforschung,' and Sachs' 'Beiträge zur Sprach u. Alterthumsforschung,' 1852, to the admirable works of Luzzatto, Zunz,[v] and Fürst on Jewish literature, and to the carefully edited Rabbinic treatises which have been recently published.[w] A brighter day is surely dawning on this interesting study. 'Omnes aliquando linguæ linguam sanctam corona sua cingent, et hanc, sicut manipuli illi Josefi manipulum, consalutantes se inclinabunt; omnia studia verbum divinum suis luminibus circumdabunt, et circa hunc solem lucidis continuisque cursibus circumferentur.'[x]

Nor is the study of Hebrew solely indebted to those eminent scholars to whom it has been our privilege to refer. The grammar and lexicography of the language owe much to the commentators, whose works are constantly appearing. So numerous are they, that it is scarcely possible to gain an acquaintance with all; and yet they will, as far as philology is concerned, amply repay a careful perusal. We have lying before us five commentaries on Job, published since 1847, all of them characterised by a thorough acquaintance with the original.[y] From these works and others great assistance in mastering the language can be obtained. Maurer, a follower of Gesenius, is, for instance, an admirable guide to those who are commencing the *critical* study of the Hebrew Scriptures. Hengstenberg, in his various works, has rendered invaluable aid to the student.[z] His examination of difficult words

---

[u] Delitzsch justly says of this eminent Professor of Padua : ' Qui historia grammaticæ hebraicæ cognitione nostratibus multo antecellit.'

[v] Zunz's works are of the very greatest value. No account of the Targums can be considered as complete which has not been preceded by the careful study of this author's ' Gottesdienstliche Vorträge der Juden,' and ' Zur Geschichte u. Literatur.'

[w] The ' Liber Jesod Olam,' edited by Goldberg and Rosenkranz, 1849; Kimchi, ' Radicum Liber,' by Biesenthal and Lebrecht, 1848; the Talmud Balbi, by Dr. Pinner ; &c. &c.

[x] Delitzsch, Jesurun, p. 40.

[y] Heiligstedt's ' Commentarius Gram. Hist. Crit. in Jobum,' 1847; ' Das Buch Job übersetzt u. erklärt von D. B. Welte,' 1849; Schlottmann, ' Das Buch Hiob,' 1850-1851; Hahn's ' Commentar üb. das Buch Hiob,' 1850; and Hirzel's ' Hiob,' 2 Ant. durchgesehen v. D. J. Olshausen, 1852. The care and labour bestowed on many German Commentaries is astonishing. Thenius, in preparing his Commentary, ' Die Bücher Samuels,' 1842, compared the Masoretic text of Samuel with the Seventy *four several times, word for word.* Thiersch, in collecting matter for his ' De Pentateuchi Vers. Alex.' devoted himself exclusively for *two years* to the comparison of the Heb. Pent. with the Seventy.

[z] Our references are in every instance to the English translation.

is generally very masterly, see תִּימָרוֹת, Christology, iii. 132 ; חָלַל, Ib.
iii. 474 ; חָלָה, Commentary on Psalms ii. 140 ; אֱלֹהִים, on Pentateuch,
i. 265-273.   The synonymes of the language receive great attention from him.[a]   His remarks on verbs with prepositions,[b] on the
emphatic plural,[c] and on the change of tense,[d] will well repay
careful study.   Baur (Der Prophet Amos erk   t) has much that
is truly excellent in his exhaustive work ;[e] so has Keil in his very
learned commentaries on Joshua and Kings ; and so have
Havernick, Hitzig, Delitzsch,[f] and Thenius.[g]   Indeed it were an
endless task to specify all that is *philologically* valuable in German
commentaries.   With their theology we have now nothing to do : it
is often bad enough, alas ! too bad—impious, though we must utter
our protest against the reckless and wholesale anathemas of some
of our writers and reviewers, who ignorantly class such men as
Stier, Hengstenberg, Havernick, Keil, and Tholuck with Ammon,
Paulus, and Strauss, and think they are doing no injustice.

Many valuable ideas are also to be found in other works.
J. v. Gumpach has a good article on אַן (*Alttestamentliche Studien*, 1852, pp. 206—223).   Stier well points out the existence in
Hebrew of a sort of middle formation between the stat. const.
and the absol., as in עַנְוָה־צֶדֶק, Ps. xlv. 5 ; the whole forming a
kind of compound noun.   Dietrich (*Abhandlungen z. Heb. Gram.*
1846) has some excellent remarks on the Hebrew plural (i. 90) ;
the nominal forms in ת (159—172), and on negation (197—262).
Knobel, in his *Prophetismus*, i. 406, &c., has well collected the
paronomasia in the prophets, and Hirzel (*De Chaldaismi Biblici
Orig., &c.*, 1830) the Chaldaisms in the Bible.   Thiersch and
Frankel have given us the best works we possess on the Septuagint
and its relation to the Masoretic text.   The latter scholar has still
more recently followed up his researches in his work *Ueber d.
Einfluss der Palästin Exegese auf die Alexandrin. Hermeneutik.*

---

[a] See Christology, ii. 128 ; iii. 204, 409. Com. on Ps. i. 130, 390, &c.

[b] ' עָרַג, to pant, with עַל, in so far as the desire hangs over its object, rests upon
it, with אֶל, in so far as it is directed upon that.' Com. on Ps. ii. 90 ; and so in very
many instances too numerous to mention.

[c] Com. on Ps. i. 324, 472, 405 ; ii. 96, &c.

[d] Com. on Ps. i. 418, 445, 455, &c.

[e] For instance, his account of the difference in meaning between רָאָה and חָזָה,
יָבֵשׁ and בּוּשׁ, דּוּשׁ and דָּרַשׁ.

[f] See, for instance, his important remark (Der Prophet Habakuk, p. 77). After
referring to Ewald, § 621, Schulgr. § 337, he says, ' It belongs to the fineness of the
Hebrew diction to make *verba finita* follow the participle bearing the tone; they,
through the influence of the relative idea concentred in the participle, are to be
treated as conditional statements.' See Isa. xxxi. 1. So also Rev. i. 5: τῷ ἀγα-
πῶντι . . . λούσαντι . . . καὶ ἐποίησεν.

[g] See Thenius (Die Bücher Samuels) on אֵת as a sign of the nominative, p. 71,
and in five other places.

Having thus considered the present state of Hebrew learning in Germany as far as the publications on the language are concerned, it becomes us to refer directly to the interest which the study is exciting among the students of that country, and to the attainments in Hebrew which its candidates for the ministry must possess.

Hebrew is taught in many of the schools of Germany. Niebuhr learned it at school (*Life and Letters*, i. 27), and since then the study has rapidly advanced; so much so that very many of the elementary works on the language are for the use of schools. Biesenthal (1837) and Fürst (1842) have not thought it beneath them carefully to prepare Hebrew lexicons with this end in view.[h]

From the school the student proceeds to the Gymnasium, and, if intended for the study of theology, he there prosecutes the study in question, since in the first two and often in the first three classes that language is taught. For such students many works have been prepared,[i] and in some Gymnasiums lectures are given during term-time. We have before us a list of the lectures given at the Gymnasium in Hamburg, 1847-1848. Among these we find lectures by Redslob[k] on the *Book of Job*, every Monday, Tuesday, Thursday, and Friday. After having attended to Hebrew more or less during four years at least, the student has to pass a final examination in the language before he can enter the University as a theological student. This examination extends over the whole of the historic books of the Old Testament, and sometimes even the Psalms and Job are chosen. At any rate, the student to pass must be able to read any passage in prose Hebrew. It is conducted *viva voce*, and also by the imposition of exercises to be performed without books in a locked-up chamber.

Thus grounded in the language, the student on repairing to the University is fully able to understand and appreciate the lectures which it is his duty and privilege to attend.[m] These lectures on different books of the Old Testament are given five or six times a week during the session. There are besides courses delivered by

---

[h] The lexicons of Biesenthal and Fürst have been used by us for years, and almost always with profit. Goldstein's 'Schul-Grammatik der Ebräischer Sprache,' 1848, is an excellent work.

[i] Uhlemann has published a course of three or four years' study for the use of students in the gymnasium, 1829, 1841. So has Sonne, 1830.

[k] Some of the teachers in the gymnasiums are among the first scholars in Germany. Redslob is a fine Hebraist. His review of Ewald's Grammar in Jahn's Jahrbücher, xx. 1837, is valuable. He has written several other articles.

[m] In the directions given to students at Halle, 1827, we find the following language: 'A grammatical acquaintance with Hebrew may reasonably be expected to have been obtained at the preparatory schools.' So also in the directions given to the Leipsic students.

the ' extraordinary professors,' and lessons taught by the *pri-vatim docentes.*" In 1830, while Gesenius, Prof. Ord., was lec-turing on Isaiah, in the same University, Stange was going through Genesis, Schott the Psalms, Roediger the Minor Pro-phets, and Wahl Job. In 1835 Hengstenberg, the Prof. Ord. of Theology in Berlin University, was lecturing on the Psalms; Bellerman and Benary, Prof. Extraord., delivered lectures on Job and Isaiah, and Uhlemann and Vatke, Privatim docentes, on the Messianic Psalms and Genesis. In the same year, in the University of Gottingen, Ewald, Prof. Ord., took Isaiah, and Wüstenfeld and Klener, Priv. docentes, the Minor Prophets. To these must be added lectures on Biblical Archæology, and on the Historical and Critical Introduction to the Old Testament, besides those on the cognate dialects.

Nor does the instruction imparted to the student end here. In the Universities of Berlin, Bonn, Breslau, Greifswalde, Halle, and Königsberg there are ' seminaries '—societies among the students, under the guidance of a professor, for the more careful and familiar study of theology and philology. The seminary of Halle consists of five divisions ; that on the exegesis of the Old Testament under the direction of Hupfeld. While Gesenius lived he presided over the meetings of the students, sometimes exercising them in the writing of Hebrew, sometimes engaging them in discussions on grammar, and sometimes calling upon them to interpret difficult passages. These seminaries meet every week, and are productive of the best results. The royal theo-logical seminarium of Berlin is, in the division of Biblical exe-gesis, under the care of Hengstenberg. While Ewald was first at Gottingen an exegetical society used to meet at his house. In addition to this the students often meet among themselves. The note-books in which the students record everything valuable are always among their choicest treasures. We once knew a student who, when at the close of his University career, he was robbed of these books, entered again. A pupil of Hengstenberg's, after-wards German chaplain at Buenos Ayres, once showed to us with deepest interest these memorials of his University course, and of his successful efforts.

The enthusiasm excited by so many students of the same branches as meet together in the Universities of Germany is very great. In 1846 there were in Berlin 279 theological students, at Leipsic 187, at Bonn 213, at Tubingen 289, and at Halle 457.

ⁿ The three orders of teachers in German universities are, first, the *professores publici ordinarii*, who are bound to give one lecture gratis ; secondly, the *professores extraordinarii* ; and, thirdly, the *privatdocenten*. Of the first class there are at least forty in Leipsic.

About 4000 are at once studying theology in the German Universities. All these *necessarily* pursue the study of Hebrew, not merely from a fondness for philological pursuits, but also because they *must* undergo two, in Hanover three, examinations in the language before they are admitted into the ministry. These examinations are very thorough, and many a student receives a *zero* in Hebrew.

All these scholars are under the most eminent Hebrew scholars in the world, hear that ancient tongue constantly and fluently spoken in the course of lecturing, and catch the enthusiasm of the well-known and justly-celebrated teachers at whose feet they sit. Maurer, Tuch, and Fürst at Leipsic; Hupfeld and Roediger at Halle; Hengstenberg, Sachs, and Biesenthal in Berlin; Hitzig at Zurich; Knobel and Baur at Giessen; Keil at Dorpat; Ewald at Gottingen; Bernstein at Breslau; Delitzsch at Rostock; Thiersch and Dietrich at Marburg; Meier at Tubingen; Bottcher at Dresden, and Ullmann and Umbreit at Heidelberg, are the men, with others, whose instructions in Hebrew the students of Germany enjoy—men who will have thoroughness, and who will encourage effort.

The revival of Hebrew learning in Germany was soon felt, to some extent at least, in other countries. To America doubtless belongs the honour of having first, among the Anglo-Saxon races, caught the influence. In this republic Professor Stuart led the way, and, were it for nought but this, his name would deserve to be held in honour by all biblical students. In 1810 he was appointed Professor of Sacred Literature at Andover, which office he held for thirty-eight years with much credit to himself, and with advantage to hundreds of students. ' The good sense and ardour of Professor Stuart,' says his pupil Dr. Robinson, ' early led him to adopt the philological principles and results of Gesenius, and to apply them zealously and successfully in the wide field of his own labour. His Hebrew Grammar, first published in 1821, was founded on those principles, and the successive issue of six editions testifies to the spirit awakened, and the results produced, by his efforts in this department of theology.' His generous disposition and enthusiastic love of learning attracted multitudes of students to Andover, which became indeed the Halle of America, while his numerous elementary works on the language served still further to extend his influence, and to excite a taste for Oriental pursuits. Often did he, through the periodical press, urge the claims of Hebrew on the attention of all. ' How is it,' wrote he, ' that believing the Hebrew Scriptures to contain a revelation from heaven, they are not to be counted worthy of our study . . . *as a sword in my bones, I feel the bitter reproach of such a question.'* [o] So successfully did Professor Stuart labour that in his own institution 'some acquaintance with Hebrew was required in *order to admission.'* [p]

Nor were the labours of Gesenius unappreciated elsewhere. Professor Gibbs of Yale in 1824 translated his Hebrew and German Manual. Many of the pupils of the American Hebraist have extended still further the scientific principles of German philology. Mr. Riggs translated 'Winer's Manual of the Chaldee language,' 1832, a volume which was issued by the publishers 'without any expectation of pecuniary remuneration.' In 1836 Dr. Robinson translated the Latin Manual of Gesenius. This edition of 3000 was sold off in six years. Of all the editions of this admirable work, published by the same firm in Boston, 7500 copies have been sold. Two years after, Nordheimer published the first volume of his valuable 'Critical Grammar,' a second edition of which volume has since appeared. The same year his 'Hebrew Chrestomathy' was printed, and in 1841 the second volume of his Grammar. The influence thus excited at Andover was not confined to any one body of Christians. 'In our own country,' say a society of clergymen of the American Episcopal Church, in 1829, 'there is an increasing interest in sacred literature; and the clergy of all denominations are more and more impressed with the importance of searching the Scriptures .... our seminaries of theology are directing the attention of their students to the careful study of the Bible in its original languages.' Dr. Turner, Professor of Biblical Learning in the Protestant Episcopal Theological Seminary, has done much to foster this study in his own denomination. His translation of Jahn's 'Introduction to the Old Testament,' 1827, and his work on Genesis, 1841, are well known. Dr. Keith, of the Episcopal Theological Seminary of Virginia, has done good service by translating Hengstenberg's 'Christology,' 1836. Among the Baptists, Dr. Conant and Professor Hackett are worthily distinguished by their eminent attainments. The former scholar, one of the best Hebraists in America, translated the Grammar of Gesenius in 1839. This work reached its third edition in 1842, of which edition 1500 copies were sold. In 1846 a new edition (from the fourteenth edition of Gesenius) of 1200 appeared. About the same time Professor Stuart translated the same edition of Gesenius, of which translation 1500 were printed. This work was ably and severely criticised by Dr. Conant.[q]

---

[o] Quarterly Register and Journal of the Amer. Educ. Society, April, 1829, p. 198.

[p] In the 'Terms of Admission' we find the following language: 'Every candidate is to be examined by the Faculty with reference .... to his knowledge of Hebrew grammar, and of the Hebrew Chrestomathy of Professor Stuart, so far as the extracts from Genesis and Exodus extend.'

[q] As a piece of searching criticism, Dr. Conant's 'Defence of the Hebrew Gram-

Professor Hackett translated in 1845 the edition of Winer's
'Chaldee Grammar,' which appeared in 1842, and in 1847 published his useful and excellent 'Hebrew Exercises.' Even among
the Methodists in the States, a people not generally devoted to
biblical literature, the impulse given to Hebrew learning is felt.
The editor of the 'Methodist Quarterly Review,' Dr. M'Clintock,
is a good Hebrew scholar, and has, in this respect as well as in
others, much raised the character of that excellent periodical.

Until very recently the whole supply of Hebrew Bibles was re-
ceived from Germany, with the exception of some few from England.
In October, 1831, Hahn's 'Hebrew Bible' made its appearance.
In April, 1832, 200 copies had already been sold in the vicinity of
Andover. Since then the sale of this admirable edition has averaged
500 copies a year. In 1849 a reprint of this work was issued by
J. Wiley of New York and J. W. Moore of Philadelphia.

The interest thus excited was deepened by the frequency with
which American students repaired to the German Universities. In
1829 Dr. Robinson was a pupil of Gesenius; subsequently Professors Edwards, Hackett, and others repaired thither. 'Indeed,' says
Dr. Pusey, in a letter to Dr. Robinson, dated 1832, 'I have been
looking with anxiety to America ever since I learned to what extent
the education of your young divines was carried on in Germany.'

The whole number of theological Institutions in the States is
41. The number of students belonging to them in 1849 was
about 1300. In nearly all of them the course of study is much
the same, the exegesis of the Old Testament being pursued more
or less during the three years' course. Princeton ranks first in
the number of its theological students. The well-earned celebrity
of Dr. Alexander, the talented author of 'The Prophecies of
Isaiah,' is probably the cause of this. One hundred and fifty students are now within its walls. The Union Seminary, New York,
has ninety-one; Andover, ninety. In many of these institutes
there is also an assistant Hebrew teacher. Voluntary classes are
formed for the study of Chaldee, Syriac, and Arabic, and for instruction in German, by means of which 'many of the students are
able to avail themselves of the German helps which are now so
bountifully provided.'

In looking at the present state of Hebrew learning in America
we cannot but admire the exact scholarship and successful efforts
of many eminent men there. All honour to them! Although
they are outstripping us in the study of the Hebrew Scriptures, we
acknowledge no rivalry but a holy one, and feel no ambition but
that of co-operating with them in their noble labours. The

---

mar of Gesenius against Professor Stuart's Translation, 1847,' is worthy of being
carefully read.

influence these learned men are exerting on the students for the ministry committed to their charge cannot but be most healthful, and many a youthful scholar is now preparing himself, by thorough training and fundamental research, for future and extensive usefulness. We shall, however, be labouring under a great mistake if we suppose that all, or even a majority, of those who study Hebrew at the theological institutes of the State, become accomplished Hebrew scholars. Far otherwise. With very many no foundation is laid before entering the institution ; and as, while there, Hebrew and Greek exegesis, Church History, Theology, Homiletics, Rhetoric, &c., are, in too many instances, crowded into the three-years' course, but little thorough acquaintance with any branch of study is gained. The whole period is one of wearying struggle with that which is elementary. No mastery is acquired ; no habit of successful investigation stimulates to life-long effort. The consequence is that, amidst the pressure of duties in this age of lectures and Bible classes, the young minister too frequently throws aside his Hebrew studies, and rejoices in his freedom from those labours, which no long and successful pursuit had rendered at once easy, delightful, and profitable. It is no doubt on this account that a writer, in one of the public journals of the United States, urges the abandonment of the study of Hebrew in the theological seminaries. On this subject, however, it becomes us to say but little, as, alas ! the remarks now made are still more applicable to ourselves.

It now remains for us to consider the progress of Hebrew learning in our own country. We turn first to our Universities. On the statute-books of these seats of learning Hebrew study holds its proper place ; the statutes of the Universities demanding that candidates for the B. D. degree shall study the original Scriptures, and those of several of the colleges requiring a knowledge of Hebrew in order to the enjoyment of a fellowship — indeed, within the precincts of Jesus College, all B. A.'s are required to talk Latin, Greek, or Hebrew ! Out of these the study thirty years ago had scarcely any existence whatever either at Cambridge or Oxford. ' Prior to 1819,' writes Dr. Lee in a letter to the writer, ' when I had the honour of being elected Arabic Professor at Cambridge, ' not a lecture had been delivered on either Hebrew or Arabic learning at either of our Universities for perhaps the preceding hundred years. The endowments at Cambridge were too small to induce able and inquiring men to attend to studies of this sort, being only 40*l.* a year : besides, scriptural learning was not greatly in request in those times. Upon my election to the Arabic chair, I was requested to set up a lecture on both the Arabic and Hebrew. I did so forthwith, and a considerable number of the Masters of Arts, and even some

Heads of Houses, attended the Hebrew lecture—a few students
the Arabic. This was very encouraging. All, however, was not
smooth sailing, for there were a few who made it their business to
cry down these pursuits as useless and unnecessary, and even to
press upon the consideration of some of my pupils the danger
there would be of losing the preferment necessary to their future
well-doing. This was not to be wondered at. I took courage,
nevertheless, and persevered, judging that, without some conflict,
no victory worth having ever was, or ever would be, obtained. In
the very first year of this my undertaking, moreover, a very fortunate circumstance happened. A fellow of one of the colleges
died, bequeathing to the University the sum of 4000*l*., to be
applied for the furtherance of Hebrew learning. A scholarship of
50*l*. a year, to be holden for three years, was immediately established. Five able candidates presented themselves for examination, and the number of attendants at my lecture increased, as
might be expected. We have since then never failed to send
out one good scholar yearly, and sometimes two or three, who
would do credit to any age or nation. At first we had considerable difficulty to find examiners, as might be expected under
such circumstances. After the first two or three years, however,
this difficulty vanished: and I feel that I can safely say that we
now have in almost every part of England one or two of our
scholars located. Some of them are head masters of public schools,
and the consequence is, not a few of these make Hebrew a part of
their pupils' training.' Under Dr. Lee the students were required
to translate, explain, and illustrate any part of the Hebrew Bible
that might be put before them, with extracts from the Rabbinical
Commentaries, as well as to translate into Hebrew, with the
vowels and accents, some parts of the Greek Testament, or of the
Greek apocryphal writings. The example set at Cambridge was
soon followed at Oxford. Mrs. Kennicott, widow of the celebrated
Dr. Kennicott, bequeathed in 1828 sums for founding two scholarships of 70*l*. each for four years; and P. Pusey, Esq., Dr. Pusey,
and Dr. Ellerton, in 1832, founded three of 30*l*. each for three
years. Yet, notwithstanding all these advantages, the study in
question languished at the Universities. 'Hebrew learning in
England,' says a writer in the 'Churchman's Monthly Review' for
February, 1847, 'appears to have fallen into a state of utter decay
and neglect, which the foundation of the Tyrwhitt scholarship at
Cambridge, and some other encouragements during the present
century, have been unable to revive.' This has been partly owing
doubtless to the progress of Tractarianism. 'The Oxford movement,' writes Dr. Lee in a letter dated September, 1847, 'certainly
had a very bad effect on the Hebrew studies of this country.
Young men, who had intended to make Hebrew an important part

of their reading, were induced to have recourse to the theological writers of the dark ages, as Aquinas, Durandus, and others : and I myself have been informed, at the first hand, that the Oxford Professor of Hebrew actually inculcated the belief that nothing certain was to be found in Hebrew literature; that translators, following implicitly their own judgments, could not but be perpetually differing, and that it was in the writers of the Church alone that anything like unanimity was to be found. This check in the progress of Hebrew literature some of our booksellers felt grievously, and one, I have reason to believe, retired from business in consequence of it.' The low state of Hebrew learning at Cambridge and Oxford must, however, be mainly attributed to the fact that the studies and examinations are voluntary, not binding, and that very few of the bishops, if any, require any knowledge of the language in candidates for holy orders. Even now, although the study seems on the increase, the examination for a Hebrew scholarship in the Universities is not so thorough as that which the youth of Germany pass on leaving the Gymnasium for the college.[a] Bishop Heber's language to Rev. Mr. Oxlee is still too true :—' It is remarkable that England is, of all Protestant countries, that where the importance and riches of Hebrew literature are least known.' [b]

In the Universities of Durham and London voluntary examinations in Hebrew are held. An attempt was made in the year 1847, in connection with the latter University, to make the study of Hebrew somewhat binding on all candidates for the B.A. degree, but without success.[c]

The study of Hebrew in the dissenting theological institutions is much more successfully prosecuted. This improvement is, however, of recent date. In 1831 Dr. Henderson, writing to Professor Stuart on his Grammar, says, ' It is, I am sorry to say, too formidable for most of my countrymen, who have got so spoiled by the habit of learning the language without points, or with them so superficially, that I fear few copies will be in demand.' Since then the use of Professor Stuart's elementary works, and especially the introduction of the Grammars and Lexicons of Gesenius and Ewald, have proved highly beneficial. In most of these institutions the study of Hebrew is more or less prosecuted throughout the three years' course, and in several of them the instruction is

---

[a] Subject for voluntary Hebrew examination, 1852, at Cambridge :—' The first twelve chapters of the second book of Samuel; and the first book of Chronicles, from the thirteenth to the twentieth chapters inclusive.'

[b] Quarterly Review for 1830, vol. xliii. 391.

[c] The following is the notice of the withdrawn motion :—' That all candidates for the B.A. degree shall be examined either in one of the books of the Pentateuch in the original Hebrew, or in one of the Four Gospels or the Acts of the Apostles in the original Greek.'

imparted by some of the best Hebraists in England. Yet, alas! it is too seldom followed up by careful study. 'For myself,' writes Dr. Henderson to us (May, 1847), 'I can say that I prepare annually as great a number of competent Hebrew scholars as I ever did; but most of them are under the necessity of afterwards contenting themselves with a simple consultation of the original text, or, at the utmost, reading a small portion daily for the purpose of keeping up their acquaintance with the language. The cause is obvious. The moment they enter the ministry, they are obliged to undertake not only ordinary pastoral duty, which of itself not unfrequently not a little tasks young men, but Bible classes and transactions connected with the committees of Bible, Tract, Missionary, Education, and various other societies, which leave them no time for the prosecution of literary studies.'[d]

The real progress of the study may, however, best be learned from the demand for Hebrew works. Messrs. S. Bagster and Sons, the eminent publishers, have kindly informed us that 'the study of Hebrew in this country is certainly spreading.' 'Gesenius's Grammar,' they wrote (April 26, 1852), 'is in its second edition: Gesenius's Lexicon is about to enter its third edition: the Analytical Lexicon will soon be in its second edition. Of the smaller lexicons, lesson-books, &c., a moderate but steady sale has been secured.' We are glad to learn that, while about fifty copies of Bagster's small Hebrew Bible, with points, are sold every year, only about half-a-dozen are sold without points. Messrs. Ward and Co., the publishers of Conant's Gesenius, have sold, since 1841, 4000 copies at 9*s.*, and about 1000 at 6*s.* 6*d.*, the reduced price. Of Dr. Lee's Hebrew Grammar three very large editions have been sold off since 1827, and another published, while the sale of that eminent scholar's Lexicon has reached from 1000 to 1500. Three editions of Hurwitz's Hebrew Grammar have been sold off, and another is out. Professor Gibbs' translation of Gesenius's Lexicon, printed by Mr. Duncan about twenty years ago, is out of print. There is also a steady sale for Dr. Robinson's Gesenius's Lexicon. Of Dr. M'Caul's Hebrew Primer, published about 1828, there were sold up to 1845 about 2000 copies, and since then about 1250. Talboys' Oxford editions of Professor Stuart's Grammar and Chrestomathy have sold somewhat largely.[e] Besides the large sale of Hebrew works printed in

[d] Drs. Pye Smith and Henderson, the one now no more, the other retired from College duties, were among these capable and earnest instructors. Dr. Davidson, Professor Gotch, Hebrew examiner at London University, and others, eminently qualified to raise the study of Hebrew amongst us, are still actively engaged. Would that our learned friend Dr. Davies, translator of Roediger's Gesenius's Grammar, were in a situation to extend to us his valuable aid!

[e] We are glad to see that Mr. R. Young of Edinburgh has received sufficient encouragement to publish several very useful Oriental works.

this country, very many are imported from Germany. Bohn, the purchaser of Vanderhooght's Hebrew Bible, offered to supply the Bible Society with his edition at sixpence a copy over cost price, but they declined his offer and went to Germany. Indeed, many booksellers, not only in London but elsewhere, correspond directly with German houses, and obtain at once Hahn's Hebrew Bible, Theile's Biblia Hebraica, &c.

As far, then, as the sale of Hebrew books is concerned, the prospect is most encouraging. May we not, notwithstanding many discouragements and much, very much, superficial acquaintance with the language,[f] indulge the hope that in process of time the disgrace, which is verily ours, of encouraging Oriental literature less than almost any other country,[g] will belong to us no more. We had an honourable name two centuries ago for biblical learning; may we merit it again and keep it. 'My knowledge of the Hebrew language,' said Luther, ' is but limited, yet I would not barter it for all the treasures of the world.'

We close with the remarks of the Quarterly Reviewer (vol. xliii. p. 391) :—' It is not a little extraordinary that, at a period of so much religious excitement, and while the Scriptures are disseminated and translated into foreign languages with such unceasing and meritorious activity, our Hebrew biblical learning should be at so low an ebb. We might almost assert that a single Leipsic fair produces more Hebrew critical works than have issued from the English press for half a century. . . . . . This great school (the German) of Hebrew literature, the only one in Europe, it is well known, has adopted a system of interpretation in diametrical and, it is generally esteemed, dangerous opposition to that which has long and universally prevailed in this country. . . . . We are far from desiring to set ourselves up as arbiters in this great controversy : our only object is to express our regret that the opponents of this school do not take higher ground, and meet their antagonists more fully in the field. It surely would be a more dignified course, instead of passing a hasty and sweeping condemnation on the whole school, and placing their works in an index expurgatorius, to array ourselves in their armour, to wrest their weapons from their hands, and so, in fair fight, win the field from adversaries, to conquer whom might certainly do honour to the most redoubted champion of learning.'   F. B.

---

[f] Why has not Dr. Nicholson received encouragement enough to bring out a second edition of his translation of Ewald's Grammar, from an English press? Nearly twenty years have passed since the first edition was printed at Gottingen. Our quotations from Ewald are taken from Dr. Nicholson's translation.

[g] 'Oriental literature, I am sorry to say, is in no country so little encouraged as in this.'—Dr. Lee, in the ' British Magazine' for March, 1847, p. 291.

WHO ARE THE 'SPIRITS IN PRISON?'

1 PETER iii. 18-22.

"Ὅτι καὶ Χριστὸς ἅπαξ περὶ ἁμαρτιῶν ἔπαθε, δίκαιος ὑπὲρ ἀδίκων, ἵνα ἡμᾶς προσαγάγῃ τῷ Θεῷ, θανατωθεὶς μὲν σαρκὶ, ζωοποιηθεὶς δὲ πνεύματι, ἐν ᾧ καὶ τοῖς ἐν φυλακῇ πνεύμασι πορευθεὶς ἐκήρυξεν, ἀπειθήσασί ποτε ὅτε ἀπεξεδέχετο ἡ τοῦ Θεοῦ μακροθυμία ἐν ἡμέραις Νῶε, κατασκευαζομένης κιβωτοῦ, εἰς ἣν ὀλίγαι τουτέστιν ὀκτὼ ψυχαὶ διεσώθησαν δι' ὕδατος, ὃ καὶ ἡμᾶς ἀντίτυπον νῦν σώζει βάπτισμα, οὐ σαρκὸς ἀπόθεσις ῥύπου, ἀλλὰ συνειδήσεως ἀγαθῆς ἐπερώτημα εἰς Θεὸν, δι' ἀναστάσεως Ἰησοῦ Χριστοῦ.ᵃ

AUTHORIZED VERSION.—' For Christ also hath once suffered for sins, the just for the unjust, that he might bring us to God, being put to death in the flesh, but quickened by the Spirit: by which also he went and preached unto the spirits in prison; which sometime were disobedient, when once the longsuffering of God waited in the days of Noah, while the ark was a preparing, wherein few, that is, eight souls were saved by water. The like figure whereunto *even* baptism doth also now save us (not the putting away of the filth of the flesh, but the answer of a good conscience toward God,) by the resurrection of Jesus Christ.'

THERE is probably no sentence in the New Testament which has so little the appearance of coherent writing, or in which it is so difficult to trace the unity of thought, as the one which we have above transcribed. Relative terms connect both the 19th and 21st verses with those immediately preceding; but so little do the ordinary laws of mental association explain the connection, that, probably, each of the transitions, on a first perusal of the sentence, strikes the mind with a feeling of surprise.

It appears to us, after a careful consideration of the passage, that a clue to the continuity of the writer's ideas may be found in the practical argument which he is enforcing, and that is, the duty of Christians to be patient under provocation—not to attempt to retaliate the injuries they suffer from the wicked, much less to be seduced by their wickedness, but calmly, cheerfully, and resolutely to pursue an even tenour of upright conduct, to whatever treatment it may subject them. Such conduct, it appears to us, the writer is recommending by a reference, in the former part of the passage, to the *sacerdotal* character of our Saviour, and in the latter to his *prophetical* character; an additional illustration of the course recommended being further drawn in the last case from a distinguished patriarch's example. It is obvious that the main stress of the difficulty of the passage lies in this second line of argument; the obscure points being, first, the relation of the *spirits in prison*, whether we identify these, or not, with the antediluvians forthwith

---

ᵃ The text which we have given above is that of Griesbach (Lond., 1818), in which it will be observed that there is no periodic break at verses 19 and 20.

mentioned, to our Lord's preaching, and next, the relation of the ordinance of baptism to the antediluvians.

We shall endeavour, first of all, to ascertain the nature of the *nexus* between the 18th and 19th verses, a discussion which will turn mainly on the point, who 'the spirits in prison' are. Three principal hypotheses, among those which have been broached on this question, may be said to be current now :—the one which finds in this phrase nothing but a description of unregenerate men—the second, which considers antediluvian *penitents* to be denoted by it—and the third, which refers it to antediluvian *impenitents*. Although the evidence is to our minds very convincing, which shows that the last class only can be intended, it will be requisite to glance at the chief arguments urged for the former two hypotheses.

We will take our exhibition of the nature and force of the first of these partly from the expository lectures on 1 Peter, lately published by the Rev. Dr. Brown, and partly from the recent Biblical Cyclopædia of Dr. Eadie. These writers consider that the preaching intended is that of our Lord and his apostles to the sinners of their times. They think that the unregenerate of every age may be properly described as *spirits in prison*, and that they were in fact so described by our Lord at his entrance on his personal ministry. (See Luke iv. 19, and compare Isaiah lxi. 1.) They refer further to the language of such passages as Isaiah xlii. 7 ; xlix. 9, where, in predictions of the office and work of our Lord, almost the identical terms of our text occur. The former of these passages describes his destination as being ' to open blind eyes, to bring out prisoners from the prison, and them that sit in darkness out of the prison-house,' and the latter represents him as saying ' to the prisoners, Go forth to them that are in darkness, Show yourselves.' These passages, conjoined with the later prophecy of the same author (see lxi. 1), which attributes our Lord's fitness for these great functions to the Spirit, furnishes, our authors think, all the parallelism which is wanted for their exposition.

We should ourselves, perhaps, be disposed to think so, were the quotations in question taken from any other than a prophetical author ; but the language of poetry is of one character, that of prose of another. We do not at this moment recollect any passage in the New Testament in which a description, thus highly figurative, is employed in plain, didactic argument ; and though incidentally similar metaphors no doubt occur in the apostolic writings, some of them being indeed so frequent as almost to cease to be metaphors, it will be found in general, we apprehend, that, where employed by the writer, they are introduced for the purpose of direct emphasis. See Eph. ii. 1 ; iv. 18 ; 1 Thessal. v. 6 ; or in our own epistle, ch. ii. 5, 9.

A much stronger objection, however, to this exposition is its entire failure, as we conceive, to account for the specification of a particular class of the unregenerate in the following verse. If the evangelical ministry of the apostles was intended, why mention the sinners of a former age? Dr. Brown considers that they are brought forward simply as the prototypes, or, as we might say, the ancestors of sinners in succeeding ages. He contends that the following would be an analogous statement. 'God sent the gospel to the Britons, who, in the days of Cæsar, were painted savages.' But is it not plain, in this proposed sentence, that the latter circumstance would be wholly without point unless it involved some dissimilarity or contrast? A reference to the Picts of Cæsar's days would be worse than irrelevant if the inhabitants of the island were Picts still. The disobedience mentioned in v. 20 was not more a characteristic of the unregenerate in the patriarch's age than it was of those in the apostle's; the contemporaries of the one were as *hard to be convinced*, to use the translation Dr. Brown prefers, as the contemporaries of the other. What additional information, then, is gained or given by this historical reference? According to the hypothesis before us, the reference is *historical in form* only, but is *in fact* simply *descriptive*.

The station and talents of the late Bishop Horsley have given to the second hypothesis which we noticed, somewhat more of éclat than its intrinsic merits would secure for it. He considers that 'spirits in *prison*' are no more than 'spirits in *safe keeping*,' and that the spirits meant are those of departed penitents, to whom our Lord, in the brief interval which ensued between his death and resurrection, went personally with the news of his redemption. The Bishop takes up the passage as a proof-text for one of the articles of the Anglican creed, viz., our Lord's *descent into hell*—which latter term he accordingly explains to signify simply the *invisible state*—the state of departed spirits. Our Lord's *spirit*, in v. 19, he of course makes to denote simply his *human soul*, which sense he contends that the antithesis in which it is placed in v. 18 to his *flesh*, or body, obliges us absolutely to put on the word. The temporary sojourn of our Lord's soul in the receptacle of departed spirits, he thinks to be only a necessary part of his satisfaction for us. As our substitute unto death, he holds it to have been as essential that his spirit should pass, after decease, where ordinary spirits go, as that his body should become motionless and insensible. Without this twofold identification of condition, he maintains that our Lord would not have borne the full penalty of our guilt—that he would not have been, as it behoved him to be, 'in all points as we are.' (See Heb. ii. 17.) And although the mission attributed to our Lord would naturally be to departed saints in general, the Bishop deems it probable that the antediluvians are specified to relieve our minds in some measure with regard to their doom.   Charity, he suggests, would incline us to hope and believe that all who perished in the waters of the deluge did not perish everlastingly also. Some encouragement, he is of opinion, is given to this supposition by passages like that in the Revelation (ch. xx. 13), where it is particularly noted that ' the sea gave up the dead which were in it.' This specification, in his view, discovers a certain tenderness of reference to the millions who were engulphed at the time of the deluge, and who, above all other departed souls, would, he urges, need that especial consolation which the message borne by our Lord was adapted to supply.

Now we hold that the most serious difficulties lie against this hypothesis, both philological and theological. As it regards the former, we wait for the production of an instance from the New Testament of any such application of the word translated prison as the Bishop would plead for. *Prison* is unquestionably the meaning of the word in the vast majority of places where it occurs[b] —a place of penal confinement; in some few passages it is applied to a division of the night—a *watch*—in one, to a military watch or ward, and in one to the private watching of a shepherd. This latter is the signification it bears in a passage of the evangelist Luke (ch. ii. 8), where the shepherds at Bethlehem are said to have been ' keeping watch over their flocks by night.' A slight analogy may perhaps be thought to exist in this passage to the signification advocated by the Bishop, but it is one which will not hold on close comparison. *Safe custody* or *keeping*, which is equivalent to *protection*, implies the presence or probability of *danger*, but what further danger is to be apprehended by those who have passed their present probation? What are the class of enemies from whom the spirits of departed saints or penitents need to be guarded? On what side is it that they are threatened with assault? Of what nature are those attempts on their happiness against which vigilance has to be exercised? *Saints are kept*, and need to be kept, *by the power of God* only *unto the salvation* (1 Peter i. 5) which awaits them on their release from this world.

Far more grave and serious, however, are the theological difficulties which lie against this view of the apostle's meaning. Such a mission of our Saviour to disembodied saints as the Bishop would extract from the passage would be, we apprehend, a perfect ἅπαξ λεγόμενον among the truths of scripture. We are at a loss whether to object most to the *fact* of this mission, or to the *nature*

---

[b] In full thirty-five instances out of forty-seven.

and *objects* of it. On what scriptural basis can a *descent* of our
Saviour to any repository of disembodied spirits be grounded? Not
surely on his assurance to the dying malefactor, ' This day thou
shalt be with me in Paradise.' (Luke xxiii. 43.) It has always
savoured to us of the dryness of verbal criticism to attempt to
locate Paradise as a region in such a repository. *Etymologically*,
no doubt Paradise is a part of Hades, *i. e.*, of the invisible world,
but in what sense is it more so than the third heaven itself, the
immediate seat of the divine royalty? If the prophecy of David
(Ps. xvi. 10) be appealed to, as quoted and reasoned on by Peter
(see Acts ii. 31), it is sufficient to reply, that in places too numerous to mention, *hell* or *Hades* signifies no more than *the grave*.
(See, among others, Gen. xlii. 38 : Ps. xlix. 15.) We feel the
strongest repugnance to the idea of the detention of our Lord one
moment in any intermediate or imperfect state of being.   As
to any supposed necessity for this from his responsibilities as
our substitute, this argument, if carried out, would require him
to have made experiment even of the miseries of the lost.   The
sentence pronounced in Eden on the original transgression was
comprehensive, unquestionably, of the second as well as of the
first death.   If the substitution undertaken by our Lord must
then be a rigorous equivalent, why will it not oblige him to descend
still lower than to the general Hades? Why will it not conclude
him, as some have been hardy enough to do, to have had a taste of
the real hell?   The truth is, this whole reasoning rests on too precise and mercantile a notion of the nature of substitution.   Our
blessed Lord's atonement was not so much of the nature of a pay-
ment for a debt, as of a satisfaction for a wrong.   It was intended
as an honour and reparation to the law and government of God.
It was a public declaration, in the eye of the universe, of the equity
of the divine demands, and of the sinner's desert of wrath and
punishment.   This is, if we mistake not, the dignified view which
the apostle gives of it, when discussing the subject in the Romans.
(See Rom. iii. 25.)   ' Whom God,' says he, ' hath set forth as a
propitiation through faith in his blood, to declare his (*i. e.*, God's)
righteousness' (εἰς ἔνδειξιν τῆς δικαιοσύνης.)   Viewed in this light,
the whole theory of the descent of our Lord to some nether and
subterraneous region, in his capacity as our surety, falls to the
ground.   In the fullest and completest sense he might say of his
undertaking as Mediator, at the moment when he breathed his
last, ' *It is finished.*' (John xix. 30.)
   The explanation which the Bishop appends of the errand which
engaged our Lord during his alleged sojourn among departed
souls, strikes us as little less than puerile. ' He went to announce
the great fact that he had completed his redemption.'   Why now,

for the first time, we are tempted to ask, the communication of such intelligence? Why not previous missions to this collection of spirits to announce important facts? Why was not, *e. g.*, the birth as well as the death of our Lord the object of such annunciation? Above all, why must our Lord be made to stoop to the office of his own herald? An angelic choir was deputed to give information to the living inhabitants of earth of his advent; could no celestial messenger be spared for its departed multitudes? A special harbinger was raised up to usher in his ministry among men; is he to be left wholly without attendance or escort on the honourable fulfilment of that ministry? Was there no other channel especially through which this stupendous fact could reach the world in question? The two prophets during their temporary rapture on the mount (see Luke ix. 31) did not appear uninformed of what would happen to our Lord; why should we suppose that other perfected spirits were kept in ignorance? The more we look at this hypothesis in its different aspects, the more crude, absurd, and unscriptural does it appear.

It is sufficient to say of the alleged repentance of those whom the Bishop would make the objects of this mission, that it is a figment without foundation from beginning to end. Whatever allusions we have in the New Testament to the religious state of the antediluvians are all adverse to the supposition that any of them left the world in a state of acceptance. Our Lord, in his reference to them, describes them as a race of careless voluptuaries to the last. (See Luke xvii. 27.) Our apostle, in his second epistle, without reservation or exception, characterizes them as *a world of ungodly.* (See 2 Peter ii. 5.) The apostle Paul similarly (Heb. xi. 7) speaks of them as *condemned* by Noah. We cannot ourselves see anything in the text from the Revelation to countervail these descriptions; rather, we should say, the reverse. The dead who were given up by the sea, were given up, it is represented, for *judgment;* almost immediately afterwards it is added, 'they were judged every man according to his works.' Here justice rules predominant; no hint of clemency or special favour. The following and closing verses are, 'And death and hell were cast into the lake of fire. This is the second death. And whosoever was not found written in the book of life was cast into the lake of fire.' (See Rev. xx. 13-15.) There is nothing assuredly here to diminish the unfavourable impression given of the antediluvians in the sequel of our passage. The utmost that can be allowed to the Bishop's hypothesis is, that it is honourable to his ingenuity and acuteness; but notwithstanding so weighty an authority, we must regard the whole notion of our Lord's descent into hell as a post-apostolic tradition, not worth retaining.

It remains to be considered what objections lie against the ordinary interpretation of the passage, and what arguments recommend its adoption. We are now speaking of that exposition which understands by the prison, the prison of hell; by the spirits within it, those of antediluvian impenitents; and by the preaching to these spirits, that of the patriarch Noah. It is a powerful presumption in favour of this view, that each of the aspects under which we have presented it was familiar to the apostle's mind. That he regarded the antediluvians as having *perished in their iniquity* (see Joshua xxii. 20), as a race, in other words, of condemned souls, is plain from the passage in the second epistle (see, again, 2 Pet. ii. 5); in the same verse he expressly styles Noah ' a preacher of righteousness.' The spirit which animated all the ancient prophets he calls, in the present epistle, the spirit of Christ (see 1 Peter i. 11), a spirit which we know from other scripture (see Nehem. ix. 20, 30) influenced them quite as much in the instructions and warnings, as in the predictions which they delivered. The last-named coincidence between the two epistles ought not to be overlooked. Peter, in the chapter of the second referred to, holds up two generations of ungodly men as beacons to succeeding ages (see 2 Peter ii. 5-9)—the antediluvians and the Sodomites: but it is only the former whom he represents as having been *preached to*. If a further ground for identifying the preaching of Noah with the preaching of Christ were wanted, it might be found in the 40th Psalm, where he who reminds Jehovah that he had a body prepared for sacrifice, proceeds to say that he had ' preached righteousness in the great congregation.' (See Ps. xl. 9.) The mention of our Lord's prophetical office follows immediately on that of his sacerdotal, as it does here.

It is objected by Dr. Brown and others to this explanation, that the *spirits in prison* preached to, must have been in prison at the time of the preaching, that is to say, to generalize the observation, that the objects of any action must always be described by their state at the time of the action. Let it be considered, however, whether the following scriptural parallel will not suffice to overthrow this canon. The apostle Paul says (1 Cor. i. 18), that the preaching of the cross is to those that perish ($\tau o \tilde{\iota} s$ $\dot{\alpha} \pi o \lambda$-$\lambda \upsilon \mu \dot{\epsilon} \nu o \iota s$) foolishness, and elsewhere (see 2 Cor. iv. 3) that ' if his gospel were hid, it was hid to those who were lost' ($\tau o \tilde{\iota} s$ $\dot{\alpha} \pi o \lambda \lambda \upsilon \mu \dot{\epsilon} \nu o \iota s$.) Here he plainly describes the despisers and rejecters of his ministry, not by their present, but their future condition. Those who deemed the preaching of the gospel folly, were not under perdition at the time of the preaching, but simply in the likely course to it. They were destined, unless they repented, to become spirits in prison—what the antediluvian impenitents now were. It appears to us that the adverb of past time (ποτε) introduced by the apostle in v. 20, is in designed contrast to an adverb of present time to be understood in the preceding verse. Those of whom he was speaking were now under penal custody, but that custody was the award of their former disobedience. Why he should describe them particularly as *spirits* in custody, it is not difficult to conjecture. It was in undesigned or designed conformity to the mention of our Lord's spirit just before. This is the explanation of Bengel, and will appear forced to no one who understands the subtle links of ideas. The whole character of the phraseology of the verse may have been determined by a tacit reference in the apostle's mind to Genesis vi. 3. Being about to speak of our Lord's ministry to the antediluvian world, he was naturally reminded of the inspired sentence which had described the Divine *spirit* as *striving with the men of that world*, for what was that striving with men but the remonstrances, counsels, and appeals which were addressed to them?

It will, however, be asked why the apostle should here single out for remark this particular exercise of our Lord's ministry? To this question we can have no hesitation in replying, that it was because of its consonance with his general argument—because it threw the same light on the character of our Lord as the great sacerdotal act which he had just mentioned. The apostle's notice of our Lord's atonement, v. 17, was with a view to the illustration of his forbearance and benignity—of his readiness to do good even to 'the unthankful and the evil.' Hence it is, we conceive, that he puts in such marked antithesis *the just and the unjust*. He had just been inculcating the lesson that we should be willing to suffer undeservedly—to suffer even for well doing, and on no account either harbour the purpose or indulge the language of retaliation. In few words, he had been impressing on his readers the necessity of *patience under provocation*. (See p. 1.) Now of this patience our Lord himself had, and that long previously to his earthly career, furnished a memorable example. He had borne with the aggravated trespasses of antediluvian sinners, he had striven with them by his Spirit, and aimed to bring them to repentance for a hundred and twenty years. (See Gen. vi. 3.) During this long period it cannot be doubted that the cry of their enormities had often risen up to his ear (see Gen. xviii. 21); that the temptation to an unsparing exercise of justice had been of daily recurrence to him: but notwithstanding this, his forbearance had held out, and his efforts to reclaim the guilty offenders not been intermitted. What higher pattern of meek composure of spirit could reproached and persecuted Christians require? Let them 'arm themselves with the same mind' (see ch. iv. 1), which the great Author of their faith had exhibited : in proportion as any indignities or wrongs they could sustain must be less outrageous than his, so would they have the stronger motive to submission.

But all impenitent generations of men have exercised the divine long-suffering, and it may therefore still be inquired why, in commending this grace to imitation, impenitence so long anterior should be specified. We think that this would be sufficiently explained by the fact of the more flagrant character of antediluvian guilt. Our apostle was evidently not singular in regarding this generation of wicked men as eminently and superlatively wicked—peculiarly bold and incorrigible. Their conduct, and that of the Sodomites after them, appear to have been looked on by inspired teachers in general as unparalleled moral phenomena. (See passages already specified, pp. 11, 13, and also Gen. vi. 5, 11-14, and Jude 7.) The more presumptuous then the sin, the greater the magnanimity which had borne with it. But there was, besides this, in the example adduced, another very instructive analogy. No disproportion between the numbers of believers and unbelievers—of persecutors and the persecuted—could be more palpable than had then obtained. The Christians of the apostle's day were liable to be discouraged by the overwhelming preponderance of vice and ungodliness around them. They were called to be 'faithful amongst the faithless'—to be holy, upright, and devout amidst innumerable examples to the contrary. Their life, they might feel, was little but a continuous warfare—a feeble effort to stem an overpowering tide. This despondency, if it existed, whether consciously or unconsciously, the apostle here meets. He virtually asks the pious few whom he was addressing, what the singularity of their position was, compared with that of Noah before them. In his time the church of God was comprised within a single family. He had to maintain his principles not merely against a predominance of corruption in society, but against its diffusion throughout the mass ; to refuse to *follow* not so much *a multitude* as a world *to do evil.* He could look nowhere for sympathy, in his fidelity to God's service, beyond the walls of his own house ; the few whom he could persuade to join with him in his precautions against impending judgment did not exceed eight ; but even with this poor minority he persevered, and therefore these ' few, that is, these eight souls were saved by water.' (See v. 20.)

We conceive that this act of pious fortitude and decision on Noah's part is not brought out so prominently as desirable, in the common translation of v. 20. According to our English version, the preservation of Noah and his family in the ark appears simply as. an *act of grace* on God's part ; in our view of the apostle's language, it is meant to appear as an *act of virtue* on his. We would render the latter part of v. 20, ‘ *into* which few, that is, eight souls *made their escape* or *saved themselves* from[c] the water.’ The verb is the same, with the sole difference of its being a compound instead of the simple form, which the apostle had used on a previous occasion, where our translators represent him as testifying and exhorting ‘ *Save yourselves* from this untoward generation.’ (See Acts ii. 40.)   It is in like manner, we think, to the voluntary separation of the patriarch and his family from their ungodly fellow-men that the apostle would here call attention.   They had resolutely ‘ sanctified the Lord God in their hearts ’ (see v. 15) in the face of opposition from thousands and tens of thousands around them ; their patient construction of the ark for so many years, and, in the first instance, their entrance within it, was a proof of this resolution ; and no self-denial to which Christians were called, no occasion for a holy and heroic superiority to danger, could exceed in difficulty this.

We are much mistaken if the point of the reference to baptism in v. 21, does not lie in the similar separation from the world, which, when duly observed, that ordinance involves.   It is commonly supposed that the apostle is comparing the waters of baptism with those of the deluge : our belief is, that he is comparing the faith and fortitude manifested in baptism, with the like qualities as exhibited in the patriarch.[d]   We should accordingly, in the translation of v. 21, propose to omit the word ‘ figure’ as needless, and to supply some such term as ‘ conduct’ or ‘ deportment.’ ‘ The like *conduct* whereunto, even baptism, doth also,’ etc. The apostle would have his fellow-believers maintain as resolute a profession of their faith as was maintained by Noah, and would remind them that, by the very act of their baptism, they were pledged to such a profession.   How familiarly baptism was considered as a solemn profession, and how inseparably the idea of disconformity to the world was associated with it, is evident from many passages of the New Testament.   To this act it is commonly, and, as we think, justly supposed that the apostle Paul alludes, when he reminds his beloved Timothy of his having (see 1 Tim. vi. 12) ‘ professed a good profession before many witnesses.’ The same apostle, by the image of death, which in another place (see Rom. vi. 3, 4) he employs to describe it, conveys, in the strongest manner,

---

[c] Regarding the δι’ as equivalent to δι’ ἐκ.—See Jelf’s Greek Grammar, Syntax, s. 127.

[d] It is true that the gender of the relative ὃ is the same as that of the immediately antecedent substantive ὕδατος, but that this may be no more than an accidental coincidence, and that the true antecedent may rather lie in the verb of the sentence will be evident from the following examples:—

Acts ii. 32. ὁ Θεὸς, οὗ ἡμεῖς ἐσμεν μάρτυρες.

Colossians ii. 16, 17. σαββατων, ἃ ἐστι σκιὰ.

the obligation which it implies, of renouncing former habits and connections. Elsewhere (see Gal. iii. 27), he represents the moral change imported by it as the assumption of a new costume. We have already remarked (see p. 15) on the exhortation with which our own apostle accompanied his call on the first Christian converts to be baptized. That they should separate themselves, in life and manners, from their unbelieving neighbours was, in fact, a duty coincident with their baptism. Thus to separate themselves would be also to *save* themselves. It is not peculiar to our apostle to represent baptism, as he does in the text before us, as a saving ordinance. The baptized on the day of Pentecost are shortly afterwards described as *the saved*—οἱ σωζόμενοι—(see Acts ii. 47.) The newly converted Saul was exhorted by Ananias to 'wash away his sins' in and by baptism, 'calling on the name of the Lord.' (See Acts xxii. 16.) The analogy therefore between the case of Noah and that of the Christians whom the apostle was addressing was of a twofold nature. The faith and fortitude of Noah in daring to prefer the approbation of God to that of a whole world around him, was a pattern for them to follow; and the reward which this faith and fortitude met with in the salvation of the patriarch and his family, was a blessing which they might expect. The apostle is therefore, as we conceive, in this reference, but anticipating the admonition and encouragement which he gives in the succeeding chapter, 'Beloved, think it not strange concerning the fiery trial which is to try you, as though some strange thing happened unto you; but rejoice, inasmuch as ye are partakers of Christ's sufferings; that, when his glory shall be revealed, ye may be glad also with exceeding joy.' (See ch. iv. 12, 13.) A like parallel we have in the exhortation to the Philippian Christians (see Phil. ii. 28), 'Be in nothing terrified by your adversaries, which is to them an evident token of perdition, but to you of salvation, and that of God.'

The inquiry will be natural, if it was the intention of the apostle to exhibit these special aspects of baptism, why he does not make them more prominent in his language? Why, on this supposition, does he describe baptism as an *answer of the conscience* rather than *a confession of the tongue?* We consider that in this phrase there is a reversion of thought, on the apostle's part, to the circumstances in which Christians were. From the evidence of the context it appears sufficiently that they were the subjects of much wrongful prejudice—very generally spoken against as evil-doers. Insubordination to civil authority and hostility to the reigning powers were, it is not unlikely, as at other times, imputed to them; it may be also, the secret practice of licentious rites. There were many who anxiously watched for their falling; as many who miscon-

strued their singularity. Altogether, their assumption of the
Christian name and discipleship was misunderstood, and their
religious profession regarded as a cloak of hypocrisy. The testimony of a 'good conscience' was, under these circumstances, indispensable to them. It was incumbent on them that they should
have the answer of a good conscience *towards men*—that when
questioned by any as to their new ways and opinions, they should
be able to give a ' reason of the hope that was in them with meek-
ness and fear.' (See vv. 15, 16.) It was not less incumbent on
them that they should have such an answer *towards God*—that they
should be able to appeal from the calumnies and censures of the
ignorant or malicious to the Searcher of hearts. Their baptismal
profession came thus to be a sort of *protestation* or *appeal*. It was
such an *answer* or *appeal* as the apostle John speaks of in his first
epistle : ' For,' says he, ' if our heart condemn us, God is greater
than our heart, and knoweth all things. Beloved, if our heart
condemn us not, then have we confidence towards God.' (See
1 John iii. 20, 21.)

It only remains to be added, that we connect the mention of the
resurrection in this latter verse, with that of the quickening of the
spirit of Christ in v. 17, regarding all the intermediate matter as
parenthetical.[e] By *quickened* we there understand *restored* to life,
so that we have, at the close of the apostle's sentence, only a resump-
tion of the idea with which he set out at the commencement. This
reiterated advertence to the resurrection of Christ is intended, we
apprehend, to show that he was no loser by his great act of disinterested kindness. The malice of his enemies only partially took
effect upon him, even on the inferior part of his nature. It took
effect on this even only for a time : his submission to the power
of death was but temporary ; his subsequent exaltation would be
permanent. By his resurrection he was advanced from the grave
to the right hand of majesty and power, no longer subject to sinners, but having principalities subject to him. Thus, the apostle
argues, suffering in his cause, and suffering even to death, would
be attended with ultimate benefit. Whosoever should thus ' suffer
in the flesh would cease from sin' (see ch. iv. 1) ; he would, that
is to say, if we rightly catch the apostle's meaning, *be* thenceforward *beyond the power of sinners*. He would, by such self-sacrifice,
become the member of a kingdom 'where the wicked cease from
troubling and where the weary are at rest.' He would be united
with his great Master in his heavenly reward, illustrating with him
the divine truth that honour succeeds humility.

---

[e] The use of the noun (Χριστοῦ) rather than of the pronoun (αὐτοῦ) in the latter
verse arises naturally from the length of the period interposed.

We have thus found a thread of consistent argument running through the whole of this long period. We have discovered in it a unity of hortatory purpose. We have seen the relevancy and force of even the minor strokes of description which it contains. We have traced the link which connected in the writer's mind dispensations apparently the most remote together, and have found him never losing sight of the lesson he would inculcate. In his case, as in many admired classical writers, we must make liberal allowance for the frequent suddenness and rapidity of mental action. The father of Grecian literature, both in his images and episodes, often surprises us by the extent of his divergences, but he seldom fails, before reverting to his main topic, to gather up all his loose ends. The relation of large portions of the lyrics of Pindar to his immediate subject is also often of this slight character. Shallow and indolent criticism may be repelled by the difficulty found in unravelling such intricacies; but here, as in most other matters, patient research will be fully recompensed.

J. T. G.

HIPPOLYTUS AND HIS AGE.

Origenis Philosophumena sive omnium haeresium Refutatio. E codice Parisino nunc primum edidit EMMANUEL MILLER. pp. xii. and 348. 8vo. Oxonii, 1851.

Hippolytus and his Age; or, the Doctrine and Practice of the Church of Rome under Commodus and Alexander Severus: and Ancient and Modern Christianity and Divinity compared. By CHRISTIAN CHARLES JOSIAS BUNSEN, D.C.L. 4 vols. post 8vo. London. 1852.

IN the Bibliothèque du Roi at Paris, is a Greek MS. of the fourteenth century, written on cotton paper, and registered as a treatise 'on all heresies.' The MS. was deposited there in 1842, having been brought from Mount Athos by Myna, a Greek, along with other treasures of a similar kind. In 1851, Emmanuel Miller, one of the librarians, edited the work, which was printed by and at the expense of the University of Oxford. The title we have given above.

Soon after its appearance, Dr. Bunsen carefully perused it; and the result has been the work, whose title-page stands in the second place, at the head of this article.

The editor and the commentator differ in opinion as to the author of the treatise, the former believing it to be an authentic production of Origen, the latter of Hippolytus. Few will hesitate to agree with the Prussian.

Let us examine the four volumes which the long lost work of Hippolytus has been the means of calling forth.

The first contains five letters addressed to Archdeacon Hare, relating immediately and directly to the bishop of Portus and his recovered treatise. In the opening one, the author undertakes to prove that the work now printed, though authentic, was not written by Origen, nor even by Caius of Rome; but that it is the production of Hippolytus, bishop of Portus and presbyter of the Roman church. This proof is continued in the second letter, where the plan of the treatise is described, and the contents of its principal part given. Here Photius's statement about a composition of Hippolytus with the same title as ours, is compared and found to agree with the present book. In the third letter, the government and condition of the Church of Rome under Zephyrinus and Callistus (199-222), as gathered from Hippolytus, is given. The fourth letter is occupied with Hippolytus's own confession of faith, *i. e.* the tenth book, in which the worthy bishop speaks of the one God, the Logos, &c. &c. Unfortunately the conclusion of the tenth book is wanting in the MS. But Bunsen conjectures that we have it at the end of the epistle to Diognetus usually printed with Justin Martyr's works. This is a bold conjecture, the probability of which we shall not stop to discuss. He prints however the entire second fragment at the end of the epistle, re-arranged and amended, with an English version by its side, to show that it forms a suitable and appropriate termination to the tenth book of Hippolytus now imperfect. The last letter in the volume discusses Hippolytus's life and writings, concluding with a picture of his character and the time in which he lived. This is the largest, and in many respects the most valuable letter. Two postscripts and an index complete the volume.

The second volume commences with a series of Aphorisms on the philosophy of the history of mankind, and in particular on the history of religion ; succeeded by what are termed ' historical fragments' on the life and consciousness of the ancient Church, especially the age of Hippolytus. The volume closes with two appendixes ' on the Christian sacrifice' and ' the Constitutions and Canons of the Apostles.'

The third volume, dedicated to the memory of Thomas Arnold, exhibits the documents of early Christianity, in which the consciousness and Christian life of that age are recorded, followed by their interpretation and application. Here the writer exhibits the ' Church and house-book' of the early Christians, and the ' Law-book' of the ante-Nicene Churh, with learned notes.

The fourth volume contains ' the Apology of Hippolytus addressed to the people of England,' with short notes ; while the second part, which is much the larger portion of the volume, presents the genuine liturgies of the ancient Church. The volume concludes with an appendix, containing a critical epistle in Latin from Bernays, Professor at Bonn, in which a laudable attempt is made to amend various parts of Hippolytus's treatise as published by Miller.

We have thus tried to give a very concise summary of the contents of these four volumes, because it is necessary to any tolerable appreciation of the entire work. Whoever would determine the value attaching to the book must carefully peruse the whole, and found his estimate upon that. And yet it is possible that this analysis will fail to make the reader acquainted with the extent of the ground traversed, or the manifold materials exhibited to his view. The book itself must be *studied* in its entireness. It demands and deserves a most careful perusal. None can have an adequate idea of it without the most diligent examination.

After patiently following the learned writer through the volumes, the first impression made upon our mind was the multifariousness of the matters discussed. We had an overpowering sense of the vast storehouse unfolded to view, and felt the hopelessness of setting fully before the reader the variety and value of all the investigations, in the compass of a review intended for general readers, or even within the bounds of an article of moderate length and a more critical nature. We are persuaded that a rightful appreciation of the worth belonging to the treatise depends on the perusal of itself; and despair of doing it full justice. In truth, great difficulty to the reviewer is created by it. In consequence of the subjects discussed, and the point of view from which they are contemplated, very few scholars in this country are capable of sitting in judgment upon it. We do not know half a dozen individuals whom we should consider competent, by natural ability and acquired learning, to give a critical estimate of its exact value. In such circumstances, and because of the very various topics discussed or touched upon, we can only give a general character of it, indicating the mode in which the topics are treated, and some defects that lie on its surface.

The volumes afford unquestionable evidence of high intellectual ability. The criticism is philosophical and comprehensive. It is not merely philological; philology and philosophy are united. The writer moves freely as one at home in the department of Church history, at least in that period of it which comes immediately under review. Nor is he less familiar with the domain of dogmatic theology and the higher criticism of the records of revelation. Whatever question arises, he treats with the touch of a master, evincing a minute knowledge of its nature, which the great majority of professed theologians are strangers to. Like a true German, the subjective element is strong within him; but not so excessive as to overlay and smother the objective. He belongs, therefore, to the best school of German critics, reminding one in many respects of Schleiermacher. We should class him with such men as Neander, Nitzsch, Rothe, Dorner, Lücke, &c., in theology. Perhaps in him the proportion between the subjective and objective is juster than in these scholars; but he stands on the same platform and partakes of their characteristic excellences. On the whole, the work is a very favourable specimen of that kind of criticism for which Germany is pre-eminent at the present time. We are aware of the strong prejudice in certain quarters against any thing and every thing German; but it is a happiness to know, that they spring from sheer ignorance. Well-meaning men there are, who look with distrust on the productions of our Teutonic brethren, because of the aberrations and destructive tendencies which some exhibit; but that is no reason for turning a deaf ear to the earnest words and profound speculations of a large class in that country, who have certainly advanced the science of a critical and philosophical theology. The thinkers of Germany deserve an impartial hearing. But the English mind is obtuse to their disquisitions. It is so practical as to be generally unfit for the region of a high philosophy. Yet surely works like the present are calculated to conciliate a candid hearing both for itself and others of cognate nature proceeding from the same school. If any one turns aside from them with indifference or disdain, it is his fault and loss. In the spirit of a narrow exclusiveness he may not wish to read them; but that shews no more than a self-complacent ignorance which will not learn. It is nothing but absolute folly to anathematise German theology and its manifestations. Besides being unphilosophical, it is most injurious. The emanations of earnest spirits are passed by. Ardent longings after a high and pure region are nowhere more felt than in Germany; nor is there any country where these longings find utterance in works breathing a more healthy spirit of piety. The authors who influence there the current of theological thought are in the main on the side of faith. They have almost succeeded in solving a problem for which England has done but little—the true philosophy of religion. But it is in the region of criticism they excel, as all who are conversant with their writings know: and the present is properly a critical work in the region of patristic literature. There it takes a high place. It throws much light on an early Christian age. The reader is struck not merely or most with its masterly delineation of the peculiarities of Hippolytus's treatise on all heresies, but its comprehensive glances into the ante-Nicene period—the picture given of that age which intervened between the last apostle and the council of Nice. The entire life of the ancient church is described. Christian education, baptism, worship, polity, discipline, and social relations are brought into contrast with present dogmas and forms. We are introduced into a period of the church's existence long gone by, and behold in the mirror of opinions and practices then prevalent, the western theology and worship of our own time. To do this is no easy task; yet the critic of Hippolytus has done it in the style of a master. His acquaintance with the works of the early fathers is uncommon. The best productions of the German theological school are familiar to him; and he knows all the English books relating to his subject. Our readers will therefore find in the volumes an intellectual repast. The general style of the English is very good, often elevated and eloquent. Doubtless the work will always be referred to as having materially advanced our knowledge of some

most important topics.   We sincerely congratulate the esteemed
writer on this most valuable production of his pen.   Rich, indeed,
is the contribution he has made towards a reorganisation of the
Christian church, the church of the future, which he sees in the
distance, and is so anxious to accelerate.   The church of the
future ! How we desire to behold her in simple majesty, pure in
faith, childlike in love.   May the efforts of those who are now
stretching their eye into the vista of coming years, as if to catch a
glimpse of her features, be crowned with the divine favour, and
contribute to the desired consummation !

We shall now characterise the manner in which the different
parts of the work are treated.

The proof given in the first volume that Hippolytus and none
other was the author of the printed treatise is conclusive and convincing.   The question is most ably argued by the critic, who
appears to great advantage not only in the style of his emendations upon the Greek text, but also in the right appreciation of
evidence, a point where his countrymen often fail.   This part
might have been published separately.   Written as it must have
been since the Greek work was printed at Oxford, it shows the
student of antiquity well versed in the opinions and practices of
the first three centuries.   His knowledge of the earliest heresies
is surprisingly exact.   With Irenæus, Epiphanius, Tertullian,
Origen, &c., he is well acquainted.   We now know beyond all
doubt that Hippolytus was bishop of Portus, the harbour of
Rome, and nowhere else—that he was contemporary with Zephyrinus and Callistus bishops of Rome, and suffered martyrdom in
all probability under Maximin, about 236 A.D.

The learned author returns to Hippolytus at page 121 of the
second volume, and, examining him on various subjects, finds that
he was no Papist, that he was neither a Nicene nor an Athanasian
divine, nor an Arian.   His theological opinions cannot be reduced
to our Protestant formulas without losing their native beauty.   On
the doctrine of original sin ' he would have raised many a previous question both against St. Augustin and Pelagius ; and finally
have entrenched himself in his strong position—the doctrine of
the free agency of the human will.   He would have thought
Luther's theory a quaint expression of a truth which he fully
acknowledged ; but as to Calvin's Predestination, he would have
abhorred it, without thinking less highly of God's inscrutable
councils.' [a]   When Bunsen proceeds to develop the notions of
Hippolytus and his age respecting the Canon, tradition, and
inspiration, he touches delicate ground.   The chapter on the

---

[a] Vol. ii. p. 128.

canon contains some good ideas without being very satisfactory. The small space allotted to the topic hardly sufficed to do it justice. The canon of Hippolytus coincided with that contained in the fragment published by Muratori; but the fragment is imperfect and obscure. Hence Bunsen applies his critical skill to it, and conjectures that the Epistle to the Hebrews was mentioned in it between the words *Epistola sane Judae et suprascripti Joannis duae in Catholica (Catholicis) habentur,* and *Et sapientia ab amicis Salomonis in honorem ipsius scripta. Sapientia* is thought to mean the Proverbs, because the fathers designated that book by Σοφία, and the allusion to Proverbs is supposed to be the remainder of something said of a canonical work of the New Testament, the authorship of which presented some analogy with that case of the Old Testament. Such an allusion agrees, in his opinion, with the Epistle to the Hebrews. All this is exceedingly doubtful.

We differ from our author in relation to the Epistle to the Hebrews. We believe that it was written by Paul, or at least that the matter proceeded from him, Luke perhaps assisting in putting it into its present shape. With Luther, Bleek, and Bunsen attributing it to Apollos, and finding an Alexandrian element in it, we are unable to sympathise. It is not at all clear that the 'Wisdom of Solomon' is not meant by *Sapientia.* The fathers designated it as well as the Proverbs by Σοφία or *Sapientia.* Tertullian does so.[b] But we are willing to wait till the edition of the fragment prepared by the critic be published next year.

With regard to the Apocalypse, Bunsen also gives his opinion, affirming that the book was written earlier than Domitian. ' The horizon of the vision is the latter half of the year 68.' This is deduced from ch. xvii. 8 and the following verses, which, however, are susceptible of very various senses, and by no means warrant the confident allegation, ' the book itself plainly says the contrary' (to its having been written at the time of the apostle's exile under Domitian).[c] External evidence decidedly preponderates in favour of the *Domitianic* date, and any internal testimony to the contrary must be very clear to set it aside. The objections to Lücke's view here adopted by Bunsen, are strong and persuasive. Neither can we adopt our author's explanation of the number 666 in the Apocalypse, viz., that it is the name and designation of Balaam, though we are told ' this is the only one which agrees with the book itself.' All others are termed ' more or less ingenious or absurd *jeux d'esprit.*'[d] But we fear that his own,

---

[b] Adversus Valentin., cap. ii.   [c] Vol. ii. p. 141.   [d] Ibid., p. 142.

or rather Züllig's which he appropriates, is equally entitled to that appellation. Here it is as drawn out by the discoverer himself:—

$$ \text{ב} = 2; \ \text{ל} = 30; \ \text{ע} = 70; \ \text{ם} = 40; \ \text{ב} = 2; \ \text{נ} = 50; \ \text{ב} = 2; $$
$$ \text{ע} = 70; \ \text{ר} = 200; \ \text{ק} = 100; \ \text{ס} = 60; \ \text{ם} \ 40: \ = 666.^e $$

The Hebrew words are בלעם בן בער, *i. e.* 'Balaam, son of Beor,' to which is added, קסם, 'enchanter.' It is quite arbitrary to add the last word, and besides, בער should be written with *vau.*

On the views of the ancient church respecting tradition and inspiration, our critic touches but briefly. What he *does* say is good. Very properly does he remark that the 'Theopneusty, or theory of inspiration, of Gaussen would have appeared to Hippolytus as a dangerous Jewish superstition.'[f] In delineating the life of the church we wish he had been clearer and more explicit on some points. He does not make the common meals, Agapæ, and Eucharist, very intelligible, though he introduces them in various places. In common with many others he also embraces the opinion that the Jewish synagogue was the prototype of the Christian worship. What is the evidence for this? Equally destitute of foundation is the sentiment 'that St. John established or sanctioned the establishment of single rectors, called overseers, as presidents of the presbytery.'[g] Where is the ground for this notion? We deem it far more probable that the distinction between *elder* and *bishop* became more marked after the latter had been elevated by his brethren to be their president or moderator, which we cannot suppose to have been in the Johannean age.

The theses on the Eucharist, written in December, 1822, in German, are admirable: so is the succeeding chapter on the epochs of the Christian sacrifice. In these two sections profound truth is delivered, by means of which great light is thrown on the nature of the Lord's Supper and Christian sacrifice. But they must be *studied;* for the ideas unfolded in them are presented in a philosophical method. We fear that the great majority of English readers will not understand them, or rather turn away from them without trying to enter into their meaning. Were they expanded and amplified by an Englishman, they would be very acceptable to the true theologian. At present, it must be admitted that they are quite German in thought and expression, and therefore a little misty. To our apprehension they are pregnant with

---

[e] See Die Offenbarung Johannis vollständig erklärt, von Dr. Th. F. J. Züllig, vol. ii. p. 247.

[f] Vol. ii. pp. 147, 148.   [g] Ibid, p. 156.

spiritual truth, often beautifully expressed. Admirable, too, is the extract from a letter addressed to the late Dr. Nott ' on the nature of the Christian sacrifice,' and much clearer than the two preceding ones.

The remainder of the second volume is occupied with the work called the 'Apostolical Constitutions.' Here the writer shows the connection of a part of them with Hippolytus, and re-arranges their text in a critical manner, separating the genuine ante-Nicene materials from those of later origin. The 'Constitutions,' as preserved in various national churches, are all compared in their ancient texts and elucidated, as well as the Apostolic canons. Such critical researches are preparatory to the third volume, where the authentic texts of the 'Church-and-house-book of the early Christians, and of the Law-book of the ante-Nicene Church,' are given in English. The preparatory discussions to the restoration of these ancient documents in the second volume, and the notes to them in the third are full of learning, and evince the writer's skill in the higher criticism. The remaining portion of the volume contains a wide range of topics, bringing out the early picture of Christian worship, instruction, and discipline into striking contrast with modern usages. Here we have discussions respecting baptism, the Sunday service, the Communion service, the various liturgies which have been made, and other topics of interest into which we cannot enter. Very considerable is the accession to our knowledge made by the writer. In regard to the 'Apostolic Constitutions' in particular, he has done more than all his predecessors together. Indeed, as he truly remarks, they have been generally neglected. Perhaps he attributes too great a value to them. He says they are not scriptural and yet Apostolic. How so? Did John the Apostle change the government of the Church, or sanction its change? So he thinks. This is too like Rothe's idea, and accords with the expediency system. Its truth has not yet been made manifest: and it will need better proof than has been offered before it be worthy of general acceptation. At all events, a *clear* description of the Johannean Church in Asia Minor, and the constitution of the Church as it previously existed, with the differences between them, has not been given. A number of particulars are stated in which they *may have been* diverse, but in an unconnected method. We beg to call the author's attention to this interesting subject, and if he can throw more light upon it we shall gladly welcome it.

The second part of the fourth volume is properly a continuation of the third, containing the genuine liturgies of the ancient Church, which, after a general introduction, are presented in their own texts, or in Latin. This is a favourite topic of the author's, for in the dedication 'to the great name of Niebuhr' it is stated that it was begun to be prosecuted at Rome in 1817. Here it is completed, and in a manner above all praise. The task was worthy of the friend of Niebuhr, and excellently has it been accomplished. Henceforth Bunsen's name must ever be associated with the 'Apostolical Constitutions and Canons,' and the 'Ancient Liturgies of the Church.' It is in no boastful tone that he says of the latter, 'I have, in particular, exhibited, restored, and explained the really ancient elements in the Liturgies of the Churches of Antioch, Alexandria, and Constantinople, or in those of St. James, St. Mark, Cyril, Basil, and Chrysostom. I have endeavoured to reconstruct the ancient Gallican Liturgy, and have shown the canon of the Roman mass to be a patchwork, the original elements of which may be restored by a critical process.'[h] In restoring and commenting on the Apostolical Ordinances, Creeds, and Liturgies he has no rival, neither is he likely to have. Others will build upon his learned labours without superseding them. Among the philosophical critics of Germany who have investigated Christian antiquity, he must occupy a foremost place because of what he has done.

The first part of the fourth volume, which might better have followed the first, contains a speech supposed to be delivered by Hippolytus in person before a company of friends in London, in 1851. It consists of 117 pages, and is on the whole well managed. Of course the writer puts many of *his own sentiments* about the age of Hippolytus into the mouth of the martyr himself. The first twenty-two pages are not much to our taste; they are wordy and tedious, relating to the Crystal Palace, the mode of Government in England, and the English people generally. But with this exception, the Apology is a very readable and instructive document, evincing a discriminating mind. It is a better speech than Hippolytus himself would have made. Almost all questions of theology are touched upon in it, such as the Trinity, the Prologue of John's Gospel, the Nicene and Athanasian creeds, Inspiration, Baptism, Sacrifice, Propitiation, the Eucharist, Transubstantiation, the book of Daniel, the second epistle of Peter, the sentiments of the Tübingen school, &c. &c.

The first part of the second volume has little connection with what precedes or follows, containing 'philosophical aphorisms' as a contribution to the philosophy of religion. Although the speculative ability of the writer appears here in its loftiest exercise, we fear the portion before us will be generally misapprehended. Its Teutonic cast and obscurity will repel the English mind, or

---

[h] Vol. iii. p. 24.

prove an obstacle to intelligibility. And yet there is more genius here than in any other part of the work. The author moves in the highest region of philosophical history, unfolding views of profound and truthful import. Doubtless he will be called for this a 'Pantheist' by such as do not know what Pantheism is. He will be branded as a 'Transcendentalist.' And so he is. *There is a meaning in Transcendentalism.* The German transcendental philosophy may be ignored; but who can doubt that it contains much truth, however obscured or distorted. Through these aphorisms we have diligently followed our critic, and think we can apprehend his noble aim.

Having thus pointed out the manner in which the learned writer has conducted his investigations, and the general excellence that characterises them, we may allude to one or two defects which will weaken their impression on the minds of many.

The first defect is the occasional obscurity, inseparable perhaps from the German idiosyncracy, which pervades the discussions. Though the work be written in English, it is thoroughly German in texture and habit. A few parts, which were first composed in German and are now translated, betray strong evidences of Germanism liable to puzzle the reader. For example: 'But, on the other hand, this realization of God in the finite supposes the infinite process of creation by the antithesis of Will and Reason in the Divine Being; or, to speak theologically, the eternal Generation of the Word, which is the Son in the highest, that is to say, in the infinite or ideal sense.' [i]

Again: 'If the sin to be washed away were not *as much* that actually committed as original hereditary sin, a new-born child might certainly as well be baptized as one growing up; or rather, it would be the most natural and safest thing to do so.' [k] Or; 'What can be proved is, that he (Hippolytus) would no more have maintained or supported an Arian creed, than wished to see proclaimed as creed the exclusive and conventional language in which those formulas are couched.' [m]

'To make the logical process not a finite type, and a purely phenomenological reflex of the infinite, but the real essence and only reality of the consciousness of God, is the second error of Hegel.' [n]

A second defect is a dogmatic confident tone which occasionally appears in propounding things that hardly admit of it. Where evidence is contradictory or uncertain, it is unwise to assert too strongly. What he says of the time when John wrote the Apo-

---

[i] Vol. ii. p. 35.   [k] Vol. iii. p. 195.
[m] Vol. ii. p. 126.   [n] Vol. ii. p. 34.

calypse may be taken as an example. Again, in reference to the second epistle of Peter, he puts into the mouth of Hippolytus: 'The ancient churches did not know such a letter.'[o] That the epistle was written by Peter may be reasonably doubted; but some ancient churches before Hippolytus must have known it.

'I have given and restored all which remains to us of genuine sacramental texts of the Eastern and Western Churches, from the second to the sixth century.'[p]

Again: 'After the loss of national independence, and in the wane of prophetic spirit, the Ecclesiastes, a pious and philosophical author of the Persian times, &c.'[q]

Though the composition of this book be commonly placed at the end of the Persian or beginning of the Macedonian period, yet it is far from being certain that it was so. Hitzig, no mean judge, says that it 'was hardly composed in the Persian period,' and proceeds to give his reasons. He places it in the third century before Christ.[r]

In another place he puts into the mouth of Hippolytus the assertion: 'How is it that you do not read the same text (of the New Testament) which we had in our time?'[s] In a note we are told that 'all ancient authorities prove that the third and fourth verses (of the prologue to John's Gospel) were written thus:

'All things were made by Him, and without Him was not anything made. What was made is life in Him, and the life was the light of men.

'The present punctuation was made in order to combat the heresy of the Macedonians, towards the end of the fourth century. Thus it has all tradition and ancient authorities against it.'[t]

In the present instance tradition and ancient authorities are little worth, because the uncial MSS. are necessarily excluded. But Bunsen proceeds to say, that the internal evidence is as great as the external in favour of the division, which the Alexandrians adopted. How can this be when his friend Lücke decides, on internal grounds, that the common punctuation *must* be followed;[u] and when De Wette affirms that the old way 'gives no good sense?'[x]

The great merits of the work as an original one, overshadow

---

[o] Vol. iv. p. 34. [p] Vol. iii. p. xxiv. [q] Vol. ii. p. 7.

[r] See the Exegetisches Handbuch zum alten Testament, Lieferung vii., p. 121, et seqq. [s] Vol. iv. p. 31.

[t] Vol. iv. pp. 127, 128.

[u] 'Dieses nöthigt *ἐν αὐτῷ ζωὴ ἦν* als einen Satz für sich zu nehmen, und sonach *ὃ γέγονεν* mit dem vorhergehenden zu verbinden.' Commentar ueber das Evangel. des Johannes, p. 306, third edition.

[x] Exegetisches Handbuch, vol. i. part iii. p. 16, third edition.

all minor blemishes that may belong to it. With most of the views propounded we cordially agree. We can go along with the critic in his conclusions generally. Probably we should most differ on the question, whether the Apostolic Church be normal or not? He holds the negative; and even goes so far as to say 'it is no more absolutely normal than any other,' and that 'the consistent criticism of the Evangelical and Apostolical records proves that the glorious building of the Church was erected in too contracted proportions, both for its Divine founder and for humanity, to last for ever.'[y] We hold that the Apostolical Church was certainly more normal than any other, or rather, that it was normal and none other. A few statements here and there we should like to see changed, because they are either incorrect or incautiously expressed. Such things, however, are mere trifles.

There are some classes of religionists in the present day who will not welcome the book, notwithstanding its surpassing excellence.

The Tractarians, against whose formalism it is a powerful protest throughout, will do what they can to neutralise its efficacy for good. For are not the truth of God and the spiritual liberty of the Gospel here enunciated in a manly, liberal, candid spirit; and how can those in bondage to ceremonies relish these things? The ante-Nicene age of the Church is here pourtrayed; a remote antiquity is described; and are not its features widely different from those which this party would attribute to the ancient times they fondly appeal to? We know of few works better fitted to open their eyes to the sublime mission of a Christian man, the nature of Christian worship such as God accepts, and the qualities of a true Church. Probably they are too infatuated to listen to the teachings of a German. With them the name is almost tantamount to *infidel.* That they will receive the book in no friendly spirit may be inferred from a review in the 'Guardian' of November 3rd, written in a narrow, illiberal, flippant spirit, by one unable to answer the author. Else, why is misrepresentation resorted to by the anonymous writer? He denies, it is asserted, original sin and the grace of baptism. This is unfair. The very passages referred to as proof prove the unfairness. He denies, indeed, and rightly, that the children of Christian parents who die unbaptised are under damnation, from which they might have been rescued by baptism. He denies, and rightly, that the sentence of condemnation which Scripture and conscience proclaim against ungodly selfish nature striving in man for the mastery can apply to the case of infants.

[y] Vol. ii. p. 111.

He denies, and rightly, that the curse said to rest upon an infant is converted into a blessing or wholly removed by the act of sprinkling.[z] And he does *not* 'speak of that washing of regeneration which is effected by the blood of Christ as " not much more than the *taurobolia* and *criobolia*, mysteries of the last stages of heathenism, purporting to purify the neophyte by the blood of victims."' On the contrary, he speaks of the notion of external baptism possessing the efficacy of washing away sin as a superstition. Such Tractarian misrepresentations show the *animus* that prompted them.

Again; many of the Evangelical clergy, and the Evangelical dissenters too, will hardly like the book. Their creed is too sharply defined for that. They look upon religion as *dogma* rather than *life*. Hence they will view with suspicion the writer's sentiments on some momentous topics, such as the Trinity, Inspiration, the Canon, &c. Yet we are free to confess that a better explanation of the Trinity and the Prologue of John's Gospel we have no where seen. Such as have *studied* the subject of the canon impartially (how few they are) will hesitate about differing from the learned author respecting it; and in relation to Inspiration, his view would probably be found substantially correct if he explained it more distinctly and intelligibly. At present, he has done little more than throw out hints on the subject. He is right in rejecting *verbal* or *mechanical* inspiration. What philosophic mind could ever embrace such a hypothesis? There are other hypotheses approaching in their nature to the verbal one which he would doubtless reject.[a] In fact, Gaussen's ideas have a greater hold on most divines in England than they are aware of. Coleridge's view is far liker the true one.

Romanists will not relish the book. How can they, when the history of one of their bishops is here laid bare for the first time in its naked truth? Callistus, bishop of Rome, was a rogue and a convict, according to Hippolytus, a brother bishop and a member of the same presbytery. He was the moral corrupter of his Church and age. And he was not only the *moral*, but the *doctrinal* corrupter. He was a Noetian. How can Romanists like the book, when it points out so clearly the character of the ante-Nicene age in contrast with the later corrupt, and especially the mediæval age of the Church? The earliest liturgies, the Apostolic Constitutions in their oldest state, the canon law, the marriage of the clergy, the idea of sacrifice, the absence

---

[z] Comp. vol. iii. pp. 191, 192, 197, 212; and vol. ii. p. 126.
[a] See an introductory lecture delivered at the opening of New College, St. John's Wood, by Dr. Harris.

of domination over others on the part of the Roman bishops, the liberty enjoyed by bishops near Rome and in Italy in their respective spheres, with many other phenomena, are adverse to the assumption of a Papal head and sacerdotal despotism. The Romish Church in her devotional books, her laws, her practices, has grievously departed from ancient usages, and that for the worse. She cannot stand the test of antiquity itself, much less of Scripture.

But while these and other classes will doubtless dislike the book before us, some will welcome it. The Baptists will hail its appearance as corroborating their distinctive views. Paedo-baptism was unknown to Hippolytus. It was unknown in the *post-Apostolic* Church (to which Bunsen unhesitatingly adds *the Apostolic itself*) till Cyprian first established it as a principle. Baptism of *children* had only begun to be practised in some countries, being defended in the time of Tertullian and Hippolytus merely as an innovation; but *infant* baptism was not known. On this interesting point we refer to the third volume,[b] where the subject is treated more correctly than in any other work. Even Neander has failed to perceive the true sense of certain passages in Origen and Tertullian. Here, for the first time, the thing is cleared up. Tertullian speaks of the baptism of *growing children* (parvuli), and pleads for delay till they be able to take the vows upon themselves. The three classical passages in Origen relating to the subject also speak of *parvuli*, not *infants*. In accordance with this is a passage in the Alexandrian church-book which states, that the baptism of *children* is an apostolical tradition. What Tertullian and Origen oppose is the baptism of young, growing children, not of new-born infants. The latter was introduced by Cyprian and his African contemporaries at the close of the third century, who looked upon it as a washing away of the sinfulness of human nature and connected it with the ordinance of circumcision. It is unfortunate that Neander has confounded the *parvuli* of Tertullian and Origen with *infantes*, and has consequently furnished a very imperfect account of the origin of infant baptism. And it is somewhat remarkable, that Schaff has erred in the same matter, perversely deducing from Tertullian's testimony the general practice of infant baptism.[c]

But while Baptists rejoice in this testimony to the antiquity of their views, they are far from realising the picture of ancient baptism as practised in Hippolytus's time. Those immersed by them do not go through the formal, triennial instruction of catechumens.

---

[b] Pp. 179-210.
[c] *Geschichte der Christlichen Kirche,* vol. i. p. 490, et seqq.

They do not undergo a public examination at the end of their probation. The baptismal vow and immediate preparation for it are different with them, or rather, they are almost unknown. The mode of admission into the Church is different. If, therefore, they would conform to the earliest recorded practices in connection with baptism by immersion *from the time Christianity became general*, they must alter their present procedure. 'The Baptists,' says our author, 'find it difficult to understand that the idea of the German Protestant act of baptism, which concludes with the vow and benediction, corresponds exactly with the idea of the Gospel commandment, the letter of which they push to such an extent; and, under the yoke of an utterly one-sided rigid Calvinism, they are inclined to attach to their own form a superstitious power, by which the efficacy of a continually renewed faith is thrown into the background.'[d]

The opponents of the destructive criticism peculiar to the Tübingen school will hail the appearance of this work as an antidote to scepticism. For there is no question that the Tübingen ideas about the original elements of the Roman church, the late appearance of John's Gospel, and the doctrine of the Logos are discountenanced by it. This fact, which some may be weak enough to think the most important one in the four volumes, is prominently brought out in various places.[e] But it is of comparatively little moment; for the dreams of Baur, Schwegler, Zeller, and their associates have made no impression on the true critic, nor seduced the leading philosophical school of German theologians from their right path. We knew and believed that the Tübingen notions about the origination of John's Gospel toward the middle of the second century could not be correct; a belief confirmed by the light shed from the works of Hippolytus on early times.

The volumes will be acceptable to every right-minded theologian. The candid inquirer will receive them gratefully as suggesting new views, enforcing sound principles, presenting interesting pictures of the past for the instruction of the present and the guidance of the future. The tone of them is healthful and bracing. They must benefit the true spirits of the age who look to the future for a new and better era of Christianity in which the sickliness of modern piety, with the formalism, superstition, and unphilosophicalness of a selfish age shall disappear; and the true Church, the Church of believers, present the spectacle of a loving brotherhood, embodying the life of religion in forms of ever-expanding development pervaded by the intellectual and devotional in due proportions.

---

[d] Vol. iii. pp. 208, 209.   [e] See vol. i. pp. 53, 245, 280, &c. &c.

Of the many noble pieces of writing contained in the work we shall select two to serve as a fitting close to the present article :—

'The question at this moment is, not how to carry out, but how to prepare a second, grand, reconstructive Reformation. The porch of the Temple must first be more thoroughly cleansed than it was in the sixteenth, and, above all, restored more honestly than it was in the seventeenth century; and lastly, the work must be handled more practically than has yet been done by the critical German school of this age. In the meantime let every one cleanse his own heart and house as well as he can. When the feeling of the misery which is coming, and a real faith in the saving truth which is in Christ shall have thoroughly penetrated the nations, then will the Spirit of God assuredly come upon them with might, either for the reformation or the annihilation of the existing churches. Whether this crisis will end in the renewal or in the destruction of the present nations and states, will depend upon the position they take in face of the demands of the gospel and the wants of the times. For every nation and age has its time and its day of visitation, after which its fate is sealed. This great movement, however, will assuredly not lead to the destruction of Christianity, but to its establishment on a firmer basis; not to the lowering of the person of Jesus of Nazareth, but to his greater glorification; and God's kingdom of truth and liberty on earth will advance as triumphantly over the perishing as over the renovated kingdoms and states of the present world.

'My belief in this future rests upon the following convictions, which have been considerably strengthened by, and seem to me naturally to flow from, the criticism of the work of Hippolytus and of his age, and which I consider as the final result of the comparison between ancient and modern Christianity and divinity founded upon that criticism.

'Christianity is true, because free, and it is free and freeing because true; Christianity is philosophically and historically true, and it could not be true except by being so both by its thought and by its history. It is true, by the inexhaustible truth of the eternal thought which it manifests, and by the equally inexhaustible truth of the divine individuality upon which it rests—Jesus of Nazareth. It is true, by the genuineness and historical truth of the apostolic and evangelic accounts which we possess of this exalted individuality, and by the harmony of these records with the living tradition which accompanies it. This tradition is the Church, and the Church is Christianised humanity; Christianised by the Spirit of Christ, and by the Scripture which that Spirit produced.

'The great proof of the divine nature and truth of Christianity is its power of regenerating the world.

'This regenerating power has shown itself twice in an unparalleled, world-renovating change produced by the spirit of Christianity; in the moral and intellectual revival of the ancient world, after the downfall of the universal empire of Rome in the fifth Christian century; and by the moral, intellectual, and political revival of the modern world, after the downfall of the omnipotence of papal Rome in the sixteenth.'— vol. iii. pp. xxvii.-xxix.

Still finer is the following :—

'The nations of the present age want not less religion, but more; they do not wish for less community with the apostolic times, but for more: but, above all, they want their wounds healed by a Christianity showing a life-renewing vitality, allied to reason and conscience, and ready and able to reform the social relations of life, beginning with the domestic and culminating in the political. They want no negations, but positive reconstruction; no conventionality, but an honest and *bonâ fide* foundation deep as the human mind, and a structure free and organic as nature. In the meantime let no national form be urged as identical with divine truth; let no dogmatic formula oppress conscience and reason; and let no corporation of priests and no set of dogmatists sow discord and hatred in the sacred communities of domestic and national life. This aim cannot be attained without national efforts, Christian education, free institutions, and social reforms. Then no zeal will be called Christian which is not hallowed by charity, no faith Christian which is not sanctioned by reason.

'As to the future of the world, the present civilization of Europe may perish; the nations who have created it may make way for new nationalities, as the Celtic element in Ireland now visibly does for the Germanic; but that holy longing of the human mind for seeing truth realised over the earth will be satisfied earlier or later. The whole world will be Japhetised, which, in religious matters, means now pre-eminently that it must be Christianised by the agency of the Teutonic element. Japhet holds the torch of light to kindle the heavenly fire in all the other families of the one undivided and indivisible human race. Christianity enlightens now only a small portion of the globe, but it cannot be stationary, and it will advance, and is already advancing, triumphantly over the whole earth, in the name of Christ, and in the light of the Spirit.'—vol. ii. pp. 115-117.

T.

CORRESPONDENCE.

ON THE INTERPRETATION OF THE PHRASE 'EUNUCHS FOR THE KINGDOM OF HEAVEN'S SAKE' (MATT. XIX. 12).

DEAR SIR,—In your *Journal* for October last one or two remarks occur with reference to our Lord's declaration (Matt. xix. 12) that ' there be eunuchs which have made themselves eunuchs *for the kingdom of heaven's sake:*' upon which, with your permission, I desire to make a few remarks.

The passages to which I more especially refer are the following :—

' We do not think, with some writers, that the Essenes, unlike the cotemporary sects of the Pharisees and Sadducees, were *uncondemned* by our Saviour; for in Matthew xix. 11, 12, Christ, in answer to an inquiry of his disciples, says, " All men cannot receive this saying, save they to whom it is given : for there are some eunuchs (i. e. such as lived in voluntary abstinence) which were so from their mother's womb; and there are some eunuchs which were made eunuchs of men ; and there be eunuchs which have made themselves eunuchs *for the kingdom of heaven's sake.*" From this description of an existing state of things, we learn that three classes of individuals abstained from marriage, viz., those who were physically unable " from their mother's womb;" those who were, under the command of others, " made eunuchs of men ;" and lastly, those who abstained *for the sake of the kingdom.* All the best commentators are of opinion that the contemplative Essenes are here alluded to, because they abstained from the society of women, *in order to be (as they thought) better fitted for heaven.*

' Now,' continues your correspondent, ' in the above passage, does our Lord reprehend celibacy *for the sake of religion,* or does he not? If he does *not,* then the Essenes are to be considered as *uncondemned;* if, however, we answer the question in the affirmative, then one at least of the doctrines of the Essenes must be considered as *condemned* by him. That the question must be answered in the affirmative is evident, when we consider that if our Saviour did regard celibacy in itself as pre-eminently excellent, then he would have said, as was his custom on other occasions (e. g. the Sermon on the Mount), " *Blessed* are those who abstain from marriage for the kingdom of heaven's sake;" and the reason why he did not thus express himself was just because *the motive* (" for the kingdom of heaven's sake ") *was selfish, and not " such as implies the sacrifice of human feelings from love to the kingdom of God, and for the sake of rendering it more efficient service"* (Neander's Life of Christ, Bohn's edition, p. 363).'—*Journal,* p. 177.

Now, whatever may be the meaning of the expression ' *for the kingdom of heaven's sake,*' it may, I think, with confidence be asserted that our Lord is not speaking at all of the moral character of the eunuchism alluded to. He simply states a fact—making, neither directly nor by implication, any reference whatsoever to the ethics of the question. Let the occasion of his remark respecting these eunuchs be taken into consideration, and this will, I think, be evident. The disciples then, be it remembered, had expressed an opinion that if it were unlawful for a man to put away his wife except for fornication, it would, in their opinion, be better for a man that he should not marry at all. They thought, perhaps, that circumstances might arise which would render intolerably irksome an union which could be lawfully dissolved by nothing short of actual fornication ; and our Lord, to expose the folly of their thought, and to convince them of the almost universal inapplicability of their hastily-expressed opinion, replies, ' *All men* cannot receive this saying (i. e. cannot abstain, as you propose), save they to whom it is given ' (i. e. save ' eunuchs,' viz. ' eunuchs' in the sense in which the word *eunuch* is employed in the words that follow) : ' For,' says he, ' there are [some][a] eunuchs which were so born from their mother's womb ; and there are [some][a] eunuchs which were made eunuchs of men ; and there be eunuchs which have made themselves eunuchs for the kingdom of heaven's sake. He that is able to receive it (viz. *your* saying), let him receive it.' He says, in reply, this ; and he says no more. Unless therefore we interpolate our Lord's words, he neither approves nor condemns the eunuchism of which he is speaking. He merely states that as there were some that could not receive 'this saying,' viz. the saying of his disciples, so there were some that could ; and that of these there were some (whom he calls 'eunuchs,' since they lived as eunuchs?) who had ' eunuchised themselves' (ἑαυτοὺς εὐνούχισαν) ' for the kingdom of heaven's sake.'

Upon these grounds it may, I think, be fairly maintained that our Lord does not, as your correspondent supposes, condemn the eunuchism of those who (whatever may be the meaning of the expression) had eunuchised themselves *for the kingdom of heaven's sake.* Indeed his concluding words, ' He that is able to receive it' (viz. the saying of his disciples), though they give no countenance to the idea that a merely ascetic celibacy was of itself desirable or good, appear rather to approve of such an eunuchism, if circumstances demand it, and provided a man be capable of practising it, than to disapprove of it : at any rate they certainly do not condemn it.[b]

---

[a] The bracketed words are wanting in the original.

[b] I may perhaps be permitted to add, as bearing upon the interpretation of the passage, though foreign to the more immediate object of my letter, that the phrase ' to whom it is given '—a phrase which, more than any other, would to some seem to imply that the abstinence or eunuchism spoken of was ' pre-eminently excellent,' an idea against which your correspondent so earnestly and so properly protests—appears to denote simply that the power to abstain from lawful sexual intercourse was not common to men in general—that such a power was abnormal, unusual, unnatural—and that to him who could so abstain, the power to do so, like any other power, was the gift of God. But since '*every* man,' as St. Paul says, in speaking (1 Cor. vii. 7) of those who could abstain and of those who could not, ' hath his own proper gift of God, one after this manner and another after that,' the mere fact that the power to abstain was a ' given' power determines nothing as to its pre-eminence of excellence.

Also, that the phrases ' to be eunuchised' (εὐνουχίζεσθαι) and ' to eunuchise oneself' (ἑαυτον εὐνουχίζειν) will perhaps admit of a greater latitude of interpretation than the phrase ' to be made,' or ' to make oneself an eunuch.' A man may with propriety be said ' to be eunuchised,' or ' to eunuchise himself,' who lives *as an eunuch*, whether he be an eunuch in the usual acceptation of the word, or whether he be not ; but it may be doubted whether a man can with the same propriety be spoken of as made an eunuch, or as making himself such, unless he be really and strictly an eunuch—an eunuch proper, an eunuch in the sense in

The next point which calls for remark, and that to which I more especially desire to direct your attention, is the strong, unqualified, and somewhat hasty assertion on the part of your correspondent, that the interpretation given by him to our Lord's declaration that it was '*for the kingdom of heaven's sake*' that some had thus eunuchised themselves, or made themselves eunuchs, is the interpretation given to the phrase by ' *all the best commentators.*'

Now, whether the words will or will not admit of that interpretation, viz. that the individuals in question, actuated by a mistaken asceticism, were austerely denying themselves the pleasures of matrimonial life, ' *in order to be (as they thought) better fitted for heaven,*' such is not, as represented by him, the interpretation of ' all the best,' nor of anything like all.   It is not that of Grotius, nor of Calvin, nor of the present Archbishop of Canterbury, nor of Scott, nor of Henry, nor of Whitby, nor of Macknight, nor of Hammond, nor of Doddridge, nor of Beausobre, nor of Alford, nor of Davidson, nor of Kuinoel, nor of Olshausen, nor of Wolf.   Even Neander, from whom he nevertheless so quotes as to beget an impression (though doubtless without intending to do so) that Neander gave to the phrase the interpretation adopted by himself, does not so interpret it.   For Neander, in the very page of the very edition of his ' Life of Christ' from which your correspondent makes his quotation, gives it as his opinion that ' Our Lord never used this expression (viz. *for the kingdom of heaven's sake*) to denote fitting oneself for the kingdom by a contemplative life, &c., but always to denote a holy activity in its service.' [c]

It may be the interpretation of some; it is that of Dr. Adam Clarke and of Euthymius, for instance; and it may be that of some others: but the common, and, as I believe, the more correct, interpretation is, that those who had eunuchised themselves '*for the kingdom of heaven's sake*' were those who, like St. Paul, possessed that power of self-control which enabled them successfully to thwart their natural propensities, and to do violence to one of the strongest of human passions, *in order that they might thereby be at liberty to devote themselves the more fully to the preaching of the kingdom of God;* and who, having this power of self-control, exerted it.

---

which that word is commonly understood.   At any rate the verse under consideration would have been more literally translated, and less open perhaps to misconception, if translated as follows :—' All men cannot receive this saying, save they to whom it is given: for there are eunuchs which were so born from their mother's womb; and there are eunuchs who have been eunuchised of men; and there are eunuchs who have eunuchised themselves for the kingdom of heaven's sake.   He that is able to receive it (viz. your saying), let him receive it.'

[c] ' Such celibacy,' says Neander, ' and such only does Christ recognise, as implies the sacrifice of human feelings from love to the kingdom of God, and for the sake of rendering it more efficient service.   Only in this sense could he have spoken of celibacy "*for the kingdom of heaven's sake.*"   He never used this expression to denote fitting oneself for the kingdom by a contemplative life, &c., but always to denote a holy activity in its service.'—*Life of Christ,* Bohn's edit., p. 363.

The mode in which these words are quoted by your correspondent may be seen *supra,* p. 478.

Thus understood, the phrase (and the motive expressed by it) is strictly identical with that made use of in reference to those who, 'for Christ's sake and the Gospel's (ἕνεκεν Χριστοῦ καὶ τοῦ εὐαγγελίου), are represented as leaving house, brethren, sisters, father, mother, wife, children, or lands (Mark x. 29), or as doing or enduring for his sake (διὰ Χριστόν, 1 Cor. iv. 10), or for the furtherance of the knowledge of his Gospel (διὰ τὸ εὐαγγέλιον, 1 Cor. ix. 23), any other of those deeds of moral heroism of which no man is so capable as the zealous and determined missionary.

How many there were, more especially perhaps among the disciples of our Lord's forerunner, John the Baptist, who were thus willing to renounce the endearments of domestic life, in order that they might more entirely devote themselves to the preaching of the kingdom of heaven, it is of course impossible for us to say; but the probability is that their number was much greater than we are accustomed to suppose. Our Lord certainly refers not to John alone, but to others who, like him, had proclaimed that the kingdom of heaven was at hand, when (speaking to his disciples of 'others' who had preceded them) he says (John iv. 38), 'I sent you to reap that whereon ye bestowed no labour; *others laboured*, and ye are entered into their labours;' and it is to these, our Lord's forerunners, that our Lord, I conceive, more especially refers in the verse before us—*honourably speaking of them as men who had made themselves 'eunuchs for the kingdom of heaven's sake,'* not because they were really and strictly eunuchs, but because, for the kingdom of heaven's sake, that is, that they might more wholly give themselves up to the preaching of repentance and of the kingdom of God, they were content to live as such.

Which of these two interpretations is to be preferred, each one must of course determine for himself as he may best be able. I find no fault with your correspondent because the interpretation adopted by him is not that which I myself should be disposed to prefer; but I do object to his assertion that the interpretation to which he gives the preference is the interpretation given by 'all good commentators;' not merely because it is not correct to say so, but also because it tends to beget an impression on the minds of those who are unaccustomed or unable to think or to examine for themselves, that the other, and, as I believe, the more common, interpretation is altogether untenable. I can only suggest in justification, or rather in palliation of his statement, that we are almost all of us, at times, apt to be inaccurate and careless; that writers and speakers, from an over-anxiety to induce others to adopt the opinion which they themselves may happen to entertain, will not unfrequently overstate that which they wish them to believe—representing that as universal which is only general, or general which is only frequent, or frequent which is only occasional; and that this unfortunately may often be done almost without a consciousness that such statement is not thoroughly correct.

I have but one remark to add. In common with your correspondent I have throughout assumed the correctness of the non-literal interpretation of the term 'eunuch,' as applied by our Lord to those whom he represents as having made themselves such 'for the kingdom of heaven's sake.' In this respect indeed I know of no commentator (of no modern commentator at least) who is of a different opinion; but that to which I desire to invite attention, is, that it is usual to regard this word 'eunuch,' as applied to them, as an instance of 'figurative usage,' *without assigning any probable reason to account for the employment of the figure;* and that for the lack of some such reason there is no doubt but that almost every ordinary reader of the verse is often more or less tempted to regard a literal interpretation of the eunuchism spoken of as perhaps after all the most defensible, even though he may hesitate boldly to adopt that interpretation. The hypothesis suggested in the course of the above remarks, viz. that the term is applied to the parties referred to (whoever those parties were) *in honourable recognition* of the greatness of their self-denial, more especially in reference to marriage and to the comforts of domestic life in general, and as *a term of honourable mention,* may perhaps satisfactorily account for the employment of the figure, and so sufficiently vindicate the non-literal interpretation. Guided by an instinctive persuasion that eunuchism proper cannot be agreeable to the will of God, and by certain scriptural statements elsewhere made in reference to eunuchs (see Deut. xxiii. 1; Levit. xxii. 24, 25), commentators may have reason indeed to conclude that the parties referred to were not eunuchs in the literal sense of the word; but, if they were not, some such hypothesis as the above is still demanded, in order to account for the circumstance that men who, according to the common supposition, were not eunuchs in fact, should nevertheless be so spoken of as if they were.

This remark, in reference to the 'figurative usage' of the term as applied to these men, is foreign indeed to the more express object of the present letter. But bearing, as it does, upon a point, the settlement of which appears to be essential to a satisfactory interpretation of the phrase in question, its irrelevancy, if irrelevant, will, I trust, be pardoned.   J. C. K.

November 8, 1852.

HEROD AND HERODIAS.

[Notes on the Quotation from the Speech of the BISHOP OF EXETER, given in the JOURNAL OF SACRED LITERATURE for October, 1852, pp. 202-204.]

ON reading this singular passage it occurred to me that there are *three* questions to be asked, an affirmative reply to either of which will account for the rebuke of John, and nullify the Bishop of Exeter's argument.

    I. Was the former husband of Herodias still living?

    II. Was the former wife of Herod still living?

    III. Was there not too near a relation of consanguinity between Herod and Herodias?

    I. It is quite true that Tertullian assumes the death of Philip to have occurred prior to this marriage; but Tertullian can scarcely be quoted as an *authority*, and we know him to have been over credulous in matters of fact. Josephus *is* an authority, and in *Antiq.* xviii. 5, 4, he thus narrates the circumstances:—'After whose birth (Salome's) Herodias took upon her to confound the laws of our country, and divorce herself frôm her husband while he was alive, and was married to Herod (Antipas), her husband's brother by the father's side' (Whiston's translation). This is plain enough, and the inspired narrative simply calls Herodias Herod's 'brother's wife,' and not *widow*, as might have been expected if Philip was dead. Lord Denman, in a recent publication, dwells particularly on this latter point. If the Bishop had observed what Josephus says in the section before the one above quoted from, he would have been *unable* to infer Philip's decease from it. Now if the first husband was alive the marriage was unlawful.

II. That the former wife of Herod Antipas was still living is expressly affirmed by Josephus, who gives the particulars of her flight to her father Aretas, on hearing the rumour of her husband's intention to put her away and marry Herodias (*Antiq.* xviii. 5, 1). Now if his first wife was living the marriage was unlawful.

III. It is evident from Josephus that Herod Antipas was the uncle of Herodias, who was the daughter of Aristobulus. Hence she married her father's brother on each occasion, and the two Herods married their brother's daughter, which we all know to have been within the prohibited degrees. Now if this relation of consanguinity subsisted, the marriage was unlawful.

Of these three questions no notice is taken by the Bishop of the two last, whereas they are as really important as the first. It appears to me that in this marriage there was a complication of sins. There was the 'double' adultery of Herod and of Herodias, and the incest of both. This leaves the question of marriage with a deceased wife's sister, or husband's brother, where we found it; and any inference from the case before us, bearing upon that point, will be a *non sequitur*.

C. H. B.

HADES AND HEAVEN.

Sir,—In a foot-note at the commencement of the article 'Hades and Heaven,' in your last number (Oct.), you express a desire that the views propounded by the writer of that article would excite a discussion of the whole subject in the pages of the 'Journal of Sacred Literature.' Entertaining, as I do, a different opinion on the subject of the disembodied state of existence, from that set forth by the writer in question, I venture, with your permission, to make a few observations. I shall not touch upon those 'mystical' questions contained in the works which the writer reviews, but confine myself entirely to the subject of the separate state of existence. The writer has endeavoured to show from the scriptures, and from metaphysics, that the human mind will exist in a state of unconsciousness, or a kind of sleep, from the moment of death to the morning of the resurrection. In opposition to this, I shall

endeavour to prove, that the separate existence of the soul will be one
of consciousness, and, that that consciousness will be a happy or a
miserable one, according to the moral state of the subject. The *conscious* existence of a disembodied spirit has certainly something mysterious connected with it, but this is no proof against the reality and
possibility of such a state. The inability of the infant to conceive the
power of the human mind to solve the grand and sublime ideas, and to
carry on the elaborate logical processes, which *we* know that it does, is
no proof against the fact and possibility of such a power. The inability
of the illiterate man to conceive *how* the mathematician calculates the
distances of the planets, and maps out the heavens, is no proof whatever that he has not such a power, and does not exercise it. Neither
is our present inability to comprehend thoroughly the *how* of the conscious existence of the disembodied spirit, any proof against the fact or
possibility of such a state. The inability of the illiterate man to conceive the *how* of the mathematician's calculations, arises from his desti-
tution of those *elements* which are necessary to construct such a conception, derivable from mathematical knowledge. And so the inability of
man, in his present condition of existence, to comprehend the *how* of
the conscious disembodied state arises from the absence of those elements
of knowledge which *experience* alone can supply. To argue from the
present to the future, and to show that, because the mind is subject to
certain laws now, it must be subject to the same laws hereafter, is, in
my apprehension, to beg the whole question. The fact, that in the
present life the human consciousness is devoloped in connection with a
bodily organism, and to some extent is conditioned by a certain state of
that organism, is no proof that in a higher and more advanced condition
of existence, it cannot be continued and progressively developed apart
from such an organism. It may be that we cannot comprehend such
a condition of being, but this is no proof against its possibility. We
are apt to be prejudiced against such a state, by looking at it from our
present stand-point of existence. Because experience teaches us that
our present consciousness has been awakened in connection with a body,
we are apt to conclude that there can be no consciousness where there
is no body. But this is to be guilty of the fallacy of arguing from
what *is* to what *must be*. It may be that we are absolutely unable to
comprehend the *modus* of the separate existence whilst our experience
is confined to an existence of mind and body united, and that this inability is the reason why the scriptures reveal to us nothing more than
the fact of such an existence. There are many things which *in themselves* are not incomprehensible, but still require a certain stand-point
in the mind to comprehend them. The mode of consciousness in the
disembodied spirit may be, and we believe is, one of the things whose
comprehension is conditioned by actual experience. If the doctrine of
such a consciousness do not conflict with the constitution of human
nature, and with the teaching of revelation, we have no right to conclude that there can be no such a state, simply because our *present* mode
of existence does not enable us to comprehend it. There is a great
difference between what is *above* reason and what is *opposed* to it.

We have made these preliminary observations to show that we ought to be satisfied with evidence that relates to the fact, and, at farthest, the possibility of a *conscious* disembodied existence, though we may not be able to understand its *modus*.

Two sources of evidence are open to us:—viz., the Scriptures and Metaphysics, and to these we shall have recourse. First, the Scriptures. It is rather strange that the writer of the article in question has omitted in his consideration of Scripture, by far the most important and positive passage that the New Testament contains on the subject, viz., Luke xx. 37, 38; 'Now that the dead are raised, even Moses showed at the bush, when he called the Lord the God of Abraham, and the God of Isaac, and the God of Jacob. For he is not a God of the dead, but of the living: for all live unto him.'

In this passage Christ is opposing the Sadducean doctrine, that there is no future state of existence. The Sadducees admitted the authority of Moses. Christ took his stand on the teaching of Moses, and quoted a passage which necessarily implied the future and conscious separate existence of the souls of Abraham, Isaac, and Jacob, and, by necessary consequence, the conscious existence of that class of beings represented by these three patriarchs. This application of the passage completely confounded the Sadducees, for it is said, 'After that they durst not ask him any question at all.' But the argument would have force only as it proved that the words of Moses implied that the three patriarchs mentioned, lived at the time at which he spoke. And this is the only construction that can fairly be put upon the words. Moses did not say that God *would* be the God of Abraham, etc., after the resurrection of the body, but that he was their God at the time he spoke. And Christ, as if to leave no room for doubt, has added, 'For he *is* not the God of the dead, but of the living: for all live unto him.' These words of Christ convey to us the positive idea that the separate state of existence is one of consciousness. The persons who are dead, so far as their bodies are concerned, live in a disembodied condition. And what is it to live? Is it merely to *exist*, as the stone or stock? To call this life, as applied to a human being, is to abuse the meaning of words. Life reveals itself in consciousness. There can be no mental life without consciousness; and hence Christ has said in reference to the disembodied spirits, 'For all live *unto* him.' He did not say, for all *shall* live unto him, after the resurrection, but he employs the present tense—'all *do* live unto him.' Activity is ascribed to the spirits in Hades, and that activity is directed to the glory of God. Hence it follows that the separate state must be one of consciousness.

But it may be objected, that as the term *resurrection* is used in our version, Christ referred the passage to the future existence of men after the resurrection *of the body*. But it must be obvious on a moment's consideration, that here the term resurrection (ἀνάστασις) refers to the standing, or living again, of the spirit, and not of the body. The term ἀνάστασις itself, is as applicable to the future life of the soul, as it is to that of the body and soul united. Whether in any instance it must be taken as referring to the rising again of the body, must be determined by the context. The unbelief of the Sadducees referred more to the future existence of the soul, than to that of the body. It was a disbelief in all future existence beyond the present, and hence Christ adduced a passage, the authority of which they admitted, to prove to them that there was *then* a life beyond the present. Moreover, if Christ did not refer to the separate state of existence, his argument would not have had any force against the scepticism of the Sadducees. It is impossible to explain away this passage. It teaches most unequivocally, and on the authority of the Great Teacher Himself, that there is a spiritual state of existence, lying beyond the reach of sense, and this is one of consciousness.

The second passage which I adduce in proof of the consciousness of the disembodied state, is 2 Cor. v. 6-8. 'Therefore we are always confident, knowing that, whilst we are at home in the body, we are absent in the Lord. (For we walk by faith, not by sight.) We are confident, I say, and willing rather to be absent from the body, and to be present with the Lord.'

The words rendered in our version 'we are at home in the body,' are ἐνδημοῦντες ἐν τῷ σώματι, which might be rendered most literally thus,—we living in the body. In these words the body is represented as a house in which the soul lives. It is the soul that lives, and acts, and animates the body. It is the soul that is the person,—the living agent. And this soul is here represented as capable of living apart from the body. It is implied that when the soul ceases to live in the body it will live with Christ, and that such a change is an object of the Christian's desire, and is fraught with the greatest advantage to the soul. Now what is it to be with Christ?—obviously to be in Heaven. Christ, in his human nature, is in Heaven, and one of the greatest sources of blessedness to the Christian in Heaven will be the presence of Christ. Now to be with Christ in Heaven is to be conscious. If the disembodied spirit be not conscious, it can be no more said to be with Christ than the body which sleeps in the grave.

The next passage which I shall adduce is substantially the same as the preceding one: Philippians i. 23; 'For I am in a strait betwixt two, having a desire to depart and to be with Christ, which is far better.'

In writing this passage, Paul evidently believed that his spirit would go to Christ immediately on its departure from the body at death. His strait consisted in the difficulty of choosing between remaining on earth, as the faithful and useful servant of Christ and the Church, and being with Christ, which was better for him personally. Now, how could Paul be in this strait, if, at death, his spirit sank down into unconsciousness? How could he hesitate between choosing a life of activity and usefulness, in the greatest cause, and a condition of perfect unconsciousness? In fact, the words have no possible rational signification if the disembodied state be one of unconsciousness.

The next passage is Acts vii. 59; 'And they stoned Stephen, calling upon God, and saying, Lord Jesus receive my spirit.'

If this passage be read along with the verses preceding it, it cannot but be evident that Stephen expected and prayed that his spirit might be taken immediately to heaven. The 'vulgar' Christians of the present day do not express themselves more positively in reference to the separate existence of the soul than did Stephen at the moment of his martyrdom. And it is also obvious that Stephen's conception of being received by Christ, comprehended the being taken to that place, or state, where he saw, in vision a little before, 'the glory of God, and Jesus standing on the right hand of God.'

What becomes, then, of the assertion of W. H. J. that the language which expresses the notion of an immediate entrance into Heaven, is 'modern and unscriptural'?

Let us now turn to the Old Testament. We may observe at the outset, that it is generally admitted, that the doctrine of the resurrection of the body is peculiar to Christianity, and that therefore the evidence of the Old Testament for a future life has reference to the soul exclusively. Neither the heathen nor the Jew believed in the future life of the body, and, hence, we may not expect many passages discriminating, even incidentally, the future life of the soul from that of human nature, as consisting of soul and body. And yet there are passages of this kind. Ecclesiastes xii. 7 ; 'Then shall the dust return to the earth as it was ; and the spirit shall return to God who gave it.'

In this passage the spirit is represented as having come from God in a manner different from that in which the body came. The spirit is probably a creation of God, and incarnated for a time in the earthly body, and when the body returns to its mother dust the spirit ascends to God. But what is it to go to God? God is represented in the Scriptures as dwelling in Heaven, and to go to Him is to go to Heaven. God is, of course, naturally present everywhere, but he is present in Heaven in a special manner. To go to God again, must mean to go to Him in a conscious manner. In fact, the Scripture nowhere admits that man is specially near to his God, unless he is consciously in his presence. Unless the mind be consciously in the presence of God there is no difference between its relation to him and that of the body.

Psalm cxvi. 3 ; 'The sorrows of death compassed me, and the pains of hell (Sheol) gat hold upon me : I found trouble and sorrow.'

In this passage, Sheol or Hades is described as a place or state in which there will be pain, etc. Whatever may be the meaning of the passage as applied to the experience of David himself, it is clear that, in his conception, Hades was a condition in which pain might be experienced, as death is one of sorrow. But pain is itself a modification of consciousness, and therefore it is evident that the sweet singer of the old dispensation regarded the separate state as one of consciousness.

Psalm lxxiii. 24 ; 'Thou shalt guide me with thy counsel, and afterward receive me to glory.'

In this passage the Psalmist describes God as leading him through this present life and then receiving him to glory. There is not the slightest intimation in the passage that thousands of years were to intervene between the end of the course and the beginning of the glory. But the one is obviously described as succeeding the other immediately. The condition into which the soul is to be conducted is called glory.

It is not glory objectively considered merely, but glory into which the soul will be consciously received. Without the consciousness of this glory, it would not be glory to the soul, any more than to the body that descends to the grave. The Psalmist, therefore, anticipated a condition of glorious consciousness to succeed immediately the present course through which God was conducting him.

That to be in the presence of God is to be conscious, is evident, from the Psalmist's description in Psalm xvi. 11; 'Thou wilt show me the path of life: in thy presence is fulness of joy: at thy right hand there are pleasures for evermore.' Nothing can be clearer, then, than that the Psalmist had a brighter and more glorious conception of the future state than W. H. J.

The passages which this writer adduces from Eccles. (ix. 4, 5) and Psalms (vi. 5), do not seem to us to prove what he alleges they do, viz., the nothingness of Hades. Human nature is at present constituted of two great parts—body and mind. The former is the organ through which the latter attends to the things of this life, and by which it is connected with the present system of things. The latter is that which raises man above the present, and links him to another system of things. Man may therefore be contemplated from two distinct points of view—from the present earthly, and from the future spiritual. Now, death puts an end to man so far forth as his bodily and earthly being and relations are concerned. And, hence it may be said that man is dead in one sense and alive in another. He may be dead as far as the world is concerned, though he may live in another and nobler state of being. In the passage referred to, man is contemplated as an inhabitant of this world, and from his bodily and earthly relations. In this sense a pure spiritualist may say, 'The dead know not anything.' 'In death there is no remembrance of thee: in the grave who shall give thee thanks?'

All this may be said without denying that the soul may live in a conscious, disembodied state. We have selected these few passages from a large number, to show that the idea of an *immediate* entrance into a conscious state of existence at death pervades the teaching of the sacred Scriptures. The parable of Lazarus and Dives, and the words of Christ to the penitent thief, on which W. H. J. has touched, may be added to the above. The manner in which that writer has attempted to explain away the force of these two passages, indicates most clearly the weakness of his cause. He seems to think that it is sufficient to destroy the force of the parable of Lazarus and Dives to say that it *is* a parable, and therefore must be a figurative representation. It must be admitted that it is a parable, but a parable has real truth underlying its form. A parable and a real narrative do not differ in their fundamental principle, but simply in their *form*. The former employs fictitious examples to describe a general truth, the latter uses historical ones to do the same. The truth conveyed is the same in both cases. In the verses preceding this parable, Christ is teaching the danger of possessing riches. 'Ye cannot serve God and mammon.' 'That which is highly esteemed among men is abomination in the sight of God.' These are some of the weighty sayings of Christ on the subject of riches, in opposition to the views of the people generally, who valued too highly the possession of riches, and looked upon men's earthly condition as an index of their moral deserts, and the favour of God.   This parable was doubtless intended to teach more truths than one, but the leading truth appears to be this,—that the future condition of men will be according to their moral character, and not according to their outward circumstances.   And hence the poor man who was pious on earth is raised to the most glorious and happy condition, and the rich man who was impious, is degraded to misery and want.   The one is happy *immediately* after death, the other is miserable.   And, therefore, the separate state must be one of consciousness.   The writer in question, whilst admitting the difficulty of Christ's words to the thief, endeavours to weaken their force by asserting the undetermined signification of the term paradise.   It is evident, however, to those who have no theory to maintain on the subject, that the term paradise signifies a happy condition of being, and if so, a condition of consciousness.   If the souls of men sank at death into an unconscious sleep, what difference could there be between the believing and unbelieving thief on the day of their death?   And if there were no difference, the words of Christ would be mere mockery; nay, they would be false.   In no rational way, therefore, can these passages be explained, except on the principle that the soul goes immediately into a *state* of consciousness.   The term Sheol, or Hades, strictly speaking, does not, as it appears to us, designate a particular *place*, but the state of disembodied spirits.   'Abraham's bosom,' and 'paradise,' are terms of more limited application, descriptive of a happy state.   'Gehenna,' or hell fire, is that term which specially characterises the future state as one of misery.   If Heaven be considered as a particular *place*, fitted exclusively for the residence of beings possessing bodies as well as minds, the soul cannot be supposed to enter it immediately at death.   But it appears to us that it is the most general term which the Scriptures contain, to designate the future happy being of God's children, whether their happiness be realized in a purely disembodied state, or in connection with a body.   And hence, it is often said that Heaven begins on earth.   The New Testament most clearly asserts that eternal life begins in time.   'He that believeth on the Son *hath* everlasting life.'   The future life, therefore, must be a more perfect developement of that new life which Christ produces in the mind in time.

From what has just been said, it follows that the consciousness of the disembodied state will be a happy or a miserable one, according to the moral character of the subject.   The consciousness of every human being carries within itself the elements of a Heaven or a hell.   Sin not only secures, in the future, some positive and direct infliction of punishment on the subject, but also, through the laws of nature, brings punishment immediately after it, in the anarchy which it produces in the experience of the soul.   And that spiritual life which Christianity awakens in man will not only be rewarded hereafter, but it contains now, in itself, a part of the blessedness which man is destined to enjoy. So that in this present life the rewards of a righteous governor are, partially at least, bestowed upon men. The disembodied state of existence must, therefore, if, as we think it is, one of consciousness, be one of rewards and punishments. The soul will carry within itself the elements of happiness or misery, from the present condition to the future.

The writer, W. H. J., asks, if the intermediate state be one of rewards and punishments, what would be the meaning of a day of general judgment, ' where,' he says, ' we are notified that some of the wicked will be surprised at the doom they shall receive.' (Matt. vii. 22, 23; xxv. 41-46.) We have looked at these passages, and we fail to see that there is an intimation that any of the wicked will be surprised at their punishment. There is expressed in this language nothing more than the tendency in men to justify themselves by enumerating supposed virtuous deeds which they had performed. But if they will be surprised that they shall be punished, the theory of W. H. J., that the final judgment succeeds the conscious existence of this life, does not account for it. The wicked, whether they go from earth to the judgment, or from Hades, ought not to be surprised at their punishment, because their own consciences will tell them that they deserved that punishment. The objection derived from a general judgment to a conscious intermediate state, proceeds on the supposition that the *only* purpose of such a judgment has reference to the fixing of the individual destinies of men. But it is probable that that great public transaction is intended to answer important ends in reference to the moral universe at large, which could not be answered by the other mode of judgment. There is a κρίσις going on in time, and the ἐσχάτη κρίσις—the general judgment—is to perfect the whole process.

We come now to notice briefly, the teachings of Metaphysics on this subject. On this point, W. H. J. asks, ' Is it possible for a disembodied spirit to be conscious of anything exterior to itself, or, in the language of modern philosophy, can an entity, deprived of the organs of communication, receive objective knowledge?' We would suggest to this writer, that the real question which his theory required him to put is, —Is it possible for a disembodied spirit to be conscious *at all?* External perception is but *one form* of consciousness, but the question at issue has reference to the existence of consciousness in any form in the disembodied spirit. Even if he could prove that the spirit cannot attain to a knowledge of the objective material world, except through the medium of the bodily organism, this would not prove the impossibility of all consciousness. This he himself acknowledges. He admits that we might, on purely metaphysical grounds, allow the possibility of that part of consciousness which consists in the exercise of memory and reflection; but from scriptural reasons and experience, he is led to deny this. We have seen that scripture asserts, in the clearest manner, the *fact* of such consciousness; and as for experience, we know that that can teach nothing on the subject, because we have had no experience of the disembodied state. The inferences deducible from our *present* experience are identical with what the writer calls ' purely metaphysical reasons.' There are many operations of the mind that are carried on independently of the body. The ideas of God, of spirit, of eternity, of infinity, are products of reason, independent of the senses. And when the mind has obtained the elements of knowledge, through the channels of the senses, it can analyse and classify, arrange and re-arrange, mould, and modify them at pleasure, without the further aid of the senses. Now, when the soul leaves the body and enters Hades, it possesses the *elements* of almost all knowledge, and by memory and reflection it may not only live on its previous possessions, but construct for itself, out of the old materials, new forms of consciousness, even supposing it could not gain any new materials, either from the world of matter or mind. So that, from the light of our present experience, we may see the possibility of consciousness in the disembodied spirit.

The possibility of the *perceptive* consciousness to the disembodied spirit, we admit is difficult to conceive. It *may be* that the separate state is imperfect in this, that it is deprived of that knowledge and pleasure which arise from the perceptive consciousness. We do not assert it, but merely mention it as a possibility. We cannot help thinking, however, that W. H. J. changes his ground on this point, and, in changing, surrenders his original position for the purpose of meeting an objection drawn from Mesmerism. His original position was, that the spirit of man cannot be conscious without a bodily organism, and specially that he cannot perceive objective reality, except through his body, and therefore, as Hades does not contain the *bodies* of men, there can be no consciousness there. On page 47, second paragraph, he refers to the phenomena of Mesmerism, in which it is said that spirits communicate with others, without the intervention of their bodies. If these phenomena be founded in truth, they throw much light on the possibility of even the perceptive consciousness to the disembodied state. But the writer, W. H. J., in meeting this objection, maintains that Mesmerists themselves affirm that, though the communications are made without the intervention of the body, they are not effected without the intervention of *some* material media. Now, the point which his theory required him exclusively to prove is, that consciousness, and specially the perceptive, cannot exist, except in connection with a bodily organism, and not that perception is impossible except through *some* media. For if, whilst the soul is subjected to the laws of the bodily organism, in this life, it can communicate with distant objects through other media than the body, what hinders us to conceive the possibility of that soul, separated from its body in Hades, perceiving distant objects through the media that may there exist? The doctrine that the soul is conscious in Hades, does not imply that it would not employ any media in its communications, but merely that it would not employ the body.

On this point we will quote with pleasure the words of Britain's greatest metaphysical philosopher, Sir William Hamilton. In a foot note to page 246 of his edition of Reid's works, there is the following: ' However astonishing, it is now proved beyond all rational doubt, that, in certain abnormal states of the nervous organism, perceptions are possible through other than the ordinary channels of the senses.'

If this be true, and the writer W. H. J. seems to admit it, and the greatest British philosopher dogmatically asserts it, then it is proved, beyond all rational doubt, that consciousness, even the perceptive consciousness, is possible to the disembodied spirit. We care not for the assertion that this perception must be through *some* media. All that we need to prove is, that perception is possible without a *body*, to believe that perception is possible to the disembodied spirit in Hades.

We believe that the theory of the writer W. H. J. is one fraught with much evil. It obviously tends to materialism. It proclaims the inherent impotence of the human spirit, and magnifies the power and the importance of the material organism. That part of human nature that is the great agent operating through the bodily organism, and which is the source of the body's life, in which reside intelligence, reason, conscience, affection, and will, is declared to be unable to be conscious for a moment without the presence of the body. Alas, alas, for the dignity and glory of human nature, if they are dependent absolutely on the ever changing bodily organism. The materialism of Priestley does not cast a greater gloom over the destinies of humanity than does this theory. What is the spirituality of the soul worth if it is so subservient to the laws of matter? We are happy, however, that we have clear evidence from revelation, and from our present acquaintance with human nature, that this theory is not founded in truth, and that there lies before the redeemed spirit, a bright and glorious prospect of blessedness immediately after death, and perhaps a more perfect blessedness after the resurrection of the body.

N. J. E.

Sir,—I have been much pleased with the article in this quarter's Journal on 'Heaven and Hades,' by W. H. J. It, I believe, contains much truth, and that of a delightful character; and yet, there seem to be intermixed a few errors, and a remnant of 'traditionally received theology.' I would beg your attention to some observations and suggestions.

First, on Mr. Heath's 'Heaven upon earth,' introduced p. 39, and again spoken of p. 51 and onwards. Probably many who have studied these subjects will agree with W. H. J., that 'Mr. Heath may have appropriated to his Heaven many things which belong properly to the millennium.' Is it not probable that Mr. Heath has confounded passages, through their close connection in narration, when, in fact, they belong to different periods? May he not have done so in reading Isa. lxv., where the new Heavens and new earth are predicted? Before, however, noticing this, I would refer to Rev. xxi. Here we have two, almost independent, statements, in connection with the descent of the New Jerusalem. The first is introduced by,—'I saw a new Heaven and a new earth;' which language, considering the close connection of the first eight verses, seems, most emphatically, to mark the *era* of the passage; so that the characteristics which follow are those *of the* 'new Heaven and earth.' And if any passage gives a *description* of the new state, it surely must be this, for no other gives one so perfect in character as it does.

In this first part, the apostle does not appear to be raised above the earth, in order to see the city come down; but there stands until the New Jerusalem rests on its surface; and it is said, 'Behold, the tabernacle of God is with men, and he will dwell with them.' In the second part, these declarations are *not* made, and the apostle is carried to 'a great and high mountain,' for the purpose of beholding the descending city. May it not be that this second part describes what takes place at the commencement of the millennium, that the city *then* only descends into the mid-heaven, suspended as a cloud of glory over the earth, so that 'the nations shall walk in the light of it;' and, at the close of the millennium, when all things are made 'new,' the first description is realized, that it *then* descends *into* the new earth? This would fully realize Mr. Heath's doctrine of 'a sinless condition in a terrestrial locality.' Taking this view of the two parts of Rev. xxi., we have a representation of the heaven of the millennium, and the Heaven of the new earth. The thoughts here given distinctly mark a difference in the two narrations; and yet, a wider difference remains. In the first we find,—no pain—no sorrow—no death, 'For the former things are passed away.' In the second, there is not such perfection, there will be need of healing;—'the leaves of the tree were for the healing of the nations.' The only apparent difficulty is, that the order of fulfilment should be the reverse of the prophecy: but this difficulty vanishes when we remember that the same order is followed in some Old Testament prophecies, as Isa. ii., and also in others, which predict both advents; giving the second, and then returning to the first. And what, if this order be followed in Isa. lxv., and we find that what we have understood as belonging to the 'new earth,' is indeed only millennial? Is not verse 17 simply a *prediction* of the new Heaven and earth? for, mark the language of the sacred writer, 'Behold, I create new Heavens and a new earth: and the former shall not be remembered nor come into mind.' Be it known that this is the ultimate blessing intended: 'But be ye glad and rejoice for ever in that which I' first 'create: for, behold, I create Jerusalem a rejoicing, and her people a joy.' Is it possible to suppose that the succeeding verses can synchronise with Rev. xxi. 1—8, while in this we find that death, and a curse, may enter, and from that of Revelation such things are excluded? Another feature of this part of Revelation is, there will, during its period, be no sea; but during the millennium there will be sea and islands. On comparing all the passages in which the *fact* of the new Heaven and earth is declared, does it not appear that Rev. xxi. 1—8, is the only passage that gives any *description* of the 'new' state, and that all other 'descriptions' of future blessedness are but millennial?

The next passage that claims attention is p. 54, in which the writer applies Matt. xxiv. 29 to the whole period of *the treading down of Jerusalem.* Is the writer certain that any part, from the 15th verse of this chapter, applies to the past? No doubt Luke xxi. 20—23 has been fulfilled. The days of 'vengeance' belong to the whole period of

' treading down ;' and so ' the indignation' of Dan. viii. 19, which is to have a ' last end.' That last end, by the subsequent verses, it appears, belongs to the time of ' the king of fierce countenance,' who arises ' when the transgressors are come to the full ;' who will ' destroy the mighty and the holy people ;' 'shall also stand up against the Prince of princes.' Again we read of the same king in the latter part of Dan. xi., which closes with,—' He shall go forth with great fury to destroy, and utterly to make away many. And he shall plant the tabernacles of his palaces between the seas in the glorious holy mountain.—And at that time shall Michael stand up—and there shall be a time of trouble, such as never was since there was a nation even to that same time : and at that time thy people shall be delivered. And many of them that sleep in the dust of the earth shall awake.' This surely identifies the unexampled ' tribulation' with the ' last end of the indignation,' and the last end, exclusively. Verse 15 also seems to look forward to the same period ; even though traditional theology applies it to the Roman army. Luke speaks of seeing ' Jerusalem compassed with armies,' &c. Matthew speaks of seeing ' the abomination of desolation—stand in the holy place.' This the Jews could not do, for ' the holy place' was destroyed in the siege. So that the paragraphs of Matthew and Luke are not identical. A careful comparison of the two, and also of the passages in Daniel, to which they refer, brings one to the conviction that Matt. xxiv. 15—22 is altogether future. Then the argument founded on a past fulfilment (bottom of p. 55) falls ; and ' the day of the Lord' does *not* belong to the present period.

One other passage to be noticed is, on the restoration of the Jews, pp. 54, 55. Doubtless their restoration by the immediate act of God will not take place until they are converted. The writer seems to confound their being partially re-gathered while in unbelief, with their complete ' restoration' by divine interposition. Jews are there now ; why may there not be even thousands added ? That they will, to some extent, be so gathered, appears clear from Isa. ii. 6—22, as well as from Zechariah, and also, though perhaps less clearly, from Daniel and other prophets. To such only, as are found there in unbelief, can these passages in Zechariah apply (*i. e.*, xii. 7—14, and xiii. 1, 8, 9). And the remnant of these (' the third,' xiii. 8, 9) seem to be ' those that escape,' Isa. lxvi. 19. This last chapter of Isa. 20th verse, predicts the general restoration as a result of the wrathful visitation. Moreover, how can it be supposed that Zechariah, from xii. 1, to xiv. 2, alluded to what really did occur, either at or after the *first* siege of the city ? If it were a reference to a past siege, then it was no prediction ; if to that under Titus, then the predicted results, as xii. 2—8, were not realized. And that the first advent was illustrated by this passage is not strange ; we know that various predictions have a double application ; in applying to one, they ' look forward to another of greater importance ;'—' take in lesser events on their way to greater ;'—' The prophet takes in Cyrus on his way to Christ.' The preceding passage, Zech. xi. 16, 17, seems to predict some heavy calamity that shall befall the unconverted found in the land. Hitherto, no one has thus risen 'in the land,' and been received by the Jews, *in place of* the good Shepherd (verses 12, 13). 'I am come in my Father's name, and ye receive me not: if another shall come in his own name, him ye will receive.' These words of our Lord seem to look forward to the above being accomplished. This wicked shepherd may be the king before spoken of.

Many more words must not be added, but an observation on 'Babylon' being *Rome.* If the parallelism of the Beast and his Harlot, contrasting with the Lamb and his Bride, be important; would not a literal, gorgeous city, be equally striking, contrasted with the city, 'New Jerusalem?' And would not the locality of Babylon be more striking, as contrasting with that of Jerusalem, than Rome could be? Why should we not follow the simple reading of the Scriptures, and understand 'Babylon' to mean Babylon? This subject, with—the Beast, and—times or periods being literal, or mystical, are questions which, being carefully examined, comparing their characteristics with those of other Scripture passages might be of much service to the Church at large.

If entering into such subjects as this by W. H. J. were instrumental only in breaking down some of the barriers set up by our Gentile Talmudism, much good would be done.

I am Sir, yours respectfully,

J. B.

London, Nov. 25th, 1852.

NOTICES OF BOOKS.

The Greek Testament : with a Critically Revised Text ; a Digest of Various Readings ; Marginal References to Verbal and Idiomatic Usage ; Prolegomena ; and a Critical and Exegetical Commentary. For the use of Theological Students and Ministers. By HENRY ALFORD, B.D., Vicar of Wymeswold, Leicestershire, and late Fellow of Trinity College, Cambridge. Vol. II., containing the Acts of the Apostles, the Epistles to the Romans and Corinthians. pp. 84 and 687. London : Rivingtons. 1852.

IT was but recently that we noticed the first volume of Mr. Alford's Greek Testament (not, however, as a *new* work) in the pages of this Journal, and therefore many of the remarks which were made on that portion will be found to apply equally to the volume now before us. Indeed, in some respects, in our previous notice we anticipated points on which the learned editor intended, in the part of his work after the gospels, to expand and improve his plan.

In the advertisement prefixed to the volume before us we are distinctly informed as to what the points are in which its plan differs from that of its predecessor. Mr. Alford says—

' In this volume,

' 1. The text is arranged on critical principles, regard being had to the internal evidence for and against every reading, as well as to the external evidence of MSS.

' 2. The reasons for adopting or rejecting every reading are given in the Digest.

' 3. The Digest embraces a complete account of the various readings : those of the later cursive manuscripts, and those of minor import, which were excluded from vol. I., being here inserted.

' 4. The various marks, of variation from the received text, of divided manuscript authority, and of probable spuriousness, are omitted in the text of the present volume.'

It will be seen at once that these points relate simply to *textual criticism ;* so that, as far as variation from the first volume is concerned, it is on this subject that it is to be expected.

The Prolegomena consist of six chapters, the two last of which, as they refer to the subject already mentioned, may be looked at in connection with these points of variation of plan.

In chap. v. § 1, p. 58, Mr. Alford states with regard to the previously published portion of his work—

' In that volume a text was adopted, resting on purely diplomatic authority, as a provisional compromise for use in this country, between the received text, and one which should be based on a thoroughly critical examination of evidence, both external and internal.'

After stating that he now considers that the mode in which he formed his text of the gospels was a great mistake, he continues :—

' It proceeded on altogether too high an estimate of the authority of the most ancient existing MSS. as determining a reading, and too low an one of the importance of internal evidence.'

Before continuing to quote Mr. Alford's remarks, we may observe how singularly (we might almost say *amusingly*) our estimate of his text of the gospels differed from that which he now gives as his own. He now thinks that he presented a text too purely diplomatic, irrespective of internal considerations; we, on the contrary, had said that he had ' in various instances allowed internal considerations too much weight, in opposition to external testimonies.' We formed this judgment on the class of passages in which all evidence is one way, but Mr. Alford's verdict the other. Of these we said, ' Internal evidence has its value, but when relied on *alone*, or nearly so, it becomes a thing closely related to mere conjectural criticism.'

Another point in which Mr. Alford's edition of the Gospels stands in opposition to any diplomatic text, is one which he now mentions in justification of his change of plan; for he continues :—

'Besides, it overlooked many variations of reading of hardly less importance than those which were noticed. *The arrangement of words in the sentences* was by me at the time of editing the text of this volume (now nearly eight years ago) esteemed a *matter which might be passed over;* to which were added many other variations (see the list in chap. vi. § ii. of the Prolegomena) which I now consider as of great interest.'

In reading these remarks we do wonder that Mr. Alford should, in the next preceding paragraph, have styled his text of the Gospels one ' resting on purely diplomatic authority,' unless indeed he uses the terms in some peculiar sense. The text often rested on the evidence of the oldest MSS.; it often departed from such evidence, which (as Mr. Alford mentions) was not even stated; and it sometimes rested on mere internal grounds. That the editor should now perceive the importance of paying attention to the arrangement of words is no cause for surprise; it is only remarkable that it was overlooked before—a thing which could only, we think, have arisen from the criticism of the text having become necessary as an auxiliary in the carrying out of Mr. Alford's object: it seems as if textual criticism *could* not originally have been of *primary* importance in his eyes.

Mr. Alford next informs us how he has acted in the present volume :—

' *It has been attempted to construct the text on more worthy principles,* and to bring to bear on it *both the testimony of MSS.* and *those critical maxims which appear to furnish sound criteria of a spurious or genuine reading.*'

Wherein, then, would a text so formed differ from one *really* ' diplomatic'? If a reading exists at all, it must have come to us through some mode of documentary transmission; and thus to diplomatic authority we get back after all, even when using all possible means for forming a judgment amid conflicting testimonies.

Mr. Alford then remarks on the importance of understanding the kinds of *corrections* which were early introduced into MSS. He says,—

' The only sure way to detect them is by an intimate acquaintance with the general phenomena of manuscripts, the cursive as well as the uncial. Such acquaintance will enable us at once to pronounce a reading to be spurious which has yet a vast array of MS. authority in its favour—just because we know that it furnishes an instance of a correction or of an error found in other places.'

All this is very good, provided the reading in question is *proved to be an error.* Suppose that we find a reading in which some mistake *seems* to lie, and we put it down to be a transcriber's error: we look at the MS. authorities, and we find that the oldest attest the reading we condemn, with great unanimity; we turn to the versions, and we find the same thing: we then look at the early citations, and we find the reading which we are disposed to condemn, quoted, commented on, and explained: we are, therefore, compelled to conclude that the reading is very ancient, widely diffused, and (even if difficult to us) not deemed unintelligible by thoughtful and intelligent writers to whom Greek was the native tongue. But still we are told that the reading arises from *correction:* well then, what proof is there of the existence of any prior reading for the copyists to correct? It may be, we are told, that the later uncial MSS., and the mass of those in cursive letters, contain the true reading. Indeed! but *how* is this *proved?* This throws us on internal considerations, and a supposed ability to discern the corrections of scribes from our knowledge of the nature of MSS. But, let our tact in such things be what it may, still the really ancient MSS. ought to possess *some* weight of evidence; when this is confirmed by the mass of the versions, it is increased to a degree hardly capable of over-statement; and when the early citations are also found on the same side, we have such a confirmation, not resting on the voices of two or three witnesses, but of two or three classes of witnesses, that we may well ask for something positive, something anterior, something equal in weight, before we reject the reading so confirmed. If the attested reading *be* 'a correction,' who shall say what was the word contained in the uncorrected copies? 'But,' we may be told, 'look at what the later copies read, and follow *that.*' Well, but if the discussion is all about corrections, and if we are told that the old copies are corrected wrongly, what can we regard the reading of the later copies but as attempts to correct backward? Will such attempts lead us right? If we find something in a proof-sheet which strikes us as wrong, and without looking at the copy we try to correct according to our judg-ment, (or want of judgment,) few would feel any confidence in our having really restored what the author wrote; and this would be especially true if we apprehended but little of the author's mind and thoughts.

But farther: if the reading of later copies presents an easy sense, not requiring much depth of thought or consideration, and if some difficulty attaches itself to that which is well attested,—a difficulty not insur-mountable, but one which the other reading avoids,—then all sound criticism will adhere to Bengel's motto, ' Proclivi lectioni præstat ardua.'

We are aware that questions may be asked about the early copies, and whether transcribers did not quite early attempt corrections; no doubt that such bold endeavours were made by some, but, as this is no ground for the admittance of *mere conjecture,* so does it not warrant our neglecting the ancient evidence which we possess in favour of that which *may* present better readings. We must go as near the fountain head as we can, and use the testimonies which we possess. Our suppositions with regard to ' corrections' can never invalidate *facts ;* and of all phenomena connected with the *mendings* of copyists, none are more clear than those which show tendencies to make expressions *more easy,* and to produce verbal conformity of one passage with another.

Mr. Alford says,

' The object of course is, in each case, *to mount up, if possible, to the original reading from which all the variations sprung ;* in other words, *to discover* some word *or some arrangement which shall account for the variations, but for which none of the variations will account.'*

How, then, is such an object to be attained? Mr. Alford quotes at length the rules laid down by Griesbach ; but still the point remains that, unless we have *evidence* of the existence of a reading as ancient, we cannot assume that it *is* such : and if we have no proof that a reading is *ancient*, we cannot rightly assume that it is the original from which all variations have sprung.

When we have the ancient readings (proved to be such on undoubted evidence) before us, then we may use all the critical sagacity in our power to distinguish between them ; but if we let our supposed discrimination take the lead, we shall take the place of defining what the authors of Scripture should have written, and not of learning on grounds of evidence what they *did* write.

These are the limitations which we should think it needful to lay down in connection with Mr. Alford's statements. He illustrates his definitions by referring to the readings ἔχομεν and ἔχωμεν in Rom. v. 1 : there he considers the former to be certainly genuine, although he says of the other ' we can hardly conceive a reading more strongly attested by MSS. ;' and yet he rejects it on internal grounds—that is to say, on grounds which were not felt or perceived by the early translators in general, nor yet by the early fathers. The internal grounds have, then, to do with a supposed difficulty arising from some supposed exposition. Surely the united testimony of all ancient authority has *some* weight ; and then, if there be no evidence in favour of the other reading in the early centuries, might not a critical expositor pause before he adopted an explanation of the passage which *requires* the adoption of what seems to some the easier reading, and which is adopted by the *later* MSS. in contrast to the earlier? It is easy to *assume* that such a reading is a mere change from such another ; but the existence of the *supposed* original must first be demonstrated before any deductions are drawn from it. It may be well to state that not a few expositors, ancient and modern, have found no difficulty in the ancient reading ἔχωμεν. We refer to the passage simply because it has been used as an example by Mr. Alford.

From what we have said the reader will see that Mr. Alford's text is one, *generally* speaking, based on ancient authority : he attempts to trace the reason and origin of every material variation in MSS., and in this his own subjective feelings are expressed ; it is not a sphere of things into which absolute evidence can be introduced.

We are not met at every moment, as in Dr. Bloomfield's Greek

Testament (and still more in his supplementary volume), with crude assertions, casting discredit on all MSS. except those which generally accord with the modern text; and thus we find none of those severe and uncalled-for reflections with which he designates those who recur to ancient authority. All this is as it should be. There are still those who, if they see that a word or clause is omitted by three or four of the most ancient MSS. and by a few versions, immediately say, ' how *slight* is the evidence for its omission!' and they seem to state a glorious array of testimony in favour of such words or passages when they begin to *count up* the MSS. in their favour. Such *critics* think that they have disposed of an argument when they can say that even of *uncial* MSS. *twice* as many are on the side that *they* have chosen as those on the other: some, however, would inquire whether the fewer MSS. are not anterior to the eighth century? and whether the many are not *later?* If so, the triumph on the ground of *numbers* is vain, nugatory, and utterly fictitious.

We fully admit with Mr. Alford that the earliest MSS. which we have contain errors; but these errors are to be checked by the comparison of such MSS. one with another (using aid of versions and citations), and *not* from the attempts at correction found in the later MSS. Some may blame Mr. Alford for following the *orthography* of the old MSS.; they may say that this is an evident *mistake*, and, as such, to be corrected by later testimonies; but in this we should say that he has rightly adhered to that which *evidence* attests. Those whose notions of Greek do not go beyond a school grammar cannot believe in the habitual use of the νῦ ἐφελκυστικὸν, and other things of the same kind, just as they call a reading which sounds strange to them, and the meaning of which they do not instantly perceive, *an evident mistake.* But in all such cases we should pause and inquire: our knowledge of grammatical forms may increase; and we may also learn that the *conventional* meaning of particular passages, as based on a modern reading, is *not* the only sense which the passages can admit.

The advocates for the general correctness of ' the received text' find Mr. Alford no adherent of theirs; for though he would modify the value of evidence as such, he utterly repudiates the continued transmission of a reading based on the most slender authority conceivable, and that, too, of a modern date. His remarks on the orthographic peculiarities to which we have just alluded are clear and simple; he enumerates them, and then says, 'none of which are we at liberty to reduce to the ordinary standard of orthography, but must reproduce as we find them in the all but universal text of the earliest times.' *We* might wish to apply this principle more extensively, not confining it to *orthography,* but extending it to the text in general, and this Mr. Alford very often does.

Mr. Alford's *critical apparatus* is mostly taken (with full acknowledgment) from Tischendorf, with some additions from Scholz, &c. This must be borne in mind; for the authorities as given depend thus almost entirely on Tischendorf, whose statement of the readings of the *versions* is generally but a repetition; since, except the Latin, he knows nothing of any of them himself: *his* field of labour has been different. We are quite of opinion that Mr. Alford has acted wisely in simply giving various readings on the authority of others; for as the *Text* was not his original and principal object, it would probably have long occupied his sole attention had he done otherwise.

In following common printed authorities, he might, however, we think, have so verified *facts*, when contained in *printed books*, as not to leave his readers *in doubt* and *mystification*. An example will explain what we mean.

In Acts ii. 12 the common text has διηπόρουν, while other authorities read διηποροῦντο: for the former of these Mr. Alford cites (amongst other MSS.) 'A. Tisch.,' for the latter 'A. Lachm.:' there must then be a misprint in either Tischendorf or Lachmann; but in which? a moment's inspection of the printed edition of the Alexandrian MS. would have shown that it reads διηπορουντο, and thus all doubt would have been removed. We say unhesitatingly that Mr. Alford cites 'A. Tisch.' in favour of διηποροῦντο, for the word διηπόρουν (in his text) *must* be an erratum: if, however, we do not refer to some critical edition, we *could* not understand the various readings which Mr. Alford here gives.

We wish it to be distinctly understood that we do not find any fault with any critic for simply using the critical materials collected by others; for we do not think that the collector, as such, is the more qualified for *using* properly the results of his labours. Thus we agree with the remark of Dr. Davidson in his 'Biblical Criticism' (vol. ii. p. 105)—'we should rather see the collator and the editor of the text dissociated.' We do not think that the *habit of collating* does in itself aid in forming critical principles. It may be asked, what judgment then should we form of Dr. Tischendorf (whose Greek Testament has been so greeted), or of Dr. Tregelles (whose proposed edition has been treated by most with such apathy), in the department of biblical criticism? To this we answer that their labours as collators *were needful* as a basis for any operations. Tischendorf, however, learned new critical principles while engaged in collating, as any one may see who compares his first and last editions; and these principles would probably have been applied more steadily and consistently had not *collating* MSS. been his very business. Tregelles had laid down and published his critical principles before he collated a single MS., and to the work of collation was he *driven* by the discrepancies and defects in the previously published collations of most of the more ancient MSS. Thus we think that a reference to recent editors, or intended editors, only confirms the opinion that, if possible, the architect of a critical text should not have had to perform the drudgery of quarrying his building-stones.

We have thus entered into some detail with regard to *the text* of Mr. Alford's second volume, because *this point* is the one on which he states that his plan has altered since the publication of his first. Of course we agree with him that 'the object is in each case *to mount up, if possible, to the original reading from which all the variations sprung ;'* but *how* this is to be done, or by what intuition, is quite a different matter. We can carry such a case as far as *evidence* leads, and no farther ; and when that is so far unanimous that the variations are only trifling or recent, then, irrespective of our notions of what Scripture ought to be, we must accept it as it is : to do otherwise is to open the door to all licence of conjecture. When a reading is argued against on such transcendental grounds, as 'the inference becomes obvious that a reading so repugnant to the course of the apostle's argument *as every one must feel* [such or such an attested reading] to be,' the answer is at once suggested that the *supposed* unfitness (not felt by early translators and commentators) may, almost with absolute certainty, be assigned as the reason for the recent innovation. The whole question is assumed in saying that *every one must feel a reading to be repugnant :* this *constat* falls to the ground the moment that it can be shown that good and sound intrepreters have *not* so felt. It is impossible, when decisive *evidence* is treated lightly, for any one to impart his subjective feelings to the mind of another, especially if the other be one not professing to have any *à priori* knowledge of the true reading of passages of Holy Scripture. Let us discriminate between really conflicting evidence as well as we can, but where the *evidence* is clear, there textual criticism has no place, unless it be to guard against groundless innovation.

The larger portion of Mr. Alford's Prolegomena to this volume is occupied with speaking of the four books of Scripture which it contains. In discussing the authorship of the book of Acts, Mr. Alford mentions the ' *Silas hypothesis,*' as to which he refers to a paper in this Journal (Oct. 1850), as containing the ablest vindication of this peculiar opinion. It may be almost superfluous to remark that he mentions the theory in order to refute it—and this he does clearly and ably. To do this may seem to many readers to be superfluous, *agere actum :* it is, however, of the same kind as the theories by which unfledged theologians or neologians in Germany try to give themselves notoriety ; and *this opinion* (though afterwards adopted by one at least of a thoroughly different stamp) seems to have originated with enemies of revelation.

This part of the Prolegomena closes with a table of the chronology of the book of Acts: a wide and difficult subject, as to which an important turning-point is—*When* was Felix recalled? If critics could agree as to that, much difference of opinion as to other things would fall to the ground. For further information Mr. Alford refers his readers to Dr. Davidson's Introduction, vol. ii., where varied opinions are elaborately stated. The question whether St. Paul endured a *second* imprisonment at Rome is not discussed here.

It may be proper to say that with regard to St. Paul's voyage to Rome (Acts xxvii., xxviii.) Mr. Alford follows the satisfactory investigation of Mr. Smith of Jordanhill ; indeed it would be a subject for congratulation if Scripture discussions in general could receive so full and *decisive* an investigation.

In the Prolegomena to the three Epistles contained in this volume various questions connected with them are discussed, amongst others the style and language of St. Paul receives much attention.

The 'marginal references to verbal and idiomatic usage' are in themselves a monument to Mr. Alford's industry and care: whether the reader *uses* them or not, they are at least materials of a very valuable kind prepared ready to his hand.

The notes are of much the same character as those in the volume on the Gospels of which we have already spoken on a recent occasion. There is much to call for thought and consideration—much to lead the student to the force of sentences as deduced from the words and phrases themselves; there is full proof of a diligent use of recent critical writers, and that (as before) with studious pains to acknowledge all obligations.

There are many points in which the opinions expressed in this volume may lead to discussion, and on which inquiries may be raised how far the writer's own subjective opinions have or have not coloured his expositions. These we must leave for the present.

If the expository notes, &c., should be on as large a scale in the remaining part of the New Testament as they are in the portion before us, it appears doubtful to us whether the whole can be comprised in a single volume of any moderate size.

Eliana; or, a Layman's Contributions to Theology. By F. E. CHASE, M.D. In two volumes. London: W. and E. Painter, 1852.

IF a strenuous advocate of submission to the teaching of the Church, and repudiator of all liberty of private judgment, were in want of a good argument in favour of his own views, he could not try a more satisfactory experiment than that of inducing a well-meaning Protestant to draw up a system of theology derived from the Bible alone, without help from critics or commentators. It will be all the more to the purpose if he selected a man of some shrewdness, quick at discerning a truth, a half-truth, or a no-truth as it may happen, who shall be so far confident in his own powers as to be bold in recording his conclusions; and if he find that most of the creeds, confessions of faith, digests, and bodies of divinity, are at variance with his views, will not allow himself to doubt his own accuracy. The result, if we mistake not, will amply meet the expectations of the High Church theorists. It will be a creed that has hitherto found no adherent, a confession that is peculiar to its author, a body of divinity of which the world never saw the like. Now the experiment has been tried, though not, we admit, at any Jesuit's instigation. Dr. Chase is the writer in question, and 'Eliana, or the Essays of a Layman,' the document. With every desire to be liberal, we cannot but mourn over such a heterogeneous compound as is here set before us. It is alike unsatisfactory to the student, and unedifying to the unlettered Christian. There are many truths unquestionably, some of them ably vindicated, but so interwoven with uncritical and illogical deductions, that the work requires to be read with the utmost caution.

Dr. Chase claims novelty (!) in the treatment, and challenges refutation. We should be quite content to leave his work on the dusty shelf, and consign it to the oblivion that it deserves. What readers will a man find who admits one of the Sacraments and rejects the other —believes in the divinity of the Son, and explains the Spirit to be an attribute of Deity—who makes the primeval condition of man a neutral state devoid of virtue, and under no temptation to do wrong? According to Dr. Chase, we are to believe that Adam, had he refused to participate in his wife's offence, might have become the Saviour of the race; that Jesus, by taking flesh, became the Saviour of *angels ;* that our *bodies* require to be reconciled to God. To prove that Paul obtained some of his knowledge by personal effort alone, he quotes Galatians i. 12, 'I was not taught it,' omitting the remainder of the clause, ' but by the revelation of Jesus Christ.'

Now, Dr. Chase compels us to be believers in the necessity that exists, in religion, of bowing to authority. And what do we mean by the term? We do not use the definition, *Quod semper, quod ubique, quod ab omnibus ;* nor do we refer to that indefinite abstraction, the Church; but we do beg to remind Dr. Chase that in the digest of the Sacred Volume, abounding as it does in deep and dark sayings, the agreement of which is sometimes hidden, and the entire truth never to be attained by finite understanding, the labour of every judicious critic, the devout meditation of every sincere Christian, the investigation of every unbiassed commentator, all combine in the gradual establishment of a system of harmonious truth, which serves as a guide to subsequent investigators, and which cannot be discarded without danger to him who, in so doing, sacrifices truth and consistency to a supposed originality of thought. Do Augustine and Chrysostom, do Luther and Calvin, do the reformed Churches in their confessions, and modern evangelical sects in their articles, exhibit no substantial agreement? In the face of Rome we avow our conviction that they do. But Dr. Chase differs from them all.

The Hiding-Place; or the Sinner found in Christ. By the Rev. JOHN M'FARLANE, LL.D. Edinburgh. 1852.

THE author of this volume is already widely known as an instructive and attractive writer. It may not perhaps possess the brilliancy and splendour which are thrown around some of the scenes pictured forth in the delineations of his ' Mountains of the Bible,' or the pathos, and solemnity, and artistic skill which give to the biography of ' The Night-Lamp' its profound and entrancing interest ; but, while it has all these features at least in a very high degree, it has in common with the latter volume that deep-toned seriousness—that adaptation to the wants and anxieties of a mind in earnest about its salvation —which has rendered it so eminently useful to serious inquirers, and so great a favourite in the chambers of affliction and death. In this volume, however, the author takes a much wider range of thought and illustration. His object, as stated by himself, is to set before the reader such a clear and comprehensive view of the ' way to the Father by Christ Jesus,' that, if he be at all in earnest about his soul's salvation, he must rise from the perusal, if not convinced and converted, at least in no doubt of the place where and the manner in which lost sinners are to be delivered ' from the wrath to come.' In following up this design he is led to unfold the guilt and peril of the sinner, the nature of the disease under which he labours, and the remedy which the Gospel unfolds. In connection with these, the processes of conversion—of spiritual healing—the nature and privileges of pardon, purity, and peace enjoyed by believers—the glory of the prospects of which these are the blissful pledges,—all pass in review before him. The field which the author has marked out for himself is extensive, and it is trodden with ease and dignity; the objects of thought are often magnificent, always important; and they are clothed with the richest drapery, or handled with the solemn seriousness which they respectively require. There is no trifling—no nice and subtle disquisitions—no far-fetched dreamy fancies. The subjects are obviously felt to be too sacred, too solemn, and the interests at stake too weighty. The volume brings before the mind a mine of rich, massive, solemn, Scriptural truth, and cannot fail, by the blessing of God, to produce a great amount of practical good

The subjects treated in this volume, although various and diversified in some of their relations, possess a unity and interest, growing not merely out of the relation in which they stand to each other as parts of revealed truth, but from their immediate bearing on the salvation of the soul. The author, however, has very happily and ingeniously contrived to render this unity more palpable, and the interest more intense, through a succession of chapters, by arranging his illustrations under the various titles which are given to our Lord in the Old Testament which have the prefix Jehovah. ' He is Jehovah. Jehovah Jesus—the Lord our God. Jehovah Jireh—the Lord will provide. Jehovah Tsidikenu—the Lord our righteousness. Jehovah Rophi—the Lord our healer. Jehovah Shallom—the Lord our peace. Jehovah Nisi—the Lord my banner. Jehovah Shamah—the Lord is there.'

Had our space permitted, we would have given some specimens of our author's style and thought. But where all is excellent, and highly so, there would have been some difficulty in making a selection. We had marked some very striking passages in Jehovah our Healer—our peace—our banner; but our limited space forbids their insertion. The volume is dedicated to the Rev. William Kidston, D.D., the father-in-law of the author. Since its going to press that venerable man of God has been removed by death. He was in the 63rd year of his ministry, and the oldest minister of any denomination in Scotland.

Pictures from Sicily. By the Author of ' Forty Days in the Desert.'
    London: Arthur Hall, Virtue, and Co. 1853.

THIS is, unadvisedly we think, put forth by the publishers as a ' Gift Book,' and apparently with special reference to the present season. We confess to a prejudice against such books. All books should at least aim at permanency; and one that comes before us avowedly to serve a temporary use is self-degraded. Besides, all good books are gift-books; and we should advise one about to present a book especially to avoid 'gift-books,' which are usually of the flimsiest materials, and use his own judgment in the selection of some work of permanent value, instead of accepting a publisher's determination of fitness. However, the plan is designed for those who, from sloth or ignorance, are incapable of judging for themselves—and as these are the greater number, it is probably found to answer. In the present instance, however, some wrong has been inflicted on the book, by fixing it *this* speciality, which, indeed, is not done in the work itself, but only in advertisements, and in the Christmas style of ornamentation. Between pictures and print the work is well entitled to be regarded as a permanency; and as such those who wish to use it as a Gift Book have our free consent to do so. As usual with Mr. Bartlett's productions, the pictures are much better than the literature. The author handles the pencil better than the pen. The style lacks vigour, the matter is not replete with information, and the written descriptions, though accurate, are seldom graphic. But it is too much to expect any one man to be equally graphic with the pen and the pencil, and we can scarcely call to mind any one who has possessed the power of exhibiting the common object with equal force by both instruments. Between them, however, the author has, after his usual manner, made up a very acceptable volume, furnishing an interesting account of 'the largest and most beautiful island in the Mediterranean,' which is but little visited by the all-travelling English, although there is much in its history and condition, as well as in its physical character and remains, which might be expected to draw their attention to it. Mr. Bartlett has his advantage in this, the scenes and objects that he depicts being not only in general striking, but mostly new; whereas in works of this kind, including some of his own, we have only one more representation of that which has often been represented before.

There is an historical summary prefixed, which, with the historical details interwoven, will furnish reasons, even apart from the beautiful scenery of the island, and the peculiar Norman architecture of many of the remains and existing buildings—unlike anything elsewhere to be found—why English tourists should turn their steps in this direction if undeterred by bad roads, bad inns, and passport annoyances. Mr. Bartlett furnishes some indications of the religious condition of the island, showing it to be sunk in the lowest depths of Romish superstition.

Assyria; her Manners and Customs, Arts and Arms: restored from her Monuments. By PHILIP HENRY GOSSE. London: Society for Promoting Christian Knowledge. 1852.

THIS is a work of great merit, and calculated to be of much service to the Biblical student. It is necessarily founded on the materials furnished by the *plates* of Layard and Botta; but the work is by no means a compilation, the author having worked with these materials for himself, after having made a most laborious analysis of them.   His object has been ' to collect from the recovered monuments of Assyria the thousand traits of Assyrian life which they present ; to deduce, from what is expressed, much that is only implied—the unseen from the seen ; to digest the information thus acquired, and to arrange it methodically, so as to form an intelligible portraiture of the manners of the age and nation.'   Collateral sources of information have also been carefully consulted—the sculptures and paintings of Egypt, the remains of Sanscrit literature, the poets and historians of Greece ; but, the author tells us, it is to the Holy Scriptures he has chiefly looked for illustration ; and ' he trusts that the number of passages on which the light of these monuments has been brought to bear, and the living portraitures of incidents and usages therein alluded to which they present, not a few of which are singularly exact and interesting, will confer a value on the volume in the eyes of the Biblical student, and show how important an auxiliary these archæological discoveries are to sacred literature.'

These are worthy objects, and they have been worthily accomplished, so that we know not what book before the public we could with so much confidence recommend to those who wish to possess, within moderate limits, a complete and by no means superficial view of a subject on which many volumes have now been written.   Some experience in this kind of work enables us fully to appreciate the expenditure of time and labour the preparation of this book must have involved, and by the independent results of which it is honourably distinguished from the ordinary compilations which follow in the wake of a great subject. Mr. Gosse assure us in his Preface that he has in no case referred to the observations of his predecessors in inquiry, until he had first examined the particular subject in question for himself, and formed his own opinion thereon, and the work evinces throughout the correctness of this statement.   The conclusions of Mr. Gosse are sometimes different from those we have been led to entertain, but not so frequently or so materially as we might have expected.   But we cannot here go into details, and must leave the work with that general commendation to which it is well entitled.

We should add that the work is illustrated with 157 woodcuts of antiquities and scenery.

Popery in the Full Corn, the Ear, and the Blade.   By WILLIAM MARSHALL.   Edinburgh : Paton and Ritchie.   1852.

THIS book belongs to the controversy concerning Baptism, and is, therefore, beyond the scope of our publication.   The position of the author is that Romish baptism is ' Popery in the Full Corn ;' Episcopalian baptism is ' Popery in the Ear ;' and Congregational baptism is ' Popery in the Blade ;' but Presbyterian baptism is ' Popery rooted up.'   The work is therefore simply a treatise discussing the views of baptism which the author condemns, and expounding the one which he considers entitled to preference.   He disavows any intention of attacking churches or individuals ; but states that ' he has found it most convenient, because most in accordance with fact, to adopt a *denominational classification* of the views which he condemns.'

Romanism an Apostate Church. By Non-Clericus. London:
Longmans. 1852.

This author states that 'a life of some extent, with proportionate reading, reflection, and observation, has convinced the writer that no heretical form of Christianity, in any age of the world, has proved so derogatory to God, and so injurious to man, as the *Popish religion*. This is a grave charge, and requires substantial proof, such as it is believed will be found in the following pages.'

One would not expect much novelty in the proof of this; but by passing over, or only slightly noticing, some of the leading features of Popery, as having been already successfully treated by others, and by the resources of a somewhat peculiar reading, the writer has contrived to bring together a stock of materials, either fresh, or freshened by the use he makes of them; and as he deals chiefly with 'modern instances,' and produces freely the names and topics of the day, it may be said to have much of that kind of attraction which, to many, an article in a periodical possesses over a book. The writer seems to have watched vigilantly the recent movements of Popery, and his book will help to rouse others to watchfulness. This is important; for it is only through the slumber of Protestants that Rome can have any chance of gathering strength in these islands.

Nineveh; its Rise and Ruin. By the Rev. John Blackburn.
London: Partridge and Oakey.

We noticed this work on its first appearance; and we are glad to find that the commendation we then bestowed upon it has been sanctioned by the first authority—that of Mr. Layard himself, who, on being applied to by that excellent institution 'The Working Men's Educational Union,' to indicate the work which he considered best suited to connect his discoveries with the history and predictions of the Sacred Scriptures, named the present work, in consequence of which a revised and somewhat enlarged edition has been prepared. We heartily repeat our recommendation of this work to general attention.

Cyclopædia Bibliographica. Nos. II., III. Darling. 1852.

The third Number of this excellent work (described in our last) reaches to column 480, and to name Bull (G. S.). The bibliographical wealth and fulness of the catalogue grow upon us as we proceed, and we find increased occasion to admire the tact and skill with which the compiler contrives to furnish the student with the materials for judging of the degree in which any of the books here registered may be useful to him.

INTELLIGENCE.

BIBLICAL.

From Calcutta, August 4th, 1852, Mr. M. Wylie thus writes. 'I may add, with reference to Bengal, that we have been compelled to provide a gospel for the Mussulmans in a peculiar dialect. They very frequently read nothing but the Bengali character, and understand much of the Bengali language; but in many parts it is proved that their idiom is very different, and that a great number of their terms, especially their theological terms, are not Bengali, but Urdu or Persian. For this class, therefore, we are preparing the gospel of Luke: the Rev. J. Paterson, of the London Missionary Society, is performing the task, and we hope soon to see it executed.'—*British and Foreign Bible Society Extracts,* Oct. 30, 1852.

The subject of the Norrisian Prize Essay at Oxford for 1853 is announced, 'The Gospels could not have originated many or all of those forms of religious opinion which prevailed among the Jews at the time of our Saviour's incarnation.'

The prizes of 1500 francs and 500 francs offered by the Paris Religious Tract Society have been awarded as follow:—the first for the manuscript entitled 'There is a Saviour,' to M. Bartholomiss; and the second for the manuscript entitled 'On the Debasement of the Moral Sense,' to M. Bastie; 200 copies of each have been printed.

A letter from Mr. Allen, American missionary, Bombay, dated May 12, describes the progress which has been made in publishing a revised edition of the Scriptures in Mahratta. The second book of Samuel was in the press at the date of his communication. Mr. Allen fears that the Old Testament will not be completed till the spring of 1854; and another year may be necessary for the issuing of the New Testament in conformity therewith. It will be of a convenient size, making one royal 8vo volume.—*American Missionary Herald*, August.

M. Peet of Fuh-chau writes thus, February 7, 1852. 'It is a common opinion among the Chinese, that the regions of the dead are placed under the government of a single individual, who acts as criminal judge, and punishes the soul according to its sins in this life. For this purpose he is said to have eighteen places of punishment, each varying in intensity, according to the degree of the guilt of those who are consigned to them. The Chinese divide the universe into three divisions —the first including the lower regions, the second the present world, and the third the upper regions, or the dwelling-place of the gods celestial. The inhabitants of the first are called *kwúy*, "spirits" or "ghosts," and those of the third are called *shin*, "gods." In respect to the *kwúy*, it is supposed that some descend in the scale of animal existence, and are born brutes; some continue in a separate state, in the form of hungry and famishing ghosts; some are again born in a human form; while a few rise in the scale of being and become "gods." Hence the practice of presenting offerings of food to the dead, which prevails so universally among the Chinese. This is done both for the benefit of the "spirits" of the dead, and to prevent them from doing injury to the living. According to the Chinese, the three souls and seven spirits of each individual are uncreated; and, though separated from the body at death, they may again be collected and constitute another person, when they will lose all consciousness of a former life. Thus the Chinese acknowledge no Creator as the author of their existence; and, consequently, they recognise no obligation or duties to such a Being.'

At the Asiatic Society, December 4th, letters were read communicating the results of some recent investigations of Colonel Rawlinson. In a letter, dated September 4th, the Colonel announced the discovery he had made that the series of six kings named in the inscription of Van were contemporaneous with the kings of the Assyrian line from Sargon to Sennacherib. This determination gives a satisfactory evidence that the Assyrian royal series is complete in our lists. In a subsequent letter, September 25th, Colonel Rawlinson gives some account of one of the Khorsabad cylinders, which he finds to contain a list of the titles and conquests of Sargon, and a notice of the building of Khorsabad, very much like what is described on the bulls. He finds, however, some important variations, such as the carrying off the tribes of Tamud, Yanadid, Esyaman, and Gasipa, from the neighbourhood of Samaria. He feels considerable hesitation as to the correctness of these names. He also reads upon it an account of the capture of Tyre, which he has not seen among other inscriptions of Sargon. These cylinders confirm the Colonel's previous opinion that the capture of Samaria took place in the first year of Sargon's reign, B. C. 721.—*Literary Gazette*, Dec. 18.

LITERARY AND EDUCATIONAL.

The Dutch Government has just taken possession of the valuable collections bequeathed to the State by the celebrated bibliopolist, Baron Wertreenen van Tillandt, and is about to form them into a separate museum to be called the Wertreenen. They consist of a library of 10,000 rare and curious volumes on the history of typography, bibliography, archæology, and numismatics; a gallery of pictures by the oldest masters; ancient Greek and Roman sculptures, many of which are from Herculaneum and Pompeii: and a collection of ancient Greek, Roman, and Oriental coins. Of the books, 1233, it is said, bear date in the fifteenth century. There is further a collection of 385 MSS., all anterior to the fourteenth century.—*Athenæum*, Oct. 16.

A Chinese novel, in twenty-one volumes, and estimated to contain from one-sixth to one-fourth more characters than Dr. Morrison's version of the Bible, is sold in the shops for 60 cents. Mr. Williams sees no reason why the Bible in Chinese should not be afforded for half a dollar.

A family in Canton has engaged to have a set of blocks cut for a new edition of the national historians of China, a series of classical works called *the twenty-four hisiories*, which will involve an outlay of more than 100,000 dollars. It is done to shew their regard to letters, rather than with the hope of gain.—*Journal of Missions*, September, 1852.

The Vedas, next to the earliest portions of the Old Testament, are generally allowed to be the most ancient writings extant; dating, according to some able writers, in the fourteenth century before Christ. They disclose the opinions, the manners, and the institutions, social, political, and religious, of a people who were mighty twenty-five or thirty centuries ago. Till recently they have been locked up in a language known only to a few, but now three out of the four Vedas are wholly or in part before the world. While they have been thus unknown, the hundred millions of Hindoostan have bowed their minds and their hearts to their real or supposed utterances. The knowledge of their real merits, which will now be gained, will do much towards breaking this iron yoke of bondage.—*Journal of Missions*, February, 1852.

At Cambridge the Seatonian Prize Poem in English verse, the subject 'Mammon,' has been adjudged to James Mason Neale, M.A., Trinity College.

The Maitland Prize, given triennially, for the best English essay 'On some subject connected with the propagation of the gospel through missionary exertions in India and other parts of the heathen world,' has been adjudged to the Rev. C. K. Robinson, of St. Catherine's Hall. This prize was instituted from a fund raised as a memorial of respect to the memory of Lieutenant-General Maitland, K.C.B., late Commander of the Forces in South India.

The Le Bas Prize has been adjudged to Mr. B. A. Irving of Emmanuel College, the subject of the essay being ' A View of the Routes successively taken by the Commerce between Europe and the East, and of the Political Effect produced by these Changes.'—*Literary Gazette*, Nov. 6.

At the Syro-Egyptian Society, Nov. 9, portions of a letter were read from Mr. Harris of Alexandria, describing the progress of the excavations at Metrahinny. A great many small broken statues have been turned up, among them those of a lady of the time of Thothmes IV., as also a mutilated kneeling statue of the fourth son of Rameses II. Nothing could be verified anterior to that age.

Mr. Ainsworth read a paper ' On the meaning of the *Cones* in the Assyrian sculptures.' Mr. Ainsworth described the position, the attitudes, and the attributes of the different cone-bearing figures. They adorn as deities the entrance to peculiar chambers : within, they appear in the more humble guise of ministers to the king's necessities, attendants upon the cupbearer, as a drink purveyor and drink-bearers, as also in the Xanthian marbles, and as guardians of the sacred tree. The cone by itself decorates dresses, and especially the kitchen. Most of the cone-bearing figures have horned caps, or caps with horns like the followers of Bacchus, and Mr. Ainsworth dwelt particularly on tradition attributing to the Indian Bacchus, the thyrsus borne by the thyrsigers, or cone-bearers of Rome. All the cone-bearers carry a square   , which vessel, from being sometimes decorated as a basket, has been by some looked upon, but erroneously, as such. Layard says it was often made of metal. With respect to the sacred tree upon which the cone-bearing figures are attendant, or from which they obtained their cones, in most countries the cedar, or the cypress, it was in Assyria a pine, for the cone in the hands of Nisroch—·the patriarch Asshur deified, according to Rawlinson—cannot for a moment be compared with the fruit of the cedar or the cypress, the connection between which and the worship of Venus in the systems of the East, has been shewn by M. Lajard, of the Institute of Paris. On one of the society's cylinders, Hadad, the ' vivifier of mankind,' is handing over a son and heir to a king in front of the sacred tree. What then was the connection between the pine tree and the pine cone, and the ceremonies of certain chambers, the ' vivifier of mankind,' the worship of the Assyrian Venus, the tree of life, the sacred beverage of royalty, and the art of cookery? The answer is to be sought for in the uses to which the ancients applied certain products of the pine, more especially the Pissalaeon of the Greeks, and the Pissinum of the Romans, which appear to have been used as aphrodisiacs. The opinion of its power of ensuring long life is to be found in many ancient writers, and the peculiar action of the essential oils, derived from the different kinds of coniferæ, or pinaceæ, including the pines, firs, spruces, cedars, cypresses, junipers, savins, &c., are well known to medical men.—*Literary Gazette*, Nov. 20.

At the Syro-Egyptian Society, November 9th, Mr. Abington made some remarks upon the oriental cylinders engraved by Mr. Cullimore for the Society. Seven had reference to astronomical science, and had on them representations of the sun, moon, and seven stars. The well-known Assyrian and Persian representation of divine power, a disc with wings extended, occurs in two. Another symbol, like four arrow-headed characters crossing so as to form a wheel, occurs in no less than eleven cylinders. One cylinder appeared to represent the Babylonian Hercules in a Babylonian Hesperides; in another, Ashtaroth is attended upon by three priestesses; in another, a triumph of a monarch is represented. Several cylinders relate to the exploits of some mighty hunter or beast-tamer. In some the animals are monstrous; in others the man has a bird's head, Nisroch or Asshur. (?) In one Theseus is combating with the Minotaur, shewing the oriental origin of this fable. There are kings on their thrones, and a royal couple at a banquet. One royal personage is attended upon by Bel and by Derceto, or Diana. Merodach, or Mars, is represented with a weapon in his hand, and the sign Aries above him. A female divinity, of horrid aspect, apparently the Cybele of the Babylonians, stands upon a dragon, with the three keys (?) in her hand, and oak (?) leaves round her cap. In some cylinders we have apparently little children, with chaplets on their heads, being offered up to Moloch or Saturn. There are several other representations, supposed to refer to Nimrod the mighty hunter, and the prototype of Hercules, combating, as usual, lions and bulls, as in the Assyrian sculptures. There are also several cylinders on which are representations of Perseus capturing Pegasus, going on a mission, fighting griffins, and capturing ostriches; the latter,

Mr. Abington thinks, refers to the scene of the demigod's great exploit—taking of Medusa's head—being in Libya.

Mr. Bonomi read a short description of an Egyptian cylinder, which bore on a cartouche, according to Mr. Sharpe, the name of Amunmai Thor, or the conqueror beloved by Thor, the ninth king after Menes, and the last of his dynasty, though the first Theban king that is known to us.—*Literary Gazette*, November 20th.

Mr. Stern, agent of the British Society, thus represents the state of the Jews at Hamadan. 'According to the most accurate information that I could obtain, this ancient city is at present inhabited by about 500 Jewish families. They reside in a particular quarter, and in case of public commotion, which generally exposes them to the lawless rapacity of the covetous, and the malevolent persecutions of the powerful, they close the gates of their Ghetto and so enjoy some security till the storm has subsided. Their position is, however, at all times very sad and pitiable, and one cannot behold their sluggish and stooping motions, or their abject and cringing demeanour, without being struck with the terrible fulfilment of the prophetic warning. Their principal occupations are as workers in silver, weavers of silk, and sellers of old coins.'—*Jewish Herald*, October.

Mr. Hardey, of the Wesleyan Missionary Society, writing from Mysore, June 4, 1852, shews that the opinions as to the decline of the system of caste, often expressed in England, have no foundation in fact. 'So far from the chain of caste being broken, I can prove the existence, at this time, and can furnish the names, if required to do so, of 486 distinct castes among the Hindoos; of 26 distinct castes among the Jains; and of 70 distinct castes amongst the Roman Catholics. What I mean by distinct castes is, that few of them will eat together, and fewer still will intermarry. Among the Shoodras are the Gwollaru, shepherds who never weave, there are 13 castes who never intermarry with the remaining 12 castes, and of barbers there are 6 castes who never intermarry with the remaining 5 castes. These two have properly no caste at all, yet there are more quarrels between them than amongst all the other castes put together: these are the people from whom the missionary churches are always in difficulties. They complain of the higher castes not associating with them; and yet if a Pariah, who is a Christian, were to marry a Chuckler girl, who is also a Christian, it would be more than his head was worth.'—*Wesleyan Missionary Notices*, September.

The London Religious Tract Society have voted 40*l.* to assist in the publication of 3000 copies in Italian of 'Lucilla,' shewing the duty of reading the scriptures, a work admirably adapted for Italy. The proceeds of this book have enabled the Society's friends to print large editions in Italian of Dr. Malan's tracts, 'The Eldest Son,' and 'The True Cross.' They have likewise printed 1500 copies of Dr. Keith's work 'On the Evidence of Prophecy.' They have also voted 35*l.* for the publication of 'The Companion to the Bible,' and the tract by the late Rev. E. Bickersteth, 'On the Reading of the Holy Scriptures.' Through the donations of private friends, 'The Pilgrim's Progress' will shortly appear in Italian.—*Missionary Register*, October.

At a meeting of the Cambrian Archæological Association, Aug. 29, M. Moggridge, Esq., made some remarks upon a singular custom which formerly existed in Wales, in connection with deceased persons, and which he had recently discovered was noticed in an old work as being prevalent in the neighbourhood of Ross, in Herefordshire. The custom was this: when a person died, a man known by the name of 'The Sin-Eater' was called in, who placed upon the corpse a platter containing a loaf of bread and some salt; the sin-eater afterwards ate the bread, and in doing so was supposed to take upon himself the sins of the deceased person. The Rev. J. B. James reminded the meeting of the origin of this—the scape-goat. Mr. Symons wished to understand distinctly whether this custom still prevailed? and if so, to what extent? It was to be hoped that, for the credit of religion in this country, the custom was extinct.—*Gentleman's Magazine*, October, 1852.

The following extract from the Journal of the Rev. G. Matthan, Tiruwalla, India, on the slave population of Travancore, is confirmatory of what was stated in the *Journal of Sacred Literature*, p. 234. 'The Puliahs appear to be quite a distinct race—perhaps the aborigines of the country, like the Bhils, &c., in other parts of India. They do not wear the kutommy on their head, which distinguishes them from the Pariahs and other Hindu castes. They are more particular as to the kind of food they take, abstaining from the flesh of all dead animals. They are considered superior to the Pariahs who have great fear of offending them. They are thought much better servants, being more faithful to the interests of their masters. There is a division of them known by the name of Eastern Puliahs, who chiefly inhabit the hills. They are, if possible, in a more degraded state than the Western Puliahs, and the Pariahs, who would consider themselves polluted by coming in contact with them. They generally go without any other clothing than a string of leaves round their loins. . . . . With respect to their religious notions and practices, they admit the existence of a Supreme Being, but are unable to comprehend how the government of this vast world can be carried on without the assistance of subordinate agents. They believe that the spirits of dead men exist in a separate state, but do not seem to think that their happiness or misery depends upon their conduct in this world.'—*Missionary Register*, October.

Codex Leicestrensis.—This MS. (of the fourteenth century) has been from the year 1640 in the possession of the town council of Leicester. As its text is peculiar, it has often been wished that it should be more accurately collated than it is in the Greek Testaments of Mill and Wetstein. To this end G. Toller, Esq., the late mayor of Leicester, obtained the consent of the town council to transmit the MS. to Dr. Tregelles (on his giving security for its safe return) for the purpose of collation, in which he is now engaged. This MS. is partly on vellum, partly on paper—not, however, like MSS. in general, which have a variety of material, in which the paper supplies parts previously lost; for in the 'Codex Leicestrensis' the vellum and paper were made up indiscriminately into one book before the MS. was written. In some of the paper leaves, from the material being thin and spongy, the writing is on one side only. It is commonly known that this MS. originally contained the whole of the books of the New Testament; it is now defective in the former part of St. Matthew's Gospel, and the last leaves of the Apocalypse are injured. This is undoubtedly the most remarkable of the cursive MSS. preserved in English libraries.

The progress and value of the phonetic system as applied to the language of the Chinese is explained in the following extract of a letter from Mr. Cobbold, dated July 24, 1851:—'In a letter three months ago I mentioned that we had reduced the oral language of this district to writing, and were instructing some of those boys whom Providence had placed under our charge; the results have been up to the present very satisfactory. We have an elementary book nearly finished. It is cut in blocks, as the trouble of correcting the press when printing at Hong Kong or Shanghae is considerable. The original alphabet was prepared by Mr. Gough, and very nicely executed. Of these we had single types cut, about 26 in number, and soon we had those who could read our writing sufficiently well to print from it. The ease with which the method can be used for the purpose of communicating common ideas has been proved from several letters we have received from members of our household, who have written from time to time; the tailor whom we baptised got a month's work from me lately, and asked permission to go over to Chusan, where Mr. Gough was, for quiet. While there he found time to learn the alphabet and mode of spelling, and in about three weeks there came a note from him. This system is being adopted in nearly all the missionary schools here, and we hope it may spread to Shanghae.'—*Church Miss. Record*, December.

The Rev. John Simpson, Port Maria, Jamaica, thus writes respecting the Obeah and Myal superstitions which the negroes have imported from Africa:—'I go on with a few more notices of the Obeah and Myal superstitions. "Thou shalt not suffer a witch to live" (Exod. xxii. 18). Josephus, in his paraphrase on this passage, interprets it of a dealer in poisons; and this appears to have been the practice here alluded to from the word used in the Septuagint, though not the exact import of the original term, which is that of a sorceress merely. Obeah people all make use both of mineral and vegetable poisons, some of which do the work of death at once, and others by slow degrees. Obeahing in Jamaica was a capital offence, especially when poison was ascertained to be used. Mohammedans give no quarter to such characters, as I was told by one of our members, a Mandingo, but shoot them as soon as they know them to be practisers of the art. It was not necessary to use poisons at all times, as the dread of the Obeah-man was itself sufficient to entail misery and death on his victim. They were well aware of the power they exerted by the force of imaginary terrors.'—*United Presbyterian Record*, Dec. 1852.

From an address of the Rev. Mr. Waddell we extract the following:—' Besides the books already printed in the language of Calabar, and of which copies have been sent home to you, I now present the Calabar Primer, a series of progressive spelling and reading lessons systematically arranged. Mr. Goldie has his series of New Testament lessons in the press, and Mr. Anderson has sent home by me a translation of the Gospel by John to be printed in this country. All these little works are of a kind to help either in our schools or religious meetings ; and we have now many in our schools who are competent to read and understand them, as also to read and write in the English language.'—*United Presbyterian Record*, Dec. 1852.

The following items of intelligence we take from the Report of the British and Foreign Bible Society, Dec. 1852 :—

An edition of 5000 copies of the Gospels and Acts in Chinese, in the large type, has been several months in circulation, copies of which have been forwarded to Shanghai, Amoy, Canton, California, London, and Loo Choo.

Editions of the revised Chinese New Testament have been printed by the missionaries of the London Missionary Society at Hong Kong and Shanghai.

There have been forwarded to Chnia from England 200 copies of the Manchoo New Testament, and also 100 Bibles and 200 New Testaments in the Mongolian.

Upon the application of the Committee of the Wesleyan Missionary Society 10,000 copies of the Tongese New Testament have been ordered to be printed, and also an edition of 5000 copies of the New Testament in Feejee.

The Rev. Robert Moffat, of Kuruman, in a recent letter, acknowledges the receipt of a grant of 50 reams of paper, and states the progress effected in the translation of the Old Testament into the Sechuana language. He likewise mentions the issue of the books of Genesis and Exodus in Sechuana. The other books of the Pentateuch are very nearly ready. A new and revised edition (1000 copies) of the Proverbs, Ecclesiastes, and Isaiah has been printed.

At the request of the Church Missionary Society the committee have undertaken to print 500 copies of St. Luke's Gospel, the Acts of the Apostles, and the Epistles of James and Peter in the Yoruba language.

The missionaries in connection with the Bâsle Missionary Society on the English Gold Coast intimate their intention of preparing a translation of the Scriptures into the Gā or Accra language, which embraces a trading people on the coast numbering from 60,000 to 80,000, and into the Otsi, which (with Fanti and Asanti) embraces about 5,000,000 or 6,000,000.

At the request of the London Missionary Society 3000 copies of the Malagasy Scriptures have been forwarded to Mauritius, to be there in readiness for any openings that may present themselves for their distribution in the island of Madagascar.

On Sunday, Oct. 24, Mr. G. H. Nobbs, who has for 25 years gratuitously performed the offices of pastor, surgeon, and schoolmaster, among the interesting community, consisting of 170 persons, at Pitcairn's Island, was admitted into deacon's orders at St. Mary's, Islington, by the Bishop of Sierra Leone, under a special commission from the Lord Bishop of London. Mr. Nobbs had arrived in London a few days previous from Valparaiso, whither he had been brought in the ship 'Portland' by Rear-Admiral Moresby, who had been four days on Pitcairn's Island, and has confirmed the favourable accounts of the condition of the people. They are, as is generally known, descendants of the mutineers of the ' Bounty,' who landed there in 1789. The people are greatly attached to Mr. Nobbs, and parted with him at two days' notice with many tears. In the want of a duly-qualified clergyman he had baptized, married, and buried them according to the ritual of the Church of England. He has received Priest's Orders (Nov. 30) at the hands of the Lord Bishop of London, and will shortly return to the scene of his labours. The people during his absence are under the spiritual care of the Rev. Mr. Holman, chaplain of the 'Portland.'—*Eccles. Gazette*, Nov. 1852.

' The accounts of the virtue and piety of these people are by no means exaggerated. I have no doubt they are the most religious and virtuous community in the world; and during the month I have been here, I have seen nothing approaching a quarrel, but perfect peace and good will amongst all.'—*Rev. Mr. Holman.*

Mr. Bayard Taylor, in one of his letters addressed to the ' New York Tribune,' gives the following account of the oldest Hebrew manuscript in the world:—
' Nablous is noted for the existence of a small remnant of the ancient Samaritans. The stock has gradually dwindled away, and amounts to only 40 families, containing little more than 150 individuals. They live in a particular quarter of the city, and are easily distinguished from the other inhabitants in the cast of their features. They have long but not prominent noses, like the Jews; small, oblong eyes, narrow lips, and fair complexions, most of them having brown hair. They appear to be held in considerable obloquy by the Moslems. Our attendant, who was of the low class of Arabs, took the boys we met very unceremoniously by the head, calling out, " Here is another Samaritan." He then conducted us to their synagogue to see the celebrated Pentateuch which is there preserved. We were taken to a small open court, shaded by an apricot-tree, where the priest, an old man in a green robe and white turban, was seated in meditation. He had a long gray beard and black eyes that lighted up with a sudden expression of eager greed when we promised him backshish for a sight of the sacred book. He rose and took us into a sort of chapel, followed by a number of Samaritan boys. Kneeling down at a niche in the wall, he produced from behind a wooden case a piece of ragged parchment written with Hebrew characters. But the guide was familiar with this deception, and rated him so soundly that, after a little hesitation, he laid the fragment away, and produced a large tin cylinder covered with a piece of green satin embroidered in gold. The boys stooped down and reverently kissed the blazoned cover before it was removed. The cylinder, sliding open by two rows of hinges, opened at the same time the parchment scroll, which was rolled at both ends. It was indeed a very ancient MS., and in remarkable preservation: the rents have been carefully repaired, and the scroll neatly attached to another piece of parchment, covered on the outside with violet satin. The priest informed me that it was written by the son of Aaron; but this does not coincide with the fact that the Samaritan Pentateuch is different from that of the Jews. It is, however, no doubt one of the oldest parchment records in the world, and the Samaritans look upon it with unbounded faith and reverence. The Pentateuch, according to their version, contains their only form of religion: they reject everything else which the Old Testament contains. Three or four days ago was their grand feast of Sacrifice, when they made a burnt-offering of a lamb on the top of Mount Gerizim. Within a short time, it is said, they have shewn some curiosity to become acquainted with the New Testament, and the high priest sent to Jerusalem to procure Arabic copies.'

The Rev. Dr. Robinson has returned from his recent visit to Syria and the East, and has resumed his duties as Professor in the Union Theological Seminary, New York. He remained only a few days in England. He has explored various parts of the Holy Land hitherto little known, and has obtained valuable materials for the new edition of his ' Geography of [Biblical Researches in] Palestine,' which he is about to publish.—*Literary Gazette*, Oct. 16.

Dr. Robinson was accompanied in his late travels by his old friend the Rev. Dr. Smith; and it is the purpose of Dr. Robinson to compress his ' Researches ' into two volumes, and add a *third* of new matter.—*New York Literary World*, Nov. 20.

At the Royal Asiatic Society, Nov. 20, a portfolio of fine drawings from the temples of Jwullee, by Lieutenant Biggs of the Bombay army, was laid on the table. Jwullee is a village on the Malpurka river, and is wholly composed of caves and temples. Many inscriptions exist in the Canarese character, but in the older dialect, which is not understood by the people. In an inscription on a pillar in one of the caves there is a date which Dr. Bird believes to be equivalent to 932. At the town of Bedami, 15 miles from Jwullee, Lieutenant Biggs found three large caves in the precipices at the back of the town: the general style of sculpture in these and in the temples on the Malpurka river, which extend along the river in groups of twenty to thirty, is the same as Ellora, and appears to represent the same mythology, there being many figures of Vishnu in his different incarnations, and one or more of Siva and his attendant Nandi.—*Literary Gazette,* Dec. 11.

For some months the Waldenses have published a weekly journal, named ' La Buona Novella,' the annual subscription to which is about six shillings ; we would recommend it to such of our friends as love the Italian language, and wish information as to the political and religious movements of the Waldenses : the Waldenses are to be found in the Duchy of Piedmont at the foot of the Cottian Alps. About four years ago political privileges were accorded to them by their late king, the magnanimous and generous Charles Albert. They number about 23,000 souls. —*Edinburgh Christian Magazine,* December.

The Archbishop of Cologne has ordered a museum of religious antiquities, and especially of art, to be formed from the possessions of the different churches in his diocese.—*Literary Gazette,* Dec. 11.

A new Scientific and Exploring Expedition, under the conduct of Commander Lynch, known by his recent Expedition to the Dead Sea, is about to start, by orders of authority, at Washington. Its object is to examine the interior of Africa—inland from Liberia—with a view to the discovery of a tract of land, if any such exists, fitted for colonization, at a distance from the sea. The Expedition is apparently connected with the ever-accumulating difficulties of the slave question, and points to the idea of a larger exodus of the black people of the States than has hitherto been seen. Any well-prepared expedition into interior Africa would be of value, but the social interest of the inquiries to be conducted by Commander Lynch and his staff far exceeds the interest which is purely scientific.—*Athenæum,* Dec. 11.

We give the title of a work we have not yet seen, but which promises to be highly interesting in this country, and will probably find a translator—' Haay, la France Protestante ; ou Vies des Protestants Français qui se sont fait un nom dans l'histoire depuis les premiers temps de la Réformation.' 3 vols. Paris, 1852.

ANNOUNCEMENTS AND MISCELLANEOUS.

The Rev. H. Burgess, whose former work, a translation of the ' Festal Letters of Athanasius,' has procured him the degree of D.P. from Göttingen, has issued proposals for publishing translations into English of some of the ancient Metrical Hymns of the Syriac Christians, with historical and philological notes. It is presumed that such a work may be made highly interesting, concerning as it does the customs of the Early Church, and a department of literature but little cultivated.

The Rev. Professor Eadie, D.D., has in the press a thoroughly critical analysis and full illustration of the Epistle to the Ephesians. The work promises to be one of great use and interest to the real student. Its character will not be that of practical exposition on the one hand, nor of mere word-criticism, as in so many of the German commentaries, on the other. The most important differences of opinion will be noted and commented upon ; and from what we have been able to learn we should suppose the work likely to prove not only an important contribution to the literature of this Epistle, but an example of, and therefore an incentive to, the real critical study of the New Testament.

The Rev. Dr. Davidson has just published his valuable ' Treatise on Biblical Criticism.' It reached us too late for adequate consideration in the present Number of the JOURNAL ; but we expect to be enabled to give a full account of it in our next Number.

The American Bible Union has in progress a plan for the revision of the English New Testament. The revision made by any one of the scholars employed by the Union is printed with the Greek Text and Authorized Version in three parallel columns, with foot-notes shewing the authorities which sanction the alteration. In this shape it is sent round, interleaved with ruled paper, to scholars here and in the United States for criticism and suggestion; and it seems that copies embodying these criticisms are then to be prepared, and sent to the revisors of the other books, which will be returned to the revisor of the particular book. After being re-revised with these helps, a carefully prepared copy will be furnished to the Secretary of the Union—we presume for final sanction by him or the Committee. The portion which has been forwarded to us in conformity with these rules comprises the Second Epistle of Peter and the Epistles of John and Jude. It is perhaps hardly fair to give a specimen of a provisional text, but we give the two concluding verses of the Epistle of Jude:—' Now unto him who is able to keep them from falling, and to set *them* in the presence of his glory faultless with exceeding joy, unto the only wise God our Saviour *be* glory and majesty, strength and dominion, both now and unto all the ages.' We trust that after final revision the work will be produced in a shape not materially different from that in which the specimen appears. The notes will be of essential use.

In the United States Dr. Conant's version of the Scriptures is in progress. The minor Prophets may be expected to appear in the spring. Dr. Conant enjoys the reputation of being perhaps the best Hebrew scholar in America.

A prospectus has been issued making proposals for draining the Lake Fucino, situated in the kingdom of Naples on the confines of the Roman States, 15 leagues from Rome, 7 from the ancient town of Sora, 15 from Gaeta, and equidistant from the Mediterranean and the Adriatic Seas, with which the rivers Liri and Pescara connect it. The conduct and superintendence of the operations are intrusted to Mr. Charles Hutton Gregory, the son of the late Dr. Olinthus Gregory, a gentleman well known in the engineering world. Should the required capital be raised, and the works be proceeded with, the submerged towns of Valeria, Penna, and Marruvio, will be brought to light, and a mine of antiquity discovered from which a vast number of objects must be drawn, to the delight of the archæologist.—*Literary Gazette*, Nov. 20.

Professor Peterman, as we hear from Berlin, is at present engaged at Damascus in copying, with the aid of other learned men, a Syriac New Testament of the 6th century, which, it is said, there is reason to believe was itself translated verbally from one of the earliest and most authentic Greek MSS.—*Athenæum*, Dec. 25.

The medal of the Prussian Order of Merit, disposable by the death of Thomas Moore, is to be conferred on Colonel Rawlinson, the distinguished oriental scholar and traveller.

Journal of a Deputation sent to the East by the Committee of the Malta Protestant College. The Journal will contain an account of the nations of the East, including their religion, education, domestic customs, and occupations; a notice of the productions and resources of the countries they inhabit; with an outline of the doctrine and discipline of the Oriental Churches, and of the rise and decay of knowledge of the East. One volume. 8vo.

In the press, ' Prayers, chiefly adapted for Occasions of Personal Trial.' By John Sheppard, author of ' Thoughts on Private Devotion.' Fcp. 8vo.

' Some Account of the Council of Nicæa, in connection with the Life of Athanasius.' By John Bishop of Lincoln. In 8vo.

' The Christian Philanthropist. A Memorial of John Howard.' By John Stoughton. Fcp. 8vo.

' The Church of Rome in the Third Century, or the Greek Text of those Portions of the newly-discovered "Philosophumena" which relate to that subject; with an English Version and Notes, and an Introductory Inquiry into the Authorship of the Treatise, and on the Life and Works of the Writer.' By Christopher Wordsworth, D.D.

CONTEMPORARY PERIODICAL LITERATURE.

OCTOBER.

The CHRISTIAN REMEMBRANCER is but slightly theological. There is an article on Madame Ida Pfeiffer's Travels, in which the travelling character of that enterprising woman, and the quality of her ' Travels,' are well and favourably estimated. The poetical works of Dr. Moir (Delta), and of John Edmund Reade, furnish the text for the article Recent Poetry, in which the reviewer takes occasion to question some of the religious notions of the former, but not more strongly than one of our Scottish contemporaries has done. Nor does Mr. Reade escape—and we are glad to see a growing disposition in our theological periodicals, monthly and quarterly, to watch more narrowly than has been usual, the religious notions set forth in our polite literature, in prose or verse, which must necessarily have considerable influence for good or evil on large masses of the community. The reviewer thinks that ' in vigour of thought and power of language Mr. Reade far surpasses Mr. Moir ; and where he deigns to descend from the lofty heights of abstract research, we have passages of mingled beauty and strength, deserving to be ranked among the highest efforts of the poetic mind.' The article on the ' Recent election of Proctors to Convocation' speaks in strong condemnation of those who have shewn themselves opposed to the restoration of synodical action to the Church. ' Church Festivals and their Household Words ' is a short but elegant paper on the domestic influence of the Mediæval Church, as shewn in the terms describing its festivals, and the allusions to them found in the language and practice of common life. The article on ' Achilli v. Newman ' takes fair advantage of the arguments as against Rome furnished by the disclosures of that trial—even from the mouth of its own witnesses. Mr. Trench's remarkable book, ' On the Study of Words,' and Mr. Macfarlane's on ' Japan,' supply the subjects of the remaining articles.

The ENGLISH REVIEW for this quarter commences with a very interesting and able paper upon the condition of the London poor, and the necessity, usefulness, and importance of Pastoral Visitations among them. The writer, without undervaluing the services of ' lay parochial visitors,' insists that their attention to the poor is not to be substituted for ' the regular calls of the parish clergy.' This paper, which will be read with pleasure for the facts it produces and the suggestions it offers, will excite many to the thought of useful labour in the service of those whose spiritual interests are too little looked after under existing social arrangements. The late Rev. J. E. Tyler's *Sermons*, and his *Address*, in explanation and vindication of the Burial service of the Church of England, supplies a subject for the second article. The third, on the *Practical Working of the Church of Spain*, is composed chiefly of extracts from Meyrick's work with that title. It might be read profitably in connection with the article *Romanism in France* in the last Number of our own Journal. Passing over some articles of a literary or political character, we come to the last, in which the question now so warmly agitated in the Established Church—*Convocation*—receives very full attention, chiefly as regards the admission of laymen to Convocation, and the nature of their functions.

The QUARTERLY JOURNAL OF PROPHECY for October is essentially a Number of three articles, two of them continued from the previous Number. The first continues the investigation of the question, ' Is Rome the Babylon of the Apocalypse;' and the present portion is mainly applied to the settlement of ' the most difficult, the most delicate, and the most dangerous part of the subject,' being to decide ' the precise period when Rome became apostate, and the worship of the Virgin Queen, till then carried on in secret conventicles, superseded

Christianity as the avowed religion of the Roman Empire.' The result reached is, 'that the Church of Rome, itself apostatising to the worship of Astarte by A.D. 382, had drawn the whole Oriental Church into the same apostacy by A.D. 436.' The second article maintains the view that the Church of Christ is to be completed by the visible union of all believers, and that then the world, standing confronted with the Church thus united, will receive its condemnation. The third article is a continuation of a sort of commentary, chiefly practical, on Genesis, of which chap. iii. 8-14, is examined with ability and care, and much matter for profitable and suggestive thought drawn from it. We prefer this portion of the Journal, but there are tastes to which the other articles may be more acceptable.

The JOURNAL OF PSYCHOLOGICAL MEDICINE has a curious article on *Homicidal Monomania*. It is here noticed that the notorious Burke ' was very partial and kind to children. He preached religious sermons, and the whole series of his murders was suggested by his confederate Hare reading aloud one winter evening the death of Benhadad by Hazael in the second book of Kings.' We cite this for the sake of the biblical illustration in the note appended : ' This is a very curious fact. The diabolical suggestion arose from Hare reading the account given (ch. viii. 15) of the death of Benhadad, who was thus killed by Hazael: "And it came to pass on the morrow that he took a thick cloth, and dipped it in water, and spread it on his face, so that he died." Burke and Hare adopted the same plan. They made their victims drunk, and then covered the mouth and the nostrils with wet cloths; sometimes, by kneeling on the epigastrium, they forced a deep expiration, which emptied the lungs, and the wet cloths prevented the re-admission of the air. This murderous method was so physiologically scientific, that it was suspected to have been suggested by some anatomist. This was not true : the above statement came out in evidence.'

METHODIST QUARTERLY REVIEW (American). — The first article, *On the Mosaic Account of the Creation*, has for its object to shew that the Mosaic record ' is a literal account of the origin of the present order of things, in which every word is used in its ordinary obvious meaning.' It supports the prevailing theory, except that the writer does not allow that even the word ' beginning' refers to the origin of matter, as usually supposed, but holds that it refers only to the beginning of the human dispensation. The article is avowedly framed to meet the hesitancy, not to say scepticism, with which many eminent theologians regard the current explanation. An article on *The Genealogies of Christ* is a useful contribution to the literature of this perplexing subject. The other papers are upon Hannah More, the Theory of Reasoning, Jacob Abbot and his works, being reviews of books, with a memoir of Professor Merrit Caldwell, a person of some note in the religious body of which this publication is the organ. This is a good but not very striking number of an excellent periodical.

BIBLIOTHECA SACRA (American).—The first article is a translation of the first portion of the lately-published autobiography of Dr. Bretschneider. The next paper, *Vestiges of Culture in the Early Ages*, does not satisfy the expectations the title will create: and the next, *Protestant Christianity adapted to be the Religion of the World*, reminds one of Coquerel's eloquent discourse, *Christianity in Harmony with our Faculties*, of which a translation was formerly given in the JOURNAL OF SACRED LITERATURE, and which has since found many echoes. The next writer, in contemplating the phenomena which ' Islamism' exhibits, sees that ' God seems always to have wrought with a peculiarity of Providence in the East; He has wrought at long intervals, and then suddenly: continual progress, as at the West, does not seem to be the law of Oriental existence.' Dr. Enoch Pond next investigates *The Character of Infants*, informing us that ' What is your opinion as to the character of infants?' is a question very generally asked of candidates for the ministry—among the Presbyterians, we presume. The theories before the public on the subject may be reduced to two, one regarding the infant as *innocent*, the other treating him as a *sinner*. Dr. Pond of course goes with the latter; and he contends that they are sinners, not only as inheriting the taint of Adam's transgression, but as having active moral affections from the first, and these selfish and sinful. Articles on the *Alleged Disagreement between Paul and James;* on the *Life and Services of Prof. B. B. Edwards;* and a sketch of *Justin Martyr,* complete a very readable number of this valuable periodical.

PRINCETON REVIEW (American).—Nearly two-fifths of this Number is occupied with an article on the Apostles' Creed, going over ground that would seem to be less exhausted in America than here. An article on *The French Pulpit* has notices, with specimens, of Bossuet, Bourdaloue, and Massillon. There is a very interesting account of *The Gymnasium in Prussia,* which will be read with interest by those whose attention is directed to the progress and processes of high education. Papers on the *Laws of Latin Grammar,* on the *Lives of Robert and James Haldane,* and on the *Great Salt Lake of Utah,* complete this Number.

NOVEMBER.

The CHURCH OF ENGLAND MAGAZINE for November has, for part of its contents, a continuation of *Extracts from Religious Writers of Spain,* by Miss Stodart, and *A Sketch of the Life of Dr. Miles Smith,* one of the translators of the Authorized Version, and the writer of the preface.

The BIBLE AND THE PEOPLE for November continues, to use the language of the day, its useful mission in presenting to the thinking, honest doubter, and there are many such among the lower classes, short, well written articles. The first, *The Destruction or Expulsion of the Canaanites,* and an appendix to it, entitled, *The Jewish Land Scheme,* or *Jehovah's Freehold Land Scheme,* will repay perusal. All interested in getting our mechanics to think rightly with respect to the Bible and its claims ought to encourage this periodical; by so doing the talented editor might be enabled to effect some improvement in the variety of his journal; for the admission of some articles of a lighter cast would, without diminishing the substantial value of the periodical, increase the interest it might awaken.

The NORTH BRITISH REVIEW for November contains an able article by a ready and apparently practised pen, on *The Infallibility of the Bible, and Recent Theories of Inspiration.* We recommend it to all who wish to know the present state of the controversy. The writer first shews, with great force and fairness, the arrogance of the impugners of divine inspiration, and the arbitrary manner in which they set aside the positive external evidence for the Bible, that they may at once bring it down to their own standard. He next passes in review the opinions of those holding a partial inspiration, who are of course chiefly continental divines, and nothing can be finer or clearer than the manner in which these are presented to the reader, and the refutation successively of each.

With regard to a statement of Dr. Tholuck, 'here is unquestionable error,' the writer says, 'We freely acknowledge the difficulties in some cases, which, notwithstanding all efforts at summarily explaining them, still exist. In books so extensive, so ancient, so liable to error in transcription, especially in the case of resembling names and numbers, the marvel to us is, not that so many real difficulties exist, but so few, and that so many reasonable suppositions can be made, in almost every case, to effect harmony—suppositions precisely of the same kind which advocates of partial inspiration employ against those who reject supernatural revelation altogether, and which critics devoid of all Christian prejudices apply to the chronology of Herodotus and Berosus, or the narratives of Tacitus and Josephus. The infallibility of the Bible rests on its own inductive evidence, and this evidence is not abolished by such discrepancies, though the number already fairly eliminated by honest criticism is continually re-inforcing it, as is also the marvellous verification, by all antiquarian research and progress, of the minute accuracy of the Scripture where it once was questioned.' 'We should leave these outstanding difficulties as problems for criticism, and motives to fresh investigation, not shutting our minds to honest scruples, nor forcing others to swallow our premature solutions, but neither also refusing the strong historical testimony of Scripture to its own infallibility, nor doing it the injustice of shrinking from carrying through that infallibility in detail.'

The CHRISTIAN OBSERVER for November has for its first article, '*A few* (very judicious) *Words to Country Clergymen*,' on the maintenance of a habit of study. The writer says, that 'The public ministrations and private endeavours of the individual clergyman must inevitably be impaired in their power, when they proceed from a mind which is neither exercised nor replenished,' and, 'To trace the gradual development of truth, and its application to man in various stages of his progress—to discern the several parts of one great system as they are separately produced in various ages, and gradually unveiled by various hands—to follow the disclosures of the human heart under the different circumstances in which it is tested and proved— to discriminate character and motive in the complicated scenes —to catch the point of view of the speakers, and to apprehend the state of mind to which they address themselves—to perceive the light which a principle revealed in one book throws upon a transaction recorded in another—to enter into the language of types and significancy of images—to seize the connection of ideas, and link together the steps of uninterrupted argument,—these are exertions of mind incumbent upon any one who assumes the office of expositor of the Sacred Volume, and it need not be pointed out how great and extensive demand they make upon the intellectual faculties.' Two other short papers, entitled *On Afflic-tion*, and *Is Evangelical Religion compatible with Literary Taste?* will repay perusal.

In the review department is a notice of Mr. Forster's work, *The Voice of Israel from the Rocks of Sinai*, in which the writer acquiesces in Mr. Forster's conclusions, without advancing anything new.

The BRITISH QUARTERLY REVIEW for November, in an article on *China, its Civilization and Religion*, notices the dispute respecting the mode of translat-ing the words Elohim and Theos. The writer regards as conclusive the evidence produced by Dr. Legge, that 'The Chinese *have* a name indicating the true God, and *have* given it fitting expression, and that the God of our Bible is the Shang-tè of the Chinese. He removes all foundation for the belief that there are two or more Shang-tès, and furnishes us with a collection of exquisite odes, embodying the classic notions of Shang-tè's attributes, such as the creation of heaven and earth—the sustaining of the universe—fatherly love—a spiritual nature—the power to impart knowledge, and the like;' and Dr. Legge further argues, that a word which expresses 'the varied relations which God has thought fit to call into ex-istence, or to sustain towards us, is a more fitting rendering than the word Shin or spirit, which is not more true of Jehovah than of a thousand other spirits.'

Article III. is devoted to an investigation and vindication as to what the Old Testament has taught respecting God, and what it has taught respecting man in his relation to God. It is very full and clear, and its perusal will be useful to young students. Article IV. is an admirable introduction to the study of the two volumes, so long anxiously looked for, of Sir William Hamilton, the Professor of Logic and Metaphysics in the University of Edinburgh. The merits of Sir William Hamilton have not been sufficiently recognised in his own country; but now that the spirit of philosophical inquiry is reviving, these volumes will be more appreciated; and as there is no lack of works professing to base their hostility to religion upon a philosophical foundation, there ought to be a counter literature, whose philosophy, at once more profound, catholic, and vigorous, shall defend the truths of revelation. To those of our readers who may be unacquainted with the philosophy of which Sir William is partly the expounder and partly the creator, we beg to add that, 'in common with Aristotle, Descartes, and Locke, and in opposition to Reid, Stewart, and Royer Collard,' Sir William regards conscious-ness, 'not as a special faculty, holding only a co-ordinate rank with other powers of the mind, from which it can be numerically distinguished, but as the universal condition of all intelligence, underlying and sustaining every mental act, opera-tion, state, mode, modification, or by whatever other name the phenomena of the soul may be designated;' and 'it is from the due analysis of all the phenomena revealed in consciousness, together with their just classification, and an en-lightened induction, patiently and carefully drawn from them,' that Sir William confidently expects a true system of mental philosophy will emerge.

DECEMBER.

The BIBLE AND THE PEOPLE for December contains an announcement that this able little periodical will in 1853 be devoted almost exclusively to the question of modern infidelity. The price will be threepence monthly, so as to bring it within the reach of the poorest working man. We agree in the opinion which has been expressed of this periodical, ' as standing *alone* in the peculiarity of its purpose, and in adaptation to the wants of an *inquiring* age.' It aims at becoming ' a permanent manual of principles and investigation for doubters, inquirers, and intelligent believers;' and that this end has been accomplished, the volumes themselves speak. An earnest and popular advocate of atheistic infidelity declares of the editor of the *Bible and the People* ' that he is more than impartial, he is generous,' and of the periodical itself, ' it is the best of the controversial publications devoted to the maintenance of evangelical principles : the first sixteen numbers are critical as well as instructive.'

The CHRISTIAN SPECTATOR for December contains a vigorously-written paper on the *power* of the *Pulpit*; the writer truly says, ' There is one indirect result of the British pulpit which has not often been exhibited as a claim to honour and respect on its behalf, but which may most reasonably be so presented; it is the fact that it has been a centre of intellectual attraction and a power to quicken thoughtfulness in a vast number of minds which, without that, would never have found their way into the circles of literature and thought, but who, when there, and without neglect of their other work, have done eminent service, and added not lightly to the national renown. With a view to the office of a Christian teacher, men have made efforts to attain education which no merely literary consideration could have produced. In this way latent powers have found their true nourishment and their proper sphere, and as authors or as orators, on subjects of national or world-wide interest, their possessors have done most eminent service, and helped to give its character of intelligence to their nation and their age.' Again : ' Thinking, good thinking, careful studious thinking, is not all : there must accompany the thought, or rather precede it, a consciousness of the sublimity of the preacher's position, of the mightiness of the instrument he wields, of the awfulness—the blessedness of the ends at which he aims, of the power he is delegated and expected to exert. Without this, his thoughts may be beautiful and great as stars, but as distant and as cold. He must himself glow with the fire he would enkindle : he must *be* where he would lead others, and not merely point them there.'

The CHURCH OF ENGLAND MAGAZINE for December we again notice as an excellent Sunday-book; the sermons are admirably suited for family reading, and its judicious extracts for private meditation. No. 980 informs us of a religious movement in the Holy Land, which has subjected inquirers and converts to cruel persecution. After much consultation with gentlemen well acquainted with Palestine, it is thought that the best course to follow is to give judicious aid to the advancement of agriculture, and to improvements in such trades as furnish articles now forming the staple marketable commodities of Palestine. The soil of Palestine in most of the valleys is capable, with a very small amount of skill, of yielding the richest crops. The olive-oil is of the best quality in the world; but from the defective pressing machines now used, one-half of the produce remains unpressed. The Anglican Bishop of Jerusalem, who is now in England, confirms most fully the preceding statement, and entirely approves of the proposed plan as the most suitable for attaining the ends in view. It is proposed to raise £1000 to carry out this object.

The first paper in the CHRISTIAN OBSERVER for December is a short and excellent one on the *Jealousy of God*, a word which ' carries with it an aspect of sternness,' but is one ' which suggests the strongest intimation of tenderness and affection.' Secondly, ' it also supposes *obligation* in the case of him with regard to whom it is felt.' Thirdly, it intimates much as to the *nature* of the special service which we are called to render to God. .... ' The jealousy of God has a deep significance : it shews us that the mere ceremonial of religion, its pictures and processions, its fasts and festivals—all that it is fashionable to term æsthetic in the service of God—all that glitters to the eye or soothes the ear, falls infinitely short of the deep and interior demands which the feeling of jealousy makes on the creatures of God : and, lastly, it seems to explain and to justify the *character* and *extent* of the *woes* and *penalties* by which we are taught to believe that sin will be followed.'

The second article is another pleasant and judicious paper in continuation of some which have appeared in previous numbers, entitled *Words to Country Clergymen.* The writer advocates a ' free range of reading,' because it contributes in no slight degree to form a healthful and vigorous tone of mind where the opinions are already settled and the views distinct '— ministers to the mind a multitude of various materials, which the minister of Christ will know how to work up for his own purposes. A mind which is constantly giving forth has need to supply itself from every quarter with whatever it can turn to account.

The UNITED PRESBYTERIAN MAGAZINE for December contains a paper on the *Stopping of the Jordan for the Passage of the Israelites.* The writer says, ' The common opinion seems to be that the Jordan was stopped, and that by a miracle, in the neighbourhood of Jericho, where the Israelites passed it; but for this we have nothing that deserves to be called proof. .... It is clear from Ps. cxiv. that the district was convulsed by a terrible earthquake at the very time that the Jordan was stopped; and as earthquakes have stopped much larger rivers than the Jordan, by throwing barriers across their channels, it is much more probable that it was stopped in this way than by a direct manifestation of the divine power.' Searching for vestiges of such an embankment, he finds in Lieutenant Lynch's Narrative an account of the bridge of Mijamia, a Saracenic structure on the road from Jerusalem to Damascus, and nearly two miles from Beth-shan, ' the abutments of which stand on what may be supposed to be the remains of an embankment.' The writer also thinks that the modern Zerka can hardly be the Jabbok : the Zermak or Hieromax of the classical writers is much more likely.

THEOLOGICAL CRITIC.—In the first article Mr. Scudamore continues the reply to his Dublin reviewer. *Simoni Deo Sancto, or Semoni Santo,* is a reprint of the American Professor Norton's Defence of Justin Martyr's statement that Simon Magus was worshipped as a God at Rome. The next paper comprises a number of criticisms on the text of the so-called ' Philosophumena' of Origen, now shown by M. Bunsen to have been the work of Hippolytus. The translation of a portion of Thiersch's *Church in the Apostolic Age* is then continued; and we next come to a further portion of Mr. Johnstone's *Essay on the Life of Jesus Christ,* followed by a good review of Bunsen's *Hippolytus,* which seems to have attracted more attention than any other work in serious literature this season has produced. The Rev. H. Browne continues his article on the *Ignatian Controversy,* being here engaged chiefly on the Epistle to the Ephesians.

LIST OF PUBLICATIONS.

ENGLISH.

Alford (Rev. H., B. D.)—The Greek Testament; Vol. II.—Acts to Second Corinthians, with a critically-revised Text. 8vo.

Alexander (Rev. Dr.)—Moral Science. 12mo. (American.)

American Pulpit, The, containing Sermons by the most eminent Pulpit Orators of America. Post 8vo.

Anderson (Rev. J.)—Wanderings in the Land of Israel and through the Wilderness of Sinai in 1850 and 1851, with an Account of the Inscriptions on the Written Valley. 12mo. pp. 304.

Analysis (An) and Summary of the Acts of the Apostles and the Continuous History of St. Paul, with Notes. 12mo. pp. 176.

Angus (Joseph, D.D.)—Christian Life, in its Origin, Law, and End. A Prize Essay on the Life of Christ, adapted to missionary purposes. Cr. 8vo.

Arnold (Rev. T. K.)—The First Hebrew Book, on the plan of ' Henry's First Latin Book.' 12mo. A Second Part, containing the Books of Genesis and Psalms, with English Notes, is in the Press.

Barker (E. H.)—Literary Anecdotes and Contemporary Reminiscences of Professor Porson and others. 2 vols. 8vo.

Bathgate (William)—The Soul's Arena; or, Views of Man's Great Contest.

Bartlett (W. H.)—Sicily, its Scenery and its Antiquities, Greek, Saracenic, and Norman. Super-royal 8vo.

Blackie (J. S.)—Classical Literature in its Relation to the Nineteenth Century. 8vo. Sewed.

Benisch (Dr. M. A.)—Jewish School and Family Bible. Vol. II. 8vo.

Binney (The Rev. T.)—Is it possible to make the best of both Worlds? ————————————————Wellington, as Warrior, Senator, and Man. Fcp. 8vo.

Bible, Editions of the, and Parts thereof, in English, from the year MDV. to MDCCL. With an Appendix containing Specimens of Translations and Bibliographical Descriptions. Second Edition. By the Rev. Henry Cotton, D.C.L. 8vo.

Brown (Rev. John, D.D.)—Plain Discourses on Important Subjects. 12mo. pp. 424.

Brown (John, D.D.)—The Dead in Christ, their State, Present and Future, with Reflections. 18mo. pp. 176.

Clayton (George, junior) — Angelology; Remarks and Reflections touching the Ministrations of Holy Angels, with reference to their History, Rank, Titles, Attributes, &c. Post 8vo. (New York).

Cheever (G. B.)—Voices of Nature to her Foster-Child, the Soul of Man. 12mo.

Christianity, Lectures on the Evidences of, delivered at the University of Virginia during the Session of 1850-51. 8vo. New York.

Christology of the Targums, in Hebrew and Chaldee. 12mo.

Christendom—The Religious Condition of; a Series of Papers, edited by the Rev. E. Steane, D.D. Royal 8vo.

Cousin (M. Victor)—Course of the History of Modern Philosophy, translated by O. W. Wight. 2 vols. Post 8vo.

Colwell (Stephen)—New Themes for the Protestant Clergy, with Notes. Fcp. 8vo. (American.)

Conybeare (The Rev. W. J.) and Howson (the Rev. J. S.)—Life and Epistles of St. Paul, with numerous Plates. 2 vols. 4to.

Cumming (Rev. J., D.D.)—Expository Readings from the Book of Revelation. Post 8vo.

Davidson (Sam., D.D.)—A Treatise on Biblical Criticism, exhibiting a Systematic View of that Science. 2 vols. 8vo.

Donaldson (John W., D.D.)—Varronianus ; a Critical and Historical Introduction to the Ethnography of Ancient Italy, and the Philological Study of the Latin Language.

Foulke (Rev. E. S.)—A Manual of Ecclesiastical History from the First to
the Twelfth Century. 8vo.

Ford (J.)—Illustrations of St. John's Gospel. 8vo.

Fullom (S. W.)—The Marvels of Science and their Testimony to Holy
Writ. 8vo.

Greece, Macedonia, and Syria (History of), from the time of Xenophon to
the Incorporation of those States with the Roman Empire. By Dr. Mountain, Dr. Renouard,
Dean Lyall, Bishop Russell, and E. Pococke, Esq.

Gilfillan (G.)—Martyrs, Heroes, and Bards of the Scottish Covenant. 12mo.

Godwin (George)—History in Ruins ; Letters on Architecture. 12mo.

Harris (John, D.D.)—The ALTAR of the HOUSEHOLD, a Series of Services for
Domestic Worship. In Shilling Parts. Part I. Demy 4to.

HADES and the RESURRECTION ; or, A Voice to the Church of Jesus Christ.
12mo.

Havernick (H. A.)—General Historico-Critical Introduction to the Old
Testament. Translated by W. L. Alexander, D.D. 8vo. pp. 389.

Hitchcock (Edward, D.D.)—Geology of the Globe. 1 vol. 12mo.

Johnson (Rev. W. B.), Memoir of, Missionary at Sierra Leone. Fcp. 8vo.

Kingsly (Rev. C.)—Phaëton ; or, Loose Thoughts for Loose Thinkers.
Crown 8vo.

——————————— Sermons on National Subjects, preached in a Village
Church. Fcp. 8vo.

Layard (Austen H.)—Fresh Discoveries at Nineveh, and Researches at
Babylon ; being the Results of the Second Expedition to Assyria. 2 vols. 8vo.

——————————— Monuments of Nineveh. Second Series, consisting
of Sculptures, Vases, and Bronzes recently discovered, illustrating the Wars and Exploits of
Sennacherib. Folio.

Lee (Dr.), Bishop of Delaware.—The Life of the Apostle Peter. Fcp. 8vo.
pp. 352.

Maurice (Rev. F. D.)—The Prophets and Kings of the Old Testament.
Crown 8vo.

——————————— Sermons on the Sabbath-day; the Warrior; and the
Interpretation of History. Fcp. 8vo.

Macfarlane (Rev. J., LL.D.)—The Hiding Place; or, The Sinner found in
Christ. Cr. 8vo.

Meyrick (Rev. F.)—The Practical Working of the Church of Spain. Fcp. 8vo.

Muller (Dr. Julius)—The Christian Doctrine of Sin. Translated from the
Third German Edition. 8vo. pp. 380.

Nangle (The Rev. Edward)—A History of the Reformation, for Children.
3 vols. 18mo.

Paraphrase, A, and Annotations upon all the Epistles of St. Paul. A new
Edition. pp. 400. 8vo. (Oxford).

Princeton (The) Pulpit, edited by Duffield. 8vo.

Purslo (Joshua)—The Government of the Heavens. Post 8vo. With
Illustrations.

Ramsay (G.)—Introduction to Mental Philosophy. 8vo.

storation (The) of Belief. Part II. On the Supernatural Origin of
Christianity. 12mo. pp. 240.

Riddle (Rev. J. E.)—The Natural History of Infidelity and Superstition in
contrast with Christian Faith. 8vo.

Robertson (Joseph)—A History of the Jews, from the Babylonish Captivity
to the Destruction of Jerusalem. 12mo. pp. 140.

Roman Literature (History of). By several Writers. Edited by the Rev.
H. Thompson. Cr. 8vo.

Stansbury (Howard)—Expedition to the Valley of the Great Salt Lake of Utah : with an Authentic Account of the Mormon Settlement. Royal 8vo. With Illustrations and Maps.

Shepherd (The Rev. E. J.)—First Letter to the Rev. S. R. Maitland, D.D., on the Genuineness of the Writings ascribed to Cyprian. 8vo.

Seang (H. P.)—The Ceremonial Usages of the Chinese, B.C. 1121, as prescribed in the Institutes of the Chow Dynasty, strung as pearls. Translated with Notes by W. R. Gingell. 4to. pp. 116.

Smith (George, D.D.), Lord Bishop of Victoria, Hong Kong—Lew-Chew and the Lew-Chewans ; being a Narrative of a Visit to Lew-Chew in Oct. 1850.

Stoughton (Rev. John)—The Lights of the World ; or, Illustrations of Character. Royal 18mo.

Tregelles (S. P.)—Remarks on the Prophetic Visions of the Book of Daniel A new Edition, revised and greatly enlarged. Fcp. 8vo.

———————————— The Prisoners of Hope ; Letters from Florence. 12mo.

———————————— The Authenticity of the Book of Daniel. 12mo. Sewed.

Thoughts on Man in his Relations to God and to External Nature ; with Minor Poems. Fcp. 8vo.

Wardlaw (Ralph, D.D.)—On Miracles. 12mo. pp. 310.

Woodward (Rev. F. B.)—Sermons preached at Rome. Second Series. 12mo.

Williams (Rev. Isaac, B.D.)—The Apocalypse ; with Notes and Reflections. In small 8vo.

Wyld (Robert S.)—The Philosophy of the Senses ; or, Man in Connection with a Material World. 8vo. pp. 521.

Wolf (J. Robert)—A Practical Hebrew Grammar, with Exercises. Post 8vo.

FOREIGN.

Baumgarten (M.)—Die Apostelgeschichte oder der Entwicklungsgang der Kirche von Jerusalem bis Rom. Ein biblisch-historischer Versuch. 1, 2 Theil, 1 Abth. (Von Antiochia bis Korinth.) 8vo. Halle. Now complete, 2 vols. in 3, 8vo.

Düsterdieck (Z.)—Die drei johanneischen Briefe. Mit vollständigem theol. Commentar. Band 1. 8vo. cxii. and 392 pp.

Gumpach (J. von)—Die Zeitrechnung der Babylonier und Assyrer. 8vo., 170 pp.

Hengstenberg—Das hohe Lied Salmonis erklärt. 8vo.

Jaeger (Abbé)—Histoire de l'Eglise de France pendant la Révolution. 3 vols. 8vo.

Knobel—Die Genesis kritisch exegetisch erklärt. 8vo.

Köstlin (Jul.)—Die Schottische Kirche, ihr inneres Leben, und ihr Verhältniss zum Staat von der Reformation bis auf die Gegenwart. 8vo. 448 pp.

Luthardt (C. E.)—Das Johanneische Evangelium nach seiner Eigenthüm. lichkeit geschildert und erklärt. Abthl. 1. 8vo. 412 pp.

Menzel (K. A.)—Staats-und Religionsgesch. der Königreiche Israel und Juda. 8vo. 456 pp.

Mejer (O.)—Die Propaganda, ihre Provinzen und ihr Recht. Bd. 1. 8vo., 562 pp.

Meyer's Kritisch exeget. Kommentar zum N. Test. Abthl. II. Evangelium Johannis. Second edition. 8vo. 456 pp.

Neander's Leben Jesu. Fifth Edition. 8vo. 800 pp.

Remusat (Ch. de)—Saint Anselme de Cantorbéry. 8vo. 562 pp.

Reuss (Ed.)—Geschichte der heil. Schriften Neuen Testaments. Abthl. I. Second edition. 8vo. 265 pp.

Schümann (A.)—Christus oder die Lehre des A. u. N. Test. von der Person des Erlösers, biblisch-dogmatisch entwickelt. 2 vols. 8vo.

Tertulliani quae supersunt omn edidit Fr. Oehler Vols. 1 and 3. Vol. 2 will be published shortly.

OBITUARY.

At Dorpat in Livonia, Dr. Charles de Morgenstern, who had occupied the chair of Greek and Latin philology for nearly half a century. He was the creator of the Museum of Antiquities, and of the Library of the University at Halle, where he had at first professed, and the founder of the Philological Seminary, and of the Normal School at Dorpat. In his person learning had been decorated by the hands of two sovereigns, the emperors Alexander and Nicholas, and many well-known works in German and in Latin remain to attest his titles.—*Athenæum*, Oct. 16.

We have to announce the death of Dr. Scholz, one of the most distinguished Oriental scholars of Germany. He was senior member of the Faculty of Theology at Bonn, and professor in the university of that town. He studied Persian and Arabic under the celebrated Sylvestre de Sacy, of Paris, brought out a new critical edition of the New Testament, for which he consulted innumerable original documents; made a complete literary and scientific exploration of Alexandria, Cairo, Central Egypt, Palestine, Syria, and Marmarica, and published accounts thereof. He also wrote several volumes on France, Switzerland, &c. He has bequeathed his valuable collection of Egyptian, Greek, and Roman manuscripts, antiquities, coins, together with his very valuable library, to the University of Bonn.—*Literary Gazette*, Nov. 6.

On the 20th of September, from injuries received some days previous in a fall from his carriage, the aged and venerable the Right Rev. Philander Chase, D.D., Bishop of Illinois. He was born in New Hampshire about the year 1775, of an old New England stock. He was consecrated Bishop of Ohio in 1819. With indefatigable labour the Bishop—who had a constitution of extraordinary physical power and endurance—traversed his diocese in all directions, exploring his way through pathless forests, fording unbridged streams, and everywhere seeking and finding the lost sheep of his Master's fold. By the help of assistance from England, the Bishop established a College and Theological Seminary in the state of Ohio, but the immense and successful labours of the Bishop did not ensure him cordial support from his diocese or proper assistants in his school; the result of which was his resignation of the episcopate of Ohio. He was afterwards called to take charge of the diocese of Illinois, and though then an old man the Bishop vigorously commenced a repetition of his struggles and triumphs in Ohio. His Jubilee College is left on a firm basis, and will doubtless be a blessing to many generations.—*New York Literary World*, Oct. 9.

One of the most learned and accomplished scholars of his day, Mr. Henry Fynes Clinton, died last week. The 'Fasti Hellenici,' and 'Fasti Romani,' are works which entitle him to the high place he holds in modern classical literature.—*Literary Gazette*, Nov. 6.

On the 12th November, at the age of 63, died the renowned geologist, Gideon Algernon Mantell, LL.D., F.R.S. Dr. Mantell imbibed at an early period of his life a taste for natural history pursuits. In 1812-15 he commenced forming, at Lewes, the magnificent collection of 1300 specimens of fossil bones, which is now in the British Museum. In 1822 appeared his 'Fossils of the South Downs,' a large quarto work with forty plates. In 1825 Dr. Mantell was elected a Fellow of the Royal Society, and for his memoir on the Iguanodon he received the Royal Medal. In 1835 he was presented with the Wollaston Medal and Fund in consideration of his discoveries in fossil comparative anatomy generally, It is with his more popular and attractive works that his name will be chiefly remembered: 'Wonders of Geology,' 'Medals of Creation,' 'Geological Excursions round the Isle of Wight,' and 'Thoughts on a Pebble.' Dr. Mantell was a most attractive lecturer, filling the listening ears of his audience with seductive imagery, and leaving them in amazement with his exhaustless catalogue of wonders. In a philosophical point of view he had failings, but he has done much for the advancement of geology and certainly more than any man living to bring it into attractive and popular notice.—*Literary Gazette*, Nov. 13.

On September 28, in his 80th year, the Rev. Hugh Salvin. He was a ripe scholar and a good classic, and a keen and intelligent observer of all that was passing in the world. He had an insatiable thirst for knowledge and information on every subject, and possessed the rare faculty of being able to communicate to others, and to the young especially, in the most lucid and agreeable manner, the treasures of a well-stored mind. He was also an oriental scholar, conversant with Hebrew and Arabic, and with most of the modern languages of Europe he was also familiar.—*Gentleman's Magazine*, November.

On Saturday, Oct. 19, Professor Cowper. In the general applications of science to the practical purposes of life few men stood higher than Professor Cowper, but his most distinguished success was in the invention and improvement of machinery for the printing machine, which has had so important an effect in cheapening literature. In his general character Mr. Cowper was as eager in extending his knowledge to others as he was industrious in acquiring it for himself.—*Athenæum*, Oct. 23.

On Dec. 16th, at Barley Rectory, Herts, the Rev. Samuel Lee, D.D., Rector of Barley, canon of the cathedral church of Bristol, and late Regius Professor of Hebrew in the University of Cambridge.

Dr. Lee received the first rudiments of learning at a charity school at Longnor; and at twelve he was put out apprentice to a carpenter. Though he had only six shillings per week, he contrived to spare something to gratify his desire for learning, and acquired the knowledge of Latin and Greek, reading Cicero, Cæsar, Horace, Plato, Homer, and Lucian. After this, chance threw in his way the Targum of Onkelos, which he soon learned to read; then the Syriac and the Samaritan.

By this time he had attained his 25th year; and being sent into Worcestershire, on the part of his master, to superintend the repairing of a large house, he determined to relinquish the study of languages, and consider his calling as his only support. But a fire broke out in the house, and, consuming his tools, worth about 25*l.*, left him without a shilling. He then thought of some new course of life in which his former studies might prove advantageous, and he became master of a school at Shrewsbury, and afterwards the most distinguished Oriental scholar of this country.

INDEX

TO THE

THIRD VOLUME, NEW SERIES,

OF

THE JOURNAL OF SACRED LITERATURE.

A.

B.

C.

O.

P.

Q.

R.

Printed in the United States
41650LVS00013B/3-4

9 780766 1558